SERIES ON
INTERNATIONAL
LAW AND
DEVELOPMENT

The Future of the Global Economic Organizations:

An Evaluation of Criticisms Leveled at the IMF,
the Multilateral Development Banks, and the WTO

JOHN W. HEAD

Transnational Publishers

Published and distributed by Transnational Publishers, Inc.
Ardsley Park
Science and Technology Center
410 Saw Mill River Road
Ardsley, NY 10502

Phone: 914-693-5100
Fax: 914-693-4430
E-mail: info@transnationalpubs.com
Web: www.transnationalpubs.com

Library of Congress Cataloging-in-Publication Data

Head, John W. (John Warren), 1953–
    The future of the global economic organizations : an evaluation of
criticisms leveled at the IMF, the multilateral development banks, and
the WTO / John W. Head.
        p. cm. — (Series on international law and development)
    Includes bibliographical references and index.
    ISBN 1-57105-299-2
    1. International Monetary Fund—Evaluation.   2. Development
banks—Evaluation.   3. World Trade Organization—Evaluation.
4. Economic assistance—Evaluation.   5. Globalization—Economic
aspects. I. Title. II. Series.

HG3881.5.I58H43 2005
332.1'52—dc22

                                                                2005043928

Manufactured in the United States of America

SUMMARY OF CONTENTS

DETAILED CONTENTS

FOREWORD

It is a pleasure to welcome to the *International Law and Development Series* of Transnational Publishers, Inc., the present work by Professor John Head, *The Future of the Global Economic Organizations.*

The publication of Professor Head's interdisciplinary analysis of the key international institutions engaged in the formulation, articulation, and adoption of rules and standards on commerce, finance, investment, and trade comes at an auspicious time. Never before has the potential been so obvious for international institutions to do "right," to do "wrong," and sometimes to do both. The impact of organizations like the International Monetary Fund (IMF), World Bank, and World Trade Organization (WTO) goes far beyond economic indicia like capital and current account balances and gross domestic product. It extends to labor and environmental standards, and even human rights. In working on their expanded and expanding agendas, the IMF, World Bank, and WTO have come in for great scrutiny on matters such as transparency, participation, decision-making processes, and corruption. Some dedicated multilateralists hail these institutions as saviors in times of crisis, and as guardians of long-term progress for the poorest of the poor. Their anti-globalization critics decry them as unjust not only in their effect on countries like Argentina or Indonesia, but also in their purpose.

Professor Head knows well there are no "easy" answers. He takes a characteristically balanced, thoughtful approach to this debate, a debate often characterized better as a dialogue of the deaf. He marshals evidence from leading attorneys, policy officials, and scholars around the world. He brings to bear his own considerable experience as in-house counsel with the IMF and Asian Development Bank, work that has taken him to over 30 countries—and the list continues to grow. Thus, Professor Head's book has theoretical appeal tempered by practical reality. Most of all, Professor Head brings to *The Future of the Global Economic Organizations* his experience as a world-class teacher—clear, organized, provocative, and compassionate. His book is more evidence of his stature as a presence and catalyst in international business law. Not surprisingly, he is a beloved colleague at the University of Kansas School of Law.

In these and other respects, Professor Head's book fits squarely within the mission of the *International Law and Development Series.* That mission is to publish books on the intersection between international law and Third

World development. The relevant fields of international law include trade law, commercial law, foreign direct investment, banking law, securities regulation, labor law, environmental law, corporate law, competition policy, public law, human rights, and jurisprudence. The relevant aspects of development include legal, economic, or political progress in one or more Third World countries. Books in the *Series* explore the relationship between doctrines in one of these international legal specialties and events in the Third World. They also may focus on comparative aspects of their subject, including discussions of structures and trends in one or more developed countries.

Thus, books in the *International Law and Development Series* are intended for a global audience of legal practitioners, policy makers, and academicians. Professor Head's timely work is sure to be of interest to this audience.

Raj Bhala
Rice Distinguished Professor
The University of Kansas School of Law
Lawrence, Kansas

PREFACE AND ACKNOWLEDGMENTS

This book examines the international organizations that lie at the heart of globalization. The International Monetary Fund (IMF), the World Trade Organization (WTO), and the World Bank (along with its younger associates, the regional development banks) are the most powerful public inter-governmental institutions in the world economic order. The IMF and the World Bank, for example, wield enormous power over national economic policies and world financing flows because they lend (and trigger the lending of) massive amounts every year in their countries of operation—in the case of the World Bank, $20 billion in direct loan commitments last year alone. Likewise, the WTO deeply influences national economic policies and international trade flows by managing a regime of trade liberalization with "teeth" for enforcing the rules against nearly all countries of the world. The exercise of these various forms of economic power bears at least indirectly on nearly every villager in Nepal, nearly every child in Peru, nearly every shop owner in Istanbul.

It is this enormous power, of course, that, in recent years, has attracted such attention, much of it critical, toward the global economic organizations (GEOs). In this book I explore those criticisms. My approach in doing so reflects both my professional experience and my personal ideology. For about a quarter of a century I have concentrated my attention on issues of international economic law and comparative legal traditions, both in working directly with several of the GEOs themselves and in my academic teaching and writing. On the surface these two areas of interest—international economic law and comparative legal traditions—might seem to have little in common. Accordingly, the two books that I am having published almost simultaneously—this one and a book on Chinese legal history[1]—might seem, on their surface, also to have little in common.

As I see things, however, international economic law and comparative legal traditions do have important commonalities. Any efforts we might

---

[1] JOHN W. HEAD & YANPING WANG, LAW CODES IN DYNASTIC CHINA: A SYNOPSIS OF CHINESE LEGAL HISTORY IN THE THIRTY CENTURIES FROM ZHOU TO QING (Carolina Academic Press, Spring 2005). In another publication I have compared China's experience with legal codification to corresponding experiences in European civil law and in American common law traditions. *See* John W. Head, *Code, Cultures, Chaos, and Champions: Common Features of Legal Codification Experiences in China, Europe, and North America*, 13 DUKE J. COMP. & INT'L L. 1 (2003).

wage across national borders to help improve the economic and social circumstances of each other as fellow travelers on our Earth will be fruitless—
maybe even counter-productive—unless we make some credible effort to
understand both (1) the legal aspects of international economic relations
(that is, the relations of an economic character among states and international organizations) and (2) the wide variations in legal culture that shape
the way different peoples conceptualize the role that law should play in
society and governance. Even *with* some command over these subjects, we
are faced with a daunting task to beat back the ever-changing virus of economic distress that has figured so prominently in so much of the world
over the past several decades. But *without* at least an elementary understanding of these subjects, I believe we have very little hope of doing so.

Hence my efforts to contribute to an understanding of these subjects.
In particular, my aim in this book is to offer a useful and competent arm's-
length evaluation, from a legal perspective, of the main criticisms that have
been leveled recently at the key GEOs. I explain this aim more fully in
Chapter One, along with an overview of the main criticisms themselves. In
Chapter Two I offer a "nutshell" account of each of the key GEOs, so that
we may be conversant enough with their historical, legal, institutional, and
operational features to make some sense of the criticisms that have been
directed at them.

I then sift through those criticisms in Chapters Three, Four, and Five.
Those three chapters focus, respectively, on the IMF, the multilateral development banks (the World Bank being the most prominent among them),
and the WTO. In each case I provide (1) a brief summary of the criticisms,
together with extensive citations to the literature in which the criticisms
have been expressed, (2) an explanation of why I largely dismiss some of
the criticisms, (3) an explanation of why I generally endorse some of the
criticisms, and (4) a set of proposals for addressing and responding to the
criticisms I consider valid. In Chapter Six I offer some concluding observations and more general prescriptions for change.

The audiences to whom I intend to speak in this book include not only
those persons in various specialized professional positions—policymakers,
academics, government trade and finance officials, international civil servants, and others—whose work should already have made them well-versed
in the basic historical and institutional character of the GEOs, but also two
other groups: (1) those persons in national governments and politics
around the world who are responsible for establishing and implementing
their nations' foreign policy, especially as it relates to international economic relations, but do *not* already have a strong working knowledge of the
GEOs; and (2) the more general audience of curious readers on whose
involvement in civic life any society ultimately depends. It is from these two

groups, after all, that the most insistent critics of the GEOs have come. A service that I hope to be providing in this book to the persons in those two groups—that is, to governmental and political officials lacking expertise in the GEOs and to other civic-minded, questioning, intelligent, and (I hope) politically influential readers—is the combination, in a single text, of four resources: (1) a factual synopsis, in historical context, of the GEOs' aims, structures, and operations, (2) an intentionally objective survey of key criticisms leveled at the GEOs, (3) my own assessment—admittedly influenced by my ideology and experience—of those criticisms, and (4) the texts of the charters that establish and govern the GEOs, so that informed critics can consider for themselves what specific changes might best be made in the formal instruments under which those institutions are to operate. To the first audience I mentioned above—the professionals who should already be familiar with the GEOs—the first of these four resources (the factual synopsis of the GEOs) will be less important, although my experience suggests that some persons quite knowledgeable about one of the GEOs (for example, the WTO) know relatively little about the other GEOs.

The GEOs are complicated, as are the problems they were established to solve. Given their complexity, exacerbated by my own limitations, I have surely made numerous mistakes in explaining them and in evaluating the criticisms leveled against them. Moreover, I have no doubt fallen short in my effort to collect, condense, and comment on the enormous corpus of critical literature that now exists regarding the GEOs. I take responsibility, of course, for all those mistakes and shortcomings, and I welcome comments, corrections, and suggestions from any and all quarters. In particular, I would appreciate comments from harsh critics of the global economic organizations and from those whose lives are most directly affected by the operations of those organizations—the residents of economically less developed countries. From the experience I have had living, teaching, traveling, and consulting in various parts of the world, I have concluded that Americans are, in general, among the most poorly informed people regarding the global economic organizations, and that many of the voices most worth listening to regarding international economic relations live elsewhere. I have tried to reflect their voices in this book and would welcome criticisms for my shortcomings in this effort.

I could and should offer thanks to numerous people for their patience, inspiration, and guidance as I have written this book, but I shall confine myself to three individuals and one small group of colleagues. The three individuals are: Bob Hockett, whose help in commenting on a draft (and earlier versions) of this book has been invaluable; Raj Bhala, whose own energetic enthusiasm for international economic law and development has bolstered my own in the last two years; and most importantly my wife Lucia Orth, who remains my most trusted and stalwart critic and conscience. The group of colleagues whose friendship and guidance I wish to acknowledge, and to whom I dedicate this book, is the team of about two dozen lawyers I have worked most closely with in the Office of General Counsel at the Asian Development Bank over the past 20 years. These include not only those whose company I enjoyed while on the professional staff there in the 1980s—including the likes of Fred Mesch, Bruce Purdue, Peter Sullivan, Peter Kyle, Jeremy Hovland, Pierre-Marie Bouvet de Maisonneuve, Craig Wilson, Peter Pedersen, Douglas Webb, Mohan Gopal, Robert Bares, Herbert Morais, Ramdass Keswani, Moon-Soo Chung, Eisuke Suzuki, Richard Eyre, Eveline Fischer, Ross Clendon, Priya Amerasinghe, Chun Pyo Jhong, and several others—but also some whom I have worked with in more recent years, especially Philip Daltrop, Henry Pitney, and a few others. To all those persons, and for my good fortune in knowing you, I say many thanks.

Lastly, I wish to add a note of gratitude also to several research assistants who have provided such valuable help to me in the work that culminates in this book. They include in particular Alison Ranson Anway, Ashley Brown, Liz Huston, and Brooke Pyle. Support from the University of Kansas General Research Fund is also gratefully acknowledged.

J. W. Head
February 2005

GLOSSARY OF ABBREVIATIONS
AND ACRONYMS

AfDB	African Development Bank
AsDB	Asian Development Bank
AsDF	Asian Development Fund
DFI	development finance institution
DSB	Dispute Settlement Body
DSU	Dispute Settlement Understanding
EBRD	European Bank for Reconstruction and Development
EEC	European Economic Community
EFF	Extended Fund Facility
ESAF	Extended Structural Adjustment Facility
EU	European Union
GATS	General Agreement on Trade in Services
GATT 1947	General Agreement on Tariffs and Trade, 1947
GATT 1994	General Agreement on Tariffs and Trade, 1994
GCI	general capital increase
GEF	Global Environment Facility
GEO	global economic organization
GNP	gross national product
GSP	Generalized System of Preferences
IADB	Inter-American Development Bank
IBRD	International Bank for Reconstruction and Development
ICSID	International Convention/Centre for the Settlement of Investment Disputes
IDA	International Development Agency
IEO	Independent Evaluation Office (IMF)
IFI	international financial institution
ILO	International Labour Organization
IMF	International Monetary Fund
ITO	International Trade Organization (never formed)
LDC	less developed country
MDB	multilateral development bank
MFN	most-favored nation
MIGA	Multilateral Investment Guarantee Agency
NAFTA	North American Free Trade Agreement
NGO	non-government organization
NTB	non-tariff barrier

OCR	ordinary capital resources
OECD	Organization for Economic Cooperation and Development
PRGF	Poverty Reduction and Growth Facility
SAF	Structural Adjustment Facility
SCM	Subsidies and Countervailing Measures (agreement)
SDR	Special Drawing Rights
TA	technical assistance
TAA	Trade Adjustment Assistance
TRIMs	Trade-Related Investment Measures (agreement)
TRIPs	Trade-Related Aspects of International Property Rights (agreement)
U.N.	United Nations
UNCITRAL	U.N. Commission on International Trade Law
U.S.	United States
WTO	World Trade Organization

Notes on spellings and usages:

- Throughout this book, the term "state" carries the meaning it has in international law—that is, as a nation-state and not as a subsidiary political unit such as the individual domestic states that make up federal nation-states such as India or the United States or Mexico.

- I have used the spelling "Basle" throughout this book in the interest of consistency, even though the alternative spelling "Basel" appears to be more commonly used in certain contexts.

ABOUT THE AUTHOR

John Head is a professor of international and comparative law at the University of Kansas. He holds an English law degree from Oxford University (1977) and a U.S. law degree from the University of Virginia (1979). Before starting an academic career, he worked in the Washington, D.C. office of Cleary, Gottlieb, Steen & Hamilton (1980–1983), at the Asian Development Bank (AsDB) in Manila (1983–1988), and at the International Monetary Fund (IMF) in Washington (1988–1990). Both his teaching and his published works concentrate on the areas of international financial institutions, international trade regulation, international public law, comparative law, and dynastic Chinese law. He has taught in Austria, China, Hong Kong, Jordan, Mongolia, Turkey, and the United Kingdom and has undertaken special assignments in numerous locations for the AsDB, the IMF, the European Bank for Reconstruction and Development, the Agency for International Development, the United Nations Development Program, and other agencies. Mr. Head is married to Lucia Orth and has three children. He and his wife live in the quiet wooded countryside southwest of Lawrence, Kansas.

CHAPTER ONE
INTRODUCTION AND SYNOPSIS

I. WHY THIS BOOK?

My overall aim in writing this book is to offer a useful and competent arm's-length evaluation, from a legal perspective, of the main criticisms that have been leveled recently at the key global economic organizations (GEOs) —that is, those public inter-governmental institutions mainly responsible for, or at least blamed for, implementing economic globalization. In order to make the book useful, I have tried to achieve two subsidiary goals: (1) to separate the wheat from the chaff and (2) to survey the entire landscape at once. Allow me to explain these subsidiary goals, which—although they might be regarded as not being entirely consistent with each other—give this book its particular personality.

The recent increased attention on GEOs has unleashed a swarm of criticisms.[1] Many of the criticisms make little or no effort at presenting an objective assessment,[2] or are nonsensical because they rest on erroneous or even goofy assumptions and a misunderstanding of the history, character, and functions of the GEOs. I regard those criticisms as chaff. They clog the air with trash and interfere with an intelligent and reasoned debate over the appropriate role and future of the GEOs. On the other hand, many criticisms directed at the GEOs are reasonable and well-informed. They are

---

[1] Appendix A provides citations to scores of books and articles offering criticisms of the GEOs. The sources cited there are organized by the character of the criticisms being offered and by the specific institution under scrutiny. Chapters Three, Four, and Five provide summaries and explanations of those criticisms.

[2] For one recently popular work that I would place in this category, *see generally* JOSEPH E. STIGLITZ, GLOBALIZATION AND ITS DISCONTENTS (2002). In reviewing Stiglitz's book, Kevin Kennedy explains that it amounts to "nothing less than a diatribe," mainly against the IMF, in which the author, a Nobel laureate in economics and former chief economist at the World Bank, "makes no pretense of being balanced or of writing a scholarly work" but instead delivers only "rather rambling, uneven rhetoric" that includes "mean-spiritedness and ad hominem attacks." Kevin Kennedy, *A Review of Globalization and Its Discontents*, 35 GEO. WASH. INT'L L. REV. 251, 252–53 (2003). Kennedy criticizes Stiglitz's "wild hypothesizing, unsubstantiated accusations, and overheated rhetoric" and, perhaps more importantly, the glaring errors or omissions in Stiglitz's analysis of the IMF's role in the Asian financial crisis and Russia's painful economic transformation. *Id.* at 255–57. An equally critical review of Stiglitz' book came in the form of an open letter from an IMF official who noted numerous instances of Stiglitz being too short on facts and too long on ego. *See Rogoff's Discontent With Stiglitz*, 31 IMF SURVEY 209, 209–11 (July 8, 2002).

the grains of wheat. It is those that I wish to identify—to separate from the chaff—and then examine most closely.

In doing so, however, I have a strong desire to avoid losing myself or the reader in details. Numerous commentators far smarter than I am have focused on particular strengths and weaknesses of one or the other of the GEOs, and have argued for changes on the basis of specific areas of operation—the involvement, for example, of the International Monetary Fund (IMF) in the Asian financial crisis of the late 1990s, or of the WTO in interpreting international trade treaties, or of the World Bank in the resettlement of communities in the face of hydroelectric dam projects. But there are few knowledgeable writers who have taken a wider view to examine all the GEOs at once. I intend to do that here. I see merit in this effort because the criticisms and the institutions themselves are interrelated in important ways. Some of the criticisms—complaints, for example, about the so-called "democracy deficit"—obviously can be applied to all of the GEOs but with different nuances in emphasis and sting. Even those criticisms that seem, on their face, to be specific to a particular institution, such as the claim that it is anachronistic for the 60-year-old World Bank to be making loans in an age when private international capital markets are so well-developed, can, in fact, enrich the debate over the future of all the GEOs; for example, what other changes in our world's economic structure (analogous, that is, to the development of international capital markets) might make obsolete certain operations of the IMF, or even of the much more recently created WTO?

I wish to strike a balance, then, between breadth and depth in exploring the criticisms directed at the GEOs. We might imagine three wheatfields to be harvested—one field of criticisms leveled at the IMF, one field of criticisms leveled at the World Bank and the regional development banks modeled on it, and one field of criticisms leveled at the WTO. It is necessary to sift carefully through the criticisms in order to separate the wheat from the chaff. But there is also value—economies of scale, at the very least—to doing the whole process together, harvesting all the fields at once.

II. WHAT ARE THE GEOs?

In the above paragraphs I have mentioned, in passing, the institutions on which this book focuses, and I shall offer more detailed descriptions of them in later chapters.[3] It is important at this point, however, to identify precisely what institutions are being scrutinized and to explain why they warrant that scrutiny.

---

[3] *See* Chapter Two for "nutshell" descriptions of each of the GEOs. Further information about each of them also emerges from the discussions of the criticisms leveled at them, found in Chapter Three (IMF), Chapter Four (multilateral development banks), and Chapter Five (WTO).

The GEOs, for purposes of this book, are as follows:

- *The International Monetary Fund.* The IMF, formed at the Bretton Woods Conference in 1944, began its existence as the international supervisor of a system of fixed currency exchange rates (the "par value system"). That system broke down in the 1970s, and since that time the IMF has been most evident as a financing institution for countries facing heavy external debts and facing financial or economic crises. Nearly all countries are IMF members, but the wealthiest members do not borrow from it now.

- *The World Bank.* Nearly all countries also belong to the World Bank, which technically consists of two legally distinct organizations: the International Bank for Reconstruction and Development (IBRD) and the International Development Association (IDA). The IBRD was formed alongside the IMF at Bretton Woods in 1944, mainly to finance post-war reconstruction in Europe. A decade and a half later the IDA was established to provide lower cost financing to less economically developed countries, which rocketed to prominence with the demise of colonial holdings by European powers. For most practical purposes, the IBRD and the IDA operate as one institution, and they undertake mainly public-sector project lending—that is, lending to national governments (or government agencies) to finance the building of roads, irrigation systems, hospitals, power plants, schools, and the like.[4]

- *The regional multilateral development banks.* The IBRD and the IDA are multilateral development banks (MDBs) in that they muster funds on a multilateral basis to help finance projects designed to aid economic development. Complementing the work of the IBRD and the IDA, and using those institutions as their models, are four main regional development banks. Three were formed in the 1960s: the Inter-American Development Bank (IADB), the African Development Bank (AfDB),

---

[4] Another institution, the International Finance Corporation (IFC), was established in the late 1950s to provide financing (both debt and equity) to private-sector borrowers, as opposed to governments and government agencies. The IFC is an affiliate of the World Bank, in that it has close institutional ties to it. So are two other institutions formed in the 1960s and the 1980s, respectively: the International Centre for the Settlement of Investment Disputes (ICSID) and the Multilateral Investment Guarantee Agency (MIGA). These three affiliates of the World Bank, plus the two entities that comprise the World Bank itself (that is, the IBRD and the IDA) are officially referred to collectively as "the World Bank Group." For purposes of this book, the IFC, the ICSID, and the MIGA are of only tangential interest, as the criticisms assessed herein are not typically addressed to those institutions.

and the Asian Development Bank (AsDB). A fourth, the European Bank for Reconstruction and Development (EBRD), was established in 1990.[5]

- *The World Trade Organization.* The WTO was established in 1995 following the conclusion of the Uruguay Round of trade negotiations held under the aegis of the General Agreement on Tariffs and Trade (GATT). Unlike the GATT, the WTO is a true international organization (explained further below) and hence has substantially more authority to manage the system of international trade rules. Those rules, found largely in treaties that likewise emerged from the Uruguay Round, aim to encourage trade among countries by reducing or eliminating tariff and non-tariff barriers to imports. Like the World Bank and the IMF (both of which are headquartered in Washington, DC), the WTO (headquartered in Geneva) has very broad membership—currently 148 countries.

As I noted in the Preface, these GEOs are the most powerful public inter-governmental institutions in the world economic order.[6] The IMF and the MDBs wield enormous power over national economic policies and world financing flows because they lend (and trigger the lending of) massive amounts every year in their countries of operation.[7] Likewise, the WTO wields enormous power over national economic policies and international trade flows by establishing a regime of trade liberalization with "teeth" for enforcing the rules against nearly all countries of the world. The exercise of these various forms of economic power concentrated in

---

[5] I do not in this book cover any of the less prominent regional or sub-regional development banks such as the Islamic Development Bank or the Caribbean Development Bank. Information about those two particular institutions may be found on their websites: www.isdb.org and www.caribank.org, respectively. For a report on recent changes in the Islamic Development Bank, *see* Bhupinder Singh, *IDB Gears Up*, MALAYSIAN BUS., Apr. 1, 2004, at 36.

[6] They are not, of course, the only important international economic organizations. One of the paramount such organizations, and the oldest of all, is the International Labour Organization (ILO). As I note below in subsection IB of Chapter Two, the ILO can be regarded as the first major successful international economic organization, and its accomplishments are manifold. For a review of those accomplishments, and a look toward the ILO's future, *see generally* Steve Charnovitz, *The International Labour Organization in its Second Century*, appearing as Chapter 11 in STEVE CHARNOVITZ, TRADE LAW AND GLOBAL GOVERNANCE (2002). The ILO has not attracted anywhere near the level of criticism that the IMF, the MDBs, and the WTO have attracted.

[7] For example, total World Bank lending commitments in fiscal year 2004 amounted to about US$20 billion, and cumulative lending commitments amounted to about US$545 billion. *See* THE WORLD BANK, FIVE AGENCIES, ONE GROUP (offering a synopsis of operations of the entities in the World Bank Group), *available at* http://web.worldbank.org/WBSITE/EXTERNAL/EXTABOUTUS (last visited Feb. 16, 2005).

the GEOs bears at least indirectly on nearly every villager in Nepal, nearly every child in Peru, nearly every shop owner in Istanbul. And it is this enormous power, of course, that in recent years has attracted such attention, much of it critical.

III. THE SIGNIFICANCE OF HISTORY AND THE NEED FOR CRITICISM

Unfortunately, much of the criticism now being directed at the GEOs gives relatively little attention to their historical underpinnings. In my view, it is simply impossible to understand the current significance of the GEOs, let alone to offer well-grounded criticisms and suggestions about them, without appreciating those historical underpinnings, both institutional and legal. For example, why are the 1960s of huge significance to the operations of MDBs? Decolonization and the rise of the developing world. Why is the IMF in the business of bailouts? The breakdown of the par value system in the 1970s. Why does the WTO incorporate by reference (under a "single-package" approach) the score of Uruguay Round treaties? Atomization and regionalization of trade rules in the 1980s.

I shall develop these historical themes and many others later, mainly in Chapter Two. My point here is simply to underscore the importance of historical facts and trends to an understanding of the GEOs. Critics ignorant of those facts and trends can offer only unanchored views—chaff. Were the GEOs themselves unimportant, the chaff would matter little. But just the opposite is true. The influence of the GEOs is so great that they demand a rigorous and intelligent scrutiny. The opposite of such scrutiny—that is, a chaotic, uninformed, thrashing, sound-bite form of criticism—carries an extremely high price: either the criticism will be disregarded for its vacuousness (thereby giving yet more influence and less accountability to the institutions being criticized) or the criticism will trigger action that will later prove completely ineffective or even counterproductive in dealing with problems that underlie the criticisms. In short, smart and careful criticism neither defeats itself nor throws out the baby with the bath water. Ill-informed and careless criticism can do both.

IV. LEGAL ANGLE AND IDEOLOGICAL PERSPECTIVE

The GEOs are legal persons. They operate under charters that are multilateral treaties. They are subjects of international law and are subject to international law. As a legal matter, they are what their member states make them or allow them to become.[8] Great thought and energy, tempered with considerable compromise, went into creating their charters, and one of the

---

[8] Numerous explanations are available regarding the legal nature and status of public international organizations. Among these are books by Schermers and Kirgis, listed in the Bibliography.

most effective ways of both criticizing their current behavior and charting their future is to examine them from a legal angle. For example, in handling disputes with deep environmental implications, has the WTO correctly interpreted its charter provisions? Does the World Bank's shift toward poverty reduction, despite the absence of any reference to "poverty" in either the IBRD charter or the IDA charter, amount to *ultra vires* action? Does international law require the IMF to practice some sort of "symmetry in adjustment" so that rich member countries who do not borrow from the institution must hew to the same economic and financial policies that the IMF requires of countries that do borrow?

These are all legal questions, and in this book I shall take a legal angle in scrutinizing the GEOs and in assessing the criticisms leveled at them. With a few exceptions, I shall eschew an assessment of the GEOs on economic grounds—for example, on whether the specific IMF-imposed economic and financial policy conditions helped or hindered Asian countries in handling the Asian financial crisis. More important in that context, I believe, are such legal questions as whether the IMF exceeded its charter provisions in striding in so boldly to that crisis, and whether the IMF system of governance (established, of course, by its charter) provides adequately for participation by affected populations in the process by which decisions affecting them are made.

As mentioned above, I intend for this to be a useful and competent arm's-length evaluation of the main criticisms directed at the GEOs. I believe my own background of experience with several of these institutions[9] makes it possible for me to achieve this. But perhaps no evaluation, however competent and arm's-length it may try to be, emerges from an entirely unbiased perspective. In any event, this one does not, and I should explain my own perspective in examining the GEOs.

I am an internationalist, in the sense that I believe international cooperative efforts—through multilateral organizations, agreements, and initiatives—hold the best hope for civilization to navigate through the difficulties of our current age, and, in the long run, offer the only hope for humanity itself to survive. I believe the world benefitted greatly from the explosive enthusiasm that emerged in favor of multilateralism in the 1940s, when delegates from many countries created the United Nations and the Bretton Woods institutions, approved the Universal Declaration of Human Rights, outlawed genocide and war crimes, and set in motion numerous other initiatives that bore fruit in the decades that followed. And in a post-9/11 world, I believe multilateral efforts are even more important than ever.[10]

---

[9] *See* "About the Author" at the beginning of the book.

[10] For an expression of these views, *see* John W. Head, *Essay: What Has Not Changed*

V. OVERVIEW OF THE CRITICISMS

In order to study the cacophony of criticisms leveled against the GEOs—that is, to bring some order out of the chaos—I have distilled them all into 25 key complaints or assertions. Of these, seven apply to the IMF, 12 to the MDBs, and six to the WTO. A few criticisms (such as the "secrecy and opaqueness" and the "democracy deficit" criticisms) apply to more than one institution or class of institution but are enumerated separately for purposes of analysis. I have also divided the criticisms into two broad categories, which I refer to under the headings of (1) the "policies and operations" of the institution(s) under attack and (2) the "character, control, and reach" of the institution(s) under attack.

Detailed descriptions of the criticisms leveled at the GEOs will appear in later chapters. For purposes of this introductory chapter, I offer the following brief enumeration. The list here indicates the numbering system I use throughout this book for easy reference to the criticisms.

- *Criticisms of the IMF*

  IMF policies and operations

  Criticism #I-1— *Bad medicine.* "The IMF prescribes economic and financial policies that fail to cure, and that indeed often make sicker, its borrowing member countries and the entire world economy."

  Criticism #I-2— *Distributional and social injustice.* "The economic and financial policies that the IMF insists on create distributional inequities and ignore the social aspects of a country's well-being."

  Criticism #I-3— *IMF trampling of national sovereignty.* "In imposing conditionality on its loans, the IMF tramples on national sovereignty—not just in economics but increasingly in other areas of state autonomy."

  Character, control, and reach of the IMF

  Criticism #I-4— *IMF secrecy and opaqueness.* "The IMF is a closed, nontransparent organization that operates in secret, despite its insistence on transparency in the governments of its members."

  Criticism #I-5— *The IMF democracy deficit.* "Controlled by a handful of rich countries, the IMF is an unaccountable autoc-

Since September 11—The Benefits of Multilateralism, 12 KAN. J.L. & PUB. POL'Y 1, 10 (2002) (criticizing the unilateralism of the George W. Bush administration in dealing with Iraq and urging that "the United States should do what it takes to stay on the road of multilateralism . . . [which] constitutes our best hope of beating back the darkness that we saw come so vividly and menacingly on September 11").

racy in which the people most affected by its operations have far too little chance to participate."

Criticism #I-6— *IMF mission creep.* "As both a legal and a practical matter, the IMF has overstepped its authority and its competence in providing bailouts and adopting policies on a proliferation of topics."

Criticism #I-7— *Asymmetry in obligations.* "The IMF permits its rich member countries to insist that the poor borrowing member countries follow certain policies without pressuring the rich countries to follow those policies themselves."

• *Criticisms of the MDBs*

MDB policies and operations

Criticism #II-1— *Bad economic and financial policies and projects.* "The MDBs promote a flawed laissez-faire economic model, conceive of 'development' too narrowly, and support bad projects that do not help the borrowing member countries."

Criticism #II-2— *Wrong form of financial assistance.* "MDB lending operations are anachronistic now that effective international capital markets exist; so MDB financing (if continued at all) should take the form of grants, not loans."

Criticism #II-3— *Environmental degradation.* "MDB-financed projects too often have devastating effects on the environment, because the MDBs disregard environmental issues at both the project design and project implementation phases."

Criticism #II-4— *Human rights shortcomings.* "The MDBs largely disregard human rights issues and act independently of any accepted human rights norms and institutions; and the MDBs fuel, not fight, public corruption."

Criticism #II-5— *MDB trampling of national sovereignty.* "In imposing conditions on the rights of member countries to borrow, the MDBs violate the sovereignty of those countries, and in particular the principle of self-determination."

Criticism #II-6— *Incoherence in policy prescriptions.* "Because there is inadequate coordination among the MDBs—and also between the MDBs and other GEOs—countries can be subject to conflicting economic and financial mandates."

Criticism #II-7— *Weaknesses in staffing and management.* "The MDBs are poorly managed, in part because (i) staff members are not properly accountable for their performance and (ii) staff hiring and promotion rest on inappropriate criteria."

Character, control, and reach of the MDBs

Criticism #II-8— *MDB secrecy and opaqueness.* "The MDBs practice both documentary secretiveness and operational secretiveness, thereby remaining inappropriately hidden from scrutiny and insulated from external criticism."

Criticism #II-9— *The MDB democracy deficit.* "Controlled by a handful of rich countries and corporate interests, the MDBs are largely unaccountable to the people most affected by their operations."

Criticism #II-10—*Narrowness of economic focus.* "The MDBs interpret their charter mandates too rigidly by considering only strictly economic factors in assessing the development needs of their member countries and in designing projects."

Criticism #II-11—*MDB mission creep.* "The MDBs are gripped by 'policy proliferation'; they have diluted their commitment to true economic development by expanding their operations into areas in which they have no authority or competence."

Criticism #II-12—*Asymmetry in obligations.* "As in the IMF, the MDBs' rich member countries insist that the poor borrowing member countries follow certain policies, yet the rich countries can (and often do) fail to follow those policies themselves."

• **Criticisms of the WTO**

WTO policies and operations

Criticism #III-1— *Free trade's fostering of economic harm.* "The WTO's central aim is wrong, because free trade does more economic harm than good to a national society and to the world as a whole."

Criticism #III-2— *Free trade's distributional injustice.* "Even if free trade brings aggregate economic benefits, those benefits are not fairly distributed, either within a national economic system or among nations; and the WTO permits this injustice."

Criticism #III-3— *Free trade's race to the bottom.* "The WTO's free-trade agenda is wrong also because free trade causes a 'race to the bottom' in the regulatory standards for labor (worker safety and health) and environmental protection."

Criticism #III-4— *WTO disregard for labor and environmental values.* "Even if free trade does not in itself cause a race to the bottom, the WTO fails to give adequate attention to environmental and labor concerns in its operations."

Character, control, and reach of the WTO

Criticism #III-5— *WTO secrecy and opaqueness.* "The WTO is a closed, non-transparent organization that operates in secret, inappropriately hidden from scrutiny and hence insulated from external criticism."

Criticism #III-6— *The WTO democracy deficit.* "The WTO is undemocratic, both (i) in excluding participation by citizens and (ii) in having no allegiance to political authorities—and hence can impose its will arbitrarily on its member countries."

VI. SYNOPSIS OF MY VIEWS AND PRESCRIPTIONS

My evaluation of each of the key criticisms enumerated above appears in Chapters Three (IMF), Four (MDBs), and Five (WTO). In Chapter Six the focus broadens again when I give (1) a wrap-up regarding the criticisms and (2) some observations about the future of the GEOs in general. As a preview to the conclusions and prescriptions found in all four of those chapters, I offer the following points in synopsis:

Wheat and chaff. First, after separating the wheat from the chaff, I conclude that all of the GEOs have been criticized fairly in several respects. The "democracy deficit" criticism that has been leveled at all of the GEOs, for example, packs a punch when applied to all of them, although for somewhat different reasons, and should be addressed by those institutions and their member countries. Likewise, criticisms focusing on environmental protection have validity, especially as applied to the WTO and the MDBs; and similar criticisms alleging distributional and social injustice get traction when leveled against all the GEOs. By contrast, I largely dismiss several of the key criticisms, including the "mission creep" and "trampling of national sovereignty" complaints directed at some or all of the GEOs.

Proposed reforms. In order to respond to the valid criticism, the GEOs and their member countries should undertake reforms. These include some policy changes and some charter amendments aimed at shifting priorities, providing more accountability, and modernizing the institutions in various ways that will reflect contemporary views and values on issues ranging from participatory decisionmaking to environmental protection to human rights to competence in government. In addition, these efforts to reform and update the GEOs should, in my view, reflect a broader ideological renaissance—a reaffirmation of, and rededication to, multilateral solutions to global economic challenges. Such initiatives will both recognize and support the historical trends of the past sixty to eighty years; and viewed more broadly, this ideological renaissance will offer an opportunity to improve and modernize our view of how this planet should be organized and governed in the 21st century. Little of this is possible, however, without enlightened leadership, or at least intelligent acquiescence, from the United States.

CHAPTER TWO

FOUNDATIONS AND KEY FEATURES OF THE GEOs

I. HISTORICAL SURVEY

This chapter aims to provide a condensed description of the GEOs that are the subject of the criticisms being assessed in this book: the IMF, the five multilateral development banks (counting the IBRD and the IDA as a single bank), and the WTO. As indicated above in Section III of Chapter One, such a description requires at least a brief historical account, as the character and operations of these institutions simply cannot be understood without an appreciation for how and why they have developed over time. Accordingly, I begin in this Section I with a historical synopsis that sweeps all of the GEOs into a single story, before turning (in the later sections of this chapter) to a more detailed account (still somewhat simplified) of each institution.

A. GEO Timeline

The following timeline offers a chronological enumeration of some important dates in the founding and development of the GEOs. (Several of these dates, and some of the key trends they reflect, will then be developed in the text that follows the timeline.) In order to identify the three separate threads of the IMF, the MDBs, and the WTO, I have preceded each textual entry in the timeline with a notation of "EP" (economic policy, the principal focus of the IMF today), "TR" (trade regulation, the principal focus of the WTO), and "DF" (development financing, the principal focus of the MDBs).

1944 • [EP] Chartering of the IMF at the Bretton Woods conference

• [DF] Chartering of the IBRD at the Bretton Woods conference

1945 • [EP] IMF Charter enters into force

• [DF] IBRD Charter enters into force

1947 • [TR] Adoption of the GATT

• [TR] Completion of the Havana Charter, to establish the ITO— an effort later abandoned

- [EP] IMF begins operations by providing financial credit to France

1952 • [EP] IMF establishes standards and procedures for stand-by arrangements

1959 • [DF] IADB Charter adopted

1960 • [DF] IDA Charter adopted

- [TR] GATT Council created to act between the sessions of the GATT contracting parties and to act as their delegate in decisionmaking

1962 • [TR] Conclusion of the Dillon Round of GATT-sponsored trade negotiations

1963 • [DF] AfDB Charter adopted

1965 • [DF] AsDB Charter adopted

- [TR] GATT amended to add Part IV ("Trade and Development")

1967 • [TR] Conclusion of the Kennedy Round of GATT-sponsored trade negotiations

1968 • [EP] First Amendment to IMF Charter approved, to create SDRs

1969 • [EP] First Amendment to IMF Charter enters into force

1971 • [EP] Par value system collapses when US informs IMF that it will no longer freely buy and sell gold to settle international transactions

- [TR] GATT parties approve establishment of a Generalized System of Preferences, via a temporary-waiver decision (formalized in 1979)

1974 • [EP] IMF establishes Extended Fund Facility ("EFF") to provide medium-term financing to members (longer term than stand-by arrangements)

1977 • [EP] IMF holds gold auction and transfers proceeds to Trust Fund to benefit LDCs

1978 • [EP] IMF Second Amendment enters into force

- [EP] Final stand-by arrangements with industrialized countries

1979 • [TR] Conclusion of the Tokyo Round of GATT-sponsored trade negotiations

- [TR] GATT parties approve decision on differential and favorable treatment for LDCs, formalizing the Generalized System of Preferences

1981 • [EP] IMF starts using simplified basket of five currencies to set SDR value—U.S. dollar, deutsche mark, French franc, Japanese yen, and pound sterling

1982 • [EP] Debt crisis erupts with announcements by Mexico and Brazil of serious problems servicing their foreign debt

1986 • [EP] IMF establishes Structural Adjustment Facility (SAF) to provide concessional (low-cost) financing for LDCs

1987 • [EP] IMF establishes Enhanced Structural Adjustment Facility (ESAF) to expand its concessional financing for LDCs

1990 • [EP] Third Amemdment to IMF Charter approved, authorizing suspension of voting rights

• [DF] EBRD Charter adopted

• [TR] GATT panel issues *Tuna-Dolphin* decision

1992 • [EP] Third Amendment to IMF Charter enters into force

• [EP] Procedures start for bringing former Soviet Republics into IMF membership

1993 • [TR] Conclusion of the Uruguay Round of GATT-sponsored trade negotiations

1994 • [TR] GATT-1994, WTO Charter, and other Uruguay Round treaties enter into force

1995 • [EP] IMF approves largest-to-date stand-by arrangement—SDR 12.1 billion for Mexico

• [TR] WTO starts operations

1996 • [EP] IMF approves largest-to-date EFF arrangement—SDR 6.9 billion to Russia

1997 • [EP] IMF approves procedure for making public the IMF's views on members' economic and financial policies following Article IV consultations

• [EP] Asian financial crisis erupts, beginning with Thailand and spreading to Indonesia and Korea

• [EP] IMF approves largest-to-date stand-by arrangement—SDR 15.5 billion for Korea

1998 • [EP] Euro is adopted as a common currency by eleven European countries

1999 • [EP] Quotas of member countries in the IMF are increased (the most recent of several such increases) to SDR 212 billion

- [EP] The IMF's ESAF is transformed into the Poverty Reduction and Growth Facility (PRGF)

- [TR] WTO ministerial conference in Seattle attracts thousands of street protestors criticizing WTO policies and economic globalization generally

2000 • [EP] IMF approves establishment of Independent Evaluation Office (IEO)

2001 • [TR] Doha Round of WTO-sponsored trade negotiations begins

2003 • [TR] WTO ministerial conference in Cancún collapses, partly over disagreements on agricultural subsidies

2004 • [TR] WTO delegates approve proposal for further reducing agricultural subsidies

B. The Inter-War Period and Bretton Woods

Perhaps 1944 is the most important year in the history of the GEOs because it marks the birth of the first of those institutions. Indeed, it is with that year that I started the above chronological GEO timeline. However, it is in the three decades just preceding 1944 that the main roots of these institutions can be found. It is worth recounting briefly what those roots are and what emerged from them in 1944.

The history of international organizations—or at any rate of those that can be regarded as forerunners of the GEOs—is a short one. I consider that history to have started in about 1920. Although the first true public international organizations (having nation-states as members) are typically regarded as the International Telegraphic (now Telecommunications) Union and the Universal Postal Union, formed in 1865 and 1874, respectively,[1] the two public international organization established following World War I—the League of Nations and the International Labour Organization (ILO)—stand out as setting the stage for the creation of numerous international organizations following World War II. Although the League had failed to meet its aim of "achiev[ing] international peace and security,"[2] its mere creation was significant because of the breadth of issues that

---

[1] For a brief account of the history of international organizations, *see* John W. Head, *Supranational Law: How the Move Toward Multilateral Solutions Is Changing the Character of "International" Law*, 42 U. KAN. L. REV. 605, 621–32 (1994) [hereinafter *Supranational Law*]. For more extensive accounts, including a discussion of the importance of international conferences, beginning especially in the 19th century, *see* MARK JANIS, AN INTRODUCTION TO INTERNATIONAL LAW 199–207 (4th ed. 2003); MALCOLM N. SHAW, INTERNATIONAL LAW 587–89 (2d ed. 1986).

[2] Covenant of the League of Nations, preamble. The Covenant of the League of

its founding states empowered it to handle. The ILO had a narrower scope but has had a longer life; and it can be regarded as the first major successful international economic organization, as it deals with issues arising directly out of the great economic and industrial revolutions of the late 1800s and early 1900s—labor standards and conditions.

Against this institutional backdrop—that is, the 1920s experimentation with important international organizations—must be set the economic conditions that developed in the years just following the conclusion of World War I. They were difficult times. They were marked by two national economic policy trends that help explain the proposals made at Bretton Woods and beyond. First, the major states engaged in competitive raising of tariff barriers. A tariff is a tax on the importation of an article from one country into another. Such taxes can have two main effects and purposes: (1) to raise revenue for the state imposing the tariff and (2) to protect the domestic industry in that state against competition from goods produced in another state, by making the imported goods more expensive for consumers in the state imposing the tariff on those goods. In the 1920s, many states raised the levels of their tariffs. A premier example is the United States, which in the Smoot-Hawley Tariff Act of 1930 required that tariffs be paid on imported goods in amounts equivalent to 60 percent, 80 percent, and even 100 percent of the commercial value of those goods.[3]

Such high tariffs tended to stifle international trade. So did the other main national economic policy trend that became popular in the years following World War I: competitive devaluations of national currencies. Official measures by a national government to reduce the value of that state's currency against the currencies of other countries typically has the effect of making imported items more expensive for the subjects of the devaluing state and making items exported from that state more attractively priced for subjects of other states against whose currencies the exporting state's currency has been devalued. Several states engaged in the practice of currency devaluation in order to gain these short-term advantages in the terms of trade with other countries. Such currency practices, and others, provided a drag on trade among states.

By the 1940s, both of these two economic policy trends that had emerged in the inter-war years—competitive raising of tariff barriers and competitive devaluations of currencies—were regarded by many econo-

---

Nations, which came into force on January 10, 1920, constitutes Part I of the Treaty of Versailles, June 28, 1919, 225 Consol. T.S. 188, 195. M.J. BOWMAN & D.J. HARRIS, MULTI- LATERAL TREATIES: INDEX AND CURRENT STATUS 37–39 (1984).

[3] Tariff Act of 1930 (June 17, 1930), 46 Stat. 672–763, codified at 19 U.S.C. §§ 1001–1654 (1934 ed.).

mists and political leaders as dangerous to world economic stability, and therefore to the peace that was to be sought after the conclusion of World War II. Similar danger was seen in another reality brought on by the war itself: much of Europe's infrastructure had been destroyed. Such destruction had also occurred in World War I, and the reparations demands placed on Germany after that war were blamed by many people for the economic and political meltdown that had permitted Hitler and Nazism to rise and flourish.

In short, by the early 1940s, a general view had coalesced among influential policymakers that three international economic problems had to be addressed in a post-war world, in order to prevent a third world war from following on the heels of the second as quickly as the second had followed on the heels of the first. These economic problems related to (1) tariff barriers to trade among states, (2) manipulation of currency values, and (3) the economic distress of Europe. Expressed from a more general and more positive perspective, those policymakers saw it as necessary (1) to encourage international trade by reducing tariff levels and other trade barriers, (2) to encourage international trade also by stabilizing and regulating national currency values, and (3) to foster economic and political stability in Europe by rebuilding its infrastructure quickly following the war.[4]

For each of these tasks, an international organization was envisioned. For trade regulation, an International Trade Organization (ITO) was to be established; it would prescribe and enforce rules to limit tariff and non-tariff barriers to trade among states. For currency matters, the International Monetary Fund (IMF) was to be established; it would prescribe and enforce rules to stabilize currency rates and encourage currency convertibility among states. For rebuilding Europe, the International Bank for Reconstruction and Development (IBRD) was to be established; it would serve as a financial intermediary between investors in countries with wealth (mainly the United States following World War II) and the reconstruction projects in Europe.

The latter two of these two organizations—the IMF and the IBRD—were created at the July 1944 Bretton Woods conference, in the sense that their charters were drafted and approved by the delegates at that conference. Both of these charters, titled "Articles of Agreement," took the form of treaties that were later formally ratified by most of the states represented

---

[4] For further discussion of this point, *see* sources cited in Head, *Supranational Law, supra* note 1, at 630. As I expressed it there, "[t]o avoid another world war, the theory went, would require a new international economic order with (i) a multilateral system of binding rules governing international trade, (ii) a stable monetary system with predictable exchange rates and (iii) a financing system to channel the post-war wealth of the United States into profitable overseas investments." *Id.* at 630 n.156.

at the conference. The IMF Charter,[5] once it gained such formal ratification, entered into force in late December 1945, and an inaugural meeting of the Board of Governors took place in March of the following year. The IBRD Charter[6] also entered into force in late December 1945 on gaining the requisite number of ratifications.

The ITO was not established, either in 1944 or in the years immediately following. As explained below, the United States declined to agree to that organization's proposed charter, called the Havana Charter, and the gap created by the absence of the ITO was partially filled by the General Agreement on Tariffs and Trade (GATT).

C. The First 25 Years: 1945 to 1970

Just as the quarter-century preceding 1944 contains the roots of the GEOs, so the quarter-century just following that year contains the main branches of the institutions. Whereas only two GEOs—the IBRD and the IMF—existed as of 1945 (when the charter of each institution entered into force as a formal matter of international law with the requisite number of ratifications), by 1970 four more were in place. As shown above on the GEO timeline, these institutions were the International Development Association, the African Development Bank, the Inter-American Development Bank, and the Asian Development Bank.[7] These will be described more fully below, in Section III of this chapter.

In addition to these international organizations, another quasi-organization had come into existence—the GATT. As explained above, and as reflected in the above GEO timeline, the international organization that was envisioned for regulating international trade policy was the ITO; but plans to establish the ITO were aborted in the late 1940s, when the United States (for political reasons related to the Cold War) declined to agree to the Havana Charter that would have created the ITO.[8] In its stead, the

---

[5] Articles of Agreement of the International Monetary Fund, July 22, 1944, 60 Stat. 1401, 2 U.N.T.S. 39 (entered into force Dec. 27, 1945) [hereinafter Original IMF Charter]. For details on the three amendments that have been made to the Original IMF Charter, *see infra* note 12.

[6] Articles of Agreement of the International Bank for Reconstruction and Development, July 22, 1944, 60 Stat. 1440, 2 U.N.T.S. 134 (entered into force Dec. 27, 1945) [hereinafter Original IBRD Charter]. For further information on the IBRD Charter, *see infra* note 43.

[7] Numerous other organizations were also formed in this period. Among them was the International Finance Corporation (IFC), closely associated with the IBRD and the IDA. For reasons noted in Section II of Chapter One, the IFC is not a subject of significant attention in this book.

[8] Among the various reasons that have been cited for this rejection of the Havana

General Agreement on Tariffs and Trade, originally simply a treaty intended to govern the transitional period leading to the existence of the ITO, took on the trappings of an international organization itself, without such status as a formal matter. In this capacity the GATT served as the triggering influence for several rounds of negotiations among the GATT parties regarding tariff levels and other aspects of trading rules and procedures.

Another noteworthy feature of the first quarter-century of the GEOs relates specifically to the IBRD. That institution's assignment to help rebuild Europe, by serving as a financial intermediary for relatively rich investors (mainly in the United States), was, in effect, withdrawn from it only a few years after the Bretton Woods conference, when (among other things) the task of rebuilding Europe was assumed by the Marshall Plan initiated under the Truman Administration in the United States. Accordingly, the IBRD shifted its attention away from the "R" in its title (for reconstruction) and toward the "D" in its title (for the development of LDC economies), so that by the mid-1950s its new operations concentrated predominantly on the developing world.[9]

In sum, the period from 1945 to 1970 saw the IBRD and the IMF begin their operations, saw the establishment of most of the other MDBs (only the European Bank for Reconstruction and Development belongs to a later era), saw the GATT assume many of the responsibilities for trade regulation (despite its lack of institutional stature), and saw also the building of momentum and experience of all these organizations. For the most part, the organizations attracted little attention among the public at large, at least in the developed countries, before 1970.

D. Themes from 1970 to Today

As the above GEO timeline indicates, those institutions have undergone enormous change in the past three and a half decades. Some of the details of those changes are explained below in Sections II, III, and IV of

---

Charter is one that is particularly pertinent to some recommendations I make later in this book: that the Havana Charter contained what was regarded as too broad a range of goals besides trade liberalization—goals reflected in provisions relating to full employment, fair labor standards, double taxation, cooperation with the IMF, restrictive business practices, and commodity agreements. *See* Steve Charnovitz, *Linking Topics in Treaties*, appearing as Chapter 1 in STEVE CHARNOVITZ, TRADE LAW AND GLOBAL GOVERNANCE (2002), at 14 (citing William Diebold, *Reflections on the International Trade Organization*, 14 N. ILL. U. L. REV. 335 (1994)). For my recommendations on linkages of treaty obligations, *see infra* Subsection IVB of Chapter Three, Subsection IVF of Chapter Four, and Subsection IVB of Chapter Five.

[9] For a lucid account of the early years of the World Bank, *see* RICHARD PEET, UNHOLY TRINITY: THE IMF, WORLD BANK AND WTO 113–20 (2003).

this chapter. However, a few themes are worth noting in this overview. The first theme is the growing public awareness of, and concern over, the GEOs. Whereas the GEOs conducted their early lives largely outside public scrutiny or even public interest, they now find themselves constantly in the popular consciousness. The past decade in particular has seen the crescendo of criticisms that are the subject of this book. Why? In large part because the institutions have been called on to expand their operations; and this is a second theme of these years since 1970. For example, the World Bank's initiative in the 1960s in enlarging its focus to accommodate (through cheap "concessional" IDA loans) the rise of new countries following decolonization was to serve as a model for the other GEOs in the decades that followed. Now all the GEOs involved in financial assistance provide concessional financing; and when the LDC debt crisis broke out in 1982, the IMF took a lead role in handling it. In doing so, the IMF took a new lease on life after having been placed in an awkward position just a decade earlier with the collapse of the par value system.

As these dramatic changes were taking place in the areas of international development and the international monetary system, the international trading system was likewise undergoing a transformation. Trade flows increased dramatically, raising the profile of trading rules, and these ultimately resulted in two rounds of trade negotiations—the Tokyo Round ending in 1979 and the Uruguay Round ending in 1993—that created a score of binding rules as well as a new institution, the World Trade Organization. In all these ways, which will be detailed below in the later sections of this chapter, the GEOs gained prominence and influence, and attracted scrutiny, as never before.

A third theme and a fourth theme emerging from the last few decades of GEO developments both revolve around the concept of the nation-state. The third theme is this: the GEOs have been involved in the painful dance between rich countries and poor countries—that is, the handful of industrially developed nations and the vast majority of LDCs—that has occupied the attention of political and economic leaders since the mid-1960s when scores of new countries emerged from colonial rule. This is often referred to as the tension between the "North" and the "South," as reflected arrestingly in the title of a report published in 1980 on international development issues.[10] A fourth theme I see emerging from the past four decades also relates to countries and their status: the GEOs, along with multinational corporations, have gained in economic power so dramatically in this period of time that they tend to eclipse many nation-states in influence,

---

[10] *See The Report of the Independent Commission on International Development Issues Under the Chairmanship of Willy Brandt,* published as NORTH-SOUTH: A PROGRAM FOR SURVIVAL (1980). For a discussion of the terms "North" and "South," *see id.* at 31.

shaking the foundations of a system of political organization that has existed on this planet since about the mid-1600s.

Exactly what I mean by these four themes—relating respectively to how GEOs have attracted critical attention, how they have expanded their operations and influence, how they bear on the growing tensions between rich developed countries and LDCs, and what they portend for the future of the nation-state—will become clearer, I hope, in the following sections of this chapter; and I shall return to some of these themes again in Chapter Six. I invite the reader to watch for these themes to emerge as I sketch a series of "nutshell" pictures of the main GEOs.

II. THE IMF IN A NUTSHELL[11]

A. Establishment of the IMF and the Par Value System

The IMF, formed near the close of World War II along lines proposed by leading U.S. and U.K. economists and politicians, was originally designed to manage a system of fixed exchange rates. Under that system, currencies of all (or most) countries were to be made freely convertible, and the values of the currencies would be unchangeable, except within a narrow range or with prior IMF approval.[12] This system was favored by the

---

[11] This summary of the IMF is drawn from my recent article evaluating criticisms leveled at the IMF. *See* John W. Head, *Seven Deadly Sins: An Assessment of Criticisms Directed at the International Monetary Fund*, 52 U. KAN. L. REV. 521, 525–30 (2004). For more extensive footnote citations to authority, please see that article and sources listed in the Bibliography to this book. General information on the IMF also can be found in the annual IMF Survey Supplement issued, usually each September, by the IMF. In addition, both detailed and general information about the IMF and its activities is available in its annual report, available for recent years on the IMF's website, www.imf.org.

[12] The rules governing the original system of fixed exchange rates were set forth in the IMF Charter as adopted at the Bretton Woods Conference in 1944. *See* Original IMF Charter, *supra* note 5. The IMF Charter has been amended three times, as explained in my 1993 article on the IMF. *See* John W. Head, *Suspension of Debtor Countries' Voting Rights in the IMF: An Assessment of the Third Amendment to the IMF Charter*, 33 VA. J. INT'L L. 591, 592 nn.2–3 (1993) [hereinafter *Third Amendment*]. The first amendment, which dates from the late 1960s, introduced the special drawing right (SDR). *See* Amendment of Articles of Agreement of the International Monetary Fund, approved May 31, 1968, 22 U.S.T. 2775, 726 U.N.T.S. 266 (entered into force July 28, 1969). For an explanation of the SDR, *see infra* note 17 and accompanying text. A second amendment to the IMF Charter, much more far-reaching than the first, was adopted in the late 1970s. *See* Second Amendment to the Articles of Agreement of the International Monetary Fund, approved Apr. 30, 1976, 29 U.S.T. 2203, T.I.A.S. No. 8937, 15 I.L.M. 546 (entered into force Apr. 1, 1978). The third and most recent amendment to the Charter, which took effect in 1992, added a new sanction that could be imposed on a member country for failing to pay its arrears to the IMF. *See* Third Amendment of the Articles of Agreement of the International Monetary Fund, approved June 28, 1990, 31 I.L.M. 1307, 1309–10 (entered into force Nov. 11, 1992). A proposed fourth amendment, under which a special one-

countries that formed and joined the IMF because predictability in the convertibility and value of currencies would help foster trade, which itself was seen as a means of improving the international economy and, ultimately, of contributing toward peaceful relations. The fixed-value system of currency exchange rates was particularly attractive compared with the circumstances of the inter-war period (discussed above in Section IB of this chapter), in which countries competitively manipulated the values of their currencies in an effort to gain short-term trade advantages.

In order to make the system work, the IMF Charter authorized the IMF to make short-term loans available to member countries having temporary balance-of-payments difficulties,[13] as could occur when a bad crop year reduced a country's export revenues. The IMF used this authority when necessary, and the United States borrowed from the IMF for that reason as recently as the late 1970s.

B.   Collapse of the Par Value System and a Redirected IMF

The par value system of fixed exchange rates broke down in the early 1970s when the United States announced that it would no longer abide by some of its IMF Charter obligations on currency convertibility. The IMF's members radically amended the IMF Charter accordingly,[14] and the IMF's operations were correspondingly reduced. However, when the 1982 debt crisis broke out (upon the announcements by Mexico and Brazil that they would no longer be able to service their debt obligations), the IMF took a lead role that has set the stage for its operations ever since. Now its credit operations (some of which are not technically loans but coincident unilateral undertakings) focus mostly on member countries with persistent balance-of-payments problems, and occasionally on responding to crises that threaten the international monetary system as a whole. The Asian financial

---

time allocation of SDRs would take place, has not yet become effective. *See* INTERNATIONAL MONETARY FUND, ANNUAL REPORT 2003 (2003) [hereinafter IMF ANNUAL REPORT 2003], at 75. All references hereinafter to the IMF Charter reflect the text as it stands following the third amendment, unless otherwise specified. It is that form of the IMF Charter that appears as Appendix B to this book.

[13]   *See* IMF Charter, art. I(v) and art. V, § 3(a).

[14]   Perhaps the most important change appeared in Article IV of the charter. In its original formulation, Article IV provided for the establishment of a par value (expressed in terms of gold or U.S. dollars) for each member country's currency and prohibited a country from changing or departing from such par value by more than 1 percent (in most cases) without IMF approval. After the amendments of the late 1970s, Article IV permitted each member country to establish exchange arrangements of its choice and merely required a member to notify the IMF of its decision in that regard. For the text of Article IV in its original formulation, *see* STEPHEN ZAMORA & RONALD A. BRAND, I BASIC DOCUMENTS OF INTERNATIONAL ECONOMIC LAW 387 (1990).

crisis of the late 1990s is an example of the latter; the IMF lent unprece-dented amounts of money to Thailand, Indonesia, and Korea to stop that crisis from spreading further in Asia and elsewhere.

C. IMF Financing

The IMF has several different mechanisms or facilities by which it pro-vides financing to its member countries. The most common type is a stand-by arrangement (first used in 1952), under which the IMF assures a member country that it can draw up to a specified amount of money, usu-ally over 12 to 18 months, to deal with a short-term balance of payments problem. Closely related to the stand-by arrangement is funding through the Extended Fund Facility (dating from 1974), which allows a member country to draw up to a specified amount over a longer term—usually three or four years—to help it tackle structural economic problems that are caus-ing weaknesses in its balance of payments.[15] A third source of IMF financ-ing is the Poverty Reduction and Growth Facility, which gives low-interest financing to help the poorest member countries facing protracted balance of payments problems. This facility, created in 1999, replaced the earlier Enhanced Structural Adjustment Facility created in 1987, and, like that ear-lier facility, is financed with resources raised through past sales of IMF-owned gold and with loans and grants provided to the IMF for this purpose, mainly by wealthy countries. A fourth source is the Supplemental Reserve Facility (created in 1997), which provides additional short-term financing to a member country experiencing exceptional balance of pay-ments difficulty because of a sudden and disruptive loss of market confi-dence reflected in capital outflows—as was the case in the Asian financial crisis of the late 1990s. And a fifth source, also of recent origin, is the Contingent Credit Line (dating from 1999), by which the IMF provides a precautionary line of defense enabling a member country that is pursuing strong economic policies to obtain financing on a short-term basis when

---

[15] It is perhaps worth pointing out that IMF financing under a stand-by arrangement or under an extended (EFF) arrangement does not, technically and legally speaking, take the form of a loan. Instead, it consists of exchanges of currencies according to a pair of legally free-standing unilateral commitments—one by the IMF and one by the country. If, for example, the IMF approves a stand-by arrangement for Gabon, that coun-try is authorized, subject to certain conditions, to purchase from the IMF a specified amount of hard currency using Gabon's own currency. Gabon is then required to reverse the transaction not later than a specified date by repurchasing its own currency with hard currency. For further details in this regard, and an explanation of the notion of "hard currency" in this context, *see* John W. Head, *Third Amendment, supra* note 12, at 594–96. An excellent early description of stand-by arrangements was provided by Sir Joseph Gold, the person whose service to and scholarship regarding the IMF makes him even today, several years after his death, the foremost authority on the institution. *See generally* Joseph Gold, *The Law and Practice of the International Monetary Fund With Respect to "Stand-By Arrangements,"* 12 INT'L & COMP. L.Q. 1 (1963).

faced by a sudden and disruptive loss of market confidence because of contagion from difficulties in other countries. The IMF also has some other less-used financing mechanisms.

D. IMF Conditionality

In providing financing to its members under the various mechanisms and facilities enumerated above, the IMF almost always engages in "conditionality." Under conditionality, the IMF disburses money to a borrowing country only on a piecemeal basis (rather than in a single lump sum) and only if the country can demonstrate that certain economic and financial policies that the borrowing country's government committed to in advance with the IMF are, in fact, being implemented and having the desired results. The types of policies that IMF conditionality often focuses on include such rather obvious things as (1) a reduction in government spending and foreign borrowing, (2) regulation of the money supply to stop or forestall inflation, and (3) steps to strengthen banking supervision in order to protect depositors from being bilked out of their savings by dishonest or incompetent bank managers.

Conditionality also can, depending on the circumstances, reflect policies for liberalizing a country's trade and investment laws, encouraging privatization of government-owned entities or operations, and strengthening tax laws and collection—all with an eye to improving a country's overall economic stability and performance. Since the late 1990s, "in growing recognition of the adverse impact of poor governance (and the resulting corruption) on economic efficiency and growth, the IMF has turned its attention to a broader range of institutional reforms and governance issues in the reform programs it supports,"[16] and therefore in its use of conditionality. Measures to improve governance include strengthening legal frameworks and applying international standards of accounting and auditing.

E. IMF Resources

Where does the IMF get the money to make its loans? Mainly from a pool of resources formed by its members' subscriptions to the IMF's capital. The level of each member's subscription is equal to its "quota" in the

---

[16] THOMAS WOLF & EMINE GÜRGEN, IMPROVING GOVERNANCE AND FIGHTING CORRUPTION IN THE BALTIC AND CIS COUNTRIES 8–9 (Int'l Monetary Fund, Economic Issues No. 21, 2000), *available at* www.imf.org/external/pubs/ft/issues/issue21/index.htm (last visited Feb. 16, 2004). For the IMF guidelines in this area, *see* INTERNATIONAL MONETARY FUND, NEWS BRIEF NO. 97/15, IMF ADOPTS GUIDELINES REGARDING GOVERNANCE ISSUES 1 (Aug. 4, 1997), *available at* www.imf.org/external/np.sec/nb/1997/NB9715.htm (last visited Feb. 16, 2004). These governance guidelines are summarized in WOLF & GÜRGEN, *supra.*

IMF, and a member's quota—denominated in special drawing rights (SDRs) created by the IMF following the first amendment to the IMF Charter[17]—is largely determined by its economic and financial position relative to the other members. The United States, by virtue of its dominant economic strength in the world, has the largest quota, so its subscription to the IMF's capital is the largest. In addition to this source of capital, the IMF also maintains two standing borrowing arrangements with official lenders; but the IMF has not had to draw upon either of these arrangements for several years. Furthermore, the IMF is empowered to borrow from private markets but has not done so.

F. Other IMF Operations

The IMF does more than just make loans. Two other activities, in particular, warrant mention: surveillance and technical assistance. Although surveillance can take several forms, the most important form is that of country surveillance. The IMF conducts regular consultations, normally once a year, with each member country about its economic and financial policies. These consultations—referred to as "Article IV consultations" because they are required under Article IV of the IMF Charter[18]—typically culminate in the issuance of observations and recommendations by the IMF of each member country's economic and financial policy performance. In addition, of course, the IMF undertakes frequent monitoring of economic and financial factors in those countries that have borrowed funds from the IMF.

Technical assistance is another key feature of IMF operations that attracts little attention from the public at large. Representing about a quarter of the IMF's total administrative budget, IMF technical assistance helps member countries design and implement financial policies, draft and

---

[17] The SDR is an international reserve asset created in 1970 by the IMF following the first amendment to the IMF Charter, referred to *supra* note 12. The SDR is valued on the basis of a basket of key international currencies—currently the Euro (32 percent), the Japanese yen (18 percent), the pound sterling (11 percent), and the U.S. dollar (39 percent)—and serves as the unit of account of the IMF and a number of other international organizations. The SDR's value as a reserve asset derives from the commitments of member countries to hold and accept SDRs and to honor various obligations connected with the operations of the SDR system. The IMF allocates SDRs to its members in proportion to their IMF quotas. For further details, *see* INTERNATIONAL MONETARY FUND, IMF SURVEY SUPPLEMENT (2003) [hereinafter IMF SURVEY SUPPLEMENT 2003], *available at* www.imf.org/external/pubs/ft/survey/2003/091503.pdf (last visited Feb. 16, 2004).

[18] *See* IMF Charter, art. IV, § 3(b). This provision requires that the IMF "oversee the compliance of each member with its obligations" to work toward economic growth, price stability, and an orderly international monetary system, and that, to this end, the IMF adopt "principles for the guidance of all members" that respect "the domestic social and political policies of members." *Id.*

review legislation, and build institutional capacity. In fiscal year 2003, the IMF provided over 350 person-years of such technical assistance.[19]

G. IMF Structure and the Weighted Voting System

Understanding the structure of the IMF—that is, its system of internal governance, membership, capitalization, voting rights, and so forth—is essential to understanding and evaluating some of the key criticisms leveled against it. Overall authority over the IMF's activities is vested in a Board of Governors, which is composed of ministers of finance or heads of central banks from each of the IMF's members countries, of which there were 184 as of early 2005. The Governors gather officially as a body only once a year, as the day-to-day work of the IMF is conducted by a staff and a Managing Director acting under the supervision of the Executive Board. Under some changes initiated in late 1999 that will give "greater direct involvement of governments in the policy-making process" in the IMF,[20] a group of 24 Governors—the International Monetary and Financial Committee—gathers twice a year.[21] The Executive Board, based at the IMF's headquarters in Washington, D.C., consists of 24 Executive Directors appointed or elected by the IMF's member countries. The Executive Board meets about three times a week in formal session. At present five Executive Directors are appointed by the members with the largest IMF quotas—the United States, Japan, Germany, France, and the United Kingdom—and each of the other 19 Executive Directors is elected by one country or a group of countries. The Executive Board rarely makes its decisions on the basis of formal voting, relying instead on the formation of consensus among its members.

When formal voting is conducted, however, it reflects a "weighted voting" system that places most of the voting power in a handful of countries. A member country has, according to the IMF Charter, "two hundred fifty votes plus one additional vote for each part of its quota equivalent to one hundred thousand special drawing rights."[22] Under this formula, the five countries mentioned in the previous paragraph control just under 40 percent of the total voting power in the IMF.[23] If the other two countries in the

---

[19] IMF ANNUAL REPORT 2003, *supra* note 12, at iv.

[20] François Gianviti, *The Reform of the International Monetary Fund (Conditionality and Surveillance)*, 34 INT'L LAW. 107, 115 (2003).

[21] The predecessor to the International Monetary and Financial Committee (IMFC) was the Interim Committee. When the Interim Committee was transformed in 1999 into the IMFC, "it was agreed that meetings of its members, who are finance ministers or central bank governors, could be preceded by meetings of their deputies," and because of this decision the effective role of the Executive Board "is declining." *Id.*

[22] IMF Charter, art. XII, § 5(a).

[23] For a listing of the voting power for each member of the Executive Board as of

Group of Seven (G-7)[24] are included in the calculation, the aggregate voting power is over 45 percent of the total.[25] Although the basic rule is that all decisions are made by a majority of the votes cast,[26] special majorities are required for particular decisions, including the reimposition of fixed exchange rates (85 percent)[27] and the amendment of the Charter (also 85 percent),[28] including, of course, the Charter provisions establishing the weighted voting system itself.

H. Membership; Obligations; Privileges and Immunities

As noted above, the IMF had 184 member countries as of early 2005. This is nearly all the countries in the world. Before the end of the Cold War, of course, the story was different. Although the USSR had participated in the Bretton Woods conference, it did not become an IMF member in the 1940s. Only in the late 1980s, when the Soviet leader Mikhail Gorbachev was pressing for economic and political change in that country, did the Soviet Union come close to IMF membership, in the form of a proposed "associate membership" status. Once the USSR collapsed, the various former Soviet republics became IMF members one by one.[29]

In becoming an IMF member, a country undertakes certain obligations regarding economic and financial policies, including especially its management of a national currency. These obligations, commonly referred to

---

August 2003, *see* IMF SURVEY SUPPLEMENT, *supra* note 17, at 30. As indicated there, the percentages of overall voting power for those Executive Directors representing the United States, Japan, Germany, France, and the United Kingdom are 17.14 percent, 6.15 percent, 6.01 percent, 4.96 percent, and 4.96 percent, respectively. *Id.* For the most recent voting power information, *see* International Monetary Fund, IMF Members' Quotas and Voting Power, and IMF Board of Governors [hereinafter IMF Members' Quotas], *at* www.imf.org/external/np/sec/memdir/members.htm (last visited Feb. 13, 2005).

[24] The Group of Seven, or G-7, consists of the United States, Japan, Germany, the United Kingdom, France, Italy, and Canada. In recent years, the Russian Federation has been invited to G-7 meetings, and the group is now often referred to as the G-8, as reflected on its Web site, www.g8.fr.

[25] Canada's voting power in the IMF is 2.95 percent of the total, and Italy's is 3.26 percent. IMF Members' Quotas, *supra* note 23.

[26] IMF Charter, art. XII, § 5(c).

[27] *Id.* art. IV, § 4.

[28] *Id.* art. XXVIII(a). This provision also requires, in addition to the 85 percent voting majority, approval by three-fifths of the membership.

[29] The most recent of the former Soviet republics to gain IMF membership was Tajikistan, in 1993. For a listing of IMF members, and the year in which each joined, *see* the IMF website at www.imf.org/external/country/index.htm.

as the "code of good conduct,"[30] include a general duty to collaborate with the IMF and other members "to assure orderly exchange arrangements and to promote a stable system of exchange rates"[31] and more specific duties on that country to (1) pursue policies that foster "orderly economic growth with reasonable price stability," (2) pursue policies that foster "orderly underlying economic and financial conditions and a monetary system that does not tend to produce erratic disruptions," and (3) "avoid manipulating exchange rates" in order to gain an unfair competitive advantage over other members.[32] In addition, an IMF member is obligated to cooperate with the IMF in the so-called "Article IV consultations," referred to above, which the IMF is empowered to carry out with members (usually annually)[33] and to provide information requested by the IMF regarding foreign exchange holdings, exports and imports, national income, exchange controls, and the like.[34] Moreover, an IMF member is required, unless it has taken advantage of certain "grandfathering" provisions,[35] to avoid imposing restrictions on the making of payments or transfers in respect of current international transactions,"[36] which include transactions involved in paying for importation of goods,[37] and to refrain from engaging in "discriminatory currency arrangements or multiple currency practices."[38] While the content of these and other obligations of membership might seem rather narrow and technical, the monitoring of such matters constitutes a major area of IMF activity—eclipsed in the public eye by the IMF's credit operations but central to the IMF's original purpose of facilitating a stable international monetary system.

Two other obligations of membership—unrelated to exchange rates and monetary policy—warrant brief mention. First, perhaps obviously, an IMF member is obligated to repay any amount it borrows from the IMF, and to pay interest and other charges where applicable.[39] Failure to honor

---

[30] For a more detailed explanation of the "code of good conduct," *see* RICHARD W. EDWARDS, JR., INTERNATIONAL MONETARY COLLABORATION 17–22 (1985). Rich Edwards is a premier authority on the IMF, and his 1985 text is among the very best explanations of the organization's character, structure, and operations.

[31] IMF Charter, art. IV, § 1.

[32] IMF Charter, art. IV, § 1(i), (ii), and (iii).

[33] *See* IMF Charter, art. IV, § 3.

[34] *See* IMF Charter, art. VIII, § 5(a).

[35] *See* IMF Charter, art. XIV, § 2.

[36] IMF Charter, art. VIII, § 2(a).

[37] This meaning of "current transactions" is found at IMF Charter, art. XXX(d).

[38] IMF Charter, art. VIII, § 3.

[39] As noted above, some of the financing made available by the IMF does not take

this obligation can make a country ineligible to borrow further from the IMF and, if the failure persists, can lead to a suspension of the member's voting rights or even to the member's expulsion from the IMF.[40] Second, a member's obligations under the IMF Charter include a duty to grant certain privileges and immunities to the IMF itself—for example, exemption from national or local taxes, immunity from judicial process, and inviolability of archives—as well as certain privileges and immunities to IMF staff members.[41] In general, such privileges and immunities are intended to underscore the IMF's stature as an independent legal entity with some of the same attributes as states.

III.   THE WORLD BANK AND THE REGIONAL MDBs IN A NUTSHELL[42]

Having offered, in the preceding section, a synopsis of the IMF, I find it easier in this section to offer a synopsis of the MDBs, for two reasons. First, the MDBs—and particularly the two entities that comprise the World Bank—share many structural features with the IMF. Second, the MDBs are intrinsically less complicated than the IMF both in their operations and their sources of funding. Having said that, I would hasten to add that some key features of the MDBs apparently remain misunderstood by many people. Hence the need for a "nutshell" introduction here that builds on the historical sketch I offered in Section I of this chapter.

Although they differ in important ways, it is appropriate for present purposes to offer a unified picture of the six MDBs—the IBRD (chartered at the Bretton Woods conference in 1944),[43] the IDA (chartered in

---

the form, as a legal matter, of loans but instead takes the forms of exchanges of currencies. *See supra* note 15. For purposes of this nutshell account, I have omitted numerous details regarding the transactions undertaken by the IMF with its member countries.

[40] For the provisions regarding ineligibility, suspension, and expulsion, *see* IMF Charter, art. XXVI, § 2.

[41] *See* IMF Charter, art. IX, §§ 3, 5, 9.

[42] This summary of the MDBs is drawn in part from my recent article evaluating criticisms leveled at the MDBs. *See* John W. Head, *For Richer or For Poorer: Assessing the Criticisms Directed at the Multilateral Development Banks*, 52 U. KAN. L. REV. 241, 525–30 (2004) [hereinafter *Richer or Poorer*]. For more extensive footnote citations to authority, please see that article. This summary also draws from the basic information on the MDBs that can be found on their individual websites and from the websites of certain creditable NGOs. Some pertinent website addresses appear in the Bibliography at the end of this book.

[43] Like the IMF Charter, the IBRD Charter has been amended since its approval at the Bretton Woods conference, although only twice. *See* Original IBRD Charter, *supra* note 6, as amended Dec. 16, 1965, 16 U.S.T. 1942, 606 U.N.T.S. 294 (entered into force Dec. 26, 1965), and as amended effective Feb. 16, 1989. It is the amended version of the IBRD Charter that appears in Appendix C of this book. The IBRD Charter is also avail-

1960),[44] the IADB,[45] AfDB,[46] and AsDB[47] (all chartered between 1959 and 1965), and the EBRD (chartered in 1990)[48]—because they all share the

able from the World Bank website (www.world.bank.org), as is general information about the Bretton Woods conference at which the IBRD was established.

[44] Articles of Agreement of the International Development Association, Jan. 26, 1960, 11 U.S.T. 2284, 439 U.N.T.S. 249 (entered into force Sept. 24, 1960) [hereinafter IDA Charter]. The IDA Charter appears in Appendix D of this book. It is also available from the World Bank website (www.worldbank.org), as is general information about the history, purposes, and operations of the IDA.

[45] The IADB, like the IBRD and the IDA, is governed by a charter that takes the form of a treaty. *See* Agreement Establishing the Inter-American Development Bank, Apr. 8, 1959, 10 U.S.T. 3029, 389 U.N.T.S. 69 (entered into force Dec. 30, 1959), as amended Mar. 31, 1968, 19 U.S.T. 7381, and Mar. 23, 1972, TIAS No. 7437 [hereinafter IADB Charter]. (According to at least one source, the IADB Charter was also amended in 1987 and 1995.) The IADB Charter appears in Appendix E of this book. It is also available from the IADB website (www.iadb.org), as is general information about the history, purposes, and operations of the IADB. The IADB's membership comprises 47 countries, including 26 Latin American and Caribbean countries, Canada, the United States, and 19 non-regional countries. *See* INTER-AMERICAN DEVELOPMENT BANK, ANNUAL REPORT 2001 (n.p.) (2002) [hereinafter IADB ANNUAL REPORT 2001], *available at* www.iadb.org/ EXR/ar99/pdf/ eng/IA2001_Eng.pdf (last visited Nov. 17, 2003). The IADB is head-quartered in Washington, DC.

[46] *See* Agreement Establishing the African Development Bank, Aug. 4, 1963, 510 U.N.T.S. 3 (entered into force Sept. 10, 1964) [hereinafter AfDB Charter]. The AfDB Charter appears in Appendix F of this book. Curiously, and unlike the other MDB charters, it is not available from the AfDB website (www.afdb.org), although a summary of it is available there, as is general information about the history, purposes, and operations of the AfDB. The AfDB's membership comprises 53 countries in Africa and 24 non-African countries. The AfDB provides loans on non-concessional terms. However, a companion institution, the African Development Fund, established in 1973, provides loans on concessional terms to low-income member countries in the region. AFRICAN DEVELOPMENT BANK GROUP, ANNUAL REPORT 2002 viii–ix (2003) [hereinafter AfDB ANNUAL REPORT 2002], *available at* www.adfdb.org/knowledge/documents/Banks_Annual_ Report.htm (last visited Nov. 17, 2003). The AfDB, having been headquartered in Abidjan for many years, recently shifted its headquarters to Tunis.

[47] *See* Agreement Establishing the Asian Development Bank, Dec. 4, 1965, 17 U.S.T. 1418, 571 U.N.T.S. 123 (entered into force Aug. 22, 1966) [hereinafter AsDB Charter]. The AsDB Charter appears in Appendix G of this book. It is also available from the AsDB website, www.adb.org, as is general information about the history, purposes, and operations of the AsDB. For a more detailed descriptive explanation of the AsDB, *see* John W. Head, *Asian Development Bank, in* INTERNATIONAL ENCYCLOPAEDIA OF LAWS (R. Blanpain ed., 2002) [hereinafter Head, *Asian Development Bank*]. The AsDB is headquartered in Manila.

[48] Agreement Establishing the European Bank for Reconstruction and Development, May 29, 1990, 29 I.L.M. 1077 (entered into force Mar. 28, 1991) [hereinafter EBRD Charter]. The EBRD Charter appears as Appendix H to this book. It is also available from the EBRD website (www.ebrd.org), as is general information about the history, purposes, and operations of the EBRD. For further information about the history of the EBRD, *see generally* IBRAHIM F.I. SHIHATA, THE EUROPEAN BANK FOR RECONSTRUCTION AND DEVELOPMENT (1990) [hereinafter Shihata I]; Head, *Supranational Law, supra* note 1, at 635–49. The EBRD is headquartered in London.

same fundamental precepts and structures that are most important for evaluating the criticisms currently leveled against them. Most importantly, all of these institutions have economic development as their motivating aim.[49] Hence I offer in the following paragraphs a brief description intended to apply to all the MDBs.

A. Project Financing and Policy-Based Lending

The bread-and-butter work for the MDBs has traditionally been to provide financial intermediation for specific development projects, usually for constructing some form of infrastructure or productive operation. They provide loans (and some grants) to finance projects to build roads, irrigation systems, rural health clinics, wastewater treatment systems, port facilities, power plants, schools, transmission lines, fertilizer plants, pipelines, and other physical structures, and to provide for such intangible outputs as agricultural credit, teacher training, farmers' workshops, and various other forms of institutional strengthening. The loans that MDBs provide for such projects are typically made on a reimbursement basis, so that funds are transferred from the lending MDB to the borrower only against expenditures as they are actually incurred by the borrower or implementing agency, rather than as balance-of-payments loans of the type provided by the IMF.

Selection and design of a specific development project to be financed by an MDB typically occurs through a collaborative process that involves several parties and several phases. Government officials, MDB staff members, and (increasingly in recent years) local residents and groups with a particular stake in the outcome of the project will influence the planning and preparation for the project. Once designed, the proposed project is scrutinized closely by a team of MDB staff members and outside experts engaged to appraise the financial viability, economic benefit, environmental considerations, social aspects, and other features and expected effects of the project. If the project passes muster in this appraisal phase, approval will be sought from the MDB's management and governing organ for actual financing of the project (via a loan made by the MDB in hard currency) and for entering into legal agreements with the borrower (typically a national government agency) and other entities involved in implementation of the project. Once these steps have been taken, proceeds of the approved loan will be available for use (usually on a reimbursement basis, as mentioned above) in building the facilities or carrying out the activities involved in the project. This project implementation stage often takes several years, during which loan disbursements are made, progress reports are

---

[49] As explained above in Section IC of this chapter, the IBRD was originally assigned to lead the effort to finance the reconstruction of Europe after World War II but was redirected toward economic development in the LDCs in response to the start of the Marshall Plan and other economic and political developments.

issued and discussed by government and MDB officials, modifications in the project are agreed on as necessary, and ultimately the project is completed and the loan is closed.

MDBs offer several variants of such project loans, referred to as sector loans or development finance institution (DFI) loans, but the end result is generally the same: a specific package of change is carried out—facilities are built, training is undertaken, equipment is installed, etc.—for the purpose of improving the economic circumstances of the borrowing country's people.

However, as a departure from the project-lending model of financing, most or all of the MDBs also engage to some degree in "policy-based" lending. In these cases, funds are provided by the MDBs to borrowing countries to support (and in return for) the adoption by those countries' governments of certain economic and financial policies favored by the MDBs. For example, the guidelines on such policy-based lending as carried out by the AsDB require that the lending will be based on a "broad-based sector reform and development plan that will enhance sector efficiency and performance, comprising in particular policy changes and institutional development."[50] Consistent with these guidelines, the AsDB has made policy-based loans for numerous purposes—for example, financial sector reform in several of its member countries.

The loans made by the MDBs, whether they take the form of project lending or policy-based lending, are subject to terms that require the payment of interest and the repayment of the principal. In recent years the MDBs have offered increasingly complicated and sophisticated packages of terms, but it is not too much of a simplification to say that the terms typically involve (1) market-based interest rates and relatively short maturities (on the order of eight to 12 years) for the loans made to those countries that are fairly well-off economically and (2) "concessional" terms—that is, interest-free or nearly so—with long maturities (often 32 or 40 or even 50 years) for the loans made to the poorest countries.[51] These are referred to

---

[50] Operations Manual section 6/BP, "Program Lending" (as issued Apr. 16, 1997), at para. 3. Changes made to the AsDB Operations Manual in October 2003 resulted in a renumbering of the pertinent section on such "program lending," which is the term used in the ADB to refer to policy-based lending. The guidelines now appear at OM section D4.

[51] Typical terms on an IDA loan include a maturity of 40 years and a service charge of 0.75 percent. THE WORLD BANK GROUP, WORLD BANK LENDING INSTRUMENTS: RESOURCES FOR DEVELOPMENT IMPACT 24 (2001), *available at* http://www.siteresources. worldbank.org/PROJECTS/Resources/lendinginstrumentbrochure.pdf (last visited Nov. 17, 2003). Typical terms on a soft loan from the AsDB (through the Asian Development Fund) include a maturity of 32 years (if the loan applies to a project, rather than a quick-disbursing program loan) with an interest charge of 1 percent for the first few years and 1.5 percent thereafter. Head, *Asian Development Bank, supra* note 47, at 34.

as "hard" loans and "soft" loans, respectively. The funds used by the MDBs for making such loans come from different sources, as described more fully a few paragraphs below.

In their lending operations, as in the IMF's credit operations, the MDBs follow a practice of conditionality—that is, making their loans conditional upon certain commitments being made or action being taken by the borrowers. In the smaller of the two categories of lending mechanisms described above, program (policy-based) lending, the conditions operate and sometimes even look like conditions in IMF financing arrangements: they call on the borrower to implement specified economic or financial policies favored by the MDBs in order for the disbursement of loan proceeds to continue. In the larger category, project lending, the MDBs typically impose numerous conditions relating to the government's commitment of budgetary resources to support the project being financed, the need for environmental protection measures in project implementation, various reporting requirements, and so forth.

Numerous other aspects of MDB lending operations could be included in this "nutshell" account, but I shall limit myself to one more: procurement of goods and services for use in MDB-financed projects. I referred earlier in this "nutshell" to the types of projects that the MDBs finance, including the building of roads, irrigation systems, rural health clinics, wastewater treatment systems, port facilities, power plants, schools, transmission lines, fertilizer plants, pipelines, and other physical structures, and the provision of such intangible outputs as agricultural credit, teacher training, farmers' workshops, and various other forms of institutional strengthening. Such projects require enormous quantities of equipment, supplies, and expertise—valued at nearly US$5 billion in a recent year in just one of the regional MDBs.[52] As a general rule, the MDBs insist that the procurement of these goods and services conform to three basic criteria: (1) that they be supplied from eligible member countries (although the EBRD does not have such requirements); (2) that such procurement be carried out with due regard to the economic and efficient use of the proceeds of the MDB loans paying for them; and (3) that there be adequate, fair, and equal opportunity for member countries to participate in the supply of such goods and services.

The first of these three criteria is especially noteworthy, because it helps explain why economically developed countries join the MDBs. Those countries typically win a very large share of the contracts to supply goods

---

[52] *See* Head, *Asian Development Bank, supra* note 47, at 37–38 (showing about US$4.77 billion in contract awards under AsDB-financed projects in the year 2000, not including consulting services contracts).

and services for use in MDB-financed projects. Without MDB membership, those developed countries would be ineligible to bid on most such projects.

B. Technical Assistance and Other Operations

In addition to making loans to its member countries, the MDBs also offer another crucial form of development assistance financing—grant financing for technical assistance. Although some technical assistance (as explained below) is provided by the MDBs as loans, most such assistance comes in the form of grants. And the overall volume of such grants (the amounts of which are individually relatively small) results in a very substantial transfer of resources from the richer countries to the poorer countries, inasmuch as the resources relied on for such technical assistance grants come by and large from the richer countries.

A general idea of the categories of technical assistance provided by the MDBs can be gained by examining the four types of technical assistance provided by the AsDB:[53]

— PPTA (project preparatory technical assistance), used to assist in the preparation of one or more projects that will likely be funded later by a loan from the MDB. PPTA often involves a feasibility study or detailed engineering for a project, and the provision of PPTA funding helps to keep the "pipeline" of an MDB's project financing well stocked.
— PITA (project implementation technical assistance), used not to help design projects but rather to help implement them, as by training local personnel who will be working in facilities built under the project.
— ADTA (advisory technical assistance), used for institutional building. ADTA may be provided either on a stand-alone basis or in connection with a specific project, and it usually focuses on establishing or strengthening institutions, preparing national development plans, and carrying out issues-oriented studies.
— RETA (regional technical assistance), which involves activities covering more than one member country. RETA provides financing for such things as training, conferences, research, etc.

In addition to project and policy-based lending, discussed in the previous subsection, and technical assistance financing, discussed briefly above, the MDBs also engage in a limited range of other financial operations. One of these is the provision of guarantees. These take several forms, but, in general, they involve a guarantee issued by the MDB that a member country

---

[53] *See* Head, *Asian Development Bank, supra* note 47, at 43.

will repay to another lender a financial obligation made to it by that member country. Despite early expectations that guarantee operations would figure importantly in MDB operations, the volume of such operations has remained very modest.

Another operation carried out by most of the regional MDBs is the provision of financial assistance to private sector enterprises—as distinct from the financing discussed above to benefit the public sector.[54] For instance, the AsDB relies on Articles 2(i), 11(iii), 14, and 15(2) of its charter to make loans to, and equity investments in, various types of private sector enterprises.[55] The provision of such financial assistance is predicated, of course, on an MDB's overall objective to improve economic development, and this distinguishes MDB private sector financing from the financing provided by private financial institutions, whose central aim is profitmaking. Because of the development aim that their charters call on the MDBs to serve, private sector financing often (but not always) involves government guarantees by the affected member countries. Like guarantee operations, MDB private sector operations have remained modest in scope.

One further aspect of MDB financing operations warrants a brief mention. Increasingly over time, the MDBs have engaged in what is termed "co-financing." This term refers to a financing arrangement under which funds from other sources outside a borrowing country are provided, in addition to an MDB loan. Co-financing typically takes one of two forms: (1) commercial co-financing, in which the additional funding comes from private sources such as commercial banks or export credit agencies—for example, the U.S. Export-Import Bank (EXIMBANK)—and (2) official co-financing, in which the additional funding comes from governments, government agencies—such as the U.S. Agency for International Development (USAID) —or other multilateral institutions, including of course other MDBs. By helping a country arrange for such co-financing of a project, an MDB can leverage the impact of its own involvement in that project.

C. Resources and Other Financial Matters

Where do MDBs obtain the resources they need to engage in the various financial operations described in the preceding paragraphs? Despite public impressions to the contrary, most of the resources come not from public coffers, or ultimately from tax revenues of the rich countries, but rather from private sector investors. In order to understand the sources of funds on which MDBs rely, it is important to appreciate the distinction

---

[54] The World Bank—that is, the combination of the IBRD and the IDA—does not provide financing to private sector enterprises because that task is carried out by the affiliate of the IBRD and the IDA, the International Finance Corporation. *See supra* note 7.

[55] *See* Head, *Asian Development Bank, supra* note 47, at 44–45.

made earlier between "hard" loans and "soft" loans.[56] As described above, hard loans are made by the MDBs at market-based interest rates and shorter maturities than soft loans, which carry highly concessional interest rates (often around zero or one percent). In some of the MDBs, most notably the two component entities of the World Bank (*i.e.*, the IBRD and the IDA), hard loans are, as a technical and legal matter, made by one institution and soft loans are made by another. In other MDBs, such as the AsDB, a single institution makes both types of loans.

In all events, however, the resources used for soft loans are kept separate from those used for hard loans—not only because those resources have different uses but also because they have different sources. The AsDB, for example, carefully separates its Ordinary Capital Resources (OCR) from its "Special Funds" resources. The institution uses its OCR to conduct what its charter refers to as "ordinary operations"—hard loans—and its Special Funds resources to conduct what its charter refers to as "special operations"—soft loans.[57]

In general, the MDBs make hard loans from OCR and soft loans from Special Funds resources. Importantly, OCR consists largely of funds that the MDBs borrow on international capital markets. Expressed differently, hard loans are made from funds that come from investors, not from government tax revenues. Soft loans, by contrast, do come ultimately from tax revenues, in the form of contributions made by the economically developed member countries of the MDBs.

To explore these matters more fully, I offer in the following three paragraphs a synopsis of the capitalization of the MDBs, their borrowing powers and programs, and the processes by which they attract contributions for their soft-lending operations.

Typically an MDB's capital, like that of companies under many legal systems, is categorized as authorized capital, subscribed capital, paid-in capital, and callable capital. The authorized capital stock is the amount that the MDB's governing boards have empowered the MDB to issue to its members.[58] At any one time, most, but not all, of that authorized stock will actu-

---

[56] *See supra* note 51 and accompanying text.

[57] *See* AsDB Charter, arts. 19–20. Article 19.2., for example, provides that "Special Funds established by the [AsDB] . . . may be used to guarantee or make loans of high developmental priority, with longer maturities, longer deferred commencement of repayment and lower interest rates than those established by the Bank for its ordinary operations."

[58] From time to time the MDBs reassess the adequacy of their overall subscribed capital, in part because the amount of subscribed capital typically bears on the ability of an

ally have been issued to, and subscribed by, member countries. Such subscriptions are measured in shares of stock. But in subscribing to a certain number of shares of an MDB's capital, a member country is not required to pay immediately for the total amount of its subscription. Instead, a certain portion (usually a fairly small portion in recent years) is paid-in capital and the remainder is callable capital. In most of the MDBs, the proportion of the subscribed capital that consists of paid-in capital is much smaller than the proportion of the subscribed capital that is callable. The reason for this is that the MDBs typically do not rely significantly on capital from their member countries in order to engage in their day-to-day operations (including the making of loans).[59] In the case of extraordinary financial circumstances (such as a large number of nonperforming loans), the MDB might wish to make a "call" on the callable capital that member countries have pledged, but this has rarely if ever happened. (It has never happened, for example, in the IBRD or the AsDB, with which I am most familiar.)

If MDBs do not rely much on subscribed capital to make their loans to member countries, where do they get the money for this purpose? For their hard loans, the MDBs rely on borrowings that they undertake in large volumes and in many financial markets.[60] In this respect they behave much like ordinary private sector businesses or financial intermediaries: the MDBs issue various types of debt instruments (mainly medium-term and longer term bonds) that investors purchase because of the attractive rates and low risk that they present; and the MDBs use the proceeds from those borrowings to make (hard) loans to borrowers in their member countries.[61]

MDB to borrow funds on international markets. From this reassessment often comes a general capital increase (GCI) under which all the members are invited to increase their individual subscriptions in an amount that will allow each of them to maintain the same proportion of the MDB's total subscribed capital as the proportion it held before the GCI. In addition, a member country may sometimes seek and obtain approval to increase its subscription under a special capital increase (SCI) in order to reflect an expanded economic importance attained by that country.

[59] Nor do the MDBs rely on any sort of annual dues or other contributions from their member governments, as some international organizations do. Indeed, most of the MDBs, at least in their hard lending operations, earn a modest profit each year. Of course, the earning of a profit is not one of the purposes of such institutions but rather a by-product of their operations; accordingly, such profits are not returned to member countries in the way of dividends but instead are typically are (1) used to support soft lending operations, to the extent permitted under the strict separation-of-accounts provisions described above, or (2) transferred to the ordinary reserves of the institutions.

[60] It is in recognition of this source of funds that some anti-globalist activists have proposed boycotting the purchase of MDB bonds by public institutions, in an effort to "bankrupt" the MDBs—that is, to undercut their ability to raise funds for lending operations. *See* Johann Hari, *Now the Protestors Box Clever: The Anti-Globalisation Activists Have a New Idea: To Bankrupt the World Bank,* 131 NEW STATESMAN 23 (2002).

[61] When the funds obtained through an MDB's borrowing program are not needed

The story is different for soft loans. To obtain the resources they need for soft loans, MDBs rely on contributions from member country governments. Typically these contributions result from negotiations held every few years to replenish the special funds resources maintained by the MDBs. In the case of the IDA, for example, the most recent replenishment negotiations concluded in London in July 2002 and yielded commitments totalling US$23 billion over the next three years. Negotiations for another replenishment are, as of this writing, ongoing, with recent meetings held in Athens in December 2004.[62]

D. Membership in the MDBs

Like the IMF, the World Bank has nearly universal membership. Specifically, the IBRD has 184 members (as of early 2005), and the IDA has 165 members (also as of early 2005). Membership in the IBRD is dependent on membership in the IMF; that is, a country cannot be a member of the IBRD without being a member of the IMF.[63]

Membership in the regional MDBs varies, of course, in number and identity, but in all cases their membership includes both regional and non-regional member countries. (For several years the African Development Bank did not permit non-African countries to join as members, but now it does.) Typically, the non-regional member countries are economically developed countries, and their participation in any one of the regional MDBs reflects those countries' interest in the economic circumstances of the regional served by that MDB. From the perspective of an MDB, of course, the participation by non-regional members typically carries both advantages and disadvantages. A key advantage is the financial commitment that such a non-regional (usually wealthy) member country makes with its membership—not only by contributing to the subscribed capital of that MDB but also by its contribution of funds for technical assistance and soft loan operations. A key disadvantage (to an MDB of non-regional participation) is the risk that regional control over the MDB may thereby be diluted. To contain this risk, the regional MDB charters typically establish a ceiling on shareholdings by non-regional member countries.[64]

---

immediately for making disbursements under loans it has made, the MDB will invest those funds in various types of investment-grade instruments. Hence, at any one time an MDB is a borrower, a lender, and an investor.

[62] Likewise, the AsDB completed its most recent special funds resources replenishment negotiations in September 2000 with a replenishment amount of US$5.65 billion.

[63] This membership requirement appears in the IBRD Charter, art. II, sec. 1.

[64] *See, e.g.,* AsDB Charter, art. 5 (requiring that shareholdings of capital by regional members be maintained at at least 60 percent).

As noted earlier, an incentive for relatively wealthy countries to join the MDBs (from which they obviously will not be eligible to receive loans) is that membership triggers eligibility to bid on contracts for the supply of goods and services, including consulting services, for the projects being financed by those MDBs.[65] Partly as a consequence of this incentive, as well as for other reasons, the participation by economically developed countries in the membership of the regional MDBs is fairly widespread, as shown by the following table:[66]

	Regional Members	Non-Regional Members	Total Members
Regional MDB:			
IADB	28	19	47
AfDB	52	25	77
AsDB	43	20	63
EBRD	27	33	60

Two other important membership issues warrant a brief explanation. The first relates to the classification of regional developing member countries. Most of the MDBs follow a classification system that identifies which countries are eligible to receive soft loans, which are eligible to receive "blended" loans (partly soft and partly hard), and which may only receive hard loans. The classification system is based typically on per capita GNP and debt repayment capacity. In some cases developing member countries are ineligible to receive any loans (hard or soft) because they have "graduated" from eligibility based on the strength of their economic circumstances.

A second important membership issue relates to the set of privileges and immunities accorded the MDBs by their charters. Like membership in the IMF, MDB membership carries with it the obligation to grant certain privileges and immunities to the MDB itself—for example, exemption from national or local taxes, immunity from judicial process, and inviolability of archives—as well as certain privileges and immunities to MDB staff members. In general, such privileges and immunities are intended to underscore the stature of the various MDBs as independent legal entities with some of the same attributes as nation-states.

Lastly, some curiosities of MDB membership are noteworthy. For one thing, the membership of China in the MDBs now rests with the PRC rather than the Republic of China, although in the AsDB some peculiar

---

[65] This aspect of the MDBs' procurement policies is summarized in the last paragraph of Subsection IIIA of this chapter.

[66] Information provided in this table comes mainly from the websites of the four regional MDBs under discussion, and are intended to be current as of late 2004.

arrangements persist.[67] For another, a few countries in Central Asia are, for largely historical reasons, regional members of more than one regional development bank—namely, both the EBRD and the AsDB. Another interesting feature relating to MDB membership is that although most members are independent nation-states, at least one regional MDB—the AsDB—can have "dependent territories" as members; and it was under this feature that the AsDB first admitted as members Hong Kong, Papua New Guinea, Cook Islands, Fiji, Kiribati, and Solomon Islands.

E. Structure of and Decisionmaking in the MDBs

The MDBs are structured similarly to the IMF. As explained above in subsection IIG of this chapter, the weighted voting system sits at the center of that structure. Just as in the case of the IMF, the MDBs follow a weighted voting system that places most of the voting power in a handful of countries. The IBRD Charter, for example, provides that each member "shall have 250 votes plus one additional vote for each share of stock held."[68] Given the wide variation in stockholdings in the MDBs—ranging, for example, in the AsDB from (equal) 15.9 percent shareholdings by the United States and Japan to 0.3 percent for Bangladesh and several island countries—the distribution of voting power in the institutions bears no relation to population or territorial size of the member countries but rests almost solely on the share that each country was allowed to subscribe to upon gaining membership (or upon negotiating an increase in that subscription later).

In many day-to-day operations, the weighted voting system plays little role in decisionmaking[69] because the proposals to finance projects or adopt policies are typically reviewed carefully in advance, and modified as necessary, to obtain a consensus of the members before being submitted for formal approval. Nonetheless, the weighted voting system does get reflected in many tangible ways. For example, the composition of an MDB's Board of Directors (or, in some MDBs, the Board of Executive Directors) reflects the weighted voting system by having some directorships allocated to single countries—the United States in nearly all of the MDBs, for example,

---

[67] For details in this respect, *see* Head, *Asian Development Bank, supra* note 47, at 52. One rather curious aspect of the arrangements settled on when the PRC joined the AsDB in the mid-1980s is that all references in AsDB documents to the former Republic of China now are to appear as "Taiwan,China" with no space following the comma.

[68] IBRD Charter, art. V, sec. 3(a). A difference in terminology, though it is of little practical significance in this context, is that the IBRD Charter refers to shares of stock whereas the IMF Charter refers to quotas.

[69] For a detailed examination of the process in the World Bank, starting in its earliest days, of making various types of decisions by consensus rather than by formal voting, *see generally* Andrés Rigo Sureda, *Informality and Effectiveness in the Operation of the International Bank for Reconstruction and Development,* 6 J. INT'L ECON. L. 565 (2003).

and Japan and the PRC in some of the MDBs—and all other directorships shared among "constituencies" of countries with smaller voting powers. The AsDB, for instance, has three single-member seats at its Board of Directors (for the United States, Japan, and the PRC), and other seats shared by groups of other member countries ranging in number from four to nine. In the IBRD, several constituencies include more than 24 countries.

When voting does take place, a simple majority of the votes cast is adequate to take action.[70] However, super-majorities or qualified majorities are required for certain important actions, such as amending an MDB's charter[71] or increasing the size of the Board of Directors[72] or suspending a member of the MDB.[73]

In addition to resembling the IMF in terms of the weighted voting system, the MDBs resemble the IMF also in terms of structure. In each case all powers of the MDB are granted to a Board of Governors, which includes one seat for each member. Those Governors are responsible for setting the overall policy of the institution, and they typically meet once each year to do so. Actual supervision of each of the MDBs, including the approval of specific financial operations, is carried out by a smaller board, called the Board of Directors or, in some cases, the Board of Executive Directors—a distinction that, in some cases, makes a difference.[74]

The Board of Directors (or Board of Executive Directors) of an MDB typically consists of a couple dozen individuals, most of whom represent "constituencies" of member countries as described above. These boards typically meet on a weekly or twice-weekly basis most of the year, and it is in these meetings that the board members have formal interactions with the MDB's staff members. Staff members, appointed in nearly all cases by the MDB's president, range broadly in their areas of expertise—from rural credit to aquaculture development to forest protection to project engineering to country studies to accountancy to legal drafting, and so forth.

---

[70] *See, e.g.,* IBRD Charter, art. V, sec. 3(b).

[71] *See, e.g., id.* art. VIII(a) (requiring, for adoption of a charter amendment, approval by "three-fifths of the members, having eight-five percent of the total voting power").

[72] *See, e.g., id.* art. V(4)(b) (requiring, for increasing the number of executive directors, approval by "a four-fifths majority of the total voting power").

[73] *See, e.g., id.* art. VI(2) (requiring, for suspension of a member, approval "by decision of a majority of the Governors, exercising a majority of the total voting power").

[74] For example, the AsDB Charter establishes a "Board of Directors," not a "Board of Executive Directors," and partly because of that difference in terminology the AsDB Board of Directors has been rebuffed in its efforts to claim more executive authority from the President than he thought was warranted under the AsDB Charter provisions placing executive functions with the President.

Although the MDBs typically renounce any form of nationality quota system in hiring staff members, efforts are usually made to have a broad representation of members on the staff, a point that some of the MDB charters explicitly encourage.[75]

As with the IMF, the MDBs are self-contained in the sense that they do not report to or fall under the authority of any other entity, either national or international. Their governing boards have authority to interpret their charters in the same way that the IMF has authority to interpret its charter, a matter that will be explored more below in Chapters Three and Four. In recent years, however, several of the MDBs have taken initiatives to permit some form of review of their actions. In the case of the IBRD and the IDA, for example, such review function is carried out by the World Bank Inspection Panel, established in September 1993. The World Bank Inspection Panel, comprising three members acting with substantial independence from the World Bank's management, has as its primary purpose "to address the concerns of people who might be affected by [World] Bank projects and to ensure that the Bank adheres to its operational policies and procedures in the design, preparation, and implementation of such projects."[76]

F. Policies and Initiatives

From their inception the MDBs have had certain policies that reflect their character as financial institutions designed to facilitate economic development. These policies address such issues as co-financing (the process by which an MDB and a borrower will find other official or commercial sources of financial support for a project), coordination with other aid agencies, and procurement (as discussed briefly above in this "nutshell" account of the MDBs).

In recent years, however, the MDBs have experienced an explosion in the number and variety of policies and initiatives that they have adopted and undertaken to implement. Especially with the gradual expansion of MDBs' operations into the type of policy-based lending described above in Subsection IIIA of this chapter, it is common today to find the MDBs requiring their borrowing member countries to accept and adhere to prescribed policies on environmental protection, indigenous peoples, invol-

---

[75] *See, e.g.*, AsDB Charter, art. 34.6 (providing that "[i]n appointing the officers and staff, the President shall, subject to the paramount importance of securing the highest standards of efficiency and technical competence, pay due regard to the recruitment of personnel on as wide a regional geographical basis as possible").

[76] THE WORLD BANK, ACCOUNTABILITY AT THE WORLD BANK: THE INSPECTION PANEL 10 YEARS ON 3 (2003). Information about the World Bank Inspection Panel is also available at http://wbln0018.worldbank.org/ipn/ipnweb.nsf (last visited Feb. 13, 2005).

untary resettlement, governance, corruption, public participation, the role of women in development, and poverty reduction.[77]

G. The Generational Character of the MDBs

In the introductory remarks to this "nutshell" account of the MDBs, I posited that although they differ in important ways, it is appropriate to offer a unified picture of the six MDBs—the IBRD (chartered in 1944), the IDA (chartered in 1960), the IADB, AfDB, and AsDB (all chartered between 1959 and 1965), and the EBRD (chartered in 1990)—because they all share what I called there "the same fundamental precepts and structures that are most important for evaluating the criticisms currently leveled against them." In this last portion of my "nutshell" account of the MDBs, I wish to emphasize two types of important differences among the MDBs.

The first type of difference is obvious: the first two of them as listed above are global in their reach and the other four of them are regional in character. This fact has caused by far the most scrutiny and criticism to be directed toward the IBRD and the IDA, which together form the World Bank. This lopsided scrutiny might be unfortunate, because some of the regional MDBs are probably more deserving of constructive criticism than is the World Bank.

The other type of difference among the MDBs that I wish to emphasize is temporal in nature: they were established at different times, reflecting changing needs and influences. In my view, the MDBs should be viewed as "generational" in character, with three generations now having run their course, or nearly so.[78] The first generation is represented by the IBRD, born in the closing days of World War II with the reconstruction of Europe as its main priority. As noted earlier in this chapter, the fact that the U.S. government soon took over the bulk of that task under the Marshall Plan prompted (in part) the IBRD to focus its attention more on the "D" in IBRD—that is, economic development in its non-European member countries.

---

[77] For examples of such policies as promoted by the World Bank, *see* THE WORLD BANK, I THE WORLD BANK ANNUAL REPORT 2002 [hereinafter I WORLD BANK ANNUAL REPORT 2002], *available at* http://www.worldbank.org/annualreport/2002/PrintVersion. htm (last visited Feb. 13, 2005). For an explanation of the policies of the AsDB on these topics, *see* Head, *Asian Development Bank, supra* note 47, at 75–92.

[78] I first discussed this "generational" character of the MDBs about a decade ago. *See* Head, *Supranational Law, supra* note 1, at 636, 641–44. For a further discussion of this point, from which I have drawn the next three paragraphs, *see* Head, *Richer or Poorer, supra* note 42, at 250–52, 269.

A second generation began around 1960 to cater better to the needs of LDCs. With the rapid emergence of many new states following the massive decolonization of the 1940s and 1950s, the IBRD found itself unable to provide as much useful assistance as was needed in those new states because IBRD loans carried market-based interest rates. As also explained earlier, it was against this backdrop that the IDA was established in 1960 as a companion to the IBRD—yielding the two institutions we now call the World Bank—to provide cheaper money through "soft loans" available to LDCs. At about the same time (between the late 1950s and the mid-1960s), the IADB, the AfDB, and the AsDB were formed as regional sources of development financing, and all three of these regional MDBs sooner or later developed the same authority to make "soft loans" that the IDA makes.

The EBRD represents a third generation in the evolution of the MDBs. This institution, formed about four decades after the IDA and the earliest of the regional MDBs, introduced several novel features into the operations of MDBs. Instead of prohibiting any consideration of political factors, as the charters of the earlier MDBs do, the charter of the EBRD expressly adopts a political mandate requiring the institution to take concrete steps to assist the countries of its operations—originally a handful of Eastern and Central European states newly released from the Soviet sphere of influence and now a couple of dozen states reaching from Central Europe across to Central Asia—in making their transition from Communist political control to an embrace of "the principles of multiparty democracy [and] pluralism."[79] The EBRD Charter also included two other types of mandate absent from the charters of the earlier MDBs. Its economic mandate requires the EBRD "to foster the transition toward open market-oriented economies" in its countries of operation.[80] Its environmental mandate requires the EBRD to "promote in the full range of its activities environmentally sound and sustainable development."[81]

The establishment of the EBRD was a blatant manifestation of a trend that had already begun in the other MDBs. It was a trend toward using the MDBs as instruments of global policy guidance or influence—or what I would call global policy regulation. This trend is exemplified by the gradual expansion of MDB operations into policy-based lending (described in the opening paragraphs of this "nutshell" account of the MDBs) and by the wide variety of policies and initiatives they have adopted. As noted above, the policies and initiatives address environmental protection, indigenous

---

[79] EBRD Charter, art. 1.

[80] *Id.*

[81] *Id.* art. 2, para. 1 (vii).

peoples, involuntary resettlement, governance, corruption, public participation, gender issues, and poverty reduction.

Given these developments, I believe the MDBs should be regarded as having been transformed from financial institutions into regulatory agencies—that is, into agencies involved in global policy "regulation."[82] They still carry out development banking functions, of course, but those banking functions have increasingly become instruments for achieving regulatory aims. I return to this topic in Chapter Four, where I explain and evaluate the "Mission Creep" criticism directed at the MDBs.

IV. THE WTO IN A NUTSHELL[83]

As noted above in Section I of this chapter, the problems of the interwar period relating to trade—especially the competitive raising of tariff rates—were to be addressed by an international organization to be called the International Trade Organization; but the ITO was never formed and, in its stead, the General Agreement on Tariffs and Trade (GATT),[84] origi-

---

[82] In discussing these issues with me, Bob Hockett of Cornell Law School has questioned my use of the terms "regulation" and "regulatory agency" in this context, pointing out that "regulation" connotes the notion of some entity (a regulator) that is formally authorized to assert jurisdiction over some other entity (a regulatee) and that MDBs do not enjoy the same degree of such authority as regulatory agencies typically do in a national setting. I agree with those points, and I would even add another point that further differentiates MDBs from most national regulatory agencies: in the case of the MDBs, the entities to which the policy guidance applies are themselves members of the MDBs and participate in the formulation of the policies. Despite these points, however, I still believe the MDBs can usefully be regarded as "regulatory agencies," defined liberally. After all, the aims and effects of the MDBs' policy guidance are generally the same as the aims and effects of regulations issued by national regulatory agencies: to regularize conduct on a variety of topics so as to conform to formally adopted standards. I believe the fact that the MDBs have increasingly been used in recent years to announce such standards of conduct on a wide variety of topics and to apply those standards (at least vis-á-vis borrowing member countries) makes it appropriate to regard them as engaging in "regulatory" activities.

[83] This summary of the WTO is drawn in part from my 2002 article evaluating criticisms leveled at the WTO. *See* John W. Head, *Throwing Eggs at Windows: Legal and Institutional Globalization in the 21st-Century Economy*, 50 U. KAN. L. REV. 731, 740–42, 746–47 (2002). For more extensive footnote citations to authority, please see that article. Basic information on the WTO also can be found on its website, www.wto.org, and from the websites of certain creditable NGOs. Some pertinent website addresses appear in the Bibliography at the end of this book. Perhaps the best source on the WTO and the GATT-WTO system in general is my colleague Professor Raj Bhala, whose written works on the WTO are extensive; they include, in addition to numerous law journal articles, RAJ BHALA, INTERNATIONAL TRADE LAW: THEORY AND PRACTICE (2d ed. 2001), RAJ BHALA, TRADE, DEVELOPMENT, AND SOCIAL JUSTICE (2003), and RAJ BHALA, GATT LAW (2005). For another good general source of information about the GATT-WTO system, *see generally* KENT JONES, WHO'S AFRAID OF THE WTO? (2004).

[84] General Agreement on Tariffs and Trade, done at Geneva, Oct. 30, 1947, 55

nally simply a treaty intended to govern the transitional period leading to the existence of the ITO,[85] took on the trappings of an international organization itself, without such status as a formal matter. In this capacity the GATT served as the triggering influence for several rounds of negotiations among the GATT parties, including the Uruguay Round completed in 1993. It was from that Uruguay Round of negotiations that the World Trade Organization (WTO) appeared.

An understanding of the WTO therefore requires some familiarity with (1) the principles and the operations of the GATT through the 45-plus years that began with its creation in the late 1940s, (2) the WTO charter as adopted in 1994, and (3) the score or so of other treaties that also emerged from the Uruguay Round. I offer an explanation of those three points in the following paragraphs.

A. Aims and Principles of the GATT 1947

According to the GATT itself, the countries that created it recognized "that their relations in the field of trade and economic endeavour should be conducted with a view to raising standards of living, ensuring full employment and a large and steadily growing volume of real income and effective demand, developing the full use of the resources of the world and expanding the production and exchange of goods."[86] In an effort to contribute to those objectives, the countries creating the GATT announced that they were "entering into reciprocal and mutually advantageous arrangements directed to the substantial reduction of tariffs and other barriers to trade and to the elimination of discriminatory treatment in international commerce."[87] Expressed simply, boosting commercial transactions among nations was regarded as a key aim in a post-war world, and that aim was to be achieved through breaking down the barriers to trade that had been built during the inter-war years.

How were the barriers to be broken down? Through the application of four central principles established in the GATT: bound duty rates, most-favored-nation (MFN) treatment, national treatment, and an attack on non-tariff barriers. I shall briefly summarize each of these principles.

UNTS 187, 61 Stat. A11, T.I.A.S. No. 1700 (entered into force provisionally Jan. 1, 1948 under the 1947 Protocol of Provisional Application, 55 U.N.T.S. 308, 61 Stat. A 2051) [hereinafter GATT-1947].

[85] *See id.* art. XXIX (prescribing, under the heading "The Relation of this Agreement to the Havana Charter," that GATT parties were to observe certain provisions of the Havana Charter "pending their acceptance of it in accordance with their constitutional procedures").

[86] *Id.* at preamble.

[87] *Id.*

The bound-duty-rate principle appears in Article II of the GATT, which asserts that (subject to certain exceptions) each GATT party "shall accord to the commerce of the other contracting parties treatment no less favourable than that provided for in the . . . appropriate Schedule annexed to this Agreement."[88] The weighty set of Schedules then gave the details, on a country-by-country basis, of tariff ceilings that had emerged from negotiations among the parties. Under Article II, a country could charge a tariff (duty) on a particular item that was less than or equal to the rate established in that country's Schedule for that item, but it could not charge a higher tariff. Of course, any one country's tariff rate on a specific item would probably differ substantially from both (1) the tariff rate it charges on the importation of other items and (2) the tariff rate that other countries would charge on the importation of that item into their territories, but Article II binds a GATT party not to let its tariff levels rise above those it negotiated under the auspices of the GATT.

The most-favored-nation treatment principle, expressed simply, asserts that a country shall accord identical tariff treatment to imports from all other contracting parties, and that treatment must be the best that it gives to any state (GATT party or not). A state cannot give State X the benefit of an especially low tariff rate on a particular item without giving that same benefit to all GATT parties. Moreover, this non-discrimination rule, found in GATT Article I, does not turn on reciprocity: "any advantage . . . granted by any contracting party to any product originating in . . . any other country shall be accorded *immediately* and *unconditionally* to the like product originating in . . . the territories of all other contracting parties."[89]

The national-treatment principle resembles the most-favored-nation treatment principle in its central aim: to eliminate discrimination between products based on their country of origin. But whereas the most-favored-nation treatment principle prohibits a GATT party from discriminating against the goods it imports from one country versus the goods it imports from another country, the national-treatment principle prohibits a GATT party from discriminating against the goods it imports (from whatever country) in favor of the goods produced locally. Under this principle, stated most clearly in paragraph 4 of Article III of the GATT,[90] a store owner in a GATT country could not be permitted to charge a special "for-

---

[88] *Id.*, art. II, para. 1(a).

[89] GATT-1947, *supra* note 84, art. I (emphasis added).

[90] GATT-1947, *supra* note 84, art. III, para. 4: "The products of the territory of any contracting party imported into the territory of any other contracting party shall be accorded treatment no less favourable than that accorded to like products of national origin in respect of all laws, regulations and requirements affecting their internal sale, offering for sale, purchase, transportation, distribution or use."

eign goods" tax on the sale of an item, or on its transportation, merely because that item was imported. Another difference, of course, between the most-favored-nation treatment principle and the national-treatment principle is that the former operates at the point of an article being imported into a country, whereas the latter prohibits certain behavior after the point of importation.

The fourth key principle established in the GATT in 1947 is what I refer to as the "anti-NTB principle." Found in Article XI, this principle disallows (subject also to certain exceptions) a GATT party to impose non-tariff barriers (NTBs), referred to in that provision as "prohibitions or restrictions other than duties, taxes or other charges . . . on the importation of any product of the territory of any other contracting party."[91] The most obvious non-tariff barrier would be a quota imposed by a government on the importation of a particular article into its territory. Other non-tariff barriers include such things as complex or restrictive import licensing procedures, safety and environmental standards, import testing requirements, customs procedures, and valuation of goods for customs purposes.[92]

Thus, the "bound-duty-rate" principle of Article II and the "anti-NTB principle" of Article XI combine to limit a GATT party's ability to raise barriers to trade: Article II prohibits the charging of any rates above the ceilings negotiated and recorded in the applicable Schedule; and Article XI disallows an effort to circumvent that prohibition by imposing a non-tariff barrier instead. Indeed, these two principles combine with the main work of the GATT during its first three decades—the sponsoring of various rounds of trade negotiations—to establish this game plan: eliminate NTBs, put a ceiling on existing tariff rates, and gradually work to ratchet those tariff rates downward, all with the ultimate aim of increasing international commercial activity.

B. Exceptions to GATT Principles

In addition to certain specific exceptions included in the provisions establishing the four principles noted above—that is, the bound-duty-rate, most-favored-nation-treatment, national-treatment, and anti-NTB princi-

---

[91] *Id.* art. XI, para. 1.

[92] A recent example of an NTB, and of WTO action to declare it incompatible with GATT obligations, emerged from the *Beef Hormones* case, in which an EU ban on imports from Canada and the United States of beef that had been given growth-enhancing hormones met disapproval on grounds that the ban, purportedly imposed on health concerns, was not adequately supported by scientific evidence that such beef would harm humans. For a synopsis of the case, *see* RALPH H. FOLSOM, MICHAEL GORDON WALLACE & JOHN A. SPANOGLE, INTERNATIONAL TRADE AND ECONOMIC RELATIONS IN A NUTSHELL 48 (3d ed. 2004) [hereinafter NUTSHELL].

ples—the GATT also includes several more sweeping exceptions to the application of its rules for a liberalized trade regime. Six are important enough to warrant discussion even in so brief an account as this. They are the exceptions allowing for (1) the imposition of anti-dumping duties, (2) the imposition of countervailing duties to counteract subsidies, (3) the taking of emergency action in the face of a flood of imports, (4) the enforcement by GATT parties of certain types of national measures relating to health, public morality, environmental protection, and a few other categories of concern, (5) the granting of more favorable tariff treatment to countries within a free trade area, and (6) the granting of more favorable tariff treatment to less economically developed countries.

The first of these exceptions permits a GATT party to impose additional duties, even if doing so would otherwise violate the bound-duty-rate principle of Article II, in response to the "dumping" in that country's territory of foreign-made goods. For GATT purposes, "dumping" occurs not only when the imported goods are sold at less than the cost of their production (this is a fairly obvious form of "dumping") but also when the imported goods are sold in the country of importation at a price that is lower than the price at which they are sold in the country of origin (for use in that country).[93] If such pricing behavior is a contributing cause of material injury to the relevant domestic industry in the country of importation, then that country can legally impose anti-dumping duties in an amount equal to the margin of dumping.

The second of the exceptions also permits tariff increases on certain products, but in this case the issue is not price discrimination between national markets (as is the case with anti-dumping duties) but rather subsidies that artificially lower the price of imported goods and thereby give such goods an unfair advantage in competing with domestically produced goods in the country of importation. In general terms, a subsidy is a financial contribution, usually by a government entity, that provides some benefit in the production or export of an article. While recognizing that some sorts of government subsidies are appropriate, or at least inescapable, the GATT provides that a country whose relevant domestic industry suffers material injury as a result of such a subsidy may, in most cases, impose a countervailing duty (in the amount of the subsidy) so as to level the playing field in the competition between imported goods and domestically produced goods.[94]

---

[93] For the main GATT provisions relating to dumping, and the imposition of anti-dumping duties, *see* GATT-1947, *supra* note 84, art. VI, paras. 1 and 2. As noted below, extensive rules expanding on these main GATT provisions were adopted in both the Tokyo Round and the Uruguay Round of trade negotiations.

[94] For the main GATT provisions relating to subsidies and countervailing duties, *see*

At least to some people (especially domestic producers), both dumping and subsidies create unfairness in the competition between imported goods and domestically produced goods. From the perspective of consumers, of course, it would appear to be beneficial, at least in the short run, for foreign companies to dump their goods in the consumer's country, or for foreign governments to subsidize goods bound for the consumer's country, inasmuch as both dumping and subsidies would tend to lower prices to the consumer. This (short-term) consumer perspective has not prevailed, however, and the GATT clearly permits countries of importation to impose special tariffs that offset dumping and subsidies.

In the case of the third type of exception mentioned above—emergency action in the case of a flood of imports—there is no element of unfairness involved. Even if a foreign company is not dumping goods in Country X, and even if a foreign government is not subsidizing goods being sold in Country X, a rapid rise in the volume of those goods being imported into Country X can be grounds for that country's government to restrict those imports, whether by raising tariffs on them or by imposing NTBs against them such as quotas. This exception, found in GATT Article XIX,[95] acts as like a circuit breaker in a house: just as a circuit breaker prevents a sudden surge of electricity from destroying the electrical system in a house, so the "emergency action" provision prevents a sudden surge of imports from destroying a domestic industry. One difference, of course, in the two settings is that electrical power surges are usually short-lived, whereas a surge in the pressure of imports to enter a country may continue unabated, as in the case of a dramatic improvement of the exporting country's competitive advantage in producing a particular article. Article XIX, sometimes referred to as the "escape clause," allows only temporary relief from such imports, reflecting the basic ideology of the GATT that more international trade produces net benefit overall.

GATT-1947, *supra* note 84, art. VI, para. 3 and art. XVI. As noted below, extensive rules expanding on these main GATT provisions were adopted in both the Tokyo Round and the Uruguay Round of trade negotiations. As noted below, the treaty emerging from the Uruguay Round on subsidies was the Agreement on Subsidies and Countervailing Duties (SCM). In a nod in favor of environmental protection, the SCM Agreement included "environmental retrofit" provisions under which subsidies made by a government to help a company or industry replace old equipment with more environmentally friendly equipment was non-countervailable.

[95] GATT-1947, *supra* note 84, art. XIX, para. 1(a): "If . . . any product is being imported into the territory of [a] contracting party in such increased quantities . . . as to cause or threaten serious injury to domestic producers in that territory or like or directly competitive products, the contracting party shall be free . . . to suspend [its fulfilment of GATT obligations]," such as the obligation not to raise tariffs or to impose NTBs.

The fourth of the six exceptions, for our purposes, to the key GATT principles described above appears in Articles XX and XXI of the GATT. Article XX enumerates several types of national regulatory measures with which GATT obligations should not interfere. Under that provision, as long as such measures "are not applied in a manner which would constitute a means of arbitrary or unjustifiable discrimination between countries . . . , or a disguised restriction on international trade, nothing in [the GATT] shall be construed to prevent the adoption or enforcement by any contracting party" of measures necessary to protect public morals, to protect human, animal, or plant life or health, relating to the products of prison labor, imposed to protect national artistic, historic, or archaeological value, or relating to the conservation of exhaustible natural resources.[96] In addition, Article XXI provides that the GATT should not be construed to prevent any contracting party from taking action it considers "necessary for the protection of its essential security interests" in "time of war or other emergency in international relations."[97]

A fifth exception permits countries to establish free trade areas in which the participating countries give each other tariff treatment that is better than MFN treatment. Doing so would violate the MFN treatment principle but for the special permission of Article XXIV, which "recognize[s] the desirability of increasing freedom of trade by the development . . . of closer integration between the economies of the countries parties to [free trade] agreements" and therefore permits the formation of such an area so long as the tariffs and other regulations applicable to goods from non-participating countries are "not . . . higher or more restrictive" than those "existing in the . . . constituent territories prior to the formation of the free-trade area."[98] It is under the auspices of this provision that the free trade areas in Europe (today taking the form of the EU) and in North America (via the NAFTA) are GATT-legal.

Lastly, a sixth exception to the four key principles summarized above permits countries to establish preferentially low tariff rates for less developed countries (LDCs). As with free-trade areas, discussed immediately above, lowering tariff rates below the MFN level for goods from some but not all GATT parties would violate the MFN treatment principle if not for the special permission granted in the GATT to do so. In the case of LDCs, however, such special permission was not written into the GATT in 1947 but rather added a couple of decades later with the establishment of the

---

96 *Id.* art. XX, clauses (a), (b), (e), (f), and (g).

97 *Id.* art. XXI, clause (a)(iii).

98 *Id.* art. XXIV, paras. 4, 5(b).

Generalized System of Preferences (GSP).[99] Today scores of LDCs are thus eligible to have their goods enter duty free into the markets of rich countries, including the United States—although, ironically, the magnitude of this benefit has gradually diminished over time with the general lowering of MFN tariff rates worldwide.

C. Negotiating Rounds and Other Developments

One of the most visible GATT activities—or, in the past decade, WTO activities—has been the sponsorship of various "rounds" of trade negotiations. At first these negotiations focused mostly on what I referred to at the end of Subsection IA of this chapter as the "ratcheting downward" of tariff rates. Over the course of six rounds of negotiations that were conducted in the first two decades of the GATT's existence, the average tariff rates (taking into account all articles and all participating countries) were lowered substantially from the very high levels that had existed in the inter-war years.[100]

The Tokyo Round of negotiations of the late 1970s added another feature: the creation of several side agreements, referred to as "codes," that elaborated on GATT provisions, with special attention to non-tariff barriers. For example, detailed rules on the imposition of anti-dumping duties and of countervailing duties, referred to in the preceding subsection, were set forth in such codes, which all GATT parties were invited to sign and ratify. Other important Tokyo Round codes related to technical barriers to trade, government procurement, and customs valuation. Importantly, the

---

[99] *See* "Generalized System of Preferences," Decision of June 25, 1971, found at GATT, Basic Instruments and Selected Documents, 18th Supp. 24 (1972) (granting of a temporary waiver of MFN obligations for this purpose); and "Differential and More Favourable Treatment, Reciprocity and Fuller Participation of Developing Countries," Decision of Nov. 28, 1979, found at GATT, Basic Instruments and Selected Documents, 26th Supp. 203 (1980). For a brief account of the history and impact of the Generalized System of Preferences, *see Generalized System of Preferences—Analysis, in* Int'l Trade Rep. (BNA), Reference File 31:0101–0102 (2003); RALPH H. FOLSOM, MICHAEL WALLACE GORDON & JOHN A. SPANOGLE, JR., INTERNATIONAL BUSINESS TRANSACTIONS (Hornbook Series) 310–11 (2d ed. 2001).

[100] *See supra* note 3 and accompanying text (citing the U.S. Smoot-Hawley Tariff Act to illustrate those high inter-war tariff rates). These rounds in the first two decades of the GATT's existence (following the original Geneva Round in 1947) were referred to as the Annecy Round (1949, with 29 countries participating), the Torquay Round (1950–51, with 32 countries participating), the Geneva II Round (1955–56, with 33 countries participating), the Dillon Round (1960–61, with 39 countries participating), and the Kennedy Round (1963–67, with 74 countries participating). JONES, *supra* note 83, at 70. All of these except the Kennedy Round reduced tariffs on an item-by-item basis; the Kennedy Round "was noted for its achievement of across-the-board tariff reductions." NUTSHELL, *supra* note 92, at 39. *See also* the "GEO Timeline" set forth in Subsection IA of this chapter.

Tokyo Round negotiators settled on what has been called an "a la carte" approach regarding these codes: countries were invited and encouraged to adopt them, but no requirement to do so was imposed.

This approach changed with the Uruguay Round, launched in 1986 and concluded in 1993. As described more fully in the next subsection, the Uruguay Round produced about a score of treaties that were offered on a "single-package" basis: in order to become a member of the WTO (established as the institutional successor to the GATT), a country had to agree to all of the Multilateral Trade Agreements (that is, all but four of the treaties emerging from the negotiations).[101] The Uruguay Round departed also in another fashion from the preceding rounds of negotiations by covering several topics lying outside the GATT's traditional focus on trade in goods. As explained in the following subsection, these topics included trade in services, intellectual property rights, and protection of foreign investment.

The most recent round of GATT/WTO trade negotiations, the Doha Round, was launched in 2001. As of this writing, the Doha negotiations are proceeding slowly, having suffered some significant setbacks, including the collapse of a WTO ministerial conference in Cancún in 2003,[102] partly over disagreements on agricultural subsidies. Later progress was made in this area, however, and the negotiations continue. The most recent ministerial conference, held in Geneva in August 2004, was generally viewed as a smooth success.

D. The Uruguay Round Agreements

The most significant development in international trade law over the past several decades—probably since the creation of the GATT itself in 1947—is the conclusion of the Uruguay Round in 1993, for emerging from that round of negotiations was a score of treaties, a new international organization, a further general reduction of tariff levels,[103] and a recommitment

---

[101] As a legal matter, this "single-package" requirement appears in Article II, para. 2 of the WTO Charter, providing that the Multilateral Trade Agreements (which are enumerated in Annexes 1, 2, and 3 to the charter) are integral parts of the charter and binding on all members.

[102] For a summary of the collapse of trade talks in 2003, *see Cancún's Charming Outcome*, THE ECONOMIST, Sept. 20, 2003, at 11–12 (aiming a stinging rebuke at trade ministers from both rich and poor countries, and particularly at the alleged ignorance and incompetence of globophobic activist groups and LDC governments whose delight over the breakdown in the negotiations is misplaced because weakening the multilateral trading system "is going to leave most people in the world worse off—and, without a doubt, those who will suffer worst are the world's poor").

[103] For example, average tariff rates imposed by developed countries on dutiable manufactured imports were cut from 6.3 percent to 3.9 percent. NUTSHELL, *supra* note 92, at 34.

to multilateralism in international trade relations after a period in which multilateral approaches seemed to have been supplanted by regional and bilateral approaches to trade regimes.[104] One source offers this one-paragraph summary of the Uruguay Round:

> In 1986, the "Uruguay Round" of multilateral trade negotiations began at a Special Session of the GATT Contracting States. This Uruguay Round included separate negotiations on trade in goods and on trade in services, with separate groups of negotiators dealing with each topic. Subtopics for negotiation by subgroups included nontariff barriers, agriculture, subsidies and countervailing duties, intellectual property rights and counterfeit goods, safeguards, tropical products, textiles, investment policies, and dispute resolution. The negotiating sessions were extraordinarily complex, but were able to achieve a successful conclusion, giving birth to the World Trade Organization in 1995.[105]

The "successful conclusion" referred to in the quoted passage included the establishment of these treaties, all of them subject to the "single package" approach explained above:[106]

- GATT 1994
- Agreement on Agriculture
- Agreement on the Application of Sanitary and Phytosanitary Measures
- Agreement on Textiles and Clothing
- Agreement on Technical Barriers to Trade
- Agreement on Trade-Related Investment Measures (the TRIMs Agreement)

---

[104] A preference for regional trade regimes seemed apparent in the increasing strength of the European Communities (later European Union) and in the establishment of the NAFTA in the early 1990s. Bilateral approaches to trade regulation have long taken the form of bilateral "friendship, commerce, and navigation" (FCN) treaties. As GATT weaknesses became more pronounced in the 1980s, these alternatives to multilateralization gained momentum.

[105] NUTSHELL, *supra* note 92, at 40.

[106] *See supra* note 101 and accompanying text. The first 17 of the treaties listed here appear in Annexes 1A, 1B, 1C, 2, and 3 to the WTO Charter (which is the 18th treaty listed here). The charter itself, although not those 17 treaties, appears as Appendix I to this book. In addition to these Multilateral Trade Agreements, another four "Plurilateral Trade Agreements" emerged from the Uruguay Round. These were not subject to the "single package" approach described above—that is, countries could become WTO members without adopting these four treaties—and they are, for several reasons, of little direct importance to us for purposes of this summary. They are the Agreement on Trade in Civil Aircraft, the Agreement on Government Procurement, the International Dairy Agreement, and the International Bovine Meat Agreement.

- Agreement on Implementation of Article VI of the GATT 1994 (relating to customs valuation)
- Agreement on Implementation of Article VII of the GATT 1994 (relating to dumping)
- Agreement on Preshipment Inspection
- Agreement on Rules of Origin
- Agreement on Licensing Procedures
- Agreement on Subsidies and Countervailing Measures (the SCM Agreement)
- Agreement on Safeguards
- General Agreement on Trade in Services
- Agreement on Trade-Related Aspects of Intellectual Property Rights (the TRIPs Agreement)
- Understanding on Rules and Procedures Governing the Settlement of Disputes (the DSU)
- Trade Policy Review Mechanism
- Agreement Establishing the World Trade Organization

Of these treaties, the only one for which some explanation is needed here is the GATT 1994. That treaty is nearly the same as the GATT 1947 that has been described above. It has, for instance, the same four key principles and the same exceptions that were summarized in Subsections IVA and IVB of this chapter. It differs from the GATT 1947 mainly in two respects, neither of which is important for current purposes: first, the GATT 1994 excludes the Protocol of Provisional Application by which the GATT came into force in 1948; and second, it incorporates by reference numerous interpretations of and amendments to the GATT 1947.

E. The Nature of the WTO and the WTO Charter

The WTO is similar in some fundamental respects to the IMF and the MDBs. On the other hand, the WTO differs importantly from the IMF and the MDBs—and, indeed, from the ITO whose creation was envisioned but aborted in the late 1940s.

The key similarity is that the WTO, as created in 1995 following the approval of the Uruguay Round agreements, constitutes an international organization. The GATT did not. As explained above, the GATT was, as a technical matter, merely a treaty designed to have rather temporary application pending the creation of the ITO. When the plans for an ITO were scrapped, the GATT gradually took on the mantle of international trade liberalization, but it was limited as an institutional and legal matter because it lacked the status of an international organization.[107] The WTO over-

---

[107] Several initiatives were taken to address this limitation. One such initiative, as indicated in the "GEO Timeline" provided in Subsection IA of this chapter, was the creation

comes that limitation, a point made explicit in Article VIII of the WTO Charter, which provides that the WTO "shall have legal personality" and shall be accorded by its members the legal capacity and privileges and immunities appropriate to its stature as an international organization.[108]

A key difference distinguishing the WTO is the "bare-bones" nature of its charter. Instead of including in the text of the WTO Charter detailed rules regarding international trade regulation—as was the case in, say, the IMF Charter with its detailed rules relating to national currencies—the Uruguay Round negotiators kept such substantive matters as these outside the WTO Charter, in the multitude of treaties enumerated earlier, and confined the WTO Charter provisions just to those institutional and procedural matters necessary to establish and run the organization. Moreover, in doing so, the negotiators left most authority over international trade regulation with the contracting parties themselves, as opposed to granting the WTO as an institution the authority to change or add to the rules or to initiate complaints over a member country's adherence to those rules.

One source captures several of these points of similarity and difference, and summarizes the WTO's main mission, as follows:

> The duties of the World Trade Organization are to facilitate the implementation, administer the operations and further objectives of [the Uruguay Round Agreements]. Its duties also include the resolution of disputes under the agreements [discussed below], reviews of trade policy and cooperation with the International Monetary Fund (IMF) and the World Bank. To achieve these goals, the WTO Agreement provides a charter for the new organization, creating a minimalist institution with limited capabilities, and no substantive or executive competence. The WTO as an institution, for example, has no power to bring actions on its own initiative. . . . Under the provisions of the WTO Agreement, only the Members of WTO can initiate actions via the Dispute Settlement Understanding [and enforcement] of WTO obligations is primarily through permitting Members to retaliate or cross retaliate against other members, rather than by execution of WTO institutional orders.[109]

---

of the GATT Council to act between the sessions of the GATT contracting parties and to act as their delegate in decisionmaking.

[108] WTO Charter, art. VIII, paras. 1, 2.

[109] NUTSHELL, *supra* note 92, at 43–44.

F. WTO Membership and Structure

Like the IMF and the World Bank, WTO membership stretches around the world. As of late 2004, 148 countries had become WTO members, with more countries still involved in accession negotiations. These negotiations establish the details of how various Uruguay Round treaties will be implemented by the incoming member.[110] We can expect to see in the coming years the growth of WTO membership to include nearly all countries in the world.

Also like the IMF and the MDBs, the WTO has a governing structure that features several tiers.[111] The top tier in WTO governance is the Ministerial Conference, which meets biennially and is composed of representatives of all WTO members. The Ministerial Conference is responsible for authorizing new multilateral trade negotiations, to grant waivers of obligations to members in exceptional circumstances, to adopt interpretations of the trade agreements under WTO administration, and to carry out other WTO operations. As in the case of the boards of governors of the IMF and the World Bank, however, most of the functions of the Ministerial Conference are, in practice, performed by the General Council, which sits at the second tier of WTO governance. The General Council, which consists of representatives of all WTO members, has executive authority over the day-to-day operations of the WTO and meets whenever necessary.

The third tier of WTO governance consists of various councils, bodies, and committies that report to the Ministerial Conference or the General Council. These include most notably the Dispute Settlement Body and the Trade Policy Review Body. The first of these is described in the following subsection. The Trade Policy Review Body operates the Trade Policy Review Mechanism (TPRM), which aims to improve adherence to WTO agreements in part through a regular review, and public appraisal, of each WTO member's trade policies.

G. Decisionmaking and Dispute Settlement

Although some structural aspects of the WTO resemble those of the IMF and the MDBs, the rules on decisionmaking and voting differ substantially from those of the other GEOs. Whereas the IMF and the MDBs

---

[110] These details can include such matters, for example, as the status of a member as a "developing country" for purposes of special and differential treatment under particular agreements. For a discussion of this topic in respect to China's accession, and information about accession negotiations more generally, *see generally* Raj Bhala, *Enter the Dragon: An Essay on China's WTO Accession Saga*, 15 AM. U. INT'L L. REV. 1469 (2000).

[111] For a useful summary of WTO governance and decision-making, *see* NUTSHELL, *supra* note 92, at 52–54, from which material is liberally drawn for the following synopsis.

use a weighted voting system,[112] the WTO relies on a blend of consensus and a one-state-one-vote regime. The precise contours of this blend are not yet clear, because Article IX, paragraph 1 of the WTO Charter describes these two elements—consensus and the one-state-one-vote approach—in language that is too brief to be definitive:

> The WTO shall continue the practice of decision-making by consensus followed under GATT 1947. Except as otherwise provided, where a decision cannot be arrived at by consensus, the matter at issue shall be decided by voting.[113]

Although, at first glance, the WTO's reliance (at least partially) on consensus would seem to reduce the likelihood of any tough decisions actually being made—a feature of the old GATT decision-making process that attracted much criticism—in fact, this is not the case. Thus far, the most important decisions to be taken by the WTO have arisen in the context of trade complaints made between various members about each other's policies. In that context, a special form of consensus is applied; it has been referred to as an "inverted consensus" approach because (unlike the situation under the old GATT rules) the adoption of a dispute panel report (or, on appeal, an Appellate Body report) is assured unless all members of the Dispute Settlement Body (a special assembly of the WTO General Council that includes representatives of all WTO members), including the WTO member that prevailed in the dispute, decide (by "consensus") to reject such a report.[114] Such a decision to reject a report is so unlikely as to virtually guarantee that WTO determinations of trade violations will in fact take effect, thereby triggering one of several forms of "enforcement."[115] In short, the dispute settlement provisions now have "teeth" that they lacked before the Uruguay Round.

---

[112] *See supra* Subsections IIG and IIIE of this chapter for descriptions of the weighted voting system as applied in the IMF and the MDBs, respectively.

[113] WTO Charter, art. IX, para. 1. A footnote at the end of the first of these two sentences explains that "consensus" will be deemed achieved "if no Member, present at the meeting when the decision is taken, formally objects to the proposed decision."

[114] *See* Understanding on Rules and Procedures Governing the Settlement of Disputes (Annex 2 to the WTO Charter), art. 16, para. 4.

[115] In general, there are three methods by which a determination under the DSU that a country has violated its trade treaty obligations can be "enforced": (1) that country can stop the violative practice; (2) that country can, although continuing the practice, provide compensation to the prevailing party in the dispute that will offset the injury done to it by the practice; (3) the prevailing party can, in the face of failure by the losing party to take either step (1) or step (2), impose retaliatory trade measures that would otherwise be inconsistent with its own trade treaty obligations. *See id.* arts. 21, 22.

CHAPTER THREE
EVALUATING THE CRITICISMS DIRECTED AT THE IMF

I.   SURVEY OF THE CRITICISMS

In Section V of Chapter One I enumerated the 25 key criticisms directed at the GEOs. Seven of those criticisms are leveled at the IMF in particular. In the following paragraphs I explain each of those seven criticisms. In doing so, I try to express each criticism in what I consider to be its most forceful terms. As will be clear from Section II of this chapter, I do not agree with several of these criticisms, nor do I agree with some of the assumptions and value judgments on which several of them rest. Therefore, my attempt to state the criticisms persuasively here should not be taken at this stage as any endorsement of them on my part.

A.   Criticism #I-1—Bad Medicine

This is one of the most pervasive of all the criticisms leveled at the IMF, and it has taken many forms.[1] Perhaps the most common is that the economic and financial policies that the IMF prescribes for countries that come to it for financial assistance do little or no good, and often do great harm, to those countries—not just to certain segments of the population, such as the poor, within those countries (that is the subject of Criticism #I-2, "distributional and social injustice") but to those countries' overall economic health. More specifically, according to this criticism, IMF-prescribed policies—following a "Washington Consensus"[2] recipe that "typically con-

---

[1] For citations to examples in the literature of some criticisms along these lines, *see* Part I of Appendix A.

[2] The term "Washington Consensus" was used by John Williamson in 1989, in a background paper for a conference on dealing with economic policy in Latin America, as a label for ten types of reforms that Williamson said "almost everyone in Washington thought were needed in Latin America as of that date": fiscal discipline, reordering public expenditure priorities, tax reform, liberalization of interest rates, a competitive exchange rate, trade liberalization, liberalization of inward foreign direct investment, privatization, deregulation, and property rights. John Williamson, *From Reform Agenda to Damaged Brand Name*, FINANCE & DEVELOPMENT, Sept. 2003, at 10, 10. Williamson himself now calls for a new generation of reforms that will focus on (among other things) institutional reforms and income redistribution. *Id.* at 12–13. He also urges that the term "Washington Consensus" should be dropped from the vocabulary, in part because "there is no longer any agreement on the main lines of economic policy between the current

sists of reducing budget and balance of payments deficits, raising interest rates, reducing inflation, privatizing state assets, and reducing trade barriers and regulation on capital flows in and out of the country"[3]—discourage economic growth and drag down new investment. Another related version of the criticism is that the IMF serves as a collection agency for major financial institutions that are creditors either of the governments or of private-sector actors in the less-developed, debt-ridden countries.

Critics voicing these views have offered as evidence the Asian financial crisis that struck in the latter part of 1997 and more recent crises in Argentina and Russia. Although the specific circumstances differed, the IMF took action in all these cases that critics found to be inadequate, ill-suited for the circumstances, and harmful. The Asian financial crisis, in particular, was a flashpoint for complaints, with numerous commentators charging that the IMF totally mishandled the Asian financial crisis by prescribing economic and financial policies that needlessly worsened the crisis.

A form of this criticism centers on the notion of "moral hazard." Moral hazard has been explained this way:

> Moral hazard is a term often used when analyzing the effects of insurance. It refers to the idea that the very provision of insurance raises the likelihood of the event being insured against taking place. This is because insurance reduces the incentives for the insured party to take preventive actions. . . . In the financial context, economists and policy makers debate whether the availability of financial support from institutions like the [IMF] leads to moral hazard. That is, does the IMF's role as a lender to countries in financial crisis actually encourage borrowers and lenders to behave in ways that makes a crisis more likely?[4]

According to many critics, the answer is yes—that is, the IMF, in providing bailouts in Indonesia, Korea, Russia, and other countries, has created moral hazard in two ways: (1) by signaling to the governments engaging

---

U.S. administration and the international financial institutions." *Id.* at 11-12 (citing recent IMF criticisms of U.S. fiscal policy and the Bush administration's disdain for the expressions of concern about income distribution). For other observations on the "Washington Consensus" and future reforms, *see generally* Jeremy Clift, *Beyond the Washington Consensus*, FINANCE & DEVELOPMENT, Sept. 2003, at 9; Guillermo Ortiz, *Overcoming Reform Fatigue*, FINANCE & DEVELOPMENT, Sept. 2003, at 14.

[3] John V. Paddock, Comment, *IMF Policy and the Argentine Crisis*, 34 U. MIAMI INTER-AM. L. REV. 155, 158 (2002).

[4] TIMOTHY LANE & STEVEN PHILLIPS, MORAL HAZARD: DOES IMF FINANCING ENCOURAGE IMPRUDENCE BY BORROWERS AND LENDERS? 1 (Int'l Monetary Fund, Economic Issues No. 28, 2002), *available at* www.imf.org/external/pubs/ft/issues/issues28/index.htm (last visited Nov. 4, 2004).

in poor economic management that their bad performance will have no penalty (because the IMF will bail them out); and (2) by signaling to financiers investing in those countries that they can invest without risk (because the IMF will bail them out as well).

B. Criticism #I-2—Distributional and Social Injustice

According to this criticism, IMF operations hurt the poor, spoil the environment, and generally undermine social values.[5] All of those results could flow, of course, from policies that hurt the economy as a whole, as Criticism #I-1—"bad medicine"—alleges. But Criticism #I-2—"distributional and social injustice"—claims that even if the austerity programs that the IMF pressures its borrowing member countries to adopt do in fact provide net overall economic and financial benefits to those countries—by helping them to restore economic stability or to avoid defaulting on foreign debts, for example—they win those overall benefits at the expense of the poor. Specifically, IMF-mandated measures to balance a government's budget by cutting spending and raising revenues force that government (so the criticism runs) to eliminate public funding for social programs and to increase the price of social services, making health care and education unaffordable for the poor. Similarly, IMF-mandated policies to encourage foreign investment can lead to the abolition of minimum wage and collective bargaining laws.

Such results as these contribute to what these critics would identify as a particular evil: enlarging the gap between rich and poor within a society. Likewise, other evils of a social nature can also flow (according to this criticism) from IMF operations. Prominent among these is environmental degradation, because budget cuts can prevent a government from funding the enforcement of environmental protection laws.

In sum, this criticism claims that whatever good effects IMF policy prescriptions might have for a country in aggregate economic terms, they impose a cost that no society should have to bear. Particularly in African countries, it is claimed, the toll exacted by IMF-required austerity measures has brought an increase in poverty, a gutting of education and health programs, and social ruin.

C. Criticism #I-3—IMF Trampling of National Sovereignty

Expressed most briefly, this criticism claims that IMF conditionality encroaches on a country's rightful autonomy.[6] Observers voicing this criti-

---

[5] For citations to examples in the literature of some criticisms along these line, *see* Part I of Appendix A.

[6] For citations to examples in the literature of some criticisms along these line, *see* Part I of Appendix A.

cism typically invoke a cluster of related doctrines that international lawyers are familiar with but are hard-pressed to define satisfactorily. These include the doctrine of sovereignty itself as well as the principles of self-determination, non-interference, anti-colonialism, and the like. Most of these doctrines or principles have their foundations in treaties and other international legal instruments.[7] Critics of the IMF stand on those foundations to condemn the IMF's interference in the affairs of their borrowing member countries.

Typically, the critical attention regarding sovereignty falls most squarely on IMF conditionality, which is seen as the vehicle or instrument by which the IMF permits (or perhaps even wants) its operations to encroach on and steal away a country's autonomy and self-governance. This illustrates a relationship between Criticism #I-3—"trampling of national sovereignty"—and Criticism #I-6—"mission creep." Most of the alleged undermining of sovereignty occurs (according to the critics) because of the IMF's eagerness to impose its own will on matters not only of economic and financial policy but of social and cultural policy as well, such as human rights, military spending, social programs, government corruption, and environmental protection.[8]

D. Criticism #I-4—IMF Secrecy and Opaqueness[9]

According to this criticism, the IMF is a secretive organization in several respects. For one thing, it practices "documentary secretiveness": it typically does not disclose documents that describe its governing policies, its decisions, and its plans—that is, how it does things, what it has done, and what it plans to do. Moreover, the documents that the IMF does disclose under its selective disclosure policies are usually (according to this criticism) self-serving and biased, simply whitewashing over any negative aspects of its operations; and those policies often result only in the disclosure of

---

[7] *See, e.g.*, U.N. CHARTER, art. 2, para. 1 (listing among the principles on which the United Nations is founded "the principle of sovereign equality of all its Members"); U.N. CHARTER, art. 2, para. 7 (prohibiting any interference with matters "essentially within the domestic jurisdiction" of a state); International Covenant on Civil and Political Rights, Dec. 16, 1966, art. 1, S. TREATY DOC. NO. 95-2, 999 U.N.T.S. 171 [hereinafter ICCPR] (declaring the right of peoples to self-determination), *reprinted in* 6 I.L.M. 368, 369 (1967).

[8] From this perspective, Criticism #I-2 ("distributional and social injustice") may be regarded as the converse of Criticism #I-3 ("trampling of national sovereignty"): activists emphasizing the first criticism want the IMF to pay more attention to social, non-economic matters in its operations; activists emphasizing the second criticism want the IMF to pay less attention to such issues in its operations.

[9] For citations to examples in the literature of some criticisms of the IMF of this sort, *see* Part I of Appendix A.

documents that are distracting or deceptive in character, intended to keep the public occupied with largely irrelevant information. Furthermore, in some cases, the IMF allows the member countries themselves to determine whether certain documents relating to those countries will be made public, and this represents an abdication of responsibility by the IMF.

In addition to these forms of "documentary secretiveness," the IMF also practices (according to many of its critics) "operational secretiveness"; it conducts business in closed meetings that exclude the public from observing the IMF in action. Indeed, many key decisions are made through informal "insider" meetings that are off-limits both to public scrutiny and to the formalities to which public meetings are usually subject in order to ensure procedural fairness.

Taken together, these two types of secretiveness make the IMF opaque to the rest of the world, except perhaps to the few government officials in finance ministries or central banks with whom the IMF has its formal contacts. In maintaining this opaqueness, the IMF is (according to the critics) profoundly hypocritical, given the fact that the IMF demands openness and transparency from its borrowing member countries in terms of economic information and policies.

E.   Criticism #I-5—The IMF Democracy Deficit

Although this criticism takes many forms, its essence is that the IMF, controlled through the weighted voting system by a handful of rich countries, is an unaccountable autocracy in which the people most affected by its operations have no chance to participate and against whose practices no interested party may raise a legal challenge or appeal.[10] Evidence of such a "democracy deficit" is found (1) in the weighted voting system, which places a preponderance of power in the hands of a small cluster of countries (none of which borrows from the IMF),[11] (2) in the IMF Charter provision that empowers the institution itself to determine the legality of its own actions,[12] (3) in the absence of any genuinely independent tribunal or

---

[10] For citations to examples in the literature of some criticisms along these lines, *see* Part I of Appendix A.

[11] As noted in the "nutshell" account of the IMF that I provided in Section II of Chapter Two, the G-7 countries hold over 45 percent of the total voting power in the IMF.

[10] For citations to examples in the literature of some criticisms along these lines, *see* Part I of Appendix A.

[11] As noted in the "nutshell" account of the IMF that I provided in Section II of Chapter Two, the G-7 countries hold over 45 percent of the total voting power in the IMF.

[12] IMF Charter, art. XXIX (providing that "[a]ny question of interpretation of the provisions of this Agreement . . . shall be submitted to the Executive Board for its deci-

other panel in which IMF action can be challenged, and (4) in the difficulty or impossibility of any participation in decisionmaking by NGOs, purported beneficiaries, or any other groups outside the official government service. In this last respect, Criticism #I-5—"democracy deficit"—is related to Criticism #I-4—"secrecy and opaqueness."

Another point related to the "democracy deficit" criticism looks beyond the IMF to its member countries, many of which are themselves undemocratic in character. For those countries, there is no guarantee (and often little likelihood) that a government's participation in IMF decisionmaking will, in fact, reflect the views of the country's people, including, in particular, those persons most directly affected by those IMF decisions.

F. Criticism #I-6—IMF Mission Creep

This criticism, which has attracted a great deal of attention just in the past five years or so,[13] reflects some historical points summarized in the "nutshell" account of the IMF that I offered earlier in Section II of Chapter Two. As noted there, the IMF underwent a fundamental change in its mission (and its Charter was amended accordingly) in the 1970s, when the par value system of fixed exchange rates collapsed. Further changes in course, although less drastic, were made in the 1980s with the emergence of the debt crisis and in the 1990s when the IMF started giving direct attention to "governance" issues and crisis management (most dramatically with the Asian financial crisis).[14] As a result of these developments, the IMF now, according to many of its critics, has extended its operations into areas in which it has no authority and no competence.

---

sion" and may then, if a member country so requests, "be referred to the Board of Governors, whose decision shall be final"). The IMF Charter appears as Appendix B to this book. As explained in the "nutshell" account of the IMF that I provided in Section II of Chapter Two, the IMF Charter was amended in the late 1960s, the mid-1970s, and the early 1990s; this provision on IMF Charter interpretation, however, has remained unchanged from the original version dating from 1944. For an early analysis of this provision, *see generally* JOSEPH GOLD, INTERPRETATION BY THE FUND (Int'l Monetary Fund, Pamphlet Series No. 11, 1968).

[13] For citations to examples in the literature of some criticisms along these lines, *see* Part I of Appendix A.

[14] Bob Hockett, now at Cornell Law School and formerly a Tutor and Senior Research Fellow at Yale Law School (and, incidentally, a product of the international law program at the University of Kansas), has offered this summary of how the IMF's mission expanded in the 1990s: "Property law, contract rights, judicial reform, and other market-facilitating legal and institutional arrangements . . . occupied the IMF's attention [following the breakup of the former Soviet empire; and more recently,] . . . in the wake of the Asian financial crisis, the IMF has concerned itself with the laws of bankruptcy, corporate governance, and even political governance (via a concern with corruption)." Robert Hockett, *From Macro to Micro to "Mission-Creep": Defending the IMF's Emerging*

In order to appreciate fully the "mission creep" criticism, it is important to see the distinction, illuminated by Professor Daniel Bradlow of American University, between (1) those critics who argue that "the major problem with the IFIs [international financial institutions, including the IMF] is the way they have gone about expanding their mission rather than the mere fact that they have chosen to expand their mission"[15]—this is a battle over the direction and content of the mission creep—and (2) those critics who oppose any mission creep—that is, who "argue that the IFIs' 'mission creep' is tending to politicize the organizations in ways that will ultimately undermine their efficacy" and who believe "that the IFIs are now actively engaged in activities that require making judgments that rightfully belong to the sovereign member states."[16] Perhaps this distinction could be abbreviated as separating those critics who say "not this mission creep" from those who say "not any mission creep."[17]

As a practical matter, of course, these two sets of mission creep critics agree on many points. It seems that most or all of them would strip the IMF of the crisis-bailout function that it assumed in the late 1990s beginning with the Asian financial crisis, and would cut down the volume, scope, and perceived intrusiveness of IMF conditionality, especially in those areas that seem furthest removed from the IMF's domain of exchange rate collaboration and balance of payments stability.

G. Criticism #I-7—Asymmetry in Obligations

This criticism highlights the disparity between rich industrialized countries and economically less developed countries (LDCs) in terms of the obligations that their participation in the IMF entails.[18] The criticism emerges from two legal and institutional features of the IMF that are central to some of the criticisms already described above. The first of these features is the IMF's use of conditionality. As explained in the "nutshell" account of the IMF that I offered earlier in Section II of Chapter Two, lend-

---

Concern with the Infrastructural Prerequisites to Global Financial Stability, 41 COLUM. J. TRANSNAT'L L. 153, 156–57 (2002).

[15] Daniel D. Bradlow, *Should the International Financial Institutions Play a Role in the Implementation and Enforcement of International Humanitarian Law?*, 50 U. KAN. L. REV. 695, 709 (2002) [hereinafter Bradlow-I].

[16] *Id.* at 710.

[17] The critics who say "not any mission creep" might be further divided into those who complain that mission creep is wrong as a matter of law and those who complain that mission creep is wrong as a policy or a practical matter. I develop this distinction further in my assessment of the "mission creep" criticism, in Subsection IID of this chapter.

[18] For citations to examples in the literature of some criticisms along these lines, *see* Part I of Appendix A.

ing by the IMF to its member countries is typically conditioned upon their adherence to certain economic and financial policies approved by the IMF.

The second feature is the weighted voting system under which the IMF operates. As also explained above, the G-7 countries hold over 45 percent of the total voting power in the IMF. Perhaps more telling, though, than this percentage is the percentage of voting power held by all the countries that have relatively strong economies and that do not borrow from the IMF. By adding to the total G-7 votes the votes of just ten such other countries— Australia, Austria, Belgium, Denmark, Finland, Netherlands, Norway, Spain, Sweden, and Switzerland—the percentage of voting powers increases to nearly 59 percent.[19] Because these ten countries, like the G-7 countries, do not borrow from the IMF,[20] they do not face the same policy obligations that IMF conditionality imposes on those LDCs that do borrow from the IMF.

Combined, these two features of conditionality and weighted voting create an asymmetry in obligations that allows the rich industrialized countries controlling the IMF to force LDCs to adopt economic and financial policies that the rich countries themselves can disregard if they like. This asymmetry, it is alleged, is fundamentally unfair and perhaps illegal.

II. CRITICISMS I LARGELY DISMISS

Having summarized above the seven key criticisms directed at the IMF, I explain in the following paragraphs why I largely dismiss four of those criticisms. These are Criticism #I-1 (bad medicine), Criticism #I-3 (tram-

---

[19] *See* International Monetary Fund, IMF Member Quotas and Voting Power, and IMF Board of Governors [hereinafter IMF Members' Quotas] (showing the voting power percentage for Australia as 1.50 percent, Austria 0.87 percent, Belgium 2.13 percent, Denmark 0.77 percent, Finland 0.59 percent, Netherlands 2.39 percent, Norway 0.78 percent, Spain 1.42 percent, Sweden 1.11 percent, and Switzerland 1.61 percent), *at* www.imf.org/external/np/sec/memdir/members.htm (last visited Nov. 4, 2004). As noted earlier, the voting power percentage for the G-7 countries are as follows: United States 17.14 percent, Japan 6.15 percent, Germany 6.01 percent, France 4.96 percent, the United Kingdom 4.96 percent, Italy 3.26 percent, and Canada 2.95 percent. *Id.* Taken together, the voting power percentages for the G-7 countries and those of the other ten countries listed above total 58.60 percent.

[20] For representative lists of countries that do borrow from the IMF, *see* the pertinent tables appearing in the 2002 and 2003 IMF annual reports. INTERNATIONAL MONETARY FUND, 2002 ANNUAL REPORT 58 (2002) (showing the 23 countries for which IMF financial assistance was approved in fiscal year 2002), *available at* www.imf.org/external/ pubs/ft/ar/2002/eng/index.htm (last visited Nov. 4, 2004); INTERNATIONAL MONETARY FUND, ANNUAL REPORT 2003 66 (2003) [hereinafter IMF Annual Report 2003] (showing the 27 countries for which IMF financial assistance was approved in fiscal year 2003), *available at* www.imf.org/externalpubs/ft/ar/2003/eng/index.htm (last visited Nov. 4, 2004). For the corresponding information in the 2004 IMF annual report, *see* www. imf.org/external/pubs/ft/ar/2004/end/index.htm.

pling of national sovereignty), Criticism #I-4 (secrecy and opaqueness), and Criticism #I-6 (mission creep).

A. Criticism #I-1—Bad Medicine

As I summarized it above, this criticism asserts that the IMF prescribes economic and financial policies that fail to cure, and that indeed often make sicker, its borrowing member countries and the entire world economy. I find this criticism of the IMF unpersuasive, just as I find unpersuasive the corresponding criticism as directed against the MDBs.[21] Four main reasons lead me to this conclusion.

First, experts disagree about the fundamental issue of whether, on balance, countries adopting IMF-prescribed economic and financial policies have shown improvement or deterioration. For example, although numerous claims have been made of the disastrous economic repercussions suffered in several Asian countries that adopted IMF-prescribed policies during the financial crisis that gripped the region in the late 1990s, credible counter-claims have been made as well—pointing out, for instance, that currency values in those countries did stabilize after IMF-prescribed policies were put in place, and that those countries thereby escaped a "permanent burden in terms of the amount of dollars they [would have] had to pay abroad relative to the local value of the currency."[22] And more generally (that is, taking into account IMF operations in many countries and regions), serious statistical studies have reached mixed results, suggesting that while there is a correlation between IMF-prescribed policies and either neutral or negative performance "in terms of encouraging economic growth, raising investment and reducing inflation"[23] in those countries following the IMF prescription, such policies "do seem to be associated with a statistically significant improvement in the current account of the balance of payments or the overall balance of payments."[24] Significantly, most or all of the statistical studies—both those favorable to and those unfavorable to IMF-prescribed policies—rely on old data. Even a very recently published

---

[21] *See infra* Subsection IIB of Chapter Four, assessing Criticism #II-1—"bad economic and financial policies and projects"—leveled at the MDBs.

[22] Frontline, The Crash: Views and Comments on the IMF (1999) (quoting Stanley Fischer), *at* www.pbs.org/wgbh/pages/frontline/shows/crash/imf/views.html (last visited Nov. 4, 2004). *See also* Dhanestwar Ghura, *Building Financial Stability*, 29 IMF SURVEY 77, 77 (Mar. 6, 2000) ("[T]he Korean economy is again growing rapidly and output is now above its precrisis level. The won has strengthened substantially after losing half its value soon after the crisis erupted, and the stock market has registered large gains propelled in part by purchases by foreign investors.").

[23] Graham Bird, *Reforming the IMF: Should the Fund Abandon Conditionality?*, 7 NEW ECONOMY 214, 215 (2000).

[24] *Id.*

analysis critical of IMF programs[25] "uses data that end in 1990"[26]—hardly representative of IMF operations today.

Second, even if it were to be accepted, for the sake of argument, that countries adopting IMF-prescribed policies have taken a nose-dive economically, it is illogical to conclude simply from this fact that IMF-prescribed policies caused the nose-dive. For one thing, as one scholar points out, such a conclusion is "particularly troublesome because of the problem of defining the counter-factual; in other words, determining what would have happened in the absence of [an IMF-prescribed] program."[27] For another thing, it is unfair to conclude that the IMF-prescribed policies themselves were faulty if the country did not implement those policies fully.[28] And, of course, national economic fortunes and misfortunes have momentum—"[i]t is both unfair and economically unsound for a borrower to blame the IMF for economic difficulties that originated before the Fund's intervention began."[29] Likewise, little guidance as to the effects of IMF-prescribed policies can be gained by comparing the performance of countries that participate in IMF programs with those that do not, "[s]ince countries that participate in Fund programs tend to face worse economic conditions than those that do not."[30]

A third reason I find the "bad medicine" criticism unpersuasive focuses on the specific issue of "moral hazard" that I described above.[31] I question whether the financial assistance packages arranged by the IMF during the Asian financial crisis would be interpreted either by national governments or by foreign investors as an assurance that they need not be prudent in

---

[25] JAMES RAYMOND VREELAND, THE IMF AND ECONOMIC DEVELOPMENT 152 (2003) (finding that "[IMF] programs hurt economic growth and exacerbate income inequality").

[26] *Id.* at 160.

[27] Gopal Garuda, *Lender of Last Resort: Rethinking IMF Conditionality*, 20 HARV. INT'L REV. 36, 38 (1998). *See also* Bird, *supra* note 23, at 214 (noting that "[n]umerous academic studies examining [whether IMF programs] work suggest this is a very difficult question to answer . . . largely because while the outcome is known in countries that adopted Fund programmes, what might have happened if agreement had not been reached cannot be known—the so-called counter-factual problem").

[28] *See* Garuda, *supra* note 27, at 38 (noting that "borrower countries may not be implementing the programs as completely as the IMF expects"); Bird, *supra* note 23, at 215 (stating that "the majority of IMF programmes remain uncompleted" and that "conditionality is frequently not fully implemented"). Taking this and several other factors together, Bird concludes that "[a]ny definitive answer as to whether [IMF] conditionality works, is therefore premature." *Id.* at 216.

[29] Garuda, *supra* note 27, at 38.

[30] *Id.*

[31] *See supra* text accompanying note 4.

their policies or their investments. As for governments, I agree with the view expressed by the then-Deputy Managing Director of the IMF, Stanley Fischer: "To think that [government] policymakers pursue risky courses of action because they know the IMF safety net will catch them if things go badly is far-fetched. Countries try to avoid going to the [IMF]; policymakers whose countries end up in trouble generally do not survive politically."[32] Fischer's view on moral hazard for investors is also persuasive: "foreign equity investors had lost nearly three-quarters of the value of their equity holdings in some Asian markets . . . [and] the crisis has been costly for foreign commercial banks"; in short, "[i]nvestors have been hit hard, as they should have been, for lending unwisely."[33] Given this, I think the moral hazard complaint is exaggerated, at best, and perhaps even groundless.

A fourth reason I largely dismiss the "bad medicine" criticism is that the prescription has, in fact, been changed rather dramatically in just the last few years. The IMF has responded to its experience in the Asian financial crisis and to the criticisms that its intervention there and in Argentina and Russia have attracted. I would highlight two particular aspects of that IMF response: changes in its approach to crisis management and changes in its conditionality practices.

As for crisis management, the IMF has taken several initiatives that aim to prevent crises from breaking out in the first place, such as (1) creating (in 1999) the Contingent Credit Line, described in the "nutshell" account of the IMF that I offered above in Section II of Chapter Two, to recognize a member country's good economic policies by giving it special protection against the contagion of economic troubles in other countries,[34] (2) developing a system for better assessing crisis vulnerabilities in countries that could suffer rapid capital flight,[35] to provide for early warning against possible crises, and (3) enhancing the usefulness of economic data from and about member countries and the dissemination of these data to the public.[36]

---

[32] Stanley Fischer, *In Defense of the IMF*, 77 FOREIGN AFF. 103, 106 (July–Aug. 1998).

[33] *Id.* For an extensive discussion of the moral hazard question, *see generally* LANE & PHILLIPS, *supra* note 4. These authors conclude that "moral hazard's role may have been seriously overstated by some observers." *Id.* at 13.

[34] For details on the Contingent Credit Line, *see* IMF ANNUAL REPORT 2003, *supra* note 20, at 26 (describing it as providing "a better safety net for good performers").

[35] *Id.* at 21.

[36] *Id.* at 21–22, 23–24. Recently, special attention has been given to the mechanisms by which the IMF can best provide signals to official or private creditors regarding the strength of a country's economic policies. *Id.* at 25–26. The importance accorded to these and other aspects of "crisis prevention" is reflected in the fact that an entire chapter of a recent IMF annual report is dedicated to such topics. *See id.* at 21–28 (describing IMF crisis prevention policy).

In addition to these initiatives on crisis prevention, the IMF has taken several steps recently for the resolution of crises that do occur. Several of these steps respond to the insistence by some critics that principal responsibility for handling crises should remain with the governments and the markets— "[e]volving reforms of the framework for crisis resolution have been designed to reinforce incentives for countries and their creditors to reach voluntary, market-oriented solutions to their financing problems"[37]—rather than counting on an IMF bailout.[38]

The IMF's change in conditionality policies has been equally significant. The IMF's guidelines on conditionality, which had remained unchanged for many years since their adoption in 1979,[39] were changed in 2002 to reflect four principles: (1) the need to enhance the borrowing country's "ownership" of the policy reforms, (2) the need to reduce the

---

[37] *Id.* at 29. For details about such reforms, including (1) increasing the selectivity of IMF lending to countries in crisis, (2) the inclusion of collective action clauses in sovereign bond contracts, and (3) the possible establishment of a new Sovereign Debt Restructuring Mechanism (SDRM), *see id.* at 29–33. For an assessment of the proposed SDRM, *see generally* Celeste Boeri, *How to Solve Argentina's Debt Crisis: Will the IMF's Plan Work?*, 4 CHI. J. INT'L L. 245 (2003). *See also* Susanne Soederberg, *The International Dimensions of the Argentine Default: The Case of the Sovereign Debt Restructuring Mechanism*, 28 CANADIAN J. LATIN AM. & CARIBBEAN STUD. 97, 113–20 (2003) (describing debates over, and offering criticisms of, the proposed mechanism); Deepak Gopinath, *The Debt-Crisis Crisis*, INSTITUTIONAL INVESTOR, Aug. 2002, at 72, 73–76 (describing the SDRM proposal and concerns it has raised with private sector critics). For the IMF's description of its efforts at designing an SDRM "to create a framework for an equitable debt restructuring that restores sustainability and growth, without including incentives that unintentionally increase the risk of default," see generally International Monetary Fund, *Proposals for a Sovereign Debt Restructuring Mechanism (SDRM)—A Factsheet* (Jan. 2003), *at* www.imf.org/external/np/exr/facts/sdrm.htm (last visited Nov. 4, 2004).

[38] This increased emphasis on private sector involvement in crisis management began in 1998. *See* Ross B. Leckow, *The International Monetary Fund and Strengthening the Architecture of the International Monetary System*, 30 LAW & POL'Y INT'L BUS. 117, 126–28 (1999) (describing how initiatives emerging from the IMF's October 1998 annual meeting "identify the need to more effectively involve the private sector" in resolving balance-of-payments crises). Leckow, a good friend of mine at the IMF, also describes other initiatives that focus on crisis prevention, including strengthening of IMF surveillance, strengthening of member countries' financial systems, and promoting greater transparency. *Id.* at 118–25.

[39] For background information on IMF conditionality and its evolution, particularly after 1979, *see generally* ERIK DENTERS, LAW AND POLICY OF IMF CONDITIONALITY (1996); MANUEL GUITIÁN, FUND CONDITIONALITY: EVOLUTION OF PRINCIPLES AND PRACTICES (Int'l Monetary Fund, Pamphlet Series No. 38, 1981); Jacques J. Polak, *The Changing Nature of IMF Conditionality, in* 184 ESSAYS IN INTERNATIONAL FINANCE 22 (Princeton Univ. Dep't of Econ. ed., 1991); Harold James, *From Grandmotherliness to Governance: The Evolution of IMF Conditionality*, FINANCE & DEVELOPMENT, Dec. 1998, at 44; Erik Denters, *International Monetary Fund (IMF), in* INTERNATIONAL ENCYCLOPAEDIA OF LAWS 54–60 (R. Blainpain ed., 1993).

number of conditions, (3) the need to tailor the policy programs (and hence the content of the conditionalities) more closely to the borrowing country's circumstances, and (4) the need to improve clarity in the specification of conditions.[40]

An IMF "Staff Statement" appended to the new guidelines on conditionality elaborates on those four principles as follows:

> *National ownership* refers to a willing assumption of responsibility for a program of policies, by country officials who have the responsibility to formulate and carry out those policies. . . . [National ownership] is a key determinant of success, and the guidelines aim to promote ownership by ensuring that conditionality is well designed and is formulated through a mutually acceptable process led by the member. . . . [The policies covered by conditionality will pay] due regard to the domestic social and political objectives . . . of the member.

> *Parsimony* means that program-related conditions should be limited to the minimum necessary to achieve the goals of the Fund-supported program or to monitor its implementation and that the choice of conditions should be clearly focused on those goals. . . . [One of those goals involves] fostering sustainable economic growth . . . [which] is linked to the pursuit of higher living standards and a reduction of poverty.

> *Tailoring* of programs implies a recognition that the causes of balance of payments difficulties and the emphasis to be given to various program goals may differ among members. . . . [Although] most Fund-supported programs will include certain common elements [and] . . . must be applied consistently so as to maintain the uniform treatment of members . . . the specification and timing of policy adjustments and the appropriate mix of financing and adjustment will reflect the member's circumstances. . . .

---

[40] INTERNATIONAL MONETARY FUND, IMF SURVEY SUPPLEMENT 16–17 (2003) [hereinafter IMF SURVEY SUPPLEMENT], *available at* www.imf.org/external/pubs/ft/survey/2003/091503.pdf (last visited Feb. 16, 2004). For the text of the revised guidelines on conditionality, *see generally* INTERNATIONAL MONETARY FUND, GUIDELINES ON CONDITIONALITY (Sept. 25, 2002) [hereinafter IMF GUIDELINES ON CONDITIONALITY], *available at* www.imf. org/external/np/pdr/cond/2002/eng/guid/092302.pdf (last visited Nov. 4, 2004). For a commentary on the new guidelines on conditionality, *see* VIVIEN COLLINGWOOD, BRETTON WOODS PROJECT, INDISPENSABLE OR UNWORKABLE? THE IMF'S NEW APPROACH TO CONDITIONALITY (2002), *available at* www.brettonwoodsproject.org/topic/adjustment/conditionality/s32conditbrfg.pdf (last visited Nov. 4, 2004); Vivien Collingwood, *The IMF's New Approach to Conditionality: Indispensable or Unworkable?*, AFRICA NEWS, Feb. 6, 2003, LEXIS.

Clarity means that program-related conditions should be transparently distinguished from other elements of the authorities' program both in staff reports and in the member's program documents.[41]

The adoption of these changes, like some of the other initiatives referred to above regarding crisis management, demonstrates that the IMF is not— or at least wishes not to be seen as—the immovable object, stubbornly mired in an outmoded ideology, that some critics portray it to be. How the IMF will follow through on these new initiatives, of course, remains to be seen. For the moment, however, I believe the IMF should be viewed favorably for updating its approach on both crisis management and conditionality to respond to its critics and recent experience.

Taken together, these four reasons prompt me to dismiss the "bad medicine" criticism. I have seen no persuasive evidence, based on recent data, that IMF "medicine," when actually taken as prescribed, has generally made its borrowing member countries worse off than they would have been without the IMF's involvement—which, it must be remembered, includes infusions of funds as well as policy prescriptions. Moreover, the very large infusions of such funds in Asia and elsewhere cannot, I believe, be fairly seen as having created as much moral hazard as many critics would have us think. And, in any event, the "bad medicine" criticism is anachronistic because the IMF has changed course in important ways in the past few years.

Does the conclusion I have drawn in this subsection—that I am unconvinced by the claim that the "medicine" prescribed by the IMF is generally or intrinsically or ideologically wrong—mean that I view the "medicine" prescribed by the IMF as always right? No. Strong arguments can be made in retrospect that particular forms or amounts of IMF intervention were unfortunate because they hurt rather than helped a country's economic condition, at least in the short term; and indeed such arguments have been forcefully made in the cases of Korea and Argentina in particular.[42] The

---

[41] IMF GUIDELINES ON CONDITIONALITY, *supra* note 40, at 8–11 (emphasis in original).

[42] For one of many collections of writings questioning, in retrospect, the IMF's involvement in Korea—and particularly its approach to interest rate policies and to corporate and financial restructuring—*see generally* KOREA CRISIS AND RECOVERY (David T. Coe & Se-Jik Kim, eds. 2002) (papers and commentary presented at a conference co-sponsored by the IMF and the Korea Institute for International Economic Policy). For a summary of the July 2004 retrospective assessment by the IMF's Independent Evaluation Office ("IEO") of the IMF's role in Argentina in the 1990s, *see Watchdog Faults Argentina, But Also IMF*, 33 IMF SURVEY 229 (Aug. 9, 2004). The latter report concludes that the IMF was too lenient in respect of Argentina's fiscal deficits and too generous in its support of Argentina's currency exchange policies. *See* Adam Thomson, *IMF Was 'Too Lenient' Over Argentina's Deficits as Economy Headed for Crisis*, FINANCIAL TIMES, July 28, 2004, at 9.

conclusion that I have drawn is not that IMF prescriptions have always been correct but rather that Criticism #I-1—claiming that such prescriptions are intrinsically incorrect because of some fundamental ideological mistake or that they have as a general matter had no beneficial effects on the countries applying them—has not been proven. There is doubtless room for error and room for improvement, but this fact does not, in my view, warrant a wholesale castigation of IMF prescriptions as "bad medicine," at least as long as opportunities exist for individual errors to be identified and improvements to be made.

B.   Criticism #I-3—IMF Trampling of National Sovereignty

As I summarized it above, this criticism claims that in imposing conditions on its loans to member countries, the IMF tramples on their national sovereignty—not just in economics but increasingly in other areas of state autonomy. I find this criticism of the IMF unpersuasive, just as I find unpersuasive the corresponding criticism as directed against the MDBs.[43] Two main reasons lead me to this conclusion.

First, states are under no legal obligation to accept the conditions of an IMF loan, for the simple reason that states are under no legal obligation to seek an IMF loan in the first place—or, for that matter, to join the IMF. While it is true that an approval of IMF financing often triggers other official and private sector financing for a country,[44] and conversely that a country might be hard-pressed to obtain the financing it wants if it were to not accept the IMF financing (and hence the conditions that financing carries), it is also true that if a government is dead-set against adopting the economic and financial policies prescribed by the IMF, that government can reject them by rejecting IMF involvement. Proposals to do just that have emerged recently in some countries.[45]

---

[43] *See infra* Section II of Chapter Four.

[44] For an explanation of this "triggering effect," *see* John W. Head, *Suspension of Debtor Countries' Voting Rights in the IMF: An Assessment of the Third Amendment to the IMF Charter*, 33 VA. J. INT'L L. 591, 594 n.5 (1993) [hereinafter *Third Amendment*]. *See also* TREASURER'S DEPARTMENT, FINANCIAL ORGANIZATION AND OPERATIONS OF THE IMF 13 (Int'l Monetary Fund, Pamphlet Series No. 45, 2d ed., 1991) [hereinafter FINANCIAL ORGANIZATION AND OPERATIONS] (explaining that "commercial banks have generally been more willing to extend loans to a debtor country if the Fund has approved an arrangement for that country" and noting that this is one way in which the Fund serves "as a catalyst in generating additional international credit and capital for its members").

[45] *See, e.g., Indonesian NGOs Ask Gov't to Cut Ties with Int'l Organisations,* Asia Pulse, Jan. 23, 2003, LEXIS (reporting that "[v]arious non-governmental organizations (NGOs) urged the government [of Indonesia] to cut off relations with the International Monetary Fund" and other organizations on grounds that "those international institutions could only exacerbate the plight of the Indonesian economy").

Second, to the extent that this "trampling of sovereignty" criticism relies on the principle of self-determination—by claiming that the IMF interferes with a right of people within a borrowing member country to "freely determine their political status and freely pursue their economic, social and cultural development"[46]—or on some purported "right to development," the criticism rests on a misperception of those norms. Even if the principle of self-determination amounts to something more than just a slogan,[47] it surely cannot mean that a government can demand IMF loans to help it overcome the ill effects of economic and financial policies that the IMF regards as unproductive or counterproductive.[48] Likewise, international law contains no generally accepted "right to development assistance" from another country or from the IMF.[49]

In short, I find the appeals to sovereignty weak in this context. Certain elements of the "trampling of sovereignty" criticism—those that complain about the content of conditionality or that bemoan "mission creep"—are worthy of serious attention as separate issues, and I give them that attention in my assessments of Criticism #I-1 and Criticism #I-6. Standing alone, however, the claim that IMF operations impinge on sovereignty packs no serious punch.

C. Criticism #I-4—IMF Secrecy and Opaqueness

As I summarized it above, this criticism asserts that the IMF is a closed, non-transparent organization that operates in secret, despite its insistence on transparency in the governments of its members. The IMF has already responded to this criticism. Over the past five years in particular, the IMF has undertaken an impressive project to provide more information on its operations.[50] For example, between January 2001 and March 2003, infor-

---

[46] ICCPR, *supra* note 7, art. 1(1).

[47] For a brief analysis of the principle of self-determination, and the suggestion that it either amounts to a slogan or to a subsidiary principle that takes back seat to a more fundamental principle of international peace and security, *see* John W. Head, *Selling Hong Kong to China: What Happened to the Right of Self-Determination?*, 46 U. KAN. L. REV. 283, 283, 301–04 (1998).

[48] For my assessment of the principle of self-determination in the context of MDB operations, *see infra* Subsection IID of Chapter Four.

[49] For my assessment of the purported "right to development" in the context of MDB operations, *see id.*

[50] For an overview of IMF efforts in this regard, *see* International Monetary Fund, *Transparency at the IMF—A Factsheet* (Apr. 2003) [hereinafter *Transparency at the IMF*], at http://www.imf.org/external/np/exr/facts/transpar.htm (last visited Nov. 4, 2004). For further explications of the IMF's transparency policy and practice, *see generally* International Monetary Fund, *The Fund's Transparency Policy* (Sept. 25, 2002) (statement by Horst Köhler, then the IMF Managing Director), *available at* http://www.imf.org/external/np/pdr/trans/2002/eng/092502.htm (last visited Nov. 4, 2004); INTERNA-

mation as published on Executive Board action in over 80 percent of all Article IV consultations, the "Letters of Intent for 93 percent of countries' requests" for (or review of) the use of IMF resources were released, and "57 percent of stand-alone reports on IMF-supported programs were published."[51] The IMF now posts information on its website about each member's financial position with the IMF, quarterly IMF financial statements, and other information about administrative and operational aspects of the IMF.[52]

I find these responses satisfactory. That is, I believe the IMF now provides adequate information to permit interested parties to know enough about IMF operations to evaluate and criticize those operations. No doubt some further improvements in IMF transparency are warranted and will be made in coming years as pressure intensifies for yet more transparency among all public international institutions. But, for now, I largely dismiss the "secrecy and opaqueness" criticism as it applies to the IMF.

In this regard, I draw a somewhat different conclusion regarding the IMF from those I draw regarding the WTO and the MDBs—institutions that I believe should do more than they have done to facilitate public understanding of how they operate and what they plan to do.[53] This difference in my views on the IMF versus my views on those other institutions

---

TIONAL MONETARY FUND, THE FUND'S TRANSPARENCY POLICY—PROGRESS REPORT ON PUBLICATION OF COUNTRY DOCUMENTS (Apr. 4, 2003), *available at* http://www.imf.org/external/np/pdr/trans/2003/040403.htm (last visited Nov. 4, 2004); INTERNATIONAL MONETARY FUND, THE FUND'S TRANSPARENCY POLICY—ISSUES AND NEXT STEPS (Int'l Monetary Fund, Public Information Notice No. 03/122, Oct. 10, 2003), *available at* http://www.imf.org/external/np/sec/pn/2003/pn03122.htm (last visited Nov. 4, 2004).

[51] *Transparency at the IMF, supra note* 50. As explained in the "nutshell" account of the IMF that I gave in Section II of Chapter Two, Article IV consultations are the annual discussions that the IMF holds with each of its member countries regarding economic and financial developments, problems, and policies. Copies of Article IV reports and summaries are available at International Monetary Fund, List of Recent Article IV Consultations, *at* http:www.imf.org/external/np/sec/aiv/index.htm (last visited Nov. 4, 2004). To see letters of intent and similar documents by which borrowing member countries enumerate economic and financial policies that they intend to implement, *see* International Monetary Fund, Country's Policy Intentions Documents, *at* http://www.imf.org/external/np/loi/mempub.asp (last visited Nov. 4, 2004). It is worth noting that the IMF itself is prohibited by its Charter from broadcasting official IMF views on a member country's economic performance. *See* IMF Charter, art. XII, § 8 (requiring approval by a 70-percent majority of total voting power in order to "publish a report made [by the IMF] to a member regarding its monetary or economic conditions and developments which directly tend to produce a serious disequilibrium in the international balance of payments of members"). For a discussion of how this provision bears on IMF transparency practices, *see* François Gianviti, *The Reform of the International Monetary Fund (Conditionality and Surveillance)*, 34 INT'L LAW. 107, 109 (2000).

[52] Gianviti, *supra* note 51, at 109.

[53] *See infra* Section III of Chapter Four and Section III of Chapter Five.

partly reflects differences in the character of the information at issue. In the case of the MDBs, whose main business is to help propose, design, and finance specific projects in the territories of member countries, both "operational secretiveness" and "documentary secretiveness"[54] are highly objectionable because they restrict input by members of the public who could be directly affected by, and who could offer the MDBs knowledgeable and helpful views on, the proposed projects. In the case of IMF, however, which operates at the policy level—designing not physical projects but rather programs of economic and financial policy that it urges a member country to implement—there is less scope for helpful input from the general public into the deliberations of the IMF itself, and relatively more need for input from the general public into the policy decisions of their own national governments.

The essence of this difference might be captured in what I shall call the "input-information ratio": the greater the potential value and importance of the public's input into the operations of an international institution, the greater should be the volume and detail of the information made public about those operations. In my view, the recent increase in IMF transparency (regarding its own operations, that is), creates an "input-information ratio" for the IMF that is adequate.

The same is not true about the transparency of the many national governments. I hasten to add this point because the term "transparency" has been used both (1) in referring to the openness of the IMF itself and (2) in referring to the openness of its member governments regarding their own operations.[55] In my view, there is far too little of the latter—openness of national governments regarding their own operations. This point appears in my observations about some of the other criticisms—particularly those complaining of the IMF's "mission creep" (Criticism#I-6) and of its "democracy deficit" (Criticism # I-5)—and I shall return to it also in outlining recommendations in Section IV of this chapter.

D. Criticism #I-6—IMF Mission Creep

As I summarized it above, this criticism asserts that as both a legal and a practical matter, the IMF has overstepped its authority and its competence in providing bailouts and adopting policies on a proliferation of topics. As will be seen, I give a great deal of attention to the "mission creep"

---

[54] For an explanation of these two types of secretiveness, *see supra* Subsection ID of this chapter.

[55] *See, e.g., Transparency at the IMF, supra* note 50 (treating transparency as involving both "[g]reater openness on the part of member countries" and "[g]reater openness and clarity by the IMF about its own policies and the advice it provides to members").

criticism as it arises in the context of the MDBs,[56] In doing so, I emphasize the distinction between two related complaints: (1) that mission creep is wrong as a legal matter because the MDBs have acted outside their charters (*ultra vires*) by expanding their purview into such areas as environmental protection, indigenous peoples, involuntary resettlement, governance, corruption, and so forth; and (2) that mission creep, whatever its legal legitimacy, is wrong as a matter of ideology and policy.

In the context of the IMF, I believe the first of these two complaints—that the IMF acts *ultra vires* in delving into such areas as "governance" issues and crisis management—is satisfactorily laid to rest by the analysis that Bob Hockett has given in discussing the IMF's move "from macro to micro."[57] Hockett explains how the IMF has expanded its agenda to include microeconomic and structural issues—encompassing, he says, "market-facilitating legal and institutional arrangements" and, most recently, "laws of bankruptcy, corporate governance, and even political governance."[58] But Hockett rebuts the "mission creep" claim on several grounds, including the fact that the pertinent IMF Charter provisions are quite broad in their formulation—the result, Hockett explains, of an intentional effort by the persons drafting it "to incorporate a good deal of 'creative ambiguity' into the [Charter's] final draft in order to provide for future contingencies and to secure agreement."[59] I find Hockett's analysis unassailable; from a legal perspective, the "mission creep" criticism fails when directed against the IMF.[60]

Hockett also addresses the second of the two "mission creep" complaints: that mission creep, whatever its legal legitimacy, is wrong as a matter of ideology and policy. According to Hockett, the IMF's expansion of its agenda to include structural and microeconomic matters is not only right as a matter of necessity but indeed "an entirely foreseeable consequence of float-

---

[56] *See infra* Subsection IIA of Chapter Four.

[57] *See generally* Hockett, *supra* note 14 (discussing the IMF's change in mission).

[58] *Id.* at 156. *See also supra* note 14.

[59] Hockett, *supra* note 14, at 178.

[60] To conclude, as I have, that the IMF has not acted *ultra vires* in gradually incorporating various issues into its purview is not to suggest that the IMF does not face pressures to act *ultra vires* in other respects. My own experience with such pressure came when I was working in the Legal Department of the IMF in the late 1980s and saw firsthand the attempts by representatives of the U.S. government to have the IMF impose a sanction not contemplated by the IMF Charter—a suspension of voting rights—against a few countries that had failed to repay IMF credits on time. The Legal Department, led by the General Counsel, Mr. François Gianviti, showed spine in resisting what would have been *ultra vires* action and in insisting that a suspension of voting rights was a power that the IMF could not legally exercise without an amendment to the IMF Charter. From this background emerged the Third Amendment, which I helped draft. For more details in this regard, *see generally* Head, *Third Amendment, supra* note 44.

ing exchange rates and the globalization of foreign exchange markets since the 1970s."[61] He states his point more fully in this manner:

> The pragmatic case for the Fund's shift of attention to microeconomic variables can . . . be reduced, with some perhaps regrettable crudity, to a simple "equation": floating currencies (Second amendment), plus globally liberalized currency markets (arbitrage unimpeded by technological or regulatory limitation) and the potential cross-border "spillover"or "contagion" effects of financial panic equal a colossal heightening of the global regulatory importance of domestic microeconomic or "structural" variables. Sustained market confidence and the avoidance of global panic behavior simply demand attention from monetary authorities.[62]

The IMF is not alone, of course, in recognizing the practical necessity of expanding its attention to include structural issues, including issues of governance. As I explain below in Chapter Four, the MDBs have expanded their attention in the same manner—recognizing thereby the important bearing that governance and other policy issues have on economic well-being. The IMF has explained this connection in developing its own policy on governance.[63]

Hockett's assessment should silence the mission creep critics from both a legal and a practical perspective. And it addresses both sides of the distinction Bradlow draws between those critics who say "not any mission creep" and those who say "not this mission creep."[64] That is, Hockett has explained both (1) why it is appropriate for the IMF to adapt to changing circumstances in general, and (2) why the specific direction that the IMF has taken in expanding the scope of its attention is both legal and necessary.

---

[61] Hockett, *supra* note 14, at 158.

[62] *Id.* at 176. For a shorter treatment by Hockett of the same subject, *see generally* Robert Hockett, *Legally Defending Mission Creep*, 13 INT'L LEGAL PERSP. 34 (2002).

[63] *See* James, *supra* note 39, at 46 (explaining that the IMF's willingness to take social and political matters into account in its operations "was a consequence of reflections on the collapse of communism and on the links between political and economic reform" and reflected the view "that economic efficiency depends on a functioning civil society, on the rule of law, and on respect for private property"). The IMF's guidance note on governance, adopted by its Executive Board in July 1997, asserted that "it is legitimate for management to seek information about the political situation in member countries as an essential element in judging the prospects for policy implementation." INTERNATIONAL MONETARY FUND, GOOD GOVERNANCE: THE IMF'S ROLE 5 (Aug. 1997), *available at* http://www.imf.org/external/pubs/ft/exrp/govern/govern.pdf (last visited Nov. 4, 2004).

[64] *See supra* notes 15–17 and accompanying text.

This analysis prompts a follow-up question: has the IMF gone far enough? Has it expanded and adapted the scope of its attention to include all the issues that it should take into account in order to fulfill its functions? I believe not. In particular, I believe the IMF needs to place more emphasis on social aspects of its operations, a matter that I discuss in my analysis of Criticism #II-2—"distributional and social injustice." That discussion follows immediately below, as I turn to those criticisms that I generally endorse.

III. CRITICISMS I GENERALLY ENDORSE

The four criticisms that I have assessed above—Criticisms #I-1, #I-3, #I-4, and #I-6—appear unpersuasive in most respects, although I have identified some elements of those criticisms that I believe do make some sense and should be taken seriously. Just the opposite is true of the remaining three criticisms leveled at the IMF. That is, I find these other three criticisms generally persuasive, although there are some elements to most of them that are unconvincing on closer inspection. I offer my views below on those three criticisms: Criticism #I-2 (distributional and social injustice), Criticism #I-5 (democracy deficit), and Criticism #II-7 (asymmetry in obligations).

A. Criticism #I-2—Distributional and Social Injustice

As noted above, this criticism can be summarized as follows: the economic and financial policies that the IMF insists on create distributional inequities and ignore the social aspects of a country's well-being. Expressed in such a blunt manner as that, this criticism strikes me as inaccurate because it both overstates and understates the IMF's role. It overstates the IMF's role by suggesting that the IMF-prescribed policies are so detailed as to dictate specific budgetary decisions by the governments of borrowing countries. A survey of the actual documentation of those policies belies that suggestion. For example, the letter of intent submitted by the government of Indonesia in late October 1997, when the Asian financial crisis had hit that country, did not dictate specific budget cuts.[65] It did, however, specifically state that "it is imperative that the adjustment program does not result in a worsening of [the] economic and social conditions [of the poor] . . . Measures necessary to achieve fiscal targets will protect expenditures on

---

[65] Letter of Intent and Memorandum on Economic and Financial Policies from Government of Indonesia, to Michael Camdessus, Managing Director, IMF (n.p.) (Oct. 31, 1997) [hereinafter Indonesia Letter of Intent), *at* http://www.imf.org/external/np/loi/103197.htm (last visited Nov. 4, 2004). The letter of intent, or more precisely the "Memorandum of Economic and Financial Policies" attached to the letter of intent, simply refers to the government's "intentions to cut spending" by postponing "major state enterprise infrastructure projects and development expenditures." *Id.* ¶ 10. *See also* Garuda, *supra* note 27, at 36 (noting the IMF's assertion that "it does not dictate the specific details of reform programs, such as specifying the exact source of budget cuts").

health and education . . . [and] budgetary allocation for social spending will be increased."[66]

In addition to overstating the IMF's role, the blanket criticism that the IMF insists on financial policies that create distributional inequities and ignore the social aspects of a country's well-being is inaccurate in another way: it understates the degree of attention that the IMF has given in recent years to the social aspects of a country's well-being. For well over a decade, numerous IMF-supported programs have been designed to provide specific protections for the poorest consumers and workers in borrowing member countries.[67] In urging governments to provide such protections, the IMF has advanced the view that one of the elements in a "strategy of high-quality growth" for a country is "sound social policies, including social safety nets to protect the poor during the period of economic reform, cost-effective basic social expenditures, and employment-generating labor market policies."[68] In a recent annual report, the IMF offered this description of how social issues bear on its operations:

The IMF is committed to integrating poverty and social impact analysis in programs supported by lending under the [IMF's Poverty Reduction and Growth Facility]. The purpose of this analysis is to assess the implications of key policy measures on the well-being of different social groups, especially the vulnerable and the poor.

When analysis indicates that a particular measure (for example, currency devaluation) may harm the poor, the impact is

[66] Indonesia Letter of Intent, *supra* note 65, ¶ 45. Similarly, the letter of intent submitted by the government of Indonesia in mid-January 1998, when the crisis had deepened, did not indicate particular budget cuts, and specifically called for the removal of subsidies to include exemptions "for prices of kerosene and diesel fuel, where increases will be kept to a minimum so as to protect the poor." Government of Indonesia, *Indonesia—Memorandum of Economic and Financial Policies* (Jan. 15, 1998), *at* http://www.imf/org/external/np/loi/011598.htm (last visited Nov. 4, 2004).

[67] *See, e.g.*, INTERNATIONAL MONETARY FUND, SOCIAL DIMENSIONS OF THE IMF'S POLICY DIALOGUE 16 (Int'l Monetary Fund, Pamphlet Series No. 47, 1995) (describing policies in Jordan in 1990 to target consumer subsidies for basic food items more narrowly through a food coupon system that retained the subsidies on sugar, rice, and powdered milk for the poorest people); *id.* at 17 (describing a program of phased increases in bread prices in Kyrgyz Republic in the early 1990s that "replaced the consumer subsidy for bread with targeted cash transactions to pensioners and families with three or more children under the age of 16" in order to reduce the fiscal deficit by driving down the "benefits to the better-off" people in the country); *id.* at 18 (describing a program in Ghana to reduce the size of the civil service by 10 percent but to provide severance payments, retraining, credit, and food-for-work opportunities in order to alleviate the financial impact on those losing their civil service jobs).

[68] *Id.* at 1.

addressed through the choice or timing of policies, the development of countervailing measures, or social safety nets.[69]

In short, the IMF does, in fact, pay a great deal of attention today to social issues and distributional fairness.[70] That being the case, why do I place Criticism #I-2—"distributional and social injustice"—in the category of criticisms that I generally endorse? Because I believe the IMF still is not doing enough in these areas. In other words, although I believe the criticism is inaccurate when expressed in its bluntest form (that the IMF forces inequity and ignores social issues), I do believe a more nuanced version of the criticism is valid: the IMF still does not give enough attention to issues of distributional and social justice.

I see two reasons for this shortcoming. First, any efforts by the IMF to wade into issues of poverty, social justice, or distribution of wealth run the risk of being rebuffed by the governments that the IMF is supposed to serve. Second, any such efforts can expose the IMF to claims that it is biased toward some groups and their interests and dismissive of others. This possibility of double attack has been described in this way:

> Almost paradoxically, the Fund faces a great deal of opposition when it tries to mitigate the effects of adjustment programs on the poor. Many countries resent a perceived violation of national sovereignty, viewing external involvement in sensitive issues of poverty and income distribution as paternalistic gestures by the West. On the IMF's side, some staff members are hesitant to move away from their traditional posture of neutrality toward distributional issues, since involvement can lead to accusations of bias in favor of spe-

---

[69] IMF ANNUAL REPORT 2003, *supra* note 20, at 44. The report goes on to list some of the safety nets built into IMF-supported programs: "subsidies or cash compensation for particularly vulnerable groups; improved distribution of essential commodities, such as medicines; temporary price controls on some essential commodities; severance pay and retraining for public sector employees who' have lost their jobs; and employment through public works programs." *Id.*

[70] For further information about IMF policies in this regard, *see generally* International Monetary Fund, *Social Impact Analysis of Economic Policies—A Factsheet* (Aug. 2001), *at* http://www.imf/org/external/np/exr/facts/sia/htm (last visited Nov. 4, 2004); *International Monetary Fund, Social Dimensions of the IMF's Policy Dialogue—A Factsheet* (Mar. 2001), *at* http:www.imf/org/external/np/exr/facts/social.htm (last visited Nov. 4, 2004). For a discussion of issues relating to distributional justice, *see generally* IMF FISCAL AFFAIRS DEPARTMENT, SHOULD EQUITY BE A GOAL OF ECONOMIC POLICY? (Int'l Monetary Fund, Economic Issues No. 16, 1998). It is perhaps worth noting that IMF attention to such issues dates back more than 15 years. *See generally* Peter S. Heller, A. Lans Bovenberg, Thanos Catsambas, Ke-Young Chu & Partharsarathi Shome, *The Implications of Fund-Supported Adjustment Programs for Poverty* (Int'l Monetary Fund Occasional Paper Series No. 58, 1988).

cific groups. This dilemma is especially evident when the Fund is pressured to consider issues ranging from environmental degradation to human rights.[71]

In my view, the IMF should wade more robustly into these issues than it has so far, mainly by placing more pressure on borrowing governments to implement IMF prescriptions for economic discipline in a way that provides solid protection of the poor, the disadvantaged, the working class, and the human and physical environment in which they live. In Section IV of this chapter I offer some details in this regard, emphasizing, in particular, why such an approach is appropriate and how it might be accomplished through a combination of charter revisions and new policies.

B. Criticism #I-5—The IMF Democracy Deficit

Some of the most insightful observations about this criticism—and about others mentioned above—come from Professor Daniel Bradlow. I would emphasize two specific points he makes about how the structure and management of the IMF contribute to a democracy deficit in that institution. First, Bradlow draws an important distinction between two groups of IMF member states: "IMF supplier states" and "IMF consumer states."[72] The IMF supplier states are "those countries which, because of their wealth, their access to alternative sources of funds, and for political reasons, have no intention of using the IMF's services in the foreseeable future, and so do not need to pay particular attention to the views of the IMF," whereas the IMF consumer states are those "that need or know they may need IMF financing in the foreseeable future" and therefore "must pay careful attention to the views of the IMF because these views will influence the conditions the IMF will attach to the funds it disburses."[73]

The fact that this distinction exists between IMF supplier states and IMF consumer states, and that the latter need to listen to the IMF and the former do not, would not in itself make the IMF unaccountable or undemocratic but for another fact: the IMF supplier states dominate decision-

---

[71] Garuda, *supra* note 27, at 39. Garuda also emphasizes how difficult it is to know exactly what effects IMF-prescribed policies will have on the poor. The elimination of food subsidies, for example, might actually help the poor, or at least many of them, "by increasing the incomes of rural farmers," which make up a large fraction of the poor in many developing countries. *Id.* at 36.

[72] Daniel D. Bradlow, *Rapidly Changing Functions and Slowly Evolving Structures: The Troubling Case of the IMF*, 94 AM. SOC'Y INT'L L. PROC. 152, 153 (2000) [hereinafter Bradlow-II]. Bradlow sounds many of the same themes in another article. *See generally* Daniel D. Bradlow, *Stuffing New Wine Into Old Bottles: The Troubling Case of the IMF*, 3 J. INT'L BANKING REG. 9 (2001).

[73] *Id.*

making in the IMF, and their domination has in fact increased over the years.[74] Bradlow points out the pernicious result of this situation:

> The result is that, de facto, the G-7 countries control the policy agenda in the IMF even though they do not have to live with the consequences of the policies they make for the IMF's operations. This means that they make policy that is only of limited interest to their own citizens. The policy is, of course, of immense interest to people in developing countries who have no ability to hold the G-7 countries accountable for their decisions or actions. This situation of decision makers having power with accountability to people who do not have to live with the consequences of their decisions but without accountability to those most affected by their decisions is a situation ripe with potential for abuse.[75]

This form of unaccountability, emanating from voting-and-control aspects of the IMF's structure, also bears importantly on Criticism #I-7—"asymmetry in obligations." I assess that criticism below in Subsection IIIC of this chapter.

Bradlow also explains other forms of unaccountability in IMF operations. For one thing, he says, the IMF "has not established any mechanism through which the citizens of its consuming countries can hold the IMF or its management accountable for their actions as decision makers" in helping develop policies in those countries.[76] If part of the IMF's insistence on good governance requires its borrowing member countries to make their own policymakers accountable for their actions, Bradlow reasons, there is "no obvious reason why the IMF, when it 'descends' into the national policy-making process, should be less accountable to those people affected by its decisions than [are] other actors in this process."[77] But such accountability is almost totally lacking for two related reasons: (1) "the IMF does

---

[74] *Id.* at 154. In explaining the source and growth of this domination, Bradlow emphasizes these factors: (1) the number of IMF Executive Directors has grown more slowly than the number of IMF member states, resulting in an increase in the number of "consumer states" that must be represented by shared Executive Directors, and thus diluting (in relative terms) the effective voice of those countries relative to the "supplier states," several of which have their own unshared Executive Director; (2) those shared Executive Directors who represent both consumer states and supplier states are always from supplier states, so that 11 of the IMF's 24 Executive Directors are from industrialized countries; and (3) the permanency of supplier state representation on the Executive Board gives those states negotiating and agenda-setting advantages. *Id.*

[75] *Id.* at 155.

[76] *Id.* at 156.

[77] *Id.*

not have a set of publicly available operating rules and procedures," and (2) even if there were some established standards against which to challenge IMF operations, there is no effective process or entity through which such a challenge could be mounted.[78]

It is worth noting that the IMF has taken some important steps recently in addressing this particular aspect of the "democracy deficit" criticism. Two stand out.

First, an Independent Evaluation Office (IEO) was established in July 2001[79] (after Bradlow's views, excerpted above, were published) in order "to conduct objective and independent assessments of issues of relevance to the mandate of the IMF."[80] The IEO has already undertaken several evaluation projects, including an evaluation of the IMF's role in the economic crises in Brazil, Indonesia, and Korea.[81] Although it is too early to assess the long-term impact of the IEO's work, its very creation does signal a willing-

---

[78] *Id.* The Executive Board, Bradlow says, would theoretically be an appropriate forum for challenging the actions of the IMF's management, but it is unrepresentative for reasons discussed above; and the Board of Governors would be neither an appropriate nor an effective forum at which to raise such a challenge. *Id.*

[79] IMF ANNUAL REPORT 2003, *supra* note 20, at 60.

[80] *Id.* For further information about the IEO's history, purpose, structure, and operations, see materials *available at* http://www.imf.org/external/np/ieo/ (last visited Nov. 4, 2004), including INTERNATIONAL MONETARY FUND, INDEPENDENT EVALUATION OFFICE ANNUAL REPORT 2003 (2003) [hereinafter IEO ANNUAL REPORT 2003], *available at* http://www.imf.org/External/NP/ieo/2003/ar/index.htm. *See also* IMF SURVEY SUPPLEMENT, *supra* note 40, at 32 (noting that the IEO "undertake[s] wide-ranging outreach efforts, including building ties with the academic and aid evaluation communities and with representatives of civil society"). For updated information on the IEO, and assessments of its performance as of mid-2004, *see generally* four short articles by (respectively) an academic, two former IMF Executive Directors, and a senior official of the NGO Friends of the Earth: Peter B. Kenen, *Appraising the IMF's Performance,* FINANCE & DEVELOPMENT, Sept. 2004, at 41; Karin Lissakers, *Blunt Approach Does the Trick, id.* at 46; Jean-Claude Milleron, *Enhancing the Learning Culture, id.* at 48; Carol Welch, *Credible Start, Untested Impact, id.* at 50.

[81] IMF SURVEY SUPPLEMENT, *supra* note 40, *at* 32. For the text of the IEO Evaluation Report on the IMF's operations in those three countries, *see generally* INTERNATIONAL MONETARY FUND, IMF AND RECENT CAPITAL ACCOUNT CRISIS: INDONESIA, KOREA, BRAZIL (2003), *available at* http://www.imf.org/external/np/ieo/2003/cac/pdf/all.pdf (last visited Nov. 4, 2004). For a summary of the report, *see Findings and Recommendations,* 32 IMF SURVEY 220, 220–21 (Aug. 4, 2003) (noting, for example, the IEO's finding that "the IMF's response was inadequate in some respects" in responding to the crisis in Indonesia during the Asian financial crisis, and the IEO's recommendations for specific improvements in IMF surveillance, in program flexibility, and in crisis coordination). For a synopsis of recommendations emerging from that evaluation and the response of the IMF Executive Board to those recommendations, *see* IEO ANNUAL REPORT 2003, *supra* note 80, at 38–40.

ness on the part of the IMF to provide increased public accountability. In its current formulation, the IEO is largely an internal organ of the IMF, given the fact that the Director of the IEO is appointed by the IMF Executive Board, may be dismissed at any time by the Executive Board, hires other IEO officers on terms and conditions determined by the Board, depends on the Executive Board for budgetary funding, and reports to the Board.[82] Although the IEO's terms of reference call for it to "be independent of Fund management and staff"[83]—a requirement that is given some force by (1) requiring that a majority of IEO personnel come from outside the IMF and (2) prohibiting the IEO Director from being appointed to a regular IMF staff position at the end of his or her term of office[84]—the IEO, nevertheless, falls short of being an external organ broadly representative in character, empowered to exercise a fully objective review of IMF operations and to issue binding orders if it judges those operations to be improper or *ultra vires*.

A second recent IMF initiative—or, more precisely, a cluster of related initiatives—to increase the institution's accountability to the citizens of IMF consumer countries centers on the notion of "voice." In order to increase the "voice" (without tampering with voting strengths) of member governments in IMF deliberations—and, hence, presumably reducing the relative influence of the IMF's management and staff—the International Monetary and Financial Committee has been given broader authority,[85] thereby providing "greater direct involvement of governments in the policy-making process within the Fund."[86] In a similar effort to strengthen the "voice" of developing countries, the IMF's Executive Board is continuing to develop the IMF's Poverty Reduction Strategy Paper (PRSP) process,[87] introduced in 1999, by which written plans for reducing poverty "are prepared by low-income countries through a participatory process involving domestic stakeholders and external development partners, and are endorsed by the IMF and the World Bank."[88] As another effort to strengthen the "voice" of the

---

[82] *See* IEO ANNUAL REPORT, *supra* note 80, at 27 (setting forth the terms of reference of the IEO). Indeed, the Executive Board has authority to quash the publication of IEO reports. *Id.*

[83] *Id.*

[84] *Id.* at 2 (enumerating various aspects of IEO independence).

[85] The increasing role of the International Monetary and Financial Committee is noted above in Subsection IIG of Chapter Two, as part of my "nutshell" description of the IMF.

[86] Gianviti, *supra* note 51, at 115.

[87] IMF ANNUAL REPORT 2003, *supra* note 20, at 61.

[88] *Id.* at 40. For further details on the PRSP process, including its introduction in 1999, *see* International Monetary Fund, *Poverty Reduction Strategy Papers—A Factsheet* (Sept. 2003), *at* http://www.imf.org/external/np/exr/facts/prsp.htm (last visited Nov. 4, 2004).

most thinly represented countries, the IMF's Executive Board is undertaking efforts to "address staffing and technological constraints of the two sub-Saharan African constituencies" on the Executive Board.[89]

In sum, the IMF has taken some substantive steps recently that respond in part to the complaint that it is unaccountable to the citizens of IMF consumer countries. These steps, although rather modest in scope so far, are laudable.

Another form of unaccountability emerges from the IMF's legal authority to interpret its own charter.[90] One self-described "third-world scholar" has offered the following critical description of that authority:

> [Under the pertinent provision,] an essentially legal question is decided by a non-legal body which appears to be under no obligation to decide the matter according to legal considerations. Furthermore, given that it is action by the Executive Directors that is most often in dispute, this system provides little remedy at all for the situation. In fact, the provision . . . represents a fundamental departure from the "rule of law"—a basic premise of which is that executive actions should be subject to review by an independent judicial process.[91]

Another thoughtful, recent discussion of the "democracy deficit" comes from Ngaire Woods,[92] a Fellow in Politics and International Relations at University College, Oxford (where, coincidentally, I first studied law in the 1970s). Ms. Woods examines several aspects of the problem, which she calls (probably more aptly) the "accountability deficit,"[93] and traces it to several factors.

---

[89] IMF ANNUAL REPORT 2003, *supra* note 20, at 61.

[90] For the text of the IMF Charter provision granting this authority, *see supra* note 12.

[91] Antony Anghie, *Time Present and Time Past: Globalization, International Financial Institutions, and the Third World*, 32 N.Y.U. J. INT'L L. & POL. 243, 270–71 (2000). Although the specific provision to which Anghie refers is Article IX(a) of the charter of the International Bank for Reconstruction and Development (IBRD), that provision is virtually identical to Article XXIX of the IMF Charter. That Anghie intends for his comments to apply both to the IBRD and to the IMF is evident from the next sentence in the passage quoted above: "Basically, then, the IFIs [international financial institutions] appear not to be subject to any external scrutiny as to their adherence to the rule of law." *Id.* at 271.

[92] Ngaire Woods, *Making the IMF and the World Bank More Accountable*, 77 INT'L AFF. 83 (2001).

[93] *Id.* at 100.

First, she says, the representation of member countries on the Executive Board of the IMF (and on that of the World Bank) is too unequal now, partly because of changes in members' quotas: whereas the proportion of "basic votes" to total votes in the IMF in earlier years provided some equality among the members (that proportion was 14 percent, for example, in 1955), now the "basic votes" amount to a tiny proportion (about 3 percent, according to Woods).[94]

Second, Woods says, the Executive Board does not adequately hold staff and management to account, for several reasons, including the rapid rotation of Executive Directors, their protectiveness toward the countries they represent, the tendency of the staff and management not to divulge internal disagreements to the Executive Board, and the practice of reaching decisions prior to Executive Board meetings.[95]

Third, Woods explains that the heads of both the Bretton Woods institutions—the Managing Director of the IMF and the President of the World Bank—"are selected by a non-transparent process which excludes most member countries"[96] because of a long-standing compromise by which "the head is appointed by convention according to the wishes of the United States (in respect of the World Bank) or western Europe (in respect of the IMF)."[97]

A fourth element of the democracy deficit, or accountability deficit, that Woods highlights relates to the "mission creep" criticism. She asserts

---

[94] *Id.* at 87. Bradlow has also emphasized the importance of this decline in the significance of "basic votes." Bradlow-II, *supra* note 72, at 155 (giving proportions for 1946, 1982, and 2000 as 11.3 percent, 5.6 percent, and 2.2 percent, respectively). The IMF's former Secretary, Leo Van Houtven, also recently pointed out the decline in the significance of "basic votes," which he says represent "barely 2 percent" of total votes. Leo Van Houtven, *Rethinking IMF Governance*, FINANCE & DEVELOPMENT, Sept. 2004, at 19. As explained above in the "nutshell" account that I gave of the IMF in Section II of Chapter Two, each IMF member country has an allotment of 250 basic votes plus one additional vote for each part of its quota equivalent to 100,000 SDRs. As of late August 2003, the IMF had 184 member countries, and the total voting power of those member countries was 2,168,501 votes. IMF SURVEY SUPPLEMENT, *supra* note 40, at 30. With 250 basic votes per member, the total number of basic votes for all members would be 250 x 184 = 46,000 basic votes. Thus, the current proportion of "basic votes" (46,000) to total votes (2,168,501) is 2.1 percent. For details about each member country's voting power, *see generally* International Monetary Fund, IMF Members' Quotas and Voting Power, and IMF Board of Governors *at* http://www.imf.org/external/np/sec/memdir/members.htm (last visited Nov. 4, 2004).

[95] Woods, *supra* note 92, at 87–88.

[96] *Id.* at 88.

[97] *Id.*

that "[t]he role of the IMF and World Bank has expanded; their account-ability has not."[98] Indeed, she says, "the IMF and the World Bank were nei-ther created nor structured to undertake or to be accountable for such far-reaching activities."[99]

I have identified in the preceding paragraphs a variety of important factors that contribute to the IMF's "democracy deficit." They are impor-tant enough to warrant a brief summation: (1) control over the IMF by the supplier states (G-7 countries and other industrialized countries) results in policies that the people in consumer states have no ability to influence; (2) likewise, people in consumer states have no adequate mechanism for hold-ing the IMF itself (as distinct from the IMF's controlling states) account-able for its decisions, because the IMF has neither an adequate set of publicly available operating rules against which to challenge its actions nor an adequately independent process or entity through which a challenge could be mounted (although the IEO must be regarded as a good start in that direction[100]); (3) the power of the IMF's Executive Board to interpret the IMF Charter (and, hence, to judge the legality of its own actions there-under) also prevents any formal external accountability or democratic influence; (4) representation of member countries on the IMF's Executive Board has actually become progressively more unequal in recent years because of the dilution of "basic votes"; (5) the Executive Board is not in a position to hold IMF staff and management adequately accountable for their actions, because of (among other things) the rapid rotation of direc-tors; (6) the IMF's Managing Director is selected by a non-transparent process that excludes most member countries; and (7) the effects of all these aspects of unaccountability are only aggravated by the IMF's expan-sion into a broader range of activities.

Given these various factors, it should come as no surprise that the "democracy deficit" criticism has been directed at the IMF. I find it gener-ally valid. I believe that although it would be impossible to overcome all aspects of an IMF "democracy deficit" in a world composed of countries

---

[98] *Id.* Woods refers to two points already mentioned above: (1) the broadened scope of policy matters in which the IMF involves itself (noting that "both the IMF and the World Bank now embrace areas of policy it was inconceivable they would touch prior to the 1980s"); and (2) the increase in the number of conditions placed on IMF loans (averaging, by one survey, "between 6 and 10 measures in the 1980s, as contrasted with around 26 measures in the 1990s"). *Id.*

[99] *Id.* at 89.

[100] My favorable impression of the IEO is consistent with a view expressed recently by Jeffrey Sachs, a frequent commentator on the IMF. *See* Jeffrey D. Sachs, *How to Run the International Monetary Fund*, 143 FOREIGN POL'Y 60 (2004) (referring to the IEO as "a valuable recent addition to the fund's institutional design that objectively assesses IMF operations").

that are dramatically unequal in economic terms,[101] and although we should not lose sight of the important efforts the IMF has already made to overcome some aspects of the "democracy deficit,"[102] much remains to be done to make the IMF itself, and the countries that control it, more accountable to all people whose lives the IMF affects—or, expressed in simple terms, to bring a much greater measure of democracy to the IMF.

How can this be done? I believe the answer lies in expanding several existing forms of IMF accountability and inventing new ones. I outline some specific recommendations in this regard in Section IV of this chapter.

C. Criticism #I-7—Asymmetry in Obligations

In a sentence, this criticism complains that a handful of rich countries, whose control over the IMF allows them to insist (through conditionality) that the poor borrowing member countries follow certain economic and financial policies, are under no real pressure to follow those policies themselves. This criticism—which attaches both to the IMF's rich controlling members themselves for insisting on the one-sided obligations and to the IMF for permitting itself to be used as the enforcer of such obligations—is less widely voiced than many others I have discussed in this chapter, perhaps because it is rather complex in character, resulting as it does from a combination of elements that attract plenty of attention on their own: conditionality and weighted voting.

I view this criticism as one of the most serious facing the IMF, and I have drawn attention to it before.[103] It also faces the MDBs, and much of the reasoning I explain below applies equally to those institutions.

---

[101] *See* Gianviti, *supra* note 51, at 116 (noting "how difficult it is for a monetary institution to reconcile the principle of equality of nations under international law with the reality of their unequal economic and financial weights").

[102] These include, as discussed above, the establishment of the IEO and a variety of initiatives to strengthen the "voice" of member governments in IMF deliberations. IMF efforts to address some aspects of the "democracy deficit" complaints are acknowledged by outside observers. *See, e.g.,* Garuda, *supra* note 27, at 39 (noting the IMF "has improved its coordination with non-governmental organizations . . . , donor countries, and other institutions").

[103] *See* Head, *Third Amendment, supra* note 44, at 642 (noting the perceived unfairness in the fact that "whereas LDCs are obliged to follow IMF economic policy prescriptions because of their need for external financing, the United States can continue to disregard such prescriptions"). I also discussed this criticism, and others discussed in this chapter, in my most recent article from which much of this chapter is drawn. *See generally* John W. Head, *Seven Deadly Sins: An Assessment of Criticisms Directed at the International Monetary Fund,* 52 U. KAN. L. REV. 521 (2004).

Independently, both the weighted voting system and conditionality strike me as appropriate in the context of IMF operations. After all, why shouldn't those countries providing the most financial backing for an institution have the most control over its policies: and why shouldn't a financial institution that depends on repayments of loans in order to stay alive be permitted (indeed, required) to ensure that the borrower takes action likely to enable that borrower to repay the loan?

However, although each of the two features (weighted voting and conditionality) standing alone is legal and desirable, the two of them combined in the context of actual IMF operations can be nettlesome. Why? Because they result in asymmetrical obligations: the countries that control (through the weighted voting system) the IMF's policies in imposing conditionality are the very countries that do not borrow from the IMF and to whom the policies prescribed by the IMF do not apply. Thus, the actual operation of conditionality smacks of unfairness and hypocrisy. What is sauce for the goose should, it seems, be sauce for the gander.

The sense of unfairness and hypocrisy gets stronger when the two countries that have the most votes in the IMF—the United States and Japan[104]—regularly engage in behavior that seems inconsistent with the economic and financial policies on which the IMF insists. Those economic and financial policies that the IMF insists on include such things as avoiding large budget deficits, imposing tough supervision of financial institutions to avoid sharp or imprudent practices, closing or restructuring troubled financial institutions, liberalizing trade policies, and opening up investment opportunities for foreigners.[105] Some policies and develop-

---

[104] As noted above in Subsection IIG of Chapter Two, the United States controls 17.14 percent of total voting power in the IMF, and Japan controls 6.15 percent.

[105] Most of these types of policies appeared in the conditions attached to the "bailout" package of loans made in late 1997 to Korea under the Leadership of the IMF. *See* John W. Head, *Lessons from the Asian Financial Crisis: The Role of the IMF and the United States*, 7 KAN. J.L. & PUB. POL'Y 70, 73–74 (1998) (describing the Korean economy's crash and the IMF "bailout" package). *See also* Republic of Korea, *IMF Stand-By Arrangement— Summary of the Economic Program* (Dec. 5, 1997) (enumerating policies calling for balancing the budget, consolidating supervision of banks, closing troubled banks, and a liberalized investment and trade environment), *at* http://www.imf.org/external/np/oth/korea.htm (last visited Nov. 4, 2004). Several of these also appeared in the conditions attached to the September 2003 stand-by arrangement for Argentina. *See* Letter of Intent, Memorandum of Economic and Financial Policies, and Technical Memorandum of Understanding from Government of Argentina, to Horst Köhler, Managing Director, IMF 3–6, 12–13, 15 (Sept. 10, 2003) (enumerating policies on budget, bank restructuring, and investment reforms), *at* http://www.imf.org/external/np/loi/2003/arg/03/index.htm (last visited Nov. 4, 2004). *See also* Press Release No. 03/160, International Monetary Fund, IMF Approves US$12.55 Billion Three-Year Stand-By Credit for Argentina (Sept. 20, 2003) (corrected Oct. 15, 2003) (referring to

ments in the United States and Japan in recent years—the U.S. savings-and-loan crisis of the 1980s, lax standards on corporate governance more recently, accounting and auditing scandals (leading to such scandals as that involving Enron), Japan's much-criticized handling of its banking institutions, both countries' frequent budget deficits, and trade protectionism in steel and agriculture[106]—would almost surely have run afoul of IMF conditionalities had either of those countries sought to borrow from the IMF.

Indeed, in early 2004, U.S. economic practices received intense criticism in an IMF staff report that gained front-page headlines in *The New York Times*.[107] The *Times* article offered this summation:

> With its rising budget deficit and ballooning trade imbalance, the United States is running up a foreign debt of such record-breaking proportions that it threatens the financial stability of the global economy, according to a report released [on January 6, 2004] by the International Monetary Fund.
>
> Prepared by a team of I.M.F. economists, the report sounded a loud alarm about the shaky fiscal foundation of the United States, questioning the wisdom of the Bush administration's tax cuts and warning that large budge deficits pose "significant risks" not just for the United States but for the rest of the world.
>
> [M]any international economists said they were pleased that the report raised the issue.[108]

If such a report were issued about a country wishing to borrow from the IMF, that country's government would obviously need to change its

---

banking system strengthening, including bank restructuring, improving the investment climate, and budget surplus), *available at* http://www.imf.org/external/np/sec/pr/2003/pr03160.htm (last visited Nov. 4, 2004).

[106] For examples of critical discussions within the IMF of economic and financial policies followed by the United States and Japan, *see* the report of IMF Article IV consultations with those countries, available on the IMF website: International Monetary Fund, *United States and the IMF, at* http://www.imf.org/external/country/USA/index.htm (last visited Nov. 4, 2004); International Monetary Fund, *Japan and the IMF, at* http://www.imf.org/external/country/JPN/index.htm (last visited Nov. 4, 2004).

[107] Elizabeth Becker & Edmund L. Andrews, *I.M.F. Says Rise in U.S. Debts Is Threat to World's Economy*, N.Y. TIMES, Jan. 8, 2004, at A1. For the overview of the IMF staff report itself, *see* INTERNATIONAL MONETARY FUND, U.S. FISCAL POLICIES AND PRIORITIES FOR LONG-RUN SUSTAINABILITY 1 (Martin Mühleisen & Christopher Towe eds., Occasional Paper No. 227, Jan 7, 2004), *available at* http://www.imf.org/external/pubs/nft/op/227/index.htm (last visited Nov. 4, 2004).

[108] Becker & Andrews, *supra* note 107, at A1.

policies. However, "White House officials dismissed the report as alarmist."[109]

I believe it is important to find ways of reducing this asymmetry in obligations. I outline some suggestions for this below in Section IV of this chapter.

IV. REFORMS I SUGGEST

I have identified in Section III of this chapter three criticisms that I generally endorse. They focus on "distributional and social injustice" (Criticism #I-2), the IMF's "democracy deficit" (Criticism #I-5), and "asymmetry in obligations" (Criticism #I-7). Although some critics of the IMF would assert that these three criticisms provide sufficient reason for doing away with the IMF, on grounds that it is so deeply flawed as to be irreparable, I do not take that view. Instead, I believe the IMF, as well as the other GEOs that I scrutinize in this book, are worth saving and are capable of being saved—for reasons I discuss below in Chapter Six. Accordingly, in this final section of this Chapter, I recommend some reforms that I believe would help respond to and overcome those three criticisms in order to strengthen and improve the IMF.

Before proceeding to that summary of suggested reforms, however, it is worth pausing to note that the various types of work that the IMF does that have *not* attracted substantial criticism. As noted above in my "nutshell" account of the IMF,[110] although its lending operations are the most visible aspect of the institution's activities, the IMF carries out numerous other functions. These include providing technical assistance[111] and conducting Article IV consultations,[112] as well as undertaking an enormous volume of valuable research.[113] These activities should continue (with ongoing

---

[109] *Id.* For a scathing criticism of the Bush administration's economic policies, paralleling in several respects the IMF staff report referred to above, *see* Paul Krugman, *Rubin Gets Shrill,* N.Y. TIMES, Jan. 6, 2004, at A27.

[110] *See supra* Section II of Chapter Two.

[111] For a summary of the IMF's technical assistance operations, *see* International Monetary Fund, *Technical Assistance—A Factsheet* (Mar. 2003), *at* http://www.imf.org/external/np/exr/facts/tech.htm (last visited Feb. 13, 2005). *See also supra* Subsection II F of Chapter Two.

[112] For a summary of the IMF's surveillance under Article IV, *see* International Monetary Fund, *IMF Surveillance—A factsheet* (Apr. 2003), *at* http://www.imf.org/external/np/exr/facts/surv.htm (last visited Feb. 13, 2005).

[113] For a description of the aims and scope of the IMF's research program, and the information coming out of it to aid policymakers, regulators, and other researchers, *see* the list of Staff Papers and similar publications available from the IMF. International Monetary Fund, Research at the IMF, *at* http://www.imf.org/external/pubs/res/index.htm (last visited Feb. 16, 2005). For an evaluation of the IMF's track record in one

scrutiny, of course, as to how they might be improved).[114] Indeed, under the reforms I outline below, each of them would assume a somewhat more prominent place in IMF operations.

It is also important to bear in mind the very substantial transfer of resources from rich countries to poor countries that the IMF has encouraged and presided over. A first example of this came in the 1970s. A political compromise struck in the negotiations of the Second Amendment to the IMF Charter provided that the IMF would sell 50 million ounces of gold, with the profit from half that amount earmarked for less developed countries. Part of the profit was to be remitted to each such country directly, and part was to be set aside for the benefit of specified, especially needy less developed countries. To that end, the IMF established a Trust Fund separate from its other holdings.[115] Loans made by the IMF from that Trust Fund carried "[a] highly concessional interest rate, equal to one-half of 1 percent."[116] In the late 1970s and early 1980s a total of SDR 2.9 billion was made available to less developed countries from that Trust Fund.[117] In a similar vein, special funding was made available again beginning in the

aspect of its research work (forecasting government deficits for each of the G-7 countries), *see generally* Michael Artis & Massimiliano Marcelino, *Fiscal Forecasting: The Track Record of the IMF, OECD and EC*, 4 ECONOMETRICS J. S20 (2001).

[114] For a critical assessment of what I consider one of the most important forms of IMF technical assistance—helping prepare banking legislation—see generally Gary A. Gegenheimer, *Technical Assistance or Excessive Technicality? A Critique of the International Monetary Fund's Model Commercial Banking Law for Transition Economies*, 20 ANN. REV. BANKING L. 143 (2001). According to that assessment, the model banking law that has been developed by the IMF and used in helping authorities in various transition economies write national banking legislation "is seriously flawed" because it emphasizes form over substance and grants excessively broad authority to banking supervisory authorities to shut down banks. *Id.* at 145. Based on my own involvement in this form of technical assistance over the past fifteen years, I disagree with this assessment, especially the latter point. For my views on the reasons for providing broad authority to banking supervisory authorities to shut down insolvent banks, see ROBERT LEE RAMSEY & JOHN W. HEAD, PREVENTING FINANCIAL CHAOS: AN INTERNATIONAL GUIDE TO LEGAL RULES AND OPERATIONAL PROCEDURES FOR HANDLING INSOLVENT BANKS 14–16, 31–38 (2000).

[115] RICHARD W. EDWARDS, JR., INTERNATIONAL MONETARY COLLABORATION 294–95 (1985). *See also* INTERNATIONAL MONETARY FUND, PROPOSED SECOND AMENDMENT TO THE ARTICLES OF AGREEMENT OF THE INTERNATIONAL MONETARY FUND 42–43 (Mar. 1976) (describing the proposed sale of gold and distribution of part of the proceeds to less developed countries, and the establishment of a Trust Fund to facilitate this process); Joseph Gold, *Trust Funds in International Law: The Contribution of the International Monetary Fund to a Code of Principles*, 72 AM. J. INT'L L. 856, 860–61 (1978) (referring to the sale of gold and the establishment of the Trust Fund, with the aim of assisting countries with the low per capita income).

[116] FINANCIAL ORGANIZATION AND OPERATIONS, *supra* note 44, at 113.

[117] *Id.* at 84. For a year-by-year breakdown of the disbursements from Trust Fund loans, see IMF ANNUAL REPORT 2003, *supra* note 20, at 106.

late 1980s for the benefit of less developed countries. The Structural Adjustment Facility (SAF) and the Enhanced Structural Adjustment Facility (ESAF) were established in March 1986 and December 1987, respectively, to provide assistance on concessional terms to low-income IMF member countries facing protracted balance-of-payments problems.[118] Between 1987 and 2003, a total of SDR 12.3 billion was disbursed by the IMF in loans made under the SAF or the ESAF—or under the Poverty Reduction and Growth Facility (PRGF),[119] which in the late 1990s became the successor to the ESAF.[120] Combining these figures for Trust Fund loans (SDR 2.9 billion) and SAF/ESA/PRGF loans (SDR 12.3 billion) and expressing them in U.S. dollars at the current SDR value[121] yields a total of nearly US$30 billion that has been provided to less developed countries on very attractive terms—illustrated by the current PRGF terms of 0.5 percent interest rate and repayment stretched over about five years with repayment starting five and one-half years after disbursement.[122]

In short, the IMF has performed several functions that are largely uncontroversial and that have inured to the benefit of the less developed countries that make up the bulk of its membership. It is partly to strengthen the ability of the IMF to perform those important functions, as well as to overcome some of the shortcomings in its structure and its lending operations, that I offer below several specific suggestions for bringing reform both (1) to the IMF itself and (2) to the relations the IMF has with its member countries

A. Structural and Operational Changes in the IMF

The following enumeration of nine specific proposals for reform emerges from my analysis in Section III of this chapter regarding those criticisms that I generally endorse regarding the IMF. The list also draws in part from the valuable work done by Professor Daniel Bradlow and Ms. Ngaire Woods referred to earlier,[123] as well as a few others. All of the

---

[118] FINANCIAL ORGANIZATION AND OPERATIONS, *supra* note 44, at 78, 80. For more details on the ESAF, *see* International Monetary Fund, *IMF Concessional Financing through ESAF* (Sept. 5, 1999), *at* http://www.imf.org/external/np/exr/facts/esaf.htm (last visited Feb. 13, 2005).

[119] *See* IMF ANNUAL REPORT 2003, *supra* note 20, at 106 (showing year-by-year disbursements under various types of ADB arrangements).

[120] For some details on the PRGF, *see* IMF SURVEY SUPPLEMENT, *supra* note 40, at 17–18.

[121] The value of the SDR, expressed in U.S. dollars, was about $1.51 as of early February 2005. The current value of the SDR may be found on the IMF's website at http://www.imf.org/external/fin.htm (last visited Feb. 7, 2005).

[122] IMF SURVEY SUPPLEMENT, *supra* note 40, at 15.

[123] *See generally* Bradlow-II, *supra* note 72; Woods, *supra* note 92.

changes outlined below would address the "democracy deficit" criticism; the last change suggested below would also address the "asymmetry in obligations" criticism. (My suggestions for addressing the "distributional and social injustice" criticism appears in Subsection IVB, below).

First, the IMF management could create, and submit to the Executive Board for formal approval, a relatively comprehensive Operational Manual, similar to that used in the World Bank,[124] compiling in one place the various policies that have been adopted by the Executive Board and the Board of Governors. These would most effectively appear in two categories: (1) policies governing the IMF's internal operations; and (2) policies that IMF members are expected to follow in their own financial, economic, and structural matters and in their relations with the IMF. The first category would include IMF policies on transparency (of the IMF itself), the terms applicable to various types of financial facilities available to member countries, the new guidelines on conditionality, rules on consulting with civil society groups, procedures for carrying out regional and global surveillance, policies on collaborating with the World Bank and other institutions, and so forth. The second category would include policies regarding the minimum standards that IMF member countries should be required to meet in a variety of areas crucial to the well-being of their people. I describe this second category more fully in subsection IVB below.

Second, the Executive Board could adopt, after consultation and an opportunity for public comment, formal decisions that would determine and announce certain aspects of their constitutional authority; specifically, these decisions would (1) define the scope of the IMF's mandate,[125] so it will be easier "for outsiders to understand why the IMF is willing to address certain issues but not other issues,"[126] and (2) construe the meaning of Article IV, Section 3(b) of the IMF Charter,[127] which provides that in its surveillance activities, the IMF shall "respect the domestic social and political policies of members."[128]

Third, the IMF management could put in place formal procedures to ensure that IMF staff working with government authorities interact with a range of persons and agencies—that is, that IMF staff not limit such interactions only to authorities of the central bank or ministry of finance in those countries requesting financial assistance from the IMF. The formal

---

[124] *See* The World Bank Group, Operational Manual, *at* http://wbln0018.worldbank.org/institutional/manuals/opmanual.nsf (last visited Feb. 16, 2005).

[125] Bradlow-II, *supra* note 72, at 159.

[126] *See id.* at 157.

[127] *See id.* at 157, 159.

[128] *See* IMF Charter, art. IV, § 3(b).

procedures in this regard might call for consultations with, as Bradlow suggests, "government ministries whose budgets will be affected by the specific actions [the IMF] is advocating, with the legislators who will need to pass the laws [if any] that follow from the IMF's proposed policies, and with [certain relevant] actors in civil society."[129]

Fourth, the Board of Governors could revise the structure of the Independent Evaluation Office to make the IEO more genuinely independent of the IMF Executive Board.[130] For example, the following modifications might be considered:[131] (1) providing for appointment of one or more IEO panel members by some entity (or entities) other than the IMF Executive Board; (2) providing procedures by which cases alleging IMF breach of its own policies or of the IMF Charter could be brought more directly before the IEO without review of the IEO's work program by the IMF Executive Board; (3) creating (perhaps for that purpose) a position of ombudsman "who has the power to receive and investigate complaints from any person, organization, or state that feels that the IMF has not been acting in conformity with its mandate";[132] (4) requiring that the IEO's hearings (although not all of its meetings) be open to the public (subject to valid confidentiality concerns); and (5) requiring that either the IMF's management or its Executive Board must issue a public response to each recommendation emerging form an IEO evaluation.[133]

---

[129] Bradlow-II, *supra* note 72, at 155. *See also* CAROL WELCH, THE IMF AND GOOD GOVERNANCE 3 (Interhemispheric Research Center & Institute for Policy Studies, Foreign Policy in Focus No. 33, Oct. 1998) (asserting that "discussions between the IMF and a borrowing country, to the greatest extent possible, must involve the full range of cabinet ministers and parliamentary leaders" and that there should be "consultation with the public by the government through regular interactive meetings, hearings, and workshops"). It is worth pointing out that the intensity of interaction I am suggesting here between the IMF and the public—including, for example, NGOs—is substantially less than the intensity of interaction between NGOs and the MDBs. *See, e.g., infra* Subsection IVB of Chapter Four. This difference reflects the difference in operations between the IMF and the MDBs; the latter institutions, at least in their bread-and-butter project lending operations, make decisions that the public, sometimes best represented by NGOs, can effectively participate in and influence. I make a similar distinction in Chapter Five by pointing out that the level of citizen involvement in WTO affairs should, in my view, be limited given the technical nature of WTO work. *See infra* Subsection IIID of Chapter Five.

[130] For details about the degree of control that the Executive Board can exercise over the IEO, see *supra* note 82 and accompanying text.

[131] For several of these points I draw liberally from WELCH, *supra* note 129, at 3.

[132] Bradlow-II, *supra* note 72, at 158.

[133] The Executive Board did issue responses to each of the first three evaluation reports issued by the IEO. *See* IEO ANNUAL REPORT 2003, *supra* note 80, at 34–43 (outlining pertinent IEO recommendations, the Executive Board responses, Staff Task Force recommendations, and any follow-up). However, it does not appear that the IEO's terms

Fifth, the Board of Governors could continue to place more responsibilities with the International Monetary and Financial Committee—beyond those that, as described earlier, have already been given to it recently[134]—to transform it even more "into a decision making council for the major strategic orientations of the world economy."[135] In addition, its membership might be expanded to enhance further its ability to reflect the broad interests of its shareholders.

Sixth, the membership of the IMF could revise the IMF Charter "to increase the basic votes to at least their original proportion" of the total voting strength in the IMF.[136] The aim of such a change would be to restore the degree of equality among members (despite the weighted voting system) that was envisioned by the IMF's creators.[137]

Seventh, the next General Review of Quotas[138] could be conducted under terms of reference that expressly require a response to the suggestion made by some LDCs and emerging economies that they be allowed to increase their quotas in the IMF,[139] and therefore their voting powers. If the

---

of reference require such responses. *See id.* at 27–28 (describing the IEO's duties and the flexibility the Executive Board has in issuing responses). Following the IEO's assessment of the IMF's handling of the crisis in Argentina, the IMF staff and the IMF management issued responses to the IEO report (which itself was released in late July 2003), but the Executive Board did not. *See Watchdog Faults Argentina, But Also IMF*, 33 IMF SURVEY 220, 232 (Aug. 9, 2004) (reprinting the IMF staff response, referring to the IMF management response, and citing "the summing up of the Executive Board's discussion of the [IEO] report").

[134] For a description of the IMFC and its functions, see *supra* Subsection IIG of Chapter Two.

[135] Michel Camdessus, *The IMF at the Beginning of the Twenty-First Century: Can we Establish a Humanized Globalization?*, 7 GLOBAL GOVERNANCE 363, 369 (2001).

[136] Bradlow-II, *supra* note 72, at 158. An alternative would be to increase the basic votes to a higher level than originally set; this was perhaps supported by the immediate past IMF Managing Director, Mr. Köhler, in calling for "increasing so-called basic voting rights, which would favor small, low-income members." *How Should the IMF Be Reshaped?*, FINANCE & DEVELOPMENT, Sept. 2004, at 27, 29.

[137] For an explanation of "basic votes" and their purpose, *see supra* note 94 and Subsection IIG of Chapter Two.

[138] Article III, Section 2(*a*) of the IMF Charter requires that the Executive Board undertake a general review of quotas every five years.

[139] For an example of such a suggestion, *see* YUNG CHUL PARK & YUNJONG WANG, REFORM OF THE INTERNATIONAL FINANCIAL SYSTEM AND INSTITUTIONS IN LIGHT OF THE ASIAN FINANCIAL CRISIS (2000) at 20 (asserting that "[i]n order to redress the imbalance between industrial countries and [emerging market economies such as Korea] in managing the IMF, [emerging market economies] and [LDCs] should be given the opportunity . . . to contribute more resources for the operation of the IMF" and be "accorded greater representation both on the board of directors and in management" of the insti-

60-year-old domination of the IMF by a handful of countries is to be regarded as legitimate, a strong justification should be offered; and if it cannot be offered, other countries should be permitted to have greater influence if they are willing to contribute the resources necessary to warrant such influence.[140]

Eighth, in a change that could add the IMF's transparency as well as cut the "democracy deficit," the IMF could "mov[e] . . . away from its current practice of making decisions on the basis of consensus to making decisions on a basis that better reveals the preferences of those states which will be most affected by the decisions."[141]

Ninth, in order to help address the "symmetry in obligations" criticism, the membership could revise the IMF Charter to link some portion of each member's voting power to its economic and financial policies and performance. This is a rather radical proposal, of course,[142] and I make it also in

---

tution). That same publication asserts that "[t]he rule requiring an 85 per cent supermajority for important changes in IMF policy should be changed as well." *Id.* at 21. The stranglehold of control by creditor countries in the IMF was also sharply criticized recently by a former IMF Executive Director. *See* Cyrus Rustomjee, *Why Developing Countries Need a Stronger Voice*, FINANCE & DEVELOPMENT, Sept. 2004, at 21, 23 (asserting that "[t]he current margin of voting shares in favor of creditors . . . weakens the institution, reduces operational efficiency, gnaws at the institution's legitimacy, erodes ownership of programs and policies by the collective membership, . . . and has bred understandable resentment in the debtor group").

[140] The former Secretary of the IMF recently recommended that the allocation of quotas be revised (perhaps at the next General Quota Review) in order to obtain more equity in voting power. *See* Van Houtven, *supra* note 94, at 19–20. In particular, he pointed out that the EU quota and voting power could legitimately be reduced by "the exclusion of intra-EU trade from the quota calculations, which would be appropriate for an economic union," and this would reduce EU voting power by approximately nine percentage points (it is now around 32 percent). *Id.* at 19. In addition, Van Houtven suggested having a single EU chair at the Executive Board, which would help reduce the size of the Executive Board from 24 chairs to around 18. *Id.* at 20. In the same issue of *Finance & Development*, two of the three immediate past IMF Managing Directors reacted favorably to the idea of consolidating EU representation into a single chair on the Executive Board. *See How Should the IMF Be Reshaped?*, *supra* note 136, at 29.

[141] Bradlow-II, *supra* note at 158. Bradlow suggests that the IMF might "require separate votes by those executive directors who represent consumer countries and those who represent supplier countries," and then "[a]ny decisions would only be adopted if it commanded a majority of both groups." *Id.* Some assumptions on which this suggestion rests—that the "consumer countries" are more affected by IMF decisions than "supplier countries" and that the former are entitled to equal, or more, influence over such decisions—warrant further consideration. I am indebted to Bob Hockett for raising this point with me.

[142] For my views of how proposals of this sort, which would impose potentially serious restrictions on the power of those countries (including the United States) that currently exercise such dominance over the IMF, see *infra* Subsection IIC of Chapter Six—the final subsection of this book.

the context of the MDBs.[143] Under this approach, if an IMF member country were to depart substantially and chronically from economic and financial policies agreed to with the IMF, that member country's voting power could be suspended until the member country corrects is behavior. Such agreements with the IMF regarding economic and financial policies would probably come in the context of Article IV consultations for those member countries that do not borrow form the IMF; and for those member countries that do borrow from the IMF, the agreements could come in the context of Article IV consultations or in the context of the discussions leading to a letter of intent or a memorandum of economic and financial policies. (Borrowing member countries, of course, already face the consequences of an interruption of disbursements under their IMF loans if they fail to hew to the agreed-upon policies.)

This possible remedy—suspension of voting power—has a clear precedent in the IMF. The Third Amendment to the IMF Charter, forced on most of the membership by the United States in the early 1990s, calls for a suspension of a member country's voting rights in certain cases of its failure to repay loans to the IMF on time.[144] Like the addition of that new suspension remedy in the early 1990s for failure to repay IMF loans, the addition of this suspension remedy for failure to live up to the accepted economic and financial policies would require formal amendment of the IMF Charter— presumably in Article IV, Section 3 (on the basis of which the Article IV consultations take place), and perhaps with a cross-reference there to Article XXVI, Section 2(b) (referring to suspension of voting rights).

B. Enhancing Competence in National Governance

The nine specific reform proposals summarized above relate to structural and operational changes in the IMF. A second set of suggested reforms would focus not on the IMF itself but instead on the IMF's relationship with its member countries—and, in particular, on how the IMF can help enhance economic stability in the world by (1) demanding more of its member countries and (2) providing more to them in the way of technical assistance.

My views regarding the role of the IMF vis-a-vis its member countries rest on three related points. First, today's world requires dramatically more competent national governance, especially in the areas of economics and

---

[143] *See infra* Section IVE of Chapter Four. For this purpose, I suggest that the MDBs apply certain standardized economic and financial criteria. As I point out in that discussion, this remedial function—triggering a suspension of voting power for poor performance—has analogs in domestic laws governing corporate entities. *See id.*

[144] *See* Head, *Third Amendment, supra* note 44, at 630–35 (explaining the details of the Third Amendment) and 639–40 (noting the only grudging acceptance of the Third Amendment by most less developed countries).

finance, than it ever has before. Second, today's world has many national governments that are corrupt and incompetent. Third, the best hope for rectifying this mismatch—that is, the mismatch between (1) the need for better national governance and (2) the reality of wretched national governance—lies in cooperative action through multilateral institutions.

The first of these three points, that national governments have a higher duty of care now than ever before to manage their economies competently, was expressed by former IMF Managing Director Michel Camdessus a couple of years ago:

> Whether a country is large or small, [economic] crises can now become systemic through contagion. Domestic economic policy must take into account its potential worldwide impact; a duty of universal responsibility is incumbent, making each country responsible for the stability and quality of world growth. . . .

> This adds a new dimension to the duty of excellence and rectitude that is required of every government in the management of its economy. Globalization is a prodigious factor in accelerating and spreading the international repercussions of domestic policies. Thus, the IMF emphasizes three points [in dealing with its member states]: rigor and transparency, growth centered on human development, and government reform.[145]

The second of the three points I mentioned above, that many national governments are either corrupt or incompetent (or both), is reflected in this scathing broadside attack (issued by a Ghanaian) on the quality of governance in much of Africa:

> [G]overnment, as it is understood in the West, does not exist in many parts of Africa. What exists is a Mafia state—government highjacked by crooks, thugs, and gangsters, who use the instruments of state power to enrich themselves, their cronies, and their tribesmen. All others are excluded from the government. The ruling elite perceives government, not as a vehicle for reform or as a way to serve the people, but as a way to fleece the people. The institutions of the state have been taken over by the ruling elites, corrupted, and their functions perverted to serve the interests of

---

[145] Camdessus, *supra* note 135, at 364. I might qualify the point M. Camdessus makes in the first sentence quoted above by suggesting that economic crises could probably always have become systemic through contagion. The new aspect that places on national governments a higher duty of care now than ever before is the speed with which contagion spreads, thanks to modern technologies of communication. I am indebted to Bob Hockett for noting this important point.

the elite. Practices such as meritocracy, rule of law, property rights, transparency, and administrative capacity have vanished.[146]

What, then, is to be done? If both of these points are correct—(1) that our world needs, more than ever before, national governments that are competent, and (2) that our world suffers from many incompetent or corrupt national governments—what can be done to remedy the situation? I cast my vote for multilateral solutions. In my view, the best hope for the future in terms of preventing global economic storms or melt-downs, or at least limiting the damage they cause, lies with global efforts to improve the competence and effectiveness of national governments. I endorse the views expressed by Professor Harold James of Princeton. After tracing the IMF's gradual expansion of emphasis into four new areas—military spending, corruption, democracy, and transparency of national governments—James makes this observation:

> The gradual extension of the IMF into these areas [of military spending, corruption, democracy, and transparency] is an immediate result of the new consensus about economic practice and of a new world political order that it has helped to produce. But it reflects something more profound—a realization increasingly shared throughout the world that the world economy, and world institutions, can be a better guarantee of rights and of prosperity than some governments, which may be corrupt, rent-seeking, and militaristic. Economic reform and the removal of corrupt governments are preconditions both for the effective operation of markets and for greater social justice. Indeed, these two results, far from being contradictory as some critics imagine, are complementary.[147]

In my view, these three points—the increased need for competent governance, the prevalence of incompetent national governments, and the possibility of relying on multilateral solutions and institutions—yields the

---

[146] George B.N. Ayittey, *How the Multilateral Institutions Compounded Africa's Economic Crisis*, 30 L. & POL'Y INT'L BUS. 585, 589 (1999). Ayittey, highly critical of IMF and World Bank operations in Africa, calls for these institutions to support indigenous initiatives of the people (not the governments) of Africa, on grounds that political change must precede economic and institutional reform there. *Id.* at 597–600. Ayittey expressed some of these same points also in 2004, saying that most IMF-sponsored reforms in poorly run countries have "amounted to reorganising of a bankrupt company [that is, the country] and placing it, together with a massive infusion of new capital, in the hands of the same incompetent managers who ruined it in the first place [that is, the country's same government]." George B.N. Ayittey, *The Rule of Big Men or the Rule of Law?*, THE ECONOMIST, July 17, 2004, *available at* 2004 WL 620167512.

[147] James, *supra* note 39, at 47.

following principle to guide the IMF in coming years: the IMF should serve as a vehicle by which the international community both (1) insists on the adherence by all countries to certain minimal standards and (2) provides help for those countries whose governments cannot make the grade.

I begin with the first of these. I believe the IMF—as well as the MDBs and the WTO—should impose minimum standards on member countries in a variety of areas, including good governance, environmental protection, human rights, financial prudence, and investment guidelines. Such minimum standards already exist, of course, either in the form of treaties that scores of countries have already expressly accepted or in the form of guidelines developed by international entities with recognized expertise.

For example, an abbreviated list of such treaties would include the following:[148]

- Convention on International Trade in Endangered Species of Wild Fauna and Flora (CITES) (1973)
- Vienna Convention for the Protection of the Ozone Layer (1985), and pertinent provisions of the Protocols thereto and of the Amendments to those Protocols
- Basle Convention on the Control of Transboundary Movements of Hazardous Wastes and Their Disposal (1989)[149]
- Convention on Biological Diversity (1992)
- Climate Change Convention (1992)
- Kyoto Protocol on Global Warming (1998)
- International Covenant on Civil and Political Rights (1967)
- International Covenant on the Elimination of All Forms of Racial Discrimination (1966)
- Convention on the Elimination of All Forms of Discrimination Against Women (1979)
- Convention Against Torture and Other Cruel Inhuman or Degrading Treatment or Punishment (1984)
- Convention on the Rights of the Child (1989)
- OECD Convention on Combating Bribery of Foreign Public Officials in International Business Transactions (1997).

---

[148] Many of the treaties listed below, along with information about the number of states participating in them, may be found in BURNS H. WESTON ET AL., SUPPLEMENT OF BASIC DOCUMENTS IN INTERNATIONAL LAW AND WORLD ORDER app. (3d ed. 1997).

[149] As noted in the Glossary, I have used the spelling "Basle" throughout this book in the interest of consistency, even though the alternative spelling "Basel" appears more commonly used in certain contexts.

In addition to those widely accepted treaties, the following sets of guidelines and principles also set forth international minimum standards:

- Basle guidelines on capital adequacy[150]
- Basle core principles on banking supervision[151]
- OECD guidelines on corporate governance[152]
- OECD guidelines for multinational enterprises[153]
- Guidelines for treatment of foreign direct investment, adopted by the Development Committee of the World Bank[154]
- Special Data Dissemination Standard (IMF)[155]
- Code of Good Practices in Fiscal Transparency (IMF)[156]
- Code of Good Practices on Transparency in Monetary and Financial Policies (IMF).[157]

I believe the IMF should have some role in encouraging its member countries to accept and abide by the core obligations set forth in these

---

[150] The Basle guidelines on capital adequacy requirements were first established by the Basle Committee (or, by its alternative spelling, the Basel Committee) on Banking Supervision (a committee of banking supervisory authorities) in the late 1980s to assist governments in establishing regulations that would prevent financial institutions from operating in a manner that placed depositors' assets at undue risk. For an explanation of those capital adequacy guidelines, and related work of the Basle Committee, *see* RAMSEY & HEAD, *supra* note 114, at 163–68; John W. Head, *Lessons from the Asian Financial Crisis: The Role of the IMF and the Untied States,* 7 KAN. J.L. & PUB. POL'Y 70, 80, 95 n.83 (1998) [hereinafter Head, *Lessons from the Asian Financial Crisis*].

[151] Basle Committee on Banking Supervision, Core Principles for Effective banking Supervision (Sept. 1997), *available at* http://www.bis.org/publ/bcbs30a.pdf (last visited Feb. 16, 2005); *see also* RAMSEY & HEAD, *supra* note 114, at 9–10 (summarizing the core principles) and 158–62 (reprinting the core principles as of September 1997).

[152] Organization for Economic Co-operation and Development, OECD Principles of Corporate Governance (2004), *available at* http://www.oecd.org/dataoecd/32/18/31557724.pdf (last visited Feb. 13, 2005).

[153] Organization for Economic Co-operation and Development, The OECD Guidelines for Multinational Enterprises, June 27, 2000, 40 I.L.M. 237. Information about the guidelines and other related OECD documents appears on the OECD website, *at* http://www.oecd.org.

[154] *See* World Bank, Report to the Development Committee and Guidelines on the Treatment of Foreign Direct Investment, Sept. 21, 1992, 31 I.L.M. 1363 (reflecting the findings of a working group established by the Presidents of the World Bank, the IFC, and MIGA and consisting of the General Counsel of those institutions).

[155] *See* International Monetary fund, *Standards and Codes: The Role of the IMF—A Factsheet* (Apr. 2003), *at* http://www.imf.org/external/np/exr/facts/sc.htm (last visited Feb. 13, 2005).

[156] *See id.*

[157] *See id.*

treaties and guidelines and in other standards designed to promote distributional and social justice. I think I am not alone in this view. In a speech delivered at Oxford University shortly after leaving his position as IMF Managing Director, Michel Camdessus offered a long list of objectives that the IMF should focus on, through its surveillance activities and through programs it designs, to help countries "realize their global responsibilities."[158] In addition to calling for "high-quality growth [that] . . . emphasizes equity, poverty alleviation, and empowerment of the poor . . . [and that also] stresses protection of the environment and respects national cultural values,"[159] Camdessus enumerated the following issues with which the international financial institutions should concern themselves:

- encouraging participatory democracy;
- encouraging transparency, openness, and accountability;
- combating collusion, corruption, and nepotism;
- suppressing arms transfers and military expenditures;
- emphasizing poverty alleviation as the "centerpiece of economic policy";
- promoting free markets and trade liberalization;
- providing for social safety nets;
- devoting public spending to education and health care.[160]

Camdessus did not specify in his speech how the IMF should encourage its member countries to pursue these objectives. I would offer the following ideas.

First, it is worth considering making it a requirement of IMF participation—through an additional protocol or through an amendment to the IMF Charter if necessary[161]—that a country accept the core obligations in all the treaties and guidelines I listed above, along with standards designed to promote distributional and social justice. Under this approach, any country that is not already an IMF member would be barred from membership until it accepted those core obligations; and each current member country would have its membership suspended until it did so as well.[162] I

---

158 Camdessus, *supra* note 135, at 364.

159 *Id.* at 364–65.

160 *Id.* at 365–67.

161 As the IMF General Counsel has pointed out, the IMF Charter in its current form imposes some constraints on how much the IMF can insist, through conditionality, that borrowing member countries adhere to other international agreements. *See* Gianviti, *supra* note 51, at 115 (discussing constraints on conditionality).

162 This suggestion, like some others noted below (and like the suspension-of-voting-rights suggestion made above in Subsection IVA of this chapter), could have important

suggest a similar approach, with somewhat more detail, in my assessment of the MDBs in Chapter Four.[163]

Second, in designing mechanisms by which the IMF could encourage its member countries to abide by the obligations set forth in those treaties, guidelines, and standards, policymakers should take note of the distinction Bradlow has made between implementation and enforcement.[164] The scope of "implementation," under Bradlow's distinction, involves having international financial institutions "us[e] their technical assistance and information gathering capacity"[165] to collect data and share it with specialized agencies having subject-matter competence.[166] An "enforcement" role, by contrast, would be much broader—involving, for example, loan conditionalities that would result in a suspension of financial assistance if the country acted in breach of its commitments.[167]

Using that distinction between implementation and enforcement, I would then suggest a bifurcated role for the IMF. In respect of all the core obligations referred to above, the IMF could have an implementation role—that is, a role that would involve collecting information, making it public, sharing it with other specialized agencies having competence in the subject-matter of the treaty, guidelines, or standards at issue, and thereby bringing the pressure of public opinion (favorable or unfavorable, as the case may be) on how well a country has honored its obligations in those respects. But the IMF would also have an enforcement role with respect to

---

effects on some of those countries (including the United States) that currently exercise such dominance over the IMF. I am fully aware of the practical obstacles to the implementation of such suggestions. For my views in that regard, *see infra* Subsection IIC of Chapter Six—the final subsection of this book.

[163] *See infra* Section IV of Chapter Four, in which I propose that the MDB membership requirements be expanded, in much the same way that participation in the GATT was made subject to the "single package" approach agreed upon in the Uruguay Round of trade negotions, so that membership in an MDB would require that a country accept certain specified obligations in basic (existing) multilateral treaties relating to environmental protection, human rights, and good governance. Naturally, creating such strong linkages among treaty regimes covering a broad range of economic and social issues will attract criticism. For a thoughtful discussion of why such linkages should be made, *see generally* Steve Charnovitz, *Linking Topics in Treaties*, appearing as Chapter 1 in STEVE CHARNOVITZ, TRADE LAW AND GLOBAL GOVERNANCE (2002).

[164] *See* Bradlow-I, *supra* note 15, at 728 (distinguishing between enforcement and implementation of international legal obligations in examining how, if at all, international financial institutions should deal with issues of international humanitarian law).

[165] *Id.* at 729.

[166] *Id.* at 715–16.

[167] *Id.* at 726–27 (discussing the possibility of using loan conditions to enforce international humanitarian law).

those few treaties, guidelines, and standards that bear most directly on the economic well-being of the member country—including, for example, the OECD anti-bribery convention and the Basle principles on banking supervision and capital adequacy.[168]

Lastly, what would the enforcement role of the IMF involve? I suggest consideration of two types of such an enforcement role. The first is familiar: condition a member country's access to IMF financial assistance on the country's performance of its obligations. The second, which would be novel, is similar to an approach I introduced above: give more teeth to the IMF's surveillance function by linking Article IV consultations to voting power. Specifically, in those cases where the IMF finds in the course of Article IV consultations that a member country has departed substantially and chronically from its obligations under the specified treaties, guidelines, and standards (or, as suggested above, from other economic and financial policies agreed to earlier with the IMF), the member country's voting power would be suspended until the country corrects that shortcoming. Such an approach would amount to a modification of the weighted voting system, so that a member's usable voting power would be based on its subscription to capital, as under current rules, unless (and perhaps to the extent that) the member's failure to abide by its obligations triggered a suspension of that voting power.[169]

The points sketched out above have suggested how the IMF might get more *insistent* in encouraging its member countries to live up to the minimum standards that are increasingly recognized as essential for competent governance in an interconnected world. But there is also another approach that I believe should be considered to achieve this end: authorizing the IMF to get more *generous* in encouraging its member countries to live up to those minimum standards. Such generosity could come in the from of substantially increased technical assistance funded by the wealthy industrialized countries that control the IMF's operations.

---

[168] It is conceivable that the IMF could also, at some point in the future, have an enforcement role with respect to those treaties and guidelines as to which another specialized agency had requested the IMF to exert influence over a member country that had, in the expert view of that other specialized agency, failed to abide by its obligations under the treaty or guidelines at issue. But such a role for the IMF would not seem appropriate until what Camdessus calls "a new sense of world citizenship" has emerged. Camdessus, *supra* note 135, at 369.

[169] As I have summarized it here, the proposed authority to suspend voting power for failure to meet treaty obligations (or to hew to agreed-upon economic and financial policies), would be an all-or-nothing matter. A more nuanced, but more complicated, approach would be to authorize partial suspension (that is of some but not all) of a member's voting power.

Such an increase in technical assistance would permit the IMF to do much more than it does now[170] in the way of training and assisting government officials in a range of areas where many countries fall short, such as planning of budgets, setting tax policy, collecting taxes, writing economic legislation, supervising banks and other financial institutions, establishing deposit insurance systems, managing foreign reserves, issuing and trading in government securities, managing monetary policy, implementing programs of social insurance or public welfare, keeping and auditing government accounts, and conducting government procurement operations. The IMF already undertakes an extensive and varied program of technical assistance to its member countries, but "[a]s the IMF intensifies its efforts to help countries strengthen their economic policy and financial management capacities, the pressure of demand on its technical assistance resources is likely to increase further," especially under a relatively new initiative to carry out wide-ranging Technical Cooperation Action Plans, the implementation and financing of which "will greatly exceed the technical assistance resources and instruments [currently] available to the IMF."[171] The provision of such technical assistance funding by wealthy countries would be akin to the transfers of wealth that have already taken place within the context of the IMF through the Trust Fund and the ESAF and PRGF, noted above,[172] and that have taken place in other contexts through the Global Environment Facility[173] and the IDA.[174]

In short, I believe a one-two punch could be designed to encourage IMF member countries to take seriously the obligations that all countries must honor in today's world in order to meet the minimal standards of competence: the IMF would both (1) become more insistent by enforcing such obligations through conditionality and new suspension-of-voting-power rules and (2) become more generous by providing technical assis-

---

[170] For information on technical assistance provided now by the IMF, *see supra* note 111 and Subsection IIF of Chapter Two. *See also* International Monetary Fund, *Policy Statement on IMF Technical Assistance* (Apr. 1, 2001), *available at* http://www.imf.org/external/pubs/ft/psta/index.htm (last visited Feb. 13, 2005) [hereinafter TA Policy Statement].

[171] TA Policy Statement, *supra* note 170.

[172] *See supra* text accompanying notes 116–122

[173] Under the Global Environment Facility (GEF), the costs of using environmentally friendly technology and techniques in development activities can be offset with resources contributed by the richer, more industrially advanced countries. For details about the GEF, *see infra* Subsection IIIA of Chapter Four.

[174] As noted above, the IDA was established in 1960 as a companion to the IBRD to provide a mechanism for making cheaper money available to the less developed countries by relying on contributions from rich member countries to finance projects in those poorer countries.

tance that would be funded by the wealthy countries. And underlying both approaches would be a shared understanding that the economic growth and well-being of every national economy depends on competent governance, and competent governance requires meeting a wide range of challenges—not only those of a purely economic and financial nature but also those involving distributional and social justice, environmental protection, fundamental human freedoms, and participatory decisionmaking.

CHAPTER FOUR

EVALUATING THE CRITICISMS
DIRECTED AT THE MDBs

I. SURVEY OF THE CRITICISMS

Of the 25 key criticisms that I enumerated in Chapter One of this book, 12 are leveled at the MDBs in particular. In the following paragraphs I explain each of these dozen criticisms. In doing so, I try to express each criticism in what I consider to be its most forceful terms. As I emphasized at the beginning of Chapter Three, my attempt to state the criticisms persuasively here should not be taken at this stage as any endorsement of them on my part. As will be clear from Section II of this chapter, I do not agree with several of these criticisms, nor do I agree with some of the assumptions and value judgments on which several of them rest.

A. Criticism #II-1—Bad Economic and Financial Policies and Projects[1]

In its usual form, this criticism asserts that the MDBs are based on a flawed economic model—that of laissez-faire, free-market policies—and they force borrowing member countries (sometimes in a "cookie-cutter" manner) to accept that economic model instead of allowing those countries to develop their economies through pragmatic, tailored (even protectionist) policies until those countries can get on their feet economically. The MDBs' insistence on this laissez-faire model—which is part of the "Washington Consensus" that I referred to earlier in my explanation of Criticism #I-1 ("bad medicine") leveled at the IMF[2]—reflects the fact that the MDBs conceive of "development" as a narrow process of economic restructuring to stimulate economic growth. In their headlong rush to create such economic growth, the MDBs often support bad projects that do not provide long-term economic improvement in the lives of those people who are allegedly the intended beneficiaries of the projects. Indeed, some of the projects—for example, those to expand coffee production[3]—have

---

[1] For citations to examples in the literature of some criticisms along these lines, *see* Part II of Appendix A.

[2] *See supra* Subsection IA of Chapter Three.

[3] Michael Massing, *From Protest to Program*, THE AMERICAN PROSPECT, Summer 2001, at 5 (stating that "[o]ne reason there's a glut [in coffee production] is that the World Bank has for years been pushing third-world countries to grow cash crops like coffee to boost their export earnings").

led to disruption of world markets and economic distress. In addition, some of the projects and policies supported by the MDBs promote privatization in unsophisticated economies that do not yet have an adequate institutional and regulatory framework in place. As a result, the process and results of privatization are terrible; the scoundrels waltz right in to the economy, to everyone's detriment but their own. All in all, this inappropriate and unthinking adoption of, and insistence on, a Western rich-country economic model, without due attention to local conditions, has brought further impoverishment to LDCs.

The points described above may be seen as coming from "the left."[4] Sometimes complaints about the MDBs' policies and ideology come also from the other end of the political spectrum.[5] I address those complaints more fully later in this chapter because they arise most frequently in connection with claims of "Mission Creep" (Criticism #II-11).

B.   Criticism #II-2—Wrong Form of Financial Assistance[6]

According to this criticism, the MDBs should dramatically reduce, or stop entirely, their practice of making loans. MDB lending is anachronistic: the MDBs were established because, at the time, there were no global financial markets and institutions available to provide the financing necessary to

---

[4] Indeed, one of the earliest and most insightful and biting criticisms of the World Bank, published nearly a quarter of a century ago, took a socialist stand in attacking the failures of the World Bank's operations—failures the author attributed in large part to an imperialist, class- based, capitalist ideology ultimately unconcerned with the plight of the poor. *See generally* CHERYL PAYER, THE WORLD BANK: A CRITICAL ANALYSIS (1982).

[5] *See* JOINT ECONOMIC COMMITTEE, REPORT OF THE INTERNATIONAL FINANCIAL INSTITUTIONS ADVISORY COMMISSION 9 (Mar. 2000) [hereinafter MELTZER REPORT] ("Unfortunately, neither the World Bank nor the regional development banks are pursuing the set of activities that could best help the world move more rapidly toward [the objective of eradicating world poverty] or even the lesser, but more fully achievable, goal of raising living standards and the quality of life, particularly for people in the poorest nations of the world."), *available at* http://www.house.gov/jec/imf/meltzer.pdf (last visited Nov. 4, 2004). The Report of the International Financial Institutions Advisory Commission, referred to as the Meltzer Report after its chairman, Allan Meltzer, although worthy of some attention, strikes me as a document riddled with inaccuracies, sweeping generalizations, unsubstantiated suggestions, and not a little ideological hogwash suitable for cute sound bites but of no lasting significance. Dissenting views expressed by four commission members—including most notably Fred Bergsten, whose expert insight has contributed to intelligent assessment of international institutions and relations for several decades—impress me as far more credible and persuasive. *See* MELTZER REPORT, *supra*, at 111–18. *See also* C. Fred Bergsten, *The Empire Strikes Back*, THE INT'L ECON., May 2000, at 10–13, 52 (criticizing the Meltzer Report on grounds that it "unfairly maligns two highly successful international institutions").

[6] For citations to examples in the literature of some criticisms along these lines, *see* Part II of Appendix A.

facilitate the large public-works projects needed to rebuild Europe (in the case of the IBRD) and (for all the MDBs) to bring economic development to the underdeveloped countries. Now the situation is different. The global financial system is very mature. Hence, MDB loans—and therefore the public borrowings and public contributions on which those MDB loans depend—are no longer necessary.[7] If MDB financing is to continue at all, it should continue (at least predominantly) in the form of grants, so as to assist those countries and those projects that are truly needed and viable from a long-term development perspective but for which commercial financing is unavailable on reasonable terms. Indeed, if the MDBs are justified as a legal matter in their recent shift of emphasis toward poverty reduction (see the discussion below of Criticism #II-11), then this shift can only be justified as a practical or operational matter if the MDBs provide grant financing to meet that goal. Expressed differently, surely poverty alleviation is better accomplished by giving grants than by making loans.

C. Criticism #II-3—Environmental Degradation[8]

This criticism claims that some MDB-financed projects have devastating effects on the environment. For example, the MDBs favor (according to the critics) large dam- and road-building projects and reflect a general addiction to fossil fuels. The MDBs permit and promote environmentally destructive projects because the MDBs simply disregard the environmental effects of the projects at both the design and the implementation phase. Why is this the case? Partly because the MDBs are controlled by anti-environment influences, including corporate interests (see Criticism #II-9); and partly because the MDB staff and management are out of step with modern views of sustainable development (see Criticism #II-7).

D. Criticism #II-4—Human Rights Shortcomings[9]

According to this criticism, the MDBs typically give little or no regard to human rights of various types, including the right to education and the rights of indigenous people, and they act independently of any accepted human rights norms and institutions. MDB projects and policies often set the pricing of health, education, and water services out of the reach of ordinary people. Moreover; MDBs support, at least tacitly, the notion of cultural

---

[7] As indicated above in the summary of Criticism #II-1, some complaints from "the right" as to the economic policies promoted by MDBs follow this reasoning. *See supra* note 5 and accompanying text.

[8] For citations to examples in the literature of some criticisms along these lines, *see* Part II of Appendix A.

[9] For citations to examples in the literature of some criticisms along these lines, *see* Part II of Appendix A.

exceptionalism by which universal human rights norms are ignored by some countries.[10] In addition, the MDBs are ineffective at addressing corruption in government, thus disregarding the human right to effective governance (see Criticism #II-9). Indeed, the MDBs fuel corruption (according to the critics) by virtue of the huge financial flows that they control and disburse to government officials.

E.   Criticism #II-5—MDB Trampling of National Sovereignty[11]

This criticism, which corresponds to Criticism #I-3 directed against the IMF,[12] claims that in imposing conditions on the rights of member countries to borrow money from MDBs, the MDBs violate the sovereignty of those member countries, and, in particular, the principle of self-determination. In so doing, the MDBs themselves act inconsistently with settled principles of international law—for example, the principle of state sovereignty enshrined in Article 2(1) of the U.N. Charter[13] and the principle of self-determination of peoples, set forth in (among other places) Article 1 of the International Covenant on Civil and Political Rights.[14] Moreover, to the extent that loan conditionalities imposed by the MDBs require a government to adopt economic and financial policies that are contrary to those that would be adopted by the people of that country, the MDBs encourage governments to act inconsistently with the principles of participatory governance reflected in Article 25 of the ICCPR.[15]

---

[10] A curious irony, kindly pointed out to me by Bob Hockett, arises between this criticism that the MDBs support exceptionalism in the area of human rights and an element of Criticism #II-1, described above, that the MDBs reject exceptionalism in the area of economic and financial policies, by insisting on a Western rich-country economic model without due attention to local conditions.

[11] For citations to examples in the literature of some criticisms along these lines, *see* Part II of Appendix A.

[12] *See supra* Subsection IC of Chapter Three.

[13] One of the principles on which the organization is founded is "the principle of sovereign equality of all its Members." U.N. CHARTER art. 2, para. 1. The U.N. General Assembly has, by way of a resolution adopted in 1970 without recorded vote, interpreted Article 2(1) as meaning that the "political independence of the State [is] inviolable" and that "[e]ach state has the right freely to choose and develop its political, social, economic and cultural systems." *Declaration on Principles of International Law Concerning Friendly Relations and Co-operation Among States in Accordance with the Charter of the United Nations*, G.A. Res. 485, U.N. GAOR, 25th Sess., Supp. No. 28, U.N. Doc. A/8028 (1970), *reprinted in* 9 I.L.M. 1292, 1296–97 (1970).

[14] The ICCPR provision states that "[a]ll peoples have the right of self-determination. By virtue of that right they freely determine their political status and freely pursue their economic, social and cultural development." International Covenant on Civil and Political Rights, Dec. 16, 1966, art. 1(1), S. TREATY DOC. NO. 95-2, 999 U.N.T.S. 171 [hereinafter ICCPR], *reprinted in* 6 I.L.M. 368, 369 (1967).

[15] Article 25 of the ICCPR provides that every citizen shall have the right to partici-

F.   Criticism #II-6—Incoherence in Policy Prescriptions[16]

This criticism claims that there is inadequate coordination among the MDBs—and also between the MDBs and other international institutions such as the WTO or the IMF—so that some countries might be subject to several conflicting economic and financial policy requirements. This incoherence results from the relative independence of the various global economic institutions, and that independence, in turn, reflects the fact that there is no overall coordinating process or body to bring order and consistency out of all the efforts to facilitate development.

G.   Criticism #II-7—Weakness in Staffing and Management[17]

According to this criticism, the MDBs are run by persons who have numerous inadequacies, so that even if other deficiencies in the MDBs could be remedied, their operations would still be found wanting. The inadequacies take different forms. For one thing, staff appointments to and promotions within the MDBs—and even the selections of top managers— are sometimes based on the wrong grounds. Too much emphasis, for instance, is placed on nationality, so that a candidate from an "under-represented" country might be appointed to a staff position (or promoted to a higher one) despite being otherwise poorly qualified for the job, or, in any event, substantially less qualified overall than another candidate for the position. In terms of promotions, too much emphasis is placed on the volume, rather than the quality, of lending activity generated by the person. In other words, the MDBs have an "approval culture" that gives incentives to lend for lending's sake.[18]

A second form of staff inadequacy is policy anachronism: some staff members who have served in the MDBs for over a decade or two are unable or unwilling to appreciate how the theory and practice of economic development has changed in recent years, and their seniority can give them

---

pate in elections aimed at "guaranteeing the free expression of the will of the electors." *Id.* art. 25.

[16] For citations to examples in the literature of some criticisms along these lines, *see* Part II of Appendix A.

[17] For citations to examples in the literature of some criticisms along these lines, *see* Part II of Appendix A.

[18] For the complaint that the MDBs have an "'approval culture' aimed at achieving yearly lending targets," and that this gives "[i]ncentives to lend for lending's sake . . . ," *see* MELTZER REPORT, *supra* note 5, at 75. For some elaboration on this "approval culture" complaint, and on MDB responses to it, *see infra* notes 140–141. *See also* Korinna Horta, *Rhetoric and Reality: Human Rights and the World Bank*, 15 HARV. HUM. RTS. J. 227, 241 (2002) (ascribing the term "approval culture" to former World Bank Vice President Willi Wapenhans).

great influence in formulating and implementing MDB policy. A third form of staff inadequacy stems from a lack of internal accountability because of a division in responsibilities and a regular shifting of staff from one type of job to another within the organization.

H.   Criticism #II-8—MDB Secrecy and Opaqueness[19]

The first seven criticisms summarized above relate mainly to MDB policies and operations. The next five criticisms in the "dirty dozen" complaints about the MDBs focus more on the character, control, and reach of the MDBs. Most of these criticisms are closely similar to corresponding criticisms leveled at the IMF. For example, just as Criticism #I-4 claims that the IMF is a secretive organization,[20] Criticism #II-8 complains that the MDBs are also secretive in their operations, in several respects. For one thing, they practice "documentary secretiveness." They typically do not disclose documents that describe their governing policies, their decisions, and their plans—that is, how they do things, what they have done, and what they plan to do.

Moreover, the documents that the MDBs do disclose under their selective disclosure policies are usually (according to this criticism) self-serving and biased, simply whitewashing over any negative aspects of their operations, and they often result only in the disclosure of documents that are distracting or deceptive in character, intended to keep the public occupied with largely irrelevant information. Furthermore, in some cases, the MDBs allow the member countries themselves to determine whether certain documents relating to those countries will be made public, and this represents and abdication of responsibility by the MDBs. In addition to these forms of "documentary secretiveness," the MDBs are also said to practice what I have called "operational secretiveness": they conduct business in closed meetings that exclude the public from observing the MDBs in action. Indeed, many key decisions are made through informal "insider" meetings that are off-limits to public scrutiny and that dispense with the formalities to which public meetings are usually subject for the purpose of ensuring procedural fairness.[21]

---

[19] For citations to examples in the literature of some criticisms along these lines, *see* Part II of Appendix A.

[20] *See supra* Subsection ID of Chapter Three.

[21] For the related complaint that the public has inadequate influence over MDB decisions, see the discussion below of Criticism #II-9 ("democracy deficit"). Criticism #II-8 focuses only on the complaint that the public has inadequate access to information about MDB operations.

I. Criticism #II-9—The MDB Democracy Deficit [22]

According to this criticism, which corresponds directly to Criticism #I-5 directed against the IMF,[23] the MDBs lack legitimacy in today's world because they lack, as a structural or constitutional matter, any meaningful form of accountability. This criticism takes several forms, of which five are most important. I summarize these in the following paragraphs.

First, as a structural matter the MDBs make no accommodation (according to the critics) for citizen involvement. That is, not only do the MDBs operate on the basis of secrecy (see Criticism #II-8), which prevents individuals or groups from knowing how they operate, what they have done, and what they plan to do; but the MDBs provide no mechanism for influence by members of representatives of civil society. In a world in which the importance of participatory rights is broadly accepted—for example, in human rights treaties that have been ratified by over three-quarters of all countries[24]—such unaccountability is anachronistic and unacceptable.

Second, the MDBs' unaccountability is not only a structural shortcoming but also a practical shortcoming. That is, as a practical matter the MDBs actually do listen to corporate interests (say some critics) but disregard citizens' groups and non-government organizations (NGOs).[25] For example, MDB staff members are subjected to lobbying by companies that compete fiercely for billions of dollars worth of procurement contracts—that is, contracts awarded by the MDBs or by their borrowers for the supply of equipment, the building of roads and structures, and the provision of consulting services. The decisions to award such contracts are made in circumstances that invite corruption of government officials and MDB staff members, and no adequate safeguards against such corruption have been put in place. More generally, corporate interests influence the overall selection and design of projects to be financed by the MDBs, as well as the overall policy direction of the MDBs—often overshadowing the interests of the per-

---

[22] For citations to examples in the literature of some criticisms along these lines, *see* Part II of Appendix A.

[23] For a summary explanation of that criticism, *see supra* Subsection IE of Chapter Three.

[24] The ICCPR provides that "[e]very citizen shall have the right and the opportunity . . . [t]o take part in the conduct of public affairs, directly or through freely chosen representatives." ICCPR, *supra* note 34, art. 25. As of early 1997, 139 countries had ratified the ICCPR. BURNS H. WESTON ET AL., SUPPLEMENT OF BASIC DOCUMENTS IN INTERNATIONAL LAW AND WORLD ORDER app. at 1298–99 (3d ed. 1997).

[25] For citations to examples in the literature of criticisms making these two subsidiary "democracy deficit" points—that is, that the MDBs pay too much attention to corporate interests and too little to NGOs and citizens' groups, *see* Part II of Appendix A.

sons and communities whose well-being the projects and policies are supposed to serve.

At the same time that the MDBs give undue influence, according to their critics, to corporations, the MDBs give too little attention to NGOs and citizens' groups whose aim is to protect the public interest at large—sometimes referred to as "civil society" organizations. The contribution that such groups can make in the development process is ignored, the critics say, and this, in turn, prompts some of these groups to take drastic, sometimes violent, actions that pit them against the MDBs as enemies. This needless antagonism represents both (1) a squandering by the MDBs of the opportunity to benefit from the NGOs' enthusiasm and expertise and (2) a disregard by the MDBs of the recent moves within the United Nations to encourage the involvement of public interest (civil society) organizations.[26]

A third element of the "democracy deficit" criticism revolves around the weighted voting system. Under the weighted voting system, as noted earlier,[27] a country's voting power is generally proportional to that country's subscription to the MDB's capital. From their inception, the MDBs have had capital structures (similar to that of the IMF) in which a handful of countries (including most markedly the United States) has controlled the bulk of the subscribed capital. Hence, that handful of countries controls a preponderance of the votes. For example, the G-7 countries[28]—none of which borrows from the MDBs, of course—control about 43 percent of the votes in the IBRD[29] and about 41 percent of the votes in the AsDB,[30]

---

[26] For information about how the United Nations encourages in the involvement of nongovernment organizations and "civil society" organizations, *see* the U.N. website, *at* http://www.un.org/dpi/ngosection/index.html (last visited Nov. 4, 2004).

[27] See *supra* Subsection IIIE of Chapter Two.

[28] As noted earlier, the Group of 7, or G-7, consists of the United States, Japan, Germany, the United Kingdom, France, Italy, and Canada.

[29] *See* THE WORLD BANK, II THE WORLD BANK ANNUAL REPORT 2002, at 47–50 (showing percentages of voting power as of June 2002 to be 2.79 percent for Canada, 4.31 percent for France, 2.79 percent for Italy, 4.49 percent for Germany, 7.87 percent for Japan, 4.31 percent for the United Kingdom, and 16.41 percent for the United States, for a G-7 total of 42.97 percent), *available at* http://www.worldbank.org/annualreport/2002/PrintVersion.htm (last visited Nov. 4, 2004). Similar percentages appear in more recent World Bank Annual Reports. *See, e.g.,* http://www.worldbank.org/annualreport/2003/PrintVersion.htm, http://www.worldbank.org/annualreport/2004/PrintVersion.htm.

[30] *See* II THE ASIAN DEVELOPMENT BANK, THE ASIAN DEVELOPMENT BANK ANNUAL REPORT 2001, at 47–50 [hereinafter AsDB ANNUAL REPORT 2001] (showing percentages of voting power as of December 2001 to be 4.600 percent for Canada, 2.235 percent for France, 3.863 percent for Germany, 1.811 percent for Italy, 13.053 percent for Japan, 2.003 percent for the United Kingdom, and 13.053 percent for the United States, for a G-7 total of 40.618 percent), *available at* http://www.adb.org/Documents/Reports/Annual_Report/2001/default.asp (last visited Nov. 4, 2004). These percentages have remained largely unchanged since that time. For example, as of December 2003, they

and the voting power exceeds 50 percent if (as often happens) the G-7 countries are joined by a few other European countries in decisionmaking. This is one reason why the lack of symmetry in the making and enforcing of MDB policies (see Criticism #II-12, discussed below) is regarded as so venal: a handful of mainly Western countries can effectively impose economic and financial policies on most of the world's other countries, without having to hew to those policies themselves.

Fourth, another structural or charter-based peculiarity of the MDBs contributes further to their alleged unaccountability: the MDBs are not subject to any outside judicial review. In particular, the MDB charters vest in the MDBs themselves the sole authority to determine whether they are acting in compliance with their own charters.[31] Naturally, any such determination is itself made via the weighted voting system. Although steps have been taken recently by some MDBs to establish "inspection panels" to assess whether the institution has followed its own rules,[32] these steps (so the criticism runs) have been inadequate to overcome this structural deficiency.

Fifth, as if the structural deficiencies were not enough, the MDBs exhibit, according to their critics, yet another form or cause of unaccountability: many of their member states' governments, particularly in the poorer countries, are themselves undemocratic in character. Hence, even if a member country with a small capital subscription does succeed in having its voice heard in an MDB's deliberations, there is no guarantee (and often little likelihood) that that voice will reflect the views of that country's people, including the persons most directly affected by the projects or policies at issue.

J. Criticism #II-10—Narrowness of Economic Focus[33]

According to this criticism, the MDBs interpret their charter mandates too rigidly by considering only strictly economic factors in assessing the development needs of their member countries and in appraising and

---

were 4.549 percent for Canada, 2.200 percent for France, 3.817 percent for Germany, 1.780 percent for Italy, 12.942 percent for Japan, 1.970 percent for the United Kingdom, and 12.942 percent for the United States. *See* http://www.adb.org/Documents/ Reports/Annual_Report/2003/default.asp (last visited Nov. 4, 2004). For a study of how the actual application of the weighted voting system in the AsDB affects the practical influence that some member countries have in decisionmaking there, *see generally* Jonathan R. Strand, *State Power in a Multilateral Context: Voting Strength in the Asian Development Bank*, 25 INT'L INTERACTIONS 265 (1999).

[31] For references to the pertinent charter provisions, *see infra* note 49.

[32] For a description of the inspection panels or functions of some MDBs, *see infra* note 152.

[33] For citations to examples in the literature of some criticisms along these lines, *see* Part II of Appendix A.

designing projects. The MDBs should (but do not) construe their charter provisions—such as the AsDB Charter requirement that "[o]nly economic considerations shall be relevant to [its] decisions"[34]—in a flexible manner. They should do so either (1) by recognizing that modern development theory requires that various non-economic factors (for example, politics, biodiversity, and national security) be taken into account or (2) by construing the term "economic" quite broadly to encompass such things as the efficiency of governance, long-term environmental costs and benefits, and social costs and benefits.

K. Criticism #II-11—MDB Mission Creep [35]

This criticism is, at least in part, the opposite of Criticism #II-10. Instead of complaining about an excessively narrow focus on economic matters, this criticism claims that the MDBs have become far too broad and scattered in their focus, and hence less effective in their operations, because they have responded to every policy fad that has come along.[36] The result of this looseness has been both a dilution of the MDBs' commitment to true economic development and an expansion of MDB purposes and operations into areas in which they have no competence and in which, under their charters, they have no authority. This adventure into *ultra vires* activity—getting involved, for example, in judicial reform, micro-credit, women's rights, and poverty reduction—has left the MDBs too broad and too shallow. They are gripped, the critics complain, by "policy proliferation" or "policy paralysis," so something has to change to get them back on their proper (narrow) track. This criticism of the MDBs, of course, has its counterpart in Criticism #I-6 as directed against the IMF.[37]

L. Criticism #II-12—Asymmetry in Obligations[38]

This criticism of the MDBs—like the corresponding Criticism #I-7 leveled against the IMF—focuses on the disparity between rich industrialized

---

[34] AsDB Charter, art. 36(2).

[35] For citations to examples in the literature of some criticisms along these lines, *see* Part II of Appendix A.

[36] This criticism was made effectively a few years ago by a former World Bank official. *See* Jessica Einhorn, *The World Bank's Mission Creep*, 80 FOREIGN AFF. 22, 22 (Jan.–Feb. 2001) (asserting that "[b]y now, [the World Bank's] mission has become so complex that it strains credulity to portray the bank as a manageable organization."). Einhorn describes the ways in which the World Bank has gradually widened its focus to take account of environmental sustainability, equitable income distribution, institutional strengthening, debt relief, poverty reduction, financial crisis management, banking regulation, corporate governance, gender disparities, narcotics, crime, and corruption. *Id.* at 24, 27, 29–32.

[37] For a summary of that criticism, *see supra* Subsection IF of Chapter Three.

[38] For citations to examples in the literature of some criticisms along these lines, *see* Part II of Appendix A.

countries and the LDCs in terms of the obligations that their participation in the MDBs entails. The criticism emerges from two legal and institutional features of the MDBs and their operations. The first of these is the fact that in their policy-based lending[39] the MDBs insist, by way of loan conditionality, that borrowing countries implement certain economic and financial policies endorsed by the MDBs. That is, MDB financing is made available only if (and as long as) a borrowing member country accepts certain economic and financial policies prescribed by the MDBs. If the borrower rejects those policies, the financial assistance will not be available; if the borrower accepts the policies at first but then abandons them, the financial assistance will not continue.

The second feature from which this criticism emerges is the weighted voting system under which all the MDBs operate.[40] These two features, acting in tandem, result in an asymmetrical situation: the rich countries are the policy-givers because of the system of weighted voting, and the poor countries, as borrowers, are the policy-takers; and in some cases the rich countries do not follow the very policies that they insist the poor countries should follow. This asymmetry, it is alleged, is fundamentally unfair and perhaps illegal.

II. CRITICISMS I LARGELY DISMISS

In the following paragraphs I explain why I largely dismiss several of the criticisms directed at the MDBs. These are Criticism #II-1 (bad economic and financial policies and projects), Criticism #II-2 (wrong form of financial assistance), Criticism #II-5 (trampling of national sovereignty), Criticism #II-6 (incoherence in policy prescriptions), and Criticism #II-11 (mission creep). I shall start with the last of these.

A. Criticism #II-11—MDB Mission Creep

I begin with this criticism because it strikes me as the most important one of all and because addressing it requires that we examine some elementary principles. In particular, I hope that by discussing this criticism, and ultimately dismissing it, I can identify and explain some of the values and policy choices that underlie my assessment of the MDBs generally and of the criticisms now being voiced against them.

---

[39] For a reference to the policy-based lending that the MDBs have undertaken in recent years, see the "nutshell" account of the MDBs that I provided in Section III of Chapter Two.

[40] For details on how the weighted voting system places control over the MDBs in a handful of countries, *see supra* notes 29 and 30 and accompanying text.

As I mentioned above in my "nutshell" account of the MDBs, I view the evolution of the MDBs over the past 60 years in terms of three generations.[41] To summarize:

- First generation. The IBRD was established in 1944 to be, first and foremost, a reconstruction bank—that is, a financial intermediary that would facilitate Europe's reconstruction following World War II. Its founders gave relatively little focus to the "D" in IBRD (the economic development of the poorer countries), and they prohibited the IBRD from engaging in political influence.

- Second generation. The establishment of the IDA and of the first three regional development banks (all created around 1960) came in response to the rising importance of the LDCs. These institutions provided for lower cost loans and gave greater regional focus where the LDCs were located. Those institutions were still envisioned primarily as banks, however, with no mandate for influencing the overall political or economic policy choices made by their member countries.

- Third generation. The founders of the EBRD extended that institution's scope well beyond development banking by explicitly adopting three mandates—political, economic, and environmental—that had been absent from the charters of its predecessors. Under these mandates, the EBRD was to engage in the business of broad policy regulation—that is, urging borrowing member countries to take measures, beyond those relating narrowly to development financing, that the EBRD membership as a whole favored.

It is important to note that the old dogs learned new tricks. With the emergence of each new generation, the MDB(s) of the previous generation assumed an increasingly broader role. By the time the IDA was established in 1960, the IBRD had already shifted its focus to the developing world. By the time the EBRD was established in 1990, all of the MDBs that preceded it had already taken on some aspects of policy regulation that were pressing hard against the outer limits of their charters. Indeed, in the same year that the EBRD was making its first loan (1991),[42] the World Bank General Counsel published a book explaining (and defending) the evolution of the World Bank's work and emphasizing "the ability of the World Bank to adapt

---

[41] *See* Subsection IIIG of Chapter Two.

[42] *See* John W. Head, *Supranational Law: How the Move Toward Multilateral Solutions Is Changing the Character of "International" Law*, 42 U. KAN. L. REV. 605, 645 (1994) [hereinafter *Supranational Law*] (describing the very short "gestation period" of the European Bank that culminated in the approval of its first project financing in mid-1991).

its activities to variable and changing circumstances while acting within the original legal framework established by its Articles of Agreement."[43] Now, just under 15 years later, all the MDBs have, as noted above, expanded their purview to include a very broad range of policies that the institutions and their borrowing members are to follow—including such issues as environmental protection, indigenous peoples, involuntary resettlement, governance, corruption, public participation, the role of women in development, and poverty reduction.[44]

Is this policy expansion—what former World Bank official Jessica Einhorn calls "mission creep"[45]—appropriate? That question involves two subsidiary issues that must be addressed in order to provide an answer that will allow us to assess the validity or persuasiveness of Criticism #II-11. Those two subsidiary issues, in simple terms, are:

- Charter fidelity or *ultra vires*? This issue revolves around treaty interpretation. Have the MDBs been faithful to their charter provisions—especially those "political prohibitions" that apply to the first- and second-generation institutions—or have they acted outside their charters (*ultra vires*) by expanding their purview in the ways described above?
- Development banks or regulatory agencies, or both or neither? This issue is a matter not of legality but rather of ideology and policy. Is it necessary to have development banks at all in today's world of sophisticated financial markets and services? If so, is it appropriate to allow such banks to engage in global policy regulation?

In considering the first of these two issues (charter fidelity or *ultra vires*), I am attracted to the assessment that Bob Hockett has given recently

---

[43] IBRAHIM F. I. SHIHATA, I THE WORLD BANK IN A CHANGING WORLD viii (1991) [hereinafter SHIHATA-1991]. For a review of Shihata's attempt in that book to defend the World Bank against criticisms that it had been either too timid or too aggressive vis-á-vis the limitations of its founding instruments, *see* John W. Head, *The World Bank in a Changing World: Selected Essays by Ibrahim F. I. Shihata*, 87 AM. J. INT'L L. 351, 351–52 (1993) (book review). The third book in Shihata's three-volume work on the World Bank, written about a decade after the first book, offers an updated discussion regarding the "evolution of the scope of the Bank's mandate." IBRAHIM F.I. SHIHATA, III THE WORLD BANK IN A CHANGING WORLD 73 (2000). Shihata notes that the World Bank took a "holistic approach as it realized the inevitable linkage between economic and social development, the necessity of institutional development and the direct effect of the macro-economic framework on the prospects of success or failure" in its lending operations. *Id.* at 77. Taking account of these factors, Shihata asserts, is consistent with the mandate set forth in the IDA and IBRD Charters. *Id.* at 77.

[44] *See supra* Subsection IIIG of Chapter Two.

[45] *See* Einhorn, *supra* note 36, at 22.

of complaints that the IMF has acted *ultra vires* in broadening its agenda. As I explained earlier, Hockett rebuts such "mission creep" claims.[46] His defense of the legality of the IMF's evolution includes several elements, including the point that the IMF's charter vests in the IMF itself all power to interpret its own charter—a matter that raises "a nearly irrebuttable presumption in favor of formal legality" of IMF action.[47] Beyond that, however, is the fact that the IMF's charter provisions are actually quite broad in their formulation—the result, Hockett explains, of an intentional effort by the persons drafting it "to incorporate a good deal of 'creative ambiguity' into the [charter's] final draft in order to provide for future contingencies and to secure agreement."[48]

I believe the same analysis applies in respect of the MDBs. First, I believe it would be difficult to assert, as a legal matter, that the MDBs have acted *ultra vires*, given the fact that their charters (like the IMF Charter) provide for self-interpretation. That is, the charters give the MDBs' own governing bodies complete authority to decide questions of charter interpretation or application.[49] In addition, the MDB charters (again, like the IMF Charter) are drafted broadly enough, presumably on purpose, to permit the MDBs to give at least some attention to such issues as those I enumerated above—environmental protection, indigenous peoples, involuntary resettlement, governance, corruption, public participation, the role of women in development, and poverty reduction—because any and all of these can have a bearing on the central objectives prescribed for all of the MDBs in their charters.[50]

---

[46] *See supra* Section IID of Chapter Three. For Hockett's analysis, *see* Robert Hockett, *From Macro to Micro to "Mission-Creep": Defending the IMF's Emerging Concern with the Infrastructural Prerequisites to Global Financial Stability*, 41 COLUM. J. TRANSNAT'L L. 153, 177–90 (2002). Hockett, who is fast becoming a recognized expert on legal and theoretical aspects of international financial institutions, also defends the IMF against claims that, as a practical matter (as distinct from a legal matter), it has overstepped its proper bounds, and he concludes that the combination of "pragmatic and legal justifications [that he offers] . . . should put to rest the diffuse, pseudo-*ultra vires* grumblings heard from some quarters in recent years about the IMF's 'mission-creep' or incremental broadening of agenda." *Id.* at 190.

[47] *See* Hockett, *supra* note 46, at 180.

[48] *Id.* at 178. Hockett illustrates the breadth of IMF Charter provisions on surveillance, consultations, and conditionality. *Id.* at 180–90.

[49] For the provisions on charter interpretation, *see* (in the pertinent Appendices to this book) IBRD Charter, art. IX; IDA Charter, art. X; IADB Charter, art. XIII; AfDB Charter, art. VIII; AsDB Charter, art. 60; EBRD Charter, art. 57. In the context of the IMF, Bob Hockett has noted that the power of self-interpretation that such provisions grant "is most unusual in the . . . international (not to mention domestic) legal systems." Hockett, *supra* note 46, at 178–79.

[50] One of the first provisions in each of the MDB charters is a broad statement of

Given these factors, I dismiss the "mission creep" claim insofar as it is legal in character. Instead, I submit that the MDBs have, as Shihata urged us to conclude just under 15 years ago with regard to the World Bank, remained largely true to their charter provisions, especially if we are prepared to take a "purposive" or "teleological" approach to charter interpretation.[51]

A possible exception to that conclusion is of very recent vintage: within the last few years some of the MDBs have explicitly, and with much fanfare, announced what amounts to a shift in purpose—from economic development (as prescribed in their charters[52]) to poverty reduction.[53] While this

the institution's purposes. *See* IBRD Charter, art. I; IDA Charter, art. I; IADB Charter, art. I; AfDB Charter, arts. I, II; AsDB Charter, art. 1; EBRD Charter, art. 1. All of these "statement-of-purpose" provisions are drafted broadly. For example, Article 1 of the AsDB Charter states that the AsDB's purpose "shall be to foster economic growth and co-operation in the region of Asia and the Far East . . . and to contribute to the acceleration of the process of economic development of the developing member countries in the region, collectively and individually." Article 2 of the AsDB Charter, entitled "Functions," then enumerates five areas of activity—again in broad terms, such as "to promote investment in the region of public and private capital for development purposes"—and ends with an all-encompassing authority "to undertake such other activities and provide such other services as may advance its purpose."

[51] SHIHATA-1991, *supra* note 43, at 3, 69 (positing that a "purposive" or "teleological" approach is perfectly justified in the case of the charters of multilateral institutions and is consistent with well-established rules of treaty interpretation). Similar to the notion of "purposive" or "teleological" interpretation is the notion of "evolutive" interpretation, well-established in the civil law tradition because of the desire to remain true to the spirit of a written law while being responsive to changing circumstances. *See* JOHN HENRY MERRYMAN, THE CIVIL LAW TRADITION 45–46 (2d ed. 1984). For a careful examination of the considerations that the MDBs can and should take into account in interpreting their charters, *see* John D. Ciorciari, *The Lawful Scope of Human Rights Criteria in World Bank Credit Decisions: An Interpretive Analysis of IBRD and IDA Articles of Agreement,* 33 CORNELL L.J. 331, 343–69 (2001) (discussing "ordinary meaning analysis," "secondary intrinsic sources," and the *travaux préparatoires* or preparatory works).

[52] The MDBs' charters, in announcing institutional purposes, all focus explicitly on economic development. *See, e.g.,* IBRD Charter, art. I(i) (stating that the IBRD's purposes are, *inter alia,* to "assist in the reconstruction and development of territories of members by facilitating the investment of capital for productive purposes, including . . . the encouragement of the development of productive facilities and resources in less developed countries"); AsDB Charter, art. 1 (stating that the AsDB's purpose is "to foster economic growth and co-operation in the region . . . and to contribute to the acceleration of the process of economic development of developing member countries in the region").

[53] *See, e.g.,* THE WORLD BANK, I THE WORLD BANK ANNUAL REPORT 2002 [hereinafter I WORLD BANK ANNUAL REPORT 2002], *available at* http://www.worldbank.org/annualreport/2002/PrintVersion.htm (last visited Nov. 4, 2004) at 12 (asserting that the World Bank's "mission is to fight global poverty"). For similar references pertaining to the IADB, *see* The Inter-American Development Bank, Basic Facts About the IDB—Overview, at http://www.iadb.org/exr/pub/bf/bfingles/overview4.htm (last visited Nov. 4, 2004) (noting that one of the "two main objectives of the [IADB]," along with environmentally

purported shift might not elicit the same type of criticism that some other forms of MDB "mission creep" have attracted, the shift could be viewed from a legal perspective[54] as the most egregious departure to date from the MDBs' charters, none of which makes any direct reference to poverty reduction.[55]

At bottom, however, the "mission creep" criticism leveled at the MDBs probably rests less on a concern over legality than on a concern over economic ideology and the power of intergovernmental institutions. Hence, the second issue noted above: Do we want (at the multilateral level) development banks, regulatory agencies, or both, or neither?

---

sustainable growth, is "poverty reduction and social equity"). For similar references pertaining to the AfDB, *see* The African Development Bank Group, Agreement Establishing the African Development Bank (5th ed., Sept. 30, 1999), *at* http://www.afdb.org/knowledge/documents/Agreement_Establishing.htm (last visited Nov. 4, 2004) (explaining that the AfDB's mission is to assist its regional member countries to escape "the vicious cycle of poverty in which they are entrapped"). For similar references pertaining to the AsDB, *see* ASIAN DEVELOPMENT BANK, ASIAN DEVELOPMENT BANK ANNUAL REPORT 2000 284 (2001) (touting poverty reduction as that institution's "fundamental purpose"). For a commentary on this apparent shift in purpose by the AsDB, *see* John W. Head, *Asian Development Bank, in* INTERNATIONAL ENCYCLOPAEDIA OF LAWS (R. Blanpain ed., 2002) [hereinafter Head, *Asian Development Bank*], at 24. For a commentary on this apparent shift in purpose by the World Bank, including an account of the political pressures that allegedly forced the World Bank to "discover" poverty, *see* Balakrishnan Rajagopal, *From Resistance to Renewal: The Third World, Social Movements, and the Expansion of International Institutions*, 41 HARV. INT'L L.J. 529, 547–55 (2000).

54 Viewed from a practical perspective, the shift from economic development to poverty reduction might not seem to amount to much. As a former colleague of mine at the AsDB pointed out in an e-mail message to me, "[m]ost of us in ADB—and probably in other MDBs—would deny there has been any substantive 'shift' from economic development to poverty reduction. If the former does not include the latter, if we've not been pursuing elimination of poverty, what have we in ADB been doing since the start of our operations in 1967?" E-mail message from Fred Mesch to John W. Head, Aug. 20, 2003 (on file with author). However, "economic development" could easily be regarded as having a different reach, and encompassing different types of activities, from those of "poverty reduction." For example, "economic development" can include building a society's infrastructure—roads, ports, power plants—so as to boost aggregate economic activity (measured in the society's gross domestic product) without directly addressing the needs of those portions of the society that are mired in poverty. Indeed, a World Bank annual report dating from 1990 reflected this view of "economic development" in noting that the IBRD Charter provisions require that the institution "must lend only for productive purposes and must stimulate economic growth." THE WORLD BANK, THE WORLD BANK ANNUAL REPORT 1990 3 (1990). On the other hand, "poverty reduction" might include some activities—for instance, the provision of fuel subsidies or short-term disaster relief—that would not, under that traditional view, constitute "economic development."

55 None of the MDBs charter provisions prescribing the purposes of the institutions, as cited *supra* note 50, includes the word "poverty." Indeed, my electronic search of the entire texts of those charters likewise indicates that the word "poverty" does not appear anywhere in any of them.

Although critics of the MDBs seldom accompany their criticisms with a clear statement of their underlying ideologies, I believe such critics could be classified by (1) whether they generally favor or disfavor having the MDBs continue to act in their traditional role as development banks and by (2) whether they favor or disfavor having MDBs act as international regulatory agencies—that is, as agencies responsible for urging their member countries (or at least the borrowing member countries) to adopt and implement prescribed policies on a wide range of topics. It would be interesting to take a survey of the critics (or, indeed, a survey of all persons knowledgeable enough about international affairs to care) in order to determine how many of them fall into each of the four cells in this grid:

		Do you favor or disfavor the MDBs acting in their traditional role as development banks?	
		Disfavor	Favor
Do you favor or disfavor having the MDBs acting as international regulatory agencies?	Disfavor	*Cell A*	*Cell B*
	Favor	*Cell C*	*Cell D*

Persons whose answers fall in Cell A would probably call for the MDBs to be eliminated, on grounds that such institutions should not continue their operations either as development banks or as purveyors of policy. Public-sector development banks, those persons might say, are (1) anachronistic because worthy projects can now find plenty of financial support from the private sector, given the growing sophistication of the markets in recent decades, (2) ineffective in creating sustainable economic development (and indeed perhaps do more harm than good), and (3) incompetent or untrustworthy to hold any authority over the policy decisions that national governments should make. Some persons whose answers fall in Cell A would go further, claiming that the principles of national sovereignty and self-determination should bar any international entity (not just MDBs) from forcing policy decisions on national governments.

Persons whose answers fit into Cell B would generally favor the continued operation of the MDBs in their development banking role—presumably because they think MDBs can provide services that are unavailable from (or better than) the private sector[56]—but would strip the MDBs of the policy regulatory powers that they have increasingly assumed in recent

---

[56] A linkage thus exists between Cell B and what I referred to above as the "first generation" (and perhaps also the "second generation") in the development of MDBs. *See supra* text accompanying note 41.

years. These persons might argue (with some of their colleagues in Cell A) that such policy regulation belongs instead in other international entities that have more experience in the pertinent areas, or that such policy regulation is off limits entirely to international entities and should be left to the province of national governments.

Persons whose answers fit into Cell C might believe (along with those whose answers fit into Cell A) that public-sector development banking is unnecessary or ineffective but would nevertheless see a role for MDBs as international regulatory bodies, using their influence to encourage member countries to adopt and implement policies generally favored by the international community. Of course, disagreements would likely remain over the content of those policies and the process by which such content is determined.

Persons whose answers fit into Cell D would include those who find value in both roles for MDBs—as development finance institutions and as public regulatory bodies.[57] Such persons might assert that the MDBs provide services not available from the private sector, that MDBs do more good than harm (and can perhaps be improved to do even more good), and that MDBs have (or can develop) the competence to do good work in developing, announcing, prescribing, and enforcing national-level policy choices in certain areas (for example, economic stability, environmental protection, and human rights) that have transborder or even global effects and are therefore of interest to the international community as a whole.

My answers to the two questions would place me in Cell D. I am an internationalist, in the sense that I believe international cooperative efforts —through MDBs and other multilateral entities and initiatives—hold the best hope for civilization to survive the current age, and in the long run offer the only hope for humanity itself to survive.[58] As for public-supported

---

[57] A linkage thus exists between Cell D and what I referred to above as the "third generation" in the development of MDBs. *See supra* text accompanying notes 41.

[58] My views in this respect—which I have referred to above as a matter of "ideology"—reflect my experience in working with several multilateral development institutions. Perhaps that experience makes my views both informed and biased. In another venue I shall try to develop a reasoned and empirical defense of these views, but I shall not do so here. For an expression of these same basic views in another context, *see* John W. Head, *Essay: What Has Not Changed Since September 11—The Benefits of Multilateralism*, 12 KAN. J.L. & PUB. POL'Y 1, 10 (2002) [hereinafter Head, *Benefits of Multilateralism*] (criticizing the threatened unilateralism of the George W. Bush administration in dealing with Iraq and urging that "the United States should do what it takes to stay on the road of multilateralism . . . [which] constitutes our best hope of beating back the darkness that we saw come so vividly and menacingly on September 11"). Many others, of course, have also espoused the values of multilateralism. *See, e.g.*, Richard Stanley, *The Case for Multilateralism*, COURIER, Spring 2003, at 2 (asserting that "[t]he United States can best

development financing, I consider it to be just as vital (and yet just as subject to mistake and misuse) at the global level as it is at the national level. And I favor having the MDBs engage in policy regulation—urging their member countries to follow certain policies that the international community arrives at through a collaborative process—because I believe that such regulation is necessary and that the MDBs have both the leverage necessary to make such urging effective and the potential to carry out such operations competently.

I do not, however, believe that the MDBs are properly equipped now, from either a legal or an institutional perspective, to carry these two burdens of development financing and policy regulation. As explained above, I view the evolution of the MDBs as falling into three generations so far, beginning roughly in 1945, in 1960, and in 1990. I believe it is time for a fourth generation to emerge in the evolution of the MDBs, in order (1) to respond to several criticisms that are in fact valid (I discuss these below in Section III of this chapter) and (2) to make the MDBs responsive to the changed circumstances of this new century, in which international organizations must adhere to certain institutional and substantive principles (I discuss these below in Section IV of this chapter, and further in Chapter Six). I regard the past performance of the MDBs in a generally favorable light, but I think they must change or die in the coming years.

I have gone into considerable detail about this Criticism #II-11 (mission creep) in order to describe the overall ideological perspective from which I view the MDBs. My assessment of several other criticisms leveled against the MDBs reflects this perspective. I turn now to the other four of those criticisms that (like Criticism #II-11) I generally dismiss.

B. Criticism #II-1—Bad Economic and Financial Policies and Projects

For those persons whose answers to the two questions I posed above fit into Cell C or Cell D, a third issue then arises: what policies should the MDBs prescribe? As I summarized it above in Section I of this chapter, Criticism #II-1 posits (in some of its forms) that the MDBs are based on a flawed economic model—laissez-faire, free-market policies—and the MDBs

---

maintain its influence and power as a global leader and justly avoid accusations of neo-imperialism if it is committed to working multilaterally"); Chris Patten, George C. Marshall Lecture 3 (Vancouver, Washington, Oct. 4, 2002) (transcript on file with author) (praising Secretary of State Marshall because "he believed in the absolute indispensability of international co-operation to deal with global problems"); *id.* at 6 (stating that "[t]he final reason why Marshall's instinct for international co-operation was and is justified is that the multi-national institutions that [the United States] helped to create are more than ever needed today if we are to enjoy a free and prosperous world," referring specifically to the United Nations, the IMF, the World Bank, and the WTO).

actually bring more harm than benefit to their borrowing member countries because the MDBs force those countries to accept that economic model instead of allowing them to develop their economies through pragmatic, tailored (even protectionist) policies until those countries can get on their feet economically. I find this criticism of the MDBs unpersuasive, just as I find unpersuasive the corresponding criticism as directed against the IMF.[59] Two main reasons lead me to this conclusion.

First, it rests on some incorrect factual assumptions about public economics. To the extent that the criticism attacks economic liberalism—that is, a general reliance on effective market mechanisms to provide for efficient allocation of resources, rather than on central planning under which government officials direct the details of an economic activity—I think the criticism fails miserably. If we learn anything from the last half-century, we should learn that a liberal, relatively open and effective market system of economic activity works vastly better than a system of central planning.

I would hasten, however, to emphasize a point that is implicit in my reference to an "effective" market system: markets must be regulated, and it is the failure to install adequate regulations (on bank lending, on securities trading, on consumer safety, on corporate governance, etc.) that have created havoc in some countries undertaking the transformation from central planning to market-based economies. Indeed, the dangers of inappropriate deregulation are evident not only in economies in transition but also in economically developed countries such as the United States.[60] However, the market-based model that the MDBs espouse is not itself a flawed economic model, and it is altogether appropriate, in my view, that the MDBs require that governments adopt that model in order to use the resources of the international community in the course of developing the national economies for which those governments are responsible.

Second, Criticism #II-1 rests on unprovable factual assumptions about the long-term economic effects of MDB-supported projects. To claim, as some critics do, that the World Bank has brought no improvement to Africa in three or four decades of work there is to engage in preposterous rhetoric, because it is impossible to prove or disprove the claim. There is

---

[59] *See supra* Section II of Chapter Three.

[60] For an account explaining how the U.S. savings-and-loan crisis of the late 1980s and early 1990s resulted in part from overly relaxed regulation of the financial services industry, *see* WILLIAM A. LOVETT, BANKING AND FINANCIAL INSTITUTIONS LAW IN A NUTSHELL 273–78, 284 (2001). Former World Bank chief economist Joseph Stiglitz has made a similar point about deregulation more broadly in the 1990s in America: "It is no coincidence that three of the sectors involved in today's economic problems—finance, telecommunications, and electricity trading—were all subject to deregulation." Joseph Stiglitz, *The Roaring Nineties*, THE ATLANTIC MONTHLY, Oct. 2002, at 81–82.

no "control set"—no Africa without World Bank involvement—against which to compare the results.[61] It is possible, however, to evaluate how well individual MDB-financed projects have met the goals identified at the time of their planning and approval. While it is doubtless true that some MDB projects have failed to meet their stated goals (the World Bank has said as much and provided documentary support[62]), those failures have been outweighed by successes.[63] More importantly, neither of these assertions (that

---

[61] A report of the U.S. General Accounting Office on the performance of the World Bank expresses the same point this way: "It is difficult to demonstrate the impact of Bank projects on countries' overall development. . . . [I]t is not reasonable to use country macroeconomic indicators alone to judge the effectiveness of the Bank, especially since one can only speculate about the course of a country's development in the absence of Bank assistance." General Accounting Office, *World Bank: U.S. Interests Supported, but Oversight Needed to Help Ensure Improved Performance*, GAO/NSIAD-96-212, at 38 (Sept. 1996), *available at* http://www.gao.gov/archive/1996/ns96212.pdf (last visited Nov. 4, 2004).

[62] For an early acknowledgment by the World Bank that its projects "had negative environmental consequences," *see* THE WORLD BANK, THE WORLD BANK AND THE ENVIRONMENT—FIRST ANNUAL REPORT, FISCAL 1990 11 (1990). For a more recent World Bank acknowledgment of operational shortcomings, *see* I WORLD BANK ANNUAL REPORT 2002, *supra* note 53, at 56 (referring to "the unsatisfactory performance of two adjustment loans to Russia" that "significantly dampened the Bank's overall outcome rating" for operational performance in 2001).

[63] Extensive internal assessments of projects financed by the World Bank have found that a high proportion of them qualify as "satisfactory." *See, e.g.*, I WORLD BANK ANNUAL REPORT 2002, *supra* note 53, at 56 (noting that "[t]he percentage of investment projects with satisfactory outcomes rose from 69 percent in fiscal 1999 to 78 percent in fiscal 2001"). The assessments referred to are carried out by the World Bank's Operations Evaluation Department, which "is independent of management, reporting directly to the Board of Executive Directors." *Id.* at 51. Some other assessments of World Bank projects in general have also been positive. *See, e.g.*, Henry Owen, *The World Bank: Is 50 Years Enough?*, 73 FOREIGN AFF. 97, 97 (Sept.–Oct. 1994) (asserting that the "World Bank has made a difference. To take but one example, its aid has been a major factor in making India agriculturally sufficient"). Positive assessments such as these were reflected in testimony given in September 2002 regarding the proposed replenishment of IDA resources. *See Hearing Before the International Economic Policy Subcommittee of the Export and Trade Promotion Subcommittee of the Senate Foreign Relations Committee*, Sept. 12, 2002, LEXIS (testimony of James C. Orr, Executive Director of the Bretton Woods Committee, stating on behalf of this group of 700 opinion leaders working to help improve World Bank and IMF effectiveness that "of all the bilateral and multilateral programs in existence, IDA and the World Bank have been the most effective in promoting development over the last 30 or 40 years," working on "one of the most challenging problems that faces mankind today"); *id.* (testimony of Rev. David Beckmann, President of Bread for the World, noting that this NGO supports additional funding for IDA on grounds that "we think the institution has improved"). Other favorable assessments of the World Bank and of the IMF are also easy to find. Fred Bergsten, a leading figure in international economic policy, has said that the work of those institutions has contributed substantially to economic successes of the past 50 years, in which "[h]undreds of millions of the poorest people on earth have been lifted out of poverty." Bergsten, *supra* note 5, at 12.

some projects have failed and that some have succeeded) speaks to either (1) the question of causation—was it because of MDB influence that the project succeeded or failed, or was the borrower largely unmoved by the MDB's involvement in project design or policy guidance?[64]—or (2) the long-term overall economic effects of MDB operations, either on the countries in which those operations were conducted or on the global economy more generally.

Moreover, it should be borne in mind that many of the projects financed by the MDBs would (at least in the last couple of decades, after the development of the global financial markets) have been carried out with or without MDB support. That is, had MDB financing not been available, many of the roads, ports, powers plants, and other infrastructure projects would still have been undertaken with commercial bank financing. That commercial bank financing, however, would have come at a higher cost to the borrowing countries (because the banks would not have been able to rely on the expertise and the preferred creditor status of the MDBs) and would almost surely not have taken into account environmental and social considerations to the same degree as the MDBs do for such projects.[65] From that perspective, it seems highly likely that MDB involvement has worked to the benefit, not the detriment, of the borrowing member countries and their populations.

Although I largely dismiss this Criticism #II-1, I draw from it two vital points. First, the application of a market-based economic model to societies that lack the experience or legal framework necessary for such a model to succeed is at least a disservice and perhaps a recipe for disaster. For example, requiring a country to force its banks to adhere immediately to the Basle guidelines on capital adequacy[66] could bring economic meltdown if

---

[64] In this respect, it is worth observing that many governments follow their own economic, financial, or social policies notwithstanding MDB involvement. For a discussion of this point in the context of Mexico and Argentina in the 1990s, *see* CECILIA ZANETTE, THE INFLUENCE OF THE WORLD BANK ON NATIONAL HOUSING AND URBAN POLICIES (2004). The book concludes by noting that "[i]nstead of the all-powerful image of the World Bank often portrayed by critics, this analysis identifies clear limits to the ability of the Bank to influence national sector policies"; and indeed, in at least one of those countries the country's "national authorities [were able] to affect the content of operations financed by the World Bank to support their own priorities"—underscoring the fact that "the policies being implemented [by a borrowing government] are ultimately the responsibility of national leaders, a fact that is often minimized when discussing the influence of the World Bank on developing countries." *Id.* at 291.

[65] For a reference to the increasing attention that social considerations have been taken into account in MDB operations, *see infra* note 100 and accompanying text.

[66] The Basle guidelines on capital adequacy requirements were first established by the Basle Committee on Banking Supervision (a committee of banking supervisory

the country does not have in place effective rules and procedures for handling insolvent banks.[67] Accordingly, the MDBs must (1) gauge carefully the capacity of a borrowing member's economy to undertake reform, (2) design conditionalities accordingly, and (3) provide or help arrange for the technical assistance needed to help the country build the legal framework necessary for a market-based economy to prosper.

Second, the fact that some MDB-financed projects have failed to bring the intended benefits, or have brought unintended negative consequences, underscores the importance of careful project appraisal and design. The last 15 years have seen dramatic changes in the MDBs' use of environmental impact assessment and social impact assessment (a point I shall return to in assessing Criticism #II-2 and Criticism #II-3), but these efforts need further attention, especially to ensure that the social and environmental safeguards built into project designs are in fact implemented.

C. Criticism #II-2—Wrong Form of Financial Assistance

As explained earlier, this criticism posits that MDB lending operations are anachronistic now that effective international capital markets exist; so MDB financing (if continued at all) should take the form of grants, not loans. I largely reject this criticism.

While it is true that the global financial markets have changed dramatically in the past half-century and that the MDBs no longer fill as large a gap as the one that existed in the 1940s or in the 1960s, MDBs still have an important role to play as lenders, in addition to other roles that they should play. For one thing, many of the projects that MDBs help finance still fall into the category of public works projects on which commercial financial institutions typically would not wish to be the lead lender.[68] With

---

authorities working under the auspices of the Bank for International Settlements) in the late 1980s to assist governments in establishing regulations that would prevent financial institutions from operating in a manner that placed depositors' assets at undue risk. For an explanation of those capital adequacy guidelines, and related work of the Basle Committee, *see* ROBERT LEE RAMSEY & JOHN W. HEAD, PREVENTING FINANCIAL CHAOS: AN INTERNATIONAL GUIDE TO LEGAL RULES AND OPERATIONAL PROCEDURES FOR HANDLING INSOLVENT BANKS 10, 163–68 (2000); John W. Head, *Lessons from the Asian Financial Crisis: The Role of the IMF and the United States*, KAN. J. L. & PUB. POL'Y 70, 80, 95 n.83 (1998) [hereinafter Head, *Lessons from the Asian Financial Crisis*].

[67] I have seen the danger of this in several countries in which I have assisted in the development of banking and central banking legislation—Mongolia, for example, and some of the central Asian republics—and it is to guard against this danger that I have recommended the use of carefully drafted phase-in provisions regarding the adoption of international standards.

[68] For example, nearly 20 percent of AsDB lending in the past five years went to finance "social infrastructure" projects, supporting such things as education, waste man-

an MDB serving as the lead lender, however, commercial lenders will participate. It is no accident that a substantial portion of ADB and World Bank financing, for example, is provided in conjunction with co-financing by commercial lenders.[69]

There are other reasons why loans, not grants, should continue to make up the bulk of financial assistance provided by MDBs. One of the simple reasons is that the MDBs rely in large part on "reflows"—repayments of loans—for their resources.[70] Beyond that, in many of the least economically developed borrowing countries, the experience of government officials in handling national financial affairs is so skimpy that the discipline involved in taking a loan (as opposed to a grant) is better developed by working with an MDB (which typically provides extensive counseling and training in handling such affairs) than by working with a commercial lender. Besides, it is that very category of countries—least economically developed—that will be eligible for the "soft loan" terms provided from the IDA and the regional MDBs.[71]

---

agement, urban development, water supply, and reproductive health. AsDB ANNUAL REPORT 2001, *supra* note 30, at 201–03. The corresponding figure for the IADB for 2001 was nearly 40 percent. INTER-AMERICAN DEVELOPMENT BANK, ANNUAL REPORT 2001 39 (2002) (showing categories of "social" loans committed in 2001, including those dealing with sanitation, urban development, education, social investment, health, and environment) [hereinafter IADB ANNUAL REPORT 2001], *available at* http://www.iadb.org/aboutus/I/hi_ar_2001.cfm (last visited Nov. 4, 2004).

[69] Commercial co-financing for AsDB-supported projects totaled US$912 million in 2001. AsDB ANNUAL REPORT 2001, *supra* note 30, at 47. Over the three decades from 1970 through 2001, a total of 580 AsDB-supported loan projects and programs received such commercial cofinancing, amounting in aggregate to US$9.2 billion. *Id.* at 46. Commercial co- financing for World Bank-supported projects totaled US$4.7 billion in fiscal year 2002. I WORLD BANK ANNUAL REPORT 2002, *supra* note 53, at 21.

[70] Illustrating this fact is that there is a rough equality each year between the amounts that these institutions disburse and the amounts that they receive in loan repayments. *See, e.g.*, THE ASIAN DEVELOPMENT BANK, THE ASIAN DEVELOPMENT BANK ANNUAL REPORT 2002 132 (2003) (noting that "[d]isbursements in 2002 totalled $3.1 billion" and "[p]rincipal. repayments for the year were $3.3 billion"), *available at* http://www.adb.org/Documents/Reports/Annual_Report/2002/financial_statements.pdf (last visited Nov. 4, 2004). One reason the MDBs can rely mainly on such "reflows" (repayments) to fund their operations is that they suffer virtually no defaults or other losses of principal. *See, e.g.*, THE ASIAN DEVELOPMENT BANK, FINANCIAL PROFILE 2002, at 35 (stating that "[i]n its public sector ordinary operations, the A[s]DB has not suffered any losses of principal to date and follows a policy of not taking part in debt rescheduling agreements"), *available at* http://www.adb.org/Documents/Others/Financial_Profile/FinancialProfile2002.pdf (last visited Nov. 4, 2004).

[71] For a reference to the typical terms of "soft loans" offered by the IDA and the regional MDBs, *see supra* Subsection IIA of Chapter Two.

Having said this, I agree wholeheartedly that the level of grant financing made available by the MDBs should be increased,[72] along with the "soft loan" resources through regular replenishment negotiations among the wealthy countries.[73] Such grant financing can help MDB member countries in a multitude of ways that contribute to their development. For example, AsDB technical assistance grants pay for training of government officials, development of long-range development plans, preparation of projects, technology upgrades, consulting services for project management, seminars and conferences on economic and financial issues, improvement of national accounting and auditing standards, research in economics and trade, and so forth.[74]

D. Criticism #II-5—MDB Trampling of National Sovereignty

As I summarized it above in Subsection IE of this chapter, Criticism #II-5 claims that in imposing conditions on the rights of member countries to borrow money from MDBs, the MDBs violate the sovereignty of those member countries, and in particular the principle of self-determination. In so doing, the MDBs themselves act inconsistently with settled principles of international law, including some specific treaty provisions. I find this criticism unpersuasive for three reasons, the first and third of which (as explained below) are nearly identical to those I cited in dismissing the corresponding criticism directed at the IMF.

---

[72] In this one respect, I agree with suggestions made in the (majority) Meltzer Report that grant financing by the World Bank should increase. MELTZER REPORT, *supra* note 5, at 11. (I disagree, however, with the proposal that this increase in grant financing should come at the expense of loan financing. *See id.* at 6.) George Soros has endorsed the suggestion that grant financing be increased, but he has warned of a danger that "the increase in grants would get bogged down in working out the details." GEORGE SOROS, GEORGE SOROS ON GLOBALIZATION 102 (2002).

[73] A working group within the American Bar Association's Section of International Law and Practice concluded in a 1994 report that the United States "should consider increasing the level of its financial contributions to the International Development Association (IDA), the entity of the World Bank Group that provides assistance to the poorest countries of the world." Reports & Recommendations of the A.B.A. Section of International Law and Practice (as approved by the A.B.A House of Delegates in August 1995), at 1, attachment to letter from Alaire Bretz Rieffel, Staff Director, A.B.A. Section of International Law and Practice, to Members of the U.N. Working Group (Oct. 26, 1995) (on file with author).

[74] For a description of technical assistance provided by the AsDB, and the legal and operational foundation for such assistance, *see* Head, *Asian Development Bank, supra* note 53, at 42–44. As indicated there, the AsDB provided over $300 million in technical assistance support to its member countries in the two-year period of 1999–2000, financing over 600 specific projects. *Id. See also* AsDB ANNUAL REPORT 2001, *supra* note 30, at 45 (reporting that in 2001, the AsDB "approved 257 technical assistance grants totaling $146.4 million").

First, states are under no legal obligation to accept the conditions of an MDB loan, for the simple reason that states are under no legal obligation to seek an MDB loan in the first place—or, indeed, to become a member of any MDB. It is no doubt true, as a practical matter, that a government might find no financial backing for a certain type of project (for example, a project for the construction of a road or a hospital or a school) other than MDB financing, because such a project might be unattractive to any commercial financier. However, it also remains true that if a government is dead-set against adopting the economic and financial policies (or other requirements) that an MDB proposes to include in a loan agreement, that government can decide to do without the project. There is no legal obligation on the government to surrender or diminish its sovereignty.

Second, there is likewise no legal obligation on the MDBs to provide financing for whatever projects their member governments propose. International law contains no generally accepted "right to development assistance" under which a country is legally entitled to receive financial assistance from another country or from an international financial institution owned by (itself and) other countries.[75] If such a legal entitlement did exist, of course, this Criticism #II-5 might pack some punch; but notwith-

---

[75] For discussions of various aspects of the purported "right to development," *see* RUMU SARKAR, DEVELOPMENT LAW AND INTERNATIONAL FINANCE 228–34, 246–50 (1999); IGNAZ SEIDL-HOHENVELDERN, INTERNATIONAL ECONOMIC LAW 5–6 (3d ed. 1999); Isabella D. Bunn, *The Right to Development: Implications for International Economic Law*, 15 AM. U. INT'L L. REV. 1425, 1428–52 (2000); Sumudu Atapattu, *The Right to a Healthy Life or the Right to Die Polluted?: The Emergence of a Human Right to A Healthy Environment Under International Law*, 16 TUL. ENVTL. L.J. 65, 116–25 (2002). As a legal matter, it would appear that the only affirmative international obligation clearly binding on an individual state in this regard is the one stated in Article 56 of the U.N. Charter, in which all U.N. members "pledge themselves to take joint and separate action in co-operation with the [U.N.] Organization for the achievement of the purposes set forth in Article 55"— which, in turn, asserts that "the United Nations shall promote" such things as higher standards of living and conditions of economic and international cooperation, and solutions of international economic problems. Given the weakness of the Article 56 obligation, the international law scholar Cassese concludes that it imposes only a "generic duty" to cooperate. ANTONIO CASSESE, INTERNATIONAL LAW IN A DIVIDED WORLD 151 (1986). In particular, he notes that "the kind of co-operation urged by some developing countries—one-way assistance and economic aid . . . —is . . . precisely [the] kind of co-operation which developed countries . . . are reluctant to engage in for chiefly economic reasons"; and this reluctance "is responsible for the striking weakness of the principle" of cooperation. *Id. See also* SEIDL-HOHENVELDERN, *supra*, at 5–6 (asserting that as a general rule "there does not exist any right to development in the legal sense"). Another prominent authority on international law suggests that there might exist "a legal duty . . . to provide economic aid to underdeveloped countries." IAN BROWNLIE, PRINCIPLES OF PUBLIC INTERNATIONAL LAW 258 (5th ed. 1998). He describes this obligation, however (if it exists), not as an individual duty of a state but rather as "a collective duty of [U.N.] member states to take responsible action to create reasonable living standards both for their own people and for those of other states." *Id.* at 256.

standing the efforts of the 1970s to create a new international economic order,[76] preferential economic treatment for LDCs has thus far been confined to particular circumstances specially negotiated, as in the case of (1) the Generalized System of Preferences to provide lower tariffs on goods from LDCs[77] and (2) special application of new rules adopted in the Uruguay Round of trade negotiations.[78] Indeed, the establishment of the IDA, and of "soft-loan" authority for each of the regional MDBs (thereby authorizing those institutions to make long-maturity loans at zero or near-zero interest rates[79]), represents a massive transfer of resources from developed countries to LDCs—amounting in a recent year, for example, to roughly US$12 billion[80] in loan commitments—in partial response to the

---

[76] Some of the most forceful of the calls for a new international economic order took the form of U.N. General Assembly resolutions adopted around the middle of the 1970s. *See, e.g., Declaration on the Establishment of a New Economic Order,* G.A. Res. 3201 (S-VI), 6 (Special) U.N. GAOR, 6th Special Sess., Supp. No. 1, at 3, U.N. Doc. A/9559 (1974) (adopted May 1, 1974), *reprinted in* 13 I.L.M. 715 (1974); and *Charter of Economic Rights and Duties of States,* G.A. Res. 3281 (XXIX), 29 U.N. GAOR, 29th Sess., Supp. No. 31, at 50, U.N. Doc A/9631 (1975) (adopted Dec. 12, 1974), *reprinted in* 14 I.L.M. 251 (1975). *See also Declaration on the Right to Development,* G.A. Res. 41/128, U.N. GAOR, 41st Sess., 97th mtg., at 3, U.N. Doc. A/RES/41/128 (1987), *available at* http://www.un.org/documents/ga/res/41/a41r128.htm (last visited Nov. 4, 2004).

[77] For a brief explanatory reference to the GSP, *see supra* Subsection IVB of Chapter Two. *See also Generalized System of Preferences—Analysis, in* Int'l Trade Rep. (BNA), Reference File 31:0101–0102 (2003); RALPH H. FOLSOM, MICHAEL WALLACE GORDON & JOHN A. SPANOGLE, JR., INTERNATIONAL BUSINESS TRANSACTIONS (Hornbook Series) 310–11 (2d ed. 2001).

[78] *See, e.g., Decision on Measures in Favour of Least-Developed Countries,* LT/UR/D- 1/3 (Apr. 15, 1994), *available at* http://docsonline.wto.org (last visited Nov. 4, 2004). For a synopsis of the "special and differential treatment" provisions included in various Uruguay Round trade agreements, *see* RAJ BHALA, INTERNATIONAL TRADE LAW 1429–38 (2001).

[79] As noted above in Subsection IIIA of Chapter Two, typical terms on an IDA loan include a maturity of 40 years and a service charge of 0.75 percent, and typical terms on a soft loan from the AsDB (through the Asian Development Fund) include a maturity of 32 years (if the loan applies to a project, rather than a quick-disbursing program loan) with an interest charge of 1 percent for the first few years and 1.5 percent thereafter.

[80] This figure represents the total amount of "soft loans" made by IDA, the IADB, the AfDB, and the AsDB as indicated in their annual reports. *See* WORLD BANK ANNUAL REPORT 2002, *supra* note 53 (showing fiscal year 2002 lending by the IDA at $8.1 billion); IADB ANNUAL REPORT 2001, *supra* note 68, at v (showing "Fund for Special Operations" loans for 2001 totaling US$0.4 billion); AsDB ANNUAL REPORT 2001, *supra* note 30, at 5 (showing Asian Development Fund "soft loan" operations for 2001 totaling US$1.4 billion); AFRICAN DEVELOPMENT BANK GROUP, ANNUAL REPORT 2002 7 (2003) [hereinafter AfDB ANNUAL REPORT 2002] (showing AfDF "soft loan" operations for 2001 totaling US$1.7 billion), *available at* http://www.afdb.org/knowledge/documents/Banks_Annual_Report.htm (last visited Nov. 4, 2004) . The EBRD reported no separate figures for "soft loan" operations for 2001. *See* EUROPEAN BANK FOR RECONSTRUCTION AND DEVELOPMENT, ANNUAL REPORT 2001 3 (2002) (showing a single line for "EBRD financing,"

calls for special economic treatment for countries with low per capita income and high per capita debt.

Third, this criticism rests on a legal misperception about the principle of self-determination. As I explained in dismissing the corresponding criticism directed at the IMF,[81] even if the principle of self-determination amounts to something more than just a slogan, it surely cannot mean that a government can adopt economic and financial policies that are proven failures (or, even more absurdly, that a government can be subsidized through "soft-loan" support in pursuing such policies)—especially if the government itself has not emerged from what has been referred to as "internal" self-determination[82] involving free and meaningful elections in which the affected population can have a say in the selection of policies and policymakers.

It is perhaps worth noting that a concern over the alleged trampling of national sovereignty through the operations of the MDBs is surely mitigated to at least some small degree by the fact that the borrowing countries have representation on the governing boards of the MDBs. Indeed, a borrowing country typically would also enjoy the opportunity to have special representation at MDB board meetings in which loan requests regarding that country are made.[83]

E. Criticism #II-6—Incoherence in Policy Prescriptions

Although I agree with the underlying thesis of this criticism—that it is inappropriate for MDBs to be working at cross-purposes with themselves or with other global economic institutions—I doubt this problem will persist or cause great problems as these institutions mature further. Bob Hockett has explained how IMF and World Bank operations have gradually approached a mid-point in a "macro-micro" spectrum, as the World Bank has increasingly looked to broader "infrastructural" variables in its opera-

---

without distinguishing ordinary operations from special operations). Some of the MDBs use a fiscal year different from the calendar year.

[81] For my assessment of the "trampling of sovereignty" criticism directed at the IMF, *see supra* Subsection IIB of Chapter Three.

[82] *See* John W. Head, *Selling Hong Kong to China: What Happened to the Right of Self-Determination,* 46 U. KAN. L. REV. 283, 289 (1998) (capsulizing the concept of "internal" self- determination as "the right of the 'holders' [of the right of self-determination] to choose freely the form of government under which they shall live").

[83] *See, e.g.,* By-Laws of the Asian Development Bank, sec. 9, *reprinted in* Head, *Asian Development Bank, supra* note 53 (providing that a member country may, if there is not already a Director or Alternate Director of its nationality, "appoint [a] special representative" to express the views of that country at a meeting of the Board of Directors in which a request submitted by that country is being considered).

tions and the IMF has increasingly focused on matters that could be regarded as "micro" in character.[84] Like Hockett, I see no big problem in this convergence, even if it were to result in a slight overlap (what he calls "an overshooting of the mark by one or both institutions"[85]), for I think any inconsistencies or inefficiencies would be resolved relatively easily,[86] especially if the changes I suggest regarding transparency and accountability (see my assessments of Criticisms #II-8 and #II-9, below) are made. Besides, some competition among agencies and their ideas is probably a good thing.

III. CRITICISMS I GENERALLY ENDORSE

The five criticisms that I have assessed above—Criticisms #II-1, #II-2, #II-5, #II-6, and #II-11—appear unpersuasive in most respects, although I have identified some elements of those criticisms that I believe do make some sense and should be taken seriously. Just the opposite is true of the remaining seven criticisms leveled at the MDBs. That is, I find these other seven criticisms generally persuasive, although there are some elements to most of them that do not hold water on closer inspection. I offer my views below on all seven of them: Criticism #II-3 (environmental degradation), Criticism #II-4 (human rights shortcomings), Criticism #II-7 (weakness in staffing and management), Criticism #II-8 (secrecy and opaqueness), Criticism #II-9 (the democracy deficit), Criticism #II-10 (narrowness of economic focus), and Criticism #II-12 (asymmetry in obligations).

A. Criticism #II-3—Environmental Degradation

Some of this criticism is out of date. For example, those critics who complain about MDB involvement in big hydroelectric dams apparently do not realize that the MDBs are now largely out of the dam-building business.[87] Those critics who claim that the MDBs regularly disregard effects of

---

[84] Hockett, *supra* note 46, at 191.

[85] *Id.* at 192.

[86] Procedures for facilitating close coordination among aid agencies have been established for many years and have been strengthened recently. For example, in order to improve further the cooperation between the AsDB and the World Bank, those two MDBs signed an agreement in early 2002 that details procedures for coordinating country assistance strategies, harmonizes procedures, and calls for implementation of the joint "Protocol on Collaboration among Multilateral Development Banks/IMF" for preparing poverty reduction strategies. *ADB, World Bank Sign Agreement for Closer Cooperation*, M2 Presswire, Jan. 22, 2002, LEXIS. Similarly, the AsDB signed a memorandum of understanding with the International Labour Organization in November 2002 "to maximize scarce resources and their development impact." AsDB, *Social Protection Strategy Off to Good Start*, News From NARO (AsDB North American Representative Office), Nov. 2002, at 1–2.

[87] *See Statistics on the World Bank's Dam Portfolio* (November 2000), *available at* www.worldbank.org/html/extdr/pb/dams/factsheet.htm (last visited Nov. 4, 2004)

the projects they design either are engaging in intentional misinformation or are ignorant of the enormous change that has taken place over the past two decades in the mindset, the policies, and the structures of the MDBs to incorporate environmental considerations into the operations of those institutions. The World Bank recruited its first environmental advisor in 1969. By 1990 it had a total of 54 high-level staff members, assisted by over 20 consultants, working in its Environment Department and regional Environmental Divisions,[88] and it had adopted an Operational Directive on Environmental Assessment in order "to ensure that development options are environmentally sound and sustainable and that any environmental consequences are recognized early in the project cycle and taken into account in project design."[89] As of 1998 it had over five times that many environmental specialists (over 300) and had committed close to $12 billion for scores of primarily environmental projects.[90] Today the World Bank's commitment to environmental matters is reflected in several ways:[91] It has a vice presidency for Environmentally Sustainable Development, has implemented numerous operational policies on environmental and related issues, and has

---

(showing that less than 1 percent of World Bank lending in recent years has been for new dams, and that such lending has declined substantially from the 1970s and 1980s, so that World Bank funding is involved now in only about 1 percent of new dam projects worldwide). Significantly, the World Bank declined to participate in China's huge Three Gorges Dam project.

[88] John W. Head, *Environmental Conditionality in the Operations of International Development Finance Institutions*, 1 KAN. J.L. & PUB. POL'Y 15, 20 (1991) [hereinafter *Environmental Conditionality*] (citing World Bank documents).

[89] THE WORLD BANK, THE WORLD BANK AND THE ENVIRONMENT—FIRST ANNUAL REPORT, FISCAL 1990 11 (1990), cited and excerpted in Head, *Environmental Conditionality, supra* note 88, at 18, 19, 25 n.39. For information the current version of World Bank environmental assessment policies, *see* The World Bank, Operational manual, *at* http://www.wbln0018.worldbank.org/Institutional/Manuals/OpManual.nsf/toc2/9367A 2A9D9D AEED38525672C007D0972?OpenDocument (last visited Nov. 15, 2004).

[90] Charles E. Di Leva, *International Law and Development*, 10 GEO. INT'L ENVTL. L. REV. 501, 505 (1998), cited in Todd Roessler, Comment, *The World Bank's Lending Policy and Environmental Standards*, 26 N.C. J. INT'L L. & COM. REG. 105, 105 n.4 (2000).

[91] *See* Gerhard Loibl, *The World Bank Group and Sustainable Development*, appearing as chapter 25 in INTERNATIONAL ECONOMIC LAW WITH A HUMAN FACE 519–29 (Friedl Weiss, Erik Denters & Paul De Waart eds., 1998) (describing various organizational changes and other initiatives). For a current organizational chart showing the position of the vice president for Environmentally and Socially Sustainable Development (ESSD), *see* http://Inweb18.worldbank.org/ESSD/sdvext.nsf/05ByDocName/ESSDAdvisoryService (last visited Nov. 15, 2004). For a chronology of the "Greening" of the World Bank, including a suggestion that this development resulted importantly from pressure exerted on the institution by grassroots movements, *see* Rajagopal, *supra* note 53 at 555–569. For the World Bank's own assessment of its record regarding environmental issues, *see* World Bank: Focus on Sustainability 2004, *available at* http://www.worldbank.org/WBSITE/ EXTERNAL/NEWS (last visited Feb. 16, 2005).

taken a lead role in creating new funding mechanisms to support sustainable development. Similar steps have been taken at the AsDB[92] and at the IADB[93] and the AfDB.[94] In the case of the EBRD, as noted above, a specific mandate was included in the charter, requiring that institution "to promote in the full range of its activities environmentally sound and sustainable development."[95] As a consequence of these changes, the MDBs all have procedures for conducting environmental impact assessment on any proposed projects that could have any significant effect in this regard, and most of the reports of these assessments are publicly available.[96]

However, more should be done. A study undertaken for the AsDB about five years ago concluded that although that institution did a relatively good job of incorporating environmental considerations into its design and selection of projects for AsDB financing, these efforts often did not get carried through adequately to the project implementation stage.[97] That is, the best laid plans for avoiding or mitigating environmental damage often went

---

[92] For a description of measures taken at the AsDB in respect of environmental protection, *see* Head, *Asian Development Bank, supra* note 53, at 78–80. *See* also AsDB ANNUAL REPORT 2001, *supra* note 30, at 42–43 (reporting on various initiatives taken in 2001 to address issues of environmental sustainability, including the financing of various projects to fight acid rain, reduce air pollution, protect coastal resources, and mitigate emissions of greenhouse gases, as well as the signing of a memorandum of understanding with World Wide Fund for Nature). The attention given to environmental issues in the AsDB now is dramatically greater than that given in the 1980s, when I worked at the institution. At that time, the efforts mainly of one staff member, Dr. Colin Rees, succeeded in establishing an Environment Unit that consisted of merely two professional staff members as of 1988.

[93] For a description of measures taken at the IADB in respect of environmental protection, *see* the environment page of its website, *at* http://www.iadb.org/topics/ev.cfm (providing an overview of policies and links to specific projects) (last visited Nov. 4, 2004).

[94] For a description of measures taken at the AfDB in respect of environmental protection, *see* The African Development Bank Group, *Policies and Procedures: Environmental Sector Policy Paper* (1990), *at* http://www.afdb/org/projects/policies/Environmental_ Sector_Paper.htm (last visited Nov. 4, 2004); AfDB ANNUAL REPORT 2002, *supra* note 80, at 81 (describing environmental sustainability efforts of AfDB operations).

[95] EBRD Charter, art. 2, para. 1 (vii). For information on EBRD environmental protection activities, *see* the environment partnerships and initiatives page of its website, *at* http://www.ebrd.org/enviro/init/index.htm (describing EBRD environmental initiatives and providing links to training and partnership page) (last visited Nov. 4, 2004).

[96] For environmental impact assessment reports available online from the World Bank, *see* the listing of documents and reports by document type, *at* http://www-wds.world-bank.org/navigation.jsp?pcont=browdoc (last visited Nov. 4, 2004) (click "Environmental Assessment" link under "Project Documents" for an updated list of reports).

[97] *See* John W. Head & Michael Cernea, *Report and Recommendations on Improving Environmental Protection and Supervision of Resettlement Operations During Implementation of ADB-Financed Projects* v–vi, 1–6 (2000) (on file with author).

awry in the process of actually building a road or carrying out some other project work. This should be remedied.[98]

More fundamentally, however, I believe that environmental considerations should be placed at the heart of MDB operations as a legal and policy matter. The year 2002 marked the 30th anniversary of the Stockholm Conference on the Human Environment. Just as in 1972, the world remains divided on some key issues of environmental protection, although now the fault lines appear more over the issue of who should pay for environmental protection than over the question of whether a national government has an obligation to protect its environment. Fortunately, an answer to the question of payment appears in the form of the Global Environment Facility and similar regimes by which the costs of using environmentally friendly technology and techniques in development actives can be offset with resources contributed by the richer, more industrially advanced countries.[99] Such regimes need to be expanded, as I described more fully below in Section IV of this chapter. At the same time, the charters of the MDBs should be linked to the key environmental protection treaties—also as described more fully below in Section IV of this chapter.

B. Criticism #II-4—Human Rights Shortcomings

Much of what I have written above about environmental protection applies also to human rights protection. Although it is absurd to suggest that the MDBs give no regard to human rights in their operations—they

---

[98] The report mentioned above offered specific recommendations for remedying such problems, including the more careful drafting of contracts, the inclusion of environmental covenants in mandatory checklists for review missions, the more effective use of remedies for non-compliance, and other initiatives. *See generally id.*

[99] For descriptions of the Global Environmental Facility, *see* Loibl, *supra* note 91, at 527–28; Global Environment Facility, About the GEF, *at* http://www.gefweb.org/What_is_the_GEF/What_is_the_gef.html (Describing the functions and purposes of the GEF) (last visited Nov. 4, 2004). *See also* Alan S. Miller & Eric Martino, *The GEF: Financing and Regulatory Support for Clean Energy*, 15 Nat. Resources & Env't 164, 165 (2001) (describing funding sources and projects of the GEF); Alan S. Miller, *The Global Environment Facility and the Search for Financial Strategies to Foster Sustainable Development*, 24 Vt. L. Rev. 1229, 1236 (2000) (describing the evolution of the GEF, sources of funding, and governance); Adam M. Walcoff, *The Restructured Global Environment Facility: A Practical Evaluation for Unleashing the Lending Power of GEF*, 3 Widener L. Symp. J. 485 (1998) (providing sources of funding and eligibility requirements for LDCs). A similar theme—having economically developed countries provide financial wherewithal to LDCs in order to protect the environment—appears in the establishment of the Ozone Trust Fund under the Montreal Protocol on Substances that Deplete the Ozone Layer. *See* Loibl, *supra* note 91, at 528–29 (describing the Ozone Trust Fund); The Secretariat of the Multilateral Fund for the Implementation of the Montreal Protocol, General Information, *at* http://www.unmfs.org/general.htm (providing a list of contributing industrialized countries and describing fund activities) (last visited Nov. 4, 2004).

do, after all, require various types of assessments during project design and selection (1) to guard against any interference with the rights of indigenous people, (2) to enhance the role of women, and (3) to assess the impact of proposed projects on the social fabric of the communities that the project would directly affect[100]—the MDBs could and should take further steps in this regard. A linkage between the MDB charters and the key human rights treaties is one such step, as described more fully below in Section IV of this chapter.

Why should the MDBs take on additional responsibility in the area of human rights, as well as in the area of environmental protection? Because (1) these are responsibilities that deserve careful and effective attention by a public institution operating at the international level, and (2) the MDBs have the resources and the leverage to provide that careful and effective attention. I assume that the first of these points is fairly well accepted; an international consensus seems to have developed that effective action is needed at the international level to protect human rights and the environment, and evidence of this consensus appears in the work of several U.N. agencies.

That is why the second point is so important. I believe that the prime movers in defining the terms under which economic development (broadly defined) will take place—and indeed in defining a wide range of standards by which national governments will provide services and leadership to their populations—in the coming years are the global economic institutions: the WTO, the IMF, the World Bank, and the regional development banks. Unlike the global and regional regimes established to focus exclusively on human rights protection or on environmental protection, these global economic institutions have the kind of influence that seems to matter most in today's world: economic influence. This being the case, I believe the response to Criticisms #II-2 and #II-4—environmental degradation and human rights shortcomings—should not be (1) to shut down the MDBs so

---

[100] For descriptions of ADB policies and practices in this regard, *see* Head, *Asian Development Bank, supra* note 53, at 82–86. Information about the corresponding policies and practices of other MDBs is available on their websites: the World Bank, http://www.worldbank.org, the IADB, http://www.iadb.org, the AfDB, http://www.afdb.org, and the EBRD, http://www.ebrd.org. For a careful assessment of the process by which regard for social considerations generally, and discussions of "social capital" in particular, emerged within the World Bank, *see generally* Anthony Bebbington, Scott Guggenheim, Elizabeth Olson & Michal Woolcock, *Exploring Social Capital Debates at the World Bank*, 40 J. DEVEL. STUD. 33 (2004). These authors identify particular events and individuals who, largely in the 1990s, brought the "social capital debate" into the World Bank, as a result of more than a decade of building alliances around such concepts as participation, environment, sustainability, empowerment, and social capital—alliances that operate now within the World Bank and link people in the World Bank with academics, NGOs, and others outside the World Bank.

that they cannot cause any more injury to the environment or to human rights, or (2) to restrict the mission of the MDBs in a way that excludes environmental and human rights considerations, leaving such considerations to other institutions, but instead (3) to create formal and legal linkages between the MDBs and broadly accepted treaty norms on environmental protections and human rights and the entities specifically responsible for working in those areas.[101] I shall develop this point further below in Section IV of this chapter.

C. Criticism #II-7—Weakness in Staffing and Management

I am convinced from my own experience and network of acquaintances in the MDBs that those institutions are staffed by people who are, by and large, deeply dedicated to their work. Many of them have experience and expertise in dealing with extraordinarily complex problems—endemic diseases, institutional weaknesses, cultural incongruities, scarce natural resources, dysfunctional markets, currency fluctuations, mangrove protection, perishable commodities, wind propulsion, coral reef fragility, airport runway design, corrupt government officials, bank insolvencies, cross-default clauses—all in the context of a multicultural and multilingual workplace. Most of them realize the importance of their jobs, the uniqueness of the contribution they can make (or injury they can cause), and the moral duty they have to use their best efforts. I have a deep respect and fond admiration for them as a class of international civil servants, and of course for some of them whom I know personally.[102]

However, I believe the system of MDB staffing and management suffers from several weaknesses that I described above in summarizing Criticism #II-7: excessive influence ("overweighting") of nationality as a factor in staff appointments and promotion; inordinate emphasis on loan volume, rather than on loan quality, in promotions and other rewards; "policy anachro-

---

[101] For an excellent and concise article on MDB responsibilities and opportunities to contribute to the efforts to protect human rights, *see generally* Herbert V. Morais, *The Globalization of Human Rights Law and the Role of International Financial Institutions in Promoting Human Rights*, 33 GEO. WASH. INT'L L. REV. 71 (2000). Herbert Morais, a colleague and close personal friend of mine, presents in that article the best synopsis I have seen of the development of international human rights law in the 20th century; then he discusses his view of the proper role of the MDBs (and the IMF) in human rights protection, relying in part on the philosophy of Amartya Sen and concluding that the MDBs and the IMF "are well-positioned, by virtue of their vast resources and influence, to do even more in the years ahead to further promote human rights in their member countries." *Id.* at 96. I concur in his views.

[102] For similar views complimentary to MDB staff, *see* Owen, *supra* note 63, at 100 (asserting that the World Bank "is well staffed," that the "caliber of its top management and staff is high," and that one reason for this is the "attractions of international service to humanity").

nism" on the part of some senior staff members who do not give adequate attention to environmental and social dimensions of development; and lack of internal accountability.

Beyond the weaknesses noted above is another very important one: inadequacy of staff resources. Although the staff resources of MDBs have been increased in recent years to work on environmental issues, some additional staffing in that area will be needed if, as I suggest, the MDBs are to be given an expanded role in these areas. More broadly, however, MDB staff resources need to be dramatically increased in order to handle the numerous other tasks that their governing boards have laid on them, including (in addition to environmental concerns) such topics as anti-corruption, benefit monitoring and evaluation, cooperation with NGOs and other aid agencies, gender and development, governance, indigenous peoples, inspection, poverty reduction, rehabilitation assistance, resettlement, and social development.[103] In this more general regard, I consider the staff resources of the World Bank and AsDB—the two MDBs with which I am more familiar—to be woefully inadequate now. Some senior staff members in the AsDB have pointedly criticized the "policy proliferation" that has occurred in that institution (at the initiative of the Board of Directors, following instructions from their national authorities) without an adequate increase in staff resources to handle the increased responsibilities.[104] Consistent with this, in late 2003 the AsDB staff council complained formally to the AsDB Board of Directors about a "severe work overload" among rank-and-file staff members and blamed that situation for low morale among staff.[105]

I offer in Section IV of this chapter some recommendations for redressing these various weaknesses. Those recommendations revolve around these key points: an increase in staff resources; policy changes regarding staff appointments and promotions (some of which are already on track in the World Bank); mechanisms for enhanced staff and management accountability (some of which are also underway in the World Bank and

---

[103] For AsDB policies on these issues and others, *see* Asian Development Bank, Operations Manual, *at* http://www.adb.org/Documents/Manuals/Operations (last visited Feb. 16, 2005).

[104] *See, e.g.*, Strategic Challenges for the Bank (Sept. 16, 1999) (memorandum prepared by AsDB staff for AsDB management) (on file with the author). The inadequacy of AsDB staff to handle the tasks assigned to it has also been pointed out by a former AsDB director who included this point in a list of stinging criticisms when he left the institution in 2003. *See* Shawn Donnan, *Ex-Director Attacks ADB's 'Lack of Direction,'* FINANCIAL TIMES, Sept. 17, 2003, at 14 (reporting that the former director said "the bank's expert staff is 'thinly stretched, well beyond its overall capacity'").

[105] Shawn Donnan & Roel Landingin, *Asian Development Bank Moves to Address Low Morale of Staff*, FINANCIAL TIMES, Nov. 25, 2003, at 4.

the AsDB); and greatly improved and expanded cooperation with other agencies and NGOs, so that the MDBs serve as clearing-houses and coordinators for a network of subject matter specialists.

D. Criticism #II-8—MDB Secrecy and Opaqueness

As with several other criticisms, Criticism #II-8 (at least as I have summarized it in Section I, above) contains some chaff along with the wheat. For example, those who complain that the MDBs operate entirely behind a veil of secrecy are simply wrong. In the past few years, these institutions have adopted and implemented document disclosure policies that make vastly more information available about the MDBs now than evan a decade ago.[106] For example, detailed reports issued by the AsDB president to the AsDB board of Directors regarding loan proposals—enumerating the specific conditionalities accepted by a borrower—would have been almost impossible to obtain a few years ago without inside access to the AsDB. Now they can be obtained through the ADB's website.[107]

However, more should be done to facilitate public understanding of how the MDBs operate, what they have done, and what they plan to do. In this respect, the same types of "open meetings" principles adopted in many countries for the conduct of public business should be adopted within the MDBs. Records of meetings of the MDBs' governing boards should, as a general rule, be made publicly available, with exceptions and safeguards, as necessary, to guard against disclosure of information that is legitimately confidential. Further details in this regard appear below in Section IV of this chapter.

E. Criticism #II-9—The MDB Democracy Deficit

In my view, this is one of the most important and persuasive criticisms. As I described it above in Section I of this chapter, this criticism has several elements: (1) the MDBs provide little structural accommodation for citizen

---

106 *See, e.g.,* Asian Development Bank, Confidentiality and Disclosure of Information, Operations Manual § L3 (Oct. 29, 2003) (setting forth the AsDB's disclosure policy), *at* http://www.adb.org/Documents/Manuals/Operations/OML03_29oct03.pdf (last visited Nov. 4, 2004); THE WORLD BANK, THE WORLD BANK POLICY ON DISCLOSURE OF INFORMATION (June 2002) (setting forth the World Bank's disclosure policy), *available at* http://www1.worldbank.org/operations/disclosure/documents/disclosurepolicy.pdf (last visited Nov. 4, 2004).

107 *See* Asian Development Bank, Reports and Recommendations of the President, *at* http://www.adb.org/Projects/reports.asp?key+res&val=RRP (providing links to Reports and Recommendations of the President) (last visited Nov. 4, 2004); *see also* The World Bank Group, President's Reports, *at* http://www-wds.worldbank.org/navigation.jsp?pcont =browdoc (providing links to "President's Report" and "Project Appraisal Document" lists) (last visited Nov. 4, 2004).

involvement in MDB decisionmaking; (2) as a practical matter the MDBs actually do listen to corporate interests but disregard citizens' groups and NGOs; (3) the weighted voting system places control of the MDBs in the hands of a very few countries, leaving most people in borrowing member countries with virtually no influence over the actions taken by the MDBs' governing boards; (4) the operations of MDBs are not subject to any outside judicial review; and (5) the member states' governments themselves are in many cases undemocratic in character.

I begin with the second of these five elements, which (along with the third) I wish to question before noting my agreement with the other elements. I believe the assertion that MDB policies and operations are unduly influenced by corporate interests generally runs in the wrong direction. As should be obvious from reading this chapter, I believe the MDBs should be open to influence by a broad range of groups and interests, and that formal mechanisms should, in fact, be developed to facilitate the bringing of such influence to bear on MDB decisionmaking. Accordingly, I do not regard the influence that corporate interests have on MDBs (for example, on the overall selection of projects and policies) to be excessive in quantity; instead, that level of influence should be matched by the influence that other groups have. However, the complaints sometimes voiced about lobbying by companies and the possibility of corruption do merit close attention because they relate not to the quantity of the influence but rather to the quality or character of such influence.

As for lobbying, MDB staff members should be subject to the same types of standards as those that apply to civil servants in many national governments: contacts with private-sector parties wishing to influence policy or operations should be subject to scrutiny, reporting, and of course restrictions on any gifts. As for corruption, most of the MDBs have recently adopted rules and procedures to prevent corruption of their own staff officials by persons from any quarter, including corporate interests.[108] One of the more advanced of the MDBs in this regard is the AsDB, which has addressed the question of corruption aggressively by explicitly adopting an

---

[108] *See, e.g.*, IADB ANNUAL REPORT 2001, *supra* note 68, at 17 (describing the newly approved initiative for "Strengthening a Systemic Framework Against Corruption" under which IADB staff are to "act in accordance with the highest standards of integrity"). In August 2002, an MDB official made some unusually blunt remarks that underscored the importance of the fight against corruption. The chief World Bank representative in Indonesia asserted that corruption was probably that country's most serious economic problem. Jan Perlez, *World Banker Assails Indonesia's Corruption*, N.Y. TIMES, Aug. 28, 2002, at W1. For a detailed proposal regarding why and how the World Bank should take strong measures to fight corruption—written just before the World Bank promulgated a policy on that topic—*see generally* Susan Rose-Ackerman, *The Role of the World Bank in Controlling Corruption*, 29 L. & POL'Y INT'L BUS. 93 (1997).

anti-corruption policy in 1998[109] and establishing within the Office of the General Auditor an anti-corruption unit authorized to receive evidence of corruption, undertake preliminary inquiries, convene an Oversight Committee when necessary, and conduct investigations.[110] Likewise, the World Bank has in recent years given dramatically increased attention to fighting corruption.[111] Although efforts such as this require further development, they are unmistakably on the right track and will be spurred on by further transparency and accountability.

As for the complaint that the MDBs disregard citizens' groups and NGOs, I am skeptical. Given the recent upsurge in initiatives within the MDBs to broaden and strengthen their interaction with NGOs,[112] I doubt

---

[109] *See* Head, *Asian Development Bank, supra* note 53, at 19, 87–88. For the current version of the anti-corruption policy, as explained in Section C5 of the AsDB Operations Manual, *see* http://www.adb.org/Documents/Manuals/Operations/OMC05_29oct02. pdf55.asp (last visited Nov. 4, 2004). It defines corruption as "behavior on the part of officials in the public and private sectors, in which they improperly and unlawfully enrich themselves and/or those close to them, or induce others to do so, by misusing the position in which they are placed." *Id.* It then prescribes methods for fighting corruption both within the AsDB and in its member countries. In doing so, however, the policy expressly cites the "political prohibition" in its charter, Article 36(2), and notes that the AsDB's initiatives on corruption "will be grounded solely upon economic considerations and concerns of sound development management . . . [and] will not involve interference in the political affairs of a member country." *Id.*

[110] Head, *Asian Development Bank, supra* note 53, at 88. The General Auditor reports directly to the President. *Id.*

[111] For an account of World Bank efforts in this regard, *see* Murray Hiebert & John McBeth, *Stealing from the Poor*, FAR EASTERN ECON. REV., July 29, 2004, at 1 (pointing out, for example, that in 1998 the World Bank President established a Department of Institutional Integrity, which now has a staff of 50, including 30 investigators conducting 345 investigations into corruption around the world, and that World Bank efforts in this regard had led to 25 criminal convictions in national courts as well as 28 dismissals from the bank itself). Details of World Bank and other MDB initiatives to fight corruption were discussed recently before the U.S. Senate. *See* Hearing of the Senate Foreign Relations Committee on Combating Corruption in the Multilateral Development Banks, July 21, 2004. In those hearings, the U.S. Treasury Department praised the MDBs for their anti-corruption efforts. *See* Testimony of John B. Taylor, Under Secretary of the Treasury for International Affairs, *id.* (noting that "[t]he managements of the MDBs are to be commended for the positive steps they have taken in recent years to fight corruption, following the example set by the World Bank").

[112] For citations to works explaining these initiatives even as of nearly a decade ago, *see* Steve Charnovitz, *Two Centuries of Participation: NGOs and International Governance*, appearing as Chapter 15 in STEVE CHARNOVITZ, TRADE LAW AND GLOBAL GOVERNANCE (2002), at 397 n.3 [hereinafter *NGOs and International Governance*]. For further information about the World Bank's efforts to involve citizens' groups, NGOs, and other stakeholders as of the early 1990s, *see* THE WORLD BANK, THE WORLD BANK AND PARTICIPATION (1994) (out of print, on file with author). A similar publication was issued about the same time by the Office of Environment and Social Development of the AsDB. *See*

there are many NGOs that have made a reasonable effort to convey their opinions to MDBs in the past five years and found it difficult to do so. Indeed, some of the MDBs have established liaison offices within their headquarters for the express purpose of welcoming and discussing NGOs' opinions and involvement in the MDBs' work.[113]

Such NGO involvement comprises more than just communication, of course. The AsDB reports that nearly two-thirds of the public-sector projects approved for AsDB financing in 2000 involved NGOs in some significant way—as, for example, by relying on microfinance NGOs to assist flood victims in Bangladesh and by working with NGOs to develop low-cost solutions to sanitation problems in Papua New Guinea.[114] Frequent forums, workshops, and other meetings are conducted by MDBs with NGOs, and officials of NGOs regularly work in the MDBs under secondment arrangements.[115] In these and other ways, much has been done to involve NGOs and "civil society" in MDB work.[116] Protestors marching outside the World Bank headquarters during a joint annual meeting of the World Bank and the IMF are unlikely to get invited to lunch that day with a World Bank

---

ASIAN DEVELOPMENT BANK, MAINSTREAMING PARTICIPATORY DEVELOPMENT PROCESSES (undated, probably 1996).

[113] For example, the AsDB has had a formal policy of encouraging such consultation and involvement with NGOs since 1987 and expanded that policy in 1999. Head, *Asian Development Bank, supra* note 53, at 89. In keeping with that policy, the AsDB has established positions of "NGO Network Coordinator" and "NGO Liason" and has website links to facilitate communication and cooperation with NGOs. *Id.* For a more detailed account of these matters, *see* ASIAN DEVELOPMENT BANK, COOPERATION BETWEEN ASIAN DEVELOPMENT BANK AND NONGOVERNMENT ORGANIZATIONS (1999) and ASIAN DEVELOPMENT BANK, ADB-GOVERNMENT-NGO COOPERATION: A FRAMEWORK FOR ACTION, 2003–2005 (2003). All of these initiatives in the MDBs, of course, have come far later than (and perhaps still fall short of) the approach taken in the International Labour Organization (ILO), in which NGO participation has been central since its beginning. For observations as to the involvement of non- government entities in the ILO, *see* Steve Charnovitz, *The International Labour Organization in Its Second Century*, appearing as Chapter 11 in STEVE CHARNOVITZ, TRADE LAW AND GLOBAL GOVERNANCE (2002), at 269, 288, 294.

[114] *See* Head, *Asian Development Bank, supra* note 53, at 89.

[115] For information about how NGOs can work with the AsDB, and about the AsDB's NGO Center, *see* Asian Development Bank, How NGOs Can Work With ADB, *at* http://www.adb.org/NGOs/contractpoints.asp (last visited Nov. 4, 2004).

[116] According to one observer, NGOs have been able "to pressure international financial institutions such as the World Bank . . . to be transparent and accountable . . ." and have found the World Bank and other international institutions to be "soft targets for civil society. The [World] Bank has involved civil society in more than 700 of its projects since 1973." Guisai Mutume, *Development: Civil Society Seeks Greater Role in Global Finance*, Inter Press Service, Apr. 8, 2001, LEXIS.

official, but, under less confrontational circumstances, such meetings can occur. In short, I am not persuaded by complaints that the views and representatives of NGOs are systematically disregarded or excluded now by the MDBs.

I do not find the third element, regarding the weighted voting system, compelling per se. As I explain below in my assessment of Criticism #II-12—lack of symmetry in obligations—it is the combination of the weighted voting system and MDB conditionality, not the weighted voting system on its own, that raises a specter of unfairness. That specter of unfairness prompts me to offer, in Section IV of this chapter, some suggestions in this regard, involving both (1) a mechanism for reporting the national economic performance (including development performance) of non-borrowing members and (2) a linkage between voting power and national economic performance.

I find the other three elements of the "democracy deficit" criticism well-founded and compelling. Accordingly, I also suggest in Section IV of this chapter some changes that would increase citizen involvement, impose judicial review on MDBs, and authorize the MDBs to promote government reform in member countries that have not yet embraced the principles of multiparty representative governance.

F. Criticism #II-10—Narrowness of Economic Focus

At its core, this criticism is the flip side of Criticism #II-11—mission creep. Both of the criticisms raise a fundamental constitutional question: should the MDBs give a broad interpretation or a narrow interpretation to the provisions that appear in their charters (except for the EBRD Charter) requiring that the MDBs take into account only economic considerations and that they not interfere in the political affairs of their members?

For reasons summarized above in Subsection IIA of this chapter, I dismiss the "mission creep" criticism—that the MDBs have acted *ultra vires* by venturing into areas that typically would not have been regarded part of economic development work a few decades ago, such as environmental protection, social justice, governance, and the like. The gradual realization that such topics can have an important bearing on economic development, and that MDBs therefore must pay some attention to such topics, strikes me as appropriate.

However, I believe the MDBs should have a clearer and broader mandate in this area. The MDBs should be permitted and required to take into account a variety of legal and policy matters relating to the quality of the governance being provided in the member states of the MDBs. Such a permission and requirement should take the form of a new provision appearing in each of the MDBs' charters. About 14 years ago, Ibrahim Shihata defended the World Bank's involvement in governance matters as being consistent with the institution's charter. Shihata, then the World Bank's General Counsel, said that the institution had struck a "delicate balance"[117] by using conditionality to improve the overall policy environment—including, in particular, those policies that made government more efficient by reducing its size and its control over the economy—while being careful not to assert any mandate to introduce political reform or to question the political form of its borrowing member governments.[118] It is, of course, the political prohibition in the IBRD and IDA Charters that required the World Bank to strike such a "delicate balance" and prompted Shihata to defend the World Bank in that regard. Shihata drew a contrast between the IBRD and IDA Charter provisions and the political mandate given to the EBRD.[119]

In my view, the three key mandates appearing in the EBRD Charter—on political, economic, and environmental matters—should serve as models for charter amendments for the other MDBs.[120] I explained several

---

[117] SHIHATA-1991, *supra* note 43, at 53.

[118] *Id.* at 59, 61. For a detailed description and analysis of the provisions of the IBRD and IDA charters that exclude the World Bank from taking political considerations into account in its operations, *see id.* At 62–78. Shihata then turns specifically to a consideration of "Aspects of Governance Consistent with the Bank's Mandate." *Id.* at 84. He concludes in that respect that the World Bank "may . . . address issues of governance [subject to some exceptions] to the extent it deems relevant to the success of the project or program involved." *Id.* at 87. For a description of how the AsDB has justified its efforts to fight corruption with its own "political prohibition," see *supra* note 109.

[119] SHIHATA-1991, *supra* note 43, at 57–58. The EBRD's political mandate requires the institution to foster economic change "in the Central Eastern European countries committed to and applying the principles of multiparty democracy [and] pluralism." EBRD Charter art. 1.

[120] I am indebted to Fred Mesch of the AsDB for pressing me on what he calls the "Pandora's Box issue" of opening up the MDBs charters to amendment. I address that issue briefly in Subsection IVB of this chapter and again in Chapter Six. I would point out, however, that I am by no means alone in recommending that MDB charters be amended. For a similar recommendation, albeit less detailed than the ones I present below in Section IV of this chapter, *see* Carlos Santiso, *Good Governance and Aid Effectiveness: The World Bank and Conditionality*, 7 GEO. PUB. POL'Y REV. 1, 18 (2001) (noting that "[t]he time has come again to revisit and amend the [World] Bank's founding charter" in order to broaden that institution's mandate so that it explicitly addresses issues of power, politics, and democracy, rather than confining itself merely to the economic dimensions of governance). For another perspective on the possibility of amending MDB charters, *see* Heather Marquette, *Corruption, Democracy and the World Bank*, 36 CRIME, L. & SOC. CHANGE 395, 403 (2001) (suggesting that a needed broadening of World Bank attention to governance, beyond merely the economic aspects of governance, would require not only an amendment of the World Bank's Charter, which would be "a difficult and laborious process" but also a restructuring of the institution's entire culture).

paragraphs earlier, in assessing Criticisms #II-3 and II-4, why I believe the MDBs should be involved in environmental and human rights issues, and I mentioned, in particular, that there should be a linkage within the charters of the MDBs to major treaties addressing environmental and human rights issues. I would say the same for several other topics into which the MDBs have made only slight forays so far—governance, for example, and perhaps international criminal law.[121] I explain this suggestion further below in Section IV of this chapter.

I should emphasize that I do not propose that existing MDB staff and management be expected to assume the additional responsibilities of dealing with a broader array of issues and polices than they already been given. As suggested in my assessment of Criticism #II-7—weaknesses in staffing and management—I believe a substantial expansion and realignment of the staffing of the MDBs is in order. More importantly, I believe a more effective system of cooperation between MDB staff and the staff members of other international organizations, NGOs, and national governments is essential. I agree with Jessica Einhorn's observation that other organizations are better able to deal with some issues than MDB staff members are.[122] My suggestion for having the MDBs serve as focal points, at which those issues are translated into policies (and conditionalities, as appropriate), has several benefits—economies of scale, minimizing contradictory messages, and, of course, financial and institutional leverage—while at the same time using the comparative advantage that other institutions and groups have in various subject-matter areas.

G. Criticism #II-12—Asymmetry in Obligations

As explained above, this criticism emerges from two legal and institutional features of the MDBs and their operations: (1) conditionality in

---

[121] For a discussion of the propriety of MDB involvement in certain aspects of international criminal law, *see* Daniel Bradlow, *Should the International Financial Institutions Play a Role in the Implementation and Enforcement of International Humanitarian Law?*, 50 U. KAN. L. REV. 695, 697 (2002) (expressing the views that (1) "except in extreme cases, the costs of having the IFIs actively engaged in the *enforcement* of international humanitarian law outweigh the benefits," but (2) "the benefits of having the IFIs involved in the *implementation* of international humanitarian law exceed the costs"); *see also* Laurie R. Blank, *The Role of International Financial Institutions in International Humanitarian Law* (report of the International Humanitarian Law Working Group, United States Institute of Peace, Jan. 2002) (discussing the role that IFIs "can and should take" in the implementation of international humanitarian law), *available at* http://www.usip.org/pubs/peaceworks/ pwks42.pdf (last visited Feb. 13, 2005).

[122] *See* Einhorn, *supra* note 36, at 33 (suggesting, for example, that the World Bank pass the job of judicial reform "to an organization staffed by lawyers and judges" and that efforts to protect cultural heritage could likewise be "farmed out to an organization with more corresponding interest").

MDB lending and (2) the weighted voting system. This pair of elements, like the criticism they trigger, applies equally to the MDBs and to the IMF. Accordingly, my analysis of the criticism here, as it applies to the MDBs, is the same as my analysis of it in the context of the IMF—an analysis that I explained in Subsection IIIC of Chapter Three. As I explained there, I believe each of the two features at issue—conditionality and weighted voting—is completely valid and natural in its own right. After all, why shouldn't those countries providing the most financial backing for an institution have the most control over its policies; and why shouldn't a financial institution that depends on repayments of loans in order to stay alive be permitted (indeed, required) to ensure that the borrower takes action likely to enable that borrower to repay the loan?

However, although each of the two features (weighted voting and conditionality) standing alone is legal and desirable, the two of them combined in the context of actual MDB operations—or at least those operations that involve economic and financial policy prescriptions—can be nettlesome. Why? Because they result in blatantly asymmetrical obligations: the countries that control (through the weighted voting system) the MDBs' policies in imposing conditionality are, with rare exceptions, the very countries that do not borrow from the MDBs and to whom the policies on conditionality do not apply. Thus, as I asserted earlier in the context of the IMF, the actual operation of conditionality smacks of unfairness and hypocrisy; what is sauce for the goose should, it seems, be sauce for the gander.[123]

The sense of unfairness and hypocrisy gets stronger when the two countries that have, on average, the largest capital subscriptions in the MDBs—the United States and Japan—regularly engage in behavior that seems inconsistent with the economic and financial policies on which the MDBs typically insist in their policy-based lending.[124] Again, I made this point also in the context of the IMF, in Subsection IIIC of Chapter Three, so I need not repeat the details here.

---

[123] It is worth noting that asymmetry in obligations is not always inherently unfair. If, for example, the baseline distribution of wealth (and hence influence in the MDBs) among countries were generally regarded as fair, and differential loan conditionalities resulted from genuinely fair bargaining among countries, the asymmetry in applicable conditions would probably attract no criticism. I am indebted to Bob Hockett for illuminating this point.

[124] For a description of economic and financial policies that the World Bank reflects in the conditions attaching to its loans, *see* Axel Dreher, The Development and Implementation of IMF and World Bank Conditionality 10–15, 54–59 (Hamburg Inst. of Int'l Econ., HWWA Discussion Paper 165, 2002), *available at* http://www.hwwa.de/Publikationen/Discussion_Paper/2002/165.pdf (last visited Nov. 4, 2004).

However, adding further fuel to the "asymmetry in obligations" criticism, as it applies to the MDBs, is the fact that there is no mechanism in the context of those institutions for officially illuminating and discussing the mismatch between what is expected of the borrowing member countries and what is practiced by the controlling (non-borrowing) member countries. In this respect the MDBs stand in contrast to the IMF, which at least undertakes an annual review of every member's economic and financial policies and performance, in accordance with Article IV of the IMF Charter.[125]

It is worth pointing out that although the lack of symmetry at issue here is most obvious and unseemly in the context of the MDBs' policy-based lending (as distinct from their project lending), the "lack of symmetry" criticism, in fact, packs a punch in the context of all MDB operations. I stressed this point several years ago in exploring the subject of "environmental conditionality" in MDB operations.[126] I explained then that although the MDB charters do not vest the MDBs themselves with the sort of authority that Article IV of the IMF Charter grants that institution—and therefore no easy vehicle exists in the MDBs for any formal criticism of developed (non-borrowing) member countries that fail to follow the economic and financial policies that the MDBs are pressing their borrowing member countries to follow—there is still much that the MDBs and their developed member countries can do to counteract the effects of the asymmetry in obligations.[127] In that earlier article, I enumerated some initiatives that I believe the developed countries should take to improve global environmental sustainability, but I noted that "[f]or the present, the role of the [MDBs] in this area is limited by both legal and practical constraints[,]" including certain limitations in the MDBs' charters.[128]

---

[125] *See* IMF Charter, art. IV, § 3 (directing the IMF to "exercise firm surveillance over the exchange rate policies of members" and requiring each member to provide information to the IMF and to "consult with it on the member's exchange rate polices"), *available at* http://www.imf.org/external/pubs/ft/aa/aa.pdf (last visited Nov. 4, 2004). As described in my "nutshell" account of the IMF in Section II of Chapter Two, the so-called "Article IV consultations," in fact, constitute rather wide-ranging reviews of each member country's economic and financial policies, as to which the IMF often offers pointed criticisms. For example, in the 2003 Article IV consultation regarding Japan, the IMF's board of directors "stressed that serious and interrelated problems remain [in Japan's economy], and that a sustained and strong economic revival is not yet in prospect," and moreover "agreed that a more comprehensive and integrated policy approach is needed to revitalize the corporate and financial sectors, tackle deflation, and address fiscal imbalances." International Monetary Fund, IMF Concludes 2003 Article IV Consultation with Japan (Sept. 5, 2003), *at* http://www.imf.org/external/np/sec/pn/2003/pn03112.htm (last visited Nov. 4, 2004). For a description of the findings publicized following a recent Article IV consultation with the United States, see the last few paragraphs of Subsection IIIC of Chapter Three, *supra.*

[126] *See generally* Head, *Environmental Conditionality, supra* note 88.

[127] *Id.* at 23–24.

[128] *Id.* at 24.

I believe it is time to cut through those legal and practical constraints and make the burdens and obligations of economic development more symmetrical. In the closing section of this chapter, I offer some suggestions in this regard, involving both (1) a mechanism for reporting the national economic performance of non-borrowing member countries and (2) a linkage between voting power and national economic performance—with "economic performance" construed broadly to encompass social aspects of development.

IV. REFORMS I SUGGEST

I have identified in Section III of this chapter seven criticisms of the MDBs that I generally endorse. They focus on environmental and human rights shortcomings and on several structural and institutional matters, including a lack of transparency, a narrowness of economic focus, weaknesses in staffing and management, an asymmetry in obligations, and a "democracy deficit." As I observed in the introductory remarks to Section IV of Chapter Three, some critics would assert that such important defects as these provide sufficient reason for doing away with an institution (or, in the case of the MDBs, a whole class of institutions). I do not take that view. My view, instead, is that the MDBs do valuable work and can be improved in ways that can bring substantially more value to the cause of international economic development, liberally construed. I defend that view below in Chapter Six. Accordingly, in this final section of this Chapter Four I recommend some reforms that I believe would help respond to and overcome the criticisms that I find well-founded as directed against the MDBs.

In offering my recommendations, I concentrate first on structural and institutional matters. In particular, I propose that five institutional principles be formally adopted by the MDBs: (1) transparency, (2) participation, (3) legality, (4) competence, and (5) accountability. Several of the principles themselves are already supported, at least in general terms, by the MDBs, as is evident from a survey of the MDBs' websites.[129] However, my proposal goes considerably further than any of the MDBs would (or arguably could) go now, as will be evident from the description I give in Subsections A through E below. In Subsection F I turn to substantive matters, identifying certain treaties and other international standards that MDB member countries should, in my view, be required to accept, in the sense that adherence to key provisions of such treaties and standards would be a condition of membership.

---

[129] *See, e.g.,* http://www1.worldbank.org/operations/disclosure/ (referring to transparency and public disclosure in World Bank operations) (last visited Feb. 13, 2005); http://www.adb.org/Documents/Manuals/Operations/OML03_29oct03.pdf (referring to transparency and openness in all areas of AsDB operations) (last visited Feb. 13, 2005); http://www.ebrd.org/about/strategy/index.htm (stating Public Information Policy to promote transparency and good governance) (last visited Feb. 13, 2005).

A. Transparency

The principle of transparency involves making available to the public a very broad range of information about what the MDB has done, is doing, and proposes to do. Abiding by the principle of transparency would involve at least five elements.[130] First, the records of discussions and decisions at the meetings of MDB governing boards would be accessible to the public. Second, the loan agreements and related legal documents executed by an MDB with borrowers and other entities would be accessible to the public, not only through the deposit of some such agreements with the U.N. Secretary-General pursuant to Article 102 of the U.N. Charter[131] but also by immediate availability through electronic means. Third, all recommendations for financial assistance—loans, technical assistance, etc.—presented to the MDB's board of directors, along with documents relating to environmental and social assessment of such operations—would be accessible to the public through electronic means. Fourth, the MDB's governing policy and operational documents (such as the MDB's policy papers and Operations Manual) would be available, in current form, electronically. Fifth, all legal opinions issued by the General Counsel (or an MDB lawyer serving temporarily in the place of the General Counsel) to a governing board of the MDB would be accessible electronically. In all these cases, disclosure of and access to information would be subject to appropriate respect for confidentiality where necessary to protect legitimate interests of private parties. In addition, the transparency rules would apply only prospectively to most classes of documents, to avoid requiring MDBs to enter countless old documents. Moreover, because of the need for candid and lively debate in the early development of projects and policies, internal staff memoranda would typically not be publicly available.

---

[130] Several of these elements appear also in the recommendations made in 2002 by the International Law Association's Committee on Accountability of International Organizations at its New Delhi Conference. *See* INTERNATIONAL LAW ASSOCIATION, REPORT OF THE SEVENTIETH CONFERENCE 772, 775–76 (2002) (discussing basic standard of maximum possible transparency). Those recommendations also include valuable points regarding the need for international organizations to implement other policies for good governance. *See id.* at 774–79 (stating that good governance includes transparency, participation in the decision-making process, access to information, competent international civil service, sound financial management, and adequate reporting and evaluation). For a critical discussion of the fact that the meetings of the governing boards of the MDBs are closed to the public and the news media, *see* Robert Naiman, *U.S. Should Act to Open the Board Meetings of the IFIs*, 6 FOREIGN POLICY IN FOCUS, no. 38, 1 (Dec. 3, 2001), at LEXIS.

[131] *See* U.N. CHARTER, art. 102, para. 1 ("Every treaty and every international agreement entered into by any Member of the United Nations after the present Charter comes into force shall as soon as possible be registered with the Secretariat and published by it.").

B. Participation

The principle of participation involves providing for influential input by responsible parties before MDB action is finalized.[132] Abiding by the principle of participation would involve at least four elements. First, the MDBs would provide mechanisms for soliciting and considering comments from the public during a reasonable period of time before decisions are made by a governing board of the MDB on proposed financing operations or on proposed policy statements or changes.[133] This would facilitate the participation by interested parties directly, rather than only through the national government authorities of member countries. Second, the MDBs would provide mechanisms also for soliciting and considering comments on environmental assessment and social assessment of specific projects under consideration for MDB financing. This would facilitate public input into the formulation of documents evaluating the likely effects of a proposed project on the physical and human environment, at a stage before such evaluative documents are finalized and submitted to an MDB's board of directors for consideration in connection with a proposal for financial assistance. Third, the MDBs would take further steps to integrate NGOs into the establishment of MDB policies and would develop criteria for certifying which NGOs could have direct participation in MDB operations, to the extent that this does not already occur.[134] Fourth, the MDBs would strengthen the capacity of their field offices to accept comments, complaints, and other views of local residents about MDB operations, and to convey that information to the MDBs' headquarters. This could improve the responsiveness of the MDBs to local populations, whose support is essential for development assistance to work.[135]

---

[132] According to the views of some commentators, the principle of participation would also encompass the ability of the public to challenge MDB action that they believe has harmed their interests. *See, e.g.*, Chi Carmody, *Beyond the Proposals: Public Participation in International Economic Law*, 15 AM. U. INT'L L. REV. 1321, 1327–34 (2000) (describing the establishment and operations of the World Bank Inspection Panel and similar procedures in the regional MDBs). I have addressed this development under the principle of accountability, discussed below.

[133] A model for such a mechanism might be found in the American Administrative Procedure Act applicable to administrative agencies in the United States, and particularly in the "notice and comment" procedures and U.S. experience with them. *See* Richard E. Levy & Sidney A. Shapiro, *Administrative Procedure and the Decline of the Trial*, 51 U. KAN. L. REV. 473, 488–92 (2003).

[134] Other means of enriching the involvement of NGOs in MDB work could also be implemented, and the literature discussing these means is quite extensive. For example, for a detailed examination of various functions that NGOs carry out and numerous techniques of NGO participation in international governance, *see generally* Charnovitz, *NGOs and International Governance, supra* note 112.

[135] It is perhaps noteworthy that this suggestion, like several others mentioned in this paragraph to broaden public participation in the work of the MDBs, raises a perennial

C. Legality

The principle of legality involves establishing clear rules and following them. It is partly to observe this principle of legality that the MDBs should, as I suggested above in Subsection A (regarding transparency), make public all operational documents and governing policies. However, the principle of legality, as applied in the MDBs, should encompass not only (1) legality of the MDBs' activities but also (2) legality of the membership of countries in the MDBs.

The first of these aspects of legality is not new to the MDBs, although announcing it in charter amendments would provide a foundation for judicial review of MDB operations, which I explain below under the topic of accountability. However, the second of these two aspects of legality—establishing membership requirements for countries to participate in the MDBs—is largely novel. I proposed the same approach in Chapter Three with respect to the IMF.[136] Let me explain the proposal as it would apply in the case of the MDBs.

Some MDBs already have membership requirements: membership in the IBRD, for example, requires membership in the IMF,[137] and membership in the AsDB requires membership in the United Nations or certain of its agencies.[138] However, I propose that the MDB membership requirements be expanded, in much the same way that participation in the GATT (through membership in the WTO) was made subject to the "single package" approach agreed upon in the Uruguay Round of trade negotiations.[139] Under my proposal, membership in an MDB would require that a country accept certain specified obligations in basic (existing) multilateral treaties relating to environmental protection, human rights, and good governance, as well as certain other internationally accepted standards. I return to this point, and identify the treaties and other standards I am referring to, in Subsection IVF, below.

D. Competence

The principle of competence, as applied to MDBs, involves the adoption of specific policies and regulations aimed at improving the compe-

---

problem: how to balance the two competing values of (1) universality (that is, coherence and harmonization of policies) and (2) sensitivity to special needs and local conditions.

[136] *See supra* Subsection IVB of Chapter Three.

[137] IBRD Charter, art. II, para. 1.

[138] AsDB Charter, art. 3, para. 1.

[139] For a brief description of the "single package" approach, and the score of treaties that were thereby made applicable to countries joining the WTO, *see* Subsection IVD of Chapter Two.

tence of MDB staff and management, including the competence of those serving on MDB boards of directors. Specifically, I suggest that each MDB adopt regulations directing the president of the MDB to ensure (1) the competence of incoming staff, (2) that competence figures more prominently than seniority as a basis for promotions, and (3) that there is a reduction in the role of nationality in both appointments and promotions.

The first of these points, relating to incoming staff, might be facilitated by the establishment of an international civil service examination like that used in dynastic China and in some contemporary national civil service and foreign service systems. The second of these points, relating to the grounds for promotions, should involve objective methods of evaluating the quality of the staff member's performance—as is used, for example, in the work of the World Bank's Quality Assurance Group[140]—and should involve a suppression of the "approval culture" that gives undue emphasis to the volume of lending that staff members generate.[141] The third point, calling for a reduction in the role of nationality, would require a careful balancing: on the one hand, there is obvious benefit to be gained from wide geographic, national, and cultural diversity in MDB staffing (a benefit reflected, in fact, in some MDB charters);[142] on the other hand, pressure from national

---

[140] For a description of the World Bank's Quality Assurance Group, *see* its system for evaluating the quality of projects and the performance of staff members working on those projects, *at* http://web.worldbank.org/WBSITE/EXTERNAL/PROJECTS/ QAG/ 0,,pagePK:109619~theSitePK:109609,00.html (last visited Feb. 13, 2005). As described there, the World Bank's QAG initiative was launched in 1996, following internal evaluations showing "that one third of [World] Bank projects were unlikely to achieve their objectives"; to address that situation, "QAG's mandate was to increase management and staff accountability by conducting real-time assessments of the quality of the [World] Bank's performance in its major product lines." Other MDBs have also placed increasing emphasis on finding reliable methods of evaluating the quality of projects and of staff performance. *See, e.g.,* ASIAN DEVELOPMENT BANK, PROJECT QUALITY—AN AGENDA FOR ACTION (1995) [hereinafter PROJECT QUALITY AGENDA] (reporting on the proceedings of a Regional Workshop on Improving Project Quality).

[141] George Soros makes a similar point: "Performance should not be measured by the amount of loans disbursed." SOROS *supra* note 72, at 105. This point has not been lost on the MDBs. Introductory comments to the 1995 AsDB book cited earlier note that "an internal task force—the Task Force on Improving Project Quality—. . . recommended a shift away from an 'approval culture' to a new corporate culture emphasizing project quality." PROJECT QUALITY AGENDA, *supra* note 140, at xi. Research that I have carried out at the AsDB since that time indicates that the institution has followed up on this recommendation, in part by pursuing initiatives to enhance the quality of project supervision—for example, by rewarding project administration work in terms of career advancement—and thereby to reverse the so-called "approval culture."

[142] *See, e.g.,* AsDB Charter, art. 34.6 (required that the President of the AsDB, in appointing staff members, "shall, subject to the paramount importance of securing the highest standards of efficiency and technical competence, pay due regard to the recruitment of personnel on as wide a regional geographic basis as possible.").

authorities to appoint or promote a person of a particular nationality can severely damage productivity and morale[143] in a setting in which both need to be high.

In addition to these directives to the MDB president, who is typically responsible for the hiring and management of an MDB's staff,[144] regulations also should be adopted regarding the competence of those persons appointed by national authorities to serve on the boards of directors of the MDBs. It must be clear to those national authorities, and to persons serving on those boards of directors, that appointment to such service is to be based on proven professional qualifications and not on political patronage or connections. To this end, I propose that the MDBs prepare and publish detailed terms of reference describing the duties of such directors and the expected qualifications and experience of persons appointed to serve in that capacity, and that rigorous orientation and training programs for those persons, once they take up their positions at the MDBs, be put in place or strengthened. Perhaps most important, especially for those MDBs that already give serious attention to the competence of both staff and members of boards of directors, is the need to formalize and publicize MDB standards and policies in this regard, to help blunt attacks of the sort included in Criticism #II-7—weaknesses in staffing and management.

The principle of competence would also involve building a more effective network of cooperation between MDB staff and staff members of other international organizations, NGOs, and national governments. I discussed this point above,[145] and proposed that the MDBs would serve as focal points or clearinghouses for expertise that would come from other entities and be brought to bear on the MDBs' work.[146]

---

[143] I draw on my own experience as a staff member of the AsDB: pressure in the mid-1980s from Japanese authorities to hire an unqualified Japanese national seriously undermined the independence and morale of the Office of the General Counsel.

[144] *See, e.g.*, AsDB Charter, art. 34.5 ("The President shall be chief of the staff of the Bank and . . . shall be responsible for the organization, appointment and dismissal of the officers and staff in accordance with regulations adopted by the Board of Directors.").

[145] *See supra* note 122 and accompanying text. For references to existing strands in such a network of cooperation between staff members of MDBs and other international organizations, *see also infra* note 157.

[146] For a comment about the relationship between (1) this aspect of improving MDB staff competence by building a more effective network of cooperation and (2) my proposal to require that MDB member countries accept certain key obligations in fundamental treaties, *see infra* note 157.

E. Accountability

Accountability, in the context of MDBs, should mean at least two things: (1) accountability of the MDBs themselves to a wide range of interests, including the interests of the public at large; and (2) accountability of all member countries (including non-borrowers) to each other, to the MDBs, and to their own people in managing their national financial and economic affairs. I will address them in reverse order.

In generally endorsing Criticism #II-12—lack of symmetry in obligations—I pointed out that the IMF Charter requires that IMF members cooperate in Article IV consultations, an annual exercise in which the IMF studies and critiques each member country's economic and financial policies and performance. As I explained earlier, the reports issued by the IMF following the Article IV consultation are typically made public.[147] In a similar but more narrowly focused manner, I believe all MDB member countries should be required to report annually (and publicly) on their own policies and performance on economic and financial matters.

Specifically, I propose that a standardized set of objective economic and financial criteria, including, in particular, various indices of sustainable human development, be established by the MDBs, based on the kinds of requirements typically found in loan covenants and conditionalities appearing in loan documents between the MDBs and their borrowers. These criteria, in turn, would be used to evaluate the polices and performance of all MDB member countries—borrowers and non-borrowers alike. These evaluations would then be published.

What would be the use of such evaluations? For one thing, they could help blunt the complaint I described above about the mismatch between what is expected of the borrowing member countries and what is practiced by the controlling (non-borrowing) member countries. Second, such evaluations could be used for a more arresting purpose as well: in egregious cases, where a member country departed substantially and chronically from the economic and financial standards previously agreed to, that members' voting power could be suspended until it corrects its behavior.

This remedial function—triggering a suspension of voting power for poor performance—has analogs in domestic laws governing corporate entities.[148] At the international level, it might be seen as analogous to the pro-

---

[147] *See supra* Subsection IIC.

[148] For an example of statutory provisions expressly permitting limited liability companies to specify in their constitutional instruments that voting powers may be restricted or reduced in certain specified circumstances, *see* Section 151(a) of the Delaware General Corporation Law (providing that "[a]ny of the voting powers . . . of any . . . class

cedure put in place by the Third Amendment to the IMF Charter. As I explained above in Chapter Three, that Third Amendment (proposed in 1990 and adopted two years later) provided for a suspension of voting rights of a member that persisted in a failure to abide by its obligations under the IMF Charter.[149] My proposal would be somewhat different by being more objective and more automatic in its application. The system I think should be adopted would have objective criteria for measuring a country's economic and financial performance; upon substantial (defined) departure from these criteria, a member's voting power would be suspended.[150] As a consequence, the weighted voting system would be modified: a member's usable voting power would be based on its subscription to capital, as under current rules, unless the member's economic and financial performance triggered a suspension in that voting power. Even if such a suspension never occurred, the formal system providing for such an action would help address Criticism #II-12—lack of symmetry in obligations—and would help make all members accountable to each other, to the MDBs, and to their own people for the prudent management of the country's economic and financial affairs.

I turn now to the second type of accountability: accountability of the MDBs themselves. My suggestions on this point involve two elements. First, MDBs should encourage and facilitate public involvement in decision-making. I have already discussed that point above, in discussing the principle of participation.[151] Second, MDBs should submit to the jurisdiction of some external entity authorized to review the legitimacy of MDB action.

---

or series of stock may be made dependent upon facts ascertainable outside the certificate of incorporation . . . provided that the manner in which such facts shall operate upon the voting powers . . . is clearly and expressly set forth in the certificate of incorporation"; and "[t]he term 'facts,' as used in this subsection, includes . . . a determination or action by any person or body, including the corporation"). 8 DEL. CODE ANN. § 151(a) (2003). For a similar provision, *see* the Delaware Limited Liability Company Act, title 6, Section 18-502(c) of the Delaware Code (providing that "[a] limited liability company agreement may provide that the interest of any member who fails to make any contribution that the member is obligated to make shall be subject to specified penalties for . . . such failure" and that this penalty "may take the form of reducing . . . the defaulting member's proportionate interest" in the company). 6 DEL. CODE ANN. § 18-502(C) (2003).

[149] *See supra* Subsection IVE of Chapter Three. The IBRD Charter has a somewhat analogous provision for suspension of membership, which entails a suspension of voting rights, in the event that a member country fails to fulfill its obligations to that institution. IBRD Charter, art. VI, § 2.

[150] A more nuanced, but more complicated, feature could also be included in the system by providing for partial suspension. In this case the amount by which the voting power would be partially suspended would depend on the extent to which the country's economic and financial performance departed substantially from the established criteria.

[151] *See supra* Subsection B of this section.

Expressed differently, this means that MDBs should be subject to judicial review.

For this purpose, I propose the establishment of an International Tribunal for Multilateral Development Banks. Such a Tribunal would amount to an expansion of the inspection panels that some MDBs have established[152] in order to determine whether those institutions have acted consistently with the policies that they have announced. Such a tribunal would also have appellate jurisdiction over the governing boards of the MDBs in matters of charter interpretation. Judges for the tribunal could be selected mainly by the MDBs themselves—perhaps two nominated by each participating MDB and two by the President of the International Court of Justice. Providing for such judicial review would introduce some checks and balances of the sort that most national governmental structures have, by adding to the executive and legislative functions (carried out by the MDBs' management and governing boards, respectively) a judicial function responsible for checking the legality of the exercise of the other two functions. The International Tribunal for Multilateral Development Banks would accept complaints from individuals or groups alleging that an MDB had acted inconsistently with its own charter or its own announced policies and principles—including the other institutional principles discussed above and the substantive principles that I discuss below in Subsection F.

F.   Substantive Norms and Standards

Having concentrated above on structural and institutional suggestions for improving the MDBs, I now turn to a different type of proposed reform. This suggestion focuses on the substantive international legal obligations that MDB member countries undertake. I discussed a closely similar point

---

[152] For a general reference to inspection panels in the MDBs, *see supra* Subsection IIID of Chapter Two. For further descriptions and assessments of the World Bank Inspection Panel, *see generally* IBRAHIM F.I. SHIHATA, THE WORLD BANK INSPECTION PANEL (1994); THE INSPECTION PANEL OF THE WORLD BANK: A DIFFERENT COMPLAINTS PROCEDURE (Gudmundur Alfredsson & Rolf Ring eds., 2001); THE WORLD BANK, ACCOUNTABILITY AT THE WORLD BANK: THE INSPECTION PANEL 10 YEARS ON (2003). The second of the two books cited above also includes descriptions of the Inspection Policy of the AsDB, *id.* at 191–207, and the Independent Inspection Mechanism of the IADB, *id.* at 209–18. For the AsDB policies on inspection, *see* ASIAN DEVELOPMENT BANK, ADB'S INSPECTION POLICY: A GUIDEBOOK (1996), *at* http://www.adb.org/Documents/Guidelines/Inspection/default.asp (last visited Feb. 13, 2005). In June 2002, the AsDB began holding regional meetings to obtain input from NGOs, civil society, and private sector interests regarding the effectiveness and improvement of the AsDB inspection mechanism. *ADB Opens Inspection Function to Consultations*, ADB REVIEW, Sept.–Oct. 2002, at 21. The AfDB also has taken steps toward establishing an inspection function for that institution, with assistance from Professor Daniel Bradlow. *See* Bradlow's *Study on an Inspection Function for the African Development Bank Group* (2003, on file with author).

in my recommendations for improving the IMF,[153] but my recommendation as it applies to the MDBs is somewhat more extensive and detailed.

In discussing the principle of legality above in Subsection IVC of this chapter, I proposed the establishment of a new type of membership requirement for countries to participate in the MDBs: a requirement that member countries accept certain key provisions of fundamental treaties. To this end, the MDBs' charters could be amended to incorporate, by reference, those treaty provisions. A similar approach was taken in the TRIPs Agreement[154] emerging from the Uruguay Round of trade negotiations: by becoming a party to that Agreement, a country agrees to comply with certain specified provisions of various intellectual property conventions.[155]

Incorporating by reference (into the MDBs' charters) certain other treaty provisions would not only bear, however, on eligibility for membership. It would also impose a continuing requirement on member countries to adhere to those treaties. The overall aims in imposing this requirement would be (1) to announce definitively that the MDBs themselves, and their members, are committed to the key purposes of the incorporated treaties—regarding, for example, environmental protection, fundamental human rights, and responsible governance[156]—as well as (2) to provide a normative basis for imposing requirements on member countries in the form of loan covenants and conditions. Such an initiative might have another, less direct effect: further inducing compliance with the treaties to which most MDB member countries had already consented to be bound.[157]

---

[153] *See supra* Subsection IVB of Chapter Four.

[154] Agreement on Trade-Related Aspects of Intellectual Property Rights, Apr. 15, 1994, Marrakesh Agreement Establishing the World Trade Organization, Annex 1C, Legal Instruments—Results of the Uruguay Round of Multilateral Trade Negotiations, 1869 U.N.T.S. 299, 33 I.L.M. 1197 (1994).

[155] *See, e.g., id.* art. 2, (providing that WTO members "shall comply with Articles 1 through 12, and Article 19, of the Paris Convention (1967)" regarding the protection of industrial property).

[156] Other areas beyond these three could also be given similar attention. For example, I mentioned above the possibility of including international criminal law as an area in which MDBs might have some involvement. *See supra* note 121 and accompanying text.

[157] If, as a result of my proposal, treaty regimes were given a shot in the arm, it would be a gain for what has been referred to as "liberal internationalism"—an approach to international cooperation based on multilateral treaties among nation-states. *See* Kal Raustiala, *The Architecture of International Cooperation: Transgovernmental Networks and the Future of International Law*, 43 VA. J. INT'L L. 1, 2–3 (2002) (discussing liberal internationalism). However, another of the proposals I have made above is to build a more effective network of cooperation between MDB staff and staff members of other international organizations, NGOs, and national governments. *See supra* note 122 and accompanying text. This would tend to boost what has been referred to as the "transgovernmental network" model.

What substantive principles would be drawn from (existing) treaties? I propose that key substantive provisions of the following environmental, human rights, and governance treaties—the same ones I identified for a similar purpose vis-á-vis the IMF[158]—be incorporated by reference in amendments to the MDB charters:

- Convention on International Trade in Endangered Species of Wild Fauna and Flora (CITES) (1973)
- Vienna Convention for the Protection of the Ozone Layer (1985), and pertinent provisions of the Protocols thereto and of the Amendments to those Protocols
- Basle Convention on the Control of Transboundary Movements of Hazardous Wastes and Their Disposal (1989)[159]
- Convention on Biological Diversity (1992)
- Climate Change Convention (1992)[160]
- Kyoto Protocol on Global Warming (1998)
- International Covenant on Civil and Political Rights (1967)
- International Convention on the Elimination of All Forms of Racial Discrimination (1966)
- Convention on the Elimination of All Forms of Discrimination Against Women (1979)
- Convention on the Rights of the Child (1989)
- OECD Convention on Combating Bribery of Foreign Public Officials in International Business Transactions (1997).

In addition, I propose that the MDBs adopt or endorse, through actions of their governing boards, certain other substantive principles, mainly economic or financial in nature, that MDB member countries would be expected to incorporate (in a phased manner if necessary) into their own regulatory and legal frameworks. These principles would be developed by international entities with subject-matter expertise, and they

---

Raustiala, *supra*, at 4–5. Some commentators fear that this latter model might be a dangerous substitute for traditional multilateralism, but others predict that the two approaches—liberal internationalism and transgovernmentalism—will complement each other. *Id.* at 5–6. For a "history of transgovernmentalism," *see* Anne-Marie Slaughter, *The Accountability of Government Networks*, 8 IND. J. GLOBAL LEGAL STUD. 347, 350–55 (2001).

[158] *See supra* Subsection IVB of Chapter Three.

[159] As noted in the Glossary, I have used the spelling "Basle" throughout this book in the interest of consistency, even though the alternative spelling "Basel" appears more commonly used in certain contexts.

[160] For an assessment of the current legal relationship between the Climate Change Convention and the World Bank, *see generally* Wen-chen Shih, *The World Bank and Climate Change*, 3 J. INT'L ECON. L., at 633 (2000).

could include the following. Again, these are the same sets of international guidelines that I enumerated in respect of IMF membership.[161]

- the Basle guidelines on capital adequacy
- the Basle core principles on banking supervision
- the OECD Guidelines on corporate governance
- the OECD Guidelines for multinational enterprises
- the guidelines for the treatment of foreign direct investment, adopted by the Development Committee of the World Bank.

G. Charter Amendments

I have proposed in the preceding paragraphs that MDB charters be amended to include various new provisions.[162] To reiterate, the main points to be included in the amendments are:

- definition and adoption of institutional principles—transparency, participation, legality, competence, and accountability;
- environmental protection—general obligation and incorporation of key treaty provisions;
- human rights and social dimensions of development—general obligation and incorporation of key treaty provisions;
- governance—general obligation and incorporation of key treaty provisions;
- voting power—modification of weighted voting system in the MDBs in case of a member country's egregious departure from established standards of economic and financial polices and performance;
- judicial review—cross reference to the new statute establishing an International Tribunal for Multilateral Development Banks.

In Appendix I, sample language appears that might be used in effecting the sorts of amendments summarized above. For that purpose, I have used the AsDB Charter as a model. The specific format I have proposed in Appendix I is a "Draft Protocol to the AsDB Charter."

---

[161] *See supra* Subsection IVB of Chapter Three.

[162] I am fully aware of the "Pandora's Box issue" regarding charter amendments for international organizations—that is, that any attempt to open up such charters for the purpose of making amendments, however narrowly focused, might unleash a storm of proposals, demands, and rhetoric that would send the organizations into chaos. However, for reasons that I am trying to explain in this book, I believe the GEOs must change or die, and that some of the necessary changes require amendments to their charters. I address this issue more fully in Chapter Six.

CHAPTER FIVE

EVALUATING THE CRITICISMS DIRECTED AT THE WTO

I. SURVEY OF THE CRITICISMS

Of the 25 key criticisms that I enumerated in Chapter One of this book, six are leveled at the WTO in particular. In the following paragraphs I explain each of those half-dozen criticisms. In doing so, I try to express each criticism in what I consider to be its most forceful terms. As I emphasized at the beginning of Chapters Three and Four, my attempt to state the criticisms persuasively here should not be taken at this stage as any endorsement of them on my part. As will be clear from Section II of this chapter, I do not agree with several of these criticisms, nor do I agree with some of the assumptions and value judgments on which several of them rest.

A. Criticism #III-1—Free Trade's Fostering of Economic Harm[1]

According to this criticism, the WTO's central aim is wrong, because free trade does more economic harm than good to a national society and to the world as a whole. While free trade—or, more precisely, a liberal regime of trading rules in which tariffs (taxes payable on the importation of goods) are kept low and other non-tariff barriers are prohibited or discouraged—can bring some benefits in the way of lower prices, those benefits are illusory in one or more respects. For one thing (according to this criticism), the lower prices, in fact, carry a high price tag: the loss of local jobs. Instead of having a local economic base composed of industries that hire people of the community to produce the goods that the consumers in the community need, free trade outsources the production of such goods. The local industries producing the goods go out of business, which means that the worker-consumers, who held jobs in those industries, no longer have those jobs. If they are able to get other jobs, those substitute jobs often carry lower wages—not to mention lower self-esteem, thus diluting the spiritual fuel that powers any economy. If the displaced workers are not able to find other jobs, they must rely on other sources, including a typically inadequate unemployment insurance system. In either event, the standard of living for the community in general—and for the job-losers in particular—falls, all as a consequence ultimately of free trade.

---

[1] For citations to examples in the literature of some criticisms along these lines, *see* Part III of Appendix A.

This Criticism #III-1 claims that the benefits of free trade are illusory not only at an individual or community level but also at a national level. If a country subjects itself to the pressures of free trade, it will inevitably lose some industries permanently because there will always be some other countries whose economic circumstances—extremely low wage rates, for example—will make competition impossible. Having lost whole industries to the cold discipline of free trade, a country will find itself robbed of self-sufficiency. And this situation could, over the long term, lead to economic distress or even a threat to national security if the nation's economic or political relations deteriorate with the country(ies) to which its former industries have relocated.

In some cases, the benefits of free trade will, according to its critics, be illusory in yet another way as well: the comparative advantage that might prompt an industry to relocate to another country might itself be unfair or illegitimate in some way. For example, a country that permits employers to pay poverty-level wages or to ignore internationally accepted labor and workplace safety standards should not "win" in a competition to provide a home for an industry, and yet free trade allows such a country to do just that. In this respect, Criticism #III-1 (free trade's fostering of economic harm) approaches the content of Criticism #III-3 (free trade's race to the bottom), which is described below in Subsection IC of this chapter.

B. Criticism #III-2—Free Trade's Distributional Injustice[2]

This criticism claims that even if free trade can (contrary to the assertions of Criticism #III-1) be shown to bring aggregate economic benefits that exceed its costs, those benefits are not fairly distributed, either within a national economic system or among nations; and the WTO, as the institutional vehicle for free trade, permits this injustice to occur and to persist.

At work in this criticism, more than in Criticism #III-1 described above, is a concern for social justice. It is regarded as inappropriate that free trade results in some absolute losers—most obviously, those persons who lose their jobs and have no realistic expectation to be rehired in other jobs with economic or social returns equivalent to those of the jobs they have lost. Faced with this prospect of some persons who will suffer such losses as a result of free trade, critics who press this "distributional injustice" complaint would opt to stifle free trade even if free trade would bring overall economic benefit to the society in aggregate. Expressed differently, since free trade makes some people lose, the prospect that it will make more people win than lose is not good enough.

---

[2] For citations to examples in the literature of some criticisms along these lines, *see* Part III of Appendix A.

The social justice concern at work in Criticism #III-2 applies not only within a single national economic system but also to the world as a whole. In that wider context, the concern is that while free trade in general—and in particular free trade as facilitated by the WTO—can help some countries improve their economic circumstances, some other countries will either not "win" at all from free trade, or at least will not "win" as much as other countries. The great divide usually at issue in the criticism at this global level, of course, is that between the economically developed countries and the less developed countries (LDCs, or "Third World" countries[3]). What Raj Bhala has called the "anti-Third World claim," for example, asserts that international trade law as embodied in the GATT and the WTO is adverse to the interests of LDCs.[4] A variant of this complaint is that even if the rules are not unfair per se, the LDCs suffer because the economically developed countries are not playing by the rules.

C. Criticism #III-3—Free Trade's Race to the Bottom[5]

This criticism, like Criticism #III-1 and Criticism #III-2, focuses on the principles and practice of free trade, and not directly on the WTO itself but only indirectly on the WTO as the GEO responsible for administering the regime of liberal trading rules. Under Criticism #III-3, free trade should be rejected because it encourages a "race to the bottom" in the regulatory standards for labor (worker safety and health) and environmental protection.

This "race to the bottom" criticism actually has at least two versions. In one, the "race" is being run by businesses or whole industries that are relocating their manufacturing operations to countries that have especially lax regulations, or no regulations at all, relating to environmental protection or labor standards. For example, a company might easily (according to the

---

[3] For a summary on the use of the terms "less developed country" and "Third World," *see* RAJ BHALA, TRADE, DEVELOPMENT, AND SOCIAL JUSTICE xxix (2003) [hereinafter BHALA-2003]. I adopt his approach in saying that "I use the term 'Third World' *not* in any pejorative sense, but rather in an inclusive manner'." *Id.* Although Professor Bhala, a dear colleague and friend of mine here at the University of Kansas, prefers not to use the shorthand abbreviation "LDC" because it might be used to mean either "less developed country" or "least developed country," I choose to use the abbreviation throughout this book for its brevity, with two important notes: (1) I use it to mean "less developed country," which I think is by far the more common meaning ascribed to it (and for purposes of this book the distinction between less and least developed countries is of little consequence); (2) the term LDC refers only to economic development, and not to cultural or social or political development. Indeed, I regard many LDCs, especially in Asia, to be considerably more mature, sophisticated, and "developed" in many respects than my own homeland.

[4] *Id.* at 3.

[5] For citations to examples in the literature of some criticisms along these lines, *see* Part III of Appendix A.

criticism) be drawn to a "pollution haven" because the company will, in that location, incur little or no expense in treating waste products that would, in a country with adequate environmental standards, require costly treatment or abatement.

In the other version, the "race" is being run by the governments of various countries, especially LDCs, competing with each other in an effort to attract or retain businesses within their borders by applying extremely lax environmental standards or labor standards. In either version of the criticism, free trade is ultimately to blame for two complementary evils: the relocation of the industries, which results in job losses (in at least one country) and the encouragement of practices that bring injury to the environment the relocated industries foul or to the workers they employ.

D. Criticism #III-4—WTO Disregard for Labor and Environmental Values[6]

This criticism focuses on the WTO itself, alleging that even if free trade does not in itself cause a race to the bottom in environmental protection and labor standards (as claimed in Criticism #III-3), the WTO fails to give adequate attention to these matters in its operations. This criticism has generated a great deal of commentary, perhaps more than any other. Two powerful magnets for anti-WTO environmental advocates have been the *Shrimp-Turtle* and *Tuna-Dolphin* cases.[7] In the *Tuna-Dolphin* case, a GATT dispute panel found that the United States had acted contrary to its GATT obligations in banning the importation of tuna caught with purse seine nets in a manner that would kill many dolphins. In the *Shrimp-Turtle* case, a WTO dispute body likewise found a GATT violation in the U.S. embargo of shrimp imports from countries that fail to require the use of turtle exclusion devices and that therefore allow fishing methods that endanger sea turtles.[8]

---

[6] For citations to examples in the literature of some criticisms along these lines, *see* Part III of Appendix A.

[7] These cases, decided by GATT and WTO dispute panels, are described in many articles. *See, e.g.,* David M. Driesen, *What is Free Trade?: The Real Issue Lurking Behind the Trade and Environment Debate,* 41 VA. J. INT'L L. 279 (2001). *See also* Carol J. Miller & Jennifer L. Croston, *WTO Scrutiny v. Environmental Objectives: Inception of the International Dolphin Conservation Program Act* (1999) (unpublished article, on file with author). An older but insightful treatment of the *Tuna-Dolphin* case appears in Steve Charnovitz, *GATT and the Environment: Examining the Issues,* appearing as Chapter 5 in STEVE CHARNOVITZ, TRADE LAW AND GLOBAL GOVERNANCE (2002). The *Tuna-Dolphin* case emerged from a complaint lodged by Mexico. The *Shrimp-Turtle* case emerged from a complaint lodged by India, Malaysia, the Philippines, and Thailand.

[8] For extensive excerpts from, and an explanation of, these cases, *see* RAJ BHALA, INTERNATIONAL TRADE LAW: THEORY AND PRACTICE 1591–1664 (2d ed. 2001) [hereinafter BHALA-2001].

According to Criticism #III-4, such findings are inappropriate because they encourage behavior that recklessly kills other mammals and because they interfere with the sovereign right of states to adopt what I would term "externally directed" environmental protection standards—that is, standards that apply outside a country by prohibiting importation of items falling short of those standards.

Criticism #III-4 would apply to labor standards and human rights standards in roughly the same manner as it applies to environmental issues: a state should be free (according to the proponents of this criticism) to prohibit the importation of goods produced by slave labor or, more generally, to require that items imported into its territory meet certain minimum human rights standards. For the WTO to interfere with such state regulations, the critics say, both (1) violates the principles of state sovereignty[9] and (2) encourages behavior that is inconsistent with generally accepted human rights.

Criticism #III-4 has special resonance where the behavior that states purport to regulate by such "externally directed" measures (that is, restrictions on imports) is itself prohibited or discouraged by treaty law. For example, the 1982 Convention on the Law of the Sea,[10] which has been ratified by most of the international community,[11] includes extensive provisions aimed at protecting marine mammals.[12] Moreover, Criticism #III-4 draws support from the GATT itself: As explained in the "nutshell" account of the WTO that I offered in Subsection IVB of Chapter Two, GATT Article XX(b) expressly permits trade restrictions that are "necessary to protect human, animal or plant life or health," and GATT Article XX(g) permits, in specified circumstances, trade restrictions "relating to the conservation of exhaustible natural resources."[13]

---

[9] Although I have identified "trampling of national sovereignty" as a separate criticism directed both against the IMF and the MDBs (*see supra* Chapters Three and Four, respectively), I have not identified it as a separate criticism directed against the WTO. I explain the reason for this different treatment in my assessment of Criticism #III-4. *See supra* Subsection IIIB of this chapter.

[10] U.N. Convention on the Law of the Sea, done Dec. 10, 1982, at Montego Bay (entered into force Nov. 16, 1994), U.N. Doc. A/CONF.62/122, 21 I.L.M. 1261 [hereinafter CLOS].

[11] *See* http:www.un.org/Depts/los/reference_files/chronological_lists_of_ratifications.htm (indicating that 148 states had, as of Feb. 1, 2005, ratified the CLOS).

[12] *See, e.g.*, CLOS, *supra* note 10, arts. 65, 117–120, 145, 237.

[13] General Agreement on Tariffs and Trade, done at Geneva, Oct. 30, 1947, 55 U.N.T.S. 187, 61 Stat. A11, T.I.A.S. No. 1700 (entered into force provisionally Jan. 1, 1948 under the 1947 Protocol of Provisional Application, 55 U.N.T.S. 308, 61 Stat. A 2051), art. XX. The pertinent provisions, together with the *chapeau* (introductory passage) read as follows:

E. Criticism #III-5—WTO Secrecy and Opaqueness[14]

This criticism is virtually the same as Criticism #I-4 and Criticism #II-8 leveled at the IMF and the MDBs, respectively. It alleges that the WTO is a closed, non-transparent organization that operates in secret, inappropriately hidden from scrutiny and hence insulated from external criticism, and the advocates of this criticism portray the WTO as a faceless bureaucracy that holds secret meetings for clandestine purposes and decides trade cases behind closed doors. It needs no further explanation here. I offer my assessment of this criticism in Subsection IIIC of this chapter. As indicated there, although I believe the WTO has made impressive strides to improve its transparency, I nevertheless endorse the criticism generally and believe that a variety of efforts should be undertaken to respond to it.

F. Criticism #III-6—The WTO Democracy Deficit[15]

According to this criticism, the WTO is undemocratic, both (1) in excluding participation by citizens and (2) in having no allegiance to political authorities—and hence can impose its will arbitrarily on its member countries. The corresponding criticisms, as leveled against the IMF and the MDBs, are Criticism #I-5 and Criticism #II-9, respectively.

This criticism as directed at the WTO, however, is somewhat different from the ones directed at the IMF and the MDBs, perhaps because of the different organizational structure and voting system at work in the WTO. Reflecting the weighted voting system by which the IMF and the MDBs are governed, the "democracy deficit" criticisms against those institutions complain generally that they are controlled by a handful of rich countries (and,

---

Subject to the requirement that such measures are not applied in a manner which would constitute a means of arbitrary or unjustifiable discrimination between countries where the same conditions prevail, or a disguised restriction on international trade, nothing in this Agreement shall be construed to prevent the adoption or enforcement by any contracting party of measures:

. . .

(b) necessary to protect human, animal or plant life or health;

. . .

(g) relating to the conservation of exhaustible natural resources if such measures are made effective in conjunction with restriction on domestic production or consumption.

[14] For citations to examples in the literature of some criticisms along these lines, *see* Part III of Appendix A.

[15] For citations to examples in the literature of some criticisms along these lines, *see* Part III of Appendix A.

in the case of the MDBs, corporate interests) and are largely unaccountable to the people most affected by their operations. In the case of the WTO, the "democracy deficit" criticism typically conveys a different impression—not that the institution is in the pocket of a few rich countries but instead that it is politically untethered, able to visit whatever mischief it wishes to on its member countries, especially those that want to protect against job losses, environmental degradation, unethical labor practices, and so forth. According to the criticism, this institutional independence allows the WTO to ignore the involvement of NGOs and other representatives of civil society as well as the political authorities of its member states.

II. CRITICISMS I LARGELY DISMISS

Having summarized above the six key criticisms directed at the WTO, I explain in the following paragraphs why I largely dismiss two of those criticisms. These are Criticism #III-1 (free trade's fostering of economic harm) and Criticism #III-3 (free trade's race to the bottom).

A. Criticism #III-1—Free Trade's Fostering of Economic Harm

As I summarized it above, this criticism asserts that the WTO's central aim is wrong, because free trade does more economic harm than good to a national society and to the world as a whole. I reject this assertion. I am not trained as an economist, but it seems to me almost inescapably true that reducing barriers to the trading of goods among countries brings, over the long haul, an aggregate benefit to each country involved, because the lower prices that trade liberalization yields for all consumers (including domestic producers who import components) outweigh the costs imposed in the form of some lost jobs.[16]

I am not alone, of course, in rejecting the assertion that trade liberalization does more economic harm than good overall. Many studies, conducted from various perspectives and published by sources that seem trustworthy, establish that societies gain economically, in aggregate, from trade liberalization[17]—and, moreover, that this aggregate economic gain

---

[16] For a more complete, and surely more elegant, explanation of these points, *see generally* Chapter 2 of KENT JONES, WHO'S AFRAID OF THE WTO? (2004). His summation on the proposition that "Trade is Good" and that a global treaty regime facilitating trade liberalization helps neutralize special-interest political pressures that otherwise would tempt states toward protectionism, appears in the last three pages of that chapter. *See id.* at 45–47.

[17] For summaries of such studies, and the conclusions emerging from them, *see* David Dollar & Aart Kraay, *Trade Growth, and Poverty*, FINANCE & DEVELOPMENT, Sept. 2001, at 16–19 (noting that countries adopting more liberal trade policies have seen increased growth); *Profits Over People*, THE ECONOMIST, Sept. 29, 2001, in "Globalization and Its Critics: A Survey of Globalization," at 5 [hereinafter THE ECONOMIST SURVEY] (asserting

occurs even if a society embraces trade liberalization unilaterally (that is, without insisting on reciprocal liberalization of trade policies by other countries).[18] These studies confirm the common sense of Adam Smith's view of comparative advantage: it is wise for the tailor to make his shirt and buy his shoes, and for the cobbler to make his shoes and buy his shirt.[19] In this respect, I think a representative of the Center for Economic and Policy Research, writing recently for the Sierra Club magazine, is simply wrong in positing that "trade [was] originally a means to obtain what could not be produced locally."[20] Instead, trade is and always was a means of obtaining what is cheaper or better to buy than to make. To use one writer's colorful description, it is a means to "elevate the fruits of human leisure over the fruits of human labor."[21]

Having said all that, I would hasten to make four points that are all more or less related to the "economic harm" argument. These points revolve around (1) the need for "authenticity" in comparative advantage, (2) the difference between aggregate gain and individual loss from trade liberalization, (3) the gap that allegedly exists between trade liberalization's benefits to rich countries and its benefits to poor countries, and (4) the special challenges free trade poses for very small states.

---

that globalization "makes some workers worse off while making others (including the poorest ones of all, to begin with) better off" and, in the aggregate, "makes consumers . . . better off as well" so that "given freer trade, both rich-country and poor-country living standards rise," which "gives governments more to spend on welfare, education and other public services"), *available at* http://www.economist.com/surveys/displayStory. cfm?Story_id=795995 (last visited Nov. 10, 2004). *See also* EDWARD M. GRAHAM, FIGHTING THE WRONG ENEMY: ANTIGLOBAL ACTIVISTS AND MULTINATIONAL ENTERPRISES 82 (2000) (responding to the claim that one effect of free trade is to "export" jobs by arguing "that the empirical evidence does *not* support the contention that outward US investment creates or contributes to low wages or . . . to poor working conditions in developing countries" or to "a net loss of job opportunities in the United States or even [to] the destruction of jobs in high-paying industries").

18 *See Who Elected the WTO?, in* THE ECONOMIST SURVEY, *supra* note 17, at 26, 27 (deriding as "an economic fallacy" the view that lowering trade barriers is a concession [and] . . . a sacrifice for which you require compensation"). *See also* Brink Lindsey, *A New Track for U.S. Trade Policy*, CATO INST. (Center for Trade Policy Studies, Washington, D.C.), Sept. 11, 1998, at 1 (suggesting that "[f]ree traders need to take protectionist misconceptions and special interests head-on . . . and launch a campaign for the unilateral elimination of specific U.S. trade barriers"), *available at* http://www.freetrade.org/pubs/ pas/tpa-004es.html (last visited Nov. 10, 2004).

19 *See* Lindsey, *supra* note 18, at 3 (quoting Adam Smith).

20 Mark Weisbrot, *Tricks of Free Trade*, SIERRA, Sept./Oct. 2001, at 64, 64.

21 Jim Chen, *Epiphytic Economics and the Politics of Place*, 10 MINN. J. GLOBAL TRADE 1, 3 (2001).

First, it is important to recognize that trade liberalization yields its benefits in the long term only to the extent that comparative advantage is real and not illusory. Let us use Adam Smith's cobbler-and-tailor illustration of the common sense underlying free trade. What if the cobbler, in order to get the leather he uses in making shoes, is in the practice of stealing the tailor's cattle? If that were the case, it should come as little surprise that the cobbler can supply shoes at an attractive price—but we would surely hesitate to say he has a comparative advantage and that the tailor is better off buying his shoes from the cobbler.

Some critics of the current WTO-led model of trade liberalization point to specific circumstances that resemble the example I have contrived above involving the cattle-rustling cobbler. They claim that many of the costs involved in production of agricultural or manufactured goods are not adequately accounted for and paid for by those companies or countries claiming a comparative advantage in such production.[22] I agree with this claim, especially as it applies to environmental costs. I believe that deep and abiding environmental degradation occurs at alarming rates around the world at the hands of persons who, through stealth or improper influence or both, are able to engage in their rapacious behavior without cost or penalty to them.

However, I do not think this reality undercuts the economic rationale for trade liberalization. Trade flows are certainly distorted by such problems of environmental degradation and other externalities that make for unauthentic comparative advantage, but that does not mean that a liberal trade regime is itself the problem. Instead, action needs to be taken quickly to root out the underlying conditions that permit such problems to exist in the first place. I shall return to this point later in recommending much tougher environmental protections and reforms in national governance.

---

[22] One commentator has expressed it quite clearly:

> The appropriate application of comparative advantage is predicated on efficient transportation and communication, which we have, and a good accounting system which we do not have. At this time calculations of advantage do not include externalities (social costs). For example the U.S. employs the world's most environmentally and socially destructive system of agriculture. If all these costs, such as loss of top soil and mining of aquifers to grow corn in the desert, were incorporated into the cost of product, and if we quit giving out huge subsidies, would we really have a comparative advantage over many third world farmers which have the advantage of family labor inputs? I think not.

Letter from Craig S. Volland, President, Spectrum Technologists of Kansas City, Kansas, to John W. Head (Nov. 29, 2001) (on file with author), at 5.

A second point that is related to, but distinct from, the "economic harm" argument concerns the difference between aggregate economic gain for society as a whole and economic loss for some specific members of the society. This is a point at the heart of Criticism #III-2: it is obviously true that *some* groups of workers within an economic system—textile workers in the United States, for example—will almost surely suffer more than they will benefit from removing protection from (lower priced) imports. Whereas all consumers (including the textile workers themselves) can benefit from the reduced prices of textile products (because of lower tariff barriers or non-tariff barriers on imported textile products), it is naturally only the textile workers who will lose their jobs as textile workers. However, society can and should deal with that distributional problem *as* a distributional problem, not as a grounds for withholding from all consumers the benefits of lower prices. I deal with this distributional point of Criticism #III-2 in Section III of this chapter, along with the other criticisms that I endorse.

A third point that is related to the "economic harm" argument also has a distributional element to it. Some critics of the WTO-led trade liberalization regime claim that economic globalization has increased the income gap between the rich countries and the poor countries of the world. I also address this claim in Section III of this chapter, in endorsing Criticism #III-2.

Lastly, some critics assert that whatever benefits might flow from the liberalization of trade rules in and among large countries, such trade liberalization poses a special challenge to very small countries.[23] I agree. It seems unrealistic to expect trade liberalization initiatives to work in a country that has a tiny population or extraordinarily limited natural resources—and numerous countries meet one or both of these criteria, such as Andorra, Barbados, Bhutan, Cape Verde, Comoros, Dominica, Grenada, Maldives, Malta, Micronesia, Palau, St. Lucia, San Marino, Soloman Island, Tonga, and Vanuatu, to name a few. In such places, free trade might bring overall economic harm, not economic benefit. But the reason trade liberalization initiatives are, in my view, unlikely to work in such small countries is part of a bigger reality: as a more general matter, it seems entirely unrealistic to expect such small countries to have economic and political systems that are viable in a world dominated by countries with populations and economies that are larger by a factor of a hundred or even a thousand. To my mind, then, this aspect of the "economic harm" criticism—that free trade fosters economic harm in very small countries—most appropriately calls into question *not* the merits of free trade itself but instead the merits of treating such very small countries as if they were comparable to the rest of the interna-

---

[23] *See, e.g.*, Jane Kelsey, *World Trade and Small Nations in the South Pacific Region*, 14 KAN. J.L. & PUB. POL'Y 247, 247–48 (2005).

tional community, which for the most part comprises countries that are large enough to permit the development of diversified economic systems. I return to this topic briefly near the end of this book, in Subsection IIB of Chapter Six.

B. Criticism #III-3—Free Trade's Race to the Bottom

As I summarized it above, this criticism can take two forms distinguished from each other by who the runners are in the alleged "race to the bottom." First, the criticism might refer to a "race" by businesses to place their manufacturing operations in "pollution havens"—those countries that impose very light environmental requirements, or none at all. Second, it might refer to a "race" by governments themselves to relax environmental standards, presumably in a competition to attract or retain businesses within their borders.

I find the argument unpersuasive in either form, largely because (1) there seems to be little firm evidence so far that either type of "race" is in fact being run and (2) even if either of these types of "race" is being run, this would not be grounds to condemn trade liberalization as such. I explain both of these points in the following paragraphs.

As for the claim that businesses are racing to place their manufacturing operations in "pollution havens," there seems to be only inconsistent and inconclusive evidence. There are, after all, scores of specific reasons that might prompt a business to shift its operations from one place to another. According to some observers, the cost of environmental compliance is unlikely to be a dispositive reason:

> There is not much evidence, for example, that polluting industries have been migrating from developed to developing countries to take advantage of lax environmental standards. The cost of pollution control is relatively low in developed countries—"no more than 1 per cent of production costs for the average industry"—and besides, because most polluting firms are capital intensive, they tend to cluster in developed countries where capital is readily available.[24]

On the other hand, some observers challenge these assertions. Here is an example of such a challenge:

---

[24] John O. McGinnis & Mark L. Movsesian, *The World Trade Constitution*, 114 HARV. L. REV. 511, 559 (2000). *See also WTO Report: The Need for Environmental Cooperation, available at* http://docsonline/www. wto.org/gen_home.asp?language=1&_=1 (last visited Nov. 10, 2004) (asserting that the comparative advantage of environmental laws is insignificant for most industries). For a similar view, *see* JONES, *supra* note 16, at 115.

[A]verages are meaningless in this context [because] . . . [p]ollution control costs can be crucial for power plants, chemical plants, forestry and mining [which are among the types of operations that cause the most environmental damage]. Furthermore, estimates of pollution costs may not include health and safety factors governed by OSHA in the U.S. and governed by noone [*sic*] in many [less developed countries].[25]

Weighing these two perspectives, I am swayed by two points. First, despite the plausibility of the theory that businesses will "race to the bottom," especially in certain industries, the fact remains that little hard evidence is adduced showing that such a race actually takes place, at least as a general matter. Second, even if there were such a race (among businesses), it would not by itself require a stifling of trade liberalization—a point I shall return to in a few paragraphs, after examining the other type of alleged "race to the bottom," this one between countries.

Here, too, the factual foundation for the claim is uncertain. That is, the claim that countries are racing to relax their environmental standards in an effort to attract or retain pollution-prone manufacturers is the subject of contradictory evidence and analysis. On the one hand, Sierra Club officials suggest that U.S. environmental and health standards have been relaxed in response to free-trade obligations,[26] and other commentators hypothesize that developing countries fail to adopt environmentally friendly standards because they would prove costly for domestic producers,[27] or that "pollution havens" might emerge in some areas of less developed countries in order to attract coal plant construction.[28] Indeed, the

---

[25] Volland, *supra* note 22, at 4.

[26] *See* Margrete Strand, *Poisoned Workers and Poisoned Fields: Stop NAFTA's Fast-Track Expansion to South America*, *available at* http://www.sierraclub.org/trade/environment/poisoned.asp (last visited Nov. 10, 2004) (stating that the U.S. Environmental Protection Agency, in order to help U.S. growers compete with surging imports, "has increased chemical risks to farmworkers by reducing a critical safety factor—the reentry period—the time between when pesticides are sprayed on crops, and when growers can order farmworkers to reenter the fields"). *See also No Globalization Without Representation!*, *available at* http://www.sierraclub.org/trade/summit/fact.asp (last visited Nov. 10, 2004) (asserting, but without offering documentary evidence, that the United States has weakened border food inspections and developed weak standards concerning imported agricultural pests).

[27] *See, e.g.*, Lana Martin, *World Trade Organization and Environmental Protection: Reconciling the Conflict*, CURRENTS: INT'L TRADE L.J., Winter 2000, at 69 (discussing the adequacy of the WTO's environmental policies).

[28] *See* Chris Baltimore, *US Power Deregulation May Cause Trade Woes*, *available at* posting of David Orr, david@livingrivers.net, to CONS-SPST-ENERGY-FORUM@Lists.SIERRACLUB.ORG (Nov. 9, 2001) (on file with the author). That article also refers to a 2001

WTO itself has acknowledged that "[e]nvironmental measures are sometimes defeated because of competitiveness concerns."[29]

On the other hand, some observers find just the opposite trends at work. One source claims that "with respect either to safety or to environmental impact, signs of a race to the bottom are . . . hard to find. All the movement is the other way. Everywhere, the adoption [by governments] of more demanding environmental standards gathers pace as incomes rise."[30] Another asserts that "[t]he clear trend in rich and poor countries alike is for ever tighter regulation" in terms of environmental protection—as well as in terms of labor conditions, a topic often joined with environmental protection in this context—and that "[i]f globalisation has started a race in these areas, it is to the top, not the bottom."[31]

It is worth noting, in this respect, that specific steps have been taken in the context of some trade agreements to prevent governments from running a race to the bottom in an effort to attract investors seeking "pollution havens." Although the NAFTA side agreement on environmental protection—the North American Agreement on Environmental Cooperation (NAAEC)[32]—has attracted criticism as being less rigorous than it should be,[33] there can be no doubt that the side agreement represents a growing appreciation of the importance of environmental protection. That same impulse led to the inclusion of environmental protection provisions in the

---

U.S. Energy Department report "that attributed increased power plant construction in Mexico to less stringent environmental regulations." *Id.* This might be evidence of the first kind of "race to the bottom" referred to above—a move by businesses to place their operations in "pollution havens."

[29] *WTO Report, supra* note 24.

[30] *Who Elected the WTO?, supra* note 18, at 26.

[31] *A Crisis of Legitimacy,* THE ECONOMIST SURVEY, *supra* note 17, at 18, 20. *See also* JONES, *supra* note 16, at 115 (noting that empirical research "tends not to support these claims [of a race to the bottom]"); C. Fred Bergsten, *in Preface* to GRAHAM, *supra* note 17, at xii (asserting that "[w]ith respect to the environment, there is no evidence of any 'race to the bottom' where governments, in order to attract or retain direct investment, lower environmental standards; in some cases, there might even be a 'race to the top'").

[32] North American Agreement on Environmental Cooperation, Sept. 14, 1993, U.S.-Can-Mex., 32 I.L.M. 1480 (1993).

[33] *See, e.g.,* Beatriz Bugeda, *Is NAFTA Up to Its Green Expectations? Effective Law Enforcement Under the North American Agreement on Environmental Cooperation,* 32 U. RICH. L. REV. 1591, 1616 (1999) (criticizing the enforcement mechanism of the NAAEC); Paul Stanton Kibel, *The Paper Tiger Awakens: North American Environmental Law After the Cozumel Reef Case,* 39 COLUM. J. TRANSNAT'L L. 395, 472 (2001) (same). *See also* Chris Dove, Comment, *Can Voluntary Compliance Protect the Environment?: The North American Agreement on Environmental Cooperation,* 50 U. KAN. L. REV. 867, 877–83 (2001) (evaluating the strengths and weaknesses of the NAAEC).

U.S.-Jordan Free Trade Agreement of 2000[34]—as an integral part of the treaty, rather than in the form of a side agreement—and also led to the inclusion of environmental protection as an agenda item at the Doha Round of trade negotiations.[35]

It appears, then, that although more liberal trade (and investment) rules do prompt an increase in production in less developed countries (bringing with it more jobs), it is by no means clear that the other linkages or "races" that some opponents of globalization complain about are in fact real or significant.[36]

But what if they were? What if unimpeachable evidence appeared tomorrow revealing a frantic race to the bottom, in either or both of the forms described above—that is, by businesses seeking "pollution havens" or by countries wanting to attract such business? Should we then put the brakes on trade liberalization by jettisoning the key principles that I summarized earlier in my "nutshell" account of the GATT[37] and by shutting down the WTO?

Of course not. The liberal trade regime established by the GATT and the WTO rests on the proposition that general economic welfare is increased by permitting trade in goods to go forward in ways that reflect the comparative advantages enjoyed by countries or companies. One of the key principles of that liberal trade regime is that if the comparative advantage is artificial—"unauthentic," to use the term I introduced above—then a country can depart from its obligation to refrain from tariff increases or to avoid non-tariff barriers. Hence, our response to a race to the bottom, if one were to occur, should not be to abandon trade liberalization generally

---

[34] Agreement between the United States of America and the Hashemite Kingdom of Jordan or the Establishment of the Free Trade Area, Oct. 24, 2000, U.S.-Jordan, art. 5, *at* http://www.ustr.gov/assets/Trade_Agreements/Bilateral/Jordan/assets_upload_file250_5112.pdf (last visited Nov. 10, 2004). Other recent bilateral trade treaties between the United States and other countries—including those with Morocco, Australia, and Bahrain—have likewise included environmental protection provisions.

[35] *See* WTO Ministerial Declaration, WT/MIN(01)/DEC.01 (Nov. 20, 2001) ("Doha Declaration"), ¶¶ 31–33, *at* http://www.wto/org (recognizing the importance of environmental protection in developing trade) (last visited Nov. 10, 2004).

[36] On the related issue of labor standards, the Chair of the AFL-CIO International Affairs Committee offers no support for a claim of a "race to the bottom"—either in the sense of companies racing to LDCs or in the sense of LDCs racing to lower their labor standards. *See* Jay Mazur, *Labor's New Internationalism*, 79 FOREIGN AFF. 79, 88–90 (Jan.–Feb. 2000).

[37] *See supra* Section IVB of Chapter Two (explaining the most-favored-nation treatment principle, the national-treatment principle, the bound-duty-rate principle, and the anti-NTB principle).

but should instead be to pay more attention to that element of the liberal trade regime. As I explain more fully below in offering several specific recommendations, I believe our aim should be to eliminate free externalities (that is, to eliminate the possibility of businesses using public resources in their operations without paying for those resources) by strengthening multilateral environmental regulations and their enforcement.

III. CRITICISMS I GENERALLY ENDORSE

The two criticisms that I have assessed above—Criticisms #III-1 and #III-3—appear unpersuasive in most respects, although I have identified some elements of those criticisms that I believe do make some sense and should be taken seriously. Just the opposite is true of the remaining four criticisms leveled at the WTO. That is, I find these other four criticisms generally persuasive, although there are some elements to most of them that do not hold water on closer inspection. I offer my views below on all four of them: Criticism #II-2 (free trade's distributional injustice), Criticism #II-4 (disregard for labor and environmental values), Criticism #II-5 (secrecy and opaqueness), and Criticism #II-6 (democracy deficit).

A. Criticism #III-2—Free Trade's Distributional Injustice

It should come as no surprise that although an economic system as a whole benefits from trade liberalization, not every individual benefits from trade liberalization. There are both winners and losers. As noted above in Subsection IIA of this chapter, perhaps the most obvious losers are those whose jobs disappear because they were producing goods or services that, due to a comparative advantage enjoyed by another country, are cheaper to import than to make domestically.

Viewing the "winners-and-losers" equation emerging from globalization generally (that is, not focusing specifically on trade liberalization), one economics expert describes the situation like this:

> The reality is that globalization makes the world a richer place, but the wealth it creates goes disproportionately to two sorts of people. On one side are those who benefit from vastly improved access to technology and capital—which is to say, workers in developing countries. On the other are those in advanced countries who, directly or indirectly, have technology and capital to sell—which means the rich and the highly educated. Largely left out of the party, possibly even made worse off, are those who fall into neither category.[38]

---

[38] Paul Krugman, *Reckonings: The Magic Mountain*, N.Y. TIMES, Jan. 23, 2000, at 15, quoted and cited in Ewell E. Murphy, Jr., *The Lessons of Seattle: Learning from the Failed Third WTO Ministerial Conference*, 13 TRANSNAT'L LAW. 273, 286–87 (2000).

When the type of globalization at issue is trade liberalization, of course, another category of persons—so wide as to encompass nearly everyone in an economically advanced society such as the United States or Europe—also benefits: consumers. They enjoy lower prices charged on imported goods that trade liberalization welcomes into the economy. However, these lower prices on imported goods will be only faint consolation to someone who loses his or her job as a result of trade liberalization.

What, if anything, should be done about such persons—that is, those who are the losers from trade liberalization? Many people agree that the winners should share some of their winnings with the losers. One authority on international economic matters writes:

> [G]lobalization brings substantial net benefits to the American economy, . . . [but leaders] must acknowledge that globalization causes job and income losses in certain sectors, which exact significant psychological tolls. The government, therefore, has a responsibility to channel help from the winners to the losers, for humanitarian and equity reasons as well as to maintain political support for continued globalization efforts.[39]

To fulfill that obligation, the same author continues, a country "must adopt stronger safety nets, including more generous unemployment insurance eligibility and compensation levels" and other initiatives, and it must "provide better education and training programs."[40] We have tried that in the United States, with the Trade Adjustment Assistance (TAA) program that has been in existence for many years. The TAA program provides three types of financial assistance—to pay retraining expenses, job-hunting expenses, and relocation expenses—for workers who, because of import competition, lose their jobs.[41]

Unfortunately, the TAA program has never been successful.[42] It has suffered through the years from inadequate funding, which itself reflects a

---

[39] C. Fred Bergsten, *America's Two-Front Economic Conflict*, 80 FOREIGN. AFF., at 16, 26 (Mar.–Apr. 2001).

[40] *Id.* at 27. *See also* Murphy, *supra* note 38, at 287 (suggesting that "every nation must find practical ways to alleviate the insecurity of its citizens, as by providing better education, more effective job retraining and employment compensation, and health and pension coverage that employees can take from job to job").

[41] *See* 19 U.S.C. §§ 2271–2298 (codification of §§ 221–238 of the Trade Act of 1974 as amended). A similar program of financial assistance applies to workers who lose their jobs because of NAFTA. *See* 19 U.S.C. § 2331 (2000) (codifying § 250 of the Trade Act of 1974 as amended).

[42] *See, e.g.*, BHALA-2001, *supra* note 8, at 1582 (concluding that "the TAA programs have little positive impact in helping the workers and firms that lose from free trade").

lack of political support. More effective initiatives are needed. I offer some suggestions in this regard in Section IV of this chapter.

As I described it in the introductory section of this chapter, Criticism #III-2 applies not only at a national level (which is the topic of the preceding few paragraphs) but also at the global level. That is, it claims that even if free trade can be shown to bring aggregate economic benefits that exceed its costs, those benefits are not fairly distributed, either within a national economic system or among nations. For example, some critics of the WTO-led trade liberalization regime claim that economic globalization has increased the income gap between the rich countries and the poor countries of the world. They point out, for example, that "[b]y [19]93 an American [who was getting by] on the average income of the poorest 10% of the [U.S.] population was better off than two thirds of the world's people,"[43] and they note that economic growth slowed more in the past few decades for poorer countries than it did for richer countries.[44] Some such critics also emphasize that the gap between rich and poor overall in the world has increased—a fact highlighted by the 1999 U.N. Human Development Report and bemoaned by several commentators.[45]

Although these facts have led some critics to condemn economic globalism, and trade liberalization in particular,[46] I am reluctant to jump to this conclusion. There is, I think, more to the story. Some studies emphasize that the aggregate gain emerging from trade liberalization does indeed help the poor, not just the rich.[47] Some of the studies even indicate that,

---

[43] Robert Wade, *Global Inequality: Winners and Losers*, THE ECONOMIST, Apr. 28, 2001, at 72, 73.

[44] *See* CENTER FOR ECONOMIC AND POLICY RESEARCH, DIMINISHED ECONOMIC PROGRESS UNDER GLOBALIZATION (undated) (on file with author).

[45] *See, e.g.,* James W. Thomson, *Globalization: Its Defenders and Dissenters*, 106 BUS. & SOC'Y REV. 170, 176 (2001) (citing the U.N. Human Development Report for the proposition that "relative income inequality between nations has increased sharply since 1960").

[46] *See, e.g.,* Fareed Zakaria, *Some Real Street Smarts*, NEWSWEEK, July 30, 2001, at 25, 25.

[47] *See Grinding the Poor*, THE ECONOMIST SURVEY, *supra* note 17, at 10, 10–13 (disputing the view that globalization especially hurts poor workers in developing countries). Specifically, "the evidence suggests that multinational[] [corporations] . . . pay a wage premium" in low-income countries that amounts to about two times the wage paid by domestic employers in those countries. *Id.* at 13. "Separate studies on Mexico, Venezuela, China, and Indonesia have all found that foreign investors pay their local workers significantly better than other local employers." *Id.* As another commentator has observed, however, wage levels alone do not give a full picture of the economic well-being of the workers who earn them, since wages "do not account for a long list of losses that have been documented in several setting," such as "unhealthful working conditions, restrictions on personal freedom, loss of land and other assets in rural villages, damages from crime and violence (particularly to young women), disruption of families from sweatshops that employ only young women, lack of municipal infrastructure" and other

if measured correctly, "the growth benefits of increased trade are, on average, widely shared" and that those countries that have "globalized" in the last decade or so have experienced both a decline in poverty *and* a narrowing of the gap between rich and poor.[48] This suggests that even if the gap between rich and poor overall in the world has increased, the *reason* for that widening gap is not globalization but instead a failure of some countries to globalize.[49]

I wish to pursue this point one step further. Even if it were shown (contrary to the evidence I have just referred to) that trade liberalization does, in fact, contribute to a widening of the gap between rich and poor, is that a good reason to mount a broadside attack on trade liberalization? In my view, the answer should depend largely on whether the incomes of the poor—or the levels of their economic well-being generally—are rising or falling. There seems to be little question that even if the overall gap between rich and poor is widening, the economic circumstances of the poor are, in fact, improving, in that absolute poverty generally is on the decline, at least in countries that have globalized.[50] If this were not the case—that is, if economic conditions in poor countries were worsening, not improving, as a result of trade liberalization—then I would argue for quick and drastic action to stifle trade liberalization, because I believe one of the single most important challenges in today's world is to attack poverty. However, as long as trade liberalization improves economic conditions in poor countries, I would be loathe to stifle it merely out of a concern that trade liberalization is improving economic conditions faster in the rich countries. Instead, I would (and do) support continued trade liberalization but at the same time seek to understand why its benefits flow more to the already-rich countries and whether some of that differential is undeserved or unjust.

---

factors. Volland, *supra* note 22, at 5. Many problems such as these, however, do not originate with trade or investment liberalization and will not be solved or eased by stifling trade or investment liberalization.

[48] *See* Dollar & Kraay, *supra* note 17, at 17–18. These observers assert that "globalizers are narrowing the per capita income gap. Moreover, because most of the globalizers—especially China, India, and Bangladesh—were among the poorest countries in the world twenty years ago, their growth has been a force for narrowing worldwide inequality." *Id.* For another recent work on this issue, *see generally* MARTIN WOLF, WHY GLOBALIZATION WORKS (2004) (noting that globalization generally has reduced inequality and the incidence of poverty).

[49] *See* Dollar & Kraay, *supra* note 17, at 18 (stating that "[t]he real losers from globalization are those countries that have not been able to seize the opportunities to participate in this process").

[50] *See id. See also* Zakaria, *supra* note 46, at 25.

Maybe the answer lies in the rules themselves. That is, if the benefits of free trade flow more to rich countries than to LDCs, perhaps that disparity comes from the particular way the GATT-WTO rules governing trade liberalization have been established. As I explained in Section I of this chapter, where I summarized Criticism #III-2, one of the most common formulations of that criticism is what Raj Bhala has called the "anti-Third World claim"—that the rules of GATT-WTO law are adverse to the interests of LDCs.[51]

Professor Bhala has given close attention to this claim. In his masterful *Trade, Development, and Social Justice*, he examines the provisions in GATT-WTO law referred to as special and differential treatment rules—that is, those provisions expressly written into the GATT over time to benefit the Third World, such as by granting preferentially low tariff levels on goods sold from LDCs into developed countries and by providing longer periods of time for LDCs to achieve certain standards or targets regarding trade liberalization. As he explains, "[i]f the 'anti-Third World claim' has traction, then surely its traction comes from the poor design of these [special and differential treatment] rules, the failure of these rules to do their job, or both."[52] Professor Bhala analyzes those issues from several perspectives and concludes that "the claim that international trade law, specifically [that portion of international trade law found in] special and differential treatment [rules], is 'unjust' in the way it treats the Third World[,] is exaggerated" but that those preferential rules "could be more generous than they are now in GATT-WTO law."[53] Indeed, he identifies three improvements that would make them more generous: rules to enhance legal capacity among LDCs to understand and work with GATT-WTO law; a rule to eliminate conditionality on the grant of preferences to LDCs; and a rule to fund export diversification projects in LDCs. I explain and endorse these proposals in Section IV of this chapter.

Before concluding an assessment of Criticism #III-2, let me offer one additional perspective on it. I have explored above two main variants of Criticism #III-2 when applied at the global level: (1) that trade liberalization by nature (allegedly) contributes to the gap between rich and poor countries; and (2) that while trade liberalization itself may be unobjectionable from the perspective of distributional justice, the particular rules built into the WTO regime are in fact (allegedly) objectionable because they fail to deliver promised benefits to the LDCs. A third variant of Criticism #III-2 (applied still at the global level) would be that distribu-

---

[51] *See supra* note 3 and accompanying text.

[52] BHALA-2003, *supra* note 3, at 3.

[53] *Id.* at 4, 5.

tional injustice lies not in trade liberalization per se or in the WTO rules but rather in the fact that the rich and powerful countries do not play by the rules. This perspective appears in some well-written Oxfam International materials, including one paper in particular that decries "[h]ypocrisy and double standards [that allegedly] characterise the behaviour of industrialised countries towards poorer countries in world trade."[54] That paper claims that the rich countries have pursued highly protectionist policies, including high tariff barriers against imports from LDCs, high government subsidies on agricultural goods, and continued restrictions on trade in textiles and garments.[55]

In my view, some such complaints are well-founded and well-documented. Indeed, the proposition that U.S. cotton subsidies violated this country's GATT obligations was confirmed by a 2004 WTO dispute settlement panel decision.[56] Viewed more broadly, that panel ruling "confirms many of the criticisms developing countries have made in recent years: that industrialized countries have not fulfilled their commitments to open their agriculture markets and reduce the farm subsidies that distort trade."[57]

In my view, the economically developed countries should be most fastidious—not sloppy, not nonchalant, not playing fast-and-loose—about ensuring that their own policies and actions are consistent with the international trade rules that those countries themselves have been most instrumental in establishing and in urging LDCs to adopt and follow. In Section IV of this chapter I identify some specific recommendations along these lines.

B. Criticism #III-4—WTO Disregard for Labor and Environmental Values

As I summarized it above, this criticism asserts that the WTO fails to give adequate attention to environmental protection and labor standards. I also noted above what a strong negative reaction the decisions in the *Shrimp-Turtle* and *Tuna-Dolphin* cases triggered against the GATT-WTO system.[58]

---

[54] Oxfam International, *Eight Broken Promises: Why The WTO Isn't Working for the World's Poor* at front cover (Oxfam Briefing Paper No. 9, 2001), *available at* http://www.oxfam.org.uk/what_we_do/issues/trade/bp09_8broken.htm.

[55] *Id.* at 1.

[56] WTO Report of the Panel, United States Subsidies on Upland Cotton, WT/DS267/R (Sept. 8, 2004).

[57] Oxfam International, *Finding the Moral Fiber*, at 3 (Oxfam Briefing Paper No. 69, October 2004), *available at* http://www.oxfam.org.uk/what_we_do/issues/trade/bp69.cotton_htm. For details on the WTO panel decision and its wider implications, *see id.* at 27–28. *See also* Kevin Kennedy, *The Incoherence of Agricultural Trade, and Development Policy for Sub-Saharan Africa: Sowing the Seeds of False Hope for Sub-Saharan Africa's Cotton Farmers?*, 14 KAN. J.L. & PUB. POL'Y 307, 307 (2005).

[58] *See supra* Subsection ID of this chapter.

I likewise have a negative reaction to those decisions. While recognizing that the decisions themselves have attracted support on some reasonable grounds,[59] I believe they were decided incorrectly and that environmental protections should play a central role in trade policy. The first of these assertions—that the cases were decided incorrectly—turns on a fundamental point: the definition or concept of free trade. In examining this issue, David Driesen has identified three possible alternative concepts of free trade: "a concept based on the principle of non-discrimination, a concept based on an international non-coercion principle, and a concept based on a principle of laissez-faire government."[60] After demonstrating that the pertinent literature, even going back to Adam Smith and David Ricardo, offers little clear guidance on just what "free trade" means, Driesen explains the three competing concepts. Under the first—the non-discrimination concept—free trade amounts to a prohibition on any government regulations of imports that discriminate against such imports, with "discrimination" defined as "imposition of a standard or restriction on imports that one does not impose upon one's nationals."[61] Under the second—the non-coercion concept—free trade amounts to a prohibition on government regulations that attempt to coerce other countries into adopting a particular policy or practice.[62] Under the third—the laissez-faire concept—free trade means trade unencumbered by national laws that might increase prices.[63]

Driesen asserts that his three-part conceptual analysis "facilitates inquiry into which principles actually explain the decisions" in the cases mentioned above, and in other health and safety cases, "and why laissez-faire and non-coercion principles appear more troubling than facial anti-discrimination principles"[64] (that is, principles prohibiting trade practices that are discriminatory on their face). Driesen favors "focus[ing] exclusively upon free trade as trade free of discrimination" even though this would "entail some reduction in the scope of international trade law"[65] because it would per-

---

[59] *See, e.g.*, McGinnis & Movsesian, *supra* note 24, at 590–93 (asserting that the *Shrimp-Turtle* decision construed GATT provisions in ways that reflect a Madisonian view of promoting accountable government, as well as transparency).

[60] Driesen, *supra* note 7, at 285.

[61] *Id.* at 293.

[62] *Id.* at 307. Theoretical support for a non-coercion principle "comes not from economic theory, but from theories of international relations." *Id.*

[63] *Id.* at 293. Under this concept, trade would be "free of burdens." *Id.* at 291.

[64] *Id.* at 341.

[65] *Id.* at 344.

mit certain types of import regulations—such as those in the *Tuna-Dolphin* and *Shrimp-Turtle* cases—so long as they did not involve discrimination.[66]

I believe the same concept of "free trade" should be at work in cases involving labor standards, and human rights standards more generally. Under this approach, for example, it would be GATT-legal for the United States to prohibit the importation of goods that did not meet certain minimum labor standards, as long as the prohibition did not discriminate against the imported goods by imposing the minimum labor standards on the production of the imported goods but not on the production of U.S.-produced goods. And such a (non-discriminatory) prohibition could not be struck down merely because it amounted, in effect, to coercion of other countries to adopt the specified minimum labor standards or somehow ran afoul of a broad "laissez-faire" concept of free trade.

I would go further than this. Not only should more leeway be provided to national governments to implement (without discrimination) environmental protections and human rights protections in as aggressive (that is, as protective) a manner as they see fit; in addition, the relationship between GATT rules and environmental treaties and human rights treaties should be strengthened. As with the *Shrimp-Turtle* and *Tuna-Dolphin* decisions described above, this is a controversial topic. On balance, however, I believe the long-term importance of promoting environmental sustainability and human rights protections must outweigh the more immediate economic advantages of trade—or, more precisely, the long-term benefits of providing protections for the environment, for labor rights, and for human rights more generally (and the long-term costs of denying those protections) must be included in the cost-benefit calculation of trade liberalization.

In short, the substantive protections and the procedural requirements set forth in multilateral environmental and labor treaties (and certain other human rights treaties) should take precedence over GATT substantive protections and procedural requirements,[67] if and when inconsistencies arise. A first step in this direction, of course, is to strengthen the enforceability, and to broaden the acceptance, of the pertinent environ-

---

[66] For Driesen's further explanation of what "discrimination" means in this context, *see id.* at 345–52. For another discussion of issues of non-discrimination in the *Shrimp-Turtle* case, *see* GRAHAM, *supra* note 17, at 132.

[67] For an examination of this idea, and its application to other areas beyond environmental protection, *see* Marco C.E.J. Bronckers, *More Power to the WTO?*, 4 J. INT'L ECON. L. 41, 57–65 (2001). A similar idea is to "build[] labor rights, environmental protection, and social standards into trade accords." *See* Mazur, *supra* note 36, at 79 (2000). However, I question whether the actual protections themselves should appear as substantive provisions of the trade treaties. Instead, they would better be developed—as they have been up to now—in separate instruments.

mental and human rights treaties themselves.[68] Although there is a fairly extensive set of such treaties already, many of them lack effective enforcement mechanisms, and some countries—most notably the United States—have so far not seen fit to enter into several of them. Moreover, there is little indication among developing countries that further advances either in human rights or in environmental protection will be welcome or forthcoming. As for human rights, the Clinton administration's support for the Child Labor convention in December 1999 (in the midst of demonstrations calling, among other things, for better protection of workers' rights), and his call for an eventual linkage between trade sanctions and core labor rights, received a cool reception not only among developing countries but also from the European Union.[69] More worrisome yet were the comments in 1997 by Mahathir bin Mohamad, then Prime Minister of Malaysia, when he urged the United Nations to mark the 50th anniversary of the Universal Declaration of Human Rights by revising or, better, repealing it because its human rights norms focus excessively on individual rights while neglecting the rights of society and the common good.[70]

Notwithstanding these forces of resistance, I believe a stronger link should be put in place between the legal obligations relating to trade liberalization, environmental protection, and human rights.[71] In Section IV

---

[68] Amendments to some Uruguay Round trade treaties might also be needed. For a proposal that the Agreement on the Application of Sanitary and Phytosanitary Measures be "revised to more carefully articulate what the precautionary principle is" in order to address the dispute that has raged in recent years over genetically modified organism (GMOs), *see* Kevin C. Kennedy, *Implications for Global Governance: Why Multilateralism Matters in Resolving Trade-Environment Disputes*, 7 WID. L. SYMP J. 31, 62 (2001).

[69] *See* Robert Collier, *Labor Rift Widens at WTO Summit: Some Diplomats Protest Pact to Protect Children*, S.F. CHRON., Dec. 3, 1999, at A-1 (describing reaction of developing countries to President Clinton's signing of the Child Labor treaty); Murphy, *supra* note 38, at 285 (noting that the proposed linkage between trade sanctions and labor rights "enraged many of the WTO members, especially the less-developed nations"). *See also* Thomson, *supra* note 45, at 178 (explaining that "[t]he Clinton administration . . . frequently attempted to manage globalization by imposing demanding labor and environmental standards on other nations during global trade sessions . . . [and usually] the reaction from many of these nations has been immediate and rancorous"). *See also* Mark Clough, *Prospects for a New WTO Round*, 29 INT'L BUS. LAW. 146, 147 (2001) (noting that at the Seattle meeting the United States wanted "to work within the WTO on labour standards, whereas the EU and its allies strongly opposed labour rights in the WTO").

[70] *See* Thomas M. Frank, *Are Human Rights Universal?*, 80 FOREIGN AFF. 191, 196 (Jan.–Feb. 2001).

[71] It is noteworthy that a legal basis for a linkage between trade liberalization and environmental protection already exists in the WTO charter itself, which opens with an explicit recognition that improving economic conditions through trade liberalization should be achieved "while allowing for the optimal use of the world's resources in accordance with the objective of sustainable development, seeking both to protect and preserve the environment and to enhance the means for doing so." WTO Charter, at

of this chapter I offer details; they closely resemble the suggestions I have made in Chapters Three and Four to impose treaty-based membership and performance requirements on IMF and MDB member countries.

Before leaving the subject of labor and environmental complaints leveled against the WTO, it is worth pausing briefly to consider some related criticisms directed at the WTO that also involve issues of state sovereignty or social and cultural values. Critics of the *Shrimp-Turtle* and *Tuna-Dolphin* decisions, and of the WTO more generally, sometimes concentrate on state sovereignty; typically, their logic is that WTO efforts to prohibit a state from enforcing tough environmental protection laws constitute an infringement of the sovereignty of that state. This is a similar claim, of course, to Criticisms #I-3 and #II-5 discussed above—that the IMF and the MDBs, respectively, trample on the sovereignty of their members, or at least those members that borrow from them. I largely dismissed those criticisms for reasons explained in Subsection IIB of Chapter Three and Subsection IID of Chapter Four, respectively. In the context of the WTO, the suggestion that WTO actions trample state sovereignty holds even less water—so little, in fact, that I have not even treated it as a separate criticism.

The reason for this different treatment, and for my summary dismissal of the claim that the WTO infringes on state sovereignty, should be obvious if we reflect on the character of the norms whose enforcement against a state is at issue. In the case of the IMF and the MDBs, the "trampling of state sovereignty" complaint flows directly from the conditionality that attaches to IMF or MDB loans. That conditionality, critics claim, requires governments to adopt economic and financial policies (and, increasingly, other types of policies as well) that the governments do not wish to adopt. However, the WTO imposes no conditions on lending, because it does not engage in lending. The only policies that the WTO might be said to be enforcing (that is, urging its members to follow) are the very policies that the members have expressly accepted upon joining the WTO.[72] These

---

preamble. Likewise, the Ministerial Decision on Trade and Environment issued at the conclusion of the Uruguay Round reiterates the views expressed in that clause of the Preamble by noting that "there should not be, nor need [there] be, any policy contradiction between upholding and safeguarding an open, non-discriminatory and equitable multilateral trading system on the one hand, and acting for the protection of the environment, and the promotion of sustainable development on the other." Decision on Trade and Environment, adopted by Ministers on April 15, 1994, as cited in Kennedy, *supra* note 68, at 37 n.23.

[72] In responding to the claim that the WTO dictates to its member governments, a WTO pamphlet points out that "the rules of the WTO system are agreements resulting from negotiations among member governments," that "the rules are ratified by members' parliaments," and that "[t]he only occasion when a WTO body can have a direct impact on a government's policies is when a dispute is brought to the WTO and if that

include the four key principles of the GATT, the exceptions thereto, and the provisions of the various other Uruguay Round agreements. It hardly makes sense to claim that the WTO interferes with state sovereignty when it presses members to live up to obligations they have expressly accepted by way of treaty commitments.[73]

Lastly, some critics of the WTO emphasize the importance of social and cultural values. For example, some critics condemn the WTO—or, perhaps more precisely, the free trade ideology it promotes by applying the trade treaties under its administration—on grounds that the institution and the ideology bring serious non-economic harm to many societies by emasculating existing cultures and replacing them with a homogenized non-culture or with a repugnant foreign culture revolving around Western-style commercialization and consumerism. Related to this criticism, or perhaps a subsidiary of it, is the claim that free trade undercuts agrarian values in the United States.

Neither of these criticisms, in my estimation, warrants serious consideration. For one thing, I find both of them indefensible as a factual matter. Even a severe choking down of international trade would not halt cultural change; that would instead require a clampdown on the flow of information—a clampdown that itself would probably be a violation of the right of free access to information under human rights treaties accepted very broadly in the international community. As for the second (subsidiary) criticism about agrarian values, I find that point questionable also as a matter of values: even if the survival of so-called agrarian values in the United States could be assured by protecting U.S. agricultural production against competition from other countries, it seems to me deeply inappropriate to

---

leads to a ruling by the Dispute Settlement Body," in which case the ruling "is simply a judgment of whether a government has broken one of the WTO's agreements—agreements that the infringing government had itself accepted." WORLD TRADE ORGANIZATION, 10 COMMON MISUNDERSTANDINGS ABOUT THE WTO 2 (2003).

[73] Kent Jones has expressed it well:

The perceived sacrifices of national sovereignty to WTO membership . . . are not so clear [as the critics would suggest]. The WTO cannot unilaterally force its member countries to change their laws. . . . Countries join the WTO knowing full well that reciprocal market access is part of the deal. Protecting their own WTO-related trade benefits means agreeing to submit, along with everyone else, their trade-related policies to scrutiny. If a policy is inconsistent with the WTO rules that the sovereign country freely accepted and if it compromises the trade benefits of another member, then the country, by prior WTO obligation, agrees to change it. Or it can take all the steps reserved to sovereign states to avoid the obligation, and then take the consequences.

JONES, *supra* note 16, at 103.

allow that protection to work to the direct detriment of those other countries, or at least those that are LDCs.[74] If, on the other hand, the agrarian values argument boils down to a criticism of the providing of subsidies for environmentally unsustainable agribusiness practices of corporate interests in the United States and Europe, then I agree with it for reasons I identified above in discussing the "authenticity" of comparative advantage.

C. Criticism #III-5—WTO Secrecy and Opaqueness

As I summarized this criticism above, it asserts that the WTO is a closed, non-transparent organization that operates in secret, inappropriately hidden from scrutiny and, hence, insulated from external criticism. This criticism is certainly not valid when stated in its most extreme terms, because the WTO has, in recent years, taken several steps that its critics have demanded. A visit to the WTO website shows thousands of WTO documents available to the public and a range of information about how NGOs may get those documents, contact the WTO, and participate in symposia and other meetings organized by the WTO.[75]

In this respect, then, the WTO has taken some of the same steps that the MDBs have taken in the past few years—adopting a transparency or disclosure policy, making publicly available a wide range of documents on policy and operational matters, and inviting formal and informal contacts with NGOs. However, as I suggested regarding the MDBs,[76] even more should be done to facilitate public understanding of what the WTO is, how it operates, and why it reaches the decisions it does. In this respect, the same types of "open meeting" principles adopted in many countries for the conduct of public business should be adopted by the WTO. Records of meetings of the various WTO organs, for example, should, as a general rule, be made publicly available, with exceptions and safeguards to protect against the disclosure of information that is legitimately confidential. Further details in this regard appear below in Section IVC of this chapter, in which I urge that the WTO accept some of the same institutional principles that I suggested in respect of the MDBs.

---

[74] For a discussion of this "agrarian values" issue, *see* Chen, *supra* note 21, at 10–11 (2001) (asserting that clinging to agrarian values is a "destructive philosophy" whose adherents "have failed to address the severest . . . human issues facing globalized society," including widespread poverty, and that clinging to agrarian values "would stifle wealth creation and constrict political freedom across the globe, all in order to shelter incumbent economic interests in Europe, Japan, and North America").

[75] *See* http://www.wto.org (last visited Feb. 13, 2005).

[76] For my assessment of the "secrecy and opaqueness" criticism as it is directed at the MDBs, *see* Subsection IIID of Chapter Four.

There is more to this "opaqueness" criticism. A lively debate between several commentators has focused on the question of whether, and how much, NGOs should be permitted to participate in WTO policymaking and dispute settlement proceedings. This issue straddles both Criticism #III-5 (secrecy and opaqueness) and Criticism #III-6 (democracy deficit). I address it in Subsection IIID, below, in my assessment of the latter criticism.

D. Criticism #III-6—The WTO Democracy Deficit

In Chapters Three and Four, respectively, I endorsed the "democracy deficit" criticism as it is directed against the IMF and the MDBs. In respect of the WTO, I also endorse the "democracy deficit" criticism, but for very different reasons from those that apply in the case of those other GEOs. I wish to highlight these differences by first explaining some aspects of the "democracy deficit" criticism that I reject as it pertains to the WTO.

My assessment of this criticism begins with a general confession: I believe we can overdo democracy. More specifically, I do not want the WTO to be democratic, if democracy means that amateurs (I include myself in this category) have the opportunity to vote on new policies (legislating) or on the interpretation or application of existing rules (adjudicating). Trade policy—like, say, monetary policy—is complicated. I certainly do not want my 19-year-old neighbor to have a vote at WTO dispute panel deliberations, any more than I would want her to have a vote at the meetings of the U.S. Federal Reserve Board to decide on raising interest rates. Instead, the WTO should be operated by, and mostly influenced by, persons who have expertise in international economic relations, especially trade relations.[77] While this is by no means incompatible with democracy—for example, the persons selected to carry out the functions of the WTO can and typically should be appointed by authorities whose powers to do so result from democratic processes (a point on which I elaborate below)—it does not mean that decisions about WTO policies or personnel should be the result of general citizen participation or popular vote.

There is another aspect of the "democracy deficit" criticism, as directed against the WTO, that I also reject. Recall that this criticism, as I summarized it earlier, asserts that the WTO is undemocratic not only (1) in excluding participation by citizens but also (2) in having no allegiance to political authorities—with the result that the WTO can (allegedly) impose its will arbitrarily on its member countries. The latter element strikes me as

---

[77] As noted above in my assessment of Criticism #III-5, regarding secrecy and opaqueness in the WTO, it is by no means essential or even preferable that all such persons be appointed by governments; instead, some forms of participation by NGOs and other representatives of civil society is highly desirable. *See supra* Subsection IIIC of this chapter. I develop this suggestion more in later passages of this chapter.

almost completely misplaced because it does not square with reality. WTO membership is voluntary, and its management is selected by its member countries.[78] The role of the WTO Secretariat is not to make rules but to administer rules accepted by the WTO's member countries on a one-state-one-vote basis. Any major change in those rules requires consensus: "all [148] members, or at least a critical mass of" them, must agree before a new round of trade negotiations is launched,[79] as occurred in Doha in 2001.[80] Indeed, some commentators have implied that the WTO is *too* democratic, in the sense that the requirement of consensus for most policy decisions "may be a recipe for impasse, stalemate, and paralysis,"[81] and to avoid such problems some observers have suggested that a WTO Consultative Group be created to provide the same "Green Room" preparatory services carried out less formally in earlier years.[82] Whatever the merit of these views, the fact remains that there is plenty of ultimate accountability of the WTO to its constituent members—that is, the vast majority of national governments that have formed it, joined it, and remained part of it.[83]

Perhaps this latter fact—that the vast majority of states in the world have become and have remained members of the WTO—is worth emphasizing, for it suggests that none of the many criticisms leveled at the institution, including the criticisms about a democracy deficit, have prompted countries to leave the WTO.[84] Indeed, the fact that the July 2004 WTO

---

[78] *See* WTO Agreement art. XV (right of withdrawal from membership) and art. VI (appointment of Director-General). For details on issues of membership and management of the WTO, *see supra* Section IVF of Chapter II.

[79] *Playing Games with Prosperity*, THE ECONOMIST, July 28–Aug. 3, 2001, at 25, 27.

[80] *See supra* note 35.

[81] John H. Jackson, *The WTO 'Constitution' and Proposed Reforms: Seven 'Mantras' Revisited*, 3 J. INT'L ECON. L. 67, 74 (2001). Another commentator, while stopping short of worrying about paralysis, does emphasize that the requirement of consensus does provide one of the "democratic checks" within the WTO and creates "a deeply conservative bias in the decision making apparatus." Andrew T. Guzman, *Global Governance and the WTO*, 45 HARV. INT'L L.J. 303, 337–38 (2004).

[82] *See generally* Richard Blackhurst & David Hartridge, *Improving the Capacity of WTO Institutions to Fulfil Their Mandate*, 7 J. INT'L ECON. L. 705 (2004).

[83] It is this view of "ultimate accountability" (my term) that I believe underlies another author's dismissal of the "democracy deficit" criticism: "One cannot . . . assess whether a system reinforces democracy as a whole by simply summing up the democracy quotient of each of its constituent parts. The United States constitutional system has rights, and procedures for enforcing those rights, that are insulated from majority will. Yet . . . such nonmajority institutions ensure that American democracy flourishes." Such a nonmajority institution would be the Federal Reserve Board, in the somewhat sarcastic example I offered above—or, indeed, any court with an appointed judge who is expected to administer the law as formally announced by a legislature, and not to rule on the basis of popular polls about what the law should be in a particular case.

[84] As another author has expressed it (focusing specifically on the issue of sover-

meeting in Geneva was concluded with a series of congratulatory news conferences, and not with the sort of bitter bombast and recriminations that accompanied the breakdown of the 2003 WTO summit meeting in Cancún,[85] suggests that the WTO member countries do consider that the continued existence of the WTO, and their country's participation in it, remains within their countries' national self-interest.[86] Perhaps one reason for this calculation, especially from the perspective of LDCs, is that the WTO does provide a forum in which LDCs can issue formal complaints, and have won several cases, against economically powerful countries whom the LDCs claim have broken the WTO rules.[87]

Having identified some aspects of the "democracy deficit" criticism that I reject, I now explain why, on balance, I endorse the criticism. Four factors prompt me to do so.

For one thing, the WTO's democracy deficit reflects, and is partially a manifestation of, its secrecy and opaqueness. Perhaps no institution can be secret and opaque in its operations without also suffering from a democracy deficit. Correspondingly, it will be necessary for the WTO to become more transparent in order for it to become more accountable (in appropriate ways).

---

eignty, not democracy), "[c]rics of the WTO who lament countries' alleged loss of sovereignty by subjecting themselves to WTO decisions should ponder the fact that nearly every country in the world is a member or else wants to be." JONES, *supra* note 16, at 74.

[85] For a reference to these two most recent WTO ministerial conferences, *see supra* Section IVC of Chapter Two.

[86] *See* Paul Blustein, *Poor Nations Put Premium on WTO's Survival*, WASH. POST, Aug. 2, 2004 (explaining that although LDCs objected to some of the decisions taken at the Geneva meeting, and to the fact that the United States and the EU dominate the decisionmaking within the organization, LDCs "had potent reasons for wanting to keep the WTO alive and well," such as the fact that multilateral negotiation in the WTO, which requires consensus for decisionmaking, affords LDCs more leverage in dealing with big and powerful countries than bilateral negotiations of the sort that the United States is increasingly pursuing). For a different perspective on the outcome of the July 2004 Geneva meeting, *see* Oxfam International, *Arrested Development? WTO July Framework Agreement Leaves Much To Be Done, available at* http://www.oxfam.org.uk/what_we_do/issues/trade/bn_wtoframework.htm (last visited Feb. 13, 2005) (claiming that "[w]hile there are some small wins for poor countries, overall the July framework is a minimal agreement that keeps talks and the WTO afloat, but fails to bridge continuing stark disagreements between developing and developed countries, let alone guarantee a pro-development outcome").

[87] In both the *Tuna-Dolphin* case and the *Shrimp-Turtle* cases discussed above, as well as in a 1996 case brought before the WTO regarding the use of reformulated gasoline, "developing countries defeated the most powerful country in the world through the rule of law." Kennedy, *supra* note 68, at 63. The countries bringing the complaints against the United States in those three cases (in aggregate) were all LDCs from Asia and Latin America: Brazil, India, Malaysia, Mexico, the Philippines, Thailand, and Venezuela. *Id.*

Indeed, the distinction between transparency concerns and accountability concerns is fuzzy. As I noted above, views differ as to whether, and how much, NGOs should be permitted to participate in WTO policymaking and dispute settlement proceedings.[88] Pro-NGO commentators argue that NGO participation would reduce some of the mystery that surrounds the WTO and hence aid in gaining public support.[89] They also assert that the WTO must have a global perspective, which cannot be achieved solely through the input of government trade officials.[90] NGO participation, they say, could take the form of providing expert opinions and external perspectives in the course of both policymaking and dispute settlement[91]—consistent with a "stakeholder" model in which all parties with a stake in trade policy would have the opportunity for input.[92]

In opposition to expanding WTO standing or participation to include NGOs, another commentator has argued (1) that giving greater publicity to trade policy "might prove disastrous for free trade," in part because it

---

[88] *See* Jeffrey Atik, *Global Trade Issues in the New Millennium: Democratizing the WTO*, 33 GEO. WASH. INT'L L. REV. 451 (2001) (expressing "a particular style of legitimacy critique: the alleged lack of democracy within the WTO"); Philip M. Nichols, *Extension of Standing in World Trade Organization Disputes*, 17 U. PA. J. INT'L ECON. L. 295 (Spring 1996) [hereinafter Nichols I] (arguing against expanding the rules for standing before WTO dispute panels); Philip M. Nichols, *Realism, Liberalism, Values, and the World Trade Organization*, 17 U. PA. J. INT'L ECON. L. 851 (Fall 1996) [hereinafter Nichols II] (discussing issues raised regarding participation of NGOs in policy making process); G. Richard Shell, *The Trade Stakeholders Model and Participation by Nonstate Parties in the World Trade Organization*, 17 U. PA. J. INT'L ECON. L. 359 (Spring 1996) (discussing trade governance); Steve Charnovitz, *Participation of Nongovernmental Organizations in the World Trade Organization*, 17 U. PA. J. INT'L ECON. L. 331 (Spring 1996) [hereinafter Charnovitz-1996] (discussing NGO participation in the policy work of the WTO and in the WTO dispute resolution process). For an updated version of Charnovitz's views on this topic, *see* Steve Charnovitz, *Opening the WTO to Nongovernmental Interests?*, appearing as Chapter 16 in STEVE CHARNOVITZ, TRADE LAW AND GLOBAL GOVERNANCE (2002), and reprinted from Volume 24 of the *Fordham International Law Journal.*

[89] *See* Shell, *supra* note 88, at 379 (asserting that the WTO needs to allow outsiders into the process to increase support for the institution); Charnovitz-1996, *supra* note 88, at 331–34 (pointing out that the WTO is as isolated from the public as the GATT had been, because the dispute settlement panels hold closed sessions, the WTO refuses to provide biographical information about panel members, all WTO committees hold closed sessions, NGOs cannot attend regular meetings of the General Council, and minutes are kept secret for two years).

[90] Charnovitz-1996, *supra* note 88, at 334.

[91] *Id.* at 339. For an explanation of how submissions from NGOs are currently treated in WTO adjudicatory proceedings, *see* BHALA-2001, *supra* note 8, at 239 (noting that the WTO "Appellate Body held that panels should treat a brief of an NGO that is appended to the brief of a Member involved in a dispute as part of that Member's submission").

[92] Shell, *supra* note 88, at 377–78.

generally injures some domestic constituency,[93] (2) that only wealthy interest groups would be able to participate, with the result that democratic interests still would not be served,[94] and (3) that the WTO would not be able to filter out legitimate NGOs from illegitimate ones.[95]

I agree with the first set of views—that NGO participation is vital in order to build and maintain public support for trade liberalization and for the work of the WTO in particular, and that such participation can take several forms. The NGOs themselves, of course, should meet high standards of disclosure and accountability in order to gain the necessary capacity or certification to participate. I offer recommendations regarding NGO participation in Section IV of this chapter.

A second aspect of the "democracy deficit" criticism that I believe packs a punch against the WTO concerns inequality among WTO members in terms both of their influence and of their treatment in the WTO. Despite the one-state-one-vote character of the WTO's organizational structure, as a practical matter some states—the United States comes instantly to mind—enjoy much more clout than most other states have. Conversely (and curiously), some especially small states—such as some Pacific Island states—have, in effect, heavier demands placed on them than others do.[96] Perhaps there is little that can be done (immediately, at least) to counteract this, given the current geopolitical realities of the world,[97] but it is a deficiency that should be overcome in due course. Again, one step in the right direction would be to boost the transparency of WTO operations so that informed criticism can be voiced over any inappropriate efforts to circumvent the basic democratic nature of the WTO's one-state-one-vote structure.

A third aspect of the "democracy deficit" criticism also rings true when applied to the WTO: the institution is not subject to any effective and objective mechanism for adjudicating bona fide claims brought by individ-

---

[93] Nichols I, *supra* note 88, at 313.

[94] *Id.* at 318.

[95] Nichols II, *supra* note 88, at 870.

[96] For an interesting account of the latter point, *see* Kelsey, *supra* note 23, at 258–75 (describing the heavy trade and investment liberalization demands placed on Vanuatu and some other Pacific Island countries in negotiations for their accession to the WTO).

[97] In this regard I would refer, as I did above in Section IIIC of Chapter Three, to the observation made by the IMF General Counsel a few years ago about "how difficult it is for a monetary institution to reconcile the principle of equality of nations under international law with the reality of their unequal economic and financial weights." François Gianviti, *The Reform of the International Monetary Fund (Conditionality and Surveillance)*, 34 INT'L LAW. 107, 116 (2000).

uals or groups alleging that the institution has acted inconsistently with the legal rules and policies governing its operations. There is, in other words, no broadly effective outside judicial review available. In this regard the WTO lags behind the MDBs and the IMF. As explained above in Chapters Three and Four, several types of inspection panels are being developed in the MDBs to provide for this form of accountability, and the IMF's IEO (Independent Evaluation Office) represents a move in the same direction.[98] In my view, similar initiatives should occur within the WTO.

An observer familiar with the WTO might immediately reply to this suggestion by pointing out that the WTO does, in fact, have a rather effective system of court-like procedures and institutions, namely the system established under the DSU for litigating complaints raised by one country against another country's trade policies or practices. I summarized that system in Subsection IVG of Chapter Two. On balance, it strikes me as a good system as far as it goes, notwithstanding the concerns I expressed earlier over (1) the outcomes of specific cases brought before it[99] and (2) the need for greater NGO access.[100] However, that system does not go far enough in its jurisdictional reach to provide what I referred to above as an effective and objective mechanism for adjudicating bona fide claims brought by individuals or groups alleging that the WTO has acted inconsistently with the legal rules and policies governing its operations. Achieving that goal would require changes in the DSU, and probably amendments to the WTO Charter itself.

A fourth complaint related to the "democracy deficit" criticism requires some special treatment because it is not directed at the WTO per se or at the trade liberalization agenda that the WTO promotes. Instead, that related criticism is that the governments of many WTO member countries are themselves undemocratic, in the sense that they lack the institutional structures necessary to ensure that policymakers are not "captured" by a few powerful interests but instead have at least some minimal level of competence, honesty, and objectivity in establishing and conducting economic policy for their constituents.

Even though this is a criticism not of the WTO but of its member countries, I address it here because I regard it as a central reason underlying several other problems in the current regime of international trade. I gave the

---

[98] For information about MDB inspection panels, *see* Subsection IIIE of Chapter Two and Subsection IVE of Chapter Four. For information about the IMF's IEO, *see* Subsection IIIB of Chapter Three.

[99] *See supra* Subsection IIIB of this chapter (discussing the *Shrimp-Turtle* and *Tuna-Dolphin* cases).

[100] *See supra* this subsection.

matter considerable attention also in Section III of Chapter Three, so I shall not belabor the point here. Simply stated, my view is that stronger national governments would adopt economic and financial policies, including trade policies, that would better serve the populations of their states. They would, for example, enact and enforce stronger protections against the kinds of bad environmental practices and bad labor practices that many critics of the WTO condemn. Those bad practices typically come not at the hands of the governments themselves but at the hands of private sector entities that are able to persuade weak governments to permit the practices to continue.

How can governments be strengthened? I believe that a long-term commitment of resources is needed with two complementary aims in sight. First, the problems of profound poverty and economic despair—problems that exist in many countries—must be effectively attacked through a dramatic increase in development financing that will build schools, train teachers, improve health care facilities, create jobs, provide decent housing and sanitation systems, and establish social security networks. Concurrently, massive efforts must be made to build and strengthen the legal and institutional elements that are essential to the efficient running of a modern government, including effective rules on an array of economic matters—banking supervision, land registration, secured transactions, documentary payments, deposit insurance, tax collections, accounting standards, corporate governance and disclosure, business licenses, product safety, workplace standards, and so on—as well as training of officials on the administration of such rules. Special attention should be given to rules on environmental protection.

And where will the money come from for these initiatives? From a massive increase in the amounts of financial assistance provided by the rich countries, especially the United States, for international economic development. Although some Americans seem to think the United States already provides significant amounts of such assistance, the United States would, in fact, have to devote seven times as much money to economic development aid as it does now if it wanted to reach even the very modest goal (set some time ago by the United Nations) of 0.7 percent of gross domestic product.[101]

Indeed, this point about the inadequacy of U.S. development assistance is important enough to warrant further attention. A recent edition of *World Development Indicators* provides details concerning the development assistance provided by each of the 22 members of the Development

---

[101] Joseph Kahn, *U.S. Rejects Bid to Double Foreign Aid to Poor Lands*, N.Y. TIMES, Jan. 29, 2002 (reporting on the Bush administration's rejection of an international proposal to double foreign aid in the wake of the war in Afghanistan).

Assistance Committee of the OECD—these are 22 relatively rich countries including, of course, the G-7 countries and 15 others ranging from Australia to Finland to Luxembourg to Switzerland.[102] Three especially noteworthy sets of figures show how much each of those countries provides in the form of official development assistance[103]—first on a per capita basis, second as a proportion of government disbursements, and third as a proportion of gross national income.

In 2002, the most recent year reported on, the United States spent on average $46 per American on official development assistance. This put the United States 17th out of the 22 rich countries that are members of the Development Assistance Committee.[104] That is the first of the three ways of measuring how much the United States contributes to global development through official development assistance.

The second way of measuring the U.S. contribution is as a proportion of government disbursements. This set of figures puts the United States in an even less favorable light. As a percentage of general government disbursements, the United States came in dead last out of the 22 members of the Development Assistance Committee, committing only 36 hundredths of 1 percent of its government spending to providing official development assistance.[105]

The third way of measuring the flow of official development assistance is as a proportion of gross national income. Once again, the United States comes in dead last. It devoted only 13 hundredths of 1 percent of U.S. national income to global development—about half as much as the levels provided by such countries as Australia, Austria, Canada, Germany, Japan, Portugal, Spain, and Switzerland, and less than a fourth as much as is provided by Denmark, Luxembourg, the Netherlands, Norway, and Sweden.[106]

---

[102] WORLD BANK, 2004 WORLD DEVELOPMENT INDICATORS 331 (2004) [hereinafter WORLD DEVELOPMENT INDICATORS] (describing the Development Assistance Committee) and 330 (listing its members).

[103] For OECD purposes, "official development assistance" is aid provided by the official sector (typically by national governments and international organizations) on concessional terms (for example, through loans at below-market rates of interest) mainly to promote the economic development and welfare of developing countries. *Id.* at 331. Typical forms official development assistance would be the provision of financing to build schools, equip hospitals, improve irrigation systems, extend rural credit to farmers, train government officials, upgrade pollution control facilities, broaden the availability of electricity, expand port facilities, and the like.

[104] *Id.* at 332.

[105] *Id.*

[106] *Id.*

In my view, this is inadequate. I believe that as the most powerful country in the world, and in many respects the richest, the United States should be leading the way in boosting global development through official development assistance financing. Instead, this country, and the current Bush administration in particular, has fallen short.[107] This is, in my view, a breach of the American responsibility to manage and husband its resources—its economic resources, its human resources, its political influence—in a way that serves its own long-term national interest and the long-term interests of the world at large.

Unfortunately, I see this American shortcoming as part of a larger pattern of policy and ideology that I deplore and that is a gradual abandonment of the commitment made six decades ago to seek multilateral solutions for global problems in a wide array of areas, including economics, human rights, and the use of military force. I return to this point in Chapter Six.

IV. REFORMS I SUGGEST

What is to be done with the WTO, and with the free-trade ideology that underlies it? In the following paragraphs I shall summarize suggestions that I believe warrant consideration in five areas of possible reform or redirection. In doing so, I draw heavily from the criticisms that I generally endorse, as discussed above in Section III of this chapter, and I also refer to some cogent aspects of the criticisms that I largely dismiss—for, as indicated earlier, some of the criticisms that I consider generally unfounded do nevertheless have some persuasive threads or angles to them.

A. Distributional Justice and Distributional Generosity

First, I believe effective action needs to be taken to allocate some of the free trade "winnings" to the free trade "losers." Specifically, a requirement should be imposed on all WTO member countries to provide assistance to workers displaced by imports.[108] (Under such a requirement, for

---

[107] Looking at similar figures, the columnist Paul Krugman wrote a Christmas Day editorial chastising the United States for being "the Scrooge of the Western world—the least generous rich nation on the planet." Paul Krugman, *The Scrooge Syndrome*, N.Y. TIMES, December 25, 2001, as reprinted in PAUL KRUGMAN, THE GREAT UNRAVELING: LOSING OUR WAY IN THE NEW CENTURY 379–80 (2003).

[108] In late 2004 Professor Jagdish Bhagwati reminded readers of the *Financial Times* that the question of how to provide such assistance has occupied legislators and policy-makers for many years but still has not been adequately tackled. *See* Jagdish Bhagwati, *Compensating Losers in Trade Liberalisation Process*, FINANCIAL TIMES, Oct. 19, 2004, at 16. In his recent book on the WTO, Kent Jones has offered a similar recommendation, stating that "[g]overnments must develop politically effective means of softening the hardship that accompanies economic change, while promoting measures to facilitate adjustment

example, the United States would need to see that the TAA system is revised, reinvigorated, and adequately funded.) This multilateral requirement could appear in a new treaty that would also address the relationship between trade, environmental, and human rights issues (discussed further below). If necessary, substantial financial transfers, with adequate safeguards and clear conditions, should be made by rich countries to poor countries to help fund their systems of trade adjustment assistance. Such transfers could be modeled after the funding provisions for the Ozone Trust Fund or the GEF.[109]

Why should there be any interest in allocating some free trade "winnings" to the free trade "losers" within a national economy? Without going into detail, I shall identify two types of reasons: ethical and practical. As an ethical matter, providing a safety net to those displaced by trade liberalization squares with a belief that features in most religious and moral systems—to wit, that it is ethically right to provide assistance to those who find themselves in difficult circumstances, whether or not any legal claim to such assistance can be offered (hence my use of the term "distributional generosity" in the heading for this subsection). As a practical matter, providing support to free trade "losers" reduces the political support for protectionism that would constitute a drag on the economy generally. Expressed differently, oiling the squeaky wheel is much more inexpensive and effective than slowing down the entire vehicle to reduce the squeaking.

What about distributional justice and generosity at the global level? In endorsing Criticism #III-2 above (in Section IIIA of this chapter) I noted the valuable work done by Raj Bhala in examining the "anti-Third World claim" that the rules of GATT-WTO law—and, in particular, those pertaining to special and differential treatment for LDCs—are in fact unjust in their formulation, their application, or both. Professor Bhala concludes that although those rules are not unjust, they could be, and should be, more generous.[110]

---

to change." JONES, *supra* note 16, at 199. His proposal would extend beyond trade-related job losses to any job displacement. *Id. See also* AMARTYA SEN, DEVELOPMENT AS FREEDOM 240 (1999) (noting that although "global trade and commerce can bring with it . . . greater economic prosperity," "there can be losers and well as gainers, even if in the net the aggregate figures move up rather than down," and that in response, society should make "concerted efforts to make the form of globalization less destructive of employment and traditional livelihood, and to achieve gradual transition" that will include "opportunities for retraining and acquiring new skills" as well as "providing social safety nets").

[109] The Ozone Trust Fund and the Global Environment Facility are described briefly in Subsection IIIA of Chapter Four.

[110] *See* Bhala-2003, *supra* note 3, at 5, 519. Bhala grounds his recommendation in Catholic theology (with analogues in Islamic teaching); I would take a more secular approach and urge generosity toward LDCs on general ethical grounds as well as on practical grounds of national self-interest.

I fully agree, and I endorse the three specific suggestions Professor Bhala makes for achieving this improvement. The first suggestion is that every year, every rich WTO member country must pay for one year-long training program in international trade law for three lawyers from the Third World.[111] Under the second suggestion, the conditions imposed by the rich countries on eligibility of LDCs and their products for special and differential treatment—such as especially low (or zero) tariff treatment under the Generalized System of Preferences—would be largely eliminated, in part because most of those conditions typically reflect protectionist impulses anyway.[112] The third suggestion calls for each rich WTO member country to participate in an effort to help the least developed LDCs diversify their export base, at least by transferring no less than 10 U.S. cents per citizen residing in that rich country to an Export Diversification Grant Fund designed to finance industries and service providers in such LDCs seeking to commence or expand exportation of their products and services.[113]

These suggestions for imposing further obligations on rich countries to provide special and differential treatment for LDCs in the area of trade are modest in scope, perhaps even niggardly. Once these small steps are taken, however, I would hope that perceived successes of these initiatives would encourage rich countries—especially the United States, whose leadership in this area is so important—to expand dramatically the scope of their generosity.

Lastly under the topic of distributional justice and generosity, I turn to the third perspective I offered above in Subsection IIIA regarding the claim that, at the global level, the current GATT-WTO international trade regime is unfair to LDCs because the developed countries are not following the

---

[111] *Id.* at 481. For further details, *see id.* at 473. For a broader, though less specific, proposal, *see* JONES, *supra* note 16, at 200 (suggesting that "[g]overnments from the wealthier WTO countries should provide additional funding for capacity building for poorer WTO member countries, including technical and legal training for trade officials, support for participation in dispute settlement proceedings, financial assistance in maintaining a minimal representative presence in the WTO, and aid for the technical infrastructure needed to comply with WTO obligations"). For a description of efforts made thus far within the WTO to provide effective technical assistance to help with LDC capacity-building in this area, *see* FRANK J. GARCIA, TRADE, INEQUALITY, AND JUSTICE: TOWARD A LIBERAL THEORY OF JUST TRADE 182–990 (2003).

[112] Bhala-2003, *supra* note 3, at 483–91. For further details, *see id.* at 476–77. For a similar criticism of this form of conditionality in the provision of special and differential treatment, *see* GARCIA, *supra* note 111, at 162–65 (2003).

[113] Bhala-2003, *supra* note 3, at 491–98. For further details, *see id.* at 478–79. Whereas Bhala would make World Bank involvement in the administration of the Export Diversification Grant Fund optional, at the discretion of the WTO, I would make World Bank involvement mandatory, as in the case of the Global Environment Facility, which involves the World Bank, the U.N. Environment Program, and the UNDP in its administration.

rules. The anti-WTO literature unmistakably reveals this perception, and for good reason. The rebuke that the United States received in April 2004 from the WTO dispute panel deciding the cotton subsidies case should be regarded as an embarrassment to the U.S. government and a stern reminder to it and other high-subsidy-providing governments (particularly the EU) that they are standing on the wrong side of the rules that they themselves have pressed the rest of the world to adopt. In my view, the rich countries should take just the opposite approach from what the United States has taken: instead of pressing for advantage in trade competition with LDCs by trying to get away with programs that edge as close as possible to the line between GATT legality and illegality, they should instead be practicing extreme caution—even fastidiousness—in staying far away from that line, in order to avoid even the appearance of impropriety in their own adherence to the rules they have championed. The price of hypocrisy on the part of the rich countries will be an erosion of the global commitment to trade liberalization; the price of sustained hypocrisy will be a sustained erosion and eventual crumbling of that commitment.

Accordingly, I believe the United States should put an end to its participation in what even the President of the World Bank has called a "squandering" of $1 billion a day by rich countries on farm subsidies that often have devastating effects on farmers in LDCs.[114] Specifically, it should quickly reduce and eliminate agricultural subsidies that have trade-distorting effects, and it should press the EU and other wealthy members of the international community to do the same.[115] In addition, the rich countries

---

[114] *See* Edmund L. Andrews, *Rich Nations Criticized for Barriers to Trade*, N.Y. Times, Sept. 30, 2002, at A7. In a similar vein, Stanley Fischer, the former Deputy Managing Director of the IMF, is reported to have called the protectionist policies of the United States, Europe, and Japan "scandalous." *Id.* Likewise, the chief economist of the World Bank has reportedly called it "hypocrisy to encourage poor countries to open their markets while imposing protectionist measures that cater to powerful special interests." *Id.* He is also reported to have said that each day, the average European cow receives $2.50 in subsidies while 75 percent of the people in Africa are scrimping by on less than $2. Barry Bearak, *Why People Still Starve*, N.Y. TIMES MAG., July 13, 2003, at 36.

[115] In offering this suggestion, I am fully aware of some of the reasons that could be used to support the granting of agricultural subsidies, particularly subsidies on U.S. cotton production, and to support the staunch defense of such subsidies through the WTO dispute settlement system. These might include the following points: (1) agricultural subsidies can provide crucial financial support for some struggling farmers (although many persons benefitting from such subsidies are by no means struggling); (2) cotton subsidies in particular can serve important environmental aims by encouraging dry crops in a part of the United States where irrigation of (other) crops is quickly depleting aquifers; (3) a vigorous defense of such agricultural subsidies helps develop jurisprudence in an important area of law and shows respect for the WTO dispute settlement system; (4) a vigorous defense of such agricultural subsidies can also preserve bargaining chips that the rich countries can use in the tough trade negotiations that lie ahead in areas in which they have already made considerable concessions to LDCs, such as in

should take strong initiatives to dismantle other forms of protectionism that keep out imports from LDCs—barriers that UNCTAD has calculated as costing LDCs US$700 billion every year.[116]

A fairly obvious retort to my recommendations regarding distributional generosity and distributional justice would be that it would amount to a poison pill for any politician—or expressed differently, that the political climate in many countries, and especially the United States, would be so unreceptive to such recommendations that no political figure promoting them could hope to gain office or stay in office. To this retort I would simply ask that efforts be made to change that political climate. I find it deeply disappointing, even irresponsible, that political leaders in the United States in particular—given this country's special prominence and influence—do so little to promote a climate of conscientious international economic liberalism. One observer has expressed it well: "In conjunction with [the need to develop politically effective means of softening the hardship that accompanies economic change], governments should publicly promote the benefits of trade liberalization and seek to secure the broadest possible support among their industries and populations for it."[117]

B. Environmental and Human Rights Protections

A second set of suggestions for reform emerges from Criticism #III-4. In my view, the linkage should be strengthened between trade rules and environmental and human rights protections, in such a way as to ensure that trade liberalization does not act at cross-purposes with the efforts to protect the environment, labor rights, and other human rights. A recent article by Professor Andrew Guzman of Berkeley is speaking, I believe, of roughly the same thing in proposing that the WTO be changed to "eliminate the trade bias."[118] The general contours of the linkage between trade,

---

pharmaceutical intellectual property rights; (5) as a political matter, it is extremely difficult for the government of a rich country that is accustomed to providing agricultural subsidies to discontinue those subsidies without the "cover" of a ruling declaring them in violation of GATT obligations. On balance, however, I believe a better state of affairs would be one in which political will is developed within the rich countries, through strong internationally minded leadership, to lead by example in practicing what they preach in favor of trade liberalization. I am grateful to Raj Bhala for helping me consider these various ideas.

[116] *See* Oxfam International, *Is the WTO Serious About Reducing World Poverty?* (Oxfam Briefing Paper, unnumbered, 2001), at 4.

[117] JONES, *supra* note 16, at 199.

[118] Guzman, *supra* note 81, at 313–16 (2004). Professor Guzman proposes, as a means of eliminating the WTO's trade bias, "housing a range of international economic issues within a single institution," and he asserts that "a reformed WTO should be the starting point for the construction of that single institution." *Id.* at 313. I am not convinced

environmental, and human rights rules should, in my view, be similar to those I described above with respect to the IMF and the MDBs: WTO membership requirements should be expanded so that a country's membership in the WTO would require that country to accept certain specified obligations in basic (existing) multilateral treaties relating to environmental protection and human rights, especially labor standards.

To this end, new treaty obligations should be put in place—probably by means of (1) a new treaty that would be incorporated into the cluster of treaties whose implementation the WTO is responsible for facilitating, as well as (2) minor corresponding amendments as necessary to the WTO Charter—that would require WTO members to adhere to the substantive provisions of the following environmental and human rights treaties:[119]

- Convention on International Trade in Endangered Species of Wild Fauna and Flora (CITES) (1973)
- Vienna Convention for the Protection of the Ozone Layer (1985), and pertinent provisions of the Protocols thereto and of the Amendments to those Protocols
- Basle Convention on the Control of Transboundary Movements of Hazardous Wastes and Their Disposal (1989)[120]
- Convention on Biological Diversity (1992)
- Kyoto Protocol on Global Warming (1998)
- International Covenant on Civil and Political Rights (1967)
- International Convention on the Elimination of All Forms of Racial Discrimination (1966)
- Convention on the Elimination of All Forms of Discrimination Against Women (1979)
- Convention on the Rights of the Child (1989)
- OECD Convention on Combating Bribery of Foreign Public Officials in International Business Transactions (1997).

---

that the concentration of all such issues into a single institution is the best approach, but I do think that the GEOs in general should broaden their reach, as described herein.

[119] In the case of the IMF and the MDBs, I also proposed linking membership in those institutions with acceptance of certain other international standards and guidelines regarding finance and governance issues. In view of the fact that the WTO's mandate is somewhat narrower than those of the IMF and the MDBs, it strikes me as unnecessary to bring norms of those types under the WTO's purview. By contrast, for the reasons discussed above in connection with Criticisms #III-3 and #III-4, international trade does implicate a range of environmental and human rights issues.

[120] As noted in the Glossary, I have used the spelling "Basle" throughout this book in the interest of consistency, even though the alternative spelling "Basel" appears more commonly used in certain contexts.

The mechanism by which WTO membership would link trade rules to treaty rules on environmental protection and human rights standards is not novel. As noted earlier, precedent appears in (1) the "single-package" approach of the Uruguay Round treaties, by which WTO membership requires acceptance of all the multilateral treaties emerging from the Uruguay Round), and (2) the TRIPs Agreement, into which the key provisions of certain intellectual property treaties are incorporated by reference.[121]

Indeed, the TRIPs Agreement served as the point of departure for an excellent analysis of the relationship between environmental protection, labor rights, and trade liberalization in an article published in 2002 by Professor Chantal Thomas.[122] Noting the TRIPs precedent for incorporating certain "trade-related" issues into WTO law, Professor Thomas explores two possible forms of linkage between the "trade-related" issues of environmental protection and labor standards: (1) adding two new treaties—one setting forth core principles of environmental protection treaties and the other setting forth core principles of labor treaties and standards—to the set of agreements administered by the WTO,[123] as was done in the Uruguay Round with intellectual property rights; or alternatively (2) amending the language of Article XX of the GATT "to incorporate identified principles of international labor and environmental law" as set forth in multilateral treaties that would then be listed in an annex to the GATT.[124] My proposal (which I conceived before having the benefit of reading Professor Thomas' valuable contribution) would combine elements of these two approaches, in that it would involve the establishment of new treaties that would themselves incorporate, by reference, principal obligations found in major environmental and labor treaties.

The linkage I would propose between trade and environment would also have some more specific features to it. For one thing, I would propose a clarification—or, if necessary, a modification of the GATT rules—providing that import restrictions imposed by a WTO member for legitimate environmental protection purposes would not be regarded as violative of free-trade commitments so long as such restrictions are not discriminatory

---

[121] The "single package" approach and the TRIPs "incorporation-by-reference" approach are referred to in Subsections IVC and IVF, respectively, of Chapter Four, as well as in the "nutshell" account I gave of the WTO in Subsection IVD of Chapter Two.

[122] *See generally* Chantal Thomas, *Trade-Related Labor and Environment Agreements?*, 5 J. INT'L ECON. L. 791 (2002).

[123] *Id.* at 799–809. "A TRL [trade-related labor] or TRE [trade-related environment] agreement would identify and incorporate key principles of existing international labor or environmental law, and would elaborate those principles as necessary." *Id.* at 799.

[124] *Id.* at 813.

by design or effect.[125] In addition, clarifications or amendments to GATT rules should be put in place to provide that trade in goods that were manufactured under circumstances falling short of multilaterally accepted environmental standards would attract special trade barriers. Such barriers could include, for example, "environmental countervailing duties" set at levels to offset the amount of indirect subsidies enjoyed by manufacturers in producing goods in a "pollution haven." Third, a renewal and expansion of the "green light environmental retrofit" subsidies permitted under the SCM Agreement[126] should be undertaken so as to permit a country to subsidize the "greening" of its industrial base without fear of other countries reacting by imposing countervailing duties.

For both areas of environmental protection and human rights protection, efforts should be renewed to expand the coverage and the enforcement mechanisms for labor treaties and environmental protection treaties. Within the United States, for example, political pressure should be applied to trigger participation in some of the environmental and human rights treaties to which the current U.S. administration has shown so little interest. Beyond this, however, lies the question of how, if at all, the WTO dispute settlement procedures would apply to the provisions of environmental and human rights treaties. As Professor Guzman asks this question, "which obligations get [WTO] dispute resolution?"[127] My own tentative answer is, I believe, roughly the same as Professor Guzman's: trade obligations obviously "get" WTO dispute resolution, and obligations undertaken via non-trade treaties that are linked to trade treaties (in the fashion I have discussed above) should be made subject to WTO dispute resolution procedures if doing so would clarify the relationship between trade and non-trade treaty obligations, or in certain other cases with consent of the parties.[128]

---

[125] *See supra* Subsection IIIB of this chapter for a discussion of the concept of discrimination in this context, based on distinctions proposed by Driesen.

[126] For a reference to these subsidies, and the SCM Agreement itself, *see supra* Subsections IVB and IVD of Chapter Two.

[127] *See* Guzman, *supra* note 81, at 324. For Professor Guzman, the question arises in the context of his proposal to create a WTO with broader coverage. Accordingly, he poses the question in this way: "Expanding the WTO would also raise difficult questions about the proper treatment of the many existing non-WTO international obligations, the most obvious of which are the significant environmental, human rights, and labor agreements. For example, if environmental issues are brought within the WTO, should existing environmental obligations also come within the WTO's jurisdiction and, if so, should they be subject to the dispute settlement system?" *Id.* He answers the first question in the affirmative; as for the second question, he suggests that WTO dispute settlement provisions should be the "default rule" in the sense that states "should be permitted to make some agreements that have different dispute resolution provisions, or none at all." *Id.*

[128] As Professor Guzman points out, it is not the case that international agreements

C. Transparency

A third suggestion emerges from Criticism #III-5: The WTO should expand its efforts at ensuring that its operations are transparent and publicly understandable. While much has been done in this area—as is true also of the IMF and the MDBs—the WTO has such a negative image associated with it that it needs to undertake especially effective and well-publicized initiatives resulting in public access to and understanding of what the WTO has done, is doing, and proposes to do.

Such efforts should, in my view, encompass several of the various aspects of transparency that I identified in the context of the MDBs.[129] For example, to the extent that it has not already done so, the WTO should ensure that the public have electronic access (presumable through the WTO website) to (1) the records of discussions and decisions at the meetings of WTO governing bodies, (2) substantive recommendations made by member governments, WTO staff, and others offering comments to the governing bodies for their decision, (3) the WTO's governing policy, procedural, and operational documents, and (4) all legal opinions issued by the chief officer in the WTO Legal Affairs Division to a governing body of the WTO. In all these cases, disclosure of and access to information would be subject to appropriate respect for confidentiality, where necessary, to protect legitimate interests of private parties. Moreover, because of the need for candid and lively debate in the early development of negotiations and policies, internal staff memoranda would typically not be publicly available.

As noted above in Subsection IIIC, the WTO has recently begun several initiatives along these lines. These initiatives will require several years of continued effort to bear fruit.

D. Accountability

Fourth, WTO accountability should be increased dramatically, in at least two principal ways—in addition, that is, to the improvement in accountability that will naturally flow from increased transparency. The first has to do with judicial review, and the second with NGO and other public participation in WTO affairs.

---

without procedures for dispute settlement are meaningless. "In fact, the vast majority of international agreements do not have mandatory dispute resolution provisions. Making an effective dispute resolution mechanism available but not mandatory gives states a wider range of options." *Id.* at 325.

[129] *See supra* Subsection IVA of Chapter Four. As noted there, several of these aspects of transparency appear also in the recommendations made in 2002 by the International Law Association's Committee on Accountability of International Organizations at its New Delhi Conference. *See* INTERNATIONAL LAW ASSOCIATION, REPORT OF THE SEVENTIETH CONFERENCE 772, 775–76 (2002) (discussing basic standard of maximum possible transparency).

As for judicial review, I propose the establishment of an entity that will serve about the same function as the World Bank Inspection Panel—that is, to accept complaints from individuals or groups alleging that the WTO had acted inconsistently with its own charter or its own announced policies and principles. The jurisdiction of this entity would not include judicial review of WTO dispute panel or Appellate Body decisions regarding the substantive interpretation of the GATT 1994 or other Uruguay Round treaties—the DSU already provides adequate coverage of those matters, and by persons with expertise that would be hard to match.[130] The reviewing entity's jurisdiction would, however, authorize it to determine whether the WTO's actions of a procedural and institutional character passed muster when judged against the provisions of the DSU, against the decision-making provisions of Article IX of the WTO Charter, and against standards set for WTO governing bodies regarding transparency, participation, equal treatment of members, the international character of the WTO staff, and the like.

As for NGO participation: In my view, the scope of NGO participation in WTO operations—both policymaking and adjudication—should be expanded. In this regard I concur with the suggestions made by several commentators favoring such NGO participation by providing expert opinions and external perspectives. For example, as recommended by Steve Charnovitz, the WTO should "mainstream NGOs into the regular work sessions of WTO councils, committees, and bodies,"[131] perhaps by means of what Ernst-Ulrich Petersmann has referred to as "an advisory body [composed of NGO representatives and having] access to WTO documents and the right to submit recommendations to all WTO bodies subject to procedures which ensure more accountability of NGOs and check their democratic legitimacy."[132]

---

[130] In expressing this view, I realize that it conflicts with the suggestion of some observers that a veto power be created to override panel or Appellate Body decisions. *See, e.g.*, Guzman, *supra* note 81, at 348 (summarizing a proposal by Claude Barfield that a specified minority of WTO members—perhaps one-third of members accounting for at least one-quarter of trade among members—should be able to block a panel decision). While such suggestions certainly warrant serious consideration, my tentative view is that such an "override" possibility would invite too much politicization of the process.

[131] Steve Charnovitz, *WTO Cosmopolitics*, 34 N.Y.U. J. INT'L L. & POL. 299, 343 (2002) [hereinafter Charnovitz-2002].

[132] Ernst-Ulrich Petersmann, *Human Rights and International Economic Law in the 21st Century: The Need to Clarify Their Interrelationships*, 4 J. INT'L ECON. L. 3, 37 (2001), as quoted and cited in Charnovitz-2002, *supra* note 131, at 343. *See also* JONES, *supra* note 16, at 199 (suggesting that "[t]he WTO Secretariat should establish a select advisory board of NGOs for regular contact and exchanges of views with the director general" and that increased NGO participation in WTO activities should be determined through negotiations).

Another means by which the interests of NGOs and their constituencies might be served in the context of the WTO is through expanded operations of, and support for, the Advisory Centre on WTO Law (ACWL). The ACWL, established in 2001 under an agreement signed by 32 countries (including nine developed countries),[133] aims to provide LDCs with training and legal assistance in WTO matters, especially in the context of dispute settlement proceedings.[134] In my view, broad support should be provided either to the ACWL or to some other mechanism[135] for assisting entities representing the interests of LDCs—not only their government officials but also NGOs and other groups—in navigating WTO waters.[136]

An additional form of public participation in, or oversight over, WTO operations that is worth considering has been discussed by Professor Gregory Shaffer of the University of Wisconsin Law School. He has examined the possible introduction of an inter-parliamentary WTO body that would ensure parliamentary control over WTO rulemaking.[137] Although numerous practical issues would need to be addressed in order for such a plan to work well,[138] it does hold the promise of enhancing WTO accountability. Another idea warranting consideration would offer more of a "top-down" approach—the creation of a global process to review the appropriate distribution of tasks between the WTO and the U.N. agencies.[139]

---

[133] Andrea Greisberger, *Enhancing the Legitimacy of the World Trade Organization: Why the United States and the European Union Should Support the Advisory Centre on WTO Law*, 37 VAND. J. TRANSNAT'L L. 827, 840–41 (2004).

[134] *Id.* at 840. According to the ACWL sponsors, the Centre would take up all defensive panel cases (that is, where an LDC is defending itself against a complaint from a developed country) but would pursue complaints made by LDCs only in selected circumstances. *Id.*

[135] The ACWL itself has met either resistance or disinterest so far from EU and U.S. representatives. *Id.* at 853–56. The European Commission has suggested that an independent center is unnecessary. *Id.* at 854.

[136] As noted above, Kent Jones has suggested that rich countries help LDCs in various aspect of this "navigating" challenge. *See supra* note 111.

[137] *See generally* Gregory Shaffer, *Parliamentary Oversight of WTO Rule-Making: The Political, Normative, and Practical Contexts*, 7 J. INT'L ECON. L. 629 (2004).

[138] As Shaffer explains, the "primary criticisms of an inter-parliamentary WTO body are (i) that it would provide a facade of WTO legitimacy and privilege an [allegedly] illegitimate WTO process; (ii) that national parliaments . . . should focus their attention on enhancing their oversight of national positions within their own constitutional orders; (iii) that well-organized groups, such as western multinational corporations . . . , would be best-placed to lobby and advance their interests through an inter-parliamentarian body; and (iv) that adding a parliamentary dimension would add further complexity to the already difficult process of multilateral trade negotiations." *Id.* at 648.

[139] *See* Gary P. Sampson, *Is There A Need for Restructuring the Collaboration Among the*

E. Development Assistance

Fifth and finally, the wealthy countries should commit immediately to a substantial increase in resources to be made available to assist in the economic development of poor countries. Why is this point included in recommendations regarding the WTO and trade? Because of the causal link I see between economic development, good national governance, and trade. As I explained above in Subsection IIID of this chapter, when evaluating the "democracy deficit" criticism leveled at the WTO, I believe economic distress of the magnitude existing in many countries of the world makes good governance very difficult and bad governance prevalent; bad governance makes for bad policy or, at best, bad implementation of good policy—including economic, financial, and trade policy. Bad policy performance in these areas perpetuates the economic distress. In my view, a dramatic increase in the commitment of wealthy countries, including especially the United States, to improve the economic circumstances of the LDCs is essential to break this cycle of despair.

WTO and UN Agencies So As To Harness Their Complementarities?, 7 J. INT'L ECON. L. 717, 726–27 (2004). This approach is reportedly consistent with suggestions made both by Peter Sutherland, a former WTO Director-General, and the current WTO Director-General, Dr. Supachai Panitchpakdi. *Id.*

CHAPTER SIX

CONCLUSIONS AND PRESCRIPTIONS FOR CHANGE

I. COLLECTIVE ASSESSMENT OF THE GEOs

A. Propriety, Progress, and Pressure

I would offer two overarching conclusions that I draw from my study of the criticisms leveled at the GEOs. The first one is discussed in the following three paragraphs, and it may be summarized thus: in many respects, the GEOs have struck a good balance between (1) the need (as a legal and practical matter) to keep their operations within the bounds of legal propriety consistent with the charters that created them and (2) the need to respond to pressure (much of it legitimately applied) to make forward progress in responding to changing circumstances in the world.

Let me try to "unpack" that condensed conclusion. Surely nobody—or at least nobody worth listening to regarding international economic relations—would challenge the assertion that the GEOs must remain faithful to their charters. They must resist the temptation or pressure to act *ultra vires* by taking on functions not assigned them or powers not granted them. Likewise, they have an institutional obligation to exercise those functions and powers that their charters do give them. In my view, the GEOs have done a relatively good job in remaining faithful to their charters. This view is reflected in my rejection, for the most part, of the criticisms alleging that, as a legal matter, the GEOs are guilty of "mission creep." This view of charter fidelity is also reflected in my observations that most of the GEOs have been slow to incorporate environmental, human rights, labor, and other social concerns into their operations. That is, they have been slow to reflect these matters in their operations because, for the most part, their charters do not grant the GEOs clear authority to do so.[1] (I believe such authority should be clarified and broadened, as discussed more in Subsection B, below.)

---

[1] My view that the GEOs have resisted *ultra vires* action is informed partly by my own experience. About four years ago I completed a comprehensive annotation to the AsDB Charter, for use within that institution. My review of hundreds of documents, mainly legal memoranda written by lawyers in the Office of General Counsel, revealed the care taken within the AsDB to hew closely to the letter and the spirit of its charter, notwithstanding frequent pressures to stretch or exceed the limits the charter imposes on the institution.

On the other hand, although the GEOs have typically been careful to remain faithful to their charters—as they should—they have also responded to growing pressures placed on them to move forward with the times. Most of this pressure has, to my mind, come from legitimate sources, including the member countries themselves and various interest groups whose aim is to promote the interests of the intended beneficiaries of the GEOs' operations. Again I use environmental protection as an illustration. Although the charters of all the MDBs except the EBRD are silent on environmental protection, those institutions have been pressed by various groups to enlarge and update their understanding of "economic development" to provide at least some mechanisms for guarding against the most egregious environmental damage from the building of roads and ports and other infrastructure, and indeed for encouraging environmental repair and improvement in recent years. Another illustration can be seen in the increasing transparency of the GEOs. While I generally endorse the "secrecy and opaqueness" criticisms as directed against the MDBs and the WTO,[2] I also recognize (and applaud) the very substantial progress made in all the GEOs in terms of transparency in recent years. The fact that some of them should go further in this regard must not blind us to the distance they have already traveled.

In sum, I believe the GEOs have, in general, struck the balance well between (1) charter fidelity and (2) pressure to progress. It is important that the MDBs, and their observers and critics, place high value on both of these elements. Otherwise we would have GEOs that are either runaways or stick-in-the-muds.

B. To Have or Not to Have the GEOs

To conclude, as I have in the preceding paragraphs, that the GEOs have avoided either a dramatic overshooting or a dramatic undershooting of their marks does not address a more fundamental question: are the GEOs worth having at all in today's global economic system? Many critics of the GEOs would consider it faint praise, at best, to assert that these institutions have minded their Ps and Qs.[3] To those critics, the GEOs rest on

---

[2] For my assessments of this criticism as leveled against the various GEOs, *see supra* Section IIC of Chapter Three (IMF), Section IIID of Chapter Four (MDBs), and Section IIIC of Chapter Five (WTO).

[3] I wish to acknowledge the assistance provided by Arnie Feldmeier, John Thomas, and other close associates in researching the derivation of this phrase. While numerous explanations have been offered, it appears most plausible that "minding your Ps and Qs" derives from one of these sources: (1) from an admonition to a child learning letters to be careful not to mix up the handwritten lower-case letters "p" and "q"; (2) from similar advice to a printer's apprentice, for whom the backward-facing metal type letters would be especially confusing; or (3) from advice to an English barman not to confuse

ideological or structural foundations that are either obsolete or obnoxious or both. For example, the "trampling of national sovereignty" and "bad medicine" and "democracy deficit" criticisms that some observers direct at some or all of the GEOs reflect an outright rejection of the aims set forth in the charters of those institutions, and not merely a complaint as to how the institutions had construed those charters.

Should we reject those aims and kill the GEOs? My answer, as I have explained it in Chapters Three, Four, and Five, is that we should not. The aims and ideologies embedded in the charters of the IMF, the MDBs, and the WTO—such aims as international monetary collaboration, international economic development, and a liberal international trade regime— are worthy and indeed essential in the world of today and tomorrow. Moreover, these aims can be achieved only through multilateral means.

This, then, is the second of the two overarching conclusions that I draw from my study of the criticisms leveled at the GEOs: despite the shortcomings of the GEOs, some of which are quite severe and need drastic change to overcome, we are much better off with the GEOs—or some form of them—than we would be without them. Expressed differently, we should keep them, not kill them.

I hasten to add, however, that we cannot keep them as they are. So high is the tide of anti-globalist sentiment, and so well-founded are some of the criticisms of the GEOs, that if action is not taken relatively soon to improve them, the GEOs will be killed off. So to my conclusion that we should "keep them, not kill them," I add my caution that the GEOs must "change or die."

II. CLOSING PRESCRIPTIONS AND OBSERVATIONS

In Section III of each preceding chapter in which I assessed the criticisms leveled at the GEOs—Chapter Three for the IMF, Chapter Four for the MDBs, and Chapter Five for the WTO—I have offered some specific suggestions for reform. I intend here not to repeat those but to offer some general observations that apply to all of the GEOs and the environment in which they now operate. These general observations relate to (1) charter amendments, (2) the future of the nation-state, and (3) the role of the United States.

---

the letters "p" and "q" on the tally slate, on which the letters stood for the "pints" and "quarts" consumed by patrons. Although none of these explanations seems entirely satisfying, the same could be said of many things in life.

A.   Charter Amendments and Pandora's Box

As I indicated in Chapter Four, I am fully aware of the "Pandora's Box issue" regarding charter amendments for international organizations—that is, that any attempt to open up such charters for the purpose of making amendments, however narrowly focused, might unleash a storm of proposals, demands, and rhetoric that would send the organizations into chaos. I believe it is partly for this reason that proposals over the years to revise the charter of the United Nations have languished without much official attention despite the fact that some of the charter's provisions (on the use of force, for example, or the composition of the Security Council) seem clearly anachronistic. Likewise, this concern over opening the floodgates was present in my own involvement in the drafting of the Third Amendment to the IMF Charter.[4]

At some point, however, the present becomes closer to the future than to the past, and that future must be addressed by an updating of past solutions. What I mean by that high-sounding language is that the need in today's world for international institutions that can effectively facilitate economic relations among states is so great, and so imminent in nature, that the GEOs we have today—dating mostly from the 1940s and the 1960s, with the exceptions being the WTO and the EBRD—simply cannot meet that need. Too many changes have taken place in our views on environmental protection, on social aspects of economic development, on participatory structures in public institutions, and on the so-called North-South divide for the existing institutions, working within their existing charters, to be effective in a new age. As explained in the preceding chapters, I largely dismiss many criticisms leveled at the GEOs, and the criticisms that I generally endorse do not require that the charters of the GEOs be completely rewritten. They do, however, need to be amended in several respects. I have tried to outline in this book what those amendments should aim to accomplish, and why they are necessary.

I find it significant that as I am finishing this book, the United Nations has undertaken a serious review of its charter with an eye to making

---

[4] As indicated above in Subsection IID of Chapter Three, the Third Amendment to the IMF Charter authorized the IMF to impose an additional sanction—suspension of voting rights—on countries failing to repay credit provided to them by the IMF. Pressure to have the IMF impose such a sanction on the basis of the doctrine of "implied powers" (that is, without going through the exercise of amending the IMF Charter) was fueled, in part, by a concern that proposing any amendment, however narrowly targeted, could encourage efforts for a much broader review and revision of the charter. That pressure to rely on "implied powers" was resisted, the Third Amendment was drafted quite narrowly, and it did not prompt a wholesale reappraisal of the charter. I assisted in the preparation of the Third Amendment while working in the IMF Legal Department in the late 1980s.

changes that would move it closer to the future than to the past. If this sort of review is possible in the context of the United Nations, I believe it must be possible in the context of the GEOs as well, especially now that several of the GEOs have new chief executive officers.[5]

B. GEOs and Nation-States

In considering the criticisms raised against the GEOs, and in suggesting reforms, I have often referred to the relations between those institutions and their members, and I have occasionally pointed out that the stature and future of the GEOs is intrinsically connected with the stature and future of the nation-state. Indeed, in Subsection ID of Chapter Two, while identifying four themes that I would develop in the book, I posited that the GEOs (along with multinational corporations) have gained in economic power so dramatically in recent years that they tend to eclipse many nation-states in influence, shaking the foundations of a system of political organization that has existed on this planet since about the mid-1600s. This is an issue I have addressed more fully in earlier writings,[6] so I need not belabor it here. However, I do wish to draw on those earlier writings to offer three related thoughts regarding GEOs and nation-states before concluding this book.

First, the traditional conception of state sovereignty is obsolete. Globalization of the sort that the GEOs participate in and facilitate has ended any practical significance of the orthodox view of state sovereignty, dating from Jean Bodin, Machiavelli, Grotius, and other writers who were influential in the period that saw the final emergence of the nation-state as the fundamental political unit in Europe (and later the rest of the world). If that orthodox view ever held water, it has now largely evaporated. This has led some writers to announce the death or irrelevance of the nation-state itself.[7]

---

[5] As of this writing, the current IMF Managing Director, Mr. Rato, has been in office for less than a year, a new World Bank President will need to be chosen soon to succeed Mr. Wolfensohn, who recently announced his resignation at the end of two terms, the new AsDB President, Mr. Kuroda, has recently taken office, and the process is underway to select a new WTO Director General to succeed Mr. Supachai Panitchpakdi.

[6] *See generally* John W. Head, *Supranational Law: How the Move Toward Multilateral Solutions Is Changing the Character of "International" Law*, 42 U. KAN. L. REV. 605 (1994); John W. Head, *Throwing Eggs at Windows: Legal and Institutional Globalization in the 21st-Century Economy*, 50 U. KAN. L. REV. 731, esp. 736–40, 771–76 (2002). Several points, including historical references, made in the next three paragraphs are addressed or explained more fully in those two earlier articles.

[7] *See, e.g.*, Ali Khan, *The Extinction of Nation-States*, 7 AM. U. J. INT'L L. & POL'Y 197 (1992); John O. McGinnis, *The Decline of the Western Nation State and the Rise of the Regime of International Federalism*, 18 CARDOZO L. REV. 903 (1996). *See also* RUMU SARKAR, DEVELOPMENT

Second, I disagree with that "death or irrelevance" prognosis. The nation-state may be altered—and our *concept* of state sovereignty should be updated accordingly—but the nation-state itself still retains central importance in the world's (currently more complicated) political structure. Expressed differently, I hear the funeral bells not for the state itself but rather for the old notion of state sovereignty that pictured the state as a singular, impenetrable lawmaker free to do as it pleases. I believe the state itself remains strong but now shares the stage with other sources of law. As John Jackson has explained:

> The policy question really involved in the sovereignty question is: How do you want to allocate power? What decisions do you want made in Geneva, Washington, Sacramento, California, or a neighborhood in Berkeley? By viewing it as a decision about how to *allocate power*, we can disaggregate the question of sovereignty and make people think about how to correctly design that allocation.[8]

Third, when it comes to matters of international economic management, international economic development, and international trade, how policymakers decide that issue of allocating power will both bear on and depend on (1) the strength and dependability of the GEOs and (2) the strength and dependability of states. Throughout this book I have emphasized that all of the GEOs need strengthening in order for them to be dependable servants of their members and, ultimately, of the world's people. I have also emphasized that states—or, more precisely, the governments of states—also need strengthening in order for them to be dependable servants of their people and effective members of the international community.[9]

LAW AND INTERNATIONAL FINANCE 8–9 (1999) (referring to various "failures of the nation-state" reflected in its inability to deal with certain aspects of economic globalization).

[8] John H. Jackson, *The WTO 'Constitution' and Proposed Reforms: Seven 'Mantras' Revisited,* 3 J. INT'L ECON. L. 67, 72 (2001) (footnote omitted, emphasis in original). For the same theme expressed with broader application (that is, beyond the context of international trade), *see generally* Mark W. Janis, *International Law?,* 32 HARV. INT'L L.J. 363 (1991).

[9] Some of these views, and especially the view that that the nation-state will continue to be central to the functioning of our international community, but that the manner in which the nation-state is governed should or must change, may be seen in a recent conttribution to the World Bank's "Working Paper" series. *See State-Society Synergy for Accountability,* World Bank Working Paper No. 30 (2004) (opening with the statements that "[t]he contemporary era of globalization and market liberalization by no means implies the end of the state," that "[t]he institutional, technical, administrative and political capacities of the state are now as important as they ever have been," and that "[g]ood government continues to be an absolutely necessary prerequisite for successful economic growth in the developing world"). Although the copyright page of the paper notes that the conclusions expressed in it "are entirely those of the author(s) and do not necessarily reflect the views of the Board of Executive Directors of the World

C. The Role of the United States and the Prospects for Change

In Chapter Five I took the opportunity of a discussion on improving the competence of national governments to offer a strong criticism of the United States. I said there that recent U.S. policies form a pattern of policy and ideology that I deplore—that is, a gradual abandonment of the commitment made six decades ago to seek multilateral solutions for global problems in a wide array of areas, including economics, human rights, and the use of military force. That commitment to multilateral solutions represented a collegiality of spirit and a faith in the mutuality of effort. American behavior toward the GEOs and the rules that they administer constitute just one example of many in which American foreign policy has taken a turn away from that form of multilateralism and toward unilateralism—a "go-it-alone" policy.[10] Other examples, in my view, include this administration's snubbing of the international community with regard to the global warming treaty, this administration's obstructionist attitude and action vis-à-vis the International Criminal Court, and the disregard or even disdain that this administration has shown for numerous other treaty regimes dealing with environmental protection and human rights and international security. It is, I believe, a dangerous trend—this abandonment of multilateralism and regression into unilateralism—and also a shameful trend if, as I suspect, it arises out of an arrogance of wealth and an ignorance of history. I hope it is a trend that can be reversed, the sooner the better, and not only reversed but emphatically rejected and disavowed, buried with a stake driven through its heart.

The United States should, in my view, sharply reverse its recent record of international relations—a record of isolationism, unilateralism, and arrogant jinogism—and embark instead on an era of cooperative multilateralism that would bear fruit not only in the area of international economic affairs, but also in many other areas, including human rights and environmental protection.[11] Moreover, consistent with that commitment, I believe

---

Bank," that same page notes that the paper "was commissioned, developed, and produced by the Civil Society Team and the Public Sector Group for the Latin American and Caribbean Region at the World Bank" (*id.* at ii), suggesting that the views expressed in it reflect at least the views of staff members in those World Bank offices. The paper was written by John Ackerman, a Ph.D. candidate at the University of California at Santa Cruz. *Id.*

[10] The recent American turn away from multilateralism actually takes two related forms—not only the "go-it-alone" form that I mention here but also a "my-way-or-the-highway" form, in which other members of the international community are invited to join the United States in an effort that has the appearance of being multilateral (and therefore not actually "go-it-alone") in its implementation but is in fact unilateral (American-dictated) in its destination.

[11] For another expression of my views in this regard, *see generally* John W. Head,

the United States should be in the forefront (not the rear, as it is now) of national generosity directed toward improving the economic circumstances of the world's most disadvantaged people and nations.[12] Whether for ethical reasons or for reasons of self-interest alone, this country should lead efforts to provide adequate resources—financial resources, human resources, technical assistance, and technology—to treat the Earth as a shared home with broad opportunities for development and improvement.

If this change in attitude and leadership on the part of the United States were to occur, I believe the types of changes I have suggested in this book would be entirely feasible. Although many of those changes—amending charters, adopting new policies, expanding responsible NGO participation, enhancing mechanisms for judicial review, revising GEO voting structures, creating new linkages and conditionalities between the benefits of GEO participation and adherence to key environmental and human rights treaties, pressing for more competence in national governments, and so forth—surely would (and should) prompt intense debate, I believe that such changes could be accomplished if the United States, with its unique position in today's world, were to lead the way. I am not so naïve as to think that the current state of politics and ideology in the United States is conducive to such leadership being assumed now. However, I am not so pessimistic as to think that the current state of politics and ideology in the United States is permanent. With better national leadership in this country, I believe that a broad-based, intelligent, reasoned assessment of the GEOs could be undertaken and that a return to genuine multilateralism could help design a new generation of GEOs to serve the needs of our shared future. I hope this book contributes to that forward-looking enterprise.

Essay: What Has Not *Changed Since September 11—The Benefits of Multilateralism,* 12 KAN J.L. & PUB. POL'Y 1 (2002).

[12] For my discussion of the level of U.S. contributions for official development assistance, *see* Subsection IIID of Chapter Five.

APPENDIX A
SURVEY OF RECENT LITERATURE CRITICIZING THE GEOs

This appendix offers an annotated list of citations from a range of sources—law journals, books, newspapers, policy journals, websites, and others—in which the criticisms assessed in this book have appeared. I could have included these citations in the main text of the book, but that would have created some very bulky footnotes. Besides, I have tried to distill from the enormous amount of critical literature regarding the GEOs a manageable catalogue of criticisms that are worth considering in depth; for this purpose the individual writings, many of which overlap in substance, are of less interest than the main themes they reveal.

This survey of the literature is structured by criticism. That is, for each of the 25 specific criticisms that I have identified—seven for the IMF, 12 for the MDBs, and six for the WTO—I cite in this appendix several illustrations of that criticism in the literature. Then, within each of the 25 criticisms, I have organized the annotated criticisms alphabetically, with a few exceptions: in some cases I have sub-divided the literature regarding a criticism in a way that reflects the particular aspect(s) of that criticism that certain authors have focused on most closely.

It is perhaps worth emphasizing here, as I have in the main text of the book, that in providing this survey of recent literature criticizing the GEOs, I am by no means endorsing the criticisms. My own assessment of the criticisms appears in Chapters Three, Four, and Five above. In this appendix, I am simply reporting what my research into the literature reveals in terms of the criticisms leveled at the GEOs. (Likewise, several of the sources cited below report criticisms without directly endorsing those criticisms.)

I.   CRITICISMS OF THE IMF

Criticism #I-1—*Bad Medicine*

Synopsis: "The IMF prescribes economic and financial policies that fail to cure, and that indeed often make sicker, its borrowing member countries and the entire world economy."

For examples in the literature of writings that refer to this criticism generally, see:

- Graham Bird, *Reforming the IMF: Should the Fund Abandon Conditionality?*, 7 NEW ECONOMY 214, 215 (2000) (reporting the consensus among academic studies that IMF programs do seem to be associated with balance-of-payments improvements, but that they have little impact on, or might even discourage, economic growth, increases in investment, or reductions in inflation);
- Gopal Garuda, *Lender of Last Resort: Rethinking IMF Conditionality*, 20 HARV. INT'L REV. 36, 38 (1998) referring to a 1990 IMF study concluding that IMF programs tend to reduce economic growth);
- Martin Khor, *IMF Policies Make Patient Sicker, Say Critics*, THIRD WORLD ECONOMY NO. 176, n.p. (Jan. 1–15, 1998), *at* http://www.asienhaus.org/asiancrisis/imfasiakhor4.htm (last visited Nov. 14, 2004) ("Just as a patient can have his condition worsened, or even be killed, by a bad doctor or by the wrong medicine, a country whose finances have already been weakened . . . can have its economic prospects and long-term development crippled further by the IMF.");
- Arthur MacEwan, *Economic Debacle in Argentina: The IMF Strikes Again*, DOLLARS & SENSE, Mar./Apr. 2002, at 22, 24–25 (asserting that the IMF makes a policy mistake in telling governments to balance budgets in times of crisis, and to provide unrestricted access for imports and foreign investment, and to give highest priority to repaying their countries' international debts);
- Eugenia McGill, *Poverty and Social Analysis of Trade Agreements: A More Coherent Approach?*, 27 B.C. INT'L & COMP. L. REV. 371 (2004) (examining criticisms of the IMF for mis-diagnosing financial crises, for using the wrong poverty reduction strategies, for insisting on trade liberalization that destroyed conditions necessary for growth, for lacking policy coherence, and for dominating, along with the World Bank and the WTO, the world economic system at the expense of the United Nations);
- David Moberg, *How to Fix the IMF; First, Do No Harm*, IN THESE TIMES, May 15, 2000, at 9, 10 (asserting that "[t]he overall record of countries under IMF structural adjustment programs—the policies imposed as a condition for loans—has ranged from unimpressive to disastrous");
- Jason Morgan-Foster, Note, *The Relationship of IMF Structural Adjustment Programs to Economic, Social, and Cultural Rights: The Argentine Case Revisited*, 24 MICH. J. INT'L L. 577, 583 (2003) (citing studies showing that structural adjustment lending by the World Bank and the IMF in the 1980s failed to improve growth and investment);
- Richard Peet, UNHOLY TRINITY: THE IMF, WORLD BANK AND WTO 56 (2003) (arguing that the results of IMF operations have been disastrous for working people);

- Steven L. Schwarcz, *"Idiot's Guide" to Sovereign Debt Restructuring*, 53 EMORY L.J. 1189 (2004) (expressing concern over the moral hazard of IMF member states subsidizing, in effect, defaulting states and those states' creditors);
- *Sixty Years On: The Bretton Woods Twins Are Useful But Need Better Parents*, FINANCIAL TIMES, July 3, 2004, at 12 (criticizing the IMF for overlending, as well as for its democracy deficit);
- Joseph E. Stiglitz, *Failure of the Fund: Rethinking the IMF Response*, 23 HARV. INT'L REV. 14, 14 (2001) (stating that some of the IMF's policies "actually contributed to instability," in that the IMF's premature call for "capital and financial market liberalization throughout the developing world" has been "a central factor not only behind the most recent set of crises but also behind the instability that has characterized the global market over the past quarter century");
- Mark Weisbrot, *Another IMF Crash*, THE NATION, Dec. 10, 2001, at 6, 7–8 (claiming that "the neoliberal program of the IMF and the World Bank . . . has contributed to a substantial decline in economic growth over the past twenty years throughout the vast majority of low- and middle-income countries").

Numerous expressions of the "bad medicine" criticism came in the wake of the Asian financial crisis. See, for example:

- Walden Bello, DEGLOBALIZATION: IDEAS FOR A NEW WORLD ECONOMY (2004) (holding the IMF responsible for the Asian financial crisis);
- Ross P. Buckley, *A Tale of Two Crises: The Search for the Enduring Reforms of the International Financial System*, 6 UCLA J. INT'L L. & FOREIGN AFF. 1, 42–43 (2001) (referring to the IMF's bailouts of Asian debtors as "highly counterproductive" because the bailouts "rewarded creditors for investing in the most destabilizing form of debt," and concluding that "[t]he IMF made the wrong call" in providing the bailouts "because it was viewing the situation from the wrong perspective");
- Istvan Dupai, *Criticism of the IMF and the World Bank* (Oct. 4, 2000) (endorsing the view that "the IMF increased panic [in the crisis-hit Asian countries] with its public announcements that everything was wrong" and that more generally "IMF programs often incite financial panics"), *at* http:// www.dupai.com/ allforstudents/docs/00000004.html (last visited Nov. 4, 2004);
- Frontline, The Crash: Views and Comments on the IMF (1999) (quoting Jeffrey D. Sachs's assertion that in emphasizing the seriousness of financial conditions in Asia, "the IMF helped to detonate the Indonesian crisis" and took "the same

kinds of provocative steps" in Korea, and overall "made a bad mistake"), *at* http://www.pbs.org/wgbh/pages/frontline/shows/crash/imf/views.html (last visited Nov. 4, 2004);

- Khor, *supra* (endorsing the view that "by imposing a tough economic squeeze in affected [Asian] countries, the IMF risks undermining, not restoring, investor confidence," that "by insisting on faster liberalisation of capital inflows, the IMF may exacerbate financial vulnerability," and that the IMF-led "bailouts may encourage further folly, mainly by lenders");

- Catherine H. Lee, *To Thine Ownself Be True: IMF Conditionality and Erosion of Economic Sovereignty in the Asian Financial Crisis*, 24 U. PA. J. INT'L ECON. L. 875 (2003) (criticizing the IMF's alleged destruction of state sovereignty and its alleged "one size fits all" approach);

- Stiglitz, *supra*, at 15 (referring to a "general consensus that the IMF pursued excessively contractionary fiscal policies" in responding to the Asian crisis, "and that the manner in which it handled financial-sector restructuring, at least in Indonesia, was a dismal failure");

- Kevin Watkins, Oxfam International, *The IMF: Shot By Both Sides* (Apr. 2000) (referring to "the disastrous impact of IMF programmes in East Asia," attributable to the fact that "IMF budget targets and their counterpart of high interest rates can have the effect of undermining the investment on which long-run growth and poverty reduction depend") (earlier on www.bicusa.org website, now on file with author).

Other expressions of the "bad medicine" criticism came during and after economic crises in Argentina and Russia. See, for example:

- John V. Paddock, Comment, *IMF Policy and the Argentine Crisis*, 34 U. MIAMI INTER-AM. L. REV. 155, 158–59 (2002) (complaining that "the conditions imposed by the IMF on Argentina did not address the causes of the crisis, but . . . served to encourage the nation to adopt the Washington Consensus," a formula of economic and financial policies that Paddock says amounts to a "one-size-fits-all program" that the IMF has applied to Argentina, Mexico, Russia, and Asian countries despite differences in the crises faced by all those countries);

- Adam Thomson, *IMF Was 'Too Lenient' Over Argentina's Deficits as Economy Headed for Crisis*, FINANCIAL TIMES, July 28, 2004, at 9 (finding that the IMF was too lenient with its procedures in Argentina);

- Weisbrot, *supra*, at 7 (condemning the IMF in each of those crises for "burden[ing] a country with billions of dollars of debt in order to prop up an overvalued currency" and for proving itself "incapable of learning from repeated failures").

For a recent assessment of IMF policy prescriptions based on detailed economic analysis, see generally:

- James Raymond Vreeland, THE IMF AND ECONOMIC DEVELOP-MENT (2003), esp. at 152 (concluding that IMF programs "hurt economic growth and exacerbate income inequality").

Criticism #I-2—Distributional and Social Injustice

Synopsis: "The economic and financial policies that the IMF insists on create distributional inequities and ignore the social aspects of a country's well-being."

For examples in the literature of writings that refer to this criticism generally, see:

- Sarah Anderson, *The IMF and the World Bank's Cosmetic Makeover,* DOLLARS & SENSE, Jan./Feb. 2001, at 30, 30–31 (claiming that the IMF and the World Bank "have thrown millions of people deeper into poverty by promoting the same harsh economic reforms [to various countries] . . . regardless of local culture, resources, or economic context," offering specific examples of how IMF-imposed policies have hurt education, health, and environmental protection" in Haiti and Brazil, and referring to "a harsh IMF reform program [in Ecuador] that shifts the country's economic crisis onto the backs of the poor"), *available at* http://www.dollarsandsense.org/archives/2001/0101anderson. html (last visited Nov. 4, 2004);
- Mac Darrow, BETWEEN THE LIGHT AND SHADOW: THE WORLD BANK, THE INTERNATIONAL MONETARY FUND AND INTERNA-TIONAL HUMAN RIGHTS LAW 52 (2003) (finding IMF interest in human rights standards far from its focus);
- Michael O. Folorunso, *IMF: The Big Bad Wolf,* at http://www. gamji.com/NEWS2154.htm (last visited Nov. 4, 2004) (contending that the IMF and the World Bank "want to impoverish the people," that IMF policies contribute to the fall of school attendance and healthcare, and that wherever the IMF has intervened, it has "left a giant foot print of a destroyed economy, joblessness [and] more poverty than when they came in");
- Frontline, The Crash: Views and Comments on the IMF (1999) (quoting Jeffrey D. Sachs's assertion that the IMF's action in the Asian financial crisis "shift[ed] the attention away

from the real facts and from the real world that people live in" and that the IMF is "not understanding that . . . [its] actions are having such a disastrous effect on the real economy, on the jobs, the production, the exports, and the living standards of the people");

- *Id.* (quoting Jeffrey Garten's assertion, in evaluating the IMF's handling of the Asian financial crisis, that "the social cost, the cost in terms of unemployment and, you know, the sheer human misery that is created—it was too much");
- Gopal Garuda, *Lender of Last Resort: Rethinking IMF Conditionality*, 20 HARV. INT'L REV. 36, 38 (1998) (citing a study concluding that IMF-supported adjustment programs "tended to increase the percentage of people below the poverty line in sub-Saharan Africa by 10 to 15 percent");
- Arthur MacEwan, *Economic Debacle in Argentina: The IMF Strikes Again*, DOLLARS & SENSE, Mar./Apr. 2002, at 22, 24 (claiming that "IMF policies . . . often lead to . . . growing inequality" and "have a severe negative impact on low-income groups" because they increase unemployment and gut social programs);
- David Moberg, *How to Fix the IMF; First, Do No Harm*, IN THESE TIMES, May 15, 2000, at 9, 10 (complaining that "[t]he IMF pays no attention to the distribution of income and wealth" despite studies that show a link between lower levels of income inequality and higher levels of growth in nations around the world);
- Jason Morgan-Foster, Note, *The Relationship of IMF Structural Adjustment Programs to Economic, Social, and Cultural Rights: The Argentine Case Revisited*, 24 MICH. J. INT'L L. 577, 646 (2003) (asserting that the IMF is, by imposing structural adjustment requirements, preventing states from meeting some of the obligations they have under human rights treaties to provide for the economic, social, and cultural rights of their people);
- Heiner Thiessen, *Running on Empty*, ECOLOGIST, Nov. 2002, at 39, 41 (stating that the IMF's structural adjustment programs adopted by Senegal at the insistence of the IMF has "driven most of [Senegal's] small farmers out of business," has "undermined food security," has caused hunger and malnutrition to rise, has driven the unemployment rate from 25 percent to 44 percent, and has caused a rise in disease and mortality rates);
- Kevin Watkins, Oxfam International, *The IMF: Shot By Both Sides* (Apr. 2000) (claiming that "the IMF has a disastrous record in sub-Saharan Africa" in that "[c]onditions attached to its loans have destroyed livelihoods on an epic scale, [and] placed basic health and education services beyond the reach of millions of poor households," and citing a recent IMF sur-

vey showing that 12 of 16 African countries implementing IMF programs "had cut spending on basic education") (earlier on www.bicusa.org website, now on file with author);

- Mark Weisbrot, *Another IMF Crash*, THE NATION, Dec. 10, 2001, at 6, 7 (claiming that under IMF bailouts, "the people, especially the poor, are tossed overboard");
- Carol Welch, *What's Wrong with the International Monetary Fund?*, *in* CITIZEN'S GUIDE TO INTERNATIONAL FINANCIAL INSTITUTIONS 1 (CEE Bankwatch Network ed., n.d.) (asserting that IMF policies "hurt the poor and exacerbate social inequality" by requiring governments to cut spending on social programs and increase charges for social services, and that IMF policies "also hurt workers around the world" by leading to an abolition of minimum wage and collective bargaining laws), *available at* http://www.bankwatch.org/vademecum/ifis/wbgrp/cgimf.pdf (last visited Nov. 4, 2004);
- G. Pascal Zachary, *IMF: Kill it or Keep it?*, IN THESE TIMES, May 15, 2000, at 8, 9 (criticizing "the IMF's notorious practice of conditioning loans on the imposition of cuts in welfare, wages and credit"), *available at* http://www.inthesetimes.com/issue/24/12/zachary2412.html (last visited Nov. 4, 2004);
- Adam Zwass, GLOBALIZATION OF UNEQUAL NATIONAL ECONOMIES: PLAYERS AND CONTROVERSIES 248–49 (2002) (highlighting the failures of the IMF and other GEOs to prevent or even narrow the widening chasm between the ever-richer North and the poverty-ridden South).

Some critics emphasize other types of social damage, including environmental damage, allegedly done under IMF-imposed policies. In this respect, see:

- Istvan Dupai, *Criticism of the IMF and the World Bank* (Oct. 4, 2000) (citing a study claiming that programs supported by the IMF and the World Bank led to over-exploitation of forests in Ghana), *at* http://www.dupai.com/allforstudents/docs/00000004.html (last visited Nov. 4, 2004);
- Jason Tockman, AMERICAN LANDS ALLIANCE, THE IMF: FUNDING DEFORESTATION 3 (Nov. 2001) (stating that IMF operations "have caused extensive deforestation" in numerous countries);
- Welch, *supra* (asserting that "[t]he IMF turns a blind eye to the economic and social value of natural resources" and that its policies lead countries to liquidate natural resources, to cut back on conservation programs, and to lower environmental standards).

For an assertion that the IMF's policy prescriptions are founded on an ignorant misunderstanding of cultural differences between societies, see:

- Theissen, *supra*, at 39 (explaining that "Muslim life in sub-Saharan Africa involves a constant series of financial sacrifices, which peg individuals back to a natural state of cashlessness" and that IMF pressure on Senegal "to turn more and more of its agricultural land over to the production of cash crops for export" has created a cash economy that "has caused a new sense of poverty and marginalisation").

Some critics view the IMF as dismissive of non-Western values not because of ignorance but because of an actual intention to subjugate peoples of other cultures. In this respect, see:

- Timothy A. Canova, *Global Finance and the International Monetary Fund's Neoliberal Agenda: The Threat to the Employment, Ethnic Identity, and Cultural Pluralism of Latina/o Communities*, 33 U.C. DAVIS L. REV. 1547, 1549, 1562 (2000) (arguing that the IMF "systematically subordinates entire nations of color" and urging that "[t]he IMF's structural adjustment punishment should be seen as a direct threat to Latin American cultural values").

For a wide-ranging set of attacks on the IMF, including several focusing on social concerns, see generally:

- DEMOCRATIZING THE GLOBAL ECONOMY (Kevin Danaher ed., 2001).

Criticism #I-3—*IMF Trampling of National Sovereignty*

Synopsis: "In imposing conditionality on its loans, the IMF tramples on national sovereignty—not just in economics but increasingly in other areas of state autonomy."

For examples in the literature of some criticisms along these lines, see:

- Saladin Al-Jurf, *Good Governance and Transparency: Their Impact on Development*, 9 TRANSNAT'L L. & CONTEMP. PROBS. 193, 206 (1999) (recounting, in the context of anti-corruption initiatives, the criticisms that "the World Bank and IMF are perpetuating 'new colonialism,' where Western economic and cultural values are imposed upon emerging economies at the price of their sovereignty" and that "the World Bank and the IMF have failed to recognize that their programs cross the bounds of simple economic reform and encroach upon the sovereignty of member nations");

- David Asp, *Argentina's Mystery of Capital: Why the International Monetary Fund Needs Hernando de Soto*, 12 MINN. J. GLOBAL TRADE 383 (2003) (citing the allegation that the IMF intrudes on state sovereignty);

- Graham Bird, *Reforming the IMF: Should the Fund Abandon Conditionality?*, 7 NEW ECONOMY 214, 214 (2000) (noting that "[s]ome observers see IMF conditionality as overly intrusive" and that the implication of this "is that countries turning to the Fund are losing their national sovereignty over economic policy design");

- Istvan Dupai, *Criticism of the IMF and the World Bank* (Oct. 4, 2000) (claiming that the IMF "intervenes into the internal affairs of [its member] countries" and that most developing countries "have given up too much of their autonomy"), *at* http://www.dupai.com/allforstudents/docs/00000004.html (last visited Nov. 4, 2004);

- Catherine H. Lee, *To Thine Ownself Be True: IMF Conditionality and Erosion of Economic Sovereignty in the Asian Financial Crisis*, 24 U. PA. J. INT'L ECON. L. 875 (2003) (criticizing the IMF's alleged destruction of state sovereignty and its alleged "one size fits all" approach);

- Jedediah Purdy, *A World of Passions: How to Think About Globalization Now*, 11 IND. J. GLOBAL LEGAL STUD. 1 (2004) (explaining criticisms asserting that the IMF acts in a "quasi-imperial role in dictating domestic policy to governments that have little or no effective choice in the matter");

- Mary C. Tsai, *Globalization and Conditionality: Two Sides of the Sovereignty Coin*, 31 LAW & POL'Y INT'L BUS. 1317, 1318, 1329 (2000) (asserting that "globalization and [IMF and World Bank] conditionality represent a threat to state sovereignty" and positing that IMF and World Bank conditionality, when coupled with global economic integration, have placed "sovereignty . . . in a more precarious position than ever before").

Criticism #I-4—*IMF Secrecy and Opaqueness*

Synopsis: "The IMF is a closed, non-transparent organization that operates in secret, despite its insistence on transparency in the governments of its members."

For examples in the literature of some criticisms of the IMF along these lines, see:

- Andrew Balls & George Parker, *Europe Likely to Select Candidate by Next Week for IMF Vacancy*, FINANCIAL TIMES, Apr. 17, 2004, at 8 (discussing the possible candidates for IMF Managing Director and concern over the lack of transparency in the IMF);
- Istvan Dupai, *Criticism of the IMF and the World Bank* (Oct. 4, 2000) (endorsing the view that "all IMF documents, instead of being confidential, should be made public and thereby open to public scrutiny and debate" and that "[p]ast IMF programs should be formally reviewed and evaluated by independent experts"), *at* http://www.dupai.com/allforstudents/docs/00000004. html (last visited Nov. 4, 2004);
- Michael O. Folorunso, *IMF: The Big Bad World*, *at* www.gamji. com/NEWS2154.htm (last visited Nov. 4, 2004) (complaining that the IMF and the World Bank require nations "to sign secret agreements");
- Martin Khor, *IMF Policies Make Patient Sicker, Say Critics*, THIRD WORLD ECONOMY NO. 176, n.p. (Jan. 1–15, 1998) (criticizing the IMF for "work[ing] in secret, drawing up policies for the 80 countries under its control, largely without their participation and without the knowledge of the world," and operating with an "almost total lack of 'transparency' in decisions and decision-making process"), *at* http://www.asienhaus.org/asian-crisis/imfasiakhor4.htm (last visited Nov. 4, 2004);
- Joseph E. Stiglitz, *Failure of the Fund: Rethinking the IMF Response*, 23 HARV. INT'L REV. 14, 14 (2001) (stating that "the IMF conducts much of its business behind closed doors, without transparency");
- Marijke Torfs, *Reining in the IMF: The Case for Denying the IMF New Funding and Power*, MULTINATIONAL MONITOR, Jan.–Feb. 1998, at 21, 23 (pointing out that a substantial change in IMF disclosure policies, occurring after the enactment of 1994 legislation in the U.S. Congress regarding the U.S. contribution to the IMF's Enhanced Structural Adjustment Facility, represents "progress, but not a panacea," as the available documents provide only "a flavor of the nature of the program[s]" promoted by the IMF);
- Ian Vasquez, *The IMF: Bad Watchdog with a Bad Attitude* (Mar. 16, 1998) (complaining that "even as the IMF insists on full and accurate information [from Asian governments], it remains one of the world's most secretive bureaucracies"), *at* www.cato.org/dailys/3-16-98.html (last visited Nov. 4, 2004);
- Carol Welch, THE IMF AND GOOD GOVERNANCE 2 (Inter-hemispheric Res. Ctr. & Inst. for Policy Studies, Foreign Policy in Focus No. 33, Oct. 1998) (claiming that "the IMF is still too secretive" and that because "[m]ost of the loan documents

that the IMF negotiates with its borrowing members are not available to the public . . . the citizens of an affected country have little way of knowing which policies the IMF is prescribing and which policies are coming from their government"), *available at* www.fpif.org/pdf/vol3/33ifimf.pdf (last visited Nov. 4, 2004);

- *id.* at 3 (complaining that "[t]he IMF Executive Board essentially operates behind closed doors and makes agreements by consensus" rather than by formal, transparent voting, and that "board minutes are made available only after a 30-year time lag");
- Carol Welch, *What's Wrong with the International Monetary Fund?*, in CITIZEN'S GUIDE TO INTERNATIONAL FINANCIAL INSTITUTIONS 1 (CEE Bankwatch Network ed., n.d.) (complaining that although "the IMF makes more information about its programs publicly available than it used to, it remains secretive" and that "Board of Directors deliberations are secret and many staff reports and assessments are private"), *available at* http://www.bankwatch.org/vademecum/ifis/wbgrp/cgimf.pdf (last visited Nov. 4, 2004).

Criticism #I-5—*The IMF Democracy Deficit*

Synopsis: "Controlled by a handful of rich countries, the IMF is an unaccountable autocracy in which the people most affected by its operations have much too little chance to participate."

For examples in the literature of some criticisms of the IMF along these lines, see:

- Sarah Anderson, *The IMF and the World Bank's Cosmetic Makeover*, DOLLARS & SENSE, Jan./Feb. 2001, at 30, 31 (reporting that NGOs trying to enter into consultations with the IMF and the World Bank have found "either a complete lack of public consultation or mere public relations stunts that excluded groups more critical of Bank and Fund policies"), *available at* http://www.dollarsandsense.org/archives/2001/0101anderson.html (last visited Nov. 4, 2004);
- George B.N. Ayittey, *The Rule of Big Men or the Rule of Law?*, THE ECONOMIST, July 17, 2004, *available at* 2004 WL 620167512 (criticizing IMF for supporting anti-democratic governments);
- George B.N. Ayittey, *How the Multilateral Institutions Compounded Africa's Economic Crisis*, 30 L. & POL'Y INT'L BUS. 585 (1999) (same);
- Walden Bello, DEGLOBALIZATION: IDEAS FOR A NEW WORLD ECONOMY (2004) (criticizing the IMF and the other GEOs for sidestepping democracy);

- Istvan Dupai, *Criticism of the IMF and the World Bank* (Oct. 4, 2000) (pointing out that "India and China have smaller votes than the Netherlands, although . . . their population is about 60 times larger"), *at* http://www.dupai.com/allforstudents/docs/00000004.html (last visited Nov. 4, 2004);
- Sebastian Edwards, *Europe Should Give Up Its Hold on the Fund*, FINANCIAL TIMES, Mar. 17, 2004, at 19 (critically discussing the "tradition" of the IMF leader coming from Europe);
- Catherine H. Lee, *To Thine Ownself Be True: IMF Conditionality and Erosion of Economic Sovereignty in the Asian Financial Crisis*, 24 U. PA. J. INT'L ECON. L. 875 (2003) (calling for a reallocation of voting power in the IMF "to allow developing countries to have a meaningful voice in the determination of policies");
- S. Mansoob Murshed, *Perspectives on Two Phases of Globalization*, appearing as chapter 1 in S. Mansoob Murshed ed., GLOBALIZATION, MARGINALIZATION AND DEVELOPMENT 1, 4 (2002) (citing the allegedly undemocratic rules enforced by the IMF and other GEOs);
- Jedediah Purdy, *A World of Passions: How to Think About Globalization Now*, 11 IND. J. GLOBAL LEGAL STUD. 1 (2004) (explaining criticisms that the IMF acts in a "quasi-imperial role in dictating domestic policy to governments that have little or no effective choice in the matter");
- Cyrus Rustomjee, *Why Developing Countries Need a Stronger Voice*, FINANCE & DEVELOPMENT, Sept. 2004, at 21 (asserting that low-income countries, particularly in sub-Saharan Africa have too small a voice in the IMF, and proposing changes to address that problem);
- *Sixty Years On: The Bretton Woods Twins Are Useful But Need Better Parents*, FINANCIAL TIMES, July 3, 2004, at 12 (criticizing the IMF for its democracy deficit);
- Joseph E. Stiglitz, *Failure of the Fund: Rethinking the IMF Response*, 23 HARV. INT'L REV. 14, 17 (2001) (complaining that the IMF's "leaders are seldom held accountable" for the policies they pursue);
- Kevin Watkins, Oxfam International, *The IMF: Shot By Both Sides* (Apr. 2000) (asserting that "the Fund's 'one dollar, one vote' constitution" results in a "democratic deficit of staggering proportions" and asserting that "it is outrageous for the US and other industrial countries to preach the virtues of democracy and accountability in poor countries, while practicing the vices of oligarchy in the IMF") (earlier on www.bicusa.org website, now on file with author);
- Carol Welch, *What's Wrong with the International Monetary Fund?*, in CITIZEN'S GUIDE TO INTERNATIONAL FINANCIAL INSTITU-

TIONS (CEE Bankwatch Network ed., n.d.) (criticizing the IMF because it "only responds to a select group of interests in its borrowing countries" and "negotiates programs with a handful of government officials" that "excludes environmental ministries and members of parliament," and concluding that "[t]his process is fundamentally undemocratic"), *available at* http://www.bankwatch.org/vademecum/ifis/wbgrp/cgimf.pdf (last visited Nov. 4, 2004).

Criticism #I-6—*IMF Mission Creep*

Synopsis: "As both a legal and a practical matter, the IMF has overstepped its authority and its competence in providing bailouts and adopting policies on a proliferation of topics."

For examples in the literature of some criticisms of the IMF along these lines, see:

- Celeste Boeri, *How to Solve Argentina's Debt Crisis: Will the IMF's Plan Work?*, 4 CHI. J. INT'L L. 245, 245–47 (2003) (criticizing a proposal for the IMF to establish a sovereign bankruptcy system because assuming such a role could, as a practical matter, conflict with its other functions);
- David Moberg, *How to Fix the IMF; First, Do No Harm*, IN THESE TIMES, May 15, 2000, at 9, 11 (notinng that "there is growing clamor . . . to drastically scale back the IMF to focus on its original mission of managing short-term currency problems" instead of "acting as enforcers for global capital");
- Jason Morgan-Foster, Note, *The Relationship of IMF Structural Adjustment Programs to Economic, Social, and Cultural Rights: The Argentine Case Revisited*, 24 MICH. J. INT'L L. 577, 631–32 (2003) (asserting that the international financial institutions should not have a role in protecting human rights, because the subject of human rights "is not mentioned in the institutions' statutes, and promotion of human rights will require a much more active human rights policy operation than the institutions have been set up to handle");
- Joseph E. Stiglitz, *Failure of the Fund: Rethinking the IMF Response*, 23 HARV. INT'L L. REV. 14, 16–18 (2001) (observing that the IMF's mandate has changed from that of providing liquidity to "that of a bill collector for lending nations," and recommending that the IMF "be restricted to crisis management" and that "[i]ts other functions should be given to other institutions");
- James Tobin & Gustav Ranis, *Flawed Fund: The IMF's Misplaced Priorities*, THE NEW REPUBLIC, Mar. 9, 1998, at 16, 17 (arguing

that "the IMF should stick to its original mission, saving its members from disasters due to short-term illiquidity" and not getting involved in "long-run structural and developmental issues");

- Kevin Watkins, Oxfam International, *The IMF: Shot By Both Sides* (Apr. 2000) (criticizing IMF "mission creep," and observing that now "the IMF's loan conditions cover everything from monetary policy to rapid trade liberalisation, financial deregulation, and privatisation") (earlier on www.bicusa.org website, now on file with author);
- Carol Welch, THE IMF AND GOOD GOVERNANCE 2 (Interhemispheric Res. Ctr. & Inst. for Policy Studies, Foreign Policy in Focus No. 33, Oct. 1998) (complaining that the IMF's "mission creep" into the area of "good governance, taking up the issues of corruption, transparency, tax reform, and other domestic concerns" represents another example of "the IMF's power grabs of the last several decades and entrenches the IMF in the position of giving development and stabilization advice even when its qualifications are highly dubious"), *available at* www.fpif.org/pdf/vol3/33ifimf.pdf (last visited Nov. 4, 2004).

Criticism #I-7—*Asymmetry in Obligations*

Synopsis: "The IMF permits its rich member countries to insist that the poor borrowing member countries follow certain policies without pressuring the rich countries to follow those policies themselves."

For examples in the literature of some criticisms of the IMF along these lines, see:

- *An Unequal World: Fair Trade is Needed to Eradicate Poverty*, GUARDIAN (LONDON), Apr. 13, 2002, n.p. (noting that "[w]hile goods from the developing world are kept out of western markets, poor nations are pressed by the International Monetary Fund and World Bank to open their markets too rapidly"), http//www.financialtimes.com and 2002 WL 18762058;
- Alan Beattie, *Raw Deal for Poor Nations Limits Backing for Free Trade*, FINANCIAL TIMES, Apr. 12, 2002, n.p. (noting that "while the [International Monetary] [F]und and [World] Bank have the ability via their lending programs to encourage—if not compel—liberalization in poor countries, they lack a similar lever with the Group of Seven leading industrial nations"), http://www.financialtimes.com and 2002 WL 18765849.

II. CRITICISMS OF THE MDBs

Criticism #II-1—*Bad Economic and Financial Policies and Projects*

Synopsis: "The MDBs promote a flawed laissez-faire economic model, conceive of 'development' too narrowly, and support bad projects that do not help the borrowing member countries."

For examples in the literature of writings that refer to this criticism generally, see:

- Andrew Balls, *World Bank/IMF Plan to Reduce Poverty Criticized*, FINANCIAL TIMES, July 23, 2004, at 8 (finding the World Bank's poverty reduction programs lacking in prioritization of development needs);
- Timothy A. Canova, Claire Moore Dickerson & Katherine V.W. Stone, *Labor and Finance as Inevitably Transnational: Globalization Demands a Sophisticated and Transnational Lens*, 41 SAN DIEGO L. REV. 109 (2004) (asserting that the World Bank's economic policies have had little impact in improving people's lives around the world);
- Celia Dugger, *World Bank Challenged: Are the Poor Really Helped?*, N.Y. TIMES, July 28, 2004, at A4 (criticizing the World Bank on grounds that its operations are not helping the poor);
- Raymond Baker & Jennifer Nordin, *How Dirty Money Binds the Poor*, FINANCIAL TIMES, Oct. 13, 2004, at 21 (condemning the World Bank for overlooking the global economy that conspires to keep poor countries poor, and for its narrow focus on corruption only);
- Michael Massing, *From Protest to Program*, THE AMERICAN PROSPECT, Summer 2001, at 2–3 (noting that the World Bank, mirroring the interests of its most powerful members, such as the United States, "continues to push on developing nations the same market reforms criticized in its *World Development Report [2000/ 2001]*");
- Bruce R. Scott, *The Great Divide in the Global Village*, 80 FOREIGN AFF. 160, 161 (2001) (noting that "the wealthy nations must . . . acknowledge that the 'Washington consensus,' which assumes that free markets will bring about economic convergence, is mistaken [and that those interests need to] abandon the notion that their own particular strategies are the best for all countries");
- Edward Sussex, *Too Many Words and Not Enough Action on Assistance*, FINANCIAL TIMES, Oct. 21, 2004, at 14 (arguing that the World Bank and WTO have little concern for their impact on the poor).

Some of the oldest attacks on the World Bank focus on this criticism #II-1. For example:

- Walden Bello, David Kinley & Elaine Elinson, DEVELOPMENT DEBACLE: THE WORLD BANK IN THE PHILIPPINES (1982) (asserting that World Bank operations in the Philippines were aimed at (i) "pacification," to defuse rural and urban unrest, and (ii) "liberalization," to open up the country more completely to the flow of U.S. capital and commodities);
- Vivencio R. Jose ed., MORTGAGING THE FUTURE: THE WORLD BANK AND IMF IN THE PHILIPPINES (1982) (referring to the "evil power" of the World Bank and the IMF and their domination by the United States, with the ultimate goal of exploiting the natural, manpower, and financial resources of the Philippines);
- Cheryl Payer, THE WORLD BANK: A CRITICAL ANALYSIS (1982). This especially harsh attack of the World Bank, criticizing it for (among other things) its capitalist foundations, calls for the elimination of the World Bank, and the author has a colorful response to those who would criticize her for making such a demand without offering suggestions about what to put in its place: "[I]f the charges in this book of the damage done to the lives of poor and working people by the class-biased development of the World Bank have any validity, why should we need to put anything in its place? If I wrote an attack on the Mafia no one would demand to know what I would put in its place." *Id.* at 357.

Criticism #II-2—*Wrong Form of Financial Assistance*

Synopsis: "MDB lending operations are anachronistic now that effective international capital markets exist; so MDB financing (if continued at all) should take the form of grants, not loans."

For an example in the literature of some criticisms of the MDBs along these lines, see:

- JOINT ECONOMIC COMMITTEE, REPORT OF THE INTERNATIONAL FINANCIAL INSTITUTIONS ADVISORY COMMISSION 6 (Mar. 2000) [the Meltzer Report] (implying that development lending is no longer necessary because "[w]ith the development and expansion of global financial markets, capital provided by the private sector now dwarfs the volume of lending the development banks have done or are likely to do in the future"), and at 11 (suggesting that "[g]rants should replace the traditional Bank tools of loans and guarantees").

A senior advisor to the chairman of the Meltzer Commission has elaborated on the proposal to replace MDB loans with grants. See:

- Adam Lerrick, *A Better Way to Lend A Hand,* 14 THE INT'L ECONOMY 36 (2000) (downplaying concerns that focusing solely on grants would soon deplete MDB resources, and asserting that grants would overcome many shortcomings of MDB lending operations).

For observations by another commentator on this subject, see:

- George Soros, GEORGE SOROS ON GLOBALIZATION 100 (2002) (complaining that "the World Bank has only limited funds available for outright grants and technical assistance," which would be more effective forms of World Bank assistance in some areas).

*Criticism #II-3—**Environmental Degradation***

Synopsis: "MDB-financed projects too often have devastating effects on the environment, because the MDBs disregard environmental issues at both the project design and project implementation phases."

For examples in the literature of some criticisms of the MDBs along these lines, see:

- Bank Information Center, *Hot Dividends: The World Bank's Investments in Climate Changing Fossil Fuels,* Aug. 2000, at 1 (claiming that "[t]he World Bank is doling out billions annually in loans and guarantees to fossil fuel projects—the greatest contributor to climate change—in the developing world") (earlier on www.bicusa.org website, now on file with author);
- Walden Bello, DEGLOBALIZATION: IDEAS FOR A NEW WORLD ECONOMY (2002) (citing the Chad-Cameroon pipeline, with World Bank involvement, as a major environmental disaster);
- Dana L. Clark, *The World Bank and Human Rights: The Need for Greater Accountability,* 15 HARV. HUM. RTS. J. 205 (2002) (asserting that notwithstanding its stated policies to the contrary, the World Bank engages in activities that undermine efforts to protect the environment and human rights);
- Forest Peoples Programme, *Forests and the World Bank: Concern Over Bank's New Plans to Finance Commercial Logging Operations in all Types of Forests,* Sept. 2001, at 2 (stating that civil society organizations "are alarmed that the World Bank is planning to reverse its current forest Policy by lifting its proscription against financing logging in primary tropical moist forests to

enable Bank financing of commercial-scale logging operations in all types of forest") (earlier on www.bicusa.org website, now on file with author);

- Mark Hertsgaard, *The World Bank and the Global Green Deal*, OXFAM EXCHANGE, Winter 2001, at 4 (asserting that "[t]ime and time again, [the World Bank] has financed gargantuan, ill-conceived projects whose anti-poverty effects are indirect at best and whose environmental consequences are downright disastrous");

- Todd Roessler, *The World Bank's Lending Policy and Environmental Standards*, 26 N.C. J. INT'L L. & COM. REG. 105 (2000) (contending that the World Bank has not consistently implemented its environmental protection policies and that it must do so in order to convince critics that it has learned from its past mistakes);

- Kay Treakle, *Accountability at the World Bank: What Does it Take? Lessons from the Yacyreta Hydroelectric Project, Argentina/Paraguay* (Sept. 1998) (noting that in the World Bank-financed Yacyreta Hydroelectric Project, the environmental assessment was not undertaken until the project was near completion and that, although several specific environmental concerns were to have been addressed before the opening of the dam, they never were), *at* http://www.bicusa.org/bicusa/issues/misc_resources/373.php (last visited Nov. 4, 2004);

- Shannon R. Wilson, *Sustainable Aquaculture: An Organizing Solution in International Law*, 26 T. JEFFERSON L. REV. 491 (2004) (citing criticisms of World Bank projects that allegedly polluted farm land).

Criticism #II-4—*Human Rights Shortcomings*

Synopsis: "The MDBs largely disregard human rights issues and act independently of any accepted human rights norms and institutions; and the MDBs fuel, not fight, public corruption."

For examples in the literature of some criticisms of the MDBs along these lines, see:

- Bank Information Center, *Problem Project Alert #8: ADB Funded Thailand Samut Prakarn Province Wastewater Management Project*, *at* http://www.bicusa.org/bicusa/issues/bic_publications/advocsp.pdf (last visited Nov. 10, 2004) (asserting that concerns expressed by the community to be affected by the AsDB-funded Samut Prakarn Wastewater Management Project—over the necessity of the project, the design of the project, the social and environmental ramifications of the project, the allegations of corruption surrounding the project, the lack of transparency and citizen participation in the project, and the violation of Bank policies and Thai laws surrounding the project—were submitted to the AsDB but were largely ignored);

- Bank Information Center, *The ADB-funded Samut Prakarn Province Wastewater Management Project in Thailand,* at http://www.bicusa.org/bicusa/issues/bic_publications/advocsp.pdf (last visited Nov. 10, 2004) (same);

- John D. Ciorciari, *The Lawful Scope of Human Rights Criteria in World Bank Credit Decisions: An Interpretive Analysis of the IBRD and IDA Articles of Agreement,* 33 CORNELL INT'L L.J. 331, 332–35 (2001) (citing the works of several scholars calling on the World Bank to take a more proactive role in the human rights arena);

- Dana L. Clark, *The World Bank and Human Rights: The Need for Greater Accountability,* 15 HARV. HUM. RTS. J. 205 (2002) (asserting that notwithstanding its stated policies to the contrary, the World Bank engages in activities that undermine efforts to protect the environment and human rights);

- Mac Darrow, BETWEEN THE LIGHT AND SHADOW: THE WORLD BANK, THE INTERNATIONAL MONETARY FUND AND INTERNATIONAL HUMAN RIGHTS 25 (2003) (finding the World Bank's standards and instruments on human rights lacking);

- Shirin Ebadi & Amir Attaran, *When Politics Corrupts Money,* N.Y. TIMES, June 16, 2004, at A21 (criticizing the World Bank for not respecting human rights);

- Thomas M. Franck, *Are Human Rights Universal?,* 80 FOREIGN AFF. 191, 204 (2001) (arguing that the World Bank should be proactively using loan conditionalities to protect human rights against the argument of cultural exceptionalism);

- Globalization Challenge Initiative, *Growing Danger of Economic Apartheid: How the World Bank Group's Private Sector Development (PSD) Strategy Threatens Basic Service Provisions (Health, Education and Water), Debt Reduction and PRSP Processes,* Sept. 2001, at 1 (asserting that "[i]n country after country, efforts [through loan conditionalities] by the World Bank Group to privatize health, education, and water systems are pushing the costs of public services out of the reach of ordinary people") (earlier on www.bicusa.org website, now on file with author);

- Korinna Horta, *Rhetoric and Reality: Human Rights and the World Bank,* 15 HARV. HUM. RTS. J. 227 (2002) (asserting that the World Bank has inappropriately made a disingenuous distinction by separating political and civil rights from economic and social rights and has improperly insisted that the former of these lies outside of its mandate);

- David Kinley & Junko Tadaki, *From Talk to Walk: The Emergence of Human Rights Responsibilities for Corporations at International Law,* 44 VA. J. INT'L L. 931 (2004) (finding the World Bank inappropriately reluctant to adopt a human rights perspective);

- Fergus MacKay, *Universal Rights or a Universe Unto Itself? Indigenous Peoples' Human Rights and the World Bank's Draft Operational Policy 4.10 on Indigenous Peoples,* 17 AM. U. INT'L L. REV. 527, 529–30 (2002) (criticizing the World Bank for "openly disregard[ing] a whole range of rights" in a way that "runs counter to mainstream thought about the nature of human rights and attendant international obligations");

- Michael Massing, *From Protest to Program,* THE AMERICAN PROSPECT, Summer 2001, at 7 (noting that the World Bank should use conditionalities to improve socially useful categories like education, but it does not);

- Results Educational Fund, *World Bank Water Policies Undermine Public Health,* Sept. 2001, at 2 (noting that the World Bank imposes a policy of increased cost recovery on water services without protecting poor water consumers) (earlier on www.bicusa.org website, now on file with author);

- Rick Rowden, *The World Bank and User Fees,* Sept. 2001, at 1 (noting that the World Bank conditions loans upon the willingness of a borrowing country's government to impose user fees on water, health and education services, effectively locking out the poorest people from accessing them) (earlier on www.bicusa.org website, now on file with author);

- Kay Treakle, *Accountability at the World Bank: What Does it Take? Lessons from the Yacyreta Hydroelectric Project, Argentina/Paraguay* (Sept. 1998), at n.p. (noting that in the Yacyreta Hydroelectric Project, concerns over the resettlement and compensation of displaced indigenous peoples were supposed to be addressed before the opening of the dam, but they never were).

For a careful examination of the relationship between the World Bank and international human rights law, see generally:

- Sigrun I. Skogly, THE HUMAN RIGHTS OBLIGATIONS OF THE WORLD BANK AND THE INTERNATIONAL MONETARY FUND (2001).

Questions about that relationship between the World Bank and international human rights are not new; they have been the subject of debate for many years. For a 1988 symposium on international development agencies, human rights, and environmental considerations, see:

- Symposium, *International Development Agencies (IDAs), Human Rights and Environmental Considerations,* 17 DENVER J. INT'L L. & POL'Y 29 (1988).

Criticism #II-5—*MDB Trampling of National Sovereignty*

Synopsis: "In imposing conditions on the rights of member countries to borrow, the MDBs violate the sovereignty of those countries, and in particular the principle of self-determination."

For examples in the literature of some criticisms along these lines, see several of the works cited in Part I of this Appendix, relating to the IMF, as many of the critics apply the "trampling of national sovereignty" complaint to both of the Bretton Woods institutions.

In addition, for a discussion of criticisms along these lines, see:

- Kamal Malhotra, *Globalization, Private Capital Flows and the Privatization of Infrastructure,* Presentation at the "BOOT: In the Public Interest?" conference (Mar. 1998) (asserting that "[t]he weakening of the State's role partly as a result of the economic policy advice of the World Bank and IMF . . . could reduce rather than enhance a government's ability to enact and enforce effective regulation of the market in the interests of the poor and disadvantaged.") (transcript *at* http://www.signposts.uts.edu.au/articles/Generic/Economy/410.html (last updated Jan. 27, 1999));
- Martin Wolf, *Will the Nation-State Survive Globalization?,* 80 FOREIGN AFF. 178, 184–85 (2001) (noting that globalization and the global institutions that regulate globalization, such as the World Bank, are "often [seen] as destroying [national] governments' capacities to do what they want or need [to do]").

Criticism #II-6—*Incoherence in Policy Prescriptions*

Synopsis: "Because there is inadequate coordination among the MDBs—and also between the MDBs and other GEOs—countries can be subject to conflicting economic and financial mandates."

For examples in the literature of some criticisms of the MDBs along these lines, see:

- JOINT ECONOMIC COMMITTEE, REPORT OF THE INTERNATIONAL FINANCIAL INSTITUTIONS ADVISORY COMMISSION 9 (Mar. 2000) [the Meltzer Report] (noting that coherence and cooperation problems exist between the World Bank and the regional development banks);

- Lisa Jordan, *The Death of Development? The Converging Policy Agendas of the World Bank and the World Trade Organization* (Nov. 1999) (suggesting that the World Bank's alliance with the WTO violates its special responsibility to developing nations), *at* http://www.bicusa.org/bicusa/issues/misc_resources/458. php (last visited Nov. 4, 2004);

- Rick Rowden, *The IMF, World Bank and WTO: Synthesizing Trade Liberalization Goals*, Sept. 2001, at 1 (noting that, for example, sometimes "when countries seek to address balance of payment difficulties in accordance with IMF and World Bank programs [these programs] conflict with WTO membership rules") (earlier on www.bicusa.org website, now on file with author).

Criticism #II-7—*Weaknesses in Staffing and Management*

Synopsis: "The MDBs are poorly managed, in part because (1) staff members are not properly accountable for their performance and (2) staff hiring and promotion rest on inappropriate criteria."

This criticism emerges mainly from my own experience and discussions with MDB officials. I am not aware of extensive treatment of this criticism in the pertinent literature, but:

- The Meltzer Report undertaken in 1999–2000 touches on one of the points incorporated into the summary of Criticism #II-7—the complaint that the MDBs have an "'approval culture' aimed at achieving yearly lending targets," and that this gives "[i]ncentives to lend for lending's sake. . . ." JOINT ECONOMIC COMMITTEE, REPORT OF THE INTERNATIONAL FINANCIAL INSTITUTIONS ADVISORY COMMISSION 75 (Mar. 2000);

- For a scathing condemnation of World Bank president James Wolfensohn, touching on some elements of this criticism, *see* Stephen Fidler, *Who's Minding the Bank?*, FOREIGN POLY, Sept.–Oct. 2001, at 40;

- An internal memorandum from a recently departed director of the Asian Development Bank asserted that the AsDB's "expert staff is 'thinly stretched, well beyond its overall capacity'" and complained that too many of the institution's senior positions were "filled with civil servants 'parachuted' in by member governments such as Japan." Shawn Donnan, *Ex-Director Lashes Out at ADB's 'Lack of Direction,'* FINANCIAL TIMES, Sept. 17, 2003, at 4.

Criticism #II-8—*MDB Secrecy and Opaqueness*

Synopsis: "The MDBs practice both documentary secretiveness and operational secretiveness, thereby remaining inappropriately hidden from scrutiny and insulated from external criticism."

For examples in the literature of some criticisms of the MDBs along these lines, see:

- Bank Information Center, *The Ongoing Struggle for World Bank Transparency—The Outcome of the Information Disclosure Policy Review* (Nov. 4, 2001) (noting that the World Bank's "unwillingness to subject Board meetings to public oversight will continue to undermine the credibility of the Bank's governance process"), *at* http://www.bicusa.org/bicusa/issues/misc_resources/456. php (last visited Nov. 4, 2004);
- Bank Information Center, *Development Bank Transparency: Issues and Opportunities for 2002–2003*, Transparency Briefing (Mar. 2002) (discussing MDB disclosure policies), *at* http://www.bicusa.org/bicusa/issues/TransparencyBriefing19Mar02.pdf (last visited Nov. 4, 2004);
- Shalmali Guttal, *Disclosure or Deception? Multilateral Institutions and Access to Information,* Presentation at Conference on Access to Information (Mar. 2002) (concluding that the information the World Bank discloses is worthless except in its purpose to occupy the public with "sometimes interesting and largely irrelevant information while the Bank gets on with business as usual") (transcript earlier on www.bicusa.org website, now on file with author).

Criticism #II-9—*The MDB Democracy Deficit*

Synopsis: "Controlled by a handful of rich countries and corporate interests, the MDBs are largely unaccountable to the people most affected by their operations."

For examples in the literature of writings that refer to this criticism generally, see:

- Nathalie Bernasconi-Osterwalder & David Hunter, *Democratizing Multilateral Development Banks* (noting that recent protests "suggest that international financial institutions will continue to lose legitimacy unless they become more transparent and accountable to both the people affected by their projects and those whose tax money supports them"), *in* THE "NEW PUBLIC":

GLOBALIZATION OF PUBLIC PARTICIPATION 151 (2002), *available at* http://www.ciel.org/Publications/Democratizing_MDBs _NewPublic.pdf (last visited Nov. 4, 2004);

- S. Mansoob Murshed, *Perspectives on Two Phases of Globalization*, appearing as chapter 1 in S. Mansoob Murshed ed., GLOBAL- IZATION, MARGINALIZATION AND DEVELOPMENT 1, 4 (2002) (cit- ing the allegedly undemocratic rules enforced by the World Bank and other GEOs);
- Richard Falk & Andrew Strauss, *Toward Global Parliament*, 80 FOREIGN AFF. 212, 212 (2001) (positing that "[o]ne crucial aspect of the rising disaffection with globalization is the lack of citizen participation in the global institutions that shape peo- ple's daily lives").

For a thoughtful discussion of the defects in the existing structure of accountability in the two Bretton Woods institutions, see generally:

- Ngaire Woods, *Making the IMF and the World Bank More Account- able*, 77 INT'L AFF. 83 (2001) (commenting that "[a]ccount- ability, in particular, has become the catchery of officials, scholars and activists in discussing the reform of the institu- tions"). [For further references to Ms. Woods' valuable work in this areas, *see* Subsection IIIB of Chapter Three.]

Two subsidiary strains of the "democracy deficit" criticism allege that MDBs give (1) too much attention or influence to corporate interests and (2) too little attention or influence to NGOs and other citizens' groups. For examples of the first of these points, see:

- Richard Falk & Andrew Strauss, *Toward Global Parliament*, 80 FOREIGN AFF. 212, 215 (2001) (stating that "[t]hrough expand- ing trade and investment, business and banking leaders have . . . exercised extraordinary influence on global policy");
- Michael Massing, *From Protest to Program*, THE AMERICAN PROS- PECT, Summer 2001, at 3 (noting that the global regulatory structure, including the World Bank, has failed to regulate and control multinational corporations and their drive to exploit the poorest labor and most unprotected environments in order to maximize profits).

For examples of the second point—that MDBs pay too little attention to NGOs—see:

- Falk & Strauss, *supra*, at 214–15 (suggesting that MDBs incor- porate NGOs into their institutions to serve as a "voice of the citizenry" and therefore help legitimize the MDBs);

- Massing, *supra*, at 6 (asserting that the MDBs should help the NGOs pressure national governments to reign in the multinational corporations through the use of conditionalities);
- The Development Gap, *Civil Society Engages World Bank in Assessment of Structural Adjustment Programs: Hundreds of Organizations to Hold Bank Accountable to Emerging Findings*, Sept. 2000, at 1 (noting that although the World Bank has encouraged its critics to participate in evaluating the impacts of its structural adjustment policies through the Structural Adjustment Policy Review Initiative, the World Bank "has yet to demonstrate any willingness to learn from the Initiative's . . . reviews, much less integrate that learning in its policy development, programming and operations") (earlier on www.bicusa.org website, now on file with author).

For a discussion of a specific defect found to exist in the weighted voting system at the World Bank—that is, the exceptionally large voting power of the United States (reflecting the size of its capital subscription)—see:

- Jennifer N. Weidner, *World Bank Study*, 7 BUFF. HUM. RTS. L. REV. 193 (2001) (suggesting that the World Bank Inspection Panel and other possible checks on the influence of the United States are thus far inadequate and proposing that a special one-state-one-vote rule apply in the event that a single shareholder attempts to control World Bank policy on the basis of its investment in the institution).

For a more general criticism of the distribution of voting power in the World Bank, see:

- Christopher Swann, *Sixty Years On, and Still Contentious: Bretton Woods Institutions*, FINANCIAL TIMES, May 29, 2004, at 10 (finding lack of progress in addressing the inequitable method of state representation).

Criticism #II-10—Narrowness of Economic Focus

Synopsis: "The MDBs interpret their charter mandates too rigidly by considering only strictly economic factors in assessing the development needs of their member countries and in designing projects."

For examples in the literature of some criticisms of the MDBs along these lines, see:

- Daniel D. Bradlow & Claudio Grossman, *Limited Mandates and Intertwined Problems: A New Challenge for the World Bank and the*

IMF, 17 HUM. RTS. Q. 411, 439 (1995) (asserting that the political prohibition in the MDB charters should not prevent them "from incorporating all matters governed by international law, such as human rights and the . . . environment, into their operations");

- Günther Handl, *The Legal Mandate of Multilateral Development Banks as Agents for Change Toward Sustainable Development*, 92 AM. J. INT'L L. 642, 653 (1998) (noting that "the question still remains to be answered whether . . . MDBs have an international legal obligation to heed the normative implications of sustainable development generally, notwithstanding the restrictive formal language of their constituent instruments").

Criticism #II-11—*MDB Mission Creep*

Synopsis: "The MDBs are gripped by 'policy proliferation'; they have diluted their commitment to true economic development by expanding their operations into areas in which they have no authority or competence."

For examples in the literature of some criticisms of the MDBs along these lines, see:

- John D. Ciorciari, *The Lawful Scope of Human Rights Criteria in World Bank Credit Decisions: An Interpretive Analysis of the IBRD and IDA Articles of Agreement*, 33 CORNELL INT'L L.J. 331, 335 (2001) (citing some "[c]ritics of World Bank intervention in the human rights arena [who] . . . contend that the Bretton Woods institutions already overstep their proper bounds in dictating legal and political policies to less developed nations");
- Jessica Einhorn, *The World Bank's Mission Creep*, 80 FOREIGN AFF. 22, 22, 24, 27, 29–32 (2001) (asserting that "[b]y now, [the World Bank's] mission has become so complex that it strains credulity to portray the bank as a manageable organization" and describing the ways in which the World Bank has gradually widened its focus to take account of environmental sustainability, equitable income distribution, institutional strengthening, debt relief, poverty reduction, financial crisis management, banking regulation, corporate governance, gender disparities, narcotics, crime, and corruption);
- FIFTY YEARS AFTER BRETTON WOODS: THE FUTURE OF THE IMF AND THE WORLD BANK 42 (James M. Boughton & K. Sarwar Lateef eds., 1995) (recording observations by Manmohan Singh that "the World Bank of the future must return to a more focused set of priorities and activities" on ground that the proliferation of new objectives and policies "lead[s] to a

too diffused pattern of lending, whose impact on development in the recipient countries is far from certain or beneficial");

- *Sixty Years On: The Bretton Woods Twins Are Useful But Need Better Parents*, FINANCIAL TIMES, July 3, 2004, at 12 (criticizing the World Bank for having too many competing priorities and for having "petty, self-interested" shareholders).

Criticism #II-12—*Asymmetry in Obligations*

Synopsis: "As in the IMF, the MDBs' rich member countries insist that the poor borrowing member countries follow certain policies, yet the rich countries can (and often do) fail to follow those policies themselves."

For examples in the literature of some criticisms of the MDBs along these lines, see:

- *An Unequal World: Fair Trade is Needed to Eradicate Poverty*, GUARDIAN (London), Apr. 13, 2002 (noting that "[w]hile goods from the developing world are kept out of western markets, poor nations are pressed by the International Monetary Fund and World Bank to open their markets too rapidly"), *available at* http://www.financialtimes.com and 2002 WL 18762058;
- Alan Beattie, *Raw Deal for Poor Nations Limits Backing for Free Trade: A Report by Oxfam Sounds a Critical Note on Liberalization Gains That are Skewed Towards Rich Countries*, FINANCIAL TIMES, Apr. 12, 2002 (noting that "while the [International Monetary] [F]und and [World][B]ank have the ability via their lending programs to encourage—if not compel—liberalization in poor countries, they lack a similar lever with the Group of Seven leading industrial nations"), *available at* http://www.financial-times.com;
- *The Great Global Trade Robbery*, BANGKOK POST, Apr. 11, 2002 (accusing the G-7 nations of using the World Bank to "force open poor countries' markets . . . [with policies that] the rich world has itself rejected"), *available at* http://www.financial-times.com and 2002 WL 18163944.

III. CRITICISMS OF THE WTO

Criticism #III-1—*Free Trade's Fostering of Economic Harm*

Synopsis: "The WTO's central aim is wrong, because free trade does more economic harm than good to a national society and to the world as a whole."

For one of the many examples in the literature of criticisms of the WTO along these lines, see:

- Fareed Zakaria, *Some Real Street Smarts*, NEWSWEEK, July 30, 2001, at 25, 25 (condemning economic globalism, and trade liberalization in particular).

Criticism #III-2—*Free Trade's Distributional Injustice*

Synopsis: "Even if free trade brings aggregate economic benefits, those benefits are not fairly distributed, either within a national economic system or among nations; and the WTO permits this injustice."

For examples in the literature of some criticisms of the WTO and free trade along these lines, see:

- C. Fred Bergsten, *America's Two-Front Economic Conflict*, FOREIGN AFF., Mar./Apr. 2001, at 16 (pointing out that globalization causes job and income losses in certain sectors);
- Ewell E. Murphy, Jr., *The Lessons of Seattle: Learning from the Failed Third WTO Ministerial Conference*, 13 TRANSNAT'L LAW. 273 (2000) (explaining the possible economic injury that free trade causes to persons other than (1) workers in developing countries nor (2) the well-to-do in developed countries).

Criticism #III-3—*Free Trade's Race to the Bottom*

Synopsis: "The WTO's free-trade agenda is wrong also because free trade causes a 'race to the bottom' in the regulatory standards for labor (worker safety and health) and environmental protection."

For examples in the literature of some criticisms of the WTO and the free-trade "agenda" along these lines, see:

- Chris Baltimore, *US Power Deregulation May Cause Trade Woes*, *available in* posting of David Orr, david@livingrivers.net, to CONS-SPST-ENERGY-FORUM@Lists.SIERRACLUB.ORG (Nov. 8, 2001) (on file with the author) (referring to a 2001 U.S. Energy Department report "that attributed increased power plant construction in Mexico to less stringent environmental regulations" and asserting more generally that pollution havens might emerge in some areas of less developed countries in order to attract coal plant construction);
- Lana Martin, *World Trade Organization and Environmental Protection: Reconciling the Conflict*, CURRENTS: INT'L TRADE L.J., Winter

2000, at 69 (discussing the adequacy of the WTO's environmental policies);

- *No Globalization without Representation!*, available at http://www.sierraclub.org/trade/summit/fact.asp (last visited Feb. 13, 2005) (asserting that the United States has weakened border food inspections and developed weak standards concerning imported agricultural pests);

- Margrete Strand, *Poisoned Workers and Poisoned Fields: Stop NAFTA's Fast-Track Expansion to South America*, available at www.sierraclub.org/trade/environment/poisoned.asp (last visited Feb. 13, 2005) (stating that the U.S. Environmental Protection Agency, in order to help U.S. growers compete with surging imports, "has increased chemical risks to farmworkers by reducing a critical safety factor—the reentry period—the time between when pesticides are sprayed on crops, and when growers can order farmworkers to reenter the fields").

Criticism #III-4—*WTO Disregard for Labor and Environmental Values*

Synopsis: "Even if free trade does not in itself cause a race to the bottom, the WTO fails to give adequate attention to environmental and labor concerns in its operations."

For one of many examples in the literature of some criticisms of the WTO along these lines, see:

- David Kinley and Junko Tadaki, *From Talk to Walk: The Emergence of Human Rights Responsibilities for Corporations at International Law*, 44 VA. J. INT'L L. 931 (2004) (arguing that "human rights principles ought to play a more significant part in the WTO's regulation of free trade").

Criticism #III-5—*WTO Secrecy and Opaqueness*

Synopsis: "The WTO is a closed, non-transparent organization that operates in secret, inappropriately hidden from scrutiny and hence insulated from external criticism."

For examples in the literature of some criticisms of the WTO along these lines, see:

- *Invisible Government*, N.Y. TIMES, Nov. 29, 1999, at A15 (presenting a full-page advertisement by the Turning Point Project featuring a person with no facial features and warning that the WTO "is emerging as the world's first global government [but]

. . . was elected by no-one, . . . operates in secrecy, and [has a mandate to] . . . undermine the constitutional rights of sovereign nations");

- Greg Palast, *The WTO's Hidden Agenda*, Nov. 9, 2001, *at* http: www.gregpalast.com/detail.cfm?artid=105&row=1 (reporting on "[t]hree confidential documents from inside the World Trade Organization Secretariat [that] . . . reveal the extraordinary secret entanglement of industry with government in designing European and American proposals for radical pro-business changes in WTO rules");

- Arie Reich, *The WTO as a Law-Harmonizing Institution*, 25 U. PA. J. INT'L ECON. L. 321, 367–68 (2004) (noting claims that WTO rule-making is "often shrouded under a heavy veil of secrecy").

Some complaints about WTO opaqueness date from very early in the life of the institution. For example, see:

- Steve Charnovitz, *Participation of Nongovernmental Organizations in the World Trade Organization*, 17 U. PA. J. INT'L ECON. L. 331 (Spring 1996) (asserting out that the WTO is as isolated from the public as the GATT had been, because the dispute settlement panels hold closed sessions, the WTO refuses to provide biographical information about panel members, all WTO committees hold closed sessions, NGOs cannot attend regular meetings of the General Council, and minutes are kept secret for two years).

Criticism #III-6—*The WTO Democracy Deficit*

Synopsis: "The WTO is undemocratic, both (1) in excluding participation by citizens and (2) in having no allegiance to political authorities—and hence can impose its will arbitrarily on its member countries."

Recent contributions to the literature relating to this criticism appear in the September 2004 issue of the *Journal of International Economic Law*, as part of a "Mini Symposium" carrying the title of "WTO Negotiator Meet the Academics—Challenge to the Legitimacy and Efficiency of the World Trading System." Among the papers included in that symposium issue (which largely explain, more than endorse, certain criticisms about WTO accountability) are:

- Ernst-Ulrich Petersmann, *The 'Human Rights Approach' Advocated by the UN High Commissioner for Human Rights and by the International Labour Organization: Is It Relevant for WTO Law and Policy?*, 7 J. INT'L ECON. L. 605 (2004) (citing concerns about the paucity of human rights considerations in WTO operations);

- Gary P. Sampson, *Is There a Need for Restructuring the Collaboration Among the WTO and UN Agencies So As To Harness Their Complementarities?*, 7 J. INT'L ECON. L. 717 (2004) (citing criticisms claiming that WTO rules encroach on national sovereignty and impede the proper workings of democratically elected national governments);
- Gregory Shaffer, *Parliamentary Oversight of WTO Rule-Making: The Political, Normative, and Practical Contexts*, 7 J. INT'L ECON. L. 629 (2004) (discussing possible creation of an inter-parliamentary WTO body).

Another set of symposium articles relating to the alleged WTO "democracy deficit"—and focusing particularly on the appropriateness of NGO participation in WTO operations—appeared in a University of Pennsylvania law journal in 1996. They include, among others:

- Steve Charnovitz, *Participation of Nongovernmental Organizations in the World Trade Organization*, 17 U. PA. J. INT'L ECON. L. 331 (Spring 1996) (discussing NGO participation in the policy work of the WTO and in the WTO dispute resolution process);
- G. Richard Shell, *The Trade Stakeholders Model and Participation by Nonstate Parties in the World Trade Organization*, 17 U. PA. J. INT'L ECON. L. 359 (Spring 1996) (discussing trade governance and asserting that the WTO needs to allow outsiders into the process to increase support for the institution).

For other works highlighting the "democracy deficit" criticism as it relates to the WTO, see:

- Jeffrey Atik, *Democratizing the WTO*, 33 GEO. WASH. INT'L L. REV. 455 (2001) (exploring "a particular style of legitimacy critique: the alleged lack of democracy within the WTO");
- Andrew T. Guzman, *Global Governance and the WTO*, 45 HARV. INT'L L.J. 303, 336–44 (2004) (identifying three types of "democracy problems" at the WTO: the lack of direct democratic input, the risk of regulatory capture, and the fact that adjudication by WTO tribunals takes place without any opportunity for legislative or executive checks and balances);
- Arie Reich, *The WTO as a Law-Harmonizing Institution*, 25 U. PA. J. INT'L ECON. L. 321, 367–68 (2004) (noting "criticism against the WTO for not allowing NGOs . . . to participate in the legislative process").

APPENDIX B
CHARTER OF THE IMF

Citation: Articles of Agreement of the International Monetary Fund, adopted at Bretton Woods, July 22, 1944, 2 U.N.T.S. 39, 60 Stat. 1401, T.I.A.S. No. 1501 (entered into force Dec. 27, 1945), as amended in 1969, 1976, and 1990. See Amendment of Articles of Agreement of the International Monetary Fund, approved May 31, 1968, 22 U.S.T. 2775, 726 U.N.T.S. 266 (entered into force July 28, 1969); Second Amendment to the Articles of Agreement of the International Monetary Fund, approved Apr. 30, 1976, 29 U.S.T. 2203, T.I.A.S. No. 8937, 15 I.L.M. 546 (entered into force Apr. 1, 1978); Third Amendment of the Articles of Agreement of the International Monetary Fund, approved June 28, 1990, 31 I.L.M. 1307, 1309–10 (entered into force Nov. 11, 1992).

Contents

XIX.   Operations and Transactions in Special drawing Rights
    1.   Use of special drawing rights
    2.   Operations and transactions between participants
    3.   Requirement of need
    4.   Obligation to provide currency
    5.   Designation of participants to provide currency
    6.   Reconstitution
    7.   Exchange rates

XX.   Special Drawing Rights Department Interest and Charges
    1.   Interest
    2.   Charges
    3.   Rate of interest and charges
    4.   Assessments
    5.   Payment of interest, charges, and assessments

XXI.   Administration of the General Department and the Special Drawing Rights Department

XXII.   General Obligations of Participants

XXIII.   Suspension of Operations and Transactions in Special Drawing Rights
    1.   Emergency provisions
    2.   Failure to fulfill obligations

XXIV.   Termination of Participation
    1.   Right to terminate participation
    2.   Settlement on termination
    3.   Interest and charges
    4.   Settlement of obligation to the Fund
    5.   Settlement of obligation to a terminating participant
    6.   General Resources Account transactions

XXV.   Liquidation of the Special drawing Rights Department

XXVI.   Withdrawal from Membership
    1.   Right of members to withdraw
    2.   Compulsory withdrawal
    3.   Settlement of accounts with members withdrawing

XXVII.   Emergency Provisions
    1.   Temporary suspension
    2.   Liquidation of the Fund

XXVIII.   Amendments

XXIX.   Interpretation

XXX.   Explanation of Terms

XXXI.   Final Provisions
     1.   Entry into force
     2.   Signature

SCHEDULES [Not Reproduced Here]

  A.   Quotas
  B.   Transitional Provisions with Respect to Repurchase, Payment of Additional Subscriptions, Gold, and Certain Operational Matters
  C.   Par Values
  D.   Council
  E.   Election of Executive Directors
  F.   Designation
  G.   Reconstitution
  H.   Termination of Participation
  I.   Administration of Liquidation of the Special Drawing Rights Department
  J.   Settlement of Accounts with Members Withdrawing
  K.   Administration of Liquidation
  L.   Suspension of Voting Rights

Articles of Agreement of the International Monetary Fund

The Governments on whose behalf the present Agreement is signed agree as follows:

Introductory Article

(i)   The International Monetary Fund is established and shall operate in accordance with the provisions of this Agreement as originally adopted and subsequently amended.

(ii)   To enable the Fund to conduct its operations and transactions, the Fund shall maintain a General Department and a Special Drawing Rights Department. Membership in the Fund shall give the right to participation in the Special Drawing Rights Department.

(iii) Operations and transactions authorized by this Agreement shall be conducted through the General Department, consisting in accordance with the provisions of this Agreement of the General Resources Account, the

Special Disbursement Account, and the Investment Account; except that operations and transactions involving special drawing rights shall be conducted through the Special Drawing Rights Department.

Article I

Purposes

The purposes of the International Monetary Fund are:

(i) To promote international monetary cooperation through a permanent institution which provides the machinery for consultation and collaboration on international monetary problems.

(ii) To facilitate the expansion and balanced growth of international trade, and to contribute thereby to the promotion and maintenance of high levels of employment and real income and to the development of the productive resources of all members as primary objectives of economic policy.

(iii) To promote exchange stability, to maintain orderly exchange arrangements among members, and to avoid competitive exchange depreciation.

(iv) To assist in the establishment of a multilateral system of payments in respect of current transactions between members and in the elimination of foreign exchange restrictions which hamper the growth of world trade.

(v) To give confidence to members by making the general resources of the Fund temporarily available to them under adequate safeguards, thus providing them with opportunity to correct maladjustments in their balance of payments without resorting to measures destructive of national or international prosperity.

(vi) In accordance with the above, to shorten the duration and lessen the degree of disequilibrium in the international balances of payments of members.

The Fund shall be guided in all its policies and decisions by the purposes set forth in this Article.

Article II

Membership

Section 1. Original members

The original members of the Fund shall be those of the countries represented at the United Nations Monetary and Financial Conference whose governments accept membership before December 31, 1945.

Section 2. Other members

Membership shall be open to other countries at such times and in accordance with such terms as may be prescribed by the Board of Governors. These terms, including the terms for subscriptions, shall be based on principles consistent with those applied to other countries that are already members.

Article III

Quotas and Subscriptions

Section 1. Quotas and payment of subscriptions

Each member shall be assigned a quota expressed in special drawing rights. The quotas of the members represented at the United Nations Monetary and Financial Conference which accept membership before December 31, 1945 shall be those set forth in Schedule A. The quotas of other members shall be determined by the Board of Governors. The subscription of each member shall be equal to its quota and shall be paid in full to the Fund at the appropriate depository.

Section 2. Adjustment of quotas

(a) The Board of Governors shall at intervals of not more than five years conduct a general review, and if it deems it appropriate propose an adjustment, of the quotas of the members. It may also, if it thinks fit, consider at any other time the adjustment of any particular quota at the request of the member concerned.

(b) The Fund may at any time propose an increase in the quotas of those members of the Fund that were members on August 31, 1975 in proportion to their quotas on that date in a cumulative amount not in excess of amounts transferred under Article V, Section 12(f)(i) and (j) from the Special Disbursement Account to the General Resources Account.

(c) An eighty-five percent majority of the total voting power shall be required for any change in quotas.

(d) The quota of a member shall not be changed until the member has consented and until payment has been made unless payment is deemed to have been made in accordance with Section 3(b) of this Article.

Section 3. Payments when quotas are changed

(a) Each member which consents to an increase in its quota under Section 2(a) of this Article shall, within a period determined by the Fund, pay to the Fund twenty-five percent of the increase in special drawing rights, but the Board of Governors may prescribe that this payment may be made, on the same basis for all members, in whole or in part in the currencies of other members specified, with their concurrence, by the Fund, or in the member's own currency. A non-participant shall pay in the currencies of other members specified by the Fund, with their concurrence, a proportion of the increase corresponding to the proportion to be paid in special drawing rights by participants. The balance of the increase shall be paid by the member in its own currency. The Fund's holdings of a member's currency shall not be increased above the level at which they would be subject to charges under Article V, Section 8(b)(ii), as a result of payments by other members under this provision.

(b) Each member which consents to an increase in its quota under Section 2(b) of this Article shall be deemed to have paid to the Fund an amount of subscription equal to such increase.

(c) If a member consents to a reduction in its quota, the Fund shall, within sixty days, pay to the member an amount equal to the reduction. The payment shall be made in the member's currency and in such amount of special drawing rights or the currencies of other members specified, with their concurrence, by the Fund as is necessary to prevent the reduction of the Fund's holdings of the currency below the new quota, provided that in exceptional circumstances the Fund may reduce its holdings of the currency below the new quota by payment to the member in its own currency.

(d) A seventy percent majority of the total voting power shall be required for any decision under (a) above, except for the determination of a period and the specification of currencies under that provision.

Section 4. Substitution of securities for currency

The Fund shall accept from any member, in place of any part of the member's currency in the General Resources Account which in the judgment of the Fund is not needed for its operations and transactions, notes or similar obligations issued by the member or the depository designated by the member under Article XIII, Section 2, which shall be non-negotiable, non-interest bearing and payable at their face value on demand by crediting the account of the Fund in the designated depository. This Section shall apply not only to currency subscribed by members but also to any currency otherwise due to, or acquired by, the Fund and to be placed in the General Resources Account.

Article IV

Obligations Regarding Exchange Arrangements

Section 1. General obligations of members

Recognizing that the essential purpose of the international monetary system is to provide a framework that facilitates the exchange of goods, services, and capital among countries, and that sustains sound economic growth, and that a principal objective is the continuing development of the orderly underlying conditions that are necessary for financial and economic stability, each member undertakes to collaborate with the Fund and other members to assure orderly exchange arrangements and to promote a stable system of exchange rates. In particular, each member shall:

(i) endeavor to direct its economic and financial policies toward the objective of fostering orderly economic growth with reasonable price stability, with due regard to its circumstances;

(ii) seek to promote stability by fostering orderly underlying economic and financial conditions and a monetary system that does not tend to produce erratic disruptions;

(iii) avoid manipulating exchange rates or the international monetary system in order to prevent effective balance of payments adjustment or to gain an unfair competitive advantage over other members; and

(iv) follow exchange policies compatible with the undertakings under this Section.

Section 2. General exchange arrangements

(a) Each member shall notify the Fund, within thirty days after the date of the second amendment of this Agreement, of the exchange arrangements it intends to apply in fulfillment of its obligations under Section 1 of this Article, and shall notify the Fund promptly of any changes in its exchange arrangements.

(b) Under an international monetary system of the kind prevailing on January 1, 1976, exchange arrangements may include

(i) the maintenance by a member of a value for its currency in terms of the special drawing right or another denominator, other than gold, selected by the member, or

(ii) cooperative arrangements by which members maintain the value of their currencies in relation to the value of the currency or currencies of other members, or

(iii) other exchange arrangements of a member's choice.

(c) To accord with the development of the international monetary system, the Fund, by an eighty-five percent majority of the total voting power, may make provision for general exchange arrangements without limiting the right of members to have exchange arrangements of their choice consistent with the purposes of the Fund and the obligations under Section 1 of this Article.

Section 3. Surveillance over exchange arrangements

(a) The Fund shall oversee the international monetary system in order to ensure its effective operation, and shall oversee the compliance of each member with its obligations under Section 1 of this Article.

(b) In order to fulfill its functions under (a) above, the Fund shall exercise firm surveillance over the exchange rate policies of members, and shall adopt specific principles for the guidance of all members with respect to those policies. Each member shall provide the Fund with the information necessary for such surveillance, and, when requested by the Fund, shall consult with it on the member's exchange rate policies. The principles adopted by the Fund shall be consistent with cooperative arrangements by which members maintain the value of their currencies in relation to the value of the currency or currencies of other members, as well as with other exchange arrangements of a member's choice consistent with the purposes of the Fund and Section 1 of this Article. These principles shall respect the domestic social and political policies of members, and in applying these principles the Fund shall pay due regard to the circumstances of members.

Section 4. Par values

The Fund may determine, by an eighty-five percent majority of the total voting power, that international economic conditions permit the introduction of a widespread system of exchange arrangements based on stable but adjustable par values. The Fund shall make the determination on the basis of the underlying stability of the world economy, and for this purpose shall take into account price movements and rates of expansion in the economies of members. The determination shall be made in light of the evolution of the international monetary system, with particular reference to sources of liquidity, and, in order to ensure the effective operation of a system of par values, to arrangements under which both members in surplus and members in deficit in their balances of payments take prompt, effective, and symmetrical action to achieve adjustment, as well as to arrangements for intervention and the treatment of imbalances. Upon making such determination, the Fund shall notify members that the provisions of Schedule C apply.

Section 5. Separate currencies within a member's territories

(a) Action by a member with respect to its currency under this Article shall be deemed to apply to the separate currencies of all territories in respect of which the member has accepted this Agreement under Article XXXI, Section 2(g) unless the member declares that its action relates either to the metropolitan currency alone, or only to one or more specified separate currencies, or to the metropolitan currency and one or more specified separate currencies.

(b) Action by the Fund under this Article shall be deemed to relate to all currencies of a member referred to in (a) above unless the Fund declares otherwise.

Article V

Operations and Transactions of the Fund

Section 1. Agencies dealing with the Fund

Each member shall deal with the Fund only through its Treasury, central bank, stabilization fund, or other similar fiscal agency, and the Fund shall deal only with or through the same agencies.

Section 2. Limitation on the Fund's operations and transactions

(a) Except as otherwise provided in this Agreement, transactions on the account of the Fund shall be limited to transactions for the purpose of supplying a member, on the initiative of such member, with special drawing rights or the currencies of other members from the general resources of the Fund, which shall be held in the General Resources Account, in exchange for the currency of the member desiring to make the purchase.

(b) If requested, the Fund may decide to perform financial and technical services, including the administration of resources contributed by members, that are consistent with the purposes of the Fund. Operations involved in the performance of such financial services shall not be on the account of the Fund. Services under this subsection shall not impose any obligation on a member without its consent.

Section 3. Conditions governing use of the Fund's general resources

(a) The Fund shall adopt policies on the use of its general resources, including policies on stand-by or similar arrangements, and may adopt special policies for special balance of payments problems, that will assist members to solve their balance of payments problems in a manner consistent with the provisions of this Agreement and that will establish adequate safeguards for the temporary use of the general resources of the Fund.

(b) A member shall be entitled to purchase the currencies of other members from the Fund in exchange for an equivalent amount of its own currency subject to the following conditions:

  (i) the member's use of the general resources of the Fund would be in accordance with the provisions of this Agreement and the policies adopted under them;

  (ii) the member represents that it has a need to make the purchase because of its balance of payments or its reserve position or developments in its reserves;

  (iii) the proposed purchase would be a reserve tranche purchase, or would not cause the Fund's holdings of the purchasing member's currency to exceed two hundred percent of its quota;

  (iv) the Fund has not previously declared under Section 5 of this Article, Article VI, Section 1, or Article XXVI, Section 2(a) that the member desiring to purchase is ineligible to use the general resources of the Fund.

(c) The Fund shall examine a request for a purchase to determine whether the proposed purchase would be consistent with the provisions of this Agreement and the policies adopted under them, provided that requests for reserve tranche purchases shall not be subject to challenge.

(d) The Fund shall adopt policies and procedures on the selection of currencies to be sold that take into account, in consultation with members, the balance of payments and reserve position of members and developments in the exchange markets, as well as the desirability of promoting over time balanced positions in the Fund, provided that if a member represents that it is proposing to purchase the currency of another member because the purchasing member wishes to obtain an equivalent amount of its own currency offered by the other member, it shall be entitled to purchase the currency of the other member unless the Fund has given notice under Article VII, Section 3 that its holdings of the currency have become scarce.

(e) (i) Each member shall ensure that balances of its currency purchased from the Fund are balances of a freely usable currency or can be exchanged at the time of purchase for a freely usable currency of its choice at an exchange rate between the two currencies equivalent to the exchange rate between them on the basis of Article XIX, Section 7(a).

(ii) Each member whose currency is purchased from the Fund or is obtained in exchange for currency purchased from the Fund shall collaborate with the Fund and other members to enable such balances of its currency to be exchanged, at the time of purchase, for the freely usable currencies of other members.

(iii) An exchange under (i) above of a currency that is not freely usable shall be made by the member whose currency is purchased unless that member and the purchasing member agree on another procedure.

(iv) A member purchasing from the Fund the freely usable currency of another member and wishing to exchange it at the time of purchase for another freely usable currency shall make the exchange with the other member if requested by that member. The exchange shall be made for a freely usable currency selected by the other member at the rate of exchange referred to in (i) above.

(f) Under policies and procedures which it shall adopt, the Fund may agree to provide a participant making a purchase in accordance with this Section with special drawing rights instead of the currencies of other members.

Section 4. Waiver of conditions

The Fund may in its discretion, and on terms which safeguard its interests, waive any of the conditions prescribed in Section 3(b)(iii) and (iv) of this Article, especially in the case of members with a record of avoiding large or continuous use of the Fund's general resources. In making a waiver it shall take into consideration periodic or exceptional requirements of the member requesting the waiver. The Fund shall also take into consideration a member's willingness to pledge as collateral security acceptable assets having a value sufficient in the opinion of the Fund to protect its interests and may require as a condition of waiver the pledge of such collateral security.

Section 5. Ineligibility to use the Fund's general resources

Whenever the Fund is of the opinion that any member is using the general resources of the Fund in a manner contrary to the purposes of the Fund, it shall present to the member a report setting forth the views of the Fund and prescribing a suitable time for reply. After presenting such a report to a member, the Fund may limit the use of its general resources by the member. If no reply to the report is received from the member within the prescribed time, or if the reply received is unsatisfactory, the Fund may continue to limit the member's use of the general resources of the Fund or may, after giving reasonable notice to the member, declare it ineligible to use the general resources of the Fund.

Section 6. Other purchases and sales of special drawing rights by the Fund

(a) The Fund may accept special drawing rights offered by a participant in exchange for an equivalent amount of the currencies of other members.

(b) The Fund may provide a participant, at its request, with special drawing rights for an equivalent amount of the currencies of other members. The Fund's holdings of a member's currency shall not be increased as a result of these transactions above the level at which the holdings would be subject to charges under Section 8(b)(ii) of this Article.

(c) The currencies provided or accepted by the Fund under this Section shall be selected in accordance with policies that take into account the principles of Section 3(d) or 7(i) of this Article. The Fund may enter into transactions under this Section only if a member whose currency is provided or accepted by the Fund concurs in that use of its currency.

Section 7. Repurchase by a member of its currency held by the Fund

(a) A member shall be entitled to repurchase at any time the Fund's holdings of its currency that are subject to charges under Section 8(b) of this Article.

(b) A member that has made a purchase under Section 3 of this Article will be expected normally, as its balance of payments and reserve position improves, to repurchase the Fund's holdings of its currency that result from the purchase and are subject to charges under Section 8(b) of this Article. A member shall repurchase these holdings if, in accordance with policies on repurchase that the Fund shall adopt and after consultation with the member, the Fund represents to the member that it should repurchase because of an improvement in its balance of payments and reserve position.

(c) A member that has made a purchase under Section 3 of this Article shall repurchase the Fund's holdings of its currency that result from the purchase and are subject to charges under Section 8(b) of this Article not later than five years after the date on which the purchase was made. The Fund may prescribe that repurchase shall be made by a member in installments during the period beginning three years and ending five years after the date of a purchase. The Fund, by an eighty-five percent majority of the total voting power, may change the periods for repurchase under this subsection, and any period so adopted shall apply to all members.

(d) The Fund, by an eighty-five percent majority of the total voting power, may adopt periods other than those that apply in accordance with (c) above, which shall be the same for all members, for the repurchase of holdings of currency acquired by the Fund pursuant to a special policy on the use of its general resources.

(e) A member shall repurchase, in accordance with policies that the Fund shall adopt by a seventy percent majority of the total voting power, the Fund's holdings of its currency that are not acquired as a result of purchases and are subject to charges under Section 8(b)(ii) of this Article.

(f) A decision prescribing that under a policy on the use of the general resources of the Fund the period for repurchase under (c) or (d) above shall be shorter than the one in effect under the policy shall apply only to holdings acquired by the Fund subsequent to the effective date of the decision.

(g) The Fund, on the request of a member, may postpone the date of discharge of a repurchase obligation, but not beyond the maximum period under (c) or (d) above or under policies adopted by the Fund under (e) above, unless the Fund determines, by a seventy percent majority of the total voting power, that a longer period for repurchase which is consistent with the temporary use of the general resources of the Fund is justified because discharge on the due date would result in exceptional hardship for the member.

(h) The Fund's policies under Section 3(d) of this Article may be supplemented by policies under which the Fund may decide after consultation with a member to sell under Section 3(b) of this Article its holdings of the member's currency that have not been repurchased in accordance with this Section 7, without prejudice to any action that the Fund may be authorized to take under any other provision of this Agreement.

(i) All repurchases under this Section shall be made with special drawing rights or with the currencies of other members specified by the Fund. The Fund shall adopt policies and procedures with regard to the currencies to be used by members in making repurchases that take into account the principles in Section 3(d) of this Article. The Fund's holdings of a member's currency that is used in repurchase shall not be increased by the repurchase above the level at which they would be subject to charges under Section 8(b)(ii) of this Article.

(j) (i) If a member's currency specified by the Fund under (i) above is not a freely usable currency, the member shall ensure that the repurchasing member can obtain it at the time of the repurchase in exchange for a freely usable currency selected by the member whose currency has been specified. An exchange of currency under this provision shall take place at an exchange rate between the two currencies equivalent to the exchange rate between them on the basis of Article XIX, Section 7(a).

(ii) Each member whose currency is specified by the Fund for repurchase shall collaborate with the Fund and other members to enable repurchasing members, at the time of the repurchase, to obtain the specified currency in exchange for the freely usable currencies of other members.

(iii) An exchange under (j)(i) above shall be made with the member whose currency is specified unless that member and the repurchasing member agree on another procedure.

(iv) If a repurchasing member wishes to obtain, at the time of the repurchase, the freely usable currency of another member specified by the Fund under (i) above, it shall, if requested by the other member, obtain the currency from the other member in exchange for a freely usable currency at the rate of exchange referred to in (j)(i) above. The Fund may adopt regulations on the freely usable currency to be provided in an exchange.

Section 8. Charges

(a) (i) The Fund shall levy a service charge on the purchase by a member of special drawing rights or the currency of another member held in the General Resources Account in exchange for its own currency, provided that the Fund may levy a lower service charge on reserve tranche purchases than on other purchases. The service charge on reserve tranche purchases shall not exceed one-half of one percent.

(ii) The Fund may levy a charge for stand-by or similar arrangements. The Fund may decide that the charge for an arrangement shall be offset against the service charge levied under (i) above on purchases under the arrangement.

(b) The Fund shall levy charges on its average daily balances of a member's currency held in the General Resources Account to the extent that they (i) have been acquired under a policy that has been the subject of an exclusion under Article XXX(c), or (ii) exceed the amount of the member's quota after excluding any balances referred to in (i) above. The rates of charge normally shall rise at intervals during the period inwhich the balances are held.

(c) If a member fails to make a repurchase required under Section 7 of this Article, the Fund, after consultation with the member on the reduction of the Fund's holdings of its currency, may impose such charges as the Fund deems appropriate on its holdings of the member's currency that should have been repurchased.

(d) A seventy percent majority of the total voting power shall be required for the determination of the rates of charge under (a) and (b) above, which shall be uniform for all members, and under (c) above.

(e) A member shall pay all charges in special drawing rights, provided that in exceptional circumstances the Fund may permit a member to pay charges in the currencies of other members specified by the Fund, after consultation with them, or in its own currency. The Fund's holdings of a member's currency shall not be increased as a result of payments by other members under this provision above the level at which they would be subject to charges under (b)(ii) above.

Section 9. Remuneration

(a) The Fund shall pay remuneration on the amount by which the percentage of quota prescribed under (b) or (c) below exceeds the Fund's average daily balances of a member's currency held in the General Resources Account other than balances acquired under a policy that has been the subject of an exclusion under Article XXX(c). The rate of remuneration, which shall be determined by the Fund by a seventy percent majority of the total voting power, shall be the same for all members and shall be not more than, nor less than four-fifths of, the rate of interest under Article XX, Section 3. In establishing the rate of remuneration, the Fund shall take into account the rates of charge under Article V, Section 8(b).

(b) The percentage of quota applying for the purposes of (a) above shall be:

  (i) for each member that became a member before the second amendment of this Agreement, a percentage of quota corresponding to seventy-five percent of its quota on the date of the second amendment of this Agreement, and for each member that became a member after the date of the second amendment of this Agreement, a percentage of quota calculated by dividing the total of the amounts corresponding to the percentages of quota that apply to the other members on the date on which the member became a member by the total of the quotas of the other members on the same date; plus

  (ii) the amounts it has paid to the Fund in currency or special drawing rights under Article III, Section 3(a) since the date applicable under (b)(i) above; and minus

  (iii) the amounts it has received from the Fund in currency or special drawing rights under Article III, Section 3(c) since the date applicable under (b)(i) above.

(c) The Fund, by a seventy percent majority of the total voting power, may raise the latest percentage of quota applying for the purposes of (a) above to each member to:

    (i) a percentage, not in excess of one hundred percent, that shall be determined for each member on the basis of the same criteria for all members, or

    (ii) one hundred percent for all members.

(d) Remuneration shall be paid in special drawing rights, provided that either the Fund or the member may decide that the payment to the member shall be made in its own currency.

Section 10. Computations

(a) The value of the Fund's assets held in the accounts of the General Department shall be expressed in terms of the special drawing right.

(b) All computations relating to currencies of members for the purpose of applying the provisions of this Agreement, except Article IV and Schedule C, shall be at the rates at which the Fund accounts for these currencies in accordance with Section 11 of this Article.

(c) Computations for the determination of amounts of currency in relation to quota for the purpose of applying the provisions of this Agreement shall not include currency held in the Special Disbursement Account or in the Investment Account.

Section 11. Maintenance of value

(a) The value of the currencies of members held in the General Resources Account shall be maintained in terms of the special drawing right in accordance with exchange rates under Article XIX, Section 7(a).

(b) An adjustment in the Fund's holdings of a member's currency pursuant to this Section shall be made on the occasion of the use of that currency in an operation or transaction between the Fund and another member and at such other times as the Fund may decide or the member may request. Payments to or by the Fund in respect of an adjustment shall be made within a reasonable time, as determined by the Fund, after the date of adjustment, and at any other time requested by the member.

Section 12. Other operations and transactions

(a) The Fund shall be guided in all its policies and decisions under this Section by the objectives set forth in Article VIII, Section 7 and by the objective of avoiding the management of the price, or the establishment of a fixed price, in the gold market.

(b) Decisions of the Fund to engage in operations or transactions under (c), (d), and (e) below shall be made by an eighty-five percent majority of the total voting power.

(c) The Fund may sell gold for the currency of any member after consulting the member for whose currency the gold is sold, provided that the Fund's holdings of a member's currency held in the General Resources Account shall not be increased by the sale above the level at which they would be subject to charges under Section 8(b)(ii) of this Article without the concurrence of the member, and provided that, at the request of the member, the Fund at the time of sale shall exchange for the currency of another member such part of the currency received as would prevent such an increase. The exchange of a currency for the currency of another member shall be made after consultation with that member, and shall not increase the Fund's holdings of that member's currency above the level at which they would be subject to charges under Section 8(b)(ii) of this Article. The Fund shall adopt policies and procedures with regard to exchanges that take into account the principles applied under Section 7(i) of this Article. Sales under this provision to a member shall be at a price agreed for each transaction on the basis of prices in the market.

(d) The Fund may accept payments from a member in gold instead of special drawing rights or currency in any operations or transactions under this Agreement. Payments to the Fund under this provision shall be at a price agreed for each operation or transaction on the basis of prices in the market.

(e) The Fund may sell gold held by it on the date of the second amendment of this Agreement to those members that were members on August 31, 1975 and that agree to buy it, in proportion to their quotas on that date. If the Fund intends to sell gold under (c) above for the purpose of (f)(ii) below, it may sell to each developing member that agrees to buy it that portion of the gold which, if sold under (c) above, would have produced the excess that could have been distributed to it under (f)(iii) below. The gold that would be sold under this provision to a member that has been declared ineligible to use the general resources of the Fund under Section 5 of this Article shall be sold to it when the ineligibility ceases, unless the Fund decides to make the sale sooner. The sale of gold to a member under this subsection (e) shall be made in exchange for its currency and at a price equivalent at the time of sale to one special drawing right per 0.888671 gram of fine gold.

(f) Whenever under (c) above the Fund sells gold held by it on the date of the second amendment of this Agreement, an amount of the proceeds equivalent at the time of sale to one special drawing right per 0.888 671 gram of fine gold shall be placed in the General Resources Account and, except as the Fund may decide otherwise under (g) below, any excess shall be held in the Special Disbursement Account. The assets held in the Special Disbursement Account shall be held separately from the other accounts of the General Department, and may be used at any time:

(i) to make transfers to the General Resources Account for immediate use in operations and transactions authorized by provisions of this Agreement other than this Section;

(ii) for operations and transactions that are not authorized by other provisions of this Agreement but are consistent with the purposes of the Fund. Under this subsection (f)(ii) balance of payments assistance may be made available on special terms to developing members in difficult circumstances, and for this purpose the Fund shall take into account the level of per capita income;

(iii) for distribution to those developing members that were members on August 31, 1975, in proportion to their quotas on that date, of such part of the assets that the Fund decides to use for the purposes of (ii)above as corresponds to the proportion of the quotas of these members on the date of distribution to the total of the quotas of all members on the same date, provided that the distribution under this provision to a member that has been declared ineligible to use the general resources of the Fund under Section 5 of this Article shall be made when the ineligibility ceases, unless the Fund decides to make the distribution sooner.

Decisions to use assets pursuant to (i) above shall be taken by a seventy percent majority of the total voting power, and decisions pursuant to (ii) and (iii) above shall be taken by an eighty-five percent majority of the total voting power.

(g) The Fund may decide, by an eighty-five percent majority of the total voting power, to transfer a part of the excess referred to in (f) above to the Investment Account for use pursuant to the provisions of Article XII, Section 6(f).

(h) Pending uses specified under (f) above, the Fund may invest a member's currency held in the Special Disbursement Account in marketable obligations of that member or in marketable obligations of international financial organizations. The income of investment and interest received under (f)(ii) above shall be placed in the Special Disbursement Account. No investment shall be made without the concurrence of the member whose currency is used to make the investment. The Fund shall invest only in obligations denominated in special drawing rights or in the currency used for investment.

(i) The General Resources Account shall be reimbursed from time to time in respect of the expenses of administration of the Special Disbursement Account paid from the General Resources Account by transfers from the Special Disbursement Account on the basis of a reasonable estimate of such expenses.

(j) The Special Disbursement Account shall be terminated in the event of the liquidation of the Fund and may be terminated prior to liquidation of the Fund by a seventy percent majority of the total voting power. Upon termination of the account because of the liquidation of the Fund, any assets in this account shall be distributed in accordance with the provisions of Schedule K. Upon termination prior to liquidation of the Fund, any assets in this account shall be transferred to the General Resources Account for immediate use in operations and transactions. The Fund, by a seventy percent majority of the total voting power, shall adopt rules and regulations for the administration of the Special Disbursement Account.

Article VI

Capital Transfers

Section 1. Use of the Fund's general resources for capital transfers

(a) A member may not use the Fund's general resources to meet a large or sustained outflow of capital except as provided in Section 2 of this Article, and the Fund may request a member to exercise controls to prevent such use of the general resources of the Fund. If, after receiving such a request, a member fails to exercise appropriate controls, the Fund may declare the member ineligible to use the general resources of the Fund.

(b) Nothing in this Section shall be deemed:

    (i) to prevent the use of the general resources of the Fund for capital transactions of reasonable amount required for the expansion of exports or in the ordinary course of trade, banking, or other business; or

    (ii) to affect capital movements which are met out of a member's own resources, but members undertake that such capital movements will be in accordance with the purposes of the Fund.

Section 2. Special provisions for capital transfers

A member shall be entitled to make reserve tranche purchases to meet capital transfers.

Section 3. Controls of capital transfers

Members may exercise such controls as are necessary to regulate international capital movements, but no member may exercise these controls in a manner which will restrict payments for current transactions or which will unduly delay transfers of funds in settlement of commitments, except as provided in Article VII, Section 3(b) and in Article XIV, Section 2.

Article VII

Replenishment and Scarce Currencies

Section 1. Measures to replenish the Fund's holdings of currencies

The Fund may, if it deems such action appropriate to replenish its holdings of any member's currency in the General Resources. Replenishment and Scarce Currencies Account needed in connection with its transactions, take either or both of the following steps:

(i) propose to the member that, on terms and conditions agreed between the Fund and the member, the latter lend its currency to the Fund or that, with the concurrence of the member, the Fund borrow such currency from some other source either within or outside the territories of the member, but no member shall be under any obligation to make such loans to the Fund or to concur in the borrowing of its currency by the Fund from any other source;

(ii) require the member, if it is a participant, to sell its currency to the Fund for special drawing rights held in the General Resources Account, subject to Article XIX, Section 4. In replenishing with special drawing rights, the Fund shall pay due regard to the principles of designation under Article XIX, Section 5.

Section 2. General scarcity of currency

If the Fund finds that a general scarcity of a particular currency is developing, the Fund may so inform members and may issue a report setting forth the causes of the scarcity and containing recommendations designed to bring it to an end. A representative of the member whose currency is involved shall participate in the preparation of the report.

Section 3. Scarcity of the Fund's holdings

(a) If it becomes evident to the Fund that the demand for a member's currency seriously threatens the Fund's ability to supply that currency, the Fund, whether or not it has issued a report under Section 2 of this article, shall formally declare such currency scarce and shall thenceforth apportion its existing and accruing supply of the scarce currency with due regard to the relative needs of members, the general international economic situation, and any other pertinent considerations. The Fund shall also issue a report concerning its action.

(b) A formal declaration under (a) above shall operate as an authorization to any member, after consultation with the Fund, temporarily to impose limitations on the freedom of exchange operations in the scarce currency. Subject to the provisions of Article IV and Schedule C, the member shall have complete jurisdiction in determining the nature of such limitations, but they shall be no more restrictive than is necessary to limit the demand for the scarce currency to the supply held by, or accruing to, the member in question, and they shall be relaxed and removed as rapidly as conditions permit.

(c) The authorization under (b) above shall expire whenever the Fund formally declares the currency in question to be no longer scarce.

Section 4. Administration of restrictions

Any member imposing restrictions in respect of the currency of any other member pursuant to the provisions of Section 3(b) of this Article shall give sympathetic consideration to any representations by the other member regarding the administration of such restrictions.

Section 5. Effect of other international agreements on restrictions

Members agree not to invoke the obligations of any engagements entered into with other members prior to this Agreement in such manner as will prevent the operation of the provisions of this Article.

Article VIII

General Obligations of Members

Section 1. Introduction

In addition to the obligations assumed under other articles of this Agreement, each member undertakes the obligations set out in this Article.

Section 2. Avoidance of restrictions on current payments

(a) Subject to the provisions of Article VII, Section 3(b) and Article XIV, Section 2, no member shall, without the approval of the Fund, impose restrictions on the making of payments and transfers for current international transactions.

(b) Exchange contracts which involve the currency of any member and which are contrary to the exchange control regulations of that member maintained or imposed consistently with this Agreement shall be unenforceable in the territories of any member. In addition, members may, by mutual accord, cooperate in measures for the purpose of making the exchange control regulations of either member more effective, provided that such measures and regulations are consistent with this Agreement.

Section 3. Avoidance of discriminatory currency practices

No member shall engage in, or permit any of its fiscal agencies referred to in Article V, Section 1 to engage in, any discriminatory currency arrangements or multiple currency practices, whether within or outside margins under Article IV or prescribed by or under Schedule C, except as authorized under this Agreement or approved by the Fund. If such arrangements and practices are engaged in at the date when this Agreement enters into force, the member concerned shall consult with the Fund as to their progressive removal unless they are maintained or imposed under Article XIV, Section 2, in which case the provisions of Section 3 of that Article shall apply.

Section 4. Convertibility of foreign-held balances

(a) Each member shall buy balances of its currency held by another member if the latter, in requesting the purchase, represents:

  (i) that the balances to be bought have been recently acquired as a result of current transactions; or

  (ii) that their conversion is needed for making payments for current transactions.

The buying member shall have the option to pay either in special drawing rights, subject to Article XIX, Section 4, or in the currency of the member making the request.

(b) The obligation in (a) above shall not apply when:

  (i) the convertibility of the balances has been restricted consistently with Section 2 of this Article or Article VI, Section 3;

  (ii) the balances have accumulated as a result of transactions effected before the removal by a member of restrictions maintained or imposed under Article XIV, Section 2;

  (iii) the balances have been acquired contrary to the exchange regulations of the member which is asked to buy them; the currency of the member requesting the purchase has been declared scarce under Article VII, Section 3(a); or

(iv) the currency of the member requesting the purchase has been declared scarce under Article VII, Section 3(a); or

(v) the member requested to make the purchase is for any reason not entitled to buy currencies of other members from the Fund for its own currency.

Section 5. Furnishing of information

(a) The Fund may require members to furnish it with such information as it deems necessary for its activities, including, as the minimum necessary for the effective discharge of the Fund's duties, national data on the following matters:

(i) official holdings at home and abroad of (1) gold, (2) foreign exchange;

(ii) holdings at home and abroad by banking and financial agencies, other than official agencies, of (1) gold, (2) foreign exchange;

(iii) production of gold;

(iv) gold exports and imports according to countries of destination and origin;

(v) total exports and imports of merchandise, in terms of local currency values, according to countries of destination and origin;

(vi) international balance of payments, including (1) trade in goods and services, (2) gold transactions, (3) known capital transactions, and (4) other items;

(vii) international investment position, i.e., investments within the territories of the member owned abroad and investments abroad owned by persons in its territories so far as it is possible to furnish this information;

(viii) national income;

(ix) price indices, i.e., indices of commodity prices in wholesale and retail markets and of export and import prices;

(x) buying and selling rates for foreign currencies;

(xi) exchange controls, i.e., a comprehensive statement of exchange controls in effect at the time of assuming membership in the Fund and details of subsequent changes as they occur; and

(xii) where official clearing arrangements exist, details of amounts awaiting clearance in respect of commercial and financial transactions, and of the length of time during which such arrears have been outstanding.

(b) In requesting information the Fund shall take into consideration the varying ability of members to furnish the data requested. Members shall be under no obligation to furnish information in such detail that the affairs of individuals or corporations are disclosed. Members undertake, however, to furnish the desired information in as detailed and accurate a manner as is practicable and, so far as possible, to avoid mere estimates.

(c) The Fund may arrange to obtain further information by agreement with members. It shall act as a center for the collection and exchange of information on monetary and financial problems, thus facilitating the preparation of studies designed to assist members in developing policies which further the purposes of the Fund.

Section 6. Consultation between members regarding existing international agreements

Where under this Agreement a member is authorized in the special or temporary circumstances specified in the Agreement to maintain or establish restrictions on exchange transactions, and there are other engagements between members entered into prior to this Agreement which conflict with the application of such restrictions, the parties to such engagements shall consult with one another with a view to making such mutually acceptable adjustments as may be necessary. The provisions of this Article shall be without prejudice to the operation of Article VII, Section 5.

Section 7. Obligation to collaborate regarding policies on reserve assets

Each member undertakes to collaborate with the Fund and with other members in order to ensure that the policies of the member with respect to reserve assets shall be consistent with the objectives of promoting better international surveillance of international liquidity and making the special drawing right the principal reserve asset in the international monetary system.

Article IX

Status, Immunities, and Privileges

Section 1. Purposes of Article

To enable the Fund to fulfill the functions with which it is entrusted, the status, immunities, and privileges set forth in this Article shall be accorded to the Fund in the territories of each member.

Section 2. Status of the Fund

The Fund shall possess full juridical personality, and in particular, the capacity:

  (i) to contract;

(ii) to acquire and dispose of immovable and movable property; and

(iii) to institute legal proceedings.

Section 3. Immunity from judicial process

The Fund, its property and its assets, wherever located and by whomsoever held, shall enjoy immunity from every form of judicial process except to the extent that it expressly waives its immunity for the purpose of any proceedings or by the terms of any contract.

Section 4. Immunity from other action

Property and assets of the Fund, wherever located and by whomsoever held, shall be immune from search, requisition, confiscation, expropriation, or any other form of seizure by executive or legislative action.

Section 5. Immunity of archives

The archives of the Fund shall be inviolable.

Section 6. Freedom of assets from restrictions

To the extent necessary to carry out the activities provided for in this Agreement, all property and assets of the Fund shall be free from restrictions, regulations, controls, and moratoria of any nature.

Section 7. Privilege for communications

The official communications of the Fund shall be accorded by members the same treatment as the official communications of other members.

Section 8. Immunities and privileges of officers and employees

All Governors, Executive Directors, Alternates, members of committees, representatives appointed under Article XII, Section 3(j), advisors of any of the foregoing persons, officers, and employees of the Fund:

(i) shall be immune from legal process with respect to acts performed by them in their official capacity except when the Fund waives this immunity;

(ii) not being local nationals, shall be granted the same immunities from immigration restrictions, alien registration requirements, and national service obligations and the same facilities as regards exchange restrictions as are accorded by members to the representatives, officials, and employees of comparable rank of other members; and

(iii) shall be granted the same treatment in respect of traveling facilities as is accorded by members to representatives, officials, and employees of comparable rank of other members.

Section 9. Immunities from taxation

(a) The Fund, its assets, property, income, and its operations and transactions authorized by this Agreement shall be immune from all taxation and from all customs duties. The Fund shall also be immune from liability for the collection or payment of any tax or duty.

(b) No tax shall be levied on or in respect of salaries and emoluments paid by the Fund to Executive Directors, Alternates, officers, or employees of the Fund who are not local citizens, local subjects, or other local nationals.

(c) No taxation of any kind shall be levied on any obligation or security issued by the Fund, including any dividend or interest thereon, by whomsoever held:

  (i) which discriminates against such obligation or security solely because of its origin; or

  (ii) if the sole jurisdictional basis for such taxation is the place or currency in which it is issued, made payable or paid, or the location of any office or place of business maintained by the Fund.

Section 10. Application of Article

Each member shall take such action as is necessary in its own territories for the purpose of making effective in terms of its own law the principles set forth in this Article and shall inform the Fund of the detailed action which it has taken.

Article X

Relations with Other International Organizations

The Fund shall cooperate within the terms of this Agreement with any general international organization and with public international organizations having specialized responsibilities in related fields. Any arrangements for such cooperation which would involve a modification of any provision of this Agreement may be effected only after amendment to this Agreement under Article XXVIII.

Article XI

Relations with Non-Member Countries

Section 1 Undertakings regarding relations with non-member countries

Each member undertakes:

(i) not to engage in, nor to permit any of its fiscal agencies referred to in Article V, Section 1 to engage in, any transactions with a non-member or with persons in a non-member's territories which would be contrary to the provisions of this Agreement or the purposes of the Fund;

(ii) not to cooperate with a non-member or with persons in a non-member's territories in practices which would be contrary to the provisions of this Agreement or the purposes of the Fund; and

(iii) to cooperate with the Fund with a view to the application in its territories of appropriate measures to prevent transactions with non-members or with persons in their territories which would be contrary to the provisions of this Agreement or the purposes of the Fund.

Section 2. Restrictions on transactions with non-member countries

Nothing in this Agreement shall affect the right of any member to impose restrictions on exchange transactions with non-members or with persons in their territories unless the Fund finds that such restrictions prejudice the interests of members and are contrary to the purposes of the Fund.

Article XII

Organization and Management

Section 1. Structure of the Fund

The Fund shall have a Board of Governors, an Executive Board, a Managing Director, and a staff, and a Council if the Board of Governors decides, by an eighty-five percent majority of the total voting power, that the provisions of Schedule D shall be applied.

Section 2. Board of Governors

(a) All powers under this Agreement not conferred directly on the Board of Governors, the Executive Board, or the Managing Director shall be vested in the Board of Governors. The Board of Governors shall consist of

one Governor and one Alternate appointed by each member in such manner as it may determine. Each Governor and each Alternate shall serve
until a new appointment is made. No Alternate may vote except in the
absence of his principal. The Board of Governors shall select one of the
Governors as Chairman.

(b) The Board of Governors may delegate to the Executive Board authority to exercise any powers of the Board of Governors, except the powers
conferred directly by this Agreement on the Board of Governors.

(c) The Board of Governors shall hold such meetings as may be provided
for by the Board of Governors or called by the Executive Board. Meetings
of the Board of Governors shall be called whenever requested by fifteen
members or by members having one-quarter of the total voting power.

(d) A quorum for any meeting of the Board of Governors shall be a majority of the Governors having not less than two-thirds of the total voting power.

(e) Each Governor shall be entitled to cast the number of votes allotted
under Section 5 of this Article to the member appointing him.

(f) The Board of Governors may by regulation establish a procedure
whereby the Executive Board, when it deems such action to be in the best
interests of the Fund, may obtain a vote of the Governors on a specific
question without calling a meeting of the Board of Governors.

(g) The Board of Governors, and the Executive Board to the extent authorized, may adopt such rules and regulations as may be necessary or appropriate to conduct the business of the Fund.

(h) Governors and Alternates shall serve as such without compensation
from the Fund, but the Fund may pay them reasonable expenses incurred
in attending meetings.

(i) The Board of Governors shall determine the remuneration to be paid
to the Executive Directors and their Alternates and the salary and terms of
the contract of service of the Managing Director.

(j) The Board of Governors and the Executive Board may appoint such
committees as they deem advisable. Membership of committees need not
be limited to Governors or Executive Directors or their Alternates.

Section 3. Executive Board

(a) The Executive Board shall be responsible for conducting the business
of the Fund, and for this purpose shall exercise all the powers delegated to
it by the Board of Governors.

(b) The Executive Board shall consist of Executive Directors with the Managing Director as chairman. Of the Executive Directors:

    (i) five shall be appointed by the five members having the largest quotas; and

    (ii) fifteen shall be elected by the other members.

For the purpose of each regular election of Executive Directors, the Board of Governors, by an eighty-five percent majority of the total voting power, may increase or decrease the number of Executive Directors in (ii) above. The number of Executive Directors in (ii) above shall be reduced by one or two, as the case may be, if Executive Directors are appointed under (c) below, unless the Board of Governors decides, by an eighty-five percent majority of the total voting power, that this reduction would hinder the effective discharge of the functions of the Executive Board or of Executive Directors or would threaten to upset a desirable balance in the Executive Board.

(c) If, at the second regular election of Executive Directors and there-after, the members entitled to appoint Executive Directors under (b)(I) above do not include the two members, the holdings of whose currencies by the Fund in the General Resources Account have been, on the average over the preceding two years, reduced below their quotas by the largest absolute amounts in terms of the special drawing right, either one or both of such members, as the case may be, may appoint an Executive Director.

(d) Elections of elective Executive Directors shall be conducted at intervals of two years in accordance with the provisions of Schedule E, supplemented by such regulations as the Fund deems appropriate. For each regular election of Executive Directors, the Board of Governors may issue regulations making changes in the proportion of votes required to elect Executive Directors under the provisions of Schedule E.

(e) Each Executive Director shall appoint an Alternate with full power to act for him when he is not present. When the Executive Directors appointing them are present, Alternates may participate in meetings but may not vote.

(f) Executive Directors shall continue in office until their successors are appointed or elected. If the office of an elected Executive Director becomes vacant more than ninety days before the end of his term, another Executive Director shall be elected for the remainder of the term by the members that elected the former Executive Director. A majority of the votes cast shall be required for election. While the office remains vacant, the Alternate of the former Executive Director shall exercise his powers, except that of appointing an Alternate.

(g) The Executive Board shall function in continuous session at the principal office of the Fund and shall meet as often as the business of the Fund may require.

(h) A quorum for any meeting of the Executive Board shall be a majority of the Executive Directors having not less than one-half of the total voting power.

(i) (i) Each appointed Executive Director shall be entitled to cast the number of votes allotted under Section 5 of this Article to the member appointing him.

    (ii) If the votes allotted to a member that appoints an Executive Director under (c) above were cast by an Executive Director together with the votes allotted to other members as a result of the last regular election of Executive Directors, the member may agree with each of the other members that the number of votes allotted to it shall be cast by the appointed Executive Director. A member making such an agreement shall not participate in the election of Executive Directors.

    (iii) Each elected Executive Director shall be entitled to cast the number of votes which counted towards his election.

    (iv) When the provisions of Section 5(b) of this Article are applicable, the votes which an Executive Director would otherwise be entitled to cast shall be increased or decreased correspondingly. All the votes which an Executive Director is entitled to cast shall be cast as a unit.

    (v) When the suspension of the voting rights of a member is terminated under Article XXVI, Section 2(b), and the member is not entitled to appoint an Executive Director, the member may agree with all the members that have elected an Executive Director that the number of votes allotted to that member shall be cast by such Executive Director, provided that, if no regular election of Executive Directors has been conducted during the period of the suspension, the Executive Director in whose election the member had participated prior to the suspension, or his successor elected in accordance with paragraph 3(c) (i) of Schedule L or with (f) above, shall be entitled to cast the number of votes allotted to the member. The member shall be deemed to have participated in the election of the Executive Director entitled to cast the number of votes allotted to the member.

(j) The Board of Governors shall adopt regulations under which a member not entitled to appoint an Executive Director under (b) above may send a representative to attend any meeting of the Executive Board when a request made by, or a matter particularly affecting, that member is under consideration.

Section 4. Managing Director and staff

(a) The Executive Board shall select a Managing Director who shall not be a Governor or an Executive Director. The Managing Director shall be chairman of the Executive Board, but shall have no vote except a deciding vote in case of an equal division. He may participate in meetings of the Board of Governors, but shall not vote at such meetings. The Managing Director shall cease to hold office when the Executive Board so decides.

(b) The Managing Director shall be chief of the operating staff of the Fund and shall conduct, under the direction of the Executive Board, the ordinary business of the Fund. Subject to the general control of the Executive Board, he shall be responsible for the organization, appointment, and dismissal of the staff of the Fund.

(c) The Managing Director and the staff of the Fund, in the discharge of their functions, shall owe their duty entirely to the Fund and to no other authority. Each member of the Fund shall respect the international character of this duty and shall refrain from all attempts to influence any of the staff in the discharge of these functions.

(d) In appointing the staff the Managing Director shall, subject to the paramount importance of securing the highest standards of efficiency and of technical competence, pay due regard to the importance of recruiting personnel on as wide a geographical basis as possible.

Section 5. Voting

(a) Each member shall have two hundred fifty votes plus one additional vote for each part of its quota equivalent to one hundred thousand special drawing rights.

(b) Whenever voting is required under Article V, Section 4 or 5, each member shall have the number of votes to which it is entitled under (a) above adjusted

    (i) by the addition of one vote for the equivalent of each four hundred thousand special drawing rights of net sales of its currency from the general resources of the Fund up to the date when the vote is taken, or

    (ii) by the subtraction of one vote for the equivalent of each four hundred thousand special drawing rights of its net purchases under Article V, Section 3(b) and (f) up to the date when the vote is taken, provided that neither net purchases nor net sales shall be deemed at any time to exceed an amount equal to the quota of the member involved.

(c) Except as otherwise specifically provided, all decisions of the Fund shall be made by a majority of the votes cast.

Section 6. Reserves, distribution of net income, and investment

(a) The Fund shall determine annually what part of its net income shall be placed to general reserve or special reserve, and what part, if any, shall be distributed.

(b) The Fund may use the special reserve for any purpose for which it may use the general reserve, except distribution.

(c) If any distribution is made of the net income of any year, it shall be made to all members in proportion to their quotas.

(d) The Fund, by a seventy percent majority of the total voting power, may decide at any time to distribute any part of the general reserve. Any such distribution shall be made to all members in proportion to their quotas.

(e) Payments under (c) and (d) above shall be made in special drawing rights, provided that either the Fund or the member may decide that the payment to the member shall be made in its own currency.

(f) (i) The Fund may establish an Investment Account for the purposes of this subsection (f). The assets of the Investment Account shall be held separately from the other accounts of the General Department.

   (ii) The Fund may decide to transfer to the Investment Account a part of the proceeds of the sale of gold in accordance with Article V, Section 12(g) and, by a seventy percent majority of the total voting power, may decide to transfer to the Investment Account, for immediate investment, currencies held in the General Resources Account. The amount of these transfers shall not exceed the total amount of the general reserve and the special reserve at the time of the decision.

   (iii) The Fund may invest a member's currency held in the Investment Account in marketable obligations of that member or in marketable obligations of international financial organizations. No investment shall be made without the concurrence of the member whose currency is used to make the investment. The Fund shall invest only in obligations denominated in special drawing rights or in the currency used for investment.

   (iv) The income of investment may be invested in accordance with the provisions of this subsection (f). Income not invested shall be held in the Investment Account or may be used for meeting the expenses of conducting the business of the Fund.

(v)   The Fund may use a member's currency held in the Investment Account to obtain the currencies needed to meet the expenses of conducting the business of the Fund.

(vi) The Investment Account shall be terminated in the event of liquidation of the Fund and may be terminated, or the amount of the investment may be reduced, prior to liquidation of the Fund by a seventy percent majority of the total voting power. The Fund, by a seventy percent majority of the total voting power, shall adopt rules and regulations regarding administration of the Investment Account, which shall be consistent with (vii), (viii), and (ix) below.

(vii) Upon termination of the Investment Account because of liquidation of the Fund, any assets in this account shall be distributed in accordance with the provisions of Schedule K, provided that a portion of these assets corresponding to the proportion of the assets transferred to this account under Article V, Section 12(g) to the total of the assets transferred to this account shall be deemed to be assets held in the Special Disbursement Account and shall be distributed in accordance with Schedule K, paragraph 2(a)(ii).

(viii) Upon termination of the Investment Account prior to liquidation of the Fund, a portion of the assets held in this account corresponding to the proportion of the assets transferred to this account under Article V, Section 12(g) to the total of the assets transferred to the account shall be transferred to the Special Disbursement Account if it has not been terminated, and the balance of the assets held in the Investment Account shall be transferred to the General Resources Account for immediate use in operations and transactions.

(ix) On a reduction of the amount of the investment by the Fund, a portion of the reduction corresponding to the proportion of the assets transferred to the Investment Account under Article V, Section 12(g) to the total of the assets transferred to this account shall be transferred to the Special Disbursement Account if it has not been terminated, and the balance of the reduction shall be transferred to the General Resources Account for immediate use in operations and transactions.

Section 7. Publication of reports

(a) The Fund shall publish an annual report containing an audited statement of its accounts, and shall issue, at intervals of three months or less, a summary statement of its operations and transactions and its holdings of special drawing rights, gold, and currencies of members.

(b) The Fund may publish such other reports as it deems desirable for carrying out its purposes.

Section 8. Communication of views to members

The Fund shall at all times have the right to communicate its views informally to any member on any matter arising under this Agreement. The Fund may, by a seventy percent majority of the total voting power, decide to publish a report made to a member regarding its monetary or economic conditions and developments which directly tend to produce a serious disequilibrium in the international balance of payments of members. If the member is not entitled to appoint an Executive Director, it shall be entitled to representation in accordance with Section 3(j) of this Article. The Fund shall not publish a report involving changes in the fundamental structure of the economic organization of members.

Article XIII

Offices and Depositories

Section 1. Location of offices

The principal office of the Fund shall be located in the territory of the member having the largest quota, and agencies or branch offices may be established in the territories of other members.

Section 2. Depositories

(a) Each member shall designate its central bank as a depository for all the Fund's holdings of its currency, or if it has no central bank it shall designate such other institution as may be acceptable to the Fund.

(b) The Fund may hold other assets, including gold, in the depositories designated by the five members having the largest quotas and in such other designated depositories as the Fund may select. Initially, at least one half of the holdings of the Fund shall be held in the depository designated by the member in whose territories the Fund has its principal office and at least forty percent shall be held in the depositories designated by the remaining four members referred to above. However, all transfers of gold by the Fund shall be made with due regard to the costs of transport and anticipated requirements of the Fund. In an emergency the Executive Board may transfer all or any part of the Fund's gold holdings to any place where they can be adequately protected.

Section 3. Guarantee of the Fund's assets

Each member guarantees all assets of the Fund against loss resulting from failure or default on the part of the depository designated by it.

Article XIV

Transitional Arrangements

Section 1. Notification to the Fund

Each member shall notify the Fund whether it intends to avail itself of the transitional arrangements in Section 2 of this Article, or whether it is prepared to accept the obligations of Article VIII, Sections 2, 3, and 4. A member availing itself of the transitional arrangements shall notify the Fund as soon thereafter as it is prepared to accept these obligations.

Section 2. Exchange restrictions

A member that has notified the Fund that it intends to avail itself of transitional arrangements under this provision may, notwithstanding the provisions of any other articles of this Agreement, maintain and adapt to changing circumstances the restrictions on payments and transfers for current international transactions that were in effect on the date on which it became a member. Members shall, however, have continuous regard in their foreign exchange policies to the purposes of the Fund, and, as soon as conditions permit, they shall take all possible measures to develop such commercial and financial arrangements with other members as will facilitate international payments and the promotion of a stable system of exchange rates. In particular, members shall withdraw restrictions maintained under this Section as soon as they are satisfied that they will be able, in the absence of such restrictions, to settle their balance of payments in a manner which will not unduly encumber their access to the general resources of the Fund.

Section 3. Action of the Fund relating to restrictions

The Fund shall make annual reports on the restrictions in force under Section 2 of this Article. Any member retaining any restrictions inconsistent with Article VIII, Sections 2, 3, or 4 shall consult the Fund annually as to their further retention. The Fund may, if it deems such action necessary in exceptional circumstances, make representations to any member that conditions are favorable for the withdrawal of any particular restriction, or for the general abandonment of restrictions, inconsistent with the provisions of any other articles of this Agreement. The member shall be given a suitable time to reply to such representations. If the Fund finds that the member persists in maintaining restrictions which are inconsistent with the purposes of the Fund, the member shall be subject to Article XXVI, Section 2(a).

Article XV

Special Drawing Rights

Section 1. Authority to allocate special drawing rights

To meet the need, as and when it arises, for a supplement to existing reserve assets, the Fund is authorized to allocate special drawing rights to members that are participants in the Special Drawing Rights Department.

Section 2. Valuation of the special drawing right

The method of valuation of the special drawing right shall be determined by the Fund by a seventy percent majority of the total voting power, provided, however, that an eighty-five percent majority of the total voting power shall be required for a change in the principle of valuation or a fundamental change in the application of the principle in effect.

Article XVI

General Department and Special Drawing Rights Department

Section 1. Separation of operations and transactions

All operations and transactions involving special drawing rights shall be conducted through the Special Drawing Rights Department. All other operations and transactions on the account of the Fund authorized by or under this Agreement shall be conducted through the General Department. Operations and transactions pursuant to Article XVII, Section 2 shall be conducted through the General Department as well as the Special Drawing Rights Department.

Section 2. Separation of assets and property

All assets and property of the Fund, except resources administered under Article V, Section 2(b), shall be held in the General Department, provided that assets and property acquired under Article XX, Section 2 and Articles XXIV and XXV and Schedules H and I shall be held in the Special Drawing Rights Department. Any assets or property held in one Department shall not be available to discharge or meet the liabilities, obligations, or losses of the Fund incurred in the conduct of the operations and transactions of the other Department, except that the expenses of conducting the business of the Special Drawing Rights Department shall be paid by the Fund from the General Department which shall be reimbursed in special drawing rights from time to time by assessments under Article XX, Section 4 made on the basis of a reasonable estimate of such expenses.

Section 3. Recording and information

All changes in holdings of special drawing rights shall take effect only when recorded by the Fund in the Special Drawing Rights Department. Participants shall notify the Fund of the provisions of this Agreement under which special drawing rights are used. The Fund may require participants to furnish it with such other information as it deems necessary for its functions.

Article XVII

Participants and Other Holders of Special Drawing Rights

Section 1. Participants

Each member of the Fund that deposits with the Fund an instrument setting forth that it undertakes all the obligations of a participant in the Special Drawing Rights Department in accordance with its law and that it has taken all steps necessary to enable it to carry out all of these obligations shall become a participant in the Special Drawing Rights Department as of the date the instrument is deposited, except that no member shall become a participant before the provisions of this Agreement pertaining exclusively to the Special Drawing Rights Department have entered into force and instruments have been deposited under this Section by members that have at least seventy-five percent of the total of quotas.

Section 2. Fund as a holder

The Fund may hold special drawing rights in the General Resources Account and may accept and use them in operations and transactions conducted through the General Resources Account with participants in accordance with the provisions of this Agreement or with prescribed holders in accordance with the terms and conditions prescribed under Section 3 of this Article.

Section 3. Other holders

The Fund may prescribe:

   (i)   as holders, non-members, members that are non-participants, institutions that perform functions of a central bank for more than one member, and other official entities;

(ii) the terms and conditions on which prescribed holders may be permitted to hold special drawing rights and may accept and use them in operations and transactions with participants and other prescribed holders; and

(iii) the terms and conditions on which participants and the Fund through the General Resources Account may enter into operations and transactions in special drawing rights with prescribed holders.

An eighty-five percent majority of the total voting power shall be required for prescriptions under (i) above. The terms and conditions prescribed by the Fund shall be consistent with the provisions of this Agreement and the effective functioning of the Special Drawing Rights Department.

Article XVIII

Allocation and Cancellation of Special Drawing Rights

Section 1. Principles and considerations governing allocation and cancellation

(a) In all its decisions with respect to the allocation and cancellation of special drawing rights the Fund shall seek to meet the long-term global need, as and when it arises, to supplement existing reserve assets in such manner as will promote the attainment of its purposes and will avoid economic stagnation and deflation as well as excess demand and inflation in the world.

(b) The first decision to allocate special drawing rights shall take into account, as special considerations, a collective judgment that there is a global need to supplement reserves, and the attainment of a better balance of payments equilibrium, as well as the likelihood of a better working of the adjustment process in the future.

Section 2. Allocation and cancellation

(a) Decisions of the Fund to allocate or cancel special drawing rights shall be made for basic periods which shall run consecutively and shall be five years in duration. The first basic period shall begin on the date of the first decision to allocate special drawing rights or such later date as may be specified in that decision. Any allocations or cancellations shall take place at yearly intervals.

(b) The rates at which allocations are to be made shall be expressed as percentages of quotas on the date of each decision to allocate. The rates at which special drawing rights are to be cancelled shall be expressed as percentages of net cumulative allocations of special drawing rights on the date of each decision to cancel. The percentages shall be the same for all participants.

(c) In its decision for any basic period the Fund may provide, notwithstanding (a) and (b) above, that:

    (i) the duration of the basic period shall be other than five years; or

    (ii) the allocations or cancellations shall take place at other than yearly intervals; or

    (iii) the basis for allocations or cancellations shall be the quotas or net cumulative allocations on dates other than the dates of decisions to allocate or cancel.

(d) A member that becomes a participant after a basic period starts shall receive allocations beginning with the next basic period in which allocations are made after it becomes a participant unless the Fund decides that the new participant shall start to receive allocations beginning with the next allocation after it becomes a participant. If the Fund decides that a member that becomes a participant during a basic period shall receive allocations during the remainder of that basic period and the participant was not a member on the dates established under (b) or (c) above, the Fund shall determine the basis on which these allocations to the participant shall be made.

(e) A participant shall receive allocations of special drawing rights made pursuant to any decision to allocate unless:

    (i) the Governor for the participant did not vote in favor of the decision; and

    (ii) the participant has notified the Fund in writing prior to the first allocation of special drawing rights under that decision that it does not wish special drawing rights to be allocated to it under the decision. On the request of a participant, the Fund may decide to terminate the effect of the notice with respect to allocations of special drawing rights subsequent to the termination.

(f) If on the effective date of any cancellation the amount of special drawing rights held by a participant is less than its share of the special drawing rights that are to be cancelled, the participant shall eliminate its negative balance as promptly as its gross reserve position permits and shall remain in consultation with the Fund for this purpose. Special drawing rights acquired by the participant after the effective date of the cancellation shall be applied against its negative balance and cancelled.

Section 3. Unexpected major developments

The Fund may change the rates or intervals of allocation or cancellation during the rest of a basic period or change the length of a basic period or start a new basic period, if at any time the Fund finds it desirable to do so because of unexpected major developments. Section 4. Decisions on allocations and cancellations

(a) Decisions under Section 2(a), (b), and (c) or Section 3 of this Article shall be made by the Board of Governors on the basis of proposals of the Managing Director concurred in by the Executive Board.

(b) Before making any proposal, the Managing Director, after having satisfied himself that it will be consistent with the provisions of Section 1(a) of this Article, shall conduct such consultations as will enable him to ascertain that there is broad support among participants for the proposal. In addition, before making a proposal for the first allocation, the Managing Director shall satisfy himself that the provisions of Section 1(b) of this Article have been met and that there is broad support among participants to begin allocations; he shall make a proposal for the first allocation as soon after the establishment of the Special Drawing Rights Department as he is so satisfied.

(c) The Managing Director shall make proposals:

    (i) not later than six months before the end of each basic period;

    (ii) if no decision has been taken with respect to allocation or cancellation for a basic period, whenever he is satisfied that the provisions of (b) above have been met;

    (iii) when, in accordance with Section 3 of this Article, he considers that it would be desirable to change the rate or intervals of allocation or cancellation or change the length of a basic period or start a new basic period; or

    (iv) within six months of a request by the Board of Governors or the Executive Board;

provided that, if under (i), (iii), or (iv) above the Managing Director ascertains that there is no proposal which he considers to be consistent with the provisions of Section 1 of this Article that has broad support among participants in accordance with (b) above, he shall report to the Board of Governors and to the Executive Board.

(d) An eighty-five percent majority of the total voting power shall be required for decisions under Section 2(a), (b), and (c) or Section 3 of this Article except for decisions under Section 3 with respect to a decrease in the rates of allocation.

Article XIX

Operations and Transactions in Special Drawing Rights

Section 1. Use of special drawing rights

Special drawing rights may be used in the operations and transactions authorized by or under this Agreement.

Section 2. Operations and transactions between participants

(a) A participant shall be entitled to use its special drawing rights to obtain an equivalent amount of currency from a participant designated under Section 5 of this Article.

(b) A participant, in agreement with another participant, may use its special drawing rights to obtain an equivalent amount of currency from the other participant.

(c) The Fund, by a seventy percent majority of the total voting power, may prescribe operations in which a participant is authorized to engage in agreement with another participant on such terms and conditions as the Fund deems appropriate. The terms and conditions shall be consistent with the effective functioning of the Special Drawing Rights Department and the proper use of special drawing rights in accordance with this Agreement.

(d) The Fund may make representations to a participant that enters into any operation or transaction under (b) or (c) above that in the judgment of the Fund may be prejudicial to the process of designation according to the principles of Section 5 of this Article or is otherwise inconsistent with Article XXII. A participant that persists in entering into such operations or transactions shall be subject to Article XXIII, Section 2(b).

Section 3. Requirement of need

(a) In transactions under Section 2(a) of this Article, except as otherwise provided in (c) below, a participant will be expected to use its special drawing rights only if it has a need because of its balance of payments or its reserve position or developments in its reserves, and not for the sole purpose of changing the composition of its reserves.

(b) The use of special drawing rights shall not be subject to challenge on the basis of the expectation in (a) above, but the Fund may make representations to a participant that fails to fulfill this expectation. A participant that persists in failing to fulfill this expectation shall be subject to Article XXIII, Section 2(b).

(c) The Fund may waive the expectation in (a) above in any transactions in which a participant uses special drawing rights to obtain an equivalent amount of currency from a participant designated under Section 5 of this Article that would promote reconstitution by the other participant under Section 6(a) of this Article; prevent or reduce a negative balance of the other participant; or offset the effect of a failure by the other participant to fulfill the expectation in (a) above.

Section 4. Obligation to provide currency

(a) A participant designated by the Fund under Section 5 of this Article shall provide on demand a freely usable currency to a participant using special drawing rights under Section 2(a) of this Article. A participant's obligation to provide currency shall not extend beyond the point at which its holdings of special drawing rights in excess of its net cumulative allocation are equal to twice its net cumulative allocation or such higher limit as may be agreed between a participant and the Fund.

(b) A participant may provide currency in excess of the obligatory limit or any agreed higher limit.

Section 5. Designation of participants to provide currency

(a) The Fund shall ensure that a participant will be able to use its special drawing rights by designating participants to provide currency for specified amounts of special drawing rights for the purposes of Sections 2(a) and 4 of this Article. Designations shall be made in accordance with the following general principles supplemented by such other principles as the Fund may adopt from time to time:

> (i) A participant shall be subject to designation if its balance of payments and gross reserve position is sufficiently strong, but this will not preclude the possibility that a participant with a strong reserve position will be designated even though it has a moderate balance of payments deficit. Participants shall be designated in such manner as will promote over time a balanced distribution of holdings of special drawing rights among them.

> (ii) Participants shall be subject to designation in order to promote reconstitution under Section 6(a) of this Article, to reduce negative balances in holdings of special drawing rights, or to offset the effect of failures to fulfill the expectation in Section 3(a) of this Article.

> (iii) In designating participants, the Fund normally shall give priority to those that need to acquire special drawing rights to meet the objectives of designation under (ii) above.

(b) In order to promote over time a balanced distribution of holdings of special drawing rights under (a)(i) above, the Fund shall apply the rules for designation in Schedule F or such rules as may be adopted under (c) below.

(c) The rules for designation may be reviewed at any time and new rules shall be adopted if necessary. Unless new rules are adopted, the rules in force at the time of the review shall continue to apply.

Section 6. Reconstitution

(a) Participants that use their special drawing rights shall reconstitute their holdings of them in accordance with the rules for reconstitution in Schedule G or such rules as may be adopted under (b) below.

(b) The rules for reconstitution may be reviewed at any time and new rules shall be adopted if necessary. Unless new rules are adopted or a decision is made to abrogate rules for reconstitution, the rules in force at the time of review shall continue to apply. A seventy percent majority of the total voting power shall be required for decisions to adopt, modify, or abrogate the rules for reconstitution.

Section 7. Exchange rates

(a) Except as otherwise provided in (b) below, the exchange rates for transactions between participants under Section 2(a) and (b) of this Article shall be such that participants using special drawing rights shall receive the same value whatever currencies might be provided and whichever participants provide those currencies, and the Fund shall adopt regulations to give effect to this principle.

(b) The Fund, by an eighty-five percent majority of the total voting power, may adopt policies under which in exceptional circumstances the Fund, by a seventy percent majority of the total voting power, may authorize participants entering into transactions under Section 2(b) of this Article to agree on exchange rates other than those applicable under (a) above.

(c) The Fund shall consult a participant on the procedure for determining rates of exchange for its currency.

(d) For the purpose of this provision the term participant includes a terminating participant.

Article XX

Special Drawing Rights Department Interest and Charges

Section 1. Interest

Interest at the same rate for all holders shall be paid by the Fund to each holder on the amount of its holdings of special drawing rights. The Fund shall pay the amount due to each holder whether or not sufficient charges are received to meet the payment of interest.

Section 2. Charges

Charges at the same rate for all participants shall be paid to the Fund by each participant on the amount of its net cumulative allocation of special drawing rights plus any negative balance of the participant or unpaid charges.

Section 3. Rate of interest and charges

The Fund shall determine the rate of interest by a seventy percent majority of the total voting power. The rate of charges shall be equal to the rate of interest.

Section 4. Assessments

When it is decided under Article XVI, Section 2 that reimbursement shall be made, the Fund shall levy assessments for this purpose at the same rate for all participants on their net cumulative allocations.

Section 5. Payment of interest, charges, and assessments

Interest, charges, and assessments shall be paid in special drawing rights. A participant that needs special drawing rights to pay any charge or assessment shall be obligated and entitled to obtain them, for currency acceptable to the Fund, in a transaction with the Fund conducted through the General Resources Account. If sufficient special drawing rights cannot be obtained in this way, the participant shall be obligated and entitled to obtain them with a freely usable currency from a participant which the Fund shall specify. Special drawing rights acquired by a participant after the date for payment shall be applied against its unpaid charges and cancelled.

Article XXI

Administration of the General Department and the Special Drawing Rights Department

(a) The General Department and the Special Drawing Rights Department shall be administered in accordance with the provisions of Article XII, subject to the following provisions:

(i) For meetings of or decisions by the Board of Governors on matters pertaining exclusively to the Special Drawing Rights Department only requests by, or the presence and the votes of, Governors appointed by members that are participants shall be counted for the purpose of calling meetings and determining whether a quorum exists or whether a decision is made by the required majority.

(ii) For decisions by the Executive Board on matters pertaining exclusively to the Special Drawing Rights Department only Executive Directors appointed or elected by at least one member that is a participant shall be entitled to vote. Each of these Executive Directors shall be entitled to cast the number of votes allotted to the member which is a participant that appointed him or to the members that are participants whose votes counted towards his election. Only the presence of Executive Directors appointed or elected by members that are participants and the votes allotted to members that are participants shall be counted for the purpose of determining whether a quorum exists or whether a decision is made by the required majority. For the purposes of this provision, an agreement under Article XII, Section 3(i)(ii) by a member that is a participant shall entitle an appointed Executive Director to vote and cast the number of votes allotted to the member.

(iii) Questions of the general administration of the Fund, including reimbursement under Article XVI, Section 2, and any question whether a matter pertains to both Departments or exclusively to the Special Drawing Rights Department shall be decided as if they pertained exclusively to the General Department. Decisions with respect to the method of valuation of the special drawing right, the acceptance and holding of special drawing rights in the General Resources Account of the General Department and the use of them, and other decisions affecting the operations and transactions conducted through both the General Resources Account of the General Department and the Special Drawing Rights Department shall be made by the majorities required for decisions on matters pertaining exclusively to each Department. A decision on a matter pertaining to the Special Drawing Rights Department shall so indicate.

(b) In addition to the privileges and immunities that are accorded under Article IX of this Agreement, no tax of any kind shall be levied on special drawing rights or on operations or transactions in special drawing rights.

(c) A question of interpretation of the provisions of this Agreement on matters pertaining exclusively to the Special Drawing Rights Department shall be submitted to the Executive Board pursuant to Article XXIX(a) only on the request of a participant. In any case where the Executive Board has given a decision on a question of interpretation pertaining exclusively to the Special Drawing Rights Department only a participant may require that the question be referred to the Board of Governors under Article XXIX(b). The Board of Governors shall decide whether a Governor appointed by a member that is not a participant shall be entitled to vote in the Committee on Interpretation on questions pertaining exclusively to the Special Drawing Rights Department.

(d) Whenever a disagreement arises between the Fund and a participant that has terminated its participation in the Special Drawing Rights Department or between the Fund and any participant during the liquidation of the Special Drawing Rights Department with respect to any matter arising exclusively from participation in the Special Drawing Rights Department, the disagreement shall be submitted to arbitration in accordance with the procedures in Article XXIX(c).

Article XXII

General Obligations of Participants

In addition to the obligations assumed with respect to special drawing rights under other articles of this Agreement, each participant undertakes to collaborate with the Fund and with other participants in order to facilitate the effective functioning of the Special Drawing Rights Department and the proper use of special drawing rights in accordance with this Agreement and with the objective of making the special drawing right the principal reserve asset in the international monetary system.

Article XXIII

Suspension of Operations and Transactions in Special Drawing Rights

Section 1. Emergency provisions

In the event of an emergency or the development of unforeseen circumstances threatening the activities of the Fund with respect to the Special Drawing Rights Department, the Executive Board, by an eighty-five percent majority of the total voting power, may suspend for a period of not more than one year the operation of any of the provisions relating to operations and transactions in special drawing rights, and the provisions of Article XXVII, Section 1(b), (c), and (d) shall then apply.

Section 2. Failure to fulfill obligations

(a) If the Fund finds that a participant has failed to fulfill its obligations under Article XIX, Section 4, the right of the participant to use its special drawing rights shall be suspended unless the Fund otherwise decides.

(b) If the Fund finds that a participant has failed to fulfill any other obligation with respect to special drawing rights, the Fund may suspend the right of the participant to use special drawing rights it acquires after the suspension.

(c) Regulations shall be adopted to ensure that before action is taken against any participant under (a) or (b) above, the participant shall be informed immediately of the complaint against it and given an adequate opportunity for stating its case, both orally and in writing. Whenever the participant is thus informed of a complaint relating to (a) above, it shall not use special drawing rights pending the disposition of the complaint.

(d) Suspension under (a) or (b) above or limitation under (c) above shall not affect a participant's obligation to provide currency in accordance with Article XIX, Section 4.

(e) The Fund may at any time terminate a suspension under (a) or (b) above, provided that a suspension imposed on a participant under (b) above for failure to fulfill the obligations under Article XIX, Section 6(a) shall not be terminated until one hundred eighty days after the end of the first calendar quarter during which the participant complies with the rules for reconstitution.

(f) The right of a participant to use its special drawing rights shall not be suspended because it has become ineligible to use the Fund's general resources under Article V, Section 5, Article VI, Section 1, or Article XXVI, Section 2(a). Article XXVI, Section 2 shall not apply because a participant has failed to fulfill any obligations with respect to special drawing rights.

Article XXIV

Termination of Participation

Section 1. Right to terminate participation

(a) Any participant may terminate its participation in the Special Drawing Rights Department at any time by transmitting a notice in writing to the Fund at its principal office. Termination shall become effective on the date the notice is received.

(b) A participant that withdraws from membership in the Fund shall be deemed to have simultaneously terminated its participation in the Special Drawing Rights Department.

Section 2. Settlement on termination

(a) When a participant terminates its participation in the Special Drawing Rights Department, all operations and transactions by the terminating participant in special drawing rights shall cease except as otherwise permitted under an agreement made pursuant to (c) below in order to facilitate a settlement or as provided in Sections 3, 5, and 6 of this Article or in Schedule H. Interest and charges that accrued to the date of termination and assessments levied before that date but not paid shall be paid in special drawing rights.

(b) The Fund shall be obligated to redeem all special drawing rights held by the terminating participant, and the terminating participant shall be obligated to pay to the Fund an amount equal to its net cumulative allocation and any other amounts that may be due and payable because of its participation in the Special Drawing Rights Department. These obligations shall be set off against each other and the amount of special drawing rights held by the terminating participant that is used in the setoff to extinguish its obligation to the fund shall be cancelled.

(c) A settlement shall be made with reasonable despatch by agreement between the terminating participant and the Fund with respect to any obligation of the terminating participant or the Fund after the setoff in (b) above. If agreement on a settlement is not reached promptly the provisions of Schedule H shall apply.

Section 3. Interest and charges

After the date of termination the Fund shall pay interest on any outstanding balance of special drawing rights held by a terminating participant and the terminating participant shall pay charges on any outstanding obligation owed to the Fund at the times and rates prescribed under Article XX. Payment shall be made in special drawing rights. A terminating participant shall be entitled to obtain special drawing rights with a freely usable currency to pay charges or assessments in a transaction with a participant specified by the Fund or by agreement from any other holder, or to dispose of special drawing rights received as interest in a transaction with any participant designated under Article XIX, Section 5 or by agreement with any other holder.

Section 4. Settlement of obligation to the Fund

Currency received by the Fund from a terminating participant shall be used by the Fund to redeem special drawing rights held by participants in proportion to the amount by which each participant's holdings of special drawing rights exceed its net cumulative allocation at the time the currency is received by the Fund. Special drawing rights so redeemed and special drawing rights obtained by a terminating participant under the provisions of this Agreement to meet any installment due under an agreement on settlement or under Schedule H and set off against that installment shall be cancelled.

Section 5. Settlement of obligation to a terminating participant

Whenever the Fund is required to redeem special drawing rights held by a terminating participant, redemption shall be made with currency provided by participants specified by the Fund. These participants shall be specified in accordance with the principles in Article XIX, Section 5. Each specified participant shall provide at its option the currency of the terminating participant or a freely usable currency to the Fund and shall receive an equivalent amount of special drawing rights. However, a terminating participant may use its special drawing rights to obtain its own currency, a freely usable currency, or any other asset from any holder, if the Fund so permits.

Section 6. General Resources Account transactions

In order to facilitate settlement with a terminating participant, the Fund may decide that a terminating participant shall:

(i) use any special drawing rights held by it after the setoff in Section 2(b) of this Article, when they are to be redeemed, in a transaction with the Fund conducted through the General Resources Account to obtain its own currency or a freely usable currency at the option of the Fund; or

(ii) obtain special drawing rights in a transaction with the Fund conducted through the General Resources Account for a currency acceptable to the Fund to meet any charges or installment due under an agreement or the provisions of Schedule H.

Article XXV

Liquidation of the Special Drawing Rights Department

(a) The Special Drawing Rights Department may not be liquidated except by decision of the Board of Governors. In an emergency, if the Executive Board decides that liquidation of the Special Drawing Rights Department may be necessary, it may temporarily suspend allocations or cancellations and all operations and transactions in special drawing rights pending decision by the Board of Governors. A decision by the Board of Governors to liquidate the Fund shall be a decision to liquidate both the General Department and the Special Drawing Rights Department.

(b) If the Board of Governors decides to liquidate the Special Drawing Rights Department, all allocations or cancellations and all operations and transactions in special drawing rights and the activities of the Fund with respect to the Special Drawing Rights Department shall cease except those incidental to the orderly discharge of the obligations of participants and of the Fund with respect to special drawing rights, and all obligations of the Fund and of participants under this Agreement with respect to special drawing rights shall cease except those set out in this Article, ArticleXX, Article XXI(d), Article XXIV, Article XXIX(c), and Schedule H, or any agreement reached under Article XXIV subject to paragraph 4 of Schedule H, and Schedule I.

(c) Upon liquidation of the Special Drawing Rights Department, interest and charges that accrued to the date of liquidation and assessments levied before that date but not paid shall be paid in special drawing rights. The Fund shall be obligated to redeem all special drawing rights held by holders, and each participant shall be obligated to pay the Fund an amount equal to its net cumulative allocation of special drawing rights and such other amounts as may be due and payable because of its participation in the Special Drawing Rights Department.

(d) Liquidation of the Special Drawing Rights Department shall be administered in accordance with the provisions of Schedule I.

Article XXVI

Withdrawal from Membership

Section 1. Right of members to withdraw

Any member may withdraw from the Fund at any time by transmitting a notice in writing to the Fund at its principal office. Withdrawal shall become effective on the date such notice is received.

Section 2. Compulsory withdrawal

(a) If a member fails to fulfill any of its obligations under this Agreement, the Fund may declare the member ineligible to use the general resources of the Fund. Nothing in this Section shall be deemed to limit the provisions of Article V, Section 5 or Article VI, Section 1.

(b) If, after the expiration of a reasonable period following a declaration of ineligibility under (a) above, the member persists in its failure to fulfill any of its obligations under this Agreement, the Fund may, by a seventy percent majority of the total voting power, suspend the voting rights of the member. During the period of the suspension, the provisions of Schedule

L shall apply. The Fund may, by a seventy percent majority of the total voting power, terminate the suspension at any time.

(c) If, after the expiration of a reasonable period following a decision of suspension under (b) above, the member persists in its failure to fulfill any of its obligations under this Agreement, that member may be required to withdraw from membership in the Fund by a decision of the Board of Governors carried by a majority of the Governors having eighty-five percent of the total voting power.

(d) Regulations shall be adopted to ensure that before action is taken against any member under (a), (b), or (c) above, the member shall be informed in reasonable time of the complaint against it and given an adequate opportunity for stating its case, both orally and in writing.

Section 3. Settlement of accounts with members withdrawing

When a member withdraws from the Fund, normal operations and transactions of the Fund in its currency shall cease and settlement of all accounts between it and the Fund shall be made with reasonable despatch by agreement between it and the Fund. If agreement is not reached promptly, the provisions of Schedule J shall apply to the settlement of accounts.

Article XXVII

Emergency Provisions

Section 1. Temporary suspension

(a) In the event of an emergency or the development of unforeseen circumstances threatening the activities of the Fund, the Executive Board, by an eighty-five percent majority of the total voting power, may suspend for a period of not more than one year the operation of any of the following provisions:

  (i) Article V, Sections 2, 3, 7, 8(a)(i) and (e);

  (ii) Article VI, Section 2;

  (iii) Article XI, Section 1;

  (iv) Schedule C, paragraph 5.

(b) A suspension of the operation of a provision under (a) above may not be extended beyond one year except by the Board of Governors which, by an eighty-five percent majority of the total voting power, may extend a suspension for an additional period of not more than two years if it finds that the emergency or unforeseen circumstances referred to in (a) above continue to exist.

(c) The Executive Board may, by a majority of the total voting power, terminate such suspension at any time.

(d) The Fund may adopt rules with respect to the subject matter of a provision during the period in which its operation is suspended.

Section 2. Liquidation of the Fund

(a) The Fund may not be liquidated except by decision of the Board of Governors. In an emergency, if the Executive Board decides that liquidation of the Fund may be necessary, it may temporarily suspend all operations and transactions, pending decision by the Board of Governors.

(b) If the Board of Governors decides to liquidate the Fund, the Fund shall forthwith cease to engage in any activities except those incidental to the orderly collection and liquidation of its assets and the settlement of its liabilities, and all obligations of members under this Agreement shall cease except those set out in this Article, in Article XXIX(c), in Schedule J, paragraph 7, and in Schedule K.

(c) Liquidation shall be administered in accordance with the provisions of Schedule K.

Article XXVIII

Amendments

(a) Any proposal to introduce modifications in this Agreement, whether emanating from a member, a Governor, or the Executive Board, shall be communicated to the chairman of the Board of Governors who shall bring the proposal before the Board of Governors. If the proposed amendment is approved by the Board of Governors, the Fund shall, by circular letter or telegram, ask all members whether they accept the proposed amendment. When three-fifths of the members, having eighty-five percent of the total voting power, have accepted the proposed amendment, the Fund shall certify the fact by a formal communication addressed to all members.

(b) Notwithstanding (a) above, acceptance by all members is required in the case of any amendment modifying:

   (i) the right to withdraw from the Fund (Article XXVI, Section 1);

   (ii) the provision that no change in a member's quota shall be made without its consent (Article III, Section 2(d)); and

   (iii) the provision that no change may be made in the par value of a member's currency except on the proposal of that member (Schedule C, paragraph 6).

(c) Amendments shall enter into force for all members three months after the date of the formal communication unless a shorter period is specified in the circular letter or telegram.

Article XXIX

Interpretation

(a) Any question of interpretation of the provisions of this Agreement arising between any member and the Fund or between any members of the Fund shall be submitted to the Executive Board for its decision. If the question particularly affects any member not entitled to appoint an Executive Director, it shall be entitled to representation in accordance with Article XII, Section 3(j).

(b) In any case where the Executive Board has given a decision under (a) above, any member may require, within three months from the date of the decision, that the question be referred to the Board of Governors, whose decision shall be final. Any question referred to the Board of Governors shall be considered by a Committee on Interpretation of the Board of Governors. Each Committee member shall have one vote. The Board of Governors shall establish the membership, procedures, and voting majorities of the Committee. A decision of the Committee shall be the decision of the Board of Governors unless the Board of Governors, by an eighty-five percent majority of the total voting power, decides otherwise. Pending the result of the reference to the Board of Governors the Fund may, so far as it deems necessary, act on the basis of the decision of the Executive Board.

(c) Whenever a disagreement arises between the Fund and a member which has withdrawn, or between the Fund and any member during liquidation of the Fund, such disagreement shall be submitted to arbitration by a tribunal of three arbitrators, one appointed by the Fund, another by the member or withdrawing member, and an umpire who, unless the parties otherwise agree, shall be appointed by the President of the International Court of Justice or such other authority as may have been prescribed by regulation adopted by the Fund. The umpire shall have full power to settle all questions of procedure in any case where the parties are in disagreement with respect thereto.

Article XXX

Explanation of Terms

In interpreting the provisions of this Agreement the Fund and its members shall be guided by the following provisions:

(a) The Fund's holdings of a member's currency in the General Resources Account shall include any securities accepted by the Fund under Article III, Section 4.

(b) Stand-by arrangement means a decision of the Fund by which a member is assured that it will be able to make purchases from the General Resources Account in accordance with the terms of the decision during a specified period and up to a specified amount.

(c) Reserve tranche purchase means a purchase by a member of special drawing rights or the currency of another member in exchange for its own currency which does not cause the Fund's holdings of the member's currency in the General Resources Account to exceed its quota, provided that for the purposes of this definition the Fund may exclude purchases and holdings under:

    (i) policies on the use of its general resources for compensatory financing of export fluctuations;

    (ii) policies on the use of its general resources in connection with the financing of contributions to international buffer stocks of primary products; and

    (iii) other policies on the use of its general resources in respect of which the Fund decides, by an eighty-five percent majority of the total voting power, that an exclusion shall be made.

(d) Payments for current transactions means payments which are not for the purpose of transferring capital, and includes, without limitation:

    (1) all payments due in connection with foreign trade, other current business, including services, and normal short-term banking and credit facilities;

    (2) payments due as interest on loans and as net income from other investments;

    (3) payments of moderate amount for amortization of loans or for depreciation of direct investments; and

    (4) moderate remittances for family living expenses. The Fund may, after consultation with the members concerned, determine whether certain specific transactions are to be considered current transactions or capital transactions.

(e) Net cumulative allocation of special drawing rights means the total amount of special drawing rights allocated to a participant less its share of special drawing rights that have been cancelled under Article XVIII, Section 2(a).

(f) A freely usable currency means a member's currency that the Fund determines

(i) is, in fact, widely used to make payments for international transactions, and

(ii) is widely traded in the principal exchange markets.

(g) Members that were members on August 31, 1975 shall be deemed to include a member that accepted membership after that date pursuant to a resolution of the Board of Governors adopted before that date.

(h) Transactions of the Fund means exchanges of monetary assets by the Fund for other monetary assets. Operations of the Fund means other uses or receipts of monetary assets by the Fund.

(i) Transactions in special drawing rights means exchanges of special drawing rights for other monetary assets. Operations in special drawing rights means other uses of special drawing rights.

Article XXXI

Final Provisions

Section 1. Entry into force

This Agreement shall enter into force when it has been signed on behalf of governments having sixty-five percent of the total of the quotas set forth in Schedule A and when the instruments referred to in Section 2(a) of this Article have been deposited on their behalf, but in no event shall this Agreement enter into force before May 1, 1945.

Section 2. Signature

(a) Each government on whose behalf this Agreement is signed shall deposit with the Government of the United States of America an instrument setting forth that it has accepted this Agreement in accordance with its law and has taken all steps necessary to enable it to carry out all of its obligations under this Agreement.

(b) Each country shall become a member of the Fund as from the date of the deposit on its behalf of the instrument referred to in (a) above, except that no country shall become a member before this Agreement enters into force under Section 1 of this Article.

(c) The Government of the United States of America shall inform the governments of all countries whose names are set forth in Schedule A, and the governments of all countries whose membership is approved in accordance with Article II, Section 2, of all signatures of this Agreement and of the deposit of all instruments referred to in (a) above.

(d) At the time this Agreement is signed on its behalf, each government shall transmit to the Government of the United States of America one one hundredth of one percent of its total subscription in gold or United States dollars for the purpose of meeting administrative expenses of the Fund. The Government of the United States of America shall hold such funds in a special deposit account and shall transmit them to the Board of Governors of the Fund when the initial meeting has been called. If this Agreement has not come into force by December 31, 1945, the Government of the United States of America shall return such funds to the governments that transmitted them.

(e) This Agreement shall remain open for signature at Washington on behalf of the governments of the countries whose names are set forth in Schedule A until December 31, 1945.

(f) After December 31, 1945, this Agreement shall be open for signature on behalf of the government of any country whose membership has been approved in accordance with Article II, Section 2.

(g) By their signature of this Agreement, all governments accept it both on their own behalf and in respect of all their colonies, overseas territories, all territories under their protection, suzerainty, or authority, and all territories in respect of which they exercise a mandate.

(h) Subsection (d) above shall come into force with regard to each signatory government as from the date of its signature. [The signature and depositary clause reproduced below followed the text of Article XX in the original Articles of Agreement] Done at Washington, in a single copy which shall remain deposited in the archives of the Government of the United States of America, which shall transmit certified copies to all governments whose names are set forth in Schedule A and to all governments whose membership is approved in accordance with Article II, Section 2.

Done at Washington, in a single copy which shall remain deposited in the archives of the Government of the United States of America, which shall transmit certified copies to all governments whose names are set forth in Schedule A and to all governments whose membership is approved in accordance with Article II, Section 2.

[*Note:* Schedules are not reproduced here.]

APPENDIX C

CHARTER OF THE IBRD

Citation: Articles of Agreement of the International Bank for Reconstruction and Development, adopted at Bretton Woods, July 22, 1944 (entered into force Dec. 27, 1945), 60 Stat. 1440, 2 U.N.T.S. 134, T.I.A.S. No. 1507, as amended Dec. 16, 1965, 16 U.S.T. 1942, 606 U.N.T.S. 294, T.I.A.S. No. 5929 (amendment entered into force Dec. 17, 1965) and as further amended effective Feb. 16, 1989; 1 BDIEL [Basic Documents of International Economic Law] 427.

Contents

IX. Interpretation

X. Approval Deemed Given

XI. Final Provisions
   1. Entry into Force
   2. Signature
   3. Inauguration of the Bank

Articles of Agreement of the International Bank for Reconstruction and Development

The Governments on whose behalf the present Agreement is signed agree as follows:

Introductory Article

The International Bank for Reconstruction and Development is established and shall operate in accordance with the following provisions:

Article I

Purposes

The purposes of the Bank are:

(i) To assist in the reconstruction and development of territories of members by facilitating the investment of capital for productive purposes, including the restoration of economies destroyed or disrupted by war, the reconversion of productive facilities to peacetime needs and the encouragement of the development of productive facilities and resources in less developed countries.

(ii) To promote private foreign investment by means of guarantees or participations in loans and other investments made by private investors; and when private capital is not available on reasonable terms, to supplement private investment by providing, on suitable conditions, finance for productive purposes out of its own capital, funds raised by it and its other resources.

(iii) To promote the long-range balanced growth of international trade and the maintenance of equilibrium in balances of payments by encouraging international investment for the development of the productive resources of members, thereby assisting in raising productivity, the standard of living and conditions of labour in their territories.

(iv) To arrange the loans made or guaranteed by it in relation to international loans through other channels so that the more useful and urgent projects, large and small alike, will be dealt with first.

(v) To conduct its operations with due regard to the effect of international investment on business conditions in the territories of members and, in the immediate postwar years, to assist in bringing about a smooth transition from a wartime to a peacetime economy.

The Bank shall be guided in all its decisions by the purposes set forth above.

Article II

Membership in and Capital of the Bank

Section 1—Membership

(a) The original members of the Bank shall be those members of the International Monetary Fund which accept membership in the Bank before the date specified in Article XI, Section 2(e).

(b) Membership shall be open to other members of the Fund, at such times and in accordance with such terms as may be prescribed by the Bank.

Section 2—Authorized Capital

(a) The authorized capital stock of the Bank shall be $ 10,000,000,000, in terms of United States dollars of the weight and fineness in effect on July 1, 1944. The capital stock shall be divided into 100,000 shares having a par value of $ 100,000 each, which shall be available for subscription only by members.

(b) The capital stock may be increased when the Bank deems it advisable by a three-fourths majority of the total voting power.

Section 3—Subscription of Shares

(a) Each member shall subscribe shares of the capital stock of the Bank. The minimum number of shares to be subscribed by the original members shall be those set forth in Schedule A. The minimum number of shares to be subscribed by other members shall be determined by the Bank, which shall reserve a sufficient portion of its capital stock for subscription by such members.

(b) The Bank shall prescribe rules laying down the conditions under which members may subscribe shares of the authorized capital stock of the Bank in addition to their minimum subscriptions.

(c) If the authorized capital stock of the Bank is increased, each member shall have a reasonable opportunity to subscribe, under such conditions as the Bank shall decide, a proportion of the increase of stock equivalent to the proportion which its stock theretofore subscribed bears to the total capital stock of the Bank, but no member shall be obligated to subscribe any part of the increased capital.

Section 4—Issue Price of Shares

Shares included in the minimum subscriptions of original members shall be issued at par. Other shares shall be issued at par unless the Bank by a majority of the total voting power decides in special circumstances to issue them on other terms.

Section 5—Division and Calls of Subscribed Capital

The subscription of each member shall be divided into two parts as follows:

(i) 20 per cent shall be paid or subject to call under Section 7(i) of this article as needed by the Bank for its operations;

(ii) the remaining 80 per cent shall be subject to call by the Bank only when required to meet obligations of the Bank created under Article IV, Sections 1(a)(ii) and (iii).

Calls on unpaid subscriptions shall be uniform on all shares.

Section 6—Limitation on Liability

Liability on shares shall be limited to the unpaid portion of the issue price of the shares.

Section 7—Method of Payment of Subscriptions for Shares

Payment of subscriptions for shares shall be made in gold or United States dollars and in the currencies of the members as follows:

(i) under Section 5(i) of this article, two per cent of the price of each share shall be payable in gold or United States dollars, and, when calls are made, the remaining 18 per cent shall be paid in the currency of the member;

(ii) when a call is made under Section 5(ii) of this article, payment may be made at the option of the member either in gold, in United States dollars or in the currency required to discharge the obligations of the Bank for the purpose for which the call is made;

(iii) when a member makes payments in any currency under (i) and (ii) above, such payments shall be made in amounts equal in value to the member's liability under the call. This liability shall be a proportionate part of the subscribed capital stock of the Bank as authorized and defined in Section 2 of this article.

Section 8—Time of Payment of Subscriptions

(a) The two per cent payable on each share in gold or United States dollars under Section 7(i) of this article, shall be paid within 60 days of the date on which the Bank begins operations, provided that

(i) any original member of the Bank whose metropolitan territory has suffered from enemy occupation or hostilities during the present war shall be granted the right to postpone payment of one-half per cent until five years after that date;

(ii) an original member who cannot make such a payment because it has not recovered possession of its gold reserves which are still seized or immobilized as a result of the war may postpone all payment until such date as the Bank shall decide.

(b) The remainder of the price of each share payable under Section 7(i) of this article shall be paid as and when called by the Bank, provided that

(i) the Bank shall, within one year of its beginning operations, call not less than eight per cent of the price of the share in addition to the payment of two per cent referred to in (a) above;

(ii) not more than five per cent of the price of the share shall be called in any period of three months.

Section 9—Maintenance of Value of Certain Currency Holdings of the Bank

(a) Whenever (i) the par value of a member's currency is reduced, or (ii) the foreign exchange value of a member's currency has, in the opinion of the Bank, depreciated to a significant extent within that member's territories, the member shall pay to the Bank within a reasonable time an additional amount of its own currency sufficient to maintain the value, as of the time of initial subscription, of the amount of the currency of such member which is held by the Bank and derived from currency originally paid in to the Bank by the member under Article II, Section 7(i), from currency referred to in Article IV, Section 2(b), or from any additional currency furnished under the provisions of the present paragraph, and which has not been repurchased by the member for gold or for the currency of any member which is acceptable to the Bank.

(b) Whenever the par value of a member's currency is increased, the Bank shall return to such member within a reasonable time an amount of that member's currency equal to the increase in the value of the amount of such currency described in (a) above.

(c) The provisions of the preceding paragraphs may be waived by the Bank when a uniform proportionate change in the par values of the currencies of all its members is made by the International Monetary Fund.

Section 10—Restriction on Disposal of Shares

Shares shall not be pledged or encumbered in any manner whatever and they shall be transferable only to the Bank.

Article III

General Provisions Relating to Loans and Guarantees

Section 1—Use of Resources

(a) The resources and the facilities of the Bank shall be used exclusively for the benefit of members with equitable consideration to projects for development and projects for reconstruction alike.

(b) For the purpose of facilitating the restoration and reconstruction of the economy of members whose metropolitan territories have suffered great devastation from enemy occupation or hostilities, the Bank, in determining the conditions and terms of loans made to such members, shall pay special regard to lightening the financial burden and expediting the completion of such restoration and reconstruction.

Section 2—Dealings Between Members and the Bank

Each member shall deal with the Bank only through its Treasury, central bank, stabilization fund or other similar fiscal agency, and the Bank shall deal with members only by or through the same agencies.

Section 3—Limitations on Guarantees and Borrowings of the Bank

The total amount outstanding of guarantees, participations in loans and direct loans made by the Bank shall not be increased at any time, if by such increase the total would exceed 100 per cent of the unimpaired subscribed capital, reserves and surplus of the Bank.

Section 4—Conditions on Which the Bank May Guarantee or Make Loans

The Bank may guarantee, participate in, or make loans to any member or any political sub-division thereof and any business, industrial, and agricultural enterprise in the territories of a member, subject to the following conditions:

(i) When the member in whose territories the project is located is not itself the borrower, the member or the central bank or some comparable agency of the member which is acceptable to the Bank, fully guarantees the repayment of the principal and the payment of interest and other charges on the loan.

(ii) The Bank is satisfied that in the prevailing market conditions the borrower would be unable otherwise to obtain the loan under conditions which in the opinion of the Bank are reasonable for the borrower.

(iii) A competent committee, as provided for in Article V, Section 7, has submitted a written report recommending the project after a careful study of the merits of the proposal.

(iv) In the opinion of the Bank the rate of interest and other charges are reasonable and such rate, charges and the schedule for repayment of principal are appropriate to the project.

(v) In making or guaranteeing a loan, the Bank shall pay due regard to the prospects that the borrower, and, if the borrower is not a member, that the guarantor, will be in position to meet its obligations under the loan; and the Bank shall act prudently in the interests both of the particular member in whose territories the project is located and of the members as a whole.

(vi) In guaranteeing a loan made by other investors, the Bank receives suitable compensation for its risk.

(vii) Loans made or guaranteed by the Bank shall, except in special circumstances, be for the purpose of specific projects of reconstruction or development.

Section 5—Use of Loans Guaranteed, Participated in or Made by the Bank

(a) The Bank shall impose no conditions that the proceeds of a loan shall be spent in the territories of any particular member or members.

(b) The Bank shall make arrangements to ensure that the proceeds of any loan are used only for the purposes for which the loan was granted, with due attention to considerations of economy and efficiency and without regard to political or other non-economic influences or considerations.

(c) In the case of loans made by the Bank, it shall open an account in the name of the borrower and the amount of the loan shall be credited to this account in the currency or currencies in which the loan is made. The borrower shall be permitted by the Bank to draw on this account only to meet expenses in connection with the project as they are actually incurred.

Section 6—Loans to the International Finance Corporation

[*Note: This section was added by amendment in 1965*]

(a) The Bank may make, participate in, or guarantee loans to the International Finance Corporation, an affiliate of the Bank, for use in its lending operations. The total amount outstanding of such loans, participations and guarantees shall not be increased if, at the time or as a result thereof, the aggregate amount of debt (including the guarantee of any debt) incurred by the said Corporation from any source and then outstanding shall exceed an amount equal to four times its unimpaired subscribed capital and surplus.

(b) The provisions of Article III, Sections 4 and 5(c) and of Article IV, Section 3 shall not apply to loans, participations and guarantees authorized by this Section.

Article IV

Operations

Section 1—Methods of Making or Facilitating Loans

(a) The Bank may make or facilitate loans which satisfy the general conditions of Article III in any of the following ways:

  (i) By making or participating in direct loans out of its own funds corresponding to its unimpaired paid-up capital and surplus and, subject to Section 6 of this article, to its reserves.

  (ii) By making or participating in direct loans out of funds raised in the market of a member, or otherwise borrowed by the Bank.

  (iii) By guaranteeing in whole or in part loans made by private investors through the usual investment channels.

(b) The Bank may borrow funds under (a)(ii) above or guarantee loans under (a)(iii) above only with the approval of the member in whose markets the funds are raised and the member in whose currency the loan is denominated, and only if those members agree that the proceeds may be exchanged for the currency of any other member without restriction.

Section 2—Availability and Transferability of Currencies

(a) Currencies paid into the Bank under Article II, Section 7(i), shall be loaned only with the approval in each case of the member whose currency is involved; provided, however, that if necessary, after the Bank's subscribed capital has been entirely called, such currencies shall, without restriction by the members whose currencies are offered, be used or exchanged for the currencies required to meet contractual payments of interest, other charges or amortization on the Bank's own borrowings, or to meet the Bank's liabilities with respect to such contractual payments on loans guaranteed by the Bank.

(b) Currencies received by the Bank from borrowers or guarantors in payment on account of principal of direct loans made with currencies referred to in (a) above shall be exchanged for the currencies of other members or reloaned only with the approval in each case of the members whose currencies are involved; provided, however, that if necessary, after the Bank's subscribed capital has been entirely called, such currencies shall, without restriction by the members whose currencies are offered, be used or exchanged for the currencies required to meet contractual payments of interest, other charges or amortization on the Bank's own borrowings, or to meet the Bank's liabilities with respect to such contractual payments on loans guaranteed by the Bank.

(c) Currencies received by the Bank from borrowers or guarantors in payment on account of principal of direct loans made by the Bank under Section 1(a)(ii) of this article, shall be held and used, without restriction by the members, to make amortization payments, or to anticipate payment of or repurchase part or all of the Bank's own obligations.

(d) All other currencies available to the Bank, including those raised in the market or otherwise borrowed under Section 1(a)(ii) of this article, those obtained by the sale of gold, those received as payments of interest and other charges for direct loans made under Sections 1(a)(i) and (ii), and those received as payments of commissions and other charges under Section 1(a)(iii), shall be used or exchanged for other currencies or gold required in the operations of the Bank without restriction by the members whose currencies are offered.

(e) Currencies raised in the markets of members by borrowers on loans guaranteed by the Bank under Section 1(a)(iii) of this article, shall also be used or exchanged for other currencies without restriction by such members.

Section 3—Provision of Currencies for Direct Loans

The following provisions shall apply to direct loans under Sections 1(a)(i) and (ii) of this article:

(a) The Bank shall furnish the borrower with such currencies of members, other than the member in whose territories the project is located, as are needed by the borrower for expenditures to be made in the territories of such other members to carry out the purposes of the loan.

(b) The Bank may, in exceptional circumstances when local currency required for the purposes of the loan cannot be raised by the borrower on reasonable terms, provide the borrower as part of the loan with an appropriate amount of that currency.

(c) The Bank, if the project gives rise indirectly to an increased need for foreign exchange by the member in whose territories the project is located, may in exceptional circumstances provide the borrower as part of the loan with an appropriate amount of gold or foreign exchange not in excess of the borrower's local expenditure in connection with the purposes of the loan.

(d) The Bank may, in exceptional circumstances, at the request of a member in whose territories a portion of the loan is spent, repurchase with gold or foreign exchange a part of that member's currency thus spent but in no case shall the part so repurchased exceed the amount by which the expenditure of the loan in those territories gives rise to an increased need for foreign exchange.

Section 4—Payment Provisions for Direct Loans

Loan contracts under Section 1(a)(i) or (ii) of this article shall be made in accordance with the following payment provisions:

(a) The terms and conditions of interest and amortization payments, maturity and dates of payment of each loan shall be determined by the Bank. The Bank shall also determine the rate and any other terms and conditions of commission to be charged in connection with such loan. In the case of loans made under Section 1(a)(ii) of this article during the first 10 years of the Bank's operations, this rate of commission shall be not less than one per cent per annum and not greater than one and one-half per cent per annum, and shall be charged on the outstanding portion of any such loan. At the end of this period of 10 years, the rate of commission may be reduced by the Bank with respect both to the outstanding portions of loans already made and to future loans, if the reserves accumulated by the Bank under Section 6 of this article and out of other earnings are considered by it sufficient to justify a reduction. In the case of future loans the Bank shall also have discretion to increase the rate of commission beyond the above limit, if experience indicates that an increase is advisable.

(b) All loan contracts shall stipulate the currency or currencies in which payment under the contract shall be made to the Bank. At the option of the borrower, however, such payments may be made in gold, or subject to the agreement of the Bank, in the currency of a member other than that prescribed in the contract.

(i) In the case of loans made under Section 1(a)(i) of this article, the loan contracts shall provide that payments to the Bank of interest, other charges and amortization shall be made in the currency loaned, unless the member whose currency is loaned agrees that such payments shall be made in some other specified currency or currencies. These payments, subject to the provisions of Article II, Section 9(c), shall be equivalent to the value of such contractual payments at the time the loans were made, in terms of a currency specified for the purpose by the Bank by a three-fourths majority of the total voting power.

(ii) In the case of loans made under Section 1(a)(ii) of this article, the total amount outstanding and payable to the Bank in any one currency shall at no time exceed the total amount of the outstanding borrowings made by the Bank under Section 1(a)(ii) and payable in the same currency.

(c) If a member suffers from an acute exchange stringency, so that the service of any loan contracted by that member or guaranteed by it or by one of its agencies cannot be provided in the stipulated manner, the member concerned may apply to the Bank for a relaxation of the conditions of payment. If the Bank is satisfied that some relaxation is in the interests of the particular member and the operations of the Bank and of its members as a whole, it may take action under either, or both, of the following paragraphs with respect to the whole, or part, of the annual service:

(i) The Bank may, in its discretion, make arrangements with the member concerned to accept service payments on the loan in the member's currency for periods not to exceed three years upon appropriate terms regarding the use of such currency and the maintenance of its foreign exchange value; and for the repurchase of such currency on appropriate terms.

(ii) The Bank may modify the terms of amortization or extend the life of the loan, or both.

Section 5—Guarantees

(a) In guaranteeing a loan placed through the usual investment channels, the Bank shall charge a guarantee commission payable periodically on the amount of the loan outstanding at a rate determined by the Bank. During the first 10 years of the Bank's operations, this rate shall be not less than one per cent per annum and not greater than one and one-half per cent per annum. At the end of this period of 10 years, the rate of commission may be reduced by the Bank with respect both to the outstanding portions of loans already guaranteed and to future loans if the reserves accumulated by the Bank under Section 6 of this article and out of other earnings are considered by it sufficient to justify a reduction. In the case of future loans the Bank shall also have discretion to increase the rate of commission beyond the above limit, if experience indicates that an increase is advisable.

(b) Guarantee commissions shall be paid directly to the Bank by the borrower.

(c) Guarantees by the Bank shall provide that the Bank may terminate its liability with respect to interest if, upon default by the borrower and by the guarantor, if any, the Bank offers to purchase, at par and interest accrued to a date designated in the offer, the bonds or other obligations guaranteed.

(d) The Bank shall have power to determine any other terms and conditions of the guarantee.

Section 6—Special Reserve

The amount of commissions received by the Bank under Sections 4 and 5 of this article shall be set aside as a special reserve, which shall be kept available for meeting liabilities of the Bank in accordance with Section 7 of this article. The special reserve shall be held in such liquid form, permitted under this Agreement, as the Executive Directors may decide.

Section 7—Methods of Meeting Liabilities of the Bank in Case of Defaults

In cases of default on loans made, participated in, or guaranteed by the Bank:

(a) The Bank shall make such arrangements as may be feasible to adjust the obligations under the loans, including arrangements under or analogous to those provided in Section 4(c) of this article.

(b) The payments in discharge of the Bank's liabilities on borrowings or guarantees under Section 1 (a) (ii) and (iii) of this article shall be charged:

> (i) first, against the special reserve provided in Section 6 of this article;

> (ii) then, to the extent necessary and at the discretion of the Bank, against the other reserves, surplus and capital available to the Bank.

(c) Whenever necessary to meet contractual payments of interest, other charges or amortization of the Bank's own borrowings, or to meet the Bank's liabilities with respect to similar payments on loans guaranteed by it, the Bank may call an appropriate amount of the unpaid subscriptions of members in accordance with Article II, Sections 5 and 7. Moreover, if it believes that a default may be of long duration, the Bank may call an additional amount of such unpaid subscriptions not to exceed in any one year one per cent of the total subscriptions of the members for the following purposes:

(i) To redeem prior to maturity, or otherwise discharge its liability on, all or part of the outstanding principal of any loan guaranteed by it in respect of which the debtor is in default.

(ii) To repurchase, or otherwise discharge its liability on, all or part of its own outstanding borrowings.

Section 8—Miscellaneous Operations

In addition to the operations specified elsewhere in this Agreement, the Bank shall have the power:

(i) To buy and sell securities it has issued and to buy and sell securities which it has guaranteed or in which it has invested, provided that the Bank shall obtain the approval of the member in whose territories the securities are to be bought or sold.

(ii) To guarantee securities in which it has invested for the purpose of facilitating their sale.

(iii) To borrow the currency of any member with the approval of that member.

(iv) To buy and sell such other securities as the Directors by a three-fourths majority of the total voting power may deem proper for the investment of all or part of the special reserve under Section 6 of this article.

In exercising the powers conferred by this Section, the Bank may deal with any person, partnership, association, corporation or other legal entity in the territories of any member.

Section 9—Warning to be Placed on Securities

Every security guaranteed or issued by the Bank shall bear on its face a conspicuous statement to the effect that it is not an obligation of any government unless expressly stated on the security.

Section 10—Political Activity Prohibited

The Bank and its officers shall not interfere in the political affairs of any member; nor shall they be influenced in their decisions by the political character of the member or members concerned. Only economic considerations shall be relevant to their decisions, and these considerations shall be weighed impartially in order to achieve the purposes stated in Article I.

Article V

Organization and Management

Section 1—Structure of the Bank

The Bank shall have a Board of Governors, Executive Directors, a President and such other officers and staff to perform such duties as the Bank may determine.

Section 2—Board of Governors

(a) All the powers of the Bank shall be vested in the Board of Governors consisting of one governor and one alternate appointed by each member in such manner as it may determine. Each governor and each alternate shall serve for five years, subject to the pleasure of the member appointing him, and may be reappointed. No alternate may vote except in the absence of his principal. The Board shall select one of the governors as Chairman.

(b) The Board of Governors may delegate to the Executive Directors authority to exercise any powers of the Board, except the power to:

    (i)   Admit new members and determine the conditions of their admission;

    (ii)   Increase or decrease the capital stock;

    (iii) Suspend a member;

    (iv) Decide appeals from interpretations of this Agreement given by the Executive Directors;

    (v)   Make arrangements to cooperate with other international organizations (other than informal arrangements of a temporary and administrative character);

    (vi) Decide to suspend permanently the operations of the Bank and to distribute its assets;

    (vii) Determine the distribution of the net income of the Bank.

(c) The Board of Governors shall hold an annual meeting and such other meetings as may be provided for by the Board or called by the Executive Directors. Meetings of the Board shall be called by the Directors whenever requested by five members or by members having one-quarter of the total voting power.

(d) A quorum for any meeting of the Board of Governors shall be a majority of the Governors, exercising not less than two-thirds of the total voting power.

(e) The Board of Governors may by regulation establish a procedure whereby the Executive Directors, when they deem such action to be in the best interests of the Bank, may obtain a vote of the Governors on a specific question without calling a meeting of the Board.

(f) The Board of Governors, and the Executive Directors to the extent authorized, may adopt such rules and regulations as may be necessary or appropriate to conduct the business of the Bank.

(g) Governors and alternates shall serve as such without compensation from the Bank, but the Bank shall pay them reasonable expenses incurred in attending meetings.

(h) The Board of Governors shall determine the remuneration to be paid to the Executive Directors and the salary and terms of the contract of service of the President.

Section 3—Voting

(a) Each member shall have 250 votes plus one additional vote for each share of stock held.

(b) Except as otherwise specifically provided, all matters before the Bank shall be decided by a majority of the votes cast.

Section 4—Executive Directors

(a) The Executive Directors shall be responsible for the conduct of the general operations of the Bank, and for this purpose, shall exercise all the powers delegated to them by the Board of Governors.

(b) There shall be 12 Executive Directors, who need not be governors, and of whom:
  (i) five shall be appointed, one by each of the five members having the largest number of shares;
  (ii) seven shall be elected according to Schedule B by all the Governors other than those appointed by the five members referred to in (i) above.

For the purpose of this paragraph, "members" means governments of countries whose names are set forth in Schedule A, whether they are original members or become members in accordance with Article II, Section 1(b). When governments of other countries become members, the Board of Governors may, by a four-fifths majority of the total voting power, increase the total number of directors by increasing the number of directors to be elected.

Executive directors shall be appointed or elected every two years.

(c) Each executive director shall appoint an alternate with full power to act for him when he is not present. When the executive directors appointing them are present, alternates may participate in meetings but shall not vote.

(d) Directors shall continue in office until their successors are appointed or elected. If the office of an elected director becomes vacant more than 90 days before the end of his term, another director shall be elected for the remainder of the term by the governors who elected the former director. A majority of the votes cast shall be required for election. While the office remains vacant, the alternate of the former director shall exercise his powers, except that of appointing an alternate.

(e) The Executive Directors shall function in continuous session at the principal office of the Bank and shall meet as often as the business of the Bank may require.

(f) A quorum for any meeting of the Executive Directors shall be a majority of the Directors, exercising not less than one-half of the total voting power.

(g) Each appointed director shall be entitled to cast the number of votes allotted under Section 3 of this article to the member appointing him. Each elected director shall be entitled to cast the number of votes which counted toward his election. All the votes which a director is entitled to cast shall be cast as a unit.

(h) The Board of Governors shall adopt regulations under which a member not entitled to appoint a director under (b) above may send a representative to attend any meeting of the Executive Directors when a request made by, or a matter particularly affecting, that member is under consideration.

(i) The Executive Directors may appoint such committees as they deem advisable. Membership of such committees need not be limited to governors or directors or their alternates.

Section 5—President and Staff

(a) The Executive Directors shall select a President who shall not be a governor or an executive director or an alternate for either. The President shall be Chairman of the Executive Directors, but shall have no vote except a deciding vote in case of an equal division. He may participate in meetings of the Board of Governors, but shall not vote at such meetings. The President shall cease to hold office when the Executive Directors so decide.

(b) The President shall be chief of the operating staff of the Bank and shall conduct, under the direction of the Executive Directors, the ordinary business of the Bank. Subject to the general control of the Executive Directors, he shall be responsible for the organization, appointment and dismissal of the officers and staff.

(c) The President, officers and staff of the Bank, in the discharge of their offices, owe their duty entirely to the Bank and to no other authority. Each member of the Bank shall respect the international character of this duty and shall refrain from all attempts to influence any of them in the discharge of their duties.

(d) In appointing the officers and staff the President shall, subject to the paramount importance of securing the highest standards of efficiency and of technical competence, pay due regard to the importance of recruiting personnel on as wide a geographical basis as possible.

Section 6—Advisory Council

(a) There shall be an Advisory Council of not less than seven persons selected by the Board of Governors including representatives of banking, commercial, industrial, labour, and agricultural interests, and with as wide a national representation as possible. In those fields where specialized international organizations exist, the members of the Council representative of those fields shall be selected in agreement with such organizations. The Council shall advise the Bank on matters of general policy. The Council shall meet annually and on such other occasions as the Bank may request.

(b) Councellors shall serve for two years and may be reappointed. They shall be paid their reasonable expenses incurred on behalf of the Bank.

Section 7—Loan Committees

The committees required to report on loans under Article III, Section 4, shall be appointed by the Bank. Each such committee shall include an expert selected by the governor representing the member in whose territories the project is located and one or more members of the technical staff of the Bank.

Section 8—Relationship to Other International Organizations

(a) The Bank, within the terms of this Agreement, shall cooperate with any general international organization and with public international organizations having specialized responsibilities in related fields. Any arrangements for such cooperation which would involve a modification of any provision of this Agreement may be effected only after amendment to this Agreement under Article VIII.

(b) In making decisions on applications for loans or guarantees relating to matters directly within the competence of any international organization of the types specified in the preceding paragraph and participated in primarily by members of the Bank, the Bank shall give consideration to the views and recommendations of such organization.

Section 9—Location of Offices

(a) The principal office of the Bank shall be located in the territory of the member holding the greatest number of shares.

(b) The Bank may establish agencies or branch offices in the territories of any member of the Bank.

Section 10—Regional Offices and Councils

(a) The Bank may establish regional offices and determine the location of, and the areas to be covered by, each regional office.

(b) Each regional office shall be advised by a regional council representative of the entire area and selected in such manner as the Bank may decide.

Section 11—Depositories

(a) Each member shall designate its central bank as a depository for all the Bank's holdings of its currency or, if it has no central bank, it shall designate such other institution as may be acceptable to the Bank.

(b) The Bank may hold other assets, including gold, in depositories designated by the five members having the largest number of shares and in such other designated depositories as the Bank may select. Initially, at least one-half of the gold holdings of the Bank shall be held in the depository designated by the member in whose territory the Bank has its principal office, and at least 40 per cent shall be held in the depositories designated by the remaining four members referred to above, each of such depositories to hold, initially, not less than the amount of gold paid on the shares of the member designating it. However, all transfers of gold by the Bank shall be made with due regard to the costs of transport and anticipated requirements of the Bank. In an emergency the Executive Directors may transfer all or any part of the Bank's gold holdings to any place where they can be adequately protected.

Section 12—Form of Holdings of Currency

The Bank shall accept from any member, in place of any part of the member's currency, paid in to the Bank under Article II, Section 7(i), or to meet amortization payments on loans made with such currency, and not needed by the Bank in its operations, notes or similar obligations issued by the Government of the member or the depository designated by such member, which shall be non-negotiable, non-interest-bearing and payable at their par value on demand by credit to the account of the Bank in the designated depository.

Section 13—Publication of Reports and Provision of Information

(a) The Bank shall publish an annual report containing an audited statement of its accounts and shall circulate to members at intervals of three months or less a summary statement of its financial position and a profit and loss statement showing the results of its operations.

(b) The Bank may publish such other reports as it deems desirable to carry out its purposes.

(c) Copies of all reports, statements and publications made under this section shall be distributed to members.

Section 14—Allocation of Net Income

(a) The Board of Governors shall determine annually what part of the Bank's net income, after making provision for reserves, shall be allocated to surplus and what part, if any, shall be distributed.

(b) If any part is distributed, up to two per cent non-cumulative shall be paid, as a first charge against the distribution for any year, to each member on the basis of the average amount of the loans outstanding during the year made under Article IV, Section 1 (a) (i), out of currency corresponding to its subscription. If two per cent is paid as a first charge, any balance remaining to be distributed shall be paid to all members in proportion to their shares. Payments to each member shall be made in its own currency, of if that currency is not available in other currency acceptable to the member. If such payments are made in currencies other than the member's own currency, the transfer of the currency and its use by the receiving member after payment shall be without restriction by the members.

Article VI

Withdrawal and Suspension of Membership: Suspension of Operations

Section 1—Right of Members to Withdraw

Any member may withdraw from the Bank at any time by transmitting a notice in writing to the Bank at its principal office. Withdrawal shall become effective on the date such notice is received.

Section 2—Suspension of Membership

If a member fails to fulfill any of its obligations to the Bank, the Bank may suspend its membership by decision of a majority of the Governors, exercising a majority of the total voting power. The member so suspended shall automatically cease to be a member one year from the date of its suspension unless a decision is taken by the same majority to restore the member to good standing.

While under suspension, a member shall not be entitled to exercise any rights under this Agreement, except the right of withdrawal, but shall remain subject to all obligations.

Section 3—Cessation of Membership in International Monetary Fund

Any member which ceases to be a member of the International Monetary Fund shall automatically cease after three months to be a member of the Bank unless the Bank by three-fourths of the total voting power has agreed to allow it to remain a member.

Section 4—Settlement of Accounts with Governments Ceasing to be Members

(a) When a government ceases to be a member, it shall remain liable for its direct obligations to the Bank and for its contingent liabilities to the Bank so long as any part of the loans or guarantees contracted before it ceased to be a member are outstanding; but it shall cease to incur liabilities with respect to loans and guarantees entered into thereafter by the Bank and to share either in the income or the expenses of the Bank.

(b) At the time a government ceases to be a member, the Bank shall arrange for the repurchase of its shares as a part of the settlement of accounts with such government in accordance with the provisions of (c) and (d) below. For this purpose the repurchase price of the shares shall be the value shown by the books of the Bank on the day the government ceases to be a member.

(c) The payment for shares repurchased by the Bank under this section shall be governed by the following conditions:

  (i) Any amount due to the government for its shares shall be withheld so long as the government, its central bank or any of its agencies remains liable, as borrower or guarantor, to the Bank and such amount may, at the option of the Bank, be applied on any such liability as it matures. No amount shall be withheld on account of the liability of the government resulting from its subscription for shares under Article II, Section 5(ii). In any event, no amount due to a member for its shares shall be paid until six months after the date upon which the government ceases to be a member.

(ii) Payments for shares may be made from time to time, upon their surrender by the government, to the extent by which the amount due as the repurchase price in (b) above exceeds the aggregate of liabilities on loans and guarantees in (c)(i) above until the former member has received the full repurchase price.

(iii) Payments shall be made in the currency of the country receiving payment or at the option of the Bank in gold.

(iv) If losses are sustained by the Bank on any guarantees, participations in loans, or loans which were outstanding on the date when the government ceased to be a member, and the amount of such losses exceeds the amount of the reserve provided against losses on the date when the government ceased to be a member, such government shall be obligated to repay upon demand the amount by which the repurchase price of its shares would have been reduced, if the losses had been taken into account when the repurchase price was determined. In addition, the former member government shall remain liable on any call for unpaid subscriptions under Article II, Section 5(ii), to the extent that it would have been required to respond if the impairment of capital had occurred and the call had been made at the time the repurchase price of its shares was determined.

(d) If the Bank suspends permanently its operations under Section 5(b) of this article, within six months of the date upon which any government ceases to be a member, all rights of such government shall be determined by the provisions of Section 5 of this article.

Section 5—Suspension of Operations and Settlement of Obligations

(a) In an emergency the Executive Directors may suspend temporarily operations in respect of new loans and guarantees pending an opportunity for further consideration and action by the Board of Governors.

(b) The Bank may suspend permanently its operations in respect of new loans and guarantees by vote of a majority of the Governors, exercising a majority of the total voting power. After such suspension of operations the Bank shall forthwith cease all activities, except those incident to the orderly realization, conservation, and preservation of its assets and settlement of its obligations.

(c) The liability of all members for uncalled subscriptions to the capital stock of the Bank and in respect of the depreciation of their own currencies shall continue until all claims of creditors, including all contingent claims, shall have been discharged.

(d) All creditors holding direct claims shall be paid out of the assets of the Bank, and then out of payments to the Bank on calls on unpaid subscriptions. Before making any payments to creditors holding direct claims, the Executive Directors shall make such arrangements as are necessary, in their judgment, to insure a distribution to holders of contingent claims ratably with creditors holding direct claims.

(e) No distribution shall be made to members on account of their subscriptions to the capital stock of the Bank until (i) all liabilities to creditors have been discharged or provided for, and (ii) a majority of the Governors, exercising a majority of the total voting power, have decided to make a distribution.

(f) After a decision to make a distribution has been taken under (e) above, the Executive Directors may by a two-thirds majority vote make successive distributions of the assets of the Bank to members until all of the assets have been distributed. This distribution shall be subject to the prior settlement of all outstanding claims of the Bank against each member.

(g) Before any distribution of assets is made, the Executive Directors shall fix the proportionate share of each member according to the ratio of its shareholding to the total outstanding shares of the Bank.

(h) The Executive Directors shall value assets to be distributed as at the date of distribution and then proceed to distribute in the following manner:

    (i) There shall be paid to each member in its own obligations or those of its official agencies or legal entities within its territories, insofar as they are available for distribution, an amount equivalent in value to its proportionate share of the total amount to be distributed.

    (ii) Any balance due to a member after payment has been made under (i) above shall be paid, in its own currency, insofar as it is held by the Bank, up to an amount equivalent in value to such balance.

    (iii) Any balance due to a member after payment has been made under (i) and (ii) above shall be paid in gold or currency acceptable to the member, insofar as they are held by the Bank, up to an amount equivalent in value to such balance.

(iv) Any remaining assets held by the Bank after payments have been made to members under (i), (ii), and (iii) above shall be distributed pro rata among the members.

(i) Any member receiving assets distributed by the Bank in accordance with (h) above, shall enjoy the same rights with respect to such assets as the Bank enjoyed prior to their distribution.

Article VII

Status, Immunities and Privileges

Section 1—Purposes of Article

To enable the Bank to fulfill the functions with which it is entrusted, the status, immunities and privileges set forth in this article shall be accorded to the Bank in the territories of each member.

Section 2—Status of the Bank

The Bank shall possess full juridical personality, and, in particular, the capacity:

(i) to contract;

(ii) to acquire and dispose of immovable and movable property;

(iii) to institute legal proceedings.

Section 3—Position of the Bank with Regard to Judicial Process

Actions may be brought against the Bank only in a court of competent jurisdiction in the territories of a member in which the Bank has an office, has appointed an agent for the purpose of accepting service or notice of process, or has issued or guaranteed securities. No actions shall, however, be brought by members or persons acting for or deriving claims from members. The property and assets of the Bank shall, wheresoever located and by whomsoever held, be immune for all forms of seizure, attachment or execution before the delivery of final judgment against the Bank.

Section 4—Immunity of Assets from Seizure

Property and assets of the Bank, wherever located and by whomsoever held, shall be immune from search, requisition, confiscation, expropriation or any other form of seizure by executive or legislative action.

Section 5—Immunity of Archives

The archives of the Bank shall be inviolable.

Section 6—Freedom of Assets from Restrictions

To the extent necessary to carry out the operations provided for in this Agreement and subject to the provisions of this Agreement, all property and assets of the Bank shall be free from restrictions, regulations, controls and moratoria of any nature.

Section 7—Privilege for Communications

The official communications of the Bank shall be accorded by each member the same treatment that it accords to the official communications of other members.

Section 8—Immunities and Privileges of Officers and Employees

All governors, executive directors, alternates, officers and employees of the Bank

   (i) shall be immune from legal process with respect to acts performed by them in their official capacity except when the Bank waives this immunity;

   (ii) not being local nationals, shall be accorded the same immunities from immigration restrictions, alien registration requirements and national service obligations and the same facilities as regards exchange restrictions as are accorded by members to the representatives, officials, and employees of comparable rank of other members;

   (iii) shall be granted the same treatment in respect of travelling facilities as is accorded by members to representatives, officials and employees of comparable rank of other members.

Section 9—Immunities from Taxation

(a) The Bank, its assets, property, income and its operations and transactions authorized by this Agreement, shall be immune from all taxation and from all customs duties. The Bank shall also be immune from liability for the collection or payment of any tax or duty.

(b) No tax shall be levied on or in respect of salaries and emoluments paid by the Bank to executive directors, alternates, officials or employees of the Bank who are not local citizens, local subjects, or other local nationals.

(c) No taxation of any kind shall be levied on any obligation or security issued by the Bank (including any dividend or interest thereon) by whomsoever held:

   (i) which discriminates against such obligation or security solely because it is issued by the Bank; or

(ii) if the sole jurisdictional basis for such taxation is the place or currency in which it is issued, made payable or paid, or the location of any office or place of business maintained by the Bank.

(d) No taxation of any kind shall be levied on any obligation or security guaranteed by the Bank (including any dividend or interest thereon) by whomsoever held:

(i) which discriminates against such obligation or security solely because it is guaranteed by the Bank; or

(ii) if the sole jurisdictional basis for such taxation is the location of any office or place of business maintained by the Bank.

Section 10—Application of Article

Each member shall take such action as is necessary in its own territories for the purpose of making effective in terms of its own law the principles set forth in this article and shall inform the Bank of the detailed action which it has taken.

Article VIII

Amendments

(a) Any proposal to introduce modifications in this Agreement, whether emanating from a member, a governor or the Executive Directors, shall be communicated to the Chairman of the Board of Governors who shall bring the proposal before the Board. If the proposed amendment is approved by the Board the Bank shall, by circular letter or telegram, ask all members whether they accept the proposed amendment. When three-fifths of the members, having *eight-five percent of the total voting power, have accepted the proposed amendments, the Bank shall certify the fact by formal communication addressed to all members.

[*Note: "Eighty-five percent" was substituted for "four-fifths" by amendment effective February 16, 1989.*]

(b) Notwithstanding (a) above, acceptance by all members is required in the case of any amendment modifying
(i)   the right to withdraw from the Bank provided in Article VI, Section 1;

(ii) the right secured by Article II, Section 3(c);

(iii) the limitation on liability provided in Article II, Section 6.

(c) Amendments shall enter into force for all members three months after the date of the formal communication unless a shorter period is specified in the circular letter or telegram.

Article IX

Interpretation

(a) Any question of interpretation of the provisions of this Agreement arising between any member and the Bank or between any members of the Bank shall be submitted to the Executive Directors for their decision. If the question particularly affects any member not entitled to appoint an executive director, it shall be entitled to representation in accordance with Article V, Section 4(h).

(b) In any case where the Executive Directors have given a decision under (a) above, any member may require that the question be referred to the Board of Governors, whose decision shall be final. Pending the result of the reference to the Board, the Bank may, so far as it deems necessary, act on the basis of the decision of the Executive Directors.

(c) Whenever a disagreement arises between the Bank and a country which has ceased to be a member, or between the Bank and any member during the permanent suspension of the Bank, such disagreement shall be submitted to arbitration by a tribunal of three arbitrators, one appointed by the Bank, another by the country involved and an umpire who, unless the parties otherwise agree, shall be appointed by the President of the Permanent Court of International Justice or such other authority as may have been prescribed by regulation adopted by the Bank. The umpire shall have full power to settle all questions of procedure in any case where the parties are in disagreement with respect thereto.

Article X

Approval Deemed Given

Whenever the approval of any member is required before any act may be done by the Bank, except in Article VIII, approval shall be deemed to have been given unless the member presents an objection within such reasonable period as the Bank may fix in notifying the member of the proposed act.

Article XI

Final Provisions

Section 1—Entry into Force

This agreement shall enter into force when it has been signed on behalf of governments whose minimum subscriptions comprise not less that 65 per cent of the total subscriptions set forth in Schedule A and when the instruments referred to in Section 2(a) of this article have been deposited on their behalf, but in no event shall this Agreement enter into force before May 1, 1945.

Section 2—Signature

(a) Each government on whose behalf this Agreement is signed shall deposit with the Government of the United States of America an instrument setting forth that it has accepted this Agreement in accordance with its law and has taken all steps necessary to enable it to carry out all of its obligations under this Agreement.

(b) Each government shall become a member of the Bank as from the date of the deposit on its behalf of the instrument referred to in (a) above, except that no government shall become a member before this Agreement enters into force under Section 1 of this article.

(c) The Government of the United States of America shall inform the governments of all countries whose names are set forth in Schedule A, and all governments whose membership is approved in accordance with Article II, Section 1(b), of all signatures of this Agreement and of the deposit of all instruments referred to in (a) above.

(d) At the time this Agreement is signed on its behalf, each government shall transmit to the Government of the United States of America one-hundredth of one per cent of the price of each share in gold or United States dollars for the purpose of meeting administrative expenses of the Bank. This payment shall be credited on account of the payment to be made in accordance with Article II, Section 8(a). The Government of the United States of America shall hold such funds in a special deposit account and shall transmit them to the Board of Governors of the Bank when the initial meeting has been called under Section 3 of this article. If this Agreement has not come into force by December 31, 1945, the Government of the United States of America shall return such funds to the governments that transmitted them.

(e) This Agreement shall remain open for signature at Washington on behalf of the governments of the countries whose names are set forth in Schedule A until December 31, 1945.

(f) After December 31, 1945, this Agreement shall be open for signature on behalf of the government of any country whose membership has been approved in accordance with Article II, Section 1(b).

(g) By their signature of this Agreement, all governments accept it both on their own behalf and in respect of all their colonies, overseas territories, all territories under their protection, suzerainty, or authority and all territories in respect of which they exercise a mandate.

(h) In the case of governments whose metropolitan territories have been under enemy occupation, the deposit of the instrument referred to in (a) above may be delayed until one 180 days after the date on which these territories have been liberated. If, however, it is not deposited by any such government before the expiration of this period, the signature affixed on behalf of that government shall become void and the portion of its subscription paid under (d) above shall be returned to it.

(i) Paragraphs (d) and (h) shall come into force with regard to each signatory government as from the date of its signature.

Section 3—Inauguration of the Bank

(a) As soon as this Agreement enters into force under Section 1 of this article, each member shall appoint a governor and the member to whom the largest number of shares is allocated in Schedule A shall call the first meeting of the Board of Governors.

(b) At the first meeting of the Board of Governors, arrangements shall be made for the selection of provisional executive directors. The governments of the five countries to which the largest number of shares are allocated in Schedule A, shall appoint provisional executive directors. If one or more of such governments have not become members, the executive directorships which they would be entitled to fill shall remain vacant until they become members, or until January 1, 1946, whichever is the earlier. Seven provisional executive directors shall be elected in accordance with the provisions of Schedule B and shall remain in office until the date of the first regular election of executive directors which shall be held as soon as practicable after January 1, 1946.

(c) The Board of Governors may delegate to the provisional executive directors any powers except those which may not be delegated to the Executive Directors.

(d) The Bank shall notify members when it is ready to commence operations.

DONE at Washington, in a single copy which shall remain deposited in the archives of the Government of the United States of America, which shall transmit certified copies to all governments whose names are set forth in Schedule A and to all governments whose membership is approved in accordance with Article II, Section 1 (b).

[*Note:* Schedules are not reproduced here. Schedule A is titled "Subscriptions" and Section B is titled "Election of Executive Directors."]

APPENDIX D

CHARTER OF THE IDA

Citation: Articles of Agreement of the International Development Association, done at Washington, DC, Jan. 26, 1960 (entered into force September 24, 1960), 439 U.N.T.S. 249, 11 U.S.T. 2284, T.I.A.S. No. 4607.

Contents

Articles of Agreement of the International Development Association

The Governments on whose behalf this Agreement is signed,

Considering:

That mutual cooperation for constructive economic purposes, healthy development of the world economy and balanced growth of internationl trade foster international relationships conducive to the maintenance of peace and world prosperity;

That an acceleration of economic development which will promote higher standards of living and economic and social progress in the less-developed countries is desirable not only in the interests of those countries but also in the interests of the international community as a whole;

That achievement of these objectives would be facilitated by an increase in the international flow of capital, public and private, to assist in the development of the resources of the less-developed countries, do hereby agree as follows:

INTRODUCTORY ARTICLE

The INTERNATIONAL DEVELOPMENT ASSOCIATION (hereinafter called "the Association") is established and shall operate in accordance with the following provisions:

ARTICLE I
Purposes

The purposes of the Association are to promote economic development, increase productivity and thus raise standards of living in the less-developed areas of the world included within the Association's membership, in particular by providing finance to meet their important developmental requirements on terms which are more flexible and bear less heavily on the balance of payments than those of conventional loans, thereby furthering the developmental objectives of the International Bank for Reconstruction and Development (hereinafter called "the Bank") and supplementing its activities.

The Association shall be guided in all its decisions by the provisions of this Article.

ARTICLE II
Membership; Initial Subscriptions

SECTION 1. Membership

(a) The original members of the Association shall be those members of the Bank listed in Schedule A hereto which, on or before the date specified in Article XI, Section 2(c), accept membership in the Association.

(b) Membership shall be open to other members of the Bank at such times and in accordance with such terms as the Association may determine.

SECTION 2. Initial Subscriptions

(a) Upon accepting membership, each member shall subscribe funds in the amount assigned to it. Such subscriptions are herein referred to as initial subscriptions.

(b) The initial subscription assigned to each original member shall be in the amount set forth opposite its name in Schedule A, expressed in terms of United States dollars of the weight and fineness in effect on January 1, 1960.

(c) Ten percent of the initial subscription of each original member shall be payable in gold or freely convertible currency as follows: fifty percent within thirty days after the date on which the Association shall begin operations pursuant to Article XI, Section 4, or on the date on which the original member becomes a member, whichever shall be later; twelve and one-half percent one year after the beginning of operations of the Association; and twelve and one-half percent each year thereafter at annual intervals until the ten percent portion of the initial subscription shall have been paid in full.

(d) The remaining ninety percent of the initial subscription of each original member shall be payable in gold or freely convertible currency in the case of members listed in Part I of Schedule A, and in the currency of the subscribing member in the case of members listed in Part II of Schedule A. This ninety percent portion of initial subscriptions of original members shall be payable in five equal annual installments as follows: the first such installment within thirty days after the date on which the Association shall begin operations pursuant to Article XI, Section 4, or on the date on which the original member becomes a member, whichever shall be later; the second installment one year after the beginning of operations of the Association, and succeeding installments each year thereafter at annual intervals until the ninety percent portion of the initial subscription shall have been paid in full.

(e) The Association shall accept from any member, in place of any part of the member's currency paid in or payable by the member under the preceding subsection (d) or under Section 2 of Article IV and not needed by the Association in its operations, notes or similar obligations issued by the government of the member or the depository designated by such member, which shall be non-negotiable, non-interest-bearing and payable at their par value on demand to the account of the Association in the designated depository.

(f) For the purposes of this Agreement the Association shall regard as "freely convertible currency":

    (i) currency of a member which the Association determines, after consultation with the International Monetary Fund, is adequately convertible into the currencies of other members for the purposes of the Association's operations; or

    (ii) currency of a member which such member agrees, on terms satisfactory to the Association, to exchange for the currencies of other members for the purposes of the Association's operations.

(g) Except as the Association may otherwise agree, each member listed in Part I of Schedule A shall maintain, in respect of its currency paid in by it as freely convertible currency pursuant to subsection (d) of this Section, the same convertibility as existed at the time of payment.

(h) The conditions on which the initial subscriptions of members other than original members may be made, and the amounts and the terms of payment thereof, shall be determined by the Association pursuant to Section 1(b) of this Article.

SECTION 3. Limitation on Liability

No member shall be liable, by reason of its membership, for obligations of the Association.

ARTICLE III

Additions to Resources

SECTION 1. Additional Subscriptions

(a) The Association shall at such time as it deems appropriate in the light of the schedule for completion of payments on initial subscriptions of original members, and at intervals of approximately five years thereafter, review the adequacy of its resources and, if it deems desirable, shall authorize a general increase in subscriptions. Notwithstanding the foregoing, general or individual increases in subscriptions may be authorized at any time, provided that an individual increase shall be considered only at the request of the member involved. Subscriptions pursuant to this Section are herein referred to as additional subscriptions.

(b) Subject to the provisions of paragraph (c) below, when additional subscriptions are authorized, the amounts authorized for subscription and the terms and conditions relating thereto shall be as determined by the Association.

(c) When any additional subscription is authorized, each member shall be given an opportunity to subscribe, under such conditions as shall be reasonably determined by the Association, an amount which will enable it to maintain its relative voting power, but no member shall be obligated to subscribe.

(d) All decisions under this Section shall be made by a two-thirds majority of the total voting power.

SECTION 2. Supplementary Resources Provided by a Member in the Currency of Another Member

(a) The Association may enter into arrangements, on such terms and conditions consistent with the provisions of this Agreement as may be agreed upon, to receive from any member, in addition to the amounts payable by such member on account of its initial or any additional subscription, supplementary resources in the currency of another member, provided that the Association shall not enter into any such arrangement unless the Association is satisfied that the member whose currency is involved agrees to the use of such currency as supplementary resources and to the terms and conditions governing such use. The arrangements under which any such resources are received may include provisions regarding the disposition of earnings on the resources and regarding the disposition of the resources in the event that the member providing them ceases to be a member or the Association permanently suspends its operations.

(b) The Association shall deliver to the contributing member a Special Development Certificate setting forth the amount and currency of the resources so contributed and the terms and conditions of the arrangement relating to such resources. A Special Development Certificate shall not carry any voting rights and shall be transferable only to the Association.

(c) Nothing in this Section shall preclude the Association from accepting resources from a member in its own currency on such terms as may be agreed upon.

ARTICLE IV

Currencies

SECTION 1. Use of Currencies

(a) Currency of any member listed in Part II of Schedule A, whether or not freely convertible, received by the Association pursuant to Article II,

Section 2(d), in payment of the ninety percent portion payable thereunder in the currency of such member, and currency of such member derived therefrom as principal, interest or other charges, may be used by the Association for administrative expenses incurred by the Association in the territories of such member and, insofar as consistent with sound monetary policies, in payment for goods and services produced in the territories of such member and required for projects financed by the Association and located in such territories; and in addition when and to the extent justified by the economic and financial situation of the member concerned as determined by agreement between the member and the Association, such currency shall be freely convertible or otherwise usable for projects financed by the Association and located outside the territories of the member.

(b) The usability of currencies received by the Association in payment of subscriptions other than initial subscriptions of original members, and currencies derived therefrom as principal, interest or other charges, shall be governed by the terms and conditions on which such subscriptions are authorized.

(c) The usability of currencies received by the Association as supplementary resources other than subscriptions, and currencies derived therefrom as principal, interest or other charges, shall be governed by the terms of the arrangements pursuant to which such currencies are received.

(d) All other currencies received by the Association may be freely used and exchanged by the Association and shall not be subject to any restriction by the member whose currency is used or exchanged; provided that the foregoing shall not preclude the Association from entering into any arrangements with the member in whose territories any project financed by the Association is located restricting the use by the Association of such member's currency received as principal, interest or other charges in connection with such financing.

(e) The Association shall take appropriate steps to ensure that, over reasonable intervals of time, the portions of the subscriptions paid under Article II, Section 2(d) by members listed in Part I of Schedule A shall be used by the Association on an approximately pro rata basis, provided, however, that such portions of such subscriptions as are paid in gold or in a currency other than that of the subscribing member may be used more rapidly.

SECTION 2. Maintenance of Value of Currency Holdings

(a) Whenever the par value of a member's currency is reduced or the foreign exchange value of a member's currency has, in the opinion of the Association, depreciated to a significant extent within that member's territories, the member shall pay to the Association within a reasonable time an additional amount of its own currency sufficient to maintain the value, as of the time of subscription, of the amount of the currency of such member paid in to the Association by the member under Article II, Section 2(d), and currency furnished under the provisions of the present paragraph, whether or not such currency is held in the form of notes accepted pursuant to Article II, Section 2(e), provided, however, that the foregoing shall apply only so long as and to the extent that such currency shall not have been initially disbursed or exchanged for the currency of another member.

(b) Whenever the par value of a member's currency is increased, or the foreign exchange value of a member's currency has, in the opinion of the Association, appreciated to a significant extent within that member's territories, the Association shall return to such member within a reasonable time an amount of that member's currency equal to the increase in the value of the amount of such currency to which the provisions of paragraph (a) of this Section are applicable.

(c) The provisions of the preceding paragraphs may be waived by the Association when a uniform proportionate change in the par value of the currencies of all its members is made by the International Monetary Fund.

(d) Amounts furnished under the provisions of paragraph (a) of this Section to maintain the value of any currency shall be convertible and usable to the same extent as such currency.

ARTICLE V

Operations

SECTION 1. Use of Resources and Conditions of Financing

(a) The Association shall provide financing to further development in the less-developed areas of the world included within the Association's membership.

(b) Financing provided by the Association shall be for purposes which in the opinion of the Association are of high developmental priority in the light of the needs of the area or areas concerned and, except in special circumstances, shall be for specific projects.

(c) The Association shall not provide financing if in its opinion such financing is available from private sources on terms which are reasonable for the recipient or could be provided by a loan of the type made by the Bank.

(d) The Association shall not provide financing except upon the recommendation of a competent committee, made after a careful study of the merits of the proposal. Each such committee shall be appointed by the Association and shall include a nominee of the Governor or Governors representing the member or members in whose territories the project under consideration is located and one or more members of the technical staff of the Association. The requirement that the committee include the nominee of a Governor or Governors shall not apply in the case of financing provided to a public international or regional organization.

(e) The Association shall not provide financing for any project if the member in whose territories the project is located objects to such financing, except that it shall not be necessary for the Association to assure itself that individual members do not object in the case of financing provided to a public international or regional organization.

(f) The Association shall impose no conditions that the proceeds of its financing shall be spent in the territories of any particular member or members. The foregoing shall not preclude the Association from complying with any restrictions on the use of funds imposed in accordance with the provisions of these Articles, including restrictions attached to supplementary resources pursuant to agreement between the Association and the contributor.

(g) The Association shall make arrangements to ensure that the proceeds of any financing are used only for the purposes for which the financing was provided, with due attention to considerations of economy, efficiency and competitive international trade and without regard to political or other non-economic influences or considerations.

(h) Funds to be provided under any financing operation shall be made available to the recipient only to meet expenses in connection with the project as they are actually incurred.

SECTION 2. Form and Terms of Financing

(a) Financing by the Association shall take the form of loans. The Association may, however, provide other financing, either

(i) out of funds subscribed pursuant to Article III, Section 1, and funds derived therefrom as principal, interest or other charges, if the authorization for such subscriptions expressly provides for such financing; or

(ii) in special circumstances, out of supplementary resources furnished to the Association, and funds derived therefrom as principal, interest or other charges, if the arrangements under which such resources are furnished expressly authorize such financing.

(b) Subject to the foregoing paragraph, the Association may provide financing in such forms and on such terms as it may deem appropriate, having regard to the economic position and prospects of the area or areas concerned and to the nature and requirements of the project.

(c) The Association may provide financing to a member, the government of a territory included within the Association's membership, a political subdivision of any of the foregoing, a public or private entity in the territories of a member or members, or to a public international or regional organization.

(d) In the case of a loan to an entity other than a member, the Association may, in its discretion, require a suitable governmental or other guarantee or guarantees.

(e) The Association, in special cases, may make foreign exchange available for local expenditures.

SECTION 3. Modifications of Terms of Financing

The Association may, when and to the extent it deems appropriate in the light of all relevant circumstances, including the financial and economic situation and prospects of the member concerned, and on such conditions as it may determine, agree to a relaxation or other modification of the terms on which any of its financing shall have been provided.

SECTION 4. Cooperation with Other International Organizations and Members Providing Development Assistance

The Association shall cooperate with those public international organizations and members which provide financial and technical assistance to the less-developed areas of the world.

SECTION 5. Miscellaneous Operations

In addition to the operations specified elsewhere in this Agreement, the Association may:

(i) borrow funds with the approval of the member in whose currency the loan is denominated;

(ii) guarantee securities in which it has invested in order to facilitate their sale;

(iii) buy and sell securities it has issued or guaranteed or in which it has invested;

(iv) in special cases, guarantee loans from other sources for purposes not inconsistent with the provisions of these Articles;

(v) provide technical assistance and advisory services at the request of a member; and

(vi) exercise such other powers incidental to its operations as shall be necessary or desirable in furtherance of its purposes.

SECTION 6. Political Activity Prohibited

The Association and its officers shall not interfere in the political affairs of any member; nor shall they be influenced in their decisions by the political character of the member or members concerned. Only economic considerations shall be relevant to their decisions, and these considerations shall be weighed impartially in order to achieve the purposes stated in this Agreement.

ARTICLE VI

Organization and Management

SECTION 1. Structure of the Association

The Association shall have a Board of Governors, Executive Directors, a President and such other officers and staff to perform such duties as the Association may determine.

SECTION 2. Board of Governors

(a) All the powers of the Association shall be vested in the Board of Governors.

(b) Each Governor and Alternate Governor of the Bank appointed by a member of the Bank which is also a member of the Association shall ex officio be a Governor and Alternate Governor, respectively, of the Association. No Alternate Governor may vote except in the absence of his principal. The Chairman of the Board of Governors of the Bank shall ex officio be Chairman of the Board of Governors of the Association except that if the Chairman of the Board of Governors of the Bank shall represent a state which is not a member of the Association, then the Board of Governors shall select one of the Governors as Chairman of the Board of Governors. Any Governor or Alternate Governor shall cease to hold office if the member by which he was appointed shall cease to be a member of the Association.

(c) The Board of Governors may delegate to the Executive Directors authority to exercise any of its powers, except the power to:

(i) admit new members and determine the conditions of their admission;

(ii) authorize additional subscriptions and determine the terms and conditions relating thereto;

(iii) suspend a member;

(iv) decide appeals from interpretations of this Agreement given by the Executive Directors;

(v) make arrangements pursuant to Section 7 of this Article to cooperate with other international organizations (other than informal arrangements of a temporary and administrative character);

(vi) decide to suspend permanently the operations of the Association and to distribute its assets;

(vii) determine the distribution of the Association's net income pursuant to Section 12 of this Article; and

(viii) approve proposed amendments to this Agreement.

(d) The Board of Governors shall hold an annual meeting and such other meetings as may be provided for by the Board of Governors or called by the Executive Directors.

(e) The annual meeting of the Board of Governors shall be held in conjunction with the annual meeting of the Board of Governors of the Bank.

(f) A quorum for any meeting of the Board of Governors shall be a majority of the Governors, exercising not less than two-thirds of the total voting power.

(g) The Association may by regulation establish a procedure whereby the Executive Directors may obtain a vote of the Governors on a specific question without calling a meeting of the Board of Governors.

(h) The Board of Governors, and the Executive Directors to the extent authorized, may adopt such rules and regulations as may be necessary or appropriate to conduct the business of the Association.

(i) Governors and Alternate Governors shall serve as such without compensation from the Association.

SECTION 3. Voting

(a) Each original member shall, in respect of its initial subscription, have 500 votes plus one additional vote for each $ 5,000 of its initial subscription. Subscriptions other than initial subscriptions of original members shall carry such voting rights as the Board of Governors shall determine pursuant to the provisions of Article II, Section 1(b) or Article III, Section 1(b) and (c), as the case may be. Additions to resources other than subscriptions under Article II, Section 1(b) and additional subscriptions under Article III, Section 1, shall not carry voting rights.

(b) Except as otherwise specifically provided, all matters before the Association shall be decided by a majority of the votes cast.

SECTION 4. Executive Directors

(a) The Executive Directors shall be responsible for the conduct of the general operations of the Association, and for this purpose shall exercise all the powers given to them by this Agreement or delegated to them by the Board of Governors.

(b) The Executive Directors of the Association shall be composed ex officio of each Executive Director of the Bank who shall have been (i) appointed by a member of the Bank which is also a member of the Association, or (ii) elected in an election in which the votes of at least one member of the Bank which is also a member of the Association shall have counted toward his election. The Alternate to each such Executive Director of the Bank shall ex officio be an Alternate Director of the Association. Any Director shall cease to hold office if the member by which he was appointed, or if all the members whose votes counted toward his election, shall cease to be members of the Association.

(c) Each Director who is an appointed Executive Director of the Bank shall be entitled to cast the number of votes which the member by which he was appointed is entitled to cast in the Association. Each Director who is an elected Executive Director of the Bank shall be entitled to cast the number of votes which the member or members of the Association whose votes counted toward his election in the Bank are entitled to cast in the Association. All the votes which a Director is entitled to cast shall be cast as a unit.

(d) An Alternate Director shall have full power to act in the absence of the Director who shall have appointed him. When a Director is present, his Alternate may participate in meetings but shall not vote.

(e) A quorum for any meeting of the Executive Directors shall be a majority of the Directors exercising not less than one-half of the total voting power.

(f) The Executive Directors shall meet as often as the business of the Association may require.

(g) The Board of Governors shall adopt regulations under which a member of the Association not entitled to appoint an Executive Director of the Bank may send a representative to attend any meeting of the Executive Directors of the Association when a request made by, or a matter particularly affecting, that member is under consideration.

SECTION 5. President and Staff

(a) The President of the Bank shall be ex officio President of the Association. The President shall be Chairman of the Executive Directors of the Association but shall have no vote except a deciding vote in case of an equal division. He may participate in meetings of the Board of Governors but shall not vote at such meetings.

(b) The President shall be chief of the operating staff of the Association. Under the direction of the Executive Directors he shall conduct the ordinary business of the Association and under their general control shall be responsible for the organization, appointment and dismissal of the officers and staff. To the extent practicable, officers and staff of the Bank shall be appointed to serve concurrently as officers and staff of the Association.

(c) The President, officers and staff of the Association, in the discharge of their offices, owe their duty entirely to the Association and to no other authority. Each member of the Association shall respect the international character of this duty and shall refrain from all attempts to influence any of them in the discharge of their duties.

(d) In appointing officers and staff the President shall, subject to the paramount importance of securing the highest standards of efficiency and of technical competence, pay due regard to the importance of recruiting personnel on as wide a geographical basis as possible.

SECTION 6. Relationship to the Bank

(a) The Association shall be an entity separate and distinct from the Bank and the funds of the Association shall be kept separate and apart from those of the Bank. The Association shall not borrow from or lend to the Bank, except that this shall not preclude the Association from investing funds not needed in its financing operations in obligations of the Bank.

(b) The Association may make arrangements with the Bank regarding facilities, personnel and services and arrangements for reimbursement of administrative expenses paid in the first instance by either organization on behalf of the other.

(c) Nothing in this Agreement shall make the Association liable for the acts or obligations of the Bank, or the Bank liable for the acts or obligations of the Association.

SECTION 7. Relations with Other International Organizations

The Association shall enter into formal arrangements with the United Nations and may enter into such arrangements with other public international organizations having specialized responsibilities in related fields.

SECTION 8. Location of Offices

The principal office of the Association shall be the principal office of the Bank. The Association may establish other offices in the territories of any member.

SECTION 9. Depositories

Each member shall designate its central bank as a depository in which the Association may keep holdings of such member's currency or other assets of the Association, or, if it has no central bank, it shall designate for such purpose such other institution as may be acceptable to the Association. In the absence of any different designation, the depository designated for the Bank shall be the depository for the Association.

SECTION 10. Channel of Communication

Each member shall designate an appropriate authority with which the Association may communicate in connection with any matter arising under this Agreement. In the absence of any different designation, the channel of communication designated for the Bank shall be the channel for the Association.

SECTION 11. Publication of Reports and Provision of Information

(a) The Association shall publish an annual report containing an audited statement of its accounts and shall circulate to members at appropriate intervals a summary statement of its financial position and of the results of its operations.

(b) The Association may publish such other reports as it deems desirable to carry out its purposes.

(c) Copies of all reports, statements and publications made under this Section shall be distributed to members.

SECTION 12. Disposition of Net Income

The Board of Governors shall determine from time to time the disposition of the Association's net income, having due regard to provision for reserves and contingencies.

ARTICLE VII

Withdrawal; Suspension of Membership; Suspension of Operations

SECTION 1. Withdrawal by Members

Any member may withdraw from membership in the Association at any time by transmitting a notice in writing to the Association at its principal office. Withdrawal shall become effective upon the date such notice is received.

SECTION 2. Suspension of Membership

(a) If a member fails to fulfill any of its obligations to the Association, the Association may suspend its membership by decision of a majority of the Governors, exercising a majority of the total voting power. The member so suspended shall automatically cease to be a member one year from the date of its suspension unless a decision is taken by the same majority to restore the member to good standing.

(b) While under suspension, a member shall not be entitled to exercise any rights under this Agreement except the right of withdrawal, but shall remain subject to all obligations.

SECTION 3. Suspension or Cessation of Membership in the Bank

Any member which is suspended from membership in, or ceases to be a member of, the Bank shall automatically be suspended from membership in, or cease to be a member of, the Association, as the case may be.

SECTION 4. Rights and Duties of Governments Ceasing to be Members

(a) When a government ceases to be a member, it shall have no rights under this Agreement except as provided in this Section and in Article X(c), but it shall, except as in this Section otherwise provided, remain liable for all financial obligations undertaken by it to the Association, whether as a member, borrower, guarantor or otherwise.

(b) When a government ceases to be a member, the Association and the government shall proceed to a settlement of accounts. As part of such settlement of accounts, the Association and the government may agree on the amounts to be paid to the government on account of its subscription and on the time and currencies of payment. The term "subscription" when used in relation to any member government shall for the purposes of this Article be deemed to include both the initial subscription and any additional subscription of such member government.

(c) If no such agreement is reached within six months from the date when the government ceased to be a member, or such other time as may be agreed upon by the Association and the government, the following provisions shall apply:

    (i) The government shall be relieved of any further liability to the Association on account of its subscription, except that the government shall pay to the Association forthwith amounts due and unpaid on the date when the government ceased to be a member and which in the opinion of the Association are neeeded by it to meet its commitments as of that date under its financing operations.

(ii) The Association shall return to the government funds paid in by the government on account of its subscription or derived there-from as principal repayments and held by the Association on the date when the government ceased to be a member, except to the extent that in the opinion of the Association such funds will be needed by it to meet its commitments as of that date under its financing operations.

(iii) The Association shall pay over to the government a pro rata share of all principal repayments received by the Association after the date on which the government ceases to be a member on loans contracted prior thereto, except those made out of supplementary resources provided to the Association under arrangements speci-fying special liquidation rights. Such share shall be such propor-tion of the total principal amount of such loans as the total amount paid by the government on account of its subscription and not returned to it pursuant to clause (ii) above shall bear to the total amount paid by all members on account of their subscrip-tions which shall have been used or in the opinion of the Association will be needed by it to meet its commitments under its financing operations as of the date on which the government ceases to be a member. Such payment by the Association shall be made in installments when and as such principal repayments are received by the Association, but not more frequently than annu-ally. Such installments shall be paid in the currencies received by the Association except that the Association may in its discretion make payment in the currency of the government concerned.

(iv) Any amount due to the government on account of its subscription may be withheld so long as that government, or the government of any territory included within its membership, or any political sub-division or any agency of any of the foregoing remains liable, as borrower or guarantor, to the Association, and such amount may, at the option of the Association, be applied against any such lia-bility as it matures.

(v) In no event shall the government receive under this paragraph (c) an amount exceeding, in the aggregate, the lesser of the two fol-lowing: (a) the amount paid by the government on account of its subscription, or (b) such proportion of the net assets of the Association, as shown on the books of the Association as of the date on which the government ceased to be a member, as the amount of its subscription shall bear to the aggregate amount of the subscriptions of all members.

(vi) All calculations required hereunder shall be made on such basis as shall be reasonably determined by the Association.

(d) In no event shall any amount due to a government under this Section be paid until six months after the date upon which the government ceases to be a member. If within six months of the date upon which any government ceases to be a member the Association suspends operations under Section 5 of this Article, all rights of such government shall be determined by the provisions of such Section 5 and such government shall be considered a member of the Association for purposes of such Section 5, except that it shall have no voting rights.

SECTION 5. Suspension of Operations and Settlement of Obligations

(a) The Association may permanently suspend its operations by vote of a majority of the Governors exercising a majority of the total voting power. After such suspension of operations the Association shall forthwith cease all activities, except those incident to the orderly realization, conservation and preservation of its assets and settlement of its obligations. Until final settlement of such obligations and distribution of such assets, the Association shall remain in existence and all mutual rights and obligations of the Association and its members under this Agreement shall continue unimpaired, except that no member shall be suspended or shall withdraw and that no distribution shall be made to members except as in this Section provided.

(b) No distribution shall be made to members on account of their subscriptions until all liabilities to creditors shall have been discharged or provided for and until the Board of Governors, by vote of a majority of the Governors exercising a majority of the total voting power, shall have decided to make such distribution.

(c) Subject to the foregoing, and to any special arrangements for the disposition of supplementary resources agreed upon in connection with the provision of such resources to the Association, the Association shall distribute its assets to members pro rata in proportion to amounts paid in by them on account of their subscriptions. Any distribution pursuant to the foregoing provision of this paragraph (c) shall be subject, in the case of any member, to prior settlement of all outstanding claims by the Association against such member. Such distribution shall be made at such times, in such currencies, and in cash or other assets as the Association shall deem fair and equitable. Distribution to the several members need not be uniform in respect of the type of assets distributed or of the currencies in which they are expressed.

(d) Any member receiving assets distributed by the Association pursuant to this Section or Section 4 shall enjoy the same rights with respect to such assets as the Association enjoyed prior to their distribution.

ARTICLE VIII

Status, Immunities and Privileges

SECTION 1. Purposes of Article

To enable the Association to fulfill the functions with which it is entrusted, the status, immunities and privileges provided in this Article shall be accorded to the Association in the territories of each member.

SECTION 2. Status of the Association

The Association shall possess full juridical personality and, in particular, the capacity:

(i) to contract;

(ii) to acquire and dispose of immovable and movable property;

(iii) to institute legal proceedings.

SECTION 3. Position of the Association with Regard to Judicial Process

Actions may be brought against the Association only in a court of competent jurisdiction in the territories of a member in which the Association has an office, has appointed an agent for the purpose of accepting service or notice of process, or has issued or guaranteed securities. No actions shall, however, be brought by members or persons acting for or deriving claims from members. The property and assets of the Association shall, wheresoever located and by whomsoever held, be immune from all forms of seizure, attachment or execution before the delivery of final judgment against the Association.

SECTION 4. Immunity of Assets from Seizure

Property and assets of the Association, wherever located and by whomsoever held, shall be immune from search, requisition, confiscation, expropriation or any other form of seizure by executive or legislative action.

SECTION 5. Immunity of Archives

The archives of the Association shall be inviolable.

SECTION 6. Freedom of Assets from Restrictions

To the extent necessary to carry out the operations provided for in this Agreement and subject to the provisions of this Agreement, all property and assets of the Association shall be free from restrictions, regulations, controls and moratoria of any nature.

SECTION 7. Privilege for Communications

The official communications of the Association shall be accorded by each member the same treatment that it accords to the official communications of other members.

SECTION 8. Immunities and Privileges of Officers and Employees

All Governors, Executive Directors, Alternates, officers and employees of the Association

(i) shall be immune from legal process with respect to acts performed by them in their official capacity except when the Association waives this immunity;

(ii) not being local nationals, shall be accorded the same immunities from immigration restrictions, alien registration requirements and national service obligations and the same facilities as regards exchange restrictions as are accorded by members to the representatives, officials, and employees of comparable rank of other members;

(iii) shall be granted the same treatment in respect of travelling facilities as is accorded by members to representatives, officials and employees of comparable rank of other members.

SECTION 9. Immunities from Taxation

(a) The Association, its assets, property, income and its operations and transactions authorized by this Agreement, shall be immune from all taxation and from all customs duties. The Association shall also be immune from liability for the collection or payment of any tax or duty.

(b) No tax shall be levied on or in respect of salaries and emoluments paid by the Association to Executive Directors, Alternates, officials or employees of the Association who are not local citizens, local subjects, or other local nationals.

(c) No taxation of any kinds shall be levied on any obligation or security issued by the Association (including any dividend or interest thereon) by whomsoever held

(i) which discriminates against such obligation or security solely because it is issued by the Association; or

(ii) if the sole jurisdictional basis for such taxation is the place or currency in which it is issued, made payable or paid, or the location of any office or place of business maintained by the Association.

(d) No taxation of any kind shall be levied on any obligation or security guaranteed by the Association (including any dividend or interest thereon) by whomsoever held

   (i) which discriminates against such obligation or security solely because it is guaranteed by the Association; or

   (ii) if the sole jurisdictional basis for such taxation is the location of any office or place of business maintained by the Association.

SECTION 10. Application of Article

Each member shall take such action as is necessary in its own territories for the purpose of making effective in terms of its own law the principles set forth in this Article and shall inform the Association of the detailed action which it has taken.

ARTICLE IX

Amendments

(a) Any proposal to introduce modifications in this Agreement, whether emanating from a member, a Governor or the Executive Directors, shall be communicated to the Chairman of the Board of Governors who shall bring the proposal before the Board. If the proposed amendment is approved by the Board, the Association shall, by circular letter or telegram, ask all members whether they accept the proposed amendment. When three-fifths of the members, having four-fifths of the total voting power, have accepted the proposed amendments, the Association shall certify the fact by formal communication addressed to all members.

(b) Notwithstanding (a) above, acceptance by all members is required in the case of any amendment modifying

   (i)   the right to withdraw from the Association provided in Article VII, Section 1;

   (ii) the right secured by Article III, Section 1 (c);

   (iii) the limitation on liability provided in Article II, Section 3.

(c) Amendments shall enter into force for all members three months after the date of the formal communication unless a shorter period is specified in the circular letter or telegram.

ARTICLE X

Interpretation and Arbitration

(a) Any question of interpretation of the provisions of this Agreement arising between any member and the Association or between any members of the Association shall be submitted to the Executive Directors for their decision. If the question particularly affects any member of the Association not entitled to appoint an Executive Director of the Bank, it shall be entitled to representation in accordance with Article VI, Section 4 (g).

(b) In any case where the Executive Directors have given a decision under (a) above, any member may require that the question be referred to the Board of Governors, whose decision shall be final. Pending the result of the reference to the Board of Governors, the Association may, so far as it deems necessary, act on the basis of the decision of the Executive Directors.

(c) Whenever a disagreement arises between the Association and a country which has ceased to be a member, or between the Association and any member during the permanent suspension of the Association, such disagreement shall be submitted to arbitration by a tribunal of three arbitrators, one appointed by the Association, another by the country involved and an umpire who, unless the parties otherwise agree, shall be appointed by the President of the International Court of Justice or such other authority as may have been prescribed by regulation adopted by the Association. The umpire shall have full power to settle all questions of procedure in any case where the parties are in disagreement with respect thereto.

ARTICLE XI

Final Provisions

SECTION 1. Entry into Force

This Agreement shall enter into force when it has been signed on behalf of governments whose subscriptions comprise not less than sixty-five percent of the total subscriptions set forth in Schedule A and when the instruments referred to in Section 2(a) of this Article have been deposited on their behalf, but in no event shall this Agreement enter into force before September 15, 1960.

SECTION 2. Signature

(a) Each government on whose behalf this Agreement is signed shall deposit with the Bank an instrument setting forth that it has accepted this Agreement in accordance with its law and has taken all steps necessary to enable it to carry out all of its obligations under this Agreement.

(b) Each government shall become a member of the Association as from the date of the deposit on its behalf of the instrument referred to in paragraph (a) above except that no government shall become a member before this Agreement enters into force under Section 1 of this Article.

(c) This Agreement shall remain open for signature until the close of business on December 31, 1960, at the principal office of the Bank, on behalf of the governments of the states whose names are set forth in Schedule A, provided that, if this Agreement shall not have entered into force by that date, the Executive Directors of the Bank may extend the period during which this Agreement shall remain open for signature by not more than six months.

(d) After this Agreement shall have entered into force, it shall be open for signature on behalf of the government of any state whose membership shall have been approved pursuant to Article II, Section 1 (b).

SECTION 3. Territorial Application

By its signature of this Agreement, each government accepts it both on its own behalf and in respect of all territories for whose international relations such government is responsible except those which are excluded by such government by written notice to the Association.

SECTION 4. Inauguration of the Association

(a) As soon as this Agreement enters into force under Section 1 of this Article the President shall call a meeting of the Executive Directors.

(b) The Association shall begin operations on the date when such meeting is held.

(c) Pending the first meeting of the Board of Governors, the Executive Directors may exercise all the powers of the Board of Governors except those reserved to the Board of Governors under this Agreement.

SECTION 5. Registration

The Bank is authorized to register this Agreement with the Secretariat of the United Nations in accordance with Article 102 of the Charter of the United Nations and the Regulations thereunder adopted by the General Assembly.

DONE at Washington, in a single copy which shall remain deposited in the archives of the International Bank for Reconstruction and Development, which has indicated by its signature below its agreement to act as depository of this Agreement, to register this Agreement with the Secretariat of the United Nations and to notify all governments whose names are set forth in Schedule A of the date when this Agreement shall have entered into force under Article XI, Section 1 hereof.

[*Note:* Schedule A, setting forth initial subscriptions, is not reproduced here.]

APPENDIX E
CHARTER OF THE IADB

Citation: Agreement Establishing the Inter-American Development Bank, done at Washington, Apr. 8, 1959 (entered into force Dec. 30, 1959), 389 U.N.T.S. 69, 10 U.S.T. 3029, T.I.A.S. No. 4397; amended Jan. 28, 1964, 21 U.S.T. 1570, amended Mar. 31, 1968, 19 U.S.T. 7381, amended Mar. 23, 1972, T.I.A.S. 7437, amended 1987 [?], U.K.T.S. 32 (1988).

Contents

Agreement Establishing the Inter-American Development Bank

The countries on whose behalf this Agreement is signed agree to create the Inter-American Development Bank, which shall operate in accordance with the following provisions:

ARTICLE I

PURPOSE AND FUNCTIONS

Section 1. Purpose

The purpose of the Bank shall be to contribute to the acceleration of the process of economic and social development of the regional developing member countries, individually and collectively.

Section 2. Functions

(a) To implement its purpose, the Bank shall have the following functions:

    (i) to promote the investment of public and private capital for development purposes;

    (ii) to utilize its own capital, funds raised by it in financial markets, and other available resources, for financing the development of the member countries, giving priority to those loans and guarantees that will contribute most effectively to their economic growth;

    (iii) to encourage private investment in projects, enterprises, and activitiescontributing to economic development and to supplement private investment when private capital is not available on reasonable terms and conditions;

    (iv) to cooperate with the member countries to orient their development policies toward better utilization of their resources, in a manner consistentwith the objectives of making their economies more complementary and of fostering the orderly growth of their foreign trade; and

    (v) to provide technical assistance for the preparation, financing, and implementation of development plans and projects, including the study of priorities and the formulation of specific project proposals.

(b) In carrying out its functions, the Bank shall cooperate as far as possible with national and international institutions and with private sources supplying investment capital.

ARTICLE II

MEMBERSHIP IN AND CAPITAL OF THE BANK

Section 1. Membership

(a) The original members of the Bank shall be those members of the Organization of American States which, by the date specified in Article XV, Section 1(a), shall accept membership in the Bank.

(b) Membership shall be open to other members of the Organization of American States and to Canada, Bahamas and Guyana, at such times and in accordance with such terms as the Bank may determine.

Nonregional countries which are members of the International Monetary Fund, and Switzerland, may also be admitted to the Bank, at such times, and under such general rules as the Board of Governors shall have established. Such general rules may be amended only by decision of the Board of Governors by a two-thirds majority of the total number of governors, including two thirds of the governors of nonregional members, representing not less than three fourths of the total voting power of the member countries.

Section 1A. Categories of Resources

The resources of the Bank shall consist of the ordinary capital resources, provided for in this article, and the resources of the Fund for Special Operations established by Article IV (hereinafter called the Fund).

Section 2. Authorized Ordinary Capital

(a) The authorized ordinary capital stock of the Bank initially shall be in the amount of eight hundred fifty million dollars ($850,000,000) in terms of United States dollars of the weight and fineness in effect on January 1, 1959 and shall be divided into 85,000 shares having a par value of $10,000 each, which shall be available for subscription by members in accordance with Section 3 of this article.

(b) The authorized ordinary capital stock shall be divided into paid-in shares and callable shares. The equivalent of four hundred million dollars ($400,000,000) shall be paid-in, and four hundred fifty million dollars ($450,000,000) shall be callable for the purposes specified in Section 4(a)(ii) of this article.

(c) The ordinary capital stock indicated in (a) of this section shall be increased by five hundred million dollars ($500,000,000) in terms of United States dollars of the weight and fineness existing on January 1, 1959, provided that:

    (i) the date for payment of all subscriptions established in accordance with Section 4 of this article shall have passed; and

    (ii) a regular or special meeting of the Board of Governors, held as soon as possible after the date referred to in subparagraph (i) of this paragraph, shall have approved the above-mentioned increase of five hundred million dollars ($500,000,000) by a three-fourths majority of the total voting power of the member countries.

(d) The increase in capital stock provided for in the preceding paragraph shall be in the form of callable capital.

(e) Notwithstanding the provisions of paragraphs (c) and (d) of this section and subject to the provisions of Article VIII, Section 4(b), the authorized ordinary capital stock may be increased when the Board of Governors deems it advisable and in a manner agreed upon by a three-fourths majority of the total voting power of the member countries, including a three-fourths majority of the total number of governors, which includes a two-thirds majority of the governors of regional members.

Section 3. Subscription of Shares

(a) Each member shall subscribe to shares of the ordinary capital stock of the Bank. The number of shares to be subscribed by the original members shall be those set forth in Annex A of this Agreement, which specifies the obligation of each member as to both paid-in and callable capital. The number of shares to be subscribed by other members shall be determined by the Bank.

(b) In case of an increase in ordinary capital pursuant to Section 2, paragraph (c) or (e) of this article, each member shall have a right to subscribe, under such conditions as the Bank shall decide, to a proportion of the increase of stock equivalent to the proportion which its stock theretofore subscribed bears to the total capital stock of the Bank. No member, however, shall be obligated to subscribe to any part of such increased capital.

(c) Shares of ordinary capital stock initially subscribed by original members shall be issued at par. Other shares shall be issued at par unless the Bank decides in special circumstances to issue them on other terms.

(d) The liability of the member countries on ordinary capital shares shall be limited to the unpaid portion of their issue price.

(e) Shares of ordinary capital stock shall not be pledged or encumbered in any manner, and they shall be transferable only to the Bank.

Section 4. Payment of Subscriptions

(a) Payment of the subscriptions to the ordinary capital stock of the Bank as set forth in Annex A shall be made as follows:

    (i) Payment of the amount subscribed by each country to the paid-in capital stock of the Bank shall be made in three installments, the first of which shall be 20 per cent, and the second and third each 40 per cent, of such amount. The first installment shall be paid by each country at any time on or after the date on which this Agreement is signed, and the instrument of acceptance or ratification deposited, on its behalf in accordance with Article XV, Section 1, but not later than September 30, 1960. The remaining two installments shall be paid on such dates as are determined by the Bank, but not sooner than September 30, 1961, and September 30, 1962, respectively.

Of each installment, 50 per cent shall be paid in gold and/or dollars and 50 per cent in the currency of the member.

(ii) The callable portion of the subscription for ordinary capital shares of the Bank shall be subject to call only when required to meet the obligations of the Bank created under Article III, Section 4(ii) and (iii) on borrowings of funds for inclusion in the Bank's ordinary capital resources or guarantees chargeable to such resources. In the event of such a call, payment may be made at the option of the member either in gold, in United States dollars, in fully convertible currency of the member country, or in the currency required to discharge the obligations of the Bank for the purpose for which the call is made.

Calls on unpaid subscriptions shall be uniform in percentage on all shares.

(b) Each payment of a member in its own currency under paragraph (a)(i) of this section shall be in such amount as, in the opinion of the Bank, is equivalent to the full value in terms of United States dollars of the weight and fineness in effect on January 1, 1959, of the portion of the subscription being paid. The initial payment shall be in such amount as the member considers appropriate hereunder but shall be subject to such adjustment, to be effected within 60 days of the date on which the payment was due, as the Bank shall determine to be necessary to constitute the full dollar value equivalent as provided in this paragraph.

(c) Unless otherwise determined by the Board of Governors by a three-fourths majority of the total voting power of the member countries, the liability of members for payment of the second and third installments of the paid-in portion of their subscriptions to the capital stock shall be conditional upon payment of not less than 90 per cent of the total obligations of the members due for:

(i) the first and second installments, respectively, of the paid-in portion of the subscriptions; and

(ii) the initial payment and all prior calls on the subscription quotas to the Fund.

Section 5. Ordinary Capital Resources

As used in this Agreement, the term "ordinary capital resources" of the Bank shall be deemed to include the following:

(i) authorized ordinary capital, including both paid-in and callable shares, subscribed pursuant to Sections 2 and 3 of this article;

(ii) all funds raised by borrowings under the authority of Article VII, Section 1(i) to which the commitment set forth in Section 4(a)(ii) of this article is applicable;

(iii) all funds received in repayment of loans made with the resources indicated in (i) and (ii) of this section;

(iv) all income derived from loans made from the aforementioned funds or from guarantees to which the commitment set forth in Section 4(a)(ii) of this article is applicable; and

(v) all other income derived from any of the resources mentioned above.

ARTICLE III

OPERATIONS

Section 1. Use of Resources

The resources and facilities of the Bank shall be used exclusively to implement the purpose and functions enumerated in Article I of this Agreement, as well as to finance the development of any of the members of the Caribbean Development Bank by providing loans and technical assistance to that institution.

Section 2. Categories of Operations

(a) The operations of the Bank shall be divided into ordinary operations and special operations.

(b) The ordinary operations shall be those financed from the Bank's ordinary capital resources, as defined in Article II, Section 5, and shall relate exclusively to loans made, participated in, or guaranteed by the Bank which are repayable only in the respective currency or currencies in which the loans were made. Such operations shall be subject to the terms and conditions that the Bank deems advisable, consistent with the provisions of this Agreement.

(c) The special operations shall be those financed from the resources of the Fund in accordance with the provisions of Article IV.

Section 3. Basic Principle of Separation

(a) The ordinary capital resources, as defined in Article II, Section 5, and the resources of the Fund, as defined in Article IV, Section 3(h), shall at all times and in all respects be held, used, obligated, invested, or otherwise disposed of entirely separate from each other.

(b) The ordinary capital resources shall under no circumstances be charged with, or used to discharge, obligations, liabilities or losses arising out of operations for which the resources of the Fund were originally used or committed.

(c) The financial statements of the Bank shall show separately the ordinary operations and the special operations, and the Bank shall establish such other administrative rules as may be necessary to ensure the effective separation of the two types of operations.

(d) Expenses pertaining directly to ordinary operations shall be charged to the ordinary capital resources. Expenses pertaining directly to special operations shall be charged to the resources of the Fund. Other expenses shall be charged as the Bank determines.

Section 4. Methods of Making or Guaranteeing Loans

Subject to the conditions stipulated in this article, the Bank may make or guarantee loans to any member, or any agency or political subdivision thereof, to any enterprise in the territory of a member, and to the Caribbean Development Bank, in any of the following ways:

(i) by making or participating in direct loans with funds corresponding to the unimpaired paid-in ordinary capital and, except as provided in Section 13 of this article, to its reserves and undistributed surplus; or with the unimpaired resources of the Fund;

(ii) by making or participating in direct loans with funds raised by the Bank in capital markets, or borrowed or acquired in any other manner, for inclusion in the ordinary capital resources of the Bank or the resources of the Fund; and

(iii) by guaranteeing, with the ordinary capital resources or the resources of the Fund, in whole or in part loans made, except in special cases, by private investors.

Section 5. Limitations on Operations

(a) The total amount outstanding of loans and guarantees made by the Bank in its ordinary operations shall not at any time exceed the total amount of the unimpaired subscribed ordinary capital of the Bank, plus the unimpaired reserves and surplus included in the ordinary capital resources of the Bank, as defined in Article II, Section 5, exclusive of income assigned to the special reserve established pursuant to Section 13 of this article and other income of the ordinary capital resources assigned by decision of the Board of Governors to reserves not available for loans or guarantees.

(b) In the case of loans made out of funds borrowed by the Bank to which the obligations provided for in Article II, Section 4(a)(ii), are applicable, the total amount of principal outstanding and payable to the Bank in a specific currency shall at no time exceed the total amount of principal of the outstanding borrowings by the Bank for inclusion in its ordinary capital resources that are payable in the same currency.

Section 6. Direct Loan Financing

In making direct loans or participating in them, the Bank may provide financing in any of the following ways:

(a) By furnishing the borrower currencies of members, other than the currency of the member in whose territory the project is to be carried out, that are necessary to meet the foreign exchange costs of the project.

(b) By providing financing to meet expenses related to the purposes of the loan in the territories of the country in which the project is to be carried out. Only in special cases, particularly when the project indirectly gives rise to an increase in the demand for foreign exchange in that country, shall the financing granted by the Bank to meet local expenses be provided in gold or in currencies other than that of such country; in such cases, the amount of the financing granted by the Bank for this purpose shall not exceed a reasonable portion of the local expenses incurred by the borrower.

Section 7. Rules and Conditions for Making or Guaranteeing Loans

(a) The Bank may make or guarantee loans subject to the following rules and conditions:

   (i) the applicant for the loan shall have submitted a detailed proposal and the staff of the Bank shall have presented a written report recommending the proposal after a study of its merits. In special circumstances, the Board of Executive Directors, by a majority of the total voting power of the member countries, may require that a proposal be submitted to the Board for decision in the absence of such a report;

   (ii) in considering a request for a loan or a guarantee, the Bank shall take into account the ability of the borrower to obtain the loan from private sources of financing on terms which, in the opinion of the Bank, are reasonable for the borrower, taking into account all pertinent factors;

   (iii) in making or guaranteeing a loan, the Bank shall pay due regard to prospects that the borrower and its guarantor, if any, will be in a position to meet their obligations under the loan contract;

   (iv) in the opinion of the Bank, the rate of interest, other charges and the schedule for repayment of principal are appropriate for the project in question;

(v) in guaranteeing a loan made by other investors, the Bank shall receive suitable compensation for its risk; and

(vi) loans made or guaranteed by the Bank shall be principally for financing specific projects, including those forming part of a national or regional development program. However, the Bank may make or guarantee over-all loans to development institutions or similar agencies of the members in order that the latter may facilitate the financing of specific development projects whose individual financing requirements are not, in the opinion of the Bank, large enough to warrant the direct supervision of the Bank.

(b) The Bank shall not finance any undertaking in the territory of a member if that member objects to such financing.

Section 8. Optional Conditions for Making or Guaranteeing Loans

(a) In the case of loans or guarantees of loans to nongovernmental entities, the Bank may, when it deems it advisable, require that the member in whose territory the project is to be carried out, or a public institution or a similar agency of the member acceptable to the Bank, guarantee the repayment of the principal and the payment of interest and other charges on the loan.

(b) The Bank may attach such other conditions to the making of loans or guarantees as it deems appropriate, taking into account both the interests of the members directly involved in the particular loan or guarantee proposal and the interests of the members as a whole.

Section 9. Use of Loans Made or Guaranteed by the Bank

(a) Except as provided in Article V, Section 1, the Bank shall impose no condition that the proceeds of a loan shall be spent in the territory of any particular country nor that such proceeds shall not be spent in the territories of any particular member or members; provided, however, that with respect to any increase of the resources of the Bank the question of restriction of procurement by the Bank or any member with regard to those members which do not participate in an increase under the terms and conditions specified by the Board of Governors may be determined by the Board of Governors.

(b) The Bank shall take the necessary measures to ensure that the proceeds of any loan made, guaranteed, or participated in by the Bank are used only for the purposes for which the loan was granted, with due attention to considerations of economy and efficiency.

Section 10. Payment Provisions for Direct Loans

Direct loan contracts made by the Bank in conformity with Section 4 of this article shall establish:

(a) All the terms and conditions of each loan, including among others, provision for payment of principal, interest and other charges, maturities, and dates of payment; and

(b) The currency or currencies in which payment shall be made to the Bank.

Section 11. Guarantees

(a) In guaranteeing a loan the Bank shall charge a guarantee fee, at a rate determined by the Bank, payable periodically on the amount of the loan outstanding.

(b) Guarantee contracts concluded by the Bank shall provide that the Bank may terminate its liability with respect to interest if, upon default by the borrower and by the guarantor, if any, the Bank offers to purchase, at par and interest accrued to a date designated in the offer, the bonds or other obligations guaranteed.

(c) In issuing guarantees, the Bank shall have power to determine any other terms and conditions.

Section 12. Special Commission

On all loans, participations, or guarantees made out of or by commitment of the ordinary capital resources of the Bank, the latter shall charge a special commission. The special commission, payable periodically, shall be computed on the amount outstanding on each loan, participation, or guarantee and shall be at the rate of one per cent per annum, unless the Bank, by a three-fourths majority of the total voting power of the member countries, decides to reduce the rate of commission.

Section 13. Special Reserve

The amount of commissions received by the Bank under Section 12 of this article shall be set aside as a special reserve, which shall be kept for meeting liabilities of the Bank in accordance with Article VII, Section 3(b)(i). The special reserve shall be held in such liquid form, permitted under this Agreement, as the Board of Executive Directors may decide.

ARTICLE IV

FUND FOR SPECIAL OPERATIONS

Section 1. Establishment, Purpose, and Functions

A Fund for Special Operations is established for the making of loans on terms and conditions appropriate for dealing with special circumstances arising in specific countries or with respect to specific projects.

The Fund, whose administration shall be entrusted to the Bank, shall have the purpose and functions set forth in Article I of this Agreement.

Section 2. Applicable Provisions

The Fund shall be governed by the provisions of the present article and all other provisions of this Agreement, excepting those inconsistent with the provisions of the present article and those expressly applying only to other operations of the Bank.

Section 3. Resources

(a) The original members of the Bank shall contribute to the resources of the Fund in accordance with the provisions of this section.

(b) Members of the Organization of American States that join the Bank after the date specified in Article XV, Section 1(a), Canada, Bahamas and Guyana, and countries that are admitted in accordance with Article II, Section 1(b) shall contribute to the Fund with such quotas, and under such terms, as may be determined by the Bank.

(c) The Fund shall be established with initial resources in the amount of one hundred fifty million dollars ($150,000,000) in terms of United States dollars of the weight and fineness in effect on January 1, 1959, which shall be contributed by the original members of the Bank in accordance with the quotas specified in Annex B.

(d) Payment of the quotas shall be made as follows:

   (i) Fifty per cent of its quota shall be paid by each member at any time on or after the date on which this Agreement is signed, and the instrument of acceptance or ratification deposited, on its behalf in accordance with Article XV, Section 1, but not later than September 30, 1960.

   (ii) The remaining 50 per cent shall be paid at any time subsequent to one year after the Bank has begun operations, in such amounts and at such times as are determined by the Bank; pro-vided, however, that the total amount of all quotas shall be made due and payable not later than the date fixed for payment of the third installment of the subscriptions to the paid-in capital stock of the Bank.

(iii) The payments required under this section shall be distributed among the members in proportion to their quotas and shall be made one half in gold and/or United States dollars, and one half in the currency of the contributing member.

(e) Each payment of a member in its own currency under the preceding paragraph shall be in such amount as, in the opinion of the Bank, is equivalent to the full value, in terms of United States dollars of the weight and fineness in effect on January 1, 1959, of the portion of the quota being paid. The initial payment shall be in such amount as the member considers appropriate hereunder but shall be subject to such adjustment, to be effected within 60 days of the date on which payment was due, as the Bank shall determine to be necessary to constitute the full dollar value equivalent as provided in this paragraph.

(f) Unless otherwise determined by the Board of Governors by a three-fourths majority of the total voting power of the member countries, the liability of members for payment of any call on the unpaid portion of their subscription quotas to the Fund shall be conditional upon payment of not less than 90 per cent of the total obligations of the members for:

(i) the initial payment and all prior calls on such quota subscriptions to the Fund; and

(ii) any installments due on the paid-in portion of the subscriptions to the capital stock of the Bank.

(g) The resources of the Fund shall be increased through additional contributions by the members when the Board of Governors considers it advisable by a three-fourths majority of the total voting power of the member countries. The provisions of Article II, Section 3(b), shall apply to such increases, in terms of the proportion between the quota in effect for each member and the total amount of the resources of the Fund contributed by members. No member, however, shall be obligated to contribute any part of such increase.

(h) As used in this Agreement, the term "resources of the Fund" shall be deemed to include the following:

(i) contributions by members pursuant to paragraphs (c) and (g) of this section;

(ii) all funds raised by borrowing to which the commitment stipulated in Article II, Section 4(a)(ii) is not applicable, i.e., those that are specifically chargeable to the resources of the Fund;

(iii) all funds received in repayment of loans made from the resources mentioned above;

(iv) all income derived from operations using or committing any of the resources mentioned above; and

(v) any other resources at the disposal of the Fund.

Section 4. Operations

(a) The operations of the Fund shall be those financed from its own resources, as defined in Section 3(h) of the present article.

(b) Loans made with resources of the Fund may be partially or wholly repayable in the currency of the member in whose territory the project being financed will be carried out. The part of the loan not repayable in the currency of the member shall be paid in the currency or currencies in which the loan was made.

Section 5. Limitation on Liability

In the operations of the Fund, the financial liability of the Bank shall be limited to the resources and reserves of the Fund, and the liability of members shall be limited to the unpaid portion of their respective quotas that has become due and payable.

Section 6. Limitation on Disposition of Quotas

The rights of members of the Bank resulting from their contributions to the Fund may not be transferred or encumbered, and members shall have no right of reimbursement of such contributions except in cases of loss of the status of membership or of termination of the operations of the Fund.

Section 7. Discharge of Fund Liabilities on Borrowings

Payments in satisfaction of any liability on borrowings of funds for inclusion in the resources of the Fund shall be charged:

(i) first, against any reserve established for this purpose; and

(ii) then, against any other funds available in the resources of the Fund.

Section 8. Administration

(a) Subject to the provisions of this Agreement, the authorities of the Bank shall have full powers to administer the Fund.

(b) There shall be a Vice President of the Bank in charge of the Fund. The Vice President shall participate in the meetings of the Board of Executive Directors of the Bank, without vote, whenever matters relating to the Fund are discussed.

(c) In the operations of the Fund the Bank shall utilize to the fullest extent possible the same personnel, experts, installations, offices, equipment, and services as it uses for its other operations.

(d) The Bank shall publish a separate annual report showing the results of the Fund's financial operations, including profits or losses. At the annual meeting of the Board of Governors there shall be at least one session devoted to consideration of this report. In addition, the Bank shall transmit to the members a quarterly summary of the Fund's operations.

Section 9. Voting

(a) In making decisions concerning operations of the Fund, each member country of the Bank shall have the voting power in the Board of Governors accorded to it pursuant to Article VIII, Section 4(a) and (c), and each Director shall have the voting power in the Board of Executive Directors accorded to him pursuant to Article VIII, Section 4(a) and (d).

(b) All decisions of the Bank concerning the operations of the Fund shall be adopted by a three-fourths majority of the total voting power of the member countries, unless otherwise provided in this article.

Section 10. Distribution of Net Profits

The Board of Governors of the Bank shall determine what portion of the net profits of the Fund shall be distributed among the members after making provision for reserves. Such net profits shall be shared in proportion to the quotas of the members.

Section 11. Withdrawal of Contributions

(a) No country may withdraw its contribution and terminate its relations with the Fund while it is still a member of the Bank.

(b) The provisions of Article IX, Section 3, with respect to the settlement of accounts with countries that terminate their membership in the Bank also shall apply to the Fund.

Section 12. Suspension and Termination

The provisions of Article X also shall apply to the Fund with substitution of terms relating to the Fund and its resources and respective creditors for those relating to the Bank and its capital resources and respective creditors.

ARTICLE V

CURRENCIES

Section 1. Use of Currencies

(a) The currency of any member held by the Bank in its ordinary capital resources or in the resources of the Fund, however acquired, may be used by the Bank and by any recipient from the Bank, without restriction by the member, to make payments for goods and services produced in the territory of such member.

(b) Members may not maintain or impose restrictions of any kind upon the use by the Bank or by any recipient from the Bank, for payments in any country, of the following:

   (i)   gold and dollars received by the Bank in payment of the 50 per cent portion of each member's subscription to shares of the Bank's ordinary capital and of the 50 per cent portion of each member's quota for contribution to the Fund, pursuant to the provisions of Article II and Article IV, respectively;

   (ii) currencies of members purchased with the resources referred to in (i) of this paragraph;

   (iii) currencies obtained by borrowings, pursuant to the provisions of Article VII, Section 1(i), for inclusion in the capital resources of the Bank;

   (iv) gold and dollars received by the Bank in payment on account of principal, interest, and other charges, of loans made from the gold and dollar funds referred to in (i) of this paragraph; currencies received in payment of principal interest, and other charges, of loans made from currencies referred to in (ii) and (iii) of this paragraph; and currencies received in payment of commissions and fees on all guarantees made by the Bank; and

   (v)   currencies, other than the member's own currency, received from the Bank pursuant to Article VII, Section 4(d), and Article IV, Section 10, in distribution of net profits.

(c) A member's currency held by the Bank, whether in its ordinary capital resources or in the resources of the Fund, not covered by paragraph (b) of this section, also may be used by the Bank or any recipient from the Bank for payments in any country without restriction of any kind, unless the member notifies the Bank of its desire that such currency or a portion thereof be restricted to the uses specified in paragraph (a) of this section.

(d) Members may not place any restrictions on the holding and use by the Bank, for making amortization payments or anticipating payment of, or repurchasing part or all of, the Bank's own obligations, of currencies received by the Bank in repayment of direct loans made from borrowed funds Included in the ordinary capital resources of the Bank.

(e) Gold or currency held by the Bank in its ordinary capital resources or in the resources of the Fund shall not be used by the Bank to purchase other currencies unless authorized by a three-fourths majority of the total voting power of the member countries. Any currencies purchased pursuant to the provisions of this paragraph shall not be subject to maintenance of value under Section 3 of this article.

Section 2. Valuation of Currencies

Whenever it shall become necessary under this Agreement to value any currency in terms of another currency, or in terms of gold, such valuation shall be determined by the Bank after consultation with the International Monetary Fund.

Section 3. Maintenance of Value of the Currency Holdings of the Bank

(a) Whenever the par value in the International Monetary Fund of a member's currency is reduced or the foreign exchange value of a member's currency has, in the opinion of the Bank, depreciated to a significant extent, the member shall pay to the Bank within a reasonable time an additional amount of its own currency sufficient to maintain the value of all the currency of the member held by the Bank in its ordinary capital resources or in the resources of the Fund, excepting currency derived from borrowings by the Bank. The standard of value for this purpose shall be the United States dollar of the weight and fineness in effect on January 1, 1959.

(b) Whenever the par value in the International Monetary Fund of a member's currency is increased or the foreign exchange value of such member's currency has, in the opinion of the Bank, appreciated to a significant extent, the Bank shall return to such member within a reasonable time an amount of that member's currency equal to the increase in the value of the amount of such currency which is held by the Bank in its ordinary capital resources or in the resources of the Fund, excepting currency derived from borrowings by the Bank. The standard of value for this purpose shall be the same as that established in the preceding paragraph.

(c) The provisions of this section may be waived by the Bank when a uniform proportionate change in the par value of the currencies of all the Bank's members is made by the International Monetary Fund.

(d) Notwithstanding any other provisions of this section, the terms and conditions of any increase in the resources of the Fund pursuant to Article

IV, Section 3(g), may include maintenance of value provisions other than those provided for in this section which would apply to the resources of the Fund contributed by such increase.

Section 4. Methods of Conserving Currencies

The Bank shall accept from any member promissory notes or similar securities issued by the government of the member, or by the depository designated by such member, in lieu of any part of the currency of the member representing the 50 per cent portion of its subscription to the Bank's authorized ordinary capital and the 50 per cent portion of its subscription to the resources of the Fund, which, pursuant to the provisions of Article II and Article IV, respectively, are payable by each member in its national currency, provided such currency is not required by the Bank for the conduct of its operations. Such notes or securities shall be non-negotiable, non-interest-bearing, and payable to the Bank at their par value on demand. On the same conditions, the Bank shall also accept such notes or securities in lieu of any part of the subscription of a member with respect to which part the terms of the subscription do not require payment in cash.

ARTICLE VI

TECHNICAL ASSISTANCE

Section 1. Provision of Technical Advice and Assistance

The Bank may, at the request of any member or members, or of private firms that may obtain loans from it, provide technical advice and assistance in its field of activity, particularly on:

(i) the preparation, financing, and execution of development plans and projects, including the consideration of priorities, and the formulation of loan proposals on specific national or regional development projects; and

(ii) the development and advanced training, through seminars and other forms of instruction, of personnel specializing in the formulation and implementation of development plans and projects.

Section 2. Cooperative Agreements on Technical Assistance

In order to accomplish the purposes of this article, the Bank may enter into agreements on technical assistance with other national or international institutions, either public or private.

Section 3. Expenses

(a) The Bank may arrange with member countries or firms receiving technical assistance, for reimbursement of the expenses of furnishing such assistance on terms which the Bank deems appropriate.

(b) The expenses of providing technical assistance not paid by the recipients shall be met from the net income of the ordinary capital resources or of the Fund. However, during the first three years of the Bank's operations, up to three per cent, in total, of the initial resources of the Fund may be used to meet such expenses.

ARTICLE VII

MISCELLANEOUS POWERS AND DISTRIBUTION OF PROFITS

Section 1. Miscellaneous Powers of the Bank

In addition to the powers specified elsewhere in this Agreement, the Bank shall have the power to:

(i) borrow funds and in that connection to furnish such collateral or other security therefor as the Bank shall determine, provided that, before making a sale of its obligations in the markets of a country, the Bank shall have obtained the approval of that country and of the member in whose currency the obligations are denominated. In addition, in the case of borrowings of funds to be included in the Bank's ordinary capital resources, the Bank shall obtain agreement of such countries that the proceeds may be exchanged for the currency of any other country without restriction;

(ii) buy and sell securities it has issued or guaranteed or in which it has invested, provided that the Bank shall obtain the approval of the country in whose territories the securities are to be bought or sold;

(iii) with the approval of a three-fourths majority of the total voting power of the member countries, invest funds not needed in its operations in such obligations as it may determine;

(iv) guarantee securities in its portfolio for the purpose of facilitating their sale; and

(v) exercise such other powers as shall be necessary or desirable in furtherance of its purpose and functions, consistent with the provisions of this Agreement.

Section 2. Warning to be Placed on Securities

Every security issued or guaranteed by the Bank shall bear on its face a conspicuous statement to the effect that it is not an obligation of any government, unless it is in fact the obligation of a particular government, in which case it shall so state.

Section 3. Methods of Meeting Liabilities of the Bank in Case of Defaults

(a) The Bank, in the event of actual or threatened default on loans made or guaranteed by the Bank using its ordinary capital resources, shall take such action as it deems appropriate with respect to modifying the terms of the loan, other than the currency of repayment.

(b) The payments in discharge of the Bank's liabilities on borrowings or guarantees under Article III, Section 4(ii) and (iii) chargeable against the ordinary capital resources of the Bank shall be charged:

  (i) first, against the special reserve provided for in Article III, Section 13; and

  (ii) then, to the extent necessary and at the discretion of the Bank, against the other reserves, surplus, and funds corresponding to the capital paid in for ordinary capital shares.

(c) Whenever necessary to meet contractual payments of interest, other charges, or amortization on the Bank's borrowings payable out of its ordinary capital resources, or to meet the Bank's liabilities with respect to similar payments on loans guaranteed by it chargeable to its ordinary capital resources, the Bank may call upon the members to pay an appropriate amount of their callable ordinary capital subscriptions, in accordance with Article II, Section 4(a)(ii). Moreover, if the Bank believes that a default may be of long duration, it may call an additional part of such subscriptions not to exceed in any one year one per cent of the total subscriptions of the members to the ordinary capital resources, for the following purposes:

  (i) to redeem prior to maturity, or otherwise discharge its liability on, all or part of the outstanding principal of any loan guaranteed by it chargeable to its ordinary capital resources in respect of which the debtor is in default; and

  (ii) to repurchase, or otherwise discharge its liability on, all or part of its own outstanding obligations payable out of its ordinary capital resources.

Section 4. Distribution or Transfer of Net Profits and Surplus

(a) The Board of Governors may determine periodically what part of the net profits and of the surplus of the ordinary capital resources shall be distributed. Such distributions may be made only when the reserves have reached a level which the Board of Governors considers adequate.

(b) When approving the statements of profit and loss, pursuant to Article VIII, Section 2(b)(viii), the Board of Governors may by decision of a two-thirds majority of the total number of governors representing not less than three fourths of the total voting power of the member countries transfer part of the net profits for the respective fiscal year of the ordinary capital resources to the Fund.

Before the Board of Governors determines to make a transfer to the Fund, it shall have received a report from the Board of Executive Directors on the desirability of such a transfer, which shall take into consideration, inter alia, (1) whether the reserves have reached a level that is adequate; (2) whether the transferred funds are needed for the operation of the Fund; and (3) the impact, if any, on the Bank's ability to borrow.

(c) The distributions referred to in paragraph (a) of this section shall be made from the ordinary capital resources in proportion to the number of ordinary capital shares held by each member and likewise the net profits transferred to the Fund pursuant to paragraph (b) of this section shall be credited to the total contribution quotas of each member in the Fund in the foregoing proportion.

(d) Payments pursuant to paragraph (a) of this section shall be made in such manner and in such currency or currencies as the Board of Governors shall determine. If such payments are made to a member in currencies other than its own, the transfer of such currencies and their use by the receiving country shall be without restriction by any member.

ARTICLE VIII

ORGANIZATION AND MANAGEMENT

Section 1. Structure of the Bank

The Bank shall have a Board of Governors, a Board of Executive Directors, a President, an Executive Vice President, a Vice President in charge of the Fund, and such other officers and staff as may be considered necessary.

Section 2. Board of Governors

(a) All the powers of the Bank shall be vested in the Board of Governors. Each member shall appoint one governor and one alternate, who shall serve for five years, subject to termination of appointment at any time, or to reappointment, at the pleasure of the appointing member. No alternate may vote except in the absence of his principal. The Board shall select one of the governors as Chairman, who shall hold office until the next regular meeting of the Board.

(b) The Board of Governors may delegate to the Board of Executive Directors all its powers except power to:

(i) admit new members and determine the conditions of their admission;

(ii) increase or decrease the authorized ordinary capital stock of the Bank and the contributions to the Fund;

(iii) elect the President of the Bank and determine his remuneration;

(iv) suspend a member, pursuant to Article IX, Section 2;

(v) determine the remuneration of the executive directors and their alternates;

(vi) hear and decide any appeals from interpretations of this Agreement given by the Board of Executive Directors;

(vii) authorize the conclusion of general agreements for cooperation with other international organizations;

(viii) approve, after reviewing the auditors' report, the general balance sheet and the statement of profit and loss of the institution;

(ix) determine the reserves and the distribution of the net profits of the ordinary capital resources and of the Fund;

(x) select outside auditors to certify to the general balance sheet and the statement of profit and loss of the institution;

(xi) amend this Agreement; and

(xii) decide to terminate the operations of the Bank and to distribute its assets.

(c) The Board of Governors shall retain full power to exercise authority over any matter delegated to the Board of Executive Directors under paragraph (b) above.

(d) The Board of Governors shall, as a general rule, hold a meeting annually. Other meetings may be held when the Board of Governors so provides or when called by the Board of Executive Directors. Meetings of the Board of Governors also shall be called by the Board of Executive Directors whenever requested by five members of the Bank or by members having one fourth of the total voting power of the member countries.

(e) A quorum for any meeting of the Board of Governors shall be an absolute majority of the total number of governors, including an absolute majority of the governors of regional members, representing not less than three fourths of the total voting power of the member countries.

(f) The Board of Governors may establish a procedure whereby the Board of Executive Directors, when it deems such action appropriate, may submit a specific question to a vote of the governors without calling a meeting of the Board of Governors.

(g) The Board of Governors, and the Board of Executive Directors to the extent authorized, may adopt such rules and regulations as may be necessary or appropriate to conduct the business of the Bank.

(h) Governors and alternates shall serve as such without compensation from the Bank, but the Bank may pay them reasonable expenses incurred in attending meetings of the Board of Governors.

Section 3. Board of Executive Directors

(a) The Board of Executive Directors shall be responsible for the conduct of the operations of the Bank, and for this purpose may exercise all the powers delegated to it by the Board of Governors.

(b) (i) Executive directors shall be persons of recognized competence and wide experience in economic and financial matters but who shall not be governors. Agreement Establishing the Inter-American Development Bank 24

    (ii) One executive director shall be appointed by the member country having the largest number of shares in the Bank, not less than three executive directors shall be elected by the governors of the nonregional member countries, and not less than ten others shall be elected by the governors of the remaining member countries. The number of executive directors to be elected in these categories, and the procedure for the election of all the elective directors shall be determined by regulations adopted by the Board of Governors by a three-fourths majority of the total voting power of the member countries, including, with respect to provisions relating exclusively to the election of directors by nonregional member countries, a two-thirds majority of the governors of the nonregional members, and, with respect to provisions relating exclusively to the number and election of directors by the remaining member countries, by a two-thirds majority of the governors of regional members. Any change in the aforementioned regulations shall require the same majority of votes for its approval.

    (iii) Executive directors shall be appointed or elected for terms of three years and may be reappointed or re-elected for successive terms.

(c) Each executive director shall appoint an alternate who shall have full power to act for him when he is not present. Directors and alternates shall be citizens of the member countries. None of the elected directors and their alternates may be of the same citizenship, except in the case of:

(i) countries that are not borrowers; and

(ii) borrowing member countries, in cases determined by the governors of the borrowing members pursuant to a three-quarters majority of their total voting power and a two-thirds majority of their total number.

Alternates may participate in meetings but may vote only when they are acting in place of their principals.

(d) Directors shall continue in office until their successors are appointed or elected. If the office of an elected director becomes vacant more than 180 days before the end of his term, a successor shall be elected for the remainder of the term by the governors who elected the former director. An absolute majority of the votes cast shall be required for election. While the office remains vacant, the alternate shall have all the powers of the former director except the power to appoint an alternate.

(e) The Board of Executive Directors shall function in continuous session at the principal office of the Bank and shall meet as often as the business of the Bank may require.

(f) A quorum for any meeting of the Board of Executive Directors shall be an absolute majority of the total number of directors, including an absolute majority of directors of regional members, representing not less than two thirds of the total voting power of the member countries.

(g) A member of the Bank may send a representative to attend any meeting of the Board of Executive Directors when a matter especially affecting that member is under consideration. Such right of representation shall be regulated by the Board of Governors.

(h) The Board of Executive Directors may appoint such committees as it deems advisable. Membership of such committees need not be limited to governors, directors, or alternates.

(i) The Board of Executive Directors shall determine the basic organization of the Bank, including the number and general responsibilities of the chief administrative and professional positions of the staff, and shall approve the budget of the Bank.

Section 4. Voting

(a) Each member country shall have 135 votes plus one vote for each share of ordinary capital stock of the Bank held by that country, provided, however, that, in connection with any increase in the authorized ordinary capital stock, the Board of Governors may determine that the capital stock authorized by such increase shall not have voting rights and that such increase of stock shall not be subject to the preemptive rights established in Article II, Section 3(b).

(b) No increase in the subscription of any member to the ordinary capital stock shall become effective, and any right to subscribe thereto is hereby waived, which would have the effect of reducing the voting power

   (i)   of the regional developing members below 50.005 per cent of the total voting power of the member countries;

   (ii) of the member having the largest number of shares below 30 per cent of such total voting power; or (iii) of Canada below 4 per cent of such total voting power.

(c) In voting in the Board of Governors, each governor shall be entitled to cast the votes of the member country which he represents. Except as otherwise specifically provided in this Agreement, all matters before the Board of Governors shall be decided by a majority of the total voting power of the member countries.

(d) In voting in the Board of Executive Directors:

   (i)   the appointed director shall be entitled to cast the number of votes of the member country which appointed him;

   (ii) each elected director shall be entitled to cast the number of votes that counted toward his election, which votes shall be cast as a unit; and

   (iii) except as otherwise specifically provided in this Agreement, all matters before the Board of Executive Directors shall be decided by a majority of the total voting power of the member countries.

Section 5. President, Executive Vice President, and Staff

(a) The Board of Governors, by a majority of the total voting power of the member countries, including an absolute majority of the governors of regional members, shall elect a President of the Bank who, while holding office, shall not be a governor or an executive director or alternate for either.

Under the direction of the Board of Executive Directors, the President of the Bank shall conduct the ordinary business of the Bank and shall be chief of its staff. He also shall be the presiding officer at meetings of the Board of Executive Directors, but shall have no vote, except that it shall be his duty to cast a deciding vote when necessary to break a tie.

The President of the Bank shall be the legal representative of the Bank. The term of office of the President of the Bank shall be five years, and he may be reelected to successive terms. He shall cease to hold office when the Board of Governors so decides by a majority of the total voting power of the member countries, including a majority of the total voting power of the regional member countries.

(b) The Executive Vice President shall be appointed by the Board of Executive Directors on the recommendation of the President of the Bank. Under the direction of the Board of Executive Directors and the President of the Bank, the Executive Vice President shall exercise such authority and perform such functions in the administration of the Bank as may be determined by the Board of Executive Directors. In the absence or incapacity of the President of the Bank, the Executive Vice President shall exercise the authority and perform the functions of the President.

The Executive Vice President shall participate in meetings of the Board of Executive Directors but shall have no vote at such meetings, except that he shall cast the deciding vote, as provided in paragraph (a) of this section, when he is acting in place of the President of the Bank.

(c) In addition to the Vice President referred to in Article IV, Section 8(b), the Board of Executive Directors may, on recommendation of the President of the Bank, appoint other Vice Presidents who shall exercise such authority and perform such functions as the Board of Executive Directors may determine.

(d) The President, officers, and staff of the Bank, in the discharge of their offices, owe their duty entirely to the Bank and shall recognize no other authority. Each member of the Bank shall respect the international character of this duty.

(e) The paramount consideration in the employment of the staff and in the determination of the conditions of service shall be the necessity of securing the highest standards of efficiency, competence, and integrity. Due regard shall also be paid to the importance of recruiting the staff on as wide a geographical basis as possible, taking into account the regional character of the institution.

(f) The Bank, its officers and employees shall not interfere in the political affairs of any member, nor shall they be influenced in their decisions by the political character of the member or members concerned. Only economic considerations shall be relevant to their decisions, and these considerations shall be weighed impartially in order to achieve the purpose and functions stated in Article I.

Section 6. Publication of Reports and Provision of Information

(a) The Bank shall publish an annual report containing an audited statement of the accounts. It shall also transmit quarterly to the members a summary statement of the financial position and a profit-and-loss statement showing the results of its ordinary operations.

(b) The Bank may also publish such other reports as it deems desirable to carry out its purpose and functions.

ARTICLE IX

WITHDRAWAL AND SUSPENSION OF MEMBERS

Section 1. Right to Withdraw

Any member may withdraw from the Bank by delivering to the Bank at its principal office written notice of its intention to do so. Such withdrawal shall become finally effective on the date specified in the notice but in no event less than six months after the notice is delivered to the Bank. However, at any time before the withdrawal becomes finally effective, the member may notify the Bank in writing of the cancellation of its notice of intention to withdraw.

After withdrawing, a member shall remain liable for all direct and contingent obligations to the Bank to which it was subject at the date of delivery of the withdrawal notice, including those specified in Section 3 of this article. However, if the withdrawal becomes finally effective, the member shall not incur any liability for obligations resulting from operations of the Bank effected after the date on which the withdrawal notice was received by the Bank.

Section 2. Suspension of Membership

If a member fails to fulfill any of its obligations to the Bank, the Bank may suspend its membership by decision of the Board of Governors by a three-fourths majority of the total voting power of the member countries, including a two-thirds majority of the total number of governors, which, in the case of suspension of a regional member country, shall include a two-thirds majority of the governors of regional members and, in the case of suspension of a nonregional member country, a two-thirds majority of the governors of nonregional members.

The member so suspended shall automatically cease to be a member of the Bank one year from the date of its suspension unless the Board of Governors decides by the same majority to terminate the suspension.

While under suspension, a member shall not be entitled to exercise any rights under this Agreement, except the right of withdrawal, but shall remain subject to all its obligations.

Section 3. Settlement of Accounts

(a) After a country ceases to be a member, it no longer shall share in the profits or losses of the Bank, nor shall it incur any liability with respect to loans and guarantees entered into by the Bank thereafter. However, it shall remain liable for all amounts it owes the Bank and for its contingent liabilities to the Bank so long as any part of the loans or guarantees contracted by the Bank before the date on which the country ceased to be a member remains outstanding.

(b) When a country ceases to be a member, the Bank shall arrange for the repurchase of such country's capital stock as a part of the settlement of accounts pursuant to the provisions of this section; but the country shall have no other rights under this Agreement except as provided in this section and in Article XIII, Section 2.

(c) The Bank and the country ceasing to be a member may agree on the repurchase of the capital stock on such terms as are deemed appropriate in the circumstances, without regard to the provisions of the following paragraph. Such agreement may provide, among other things, for a final settlement of all obligations of the country to the Bank.

(d) If the agreement referred to in the preceding paragraph has not been consummated within six months after the country ceases to be a member or such other time as the Bank and such country may agree upon, the repurchase price of such country's capital stock shall be its book value, according to the books of the Bank, on the date when the country ceased to be a member. Such repurchase shall be subject to the following conditions:

(i) As a prerequisite for payment, the country ceasing to be a member shall surrender its stock certificates, and such payment may be made in such installments, at such times and in such available currencies as the Bank determines, taking into account the financial position of the Bank.

(ii) Any amount which the Bank owes the country for the repurchase of its capital stock shall be withheld to the extent that the country or any of its subdivisions or agencies remains liable to the Bank as a result of loan or guarantee operations. The amount withheld may, at the option of the Bank, be applied on any such liability as it matures. However, no amount shall be withheld on account of the country's contingent liability for future calls on its subscription pursuant to Article II, Section 4(a)(ii).

(iii) If the Bank sustains net losses on any loans or participations, or as a result of any guarantees, outstanding on the date the country ceased to be a member, and the amount of such losses exceeds the amount of the reserves provided therefor on such date, such country shall repay on demand the amount by which the repurchase price of its shares would have been reduced, if the losses had been taken into account when the book value of the shares, according to the books of the Bank, was determined. In addition, the former member shall remain liable on any call pursuant to Article II, Section 4(a)(ii), to the extent that it would have been required to respond if the impairment of capital had occurred and the call had been made at the time the repurchase price of its shares had been determined.

(e) In no event shall any amount due to a country for its shares under this section be paid until six months after the date upon which the country ceases to be a member. If within that period the Bank terminates operations all rights of such country shall be determined by the provisions of Article X, and such country shall be considered still a member of the Bank for the purposes of such article except that it shall have no voting rights.

ARTICLE X

SUSPENSION AND TERMINATION OF OPERATIONS

Section 1. Suspension of Operations

In an emergency the Board of Executive Directors may suspend operations in respect of new loans and guarantees until such time as the Board of Governors may have an opportunity to consider the situation and take pertinent measures.

Section 2. Termination of Operations

The Bank may terminate its operations by a decision of the Board of Governors by a three-fourths majority of the total voting power of the member countries, including a two-thirds majority of the governors of regional members. After such termination of operations the Bank shall forthwith cease all activities, except those incident to the conservation, preservation, and realization of its assets and settlement of its obligations.

Section 3. Liability of Members and Payment of Claims

(a) The liability of all members arising from the subscriptions to the capital stock of the Bank and in respect to the depreciation of their currencies shall continue until all direct and contingent obligations shall have been discharged.

(b) All creditors holding direct claims shall be paid out of the assets of the Bank and then out of payments to the Bank on unpaid or callable subscriptions. Before making any payments to creditors holding direct claims, the Board of Executive Directors shall make such arrangements as are necessary, in its judgment, to ensure a pro rata distribution among holders of direct and contingent claims.

Section 4. Distribution of Assets

(a) No distribution of assets shall be made to members on account of their subscriptions to the capital stock of the Bank until all liabilities to creditors chargeable to such capital stock shall have been discharged or provided for. Moreover, such distribution must be approved by a decision of the Board of Governors by a three-fourths majority of the total voting power of the member countries, including a two-thirds majority of the governors of regional members.

(b) Any distribution of the assets of the Bank to the members shall be in proportion to capital stock held by each member and shall be effected at such times and under such conditions, as the Bank shall deem fair and equitable. The shares of assets distributed need not be uniform as to type of assets. No member shall be entitled to receive its share in such a distribution of assets until it has settled all of its obligations to the Bank.

(c) Any member receiving assets distributed pursuant to this article shall enjoy the same rights with respect to such assets as the Bank enjoyed prior to their distribution.

ARTICLE XI

STATUS, IMMUNITIES AND PRIVILEGES

Section 1. Scope of Article

To enable the Bank to fulfill its purpose and the functions with which it is entrusted, the status, immunities, and privileges set forth in this article shall be accorded to the Bank in the territories of each member.

Section 2. Legal Status

The Bank shall possess juridical personality and, in particular, full capacity:

(a) to contract;

(b) to acquire and dispose of immovable and movable property; and

(c) to institute legal proceedings.

Section 3. Judicial Proceedings

Actions may be brought against the Bank only in a court of competent jurisdiction in the territories of a member in which the Bank has an office, has appointed an agent for the purpose of accepting service or notice of process, or has issued or guaranteed securities.

No action shall be brought against the Bank by members or persons acting for or deriving claims from members. However, member countries shall have recourse to such special procedures to settle controversies between the Bank and its members as may be prescribed in this Agreement, in the by-laws and regulations of the Bank or in contracts entered into with the Bank.

Property and assets of the Bank shall, wheresoever located and by whomsoever held, be immune from all forms of seizure, attachment or execution before the delivery of final judgment against the Bank.

Section 4. Immunity of Assets

Property and assets of the Bank, wheresoever located and by whomsoever held, shall be considered public international property and shall be immune from search, requisition, confiscation, expropriation or any other form of taking or foreclosure by executive or legislative action.

Section 5. Inviolability of Archives

The archives of the Bank shall be inviolable.

Section 6. Freedom of Assets from Restrictions

To the extent necessary to carry out the purpose and functions of the Bank and to conduct its operations in accordance with this Agreement, all property and other assets of the Bank shall be free from restrictions, regulations, controls and moratoria of any nature, except as may otherwise be provided in this Agreement.

Section 7. Privilege for Communications

The official communications of the Bank shall be accorded by each member the same treatment that it accords to the official communications of other members.

Section 8. Personal Immunities and Privileges

All governors, executive directors, alternates, officers, and employees of the Bank shall have the following privileges and immunities:

(a) Immunity from legal process with respect to acts performed by them in their official capacity, except when the Bank waives this immunity.

(b) When not local nationals, the same immunities from immigration restrictions, alien registration requirements and national service obligations and the same facilities as regards exchange provisions as are accorded by members to the representatives, officials, and employees of comparable rank of other members.

(c) The same privileges in respect of traveling facilities as are accorded by members to representatives, officials, and employees of comparable rank of other members.

Section 9. Immunities from Taxation

(a) The Bank, its property, other assets, income, and the operations and transactions it carries out pursuant to this Agreement, shall be immune from all taxation and from all customs duties. The Bank shall also be immune from any obligation relating to the payment, withholding or collection of any tax, or duty.

(b) No tax shall be levied on or in respect of salaries and emoluments paid by the Bank to executive directors, alternates, officials or employees of the Bank who are not local citizens or other local nationals.

(c) No tax of any kind shall be levied on any obligation or security issued by the Bank, including any dividend or interest thereon, by whomsoever held:

   (i) which discriminates against such obligation or security solely because it is issued by the Bank; or

   (ii) if the sole jurisdictional basis for such taxation is the place or currency in which it is issued, made payable or paid, or the location of any office or place of business maintained by the Bank.

(d) No tax of any kind shall be levied on any obligation or security guaranteed by the Bank, including any dividend or interest thereon, by whomsoever held:

   (i) which discriminates against such obligation or security solely because it is guaranteed by the Bank; or

   (ii) if the sole jurisdictional basis for such taxation is the location of any office or place of business maintained by the Bank.

Section 10. Implementation

Each member, in accordance with its juridical system, shall take such action as is necessary to make effective in its own territories the principles set forth in this article, and shall inform the Bank of the action which it has taken on the matter.

ARTICLE XII

AMENDMENTS

(a) This Agreement may be amended only by decision of the Board of Governors by a majority of the total number of governors, including two thirds of the governors of regional members, representing not less than three fourths of the total voting power of the member countries, provided, however, that the voting majorities provided in Article II, Section 1(b), may be amended only by the voting majorities stated therein.

(b) Notwithstanding the provisions of (a) above, the unanimous agreement of the Board of Governors shall be required for the approval of any amendment modifying:

(i) the right to withdraw from the Bank as provided in Article IX, Section 1;

(ii) the right to purchase capital stock of the Bank and to contribute to the Fund as provided in Article II, Section 3(b) and in Article IV, Section 3(g), respectively; and

(iii) the limitation on liability as provided in Article II, Section 3(d), and Article IV, Section 5.

(c) Any proposal to amend this Agreement, whether emanating from a member or the Board of Executive Directors, shall be communicated to the Chairman of the Board of Governors, who shall bring the proposal before the Board of Governors. When an amendment has been adopted, the Bank shall so certify in an official communication addressed to all members. Amendments shall enter into force for all members three months after the date of the official communication unless the Board of Governors shall specify a different period.

ARTICLE XIII

INTERPRETATION AND ARBITRATION

Section 1. Interpretation

(a) Any question of interpretation of the provisions of this Agreement arising between any member and the Bank or between any members of the Bank shall be submitted to the Board of Executive Directors for decision.

Members especially affected by the question under consideration shall be entitled to direct representation before the Board of Executive Directors as provided in Article VIII, Section 3(g).

(b) In any case where the Board of Executive Directors has given a decision under (a) above, any member may require that the question be submitted to the Board of Governors, whose decision shall be final. Pending the decision of the Board of Governors, the Bank may, so far as it deems it necessary, act on the basis of the decision of the Board of Executive Directors.

Section 2. Arbitration

If a disagreement should arise between the Bank and a country which has ceased to be a member, or between the Bank and any member after adoption of a decision to terminate the operation of the Bank, such disagreement shall be submitted to arbitration by a tribunal of three arbitrators. One of the arbitrators shall be appointed by the Bank, another by the country concerned, and the third, unless the parties otherwise agree, by the Secretary General of the Organization of American States. If all efforts to reach a unanimous agreement fail, decisions shall be made by a majority vote of the three arbitrators.

The third arbitrator shall be empowered to settle all questions of procedure in any case where the parties are in disagreement with respect thereto.

ARTICLE XIV
GENERAL PROVISIONS

Section 1. Principal Office

The principal office of the Bank shall be located in Washington, District of Columbia, United States of America.

Section 2. Relations with Other Organizations

The Bank may enter into arrangements with other organizations with respect to the exchange of information or for other purposes consistent with this Agreement.

Section 3. Channel of Communication

Each member shall designate an official entity for purposes of communication with the Bank on matters connected with this Agreement.

Section 4. Depositories

Each member shall designate its central bank as a depository in which the Bank may keep its holdings of such member's currency and other assets of the Bank. If a member has no central bank, it shall, in agreement with the Bank, designate another institution for such purpose.

ARTICLE XV

FINAL PROVISIONS

Section 1. Signature and Acceptance

(a) This Agreement shall be deposited with the General Secretariat of the Organization of American States, where it shall remain open until December 31, 1959, for signature by the representatives of the countries listed in Annex A. Each signatory country shall deposit with the General Secretariat of the Organization of American States an instrument setting forth that it has accepted or ratified this Agreement in accordance with its own laws and has taken the steps necessary to enable it to fulfill all of its obligations under this Agreement.

(b) The General Secretariat of the Organization of American States shall send certified copies of this Agreement to the members of the Organization and duly notify them of each signature and deposit of the instrument of acceptance or ratification made pursuant to the foregoing paragraph, as well as the date thereof.

(c) At the time the instrument of acceptance or ratification is deposited on its behalf, each country shall deliver to the General Secretariat of the Organization of American States, for the purpose of meeting administrative expenses of the Bank, gold or United States dollars equivalent to one tenth of one per cent of the purchase price of the shares of the Bank subscribed by it and of its quota in the Fund. This payment shall be credited to the member on account of its subscription and quota prescribed pursuant to Articles II, Section 4(a)(i), and IV, Section 3(d)(i). At any time on or after the date on which its instrument of acceptance or ratification is deposited, any member may make additional payments to be credited to the member on account of its subscription and quota prescribed pursuant to Articles II and IV. The General Secretariat of the Organization of American States shall hold all funds paid under this paragraph in a special deposit account or accounts and shall make such funds available to the Bank not later than the time of the first meeting of the Board of Governors held pursuant to Section 3 of this article. If this Agreement has not come into force by December 31, 1959, the General Secretariat of the Organization of American States shall return such funds to the countries that delivered them.

(d) On or after the date on which the Bank commences operations, the General Secretariat of the Organization of American States may receive the signature and the instrument of acceptance or ratification of this Agreement from any country whose membership has been approved in accordance with Article II, Section 1(b).

Section 2. Entry into Force

(a) This Agreement shall enter into force when it has been signed and instruments of acceptance or ratification have been deposited, in accordance with Section 1(a) of this article, by representatives of countries whose subscriptions comprise not less than 85 per cent of the total subscriptions set forth in Annex A.

(b) Countries whose instruments of acceptance or ratification were deposited prior to the date on which the agreement entered into force shall become members on that date. Other countries shall become members on the dates on which their instruments of acceptance or ratification are deposited.

Section 3. Commencements of Operations

(a) The Secretary General of the Organization of American States shall call the first meeting of the Board of Governors as soon as this Agreement enters into force under Section 2 of this article.

(b) At the first meeting of the Board of Governors arrangements shall be made for the selection of the executive directors and their alternates in accordance with the provisions of Article VIII, Section 3, and for the determination of the date on which the Bank shall commence operations. Notwithstanding the provisions of Article VIII, Section 3, the governors, if they deem it desirable, may provide that the first term to be served by such directors may be less than three years.

DONE at the city of Washington, District of Columbia, United States of America, in a single original, dated April 8, 1959, whose English, French, Portuguese, and Spanish texts are equally authentic.

[*Note:* Schedules are not reproduced here. Schedule A sets forth initial subscriptions to the IADB's capital stock; Schedule B sets forth contribution quotes for the Fund for Special Operations.]

APPENDIX F
CHARTER OF THE AfDB

Citation: Agreement Establishing the African Development Bank, done at Khartoum, Aug. 4, 1963 (entered into force Sept. 10, 1964), 510 U.N.T.S. 3.

Contents

NOTE: Unlike the earlier GEO charters, the AfDB Charter is divided into Chapters (I through IX) and Articles (1 through 66), numbered consecutively across chapters. The same structure appears in the charters of the AsDB and the EBRD.

IV. Borrowing and Other Additional Powers
    23. General Powers
    24. Special Borrowing Powers
    25. Warning to be Placed on Securities
    26. Valuation of Currencies and Determination of Convertibility
    27. Use of Currencies
    28. Maintenance of Value of the Currency Holdings of the Bank

V. Organization and Management
    29. Board of Governors: Powers
    30. Board of Governors: Composition
    31. Board of Governors: Procedure
    32. Board of Directors: Powers
    33. Board of Directors: Composition
    34. Board of Directors: Procedure
    35. Voting
    36. The President: Appointment
    37. The Office of the President
    38. Prohibition of Political Activity; The International Character of the Bank
    39. Office of the Bank
    40. Channel of Communications; Depositories
    41. Publication of the Agreement, Working Languages, Provision of Information and Reports
    42. Allocation of Net Income

VI. Withdrawal and Suspension of Members; Temporary Suspension and Termination of Operations of the Bank
    43. Withdrawal
    44. Suspension
    45. Settlement of Accounts
    46. Temporary Suspension of Operations
    47. Termination of Operations
    48. Liability of Members and Payment of Claims
    49. Distribution of Assets

VII. Status, Immunities, Exemptions and Privileges
    50. Status
    51. Status in Member Countries
    52. Judicial Proceedings
    53. Immunity of Assets and Archives
    54. Freedom of Assets from Restrictions
    55. Privilege for Communications
    56. Personal Immunities and Privileges
    57. Exemption from Taxation
    59. Notification of Implementation

VIII. Amendments, Interpretation, Arbitration

IX. Final Provisions

Agreement Establishing the African Development Bank

The Governments on whose behalf this Agreement is signed,

Determined to strengthen African solidarity by means of economic co-operation between African States,

Considering the necessity of accelerating the development of the extensive human and natural resources of Africa in order to stimulate economic development and social progress in that region,

Recognising that the establishment of a financial institution common to all African countries would serve these ends,

Have agreed to establish hereby the African Development Bank (hereinafter called the "Bank") which shall be governed by the following provisions:

Chapter I

PURPOSE, FUNCTIONS, MEMBERSHIP AND STRUCTURE

Article 1

Purpose

The purpose of the Bank shall be to contribute to the economic development and social progress of its members—individually and jointly.

Article 2

Functions

(1) To implement its purpose, the Bank shall have the following functions:

(*a*) To use the resources at its disposal for the financing of investment projects and programmes relating to the economic and social development of its members, giving special priority to:

    (i) Projects or programmes which by their nature or scope concern several members; and

    (ii) Projects or programmes designed to make the economies of its members increasingly complementary and to bring about an orderly expansion of their foreign trade;

(*b*) To undertake, or participate in, the selection, study and preparation of projects, enterprises and activities contributing to such development;

(*c*) To mobilize and increase in Africa, and outside Africa, resources for the financing of such investment projects and programmes;

(*d*) Generally, to promote investment in Africa of public and private capital in projects or programmes designed to contribute to the economic development or social progress of its members;

(*e*) To provide such technical assistance as may be needed in Africa for the study, preparation, financing and execution of development projects and programmes; and

(*f*) To undertake such other activities and provide such other services as may advance its purpose.

(2) In carrying out its functions, the Bank shall seek to co-operate with national, regional and sub-regional development institutions in Africa. To the same end, it should co-operate with other international organizations pursuant to a similar purpose and with other institutions concerned with the development of Africa.

(3) The Bank shall be guided in all its decisions by the provisions of articles 1 and 2 of this Agreement.

Articles 3

Membership and Geographical Area

(1) Any African country which has the status of an independent State may become a member of the Bank. It shall acquire membership in accordance with paragraph (1) or paragraph (2) of article 64 of this Agreement.

(2) The geographical area to which the membership and development activities of the Bank may extend (referred to in this Agreement as "Africa" or "African," as the case may be) shall comprise the continent of African and African islands.

Article 4

Structure

The Bank shall have a Board of Governors, a Board of Directors, a President, at least one Vice-President and such other officers and staff to perform such duties as the Bank may determine.

CHAPTER II

CAPITAL

Article 5

Authorized capital

(1) (*a*) The authorized capital stock of the Bank shall be 250,000,000 units of account. It shall be divided in 25,000 shares of a par value of 10,000 units of account each share, which shall be available for subscription by members.

   (*b*) The value of the unit of account shall be 0.88867088 gramme of fine gold.

(2) The authorized capital stock shall be divided into paid-up shares and callable shares. The equivalent of 125,000,000 units of account shall be paid up, and the equivalent of 125,000,000 units of account shall be callable for the purpose defined in paragraph (4) (*a*) of article 7 of this Agreement.

(3) The authorized capital stock may be increased as and when the Board of Governors deems it advisable. Unless that stock is increased solely to provide for the initial subscription of a member, the decision of the Board shall be adopted by a two-thirds majority of the total number of Governors, representing not less than three-quarters of the total voting power of the members.

Article 6

Subscription of shares

(1) Each member shall initially subscribe shares of the capital stock of the Bank. The initial subscription of each member shall consist of an equal number of paid-up callable shares. The initial number of shares to be subscribed by a State which acquires membership in accordance with paragraph (1) of article 64 of this Agreement shall be that set forth in its respect in annex A of this Agreement, which shall form an integral part thereof. The initial number of shares to be subscribed by other members shall be determined by the Board of Governors.

(2) In the event of an increase of the capital stock for a purpose other than solely to provide for an initial subscription of a member, each member shall have the right to subscribe, on such uniform terms and conditions as the Board of Governors shall determine, a proportion of the increase of stock equivalent to the proportion which its stock theretofore subscribed bears to the total capital stock of the Bank. No member, however, shall be obligated to subscribe to any part of such increased stock.

(3) A member may request the Bank to increase its subscription on such terms and conditions as the Board of Governors may determine.

(4) Shares of stock initially subscribed by States which acquire membership in accordance with paragraph (1) or article 64 of this Agreement shall be issued at par. Other shares shall be issued at par unless the Board of Governors by a majority of the total voting power of the members decides in special circumstances to issue them on other terms.

(5) Liability on shares shall be limited to the unpaid portion of their issue price.

(6) Shares shall not be pledged nor encumbered in any manner. They shall be transferable only to the Bank.

Article 7

Payment of subscription

(1) (*a*) Payment of the amount initially subscribed to the paid-up capital stock of the Bank by a member which acquires membership in accordance with paragraph (1) of article 64 shall be made in six instalments, the first of which shall be five per cent, the second thirty-five per cent, and the remaining four instalments each fifteen per cent of that amount.

(*b*) The first instalment shall be paid by the Government concerned on or before the date of deposit, on its behalf, of the instrument of ratification or acceptance of this Agreement in accordance with paragraph (1) of article 64. The second instalment shall become due on the last day of a period of six months from the entry into force of this Agreement or on the day of the said deposit, which is the later day. The third instalment shall become due on the last day of a period of eighteen months from the entry into force of this Agreement. The remaining three instalments shall become due successively each on the last day of a period of one year immediately following the day on which the preceding instalment becomes due.

(2) Payments of the amounts initially subscribed by the members of the Bank to the paid-up capital stock shall be made in gold or convertible currency. The Board of Governors shall determine the mode of payment of other amounts subscribed by the members to the paid-up capital stock.

(3) The Board of Governors shall determine the dates for the payment of amounts subscribed by the members of the Bank to the paid-up capital stock to which the provisions of paragraph (1) of this article do not apply.

(4) (*a*) Payment of the amounts subscribed to the callable capital stock of the Bank shall be subject to call only as and when required by the Bank to meet its obligations incurred, pursuant to paragraph (1) (*b*) and (*d*) of article 14, on borrowing of funds for inclusion in its ordinary capital resources or guarantees chargeable to such resources.

   (*b*) In the event of such calls, payment may be made at the option of the member concerned in gold, convertible currency or in the currency required to discharge the obligation of the Bank for the purpose of which the call is made.

   (*c*) Calls on unpaid subscriptions shall be uniform in percentage on all callable shares.

(5) The Bank shall determine the place for any payment under this article provided that, until the first meeting of its Board of Governors provided in article 66 of this Agreement, the payment of the first instalment referred to in paragraph (1) of this article shall be made to the Trustee referred to in article 66.

Article 8

Special Funds

(1) The Bank may establish, or be entrusted with the administration of, Special Funds which are designed to serve its purpose and come within its functions. It may receive, hold, use, commit or otherwise dispose of resources appertaining to such Special Funds.

(2) The resources of such Special Funds shall be kept separate and apart from the ordinary capital resources of the Bank in accordance with the provisions of article 11 of this Agreement.

(3) The Bank shall adopt such special rules and regulations as may be required for the administration and use of each Special Fund, provided always that:

   (*a*) Such special rules and regulations shall be subject to paragraph (4) article 7, articles 9 to 11, and those provisions of this Agreement which expressly apply to the ordinary capital resources or ordinary operations of the Bank;

(*b*) Such special rules and regulations must be consistent with provisions of this Agreement which expressly apply to special resources or special operations of the Bank; and that

(*c*) Where such special rules and regulations do not apply, the Special Funds shall be governed by the provisions of this Agreement.

Article 9

Ordinary capital resources

For the purposes of this Agreement, the expression "ordinary capital resources" of the Bank shall include:

(*a*) Authorized capital stock of the Bank subscribed pursuant to the provisions of article 6 of this Agreement;

(*b*) Funds raised by borrowing of the Bank, by virtue of powers conferred in paragraph (*a*) of article 23 of this Agreement, to which the commitment to calls provided for in paragraph (4) or article 7 of this Agreement applies;

(*c*) Funds received in repayment of loans made with the resources referred to in paragraphs (*a*) and (*b*) of this article; and

(*d*) Income derived from loans made from the aforementioned funds income from guarantees to which the commitment to calls provided for in paragraph (4) of article 7 of this Agreement applies; as well as

(*e*) Any other funds or income received by the Bank which do not form part of its special resources.

Article 10

Special resources

(1) For the purposes of this Agreement, the expression "special resources" shall refer to the resources of Special Funds and shall include:

(*a*) Resources initially contributed to any Special Fund;

(*b*) Funds borrowed for the purposes of any Special Fund, including the Special Fund provided for in paragraph (6) of article 24 of this Agreement;

(*c*) Funds repaid in respect of loans or guarantees financed from the resources of any Special Fund which, under the rules and regulations governing that Special Fund, are received by that Special Fund;

(*d*) Income derived from operations of the Bank by which any of the aforementioned resources or funds are used or committed if, under the rules and regulations governing the Special Fund concerned, that income accrues to the said Special Fund; and

(*e*) Any other resources at the disposal of any Special Fund.

(2) For the purposes of this Agreement, the expression "special resources appertaining to a Special Fund" shall include the resources, funds and incomes which are referred to in the preceding paragraph and are—as the case may be—contributed to, borrowed or received by, accruing to, or at the disposal of the Special Fund concerned in conformity with the rules and regulations governing that Special Fund.

Article 11

Separation of resources

(1) The ordinary capital resources of the Bank shall at all times and in all respects be held, used, committed, invested or otherwise disposed of, entirely separate from special resources. Each Special Fund, its resources and accounts.

(2) The ordinary capital resources of the Bank shall under no circumstances be charged with, or used to discharge, losses or liabilities arising out of operations or other activities of an Special Fund. Special resources appertaining to any Special Fund shall under no circumstances be charged with, or used to discharge, losses or liabilities arising out of operations or other activities of the Bank financed from its ordinary capital resources or form special resources appertaining to any other Special Fund.

(3) In the operations and other activities of any Special Fund, the liability of the Bank shall be limited to the special resources appertaining to that Special Fund which are at the disposal of the Bank.

CHAPTER III

OPERATIONS

Article 12

Use of resources

The resources and facilities of the Bank shall be used exclusively to implement the purpose and functions set forth in articles 1 and 2 of this Agreement.

Article 13

Ordinary and special operations

(1) The operations of the Bank shall consist of ordinary operations and of special operations.

(2) The ordinary operations shall be those financed from the ordinary capital resources of the Bank.

(3) The special operations shall be those financed from the special resources.

(4) The financial statements of the Bank shall show the ordinary operations and the special operations of the Bank separately. The Bank shall adopt such other rules and regulations as may be required to ensure the effective separation of the two types of its operations.

(5) Expenses appertaining directly to ordinary operations shall be charged to the ordinary capital resources of the Bank; expenses appertaining directly to special operations shall be charged to the appropriate special resources. Other expenses shall be charged as the Bank shall determine.

Article 14

Recipients and methods of operations

(1) In its operations, the Bank may provide or facilitate financing for any member, political sub-division or any agency thereof or for any institutions of undertaking in the territory of any member as well as for international or regional agencies or institutions concerned with the development of Africa. Subject to the provisions of this chapter, the Bank may carry out its operations in any of the following ways:

(*a*) By making or participating in direct loans out of:

(i) Funds corresponding to its unimpaired subscriber paid-up capital and except as provided in article 20 of this Agreement, to its reserves and undistributed surplus; or out of

(ii) Funds corresponding to special resources; or

(*b*) By making or participating in direct loans out of funds borrowed or otherwise acquired by the bank for inclusion in its ordinary capital resources or in special resources; or

(*c*) By investment of funds referred to in sub-paragraph (*a*) or (*b*) of this paragraph in the equity capital of an undertaking or institution; or

(*d*) By guaranteeing, in whole or in part, loans made by others.

(2) The provisions of this Agreement applying to direct loans which the Bank may make pursuant to sub-paragraph (*a*) or (*b*) of the preceding paragraph shall also apply to its participation in any direct loan undertaken pursuant to any of those sub-paragraphs. Equally, the provisions of this Agreement applying to guarantees of loans undertaken by the Bank pursuant to sub-paragraph (*d*) of the preceding paragraph shall apply where the Bank guarantees part of such a loan only.

Article 15

Limitations on operations

(1) The total amount outstanding in respect of the ordinary operations of the Bank shall not at any time exceed the total amount of its unimpaired subscribed capital, reserves and surplus included in its ordinary capital resources excepting, however, the special reserve provided for in article 20 of this Agreement.

(2) The total amount outstanding in respect of the special operations of the Bank relating to any Special Fund shall not at any time exceed the total amount of the unimpaired special resources appertaining to that Special Fund.

(3) In the case of loans made out of funds borrowed by the Bank to which the commitment to calls provided for in paragraph (4) (*a*) of article 7 of this Agreement applies, the total amount of principal outstanding and payable to the Bank in a specific currency shall not at any time exceed the total amount of principal outstanding in respect of funds borrowed by the Bank that are payable in the same currency.

(4) (*a*) In the case of investments made by virtue of paragraph (1) (c) of article 14 of this Agreement out of the ordinary capital resources of the Bank, the total amount outstanding shall not at any time exceed ten per cent of the aggregate amount of the paid-up capital stock of the Bank together with the reserves and surplus included in its ordinary capital resources excepting, however, the special reserve provided for in article 20 of this Agreement.

    (*b*) At the time it is made, the amount of any specific investment referred to in the preceding sub-paragraph shall not exceed a percentage of equity capital of the institution or undertaking concerned, which the Board of Governors shall have fixed for any investment to be made by virtue of paragraph (1) (c) of article 14 of this Agreement. In no event shall the Bank seek to obtain by such an investment a controlling interest in the institution or undertaking concerned.

Article 16

Provisions of currencies for direct loans

In making direct loans, the Bank shall furnish the borrower with currency other than the currency of the member in whose territory the project concerned is to be carried out (the latter currency hereinafter to be called "local currency") which are required to meet foreign exchange expenditure on that project provided always that the Bank may, in making direct loans, provide financing to meet local expenditure on the project concerned:

(*a*) Where it can do so by supplying local currency without selling any of its holdings in gold or convertible currencies; or

(*b*) Where in the opinion of the Bank local expenditure on that project is likely to cause undue loss or strain on the balance of payments of the county where that project is to be carried out and the amount of such financing by the Bank does not exceed a reasonable portion of the total local expenditure incurred on that project.

Article 17

Operational principles

(1) The operations of the Bank shall be conducted in accordance with the following principles:

(*a*) (i) The operations of the Bank shall, except in special circumstances provide for the financing of specific projects, or groups of projects, particularly those forming part of a national or regional development programme urgently required for the economic or social development of its members. They may however, include global loans to, or guarantees of loans made to, African national development banks or other suitable institutions, in order that the latter may finance projects of a specified type serving the purpose of the Bank within the respective fields of activities of such banks or institutions;

(ii) In selecting suitable projects, the Bank shall always be guided by the provisions of paragraph (1) (*a*) of article (2) of this Agreement and by the potential contribution of the project concerned to the purpose of the Bank rater than by the type of the project. It shall, however, pay special attention to the selection of suitable multinational projects;

(*b*) The Bank shall not provide for the financing of a project in the territory of a member if that member objects thereto;

(*c*) The Bank shall not provide for the financing of a project to the extent that in its opinion the recipient may obtain the finance or facilities elsewhere on terms that the Bank considers are reasonable for the recipient;

(*d*) Subject to the provisions of articles 16 and 24 of this Agreement, the Bank shall not impose conditions enjoining that the proceeds of any financing undertaken pursuant to its ordinary operations shall be spent in the territory of any particular country nor that such proceeds shall not be spent in the territory of any particular country;

(*e*) In making or guaranteeing a loan, the Bank shall pay due regard to the prospects that the borrower and the guarantor, if any, will be in a position to meet their obligations under the loan;

(*f*) In making or guaranteeing a loan, the Bank shall be satisfied that the rate of interest and other charges are reasonable and such rate, charges and the schedule for the repayment of principal are appropriate for the project concerned.

(*g*) In the case of a direct loan made by the bank, the borrower shall be permitted by the Bank to draw its funds only to meet expenditure in connexion with the project as it is actually incurred;

(*h*) The Bank shall make arrangements to ensure that the proceeds of any loan made or guaranteed by it are used only for the purposes for which the loan was granted, with due attention to considerations of economy and efficiency.

(*i*) The Bank shall seek to maintain a reasonable diversification in its investments in equity capital;

(*j*) The Bank shall apply sound banking principles to its operations and in particular, to its investments in equity capital. It shall not assume responsibility for managing any institution or undertaking in which it has an investment and

(*k*) In guaranteeing a loan made by other investors, the Bank shall receive suitable compensation for its risk.

(2) The Bank shall adopt such rules and regulations as are required for the consideration of projects submitted to it.

Article 18

Terms and conditions for direct loans and guarantees

(1) In the case of direct loans made by the Bank, the contract:

(*a*) Shall establish, in conformity with the operational principles set forth in paragraph (1) of article 17 of this Agreement and subject to the other provisions of this chapter, all the terms and conditions of the guarantee concerned including those relating to the fees, commission, and other charges of the Bank; and, in particular,

(*b*) Shall provide that—subject to paragraph (3) (*c*) of this article— payments to the Bank of amortization, interest, commission and other charges shall be made in the currency loaned, unless—in the case of a direct loan made as part of special operations—the rules and regulations provide otherwise.

(2) In the case of loans guaranteed by the Bank, the contract of guarantee:

(*a*) Shall establish, in conformity with the operational principles set forth in paragraph (1) of article 17 of this Agreement and subject to the other provisions of this chapter, all the terms and conditions of the guarantee concerned including those relating to the fees, commission, and other charges of the Bank; and in particular,

(*b*) Shall provide that—subject to paragraph (3) (*c*) of this article — all payments to the Bank under the guarantee contract shall be made in the currency loaned, unless—in the case of a loan guaranteed as part of special operations—the rules and regulations provide otherwise; and

(*c*) Shall also provide that the Bank may terminate its liability with respect to interest if, upon default by the borrower and the guarantor, if any, the Bank offers to purchase, at par and interest accrued to a date designated in the offer(???) the bonds or other obligations guaranteed.

(3) In the case of direct loans made or loans guaranteed by the Bank, the Bank:

(*a*) In determining the terms and conditions for the operation, shall take due account of the terms and conditions on which the corresponding funds were obtained by the Bank;

(*b*) Where the recipient is not a member, may, when it deems it advisable, require that the member in whose territory the project concerned is to be carried out, or a public agency or institution of that member acceptable to the Bank guarantee the repayment of the principal and the payment of interest and other charges on the loan;

(*c*) Shall expressly state the currency in which all payments to the Bank under the contract concerned shall be made. At the option of the borrower however, such payments may always be made in gold or convertible currency or, subject to the agreement of the Bank, in any other currency; and

(*d*) May attach such other terms or conditions, as it deems appropriate taking into account both the interest of the member directly concerned in the project and the interests of the members as a whole.

Article 19

Commission and fees

(1) The Bank shall charge a commission on direct loans made and guarantees given as part of its ordinary operations. This commission, payable periodically, shall be computed on the amount outstanding on each loan or guarantee and shall be at the rate of not less than one per cent per annum unless the Bank, after the first ten years of its operations, decides to changes this minimum rate by a majority of two-thirds of its members representing not less than three-quarters of the total voting power of the members.

(2) In guaranteeing a loan as part of its ordinary operations and the commission, fees and other charges in its special operations shall be determined by the Board of Directors.

Article 20

Special reserve

The amount of commissions received by the Bank pursuant to article 19 of this Agreement shall be set aside as a special reserve which shall be kept for meeting liabilities of the Bank in accordance with its article 21. The special reserve shall be held in such liquid form, permitted under this Agreement, as the Board of Directors may decide.

Article 21

Methods of meeting liabilities of the Bank (ordinary operations)

(1) Whenever necessary to meet contractual payments of interest, other charge or amortization on the borrowing of the Bank, or to meet its liabilities with respect to similar payments in respect of loans guaranteed by it and chargeable to its ordinary capital resources, the bank may call an appropriate amount of the unpaid subscribed callable capital in accordance with paragraph (4) of article 7 of this Agreement.

(2) In cases of default in respect of a loan made out of borrowed funds or guaranteed by the Bank as part of its ordinary operations, the Bank may, if it believes that the default may be of long duration, call an additional amount of such callable capital not exceed in any one year one per cent of the total subscriptions of the members, for the following purposes:

    (*a*) To redeem before maturity, or otherwise discharge, its liability on all or part of the outstanding principal of any loan guaranteed by it in respect of which the debtor is in default; and

    (*b*) To repurchase, or otherwise discharge, its liability on all or part of its own outstanding borrowing.

Article 22

Methods of meeting liabilities on borrowings for Special Funds

Payments in satisfaction of any liability in respect of borrowings of funds for inclusion in the special resources appertaining to a Special Fund shall be charged:

(i) First, against any reserve established for this purpose for or within the Special Fund concerned; and

(ii) Then, against any other assets available in the special resources appertaining to that Special Fund.

CHAPTER IV

BORROWING AND OTHER ADDITIONAL POWERS

Article 23

General powers

In addition to the powers provided elsewhere in this Agreement, the Bank shall have power to:

(*a*) Borrow funds in member countries or elsewhere, and in that connexion to furnish such collateral or other security as it shall determine provided always that:

   (i) Before making a sale of its obligations in the market of a member, the Bank shall have obtained its approval;

   (ii) Where the obligations of the Bank are to be denominated in the currency of a member, the Bank shall have obtained its approval; and

   (iii) Where the funds to be borrowed are to be included in its ordinary capital resources, the Bank shall have obtained, where appropriate, the approval of the members referred to in sub-paragraphs (i) and (ii) of this paragraph that the proceeds may be exchanged for any other currency without any restrictions;

(*b*) Buy and sell securities the Bank has issued or guaranteed or in which it has invested provided always that tit shall have obtained the approval of any member in whose territory the securities are to be bought or sold;

(*c*) Guarantee or underwrite securities in which it has invested in order to facilitate their sale;

(*d*) Invest funds not needed in its operations in such obligations as it may determine and invest funds held by the Bank for pensions or similar purposes in marketable securities;

(*e*) Undertake activities incidental to its operations such as, among others, the promotion of consortia for financing which serves the purpose of the Bank and comes within its functions;

(*f*) (i) Provide all technical advice and assistance which serve its purpose and come within its functions; and

(ii) Where expenditure incurred by such a service is not reimbursed, charge the net income of the Bank therewith and, in the first five years of its operations use up to one per cent of its paid-up capital on such expenditure; provided always that the total expenditure of the Bank on such services in each year of that period does not exceed one-fifth of that percentage; and

(*g*) Exercise such other powers as shall be necessary or desirable in furtherance of its purpose and functions, consistent with the provisions of this Agreement.

Article 24

Special borrowing powers

(1) The Bank may request any member to loan amounts of its currency to the Bank in order to finance expenditure in respect of goods or serves produced in the territory of that member for the purpose of a project to be carried out in the territory of another member.

(2) Unless the member concerned invokes economic and financial difficulties which, in its opinion, are likely to be provoked or aggravated by the granting of such a loan to the Bank, that member shall comply with the request of the Bank. The loan shall be made for a period to be agreed with the Bank, which shall be in relation to the duration of the project which the proceeds of the loan are designed to finance.

(3) Unless the member agrees otherwise, the aggregate amount outstanding in respect of its loans made to the Bank pursuant to this article shall not, at any time, exceed the equivalent of the amount of its subscription to the capital stock of the bank. The loan shall be made for a period to be agreed with the Bank, which shall not, at any time, exceed the equivalent of the amount of its subscription to the capital loan are designed to finance.

(4) Loans to the Bank made pursuant to this article shall bear interest, payable by the Bank to the lending member, at a rate which shall correspond to the average rate of interest paid by the Bank on its borrowings for Special Funds during a period of one year preceding the conclusion of the loan agreement. This rate shall in no event exceed a maximum rate which the Board of Governors shall determine from time to time.

(5) The Bank shall repay the loan, and pay the interest due in respect thereof, in the currency of the lending member or in a currency acceptable to the latter.

(6) All resources obtained by the Bank by virtue of the provisions of this article shall constitute a Special Fund.

Article 25

Warning to be placed on securities

Every security issued or guaranteed by the Bank shall bear on its face a conspicuous statement to the effect that it is not an obligation of any government unless it is in fact the obligation of a particular government in which case shall so state.

Article 26

Valuation of currencies and determination of convertibility

Whenever it shall become necessary under this Agreement:

  (i) To value any currency in terms of another currency, in terms of gold or of the unit of account defined in paragraph (1) (*b*) of article 5 of this Agreement, or

  (ii) To determine whether any currency is convertible,

such valuation or determination, as the case may be, shall be reasonably made by the Bank after consultation with the International Monetary Fund.

Article 27

Use of currencies

(1) members may not maintain or impose any restrictions on the holding or use by the Bank or by any recipient from the Bank, for payments anywhere of the following:

  (*a*) Gold or convertible currencies received by the Bank in payment of subscriptions to the capital stock of the Bank from its members;

  (*b*) Currencies of members purchased with the gold or convertible currencies referred to in the preceding sub-paragraph;

  (*c*) Currencies obtained by the Bank by borrowing, pursuant to paragraph (*a*) of article 23 of this Agreement, for inclusion in its ordinary capital resources

  (*d*) Gold or currencies received by the Bank in payment on account of principal, interest, dividends or other charges in respect of loans or investments made out of any of the funds referred to in sub-paragraphs (*a*) to (*c*) or in payment of commissions or fees in respect of guarantees issued by the Bank; and

(*e*) Currencies, other than its own, received by a member from the Bank in distribution of the net income of the Bank in accordance with article 42 of this Agreement.

(2) Members may not maintain or impose any restrictions on the holding or use by the Bank or by any recipient from the Bank, for payments anywhere of currency of a member received by the Bank which does not come within the provisions of the preceding paragraph, unless:

(*a*) That member declares that it desires the use of such currency to be restricted to payments for goods or services produced in its territory; or

(*b*) Such currency forms part of the special resources of the Bank and its use is subject to special rules and regulations.

(3) Members may not maintain or impose any restrictions on the holding or use by the Bank, for making amortization or anticipatory payments or for repurchasing—in whole or in part—its obligations, or currencies received by the Bank in repayment of direct loans made out of its ordinary capital resources.

(4) The Bank shall not use gold or currencies which it holds for the purchase of other currencies of its members except:

(*a*) In order to meet its existing obligations; or

(*b*) Pursuant to a decision of the Board of Directors adopted by a two-thirds majority of the total voting power of the members.

Article 28

Maintenance of value of the currency holding of the Bank

(1) Whenever the par value of the currency of a member is reduced in terms of the unit of account defined in paragraph (1) (*b*) of article 5 of this Agreement, or its foreign exchange value has, in the opinion of the Bank, depreciated to a significant extent, that member shall pay to the Bank within a reasonable time an amount of its currency required to maintain the value of all such currency held by the Bank, excepting currency derived by the Bank from its borrowing.

(2) Whenever the par value of the currency of a member is increased in terms of the said unit of account, or its foreign exchange value has, in the opinion of the Bank, depreciated to a significant extent, the Bank shall pay to that member within a reasonable time an amount of that currency

required to adjust the value of all such currency held by the Bank, excepting currency derived by the Bank from its borrowing.

(3) The Bank may waive the provisions of this article where a uniform proportionate change in the par value of the currencies of all its members takes place.

CHAPTER V

ORGANIZATION AND MANAGEMENT

Article 29

Board of Governors: Powers

(1) All the powers of the Bank shall be vested in the Board of Governors. In particular, the Board shall issue general directives concerning the credit policies of the Bank.

(2) The Board of Governors may delegate to the Board of Directors all its powers except the power to:

   (*a*) Decrease the authorized capital stock of the Bank;

   (*b*) Establish or accept the administration of Special Funds;

   (*c*) Authorize the conclusion of general arrangements for co-operation with the authorities of African countries which have not yet attained independent status or of general agreements for co-operation with African Governments which have not yet acquired membership of the Bank, as well as of such agreements with other Governments and with other international organizations;

   (*d*) Determine the remuneration of directors and their alternates:

   (*e*) Select outside auditors to certify the General Balance Sheet and the Statement of Profit and Loss of the Bank and to select such other experts as may be necessary to examine and report on the general management of the Bank;

   (*f*) Approve, after reviewing the report of the auditors, the General Balance Sheet and Statement of Profit and Loss of the Bank; and

   (*g*) Exercise such other powers as are expressly provided for that Board in this Agreement.

(3) The Board of Governors shall retain full powers to exercise authority over any matter delegated to the Board of Directors pursuant to paragraph (2) of this article.

Article 30

Board of Governors: Composition

(1) Each member shall be represented on the Board of Governors and shall appoint one governor and one alternate governor. They shall be persons of the highest competence and wide experience in economic and financial matters and shall be nationals of the member States. Each governor and alternate shall serve for five years, subject to termination of appointment at any time or to reappointment, at the pleasure of the appointing member. No alternate may vote except in the absence of his principal. At its annual meeting, the Board shall designate one of the governors as Chairman who shall hold office until the election of the Chairman at the next annual meeting of the Board.

(2) Governors and alternates shall serve as such without remuneration from the Bank, but the Bank may pay them reasonable expenses incurred in attending meetings.

Article 31

Board of Governors: Procedure

(1) The Board of Governors shall hold an annual meeting and such other meetings as may be provided for by the Board of called by the Board of Directors. Meetings of the Board of Governors shall be called, by the Board of Directors whenever requested by five members of the Bank, or by members having one quarter of the total voting power of the members.

(2) A quorum for any meeting of the Board of Governors shall be a majority of the total number of governors or their alternates, representing not less than two-thirds of the total voting power of the members.

(3) The Board of Governors may by regulation establish a procedure whereby the Board of Directors may, when it deems such action advisable, obtain a vote of the governors on a specific question without calling a meeting of the Board.

(4) The Board of Governors, and the Board of Directors to the extent authorized, may establish such subsidiary bodies and adopt such rules and regulations as may be necessary or appropriate to conduct the business of the Bank.

Article 32

Board of Directors: Powers

Without prejudice to the powers of the Board of Governors as provided in article 29 of this Agreement, the Board of Directors shall be responsible for the conduct of the general operations of the Bank and for this purpose shall, in addition to the powers provided for it expressly in this Agreement, exercise all the powers delegated to I by the Board of Governors, and in particular:

(*a*) Elect the President and, on his recommendation, one or more Vice-Presidents of the Bank and determine their terms of service;

(*b*) Prepare the work of the Board of Governors;

(*c*) In conformity with the general directives of the Board of Governors, take decisions concerning particular direct loans, guarantees, investments in equity capital and borrowing of funds by the Bank;

(*d*) Determine the rates of interest for direct loans and of commissions for guarantees;

(*e*) Submit the accounts for each financial year and an annual report for approval to the Board of Governors at each annual meeting; and

(*f*) Determine the general structure of the services of the Bank.

Article 33

Board of Directors: Composition

(1) The Board of Directors shall be composed of nine members who shall not be governors or alternate governors. They shall be elected by the Board of Governors in accordance with annex B to this Agreement, which shall form an integral part thereof. In electing the Board of Directors, the Board of Governors shall have due regard to the high competence in economic and financial matters required for the office.

(2) Each director shall appoint an alternate who shall act for him when he is not present. Director and their alternates shall be nationals of member States; but no alternate may be of the same nationality as his director. An alternate may participate in meetings of the Board but may vote only when he is acting in place of his director.

(3) Directors shall be elected for a term of three years and may be re-elected. They shall continue in office until their successors are elected. If the office of a director becomes vacant more than 1809 days before the end of his term, a successor shall be elected in accordance with annex B to this

Agreement, for the remainder of the term by the Board of Governors at its next session. While the office remains vacant the alternate of the former director shall exercise the powers of the latter except that of appointing an alternate.

Article 34

Board of Directors: Procedure

(1) The Board of Directors shall function in continuous session at the principal office of the Bank and shall meet as often as the business of the Bank may require.

(2) A quorum for any meeting fo the Board of Directors shall be a majority of the total number of directors representing not less than two-thirds of the total voting power of the members.

(3) The Board of Governors shall adopt regulations under which, there is no director of its nationality, a member may be represented at a meeting fo the Board of Directors when a request made by, or a matter particularly affecting, that member is under consideration.

Article 35

Voting

(1) Each member shall have 625 votes and, in addition, one vote for each share of the capital stock of the Bank held by that member.

(2) In voting in the Board of Governors, each governor shall be entitled to cast the votes of the member he represents. Except as otherwise expressly provided in this Agreement, all matters before the Board of Governors shall be decided by a majority of the voting power represented at the meeting.

(3) In voting in the Board of Directors, each director shall be entitled to cast the number of votes that counted towards his election, which votes shall be cast as a unit. Except as otherwise provided in this Agreement, all matters before the Board of Directors shall be decided by a majority of the voting power represented at the meeting.

Article 36

The President: Appointment

The Board of Directors, by a majority of the total voting power of the members, shall elect the President of the Bank. He shall be a person of the highest competence in matters pertaining to the activities, management and administration of the Bank and shall be a national of a member State.

While holding office, neither he nor any Vice-President shall be a governor or a director or alternate for either. The term of office of the President shall be five years. It may be renewed. He shall, however, cease to hold office if the Board of Directors so decides by a two-thirds majority of the voting power of the members.

Article 37

The Office of the President

(1) The President shall be Chairman of the Board of Directors but shall have no vote except a deciding vote in case of an equal division. He may participate in meetings of the Board of Governors but shall not vote.

(2) The President shall be chief of the staff of the Bank and shall conduct, under the direction of the Board of Directors, the current business of the Bank. He shall be responsible for the organization of the officers and staff of the Bank whom he shall appoint and release in accordance with regulations adopted by the Bank. He shall fix the terms of their employment in accordance with rules of sound management and financial policy.

(3) The President shall be the legal representative of the Bank.

(4) The Bank shall adopt regulations which shall determine who shall legally represent the Bank and perform the other duties of the President in the event that he is absent or that his office should become vacant.

(5) In appointing the officers and staff, the President shall make it his foremost consideration to secure the highest standards of efficiency, technical competence and integrity. He shall pay full regard to the recruitment of personnel among nationals of African countries, especially as far as senior posts of an executive nature are concerned. He shall recruit them on as wide a geographical basis as possible.

Article 38

Prohibition of political activity; the international character of the Bank

(1) The Bank shall not accept loans or assistance that could in any way prejudice, limit, deflect or otherwise alter its purpose or functions.

(2) The Bank, its President, Vice-Presidents, officers and staff shall not interfere in the political affairs of any member; nor shall they be influenced in their decisions by the political character of the member concerned. Only economic considerations shall be relevant to their decisions. Such considerations shall be weighed impartially in order to achieve and carry out the functions of the Bank.

(3) The President, Vice-Presidents, officers and staff of the Bank, in discharge of their offices, owe their duty entirely to the Bank and to no other authority. Each member of the Bank shall respect the international character of this duty and shall refrain from all attempts to influence any of them in the discharge of their duties.

Article 39

Offices of the Bank

(1) The principal office of the Bank shall be located in the territory of a member State. The choice of the location of the principal office of the Bank shall be made by the Board of Governors at its first meeting, taking into account the availability of facilities for the proper functioning of the Bank.

(2) Notwithstanding the provisions of article 35 of this Agreement, the choice of the location of the principal office of the Bank shall be made by the Board of Governors in accordance with the conditions that applied to the adoption of this Agreement.

(3) The Bank may establish branch offices or agencies elsewhere.

Article 40

Channel of communications; depositories

(1) Each member shall designate an appropriate authority with which the Bank may communicate in connexion with any matter arising under this Agreement.

(2) Each member shall designate its central bank or such other institution as may be agreed by the Bank, as a depository with which the Bank may keep its holdings of currency of that matter as well as other assets of the Bank.

(3) The Bank may hold its assets, including gold and convertible currencies, with such depositories as the Board of Directors shall determine.

Article 41

Publications of the Agreement, working languages, provision of information and reports

(1) The Bank shall endeavor to make available the text of this Agreement and all its important documents in the principal languages used in Africa. The working languages of the Bank shall be, if possible, African languages, English and French.

(2) Members shall furnish the Bank with all information it may request of them in order to facilitate the performance of its functions.

(3) The Bank shall publish and transmit to its members an annual report containing an audited statement of the accounts. It shall also transmit quarterly to the members a summary statement of its financial position and a profit and loss statement showing the results of its operations. The Annual Report and the Quarterly Statements shall be drawn up in accordance with the provisions of paragraph (4) of article 13 of this Agreement.

(4) The Bank may also publish such other reports as it deems desirable to carry out its purpose and functions. They shall be transmitted to the members of the Bank.

Article 42

Allocation of net income

(1) The Board of Governors shall determine annually what part of the net income of the Bank, including the net income accruing to its Special Funds, shall be allocated—after making provision for reserves—to surplus and what part, if any, shall be distributed.

(2) The distribution referred to in the preceding paragraph shall be made in proportion to the number of shares held by each member.

(3) Payments shall be made in such manner and in such currency as the Board of Governors shall determine.

CHAPTER VI

WITHDRAWAL AND SUSPENSION OF MEMBERS; TEMPORARY SUSPENSION AND TERMINATION OF OPERATIONS OF THE BANK

Article 43

Withdrawal

(1) Any member may withdraw from the Bank at any time by transmitting a notice in writing to the Bank at its principal office.

(2) Withdrawal by a member shall become effective on the date specified in its notice but in no event less than six months after the date that notice has been received by the Bank.

Article 44

Suspension

(1) If it appears to the Board of Directors that a member fails to fulfill any of its obligations to the Bank, that member shall be suspended by that Board unless the Board of Governors at a subsequent meeting, called by the Board of Directors for that purpose, decides otherwise by a decision taken by a majority of the governors exercising a majority of the total voting power of the members.

(2) A member so suspended shall automatically cease to be a member of the Bank one year from the date of suspension unless a decision is taken by the Board of Governors by the same majority to restore the member to good standing.

(3) While under suspension, a member shall not be entitled to exercise any rights under this Agreement, except the right of withdrawal, but shall remain subject to all obligations.

Article 45

Settlement of accounts

(1) After the date on which a State ceases to be a member (hereinafter in this article called the "termination date"), the member shall remain liable for its direct obligations to the Bank and for its contingent liabilities to the Bank so long as any part of the loans or guarantees contracted before the termination date is outstanding; but ti shall cease to incur liabilities with respect to loans and guarantees entered into thereafter by the Bank and to share either in the income or the expenses of the Bank.

(2) At the time a State ceases to be a member, the Bank shall arrange for the repurchase of its shares as a part of the settlement of accounts with that State in accordance with the provisions of paragraphs (3) and (4) of this article. For this purpose, the repurchase price of the shares shall be the value shown by the books of the Bank on the termination date.

(3) The payment for shares repurchased by the Bank under this article shall be governed by the following conditions:

    (*a*) Any amount due to the State concerned for its shares shall be withheld so long as the State, its central Bank or any of its agencies remains liable, as borrower or guarantor, to the Bank and such amount may, at the option of the Bank, be applied on any such liability as it matures. No amount shall be withheld on account of the liability of the State resulting from its subscription for shares in accordance with paragraph (4) of article 7 of this Agreement. In any event, no amount due to a member for its shares shall be paid until six months after the termination date.

(*b*) Payments for shares may be made from time to time, upon their surrender by the Government of the State concerned, to the extent by which the amount due as the repurchase price in accordance with paragraph (2) of this article exceeds the aggregate amount of liabilities on loans and guarantees referred to in subparagraph (*a*) of this paragraph until the former member has received the full repurchase price.

(*c*) Payments shall be made in the currency of the State receiving payment or, if such currency is not available, in gold or convertible currency.

(*d*) If losses are sustained by the Bank on any guarantees or loans which were outstanding on the termination date and the amount of such losses exceeds the amount of the reserve provided against losses on that date, the State concerned shall repay, upon demand, the amount by which the repurchase price o its shares would have been reduced, if the losses had been taken into account when the repurchase price was determined. In addition, the former member shall remain liable on any call for unpaid subscriptions in accordance with paragraph (4) of article 7 of this Agreement, to the extent that it would have been required to respond if the impairment of capital had occurred and the call had been made at the time the repurchase price of its shares was determined.

(4) If the Bank terminates its operations pursuant to article 47 of this Agreement within six months of the termination date, all rights of the State concerned shall be determined in accordance with the provisions of its articles 47 to 49.

Article 46

Temporary suspension of operations

In an emergency, the Board of Directors may suspend temporarily operations in respect of new loans and guarantees pending an opportunity for further consideration and action by the Board of Governors.

Article 47

Termination of operations

(1) The Bank may terminate its operations in respect of new loans and guarantees by a decision of the Board of Governors exercising a majority of the total voting power of the members.

(2) After such termination, the Bank shall forthwith cease all activities except those incident to the orderly realization, conservation and preservation of its assets and settlement of its obligations.

Article 48

Liability of members and payment of claims

(1) In the event of termination of the operations of the Bank, the liability of all members for uncalled subscriptions to the capital stock of the Bank and in respect of the depreciation of their currencies shall continue until all claims of creditors, including all contingent claims, shall have been discharged.

(2) All creditors holding direct claims shall be paid out of the assets of the Bank and then out of payments to the Bank on calls on unpaid subscriptions. Before making any payments to creditors holding direct claims, the Board of Directors shall make such arrangements as necessary, in its judgement, to ensure a *pro rata* distribution among holders of direct and contingent claims.

Article 49

Distribution of assets

(1) In the event of termination of operations of the Bank, no distribution shall be made to members on account of their subscriptions to the capital stock of the Bank until:

   (i) All liabilities to creditors have been discharged or provided for; and

   (ii) The Board of Governors has taken a decision to make a distribution. This decision shall be taken by the Board exercising a majority of the total voting power of the members.

(2) After a decision to make a distribution has been taken in accordance with the preceding paragraph, the Board of Directors may be a two-thirds majority vote make successive distributions of the assets of the Bank to members until all assets have been distributed. This distribution shall be subject to the prior settlement of all outstanding claims of the Bank against each member.

(3) Before any distribution of assets is made, the Board of Directors shall fix the proportionate share of each member according tot he ratio of its shareholding to the total outstanding shares of the Bank.

(4) The Board of Directors shall value the assets to be distributed at the date of distribution and then proceed to distribute in the following manner:

(*a*) There shall be paid to each member in its own obligations or those of its official agencies or legal entities within its territories, to the extend that they are available for distribution, an amount equivalent in value to its proportionate share of the total amount to be distributed.

(*b*) Any balance due to a member after payment has been made in accordance with the preceding sub-paragraph shall be paid in its currency, to the extent that it is held by the Bank, up to an amount equivalent in value to such balance.

(*c*) Any balance due to a member after payment has been made in accordance with sub-paragraph (*a*) and (*b*) of this paragraph shall be paid in gold or currency acceptable to that member, to the extent that they are held by the Bank, up to an amount equivalent in value to such balance.

(*d*) Any remaining assets held by the Bank after payments have been made to members in accordance with sub-paragraphs (*a*) to (*c*) of this paragraph shall be distributed *pro rata* among the members.

(5) Any member receiving assets distributed by the Bank in accordance with the preceding paragraph shall enjoy the same rights with respect to such assets as the Bank enjoyed before their distribution.

CHAPTER VII

STATUS, IMMUNITIES, EXEMPTIONS AND PRIVILEGES

Article 50

Status

To enable it to fulfil its purpose and the functions with which it is entrusted, the Bank shall possess full international personality. To those ends, it may enter into agreements with members, non-member States and other international organizations. To the same ends, the status, immunities, exemptions and privileges set forth in this chapter shall be accorded to the Bank in the territory of each member.

Article 51

Status in member countries

In the territory of each member the Bank shall possess full juridical personality and, in particular, full capacity:

(*a*) To contract;

(*b*) To acquire and dispose of immovable and movable property; and

(*c*) To institute legal proceedings.

Article 52

Judicial proceedings

(1) The Bank shall enjoy immunity from every form of legal process except in cases arising out of the exercise of its borrowing powers when it may be sued only in a court of competent jurisdiction in the territory of a member in which the Bank has its principal office, or in the territory of a member or non-member State where it has appointed an agent for the purpose of accepting service or notice of process or has issued or guaranteed securities. No actions shall, however, be brought by members or persons acting for or deriving claims from members.

(2) The property and assets of the Bank shall, wherever located and by whomsoever held, be immune from all forms of seizure, attachment or execution before the delivery of final judgement against the Bank.

Article 53

Immunity of assets and archives

(1) Property and assets of the Bank, wherever located and by whomsoever held, shall be immune from search, requisition, confiscation, expropriation or any other form of taking or foreclosure by executive or legislative action.

(2) The archives of the Bank and, in general, all documents belonging to it, or held by it, shall be inviolable, wherever located.

Article 54

Freedom of assets from restriction

To the extent necessary to carry out the purpose and functions of the Bank and subject to the provisions of this Agreement, all property and other assets of the Bank shall be exempt from restrictions, regulations, controls and moratoria of any nature.

Article 55

Privilege for communications

Official communications of the Bank shall be accorded by each member the same treatment that it accords to the official communications of other members.

Article 56

Personal immunities and privileges

(1) All governors, directors, alternates, officers and employees of the Bank:

    (i) Shall be immune from legal process with respect to acts performed by them in their official capacity;

    (ii) Where they are not local nationals, shall be accorded the same immunities from immigration restrictions, alien registration requirements and national service obligations, and the same facilities as regards exchange regulations as are accorded by members to the representatives, officials and employees of comparable rank of other members; and

    (iii) Shall be granted the same treatment in respect of travelling facilities as is accorded by members to representatives, officials and employees of comparable rank of other members.

(2) Experts and consultants performing missions for the Bank shall be accorded such immunities and privileges as are, in the opinion of the Bank, necessary for the independent exercise of their functions during the period their missions, including the time spent on journeys in connexion therewith.

Article 57

Exemption from taxation

(1) The Bank, its property, other assets, income and its operations and transactions shall be exempt from all taxation and from all customs duties. The Bank shall also be exempt from any obligation relating to the payment, withholding or collection of any tax or duty.

(2) No tax shall be levied on or in respect of salaries and emoluments paid by the Bank to directors, alternates, officers and other professional staff of the Bank.

(3) No tax of any kind shall be levied on any obligation or security issued by the Bank, including any dividend or interest thereon, by whomsoever held:

    (i) Which discriminates against such obligation or security solely because it is issued by the Bank; or

    (ii) If the sole jurisdictional basis for such taxation is the place or currency in which it is issued, made payable or paid, or the location of any office or place of business maintained by the Bank.

(4) No tax of any kind shall be levied on any obligation or security guaranteed by the Bank, including any dividend or interest thereon, by whomsoever held:

(i) Which discriminates against such obligation or security solely because it is guaranteed by the Bank; or

(ii) If the sole jurisdictional basis for such taxation is the location of any office or place of business maintained by the Bank.

Article 58

Notification of implementation

Each member shall promptly inform the Bank of the specific action which it has taken to make effective in its territory the provisions of this chapter.

Article 59

Application of immunities, end privileges

The immunities, exceptions and privileges provided in this chapter are granted in the interests of the Bank. The Board of Directors may waive, to such extent and upon such conditions as it may determine, the immunities and exemptions provided in articles 52, 54, 56, and 57 of this Agreement in cases where its action would in its opinion further the interests of the Bank. The President shall have the right and the duty to waive the immunity of any official in cases where, in his opinion, the immunity would impede the course of justice and can be waived without prejudice to the interests of the Bank.

CHAPTER VIII

AMENDMENTS, INTERPRETATION, ARBITRATION

Article 60

Amendments

(1) Any proposal to introduce modifications to this Agreement, whether emanating from a member, a governor or the Board of Directors, shall be communicated to the Chairman of the Board of Governors, who shall bring the proposal before that Board. If the proposed amendment is approved by the Board, the Bank shall certify the fact by formal communication addressed to the members.

(2) Notwithstanding paragraph (1) of this article, acceptance by all the members is required for any amendment modifying:

(i) The right secured by paragraph (2) of article 6 of this Agreement;

(ii) The limitation on liability provided in paragraph (5) of that article; and

(iii) The right to withdraw from the Bank provided in article 43 of this Agreement.

(3) Amendments shall enter into force for all members three months after the date of the formal communication provided for in paragraph (1) of this article unless the Board of Governors specifies a different period.

(4) Notwithstanding the provisions of paragraph (1) of this article, three years at the latest after the entry into force of this Agreement and in the light of the experience of the Bank, the rule according to which each member should have one vote shall be examined by the Board of Governors or at a meeting of Heads of State of the member countries in accordance with the conditions that applied to the adoption of this Agreement.

Article 61

Interpretation

(1) The English and French texts of this Agreement shall be regarded as equally authentic.

(2) Any question of interpretation of the provisions of this Agreement arising between any member and the Bank or between any members of the Bank shall be submitted to the Board of Directors for decision. If there is no director of its nationality on that Board, a member particularly affected by the question under consideration shall be entitled to direct representation in such cases. Such right of representation shall be regulated by the Board of Governors.

(3) In any case where the Board of Directors has given a decision under paragraph (2) of this article, any member may require that the quest be referred to the Board of Governors, whose decisions shall be sought—under procedure to be established in accordance with paragraph (3) of article 31 of this Agreement—within three months. That decision shall be final.

Article 62

Arbitration

In the case of a dispute between the Bank and the Government of a State which has ceased to be a member, or between the Bank and any member upon the termination of the operations of the Bank, such dispute shall be submitted to arbitration by a tribunal of three arbitrators. One of the arbitrators shall be appointed by the Bank, another by the Government of the State concerned, and the third arbitrator, unless the parties otherwise agree, shall be appointed by such other authority as may have been prescribed by regulations adopted by the Board of Governors. The third arbitrator shall have full power to settle all questions of procedure in any case where the parties are in disagreement with respect thereto.

CHAPTER IX

FINAL PROVISIONS

Article 63

Signature and deposit

(1) This Agreement, deposited with the Secretary-General of the United Nations (hereinafter called the "Depositary"), shall remain open until 31 December 1963 for signature by the Governments of States whose names are set forth in annex A to this Agreement.

(2) The Depositary shall communicate certified copies of this Agreement to all the Signatories.

Article 64

Ratification, acceptance, accession and acquisition of membership

(1) (*a*) This Agreement shall be subject to ratification or acceptance by the Signatories. Instruments of ratification or acceptance shall be deposited by the Signatory Governments with the Depositary before 1 July 1965. The Depositary shall notify each deposit and the date thereof to the other Signatories.

    (*b*) A State whose instrument of ratification or acceptance is deposited before the date on which this Agreement enters into force shall become a member of the Bank on that date. Any other Signatory which complies with the provisions of the preceding paragraph shall become a member on the date on which its instrument of ratification or acceptance is deposited.

(2) States which do not acquire membership of the Bank in accordance with the provisions of paragraph (1) of this article may become members—after the Agreement has entered into force—by accession thereto on such terms as the Board of Governors shall determine. The Government of any such State shall deposit, on or before a date appointed by that Board, an instrument of accession with the Depositary who shall notify such deposit and the date thereof to the Bank and to the parties to this Agreement. Upon the deposit, the State shall become member of the Bank on the appointed date.

Article 65

Entry into force

This Agreement shall enter into force upon the deposit of instruments of ratification or acceptance by twelve signatory Governments whose initial subscriptions, as set forth in annex A to this Agreement, in aggregate comprise not less than sixty-five per cent of the authorized capital stock of the Bank, provided always that 1 January 1964 shall be the earliest date on which this Agreement may enter into force in accordance with the provisions of this article.

Article 66

Commencement of operations

(1) As soon as this Agreement enters into force, each member shall appoint a governor, and the Trustee appointed for this purpose and for the purpose indicated in paragraph (5) of article 7 of this Agreement shall call the first meeting of the Board of Governors.

(2) At its first meeting, the Board of Governors:

> (*a*) Shall elect nine directors of the Bank in accordance with paragraph (1) of article 33 of this Agreement; and

> (*b*) make arrangements for the determination of the date on which the Bank shall commence its operations.

(3) The Bank shall notify its members of the date of the commencement of its operations.

Done in Khartoum, this fourth day of August nineteen hundred and sixty-three, in a single copy in the English and French languages.

[*Note:* Schedules are not reproduced here. These include information on initial subscriptions to the AfDB's capital stock.]

APPENDIX G
CHARTER OF THE AsDB

Citation: Agreement Establishing the Asian Development Bank, done at Manila, December 4, 1965 (entered into force Aug. 22, 1966), 571 U.N.T.S. 132, 17 U.S.T. 1418, T.I.A.S. No. 6103; 5 I.L.M. 262 (1966). [Available also as appended to John W. Head, Asian Development Bank, in INTERNATIONAL ENCYCLOPAEDIA OF LAWS *(2002).]*

Contents

Agreement Establishing the Asian Development Bank

THE CONTRACTING PARTIES

CONSIDERING the importance of closer economic co-operation as a means for achieving the most efficient utilization of resources and for accelerating the economic development of Asia and the Far East;

REALIZING the significance of making additional development financing available for the region by mobilizing such funds and other resources both from within and outside the region, and by seeking to create and foster conditions conducive to increased domestic savings and greater flow of development funds into the region;

RECOGNIZING the desirability of promoting the harmonious growth of the economies of the region and the expansion of external trade of member countries;

CONVINCED that the establishment of a financial institution that is Asian in its basic character would serve these ends;

HAVE AGREED to establish hereby the Asian Development Bank (hereinafter called the "Bank") which shall operate in accordance with the following:

Chapter I

PURPOSE, FUNCTIONS AND MEMBERSHIP

Article 1

PURPOSE

The purpose of the Bank shall be to foster economic growth and co-operation in the region of Asia and the Far East (hereinafter referred to as the "region") and to contribute to the acceleration of the process of economic development of the developing member countries in the region, collectively and individually. Wherever used in this Agreement, the terms "region of Asia and the Far East" and "region" shall comprise the territories of Asia and the Far East included in the Terms of Reference of the United Nations Economic Commission for Asia and the Far East.

Article 2

FUNCTIONS

To fulfil its purpose, the Bank shall have the following functions:

(i) to promote investment in the region of public and private capital for development purposes;

(ii) to utilize the resources at its disposal for financing development of the developing member countries in the region, giving priority to those regional, sub-regional as well as national projects and programmes which will contribute most effectively to the harmonious economic growth of the region as a whole, and having special regard to the needs of the smaller or less developed member countries in the region;

(iii) to meet requests from members in the region to assist them in the coordination of their development policies and plans with a view to achieving better utilization of their resources, making their economies more complementary, and promoting the orderly expansion of their foreign trade, in particular, intra-regional trade;

(iv) to provide technical assistance for the preparation, financing and execution of development projects and programmes, including the formulation of specific project proposals;

(v) to co-operate, in such manner as the Bank may deem appropriate, within the terms of this Agreement, with the United Nations, its organs and subsidiary bodies including, in particular, the Economic Commission for Asia and the Far East, and with public international organizations and other international institutions, as well as national entities whether public or private, which are concerned with the investment of development funds in the region, and to interest such institutions and entities in new opportunities for investment and assistance; and

(vi) to undertake such other activities and provide such other services as may advance its purpose.

Article 3

MEMBERSHIP

1.   Membership in the Bank shall be open to: (i) members and associate members of the United Nations Economic Commission for Asia and the Far East; and (ii) other regional countries and non-regional developed countries which are members of the United Nations or of any of its specialized agencies.

2.   Countries eligible for membership under paragraph 1 of this Article which do not become members in accordance with Article 64 of this Agreement may be admitted, under such terms and conditions as the Bank may determine, to membership in the Bank upon the affirmative vote of two-thirds of the total number of Governors, representing not less than three-fourths of the total voting power of the members.

3.   In the case of associate members of the United Nations Economic Commission for Asia and the Far East which are not responsible for the conduct of their international relations, application for membership in the Bank shall be presented by the member of the Bank responsible for the international relations of the applicant and accompanied by an undertaking by such member that, until the applicant itself assumes such responsibility, the member shall be responsible for all obligations that may be incurred by the applicant by reason of admission to membership in the Bank and enjoyment of the benefits of such membership. "Country" as used in this Agreement shall include a territory which is an associate member of the United Nations Economic Commission for Asia and the Far East.

Chapter II

CAPITAL

Article 4

AUTHORIZED CAPITAL

1.   The authorized capital stock of the Bank shall be one billion dollars ($1,000,000,000) in terms of United States dollars of the weight and fineness in effect on 31 January 1966. The dollar wherever referred to in this Agreement shall be understood as being a United States dollar of the above value. The authorized capital stock shall be divided into one hundred thousand (100,000) shares having a par value of ten thousand dollars ($ 10,000) each, which shall be available for subscription only by members in accordance with the provisions of Article 5 of this Agreement.

2.   The original authorized capital stock shall be divided into paid-in shares and callable shares. Shares having an aggregate par value of five hundred

million dollars ($ 500,000,000) shall be paid-in shares, and shares having an aggregate par value of five hundred million dollars ($ 500,000,000) shall be callable shares.

3. The authorized capital stock of the Bank may be increased by the Board of Governors, at such time and under such terms and conditions as it may deem advisable, by a vote of two-thirds of the total number of Governors, representing not less than three-fourths of the total voting power of the members.

Article 5

SUBSCRIPTION OF SHARES

1. Each member shall subscribe to shares of the capital stock of the Bank. Each subscription to the original authorized capital stock shall be for paid-in shares and callable shares in equal parts. The initial number of shares to be subscribed by countries which become members in accordance with Article 64 of this Agreement shall be that set forth in Annex A hereof. The initial number of shares to be subscribed by countries which are admitted to membership in accordance with paragraph 2 of Article 3 of this Agreement shall be determined by the Board of Governors; provided, however, that no such subscription shall be authorized which would have the effect of reducing the percentage of capital stock held by regional members below sixty (60) per cent of the total subscribed capital stock.

2. The Board of Governors shall at intervals of not less than five (5) years review the capital stock of the Bank. In case of an increase in the authorized capital stock, each member shall have a reasonable opportunity to subscribe, under such terms and conditions as the Board of Governors shall determine, to a proportion of the increase of stock equivalent to the proportion which its stock theretofore subscribed bears to the total subscribed capital stock immediately prior to such increase; provided, however, that the foregoing provision shall not apply in respect of any increase or portion of an increase in the authorized capital stock intended solely to give effect to determinations of the Board of Governors under paragraphs 1 and 3 of this Article. No member shall be obligated to subscribe to any part of an increase of capital stock.

3. The Board of Governors may, at the request of a member, increase the subscription of such member on such terms and conditions as the Board may determine; provided, however, that no such increase in the subscription of any member shall be authorized which would have the effect of reducing the percentage of capital stock held by regional members below sixty (60) per cent of the total subscribed capital stock. The Board of Governors shall pay special regard to the request of any regional member

having less than six (6) per cent of the subscribed capital stock to increase its proportionate share thereof.

4. Shares of stock initially subscribed by members shall be issued at par. Other shares shall be issued at par unless the Board of Governors by a vote of a majority of the total number of Governors, representing a majority of the total voting power of the members, decides in special circumstances to issue them on other terms.

5. Shares of stock shall not be pledged or encumbered in any manner whatsoever, and they shall not be transferable except to the Bank in accordance with Chapter VII of this Agreement.

6. The liability of the members on shares shall be limited to the unpaid portion of their issue price.

7. No member shall be liable, by reason of its membership, for obligations of the Bank.

Article 6

PAYMENT OF SUBSCRIPTIONS

1. Payment of the amount initially subscribed by each Signatory to this Agreement which becomes a member in accordance with Article 64 to The paid-in capital stock of the Bank shall be made in five (5) instalments, of twenty (20) per cent each of such amount. The first instalment shall be paid by each member within thirty (30) days after entry into force of this Agreement, or on or before the date of deposit on its behalf of its instrument of ratification or acceptance in accordance with paragraph 1 of Article 64, whichever is later. The second instalment shall become due one (1) year from the entry into force of this Agreement. The remaining three (3) instalments shall each become due successively one (1) year from the date on which the preceding instalment becomes due.

2. Of each instalment for the payment of initial subscriptions to the original paid-in capital stock:

   (a) Fifty (50) per cent shall be paid in gold or convertible currency; and

   (b) Fifty (50) per cent in the currency of the member.

3. The Bank shall accept from any member promissory notes or other obligations issued by the Government of the member, or by the depository designated by such member, in lieu of the amount to be paid in the currency of the member pursuant to paragraph 2 (b) of this Article, provided such is not required by the Bank for the conduct of its operations. Such

notes or obligations shall be non-negotiable, non-interest-bearing, and payable to the Bank at par value upon demand. Subject to the provisions of paragraph 2(ii) of Article 24, demands upon such notes or obligations payable in convertible currencies shall, over reasonable periods of time, be uniform in percentage on all such notes or obligations.

4. Each payment of a member in its own currency under paragraph 2(b) of this Article shall be in such amount as the Bank, after such consultation with the International Monetary Fund as the Bank may consider necessary and utilizing the par value established with the International Monetary Fund, if any, determines to be equivalent to the full value in terms of dollars of the portion of the subscription being paid. The initial payment shall be in such amount as the member considers appropriate hereunder but shall be subject to such adjustment, to be effected within ninety (90) days of the date on which such payment was due, as the Bank shall determine to be necessary to constitute the full dollar equivalent of such payment.

5. Payment of the amount subscribed to the callable capital stock of the Bank shall be subject to call only as and when required by the Bank to meet its obligations incurred under sub-paragraphs (ii) and (iv) of Article 11 on borrowings of funds for inclusion in its ordinary capital resources or on guarantees chargeable to such resources.

6. In the event of the call referred to in paragraph 5 of this Article, payment may be made at the option of the member in gold, convertible currency or in the currency required to discharge the obligations of the Bank for the purpose of which the call is made. Calls on unpaid subscriptions shall be uniform in percentage on all callable shares.

7. The Bank shall determine the place for any payment under this Article, provided that, until the inaugural meeting of its Board of Governors, the payment of the first instalment referred to in paragraph 1 of this Article shall be made to the Secretary-General of the United Nations, as Trustee for the Bank.

Article 7

ORDINARY CAPITAL RESOURCES

As used in this Agreement, the term "ordinary capital resources" of the Bank shall include the following:

(i) authorized capital stock of the Bank, including both paid-in and callable shares, subscribed pursuant to Article 5 of this Agreement, except such part thereof as may be set aside into one or more Special Funds in accordance with paragraph 1(i) of Article 19 of this Agreement;

(ii) funds raised by borrowings of the Bank by virtue of powers conferred by sub-paragraph (i) of Article 21 of this Agreement, to which the commitment to calls provided for in paragraph 5 of Article 6 of this Agreement is applicable;

(iii) funds received in repayment of loans or guarantees made with the resources indicated in (i) and (ii) of this Article;

(iv) income derived from loans made from the aforementioned funds or from guarantees to which the commitment to calls set forth in paragraph 5 of Article 6 of this Agreement is applicable; and

(v) any other funds or income received by the Bank which do not form part of its Special Funds resources referred to in Article 20 of this Agreement.

Chapter III

OPERATIONS

Article 8

USE OF RESOURCES

The resources and facilities of the Bank shall be used exclusively to implement the purpose and functions set forth respectively in Articles 1 and 2 of this Agreement.

Article 9

ORDINARY AND SPECIAL OPERATIONS

1. The operations of the Bank shall consist of ordinary operations and special operations.

2. Ordinary operations shall be those financed from the ordinary capital resources of the Bank.

3. Special operations shall be those financed from the Special Funds resources referred to in Article 20 of this Agreement.

Article 10

SEPARATION OF OPERATIONS

1. The ordinary capital resources and the Special Funds resources of the Bank shall at all times and in all respects be held, used, committed, invested or otherwise disposed of entirely separate from each other. The financial statements of the Bank shall show the ordinary operations and special operations separately.

2. The ordinary capital resources of the Bank shall under no circumstances be charged with, or used to discharge, losses or liabilities arising out of special operations or other activities for which Special Funds resources were originally used or committed.

3. Expenses appertaining directly to ordinary operations shall be charged to the ordinary capital resources of the Bank. Expenses appertaining directly to special operations shall be charged to the Special Funds resources. Any other expenses shall be charged as the Bank shall determine.

Article 11

RECIPIENTS AND METHODS OF OPERATION

Subject to the conditions stipulated in this Agreement, the Bank may provide or facilitate financing to any member, or any agency, instrumentality or political subdivision thereof, or any entity or enterprise operating in the territory of a member, as well as to international or regional agencies or entities concerned with economic development of the region. The Bank may carry out its operations in any of the following ways:

(i) by making or participating in direct loans with its unimpaired paid-in capital and, except as provided in Article 17 of this Agreement, with its reserves and undistributed surplus; or with the unimpaired Special Funds resources;

(ii) by making or participating in direct loans with funds raised by the Bank in capital markets or borrowed or otherwise acquired by the Bank for inclusion in its ordinary capital resources;

(iii) by investment of funds referred to in (i) and (ii) of this Article in the equity capital of an institution or enterprise, provided no such investment shall be made until after the Board of Governors, by a vote of a majority of the total number of Governors, representing a majority of the total voting power of the members, shall have determined that the Bank is in a position to commence such type of operations; or

(iv) by guaranteeing, whether as primary or secondary obligor, in whole or in part, loans for economic development participated in by the Bank.

Article 12

LIMITATIONS ON ORDINARY OPERATIONS

1. The total amount outstanding of loans, equity investments and guarantees made by the Bank in its ordinary operations shall not at any time exceed the total amount of its unimpaired subscribed capital, reserves and

surplus included in its ordinary capital resources, exclusive of the special reserve provided for by Article 17 of this Agreement and other reserves not available for ordinary operations.

2. In the case of loans made with funds borrowed by the Bank to which the commitment to calls provided for by paragraph 5 of Article 6 of this Agreement is applicable, the total amount of principal outstanding and payable to the Bank in a specific currency shall not at any time exceed the total amount of the principal of outstanding borrowings by the Bank that are payable in the same currency.

3. In the case of funds invested in equity capital out of the ordinary capital resources of the Bank, the total amount invested shall not exceed ten (10) per cent of the aggregate amount of the unimpaired paid-in capital stock of the Bank actually paid up at any given time together with the reserves and surplus included in its ordinary capital resources, exclusive of the special reserve provided for in Article 17 of this Agreement.

4. The amount of any equity investment shall not exceed such percentage of the equity capital of the entity or enterprise concerned as the Board of Directors shall in each specific case determine to be appropriate. The Bank shall not seek to obtain by such an investment a controlling interest in the entity or enterprise concerned, except where necessary to safeguard the investment of the Bank.

Article 13

PROVISION OF CURRENCIES FOR DIRECT LOANS

In making direct loans or participating in them, the Bank may provide financing in any of the following ways:

(i) by furnishing the borrower with currencies other than the currency of the member in whose territory the project concerned is to be carried out (The latter currency hereinafter to be called "local currency"), which are necessary to meet the foreign exchange costs of such project; or

(ii) by providing financing to meet local expenditures on the project concerned, where it can do so by supplying local currency without selling any of its holdings in gold or convertible currencies. In special cases when, in the opinion of the Bank, the project causes or is likely to cause undue loss or strain on the balance of payments of the member in whose territory the project is to be carried out, the financing granted by the Bank to meet local expenditures may be provided in currencies other than that of such member; in such cases, the amount of the financing granted by the Bank for this purpose shall not exceed a reasonable portion of the total local expenditure incurred by the borrower.

Article 14

OPERATING PRINCIPLES

The operations of the Bank shall be conducted in accordance with the following principles:

(i) The operations of the Bank shall provide principally for the financing of specific projects, including those forming part of a national, sub-regional or regional development programme. They may, however, include loans to, or guarantees of loans made to, national development banks or other suitable entities, in order that the latter may finance specific development projects whose individual financing requirements are not, in the opinion of the Bank, large enough to warrant the direct supervision of the Bank;

(ii) In selecting suitable projects, the Bank shall always be guided by the provisions of sub-paragraph (ii) of Article 2 of this Agreement;

(iii) The Bank shall not finance any undertaking in the territory of a member if that member objects to such financing;

(iv) Before a loan is granted, the applicant shall have submitted an adequate loan proposal and the President of the Bank shall have presented to the Board of Directors a written report regarding the proposal, together with his recommendations, on the basis of a staff study;

(v) In considering an application for a loan or guarantee, the Bank shall pay due regard to the ability of the borrower to obtain financing or facilities elsewhere on terms and conditions that the Bank considers reasonable for the recipient, taking into account all pertinent factors;

(vi) In making or guaranteeing a loan, the Bank shall pay due regard to the prospects that the borrower and its guarantor, if any, will be in a position to meet their obligations under the loan contract;

(vii) In making or guaranteeing a loan, the rate of interest, other charges and the schedule for repayment of principal shall be such as are, in the opinion of the Bank, appropriate for the loan concerned;

(viii) In guaranteeing a loan made by other investors, or in underwriting the sale of securities, the Bank shall receive suitable compensation for its risk;

(ix) The proceeds of any loan, investment or other financing under-taken in the ordinary operations of the Bank or with Special Funds established by the Bank pursuant to paragraph 1 (i) of Article 19, shall be used only for procurement in member countries of goods and services produced in member countries, except in any case in which the Board of Directors by a vote of the Directors representing not less than two-thirds of the total voting power of the members, determines to permit procurement in a non-member country or of goods and services produced in a non-member country in special circumstances making such procurement appropriate, as in the case of a non-member country in which a significant amount of financing has been provided to the Bank;

(x)   In the case of a direct loan made by the Bank, the borrower shall be permitted by the Bank to draw its funds only to meet expenditures in connexion with the project as they are actually incurred;

(xi) The Bank shall take the necessary measures to ensure that the proceeds of any loan made, guaranteed or participated in by the Bank are used only for the purposes for which the loan was granted and with due attention to considerations of economy and efficiency;

(xii) The Bank shall pay due regard to the desirability of avoiding a disproportionate amount of its resources being used for the benefit of any member;

(xiii) The Bank shall seek to maintain reasonable diversification in its investments in equity capital; it shall not assume responsibility for managing any entity or enterprise in which it has an investment, except where necessary to safeguard its investments; and

(xiv) The Bank shall be guided by sound banking principles in its operations.

Article 15

TERMS AND CONDITIONS FOR DIRECT LOANS AND GUARANTEES

1. In the case of direct loans made or participated in or loans guaranteed by the Bank, the contract shall establish, in conformity with the operating principles set forth in Article 14 of this Agreement and subject to the other provisions of this Agreement, the terms and conditions for the loan or the guarantee concerned, including those relating to payment of principal, interest and other charges, maturities, and dates of payment in respect of the loan, or the fees and other charges in respect of the guarantee, respectively. In particular, the contract shall provide that, subject to paragraph 3 of this Article, all payments to the Bank under the contract shall be made

in the currency loaned, unless, in the case of a direct loan made or a loan guaranteed as part of special operations with funds provided under paragraph 1 (ii) of Article 19, the rules and regulations of the Bank provide otherwise. Guarantees by the Bank shall also provide that the Bank may terminate its liability with respect to interest if, upon default by the borrower and the guarantor, if any, the Bank offers to purchase, at par and interest accrued to a date designated in the offer, the bonds or other obligations guaranteed.

2.   Where the recipient of loans or guarantees of loans is not itself a member, the Bank may, when it deems it advisable, require that the member in whose territory the project concerned is to be carried out, or a public agency or any instrumentality of that member acceptable to the Bank, guarantee the repayment of the principal and the payment of interest and other charges on the loan in accordance with the terms thereof.

3.   The loan or guarantee contract shall expressly state the currency in which all payments to the Bank thereunder shall be made. At the option of the borrower, however, such payments may always be made in gold or convertible currency.

Article 16

COMMISSION AND FEES

1.   The Bank shall charge, in addition to interest, a commission on direct loans made or participated in as part of its ordinary operations. This commission, payable periodically, shall be computed on the amount outstanding on each loan or participation and shall be at the rate of not less than one (1) per cent per annum, unless the Bank, after the first five (5) years of its operations, decides to reduce this minimum rate by a two-thirds majority of its members, representing not less than three-fourths of the total voting power of the members.

2.   In guaranteeing a loan as part of its ordinary operations, the Bank shall charge a guarantee fee, at a rate determined by the Board of Directors, payable periodically on the amount of the loan outstanding.

3.   Other charges of the Bank in its ordinary operations and any commission, fees or other charges in its special operations shall be determined by the Board of Directors.

Article 17

SPECIAL RESERVE

The amount of commissions and guarantee fees received by the Bank pursuant to Article 16 of this Agreement shall be set aside as a special reserve which shall be kept for meeting liabilities of the Bank in accordance with Article 18 of this Agreement. The special reserve shall be held in such liquid form as the Board of Directors may decide.

Article 18

METHODS OF MEETING LIABILITIES OF THE BANK

1. In cases of default on loans made, participated in or guaranteed by the Bank in its ordinary operations, the Bank shall take such action as it deems appropriate with respect to modifying the terms of the loan, other than the currency of repayment.

2. The payments in discharge of the Bank's liabilities on borrowings or guarantees under sub-paragraphs (ii) and (iv) of Article 11 chargeable to the ordinary capital resources shall be charged:

   (i) First, against the special reserve provided for in Article 17;

   (ii) Then, to the extent necessary and at the discretion of the Bank, against the other reserves, surplus and capital available to the Bank.

3. Whenever necessary to meet contractual payments of interest, other charges or amortization on borrowings of the Bank in its ordinary operations, or to meet its liabilities with respect to similar payments in respect of loans guaranteed by it, chargeable to its ordinary capital resources, the Bank may call an appropriate amount of the uncalled subscribed callable capital in accordance with paragraphs 6 and 7 of Article 6 of this Agreement.

4. In cases of default in respect of a loan made from borrowed funds or guaranteed by the Bank as part of its ordinary operations, the Bank may, if it believes that the default may be of long duration, call an additional amount of such callable capital not to exceed in any one (1) year one (1) per cent of the total subscriptions of the members to such capital, for the following purposes:

   (i) To redeem before maturity, or otherwise discharge, the Bank's liability on all or part of the outstanding principal of any loan guaranteed by it in respect of which the debtor is in default; and

   (ii) To repurchase, or otherwise discharge, the Bank's liability on all or part of its own outstanding borrowing.

5. If the Bank's subscribed callable capital stock shall be entirely called pursuant to paragraphs 3 and 4 of this Article, the Bank may, if necessary for the purposes specified in paragraph 3 of this Article, use or exchange the currency of any member without restriction, including any restriction imposed pursuant to paragraphs 2 (i) and (ii) of Article 24.

Article 19

SPECIAL FUNDS

1. The Bank may:

    (i) set aside, by a vote of two-thirds of the total number of Governors, representing at least three-fourths of the total voting power of the members, not more than ten (10) per cent each of the portion of the unimpaired paid-in capital of the Bank paid by members pursuant to paragraph 2(a) of Article 6 and of the portion thereof paid pursuant to paragraph 2(b) of Article 6, and establish therewith one or more Special Funds; and

    (ii) accept the administration of Special Funds which are designed to serve the purpose and come within the functions of the Bank.

2. Special Funds established by the Bank pursuant to paragraph 1(i) of this Article may be used to guarantee or make loans of high developmental priority, with longer maturities, longer deferred commencement of repayment and lower interest rates than those established by the Bank for its ordinary operations. Such Funds may also be used on such other terms and conditions, not inconsistent with the applicable provisions of this Agreement nor with the character of such Funds as revolving funds, as the Bank in establishing such Funds may direct.

3. Special Funds accepted by the Bank under paragraph 1(ii) of this Article may be used in any manner and on any terms and conditions not inconsistent with the purpose of the Bank and with the agreement relating to such Funds.

4. The Bank shall adopt such special rules and regulations as may be required for the establishment, administration and use of each Special Fund. Such rules and regulations shall be consistent with the provisions of this Agreement, excepting those provisions expressly applicable only to ordinary operations of the Bank.

Article 20

SPECIAL FUNDS RESOURCES

As used in this Agreement, the term "Special Funds resources" shall refer to the resources of any Special Fund and shall include:

(a) resources set aside from the paid-in capital to a Special Fund or otherwise initially contributed to any Special Fund;

(b) funds accepted by the Bank for inclusion in any Special Fund;

(c) funds repaid in respect of loans or guarantees financed from the resources of any Special Fund which, under the rules and regulations of the Bank governing that Special Fund, are received by such Special Fund;

(d) income derived from operations of the Bank in which any of the aforementioned resources or funds are used or committed if, under the rules and regulations of the Bank governing the Special Fund concerned, that income accrues to such Special Fund; and

(e) any other resources placed at the disposal of any Special Fund.

Chapter IV

BORROWING AND OTHER MISCELLANEOUS POWERS

Article 21

GENERAL POWERS

In addition to the powers specified elsewhere in this Agreement, the Bank shall have the power to:

(i) borrow funds in member countries or elsewhere, and in this connexion to furnish such collateral or other security therefor as the Bank shall determine, provided always that:

  (a) before making a sale of its obligations in the territory of a country, the Bank shall have obtained its approval;

  (b) where the obligations of the Bank are to be denominated in the currency of a member, the bank shall have obtained its approval;

  (c) the Bank shall obtain the approval of the countries referred to in sub-paragraphs (a) and (b) of this paragraph that the proceeds may be exchanged for the currency of any member without restriction; and

  (d) before determining to sell its obligations in a particular country, the Bank shall consider the amount of previous borrowing, if any, in that country, the amount of previous borrowing in other countries, and the possible availability of funds in such other countries; and shall give due regard to the general principle that its borrowings should to the greatest extent possible be diversified as to country of borrowing.

(ii) buy and sell securities the Bank has issued or guaranteed or in which it has invested, provided always that it shall have obtained the approval of any country in whose territory the securities are to be bought or sold;

(iii) guarantee securities in which it has invested in order to facilitate their sale;

(iv)   underwrite, or participate in the underwriting of, securities issued by any entity or enterprise for purposes consistent with the purpose of the Bank;

(v)   invest funds, not needed in its operations, in the territories of members in such obligations of members or nationals thereof as it may determine, and invest funds held by the Bank for pensions or similar purposes in the territories of members in marketable securities issued by members or nationals thereof;

(vi)   provide technical advice and assistance which serve its purpose and come within its functions, and where expenditures incurred in furnishing such services are not reimbursable, charge the net income of the Bank therewith; in the first five (5) years of its operations, the Bank may use up to two (2) per cent of its paid-in capital for furnishing such services on a non-reimbursable basis, and

(vii)   exercise such other powers and establish such rules and regulations as may be necessary or appropriate in furtherance of its purpose and functions, consistent with the provisions of this Agreement.

Article 22

NOTICE TO BE PLACED ON SECURITIES

Every security issued or guaranteed by the Bank shall bear on its face a conspicuous statement to the effect that it is not an obligation of any Government, unless it is in fact the obligation of a particular Government, in which case it shall so state.

Chapter V

CURRENCIES

Article 23

DETERMINATION OF CONVERTIBILITY

Whenever it shall become necessary under this Agreement to determine whether any currency is convertible, such determination shall be made by the Bank after consultation with the International Monetary Fund.

Article 24

USE OF CURRENCIES

1.   Members may not maintain or impose any restrictions on the holding or use by the Bank or by any recipient from the Bank, for payments in any country, of the following:

(i)   gold or convertible currencies received by the Bank in payment of subscriptions to its capital stock, other than that paid to the Bank by members pursuant to paragraph 2(b) of Article 6 and restricted pursuant to paragraphs 2(i) and (ii) of this Article;

(ii) currencies of members purchased with the gold or convertible currencies referred to in the preceding sub-paragraph;

(iii) currencies obtained by the Bank by borrowing, pursuant to sub-paragraph (i) of Article 21 of this Agreement, for inclusion in its ordinary capital resources;

(iv) gold or currencies received by the Bank in payment on account of principal, interest, dividends or other charges in respect of loans or investments made out of any of the funds referred to in sub-paragraphs (i) to (iii) of this paragraph or in payment of fees in respect of guarantees made by the Bank; and

(v)   currencies, other than the member's own currency, received by the member from the Bank in distribution of the net income of the Bank in accordance with Article 40 of this Agreement.

2.   Members may not maintain or impose any restriction on the holding or use by the Bank or by any recipient from the Bank, for payments in any country, of currency of a member received by the Bank which does not come within the provisions of the preceding paragraph, unless:

(i)   a developing member country, after consultation with and subject to periodic review by the Bank, restricts in whole or in part the use of such currency to payments for goods or services produced and intended for use in its territory; or

(ii) any other member whose subscription has been determined in Part A of Annex A hereof and whose exports of industrial products do not represent a substantial proportion of its total exports, deposits with its instrument of ratification or acceptance a declaration that it desires the use of the portion of its subscription paid pursuant to paragraph 2(b) of Article 6 to be restricted, in whole or in part, to payments for goods or services produced in its territory; provided that such restrictions be subject to periodic review by and consultation with the Bank and that any purchases of goods or services in the territory of that member, subject to the usual consideration of competitive tendering, shall be first charged against the portion of its subscription paid pursuant to paragraph 2(b) of Article 6; or

(iii) such currency forms part of the Special Funds resources of the Bank available under paragraph 1(ii) of Article 19 and its use is subject to special rules and regulations.

3.   Members may not maintain or impose any restrictions on the holding or use by the Bank, for making amortization payments or anticipatory payments or for repurchasing in whole or in part the Bank's own obligations, of currencies received by the Bank in repayment of direct loans made out of its ordinary capital resources, provided, however, that until the Bank's subscribed callable capital stock has been entirely called, such holding or use shall be subject to any limitations imposed pursuant to paragraph 2(i) of this Article except in respect of obligations payable in the currency of the member concerned.

4.   Gold or currencies held by the Bank shall not be used by the Bank to purchase other currencies of members or non-members except:

(i)   in order to meet its obligations in the ordinary course of its business; or

(ii)   pursuant to a decision of the Board of Directors adopted by a vote of the Directors representing not less than two-thirds of the total voting power of the members.

5.   Nothing herein contained shall prevent the Bank from using the currency of any member for administrative expenses incurred by the Bank in the territory of such member.

Article 25

MAINTENANCE OF VALUE OF THE CURRENCY HOLDINGS OF THE BANK

1.   Whenever (a) the par value in the International Monetary Fund of the currency of a member is reduced in terms of the dollar defined in Article 4 of this Agreement, or (b) in the opinion of the Bank, after consultation with the International Monetary Fund, the foreign exchange value of a member's currency has depreciated to a significant extent, that member shall pay to the Bank within a reasonable time an additional amount of its currency required to maintain the value of all such currency held by the Bank, excepting (a) currency derived by the Bank from its borrowings and (b) unless otherwise provided in the agreement establishing such Funds, Special Funds resources accepted by the Bank under paragraph 1(ii) of Article 19.

2.   Whenever (a) the par value in the International Monetary Fund of the currency of a member is increased in terms of the said dollar, or (b) in the opinion of the Bank, after consultation with the International Monetary Fund, the foreign exchange value of a member's currency has appreciated to a significant extent, the Bank shall pay to that member within a reasonable time an amount of that currency required to adjust the value of all such currency held by the Bank excepting (a) currency derived by the Bank from its borrowings, and (b) unless otherwise provided in the agree-

ment establishing such Funds, Special Funds resources accepted by the Bank under paragraph 1(ii) of Article 19.

3.   The Bank may waive the provisions of this Article when a uniform proportionate change in the par value of the currencies of all its members takes place.

Chapter VI

ORGANIZATION AND MANAGEMENT

Article 26

STRUCTURE

The Bank shall have a Board of Governors, a Board of Directors, a President, one or more Vice-Presidents and such other officers and staff as may be considered necessary.

Article 27

BOARD OF GOVERNORS: COMPOSITION

1.   Each member shall be represented on the Board of Governors and shall appoint one Governor and one alternate. Each Governor and alternate shall serve at the pleasure of the appointing member. No alternate may vote except in the absence of his principal. At its annual meeting, the Board shall designate one of the Governors as Chairman who shall hold office until the election of the next Chairman and the next annual meeting of the Board.

2.   Governors and alternates shall serve as such without remuneration from the Bank, but the Bank may pay them reasonable expenses incurred in attending meetings.

Article 28

BOARD OF GOVERNORS: POWERS

1.   All the powers of the Bank shall be vested in the Board of Governors.

2.   The Board of Governors may delegate to the Board of Directors any or all its powers, except the power to:

   (i)   admit new members and determine the conditions of their admission;

   (ii) increase or decrease the authorized capital stock of the Bank;

   (iii) suspend a member;

   (iv) decide appeals from interpretations or applications of this Agreement given by the Board of Directors;

(v)   authorize the conclusion of general agreements for co-operation with other international organizations;

(vi)   elect the Directors and the President of the Bank;

(vii)   determine the remuneration of the Directors and their alternates and the salary and other terms of the contract of service of the President;

(viii) approve, after reviewing the auditor's report, the general balance sheet and the statement of profit and loss of the Bank;

(ix)   determine the reserves and the distribution of the net profits of the Bank;

(x)   amend this Agreement;

(xi)   decide to terminate the operations of the Bank and to distribute its assets; and

(xii)   exercise such other powers as are expressly assigned to the Board of Governors in this Agreement.

3.   The Board of Governors shall retain full power to exercise authority over any matter delegated to the Board of Directors under paragraph 2 of this Article.

4.   For the purposes of this Agreement, the Board of Governors may, by a vote of two-thirds of the total number of Governors, representing not less than three-fourths of the total voting power of the members, from time to time determine which countries or members of the Bank are to be regarded as developed or developing countries or members, taking into account appropriate economic considerations.

Article 29

BOARD OF GOVERNORS: PROCEDURE

1.   The Board of Governors shall hold an annual meeting and such other meetings as may be provided for by the Board or called by the Board of Directors. Meetings of the Board of Governors shall be called, by the Board of Directors, whenever requested by five (5) members of the Bank.

2.   A majority of the Governors shall constitute a quorum for any meeting of the Board of Governors, provided such majority represents not less than two-thirds of the total voting power of the members.

3.   The Board of Governors may by regulation establish a procedure whereby the Board of Directors may, when the latter deems such action advisable, obtain a vote of the Governors on a specific question without calling a meeting of the Board of Governors.

4. The Board of Governors, and the Board of Directors to the extent authorized, may establish such subsidiary bodies as may be necessary or appropriate to conduct the business of the Bank.

Article 30

BOARD OF DIRECTORS: COMPOSITION

1. (i) the Board of Directors shall be composed of ten (10) members who shall not be members of the Board of Governors, and of whom:

   (a) seven (7) shall be elected by the Governors representing regional members; and

   (b) three (3) by the Governors representing non-regional members.

   Directors shall be persons of high competence in economic and financial matters and shall be elected in accordance with Annex B hereof.

   (ii) At the Second Annual Meeting of the Board of Governors after its inaugural meeting, the Board of Governors shall review the size and composition of the Board of Directors, and shall increase the number of Directors as appropriate, paying special regard to the desirability, in the circumstances at that time, of increasing representation in the Board of Directors of smaller less developed member countries. Decisions under this paragraph should be made by a vote of a majority of the total number of Governors, representing not less than two-thirds of the total voting power of the members.

2. Each Director shall appoint an alternate with full power to act for him when he is not present. Directors and alternates shall be nationals of member countries. No two or more Directors may be of the same nationality nor may any two or more alternates be of the same nationality. An alternate may participate in meetings of the Board but may vote only when he is acting in place of his principal.

3. Directors shall hold office for a term of two (2) years and may be reelected. They shall continue in office until their successors shall have been chosen and qualified. If the office of a Director becomes vacant more than one hundred and eighty (180) days before the end of his term, a successor shall be chosen in accordance with Annex B hereof, for the remainder of the term, by the Governors who elected the former Director. A majority of the votes cast by such Governors shall be required for such election. If the office of a Director becomes vacant one hundred and eighty (180) days or less before the end of his term, a successor may similarly be chosen for the remainder of the term, by the Governors who elected the former Director,

in which election a majority of the votes cast by such Governors shall be required. While the office remains vacant, the alternate of the former Director shall exercise the powers of the latter, except that of appointing an alternate.

Article 31

BOARD OF DIRECTORS: POWERS

The Board of Directors shall be responsible for the direction of the general operations of the Bank and, for this purpose, shall, in addition to the powers assigned to it expressly by this Agreement, exercise all the powers delegated to it by the Board of Governors, and in particular:

(i) prepare the work of the Board of Governors;

(ii) in conformity with the general directions of the Board of Governors, take decisions concerning loans, guarantees, investments in equity capital, borrowing by the Bank, furnishing of technical assistance and other operations of the Bank;

(iii) submit the accounts for each financial year for approval of the Board of Governors at each annual meeting; and

(iv) approve the budget of the Bank.

Article 32

BOARD OF DIRECTORS: PROCEDURE

1. The Board of Directors shall normally function at the principal office of the Bank and shall meet as often as the business of the Bank may require.

2. A majority of the Directors shall constitute a quorum for any meeting of the Board of Directors, provided such majority represents not less than two-thirds of the total voting power of the members.

3. The Board of Governors shall adopt Regulations under which, if there is no Director of its nationality, a member may send a representative to attend, without right to vote, any meeting of the Board of Directors when a matter particularly affecting that member is under consideration.

Article 33

VOTING

1. The total voting power of each member shall consist of the sum of its basic votes and proportional votes.

(i) The basic votes of each member shall consist of such number of votes as results from the equal distribution among all the members of twenty (20) per cent of the aggregate sum of the basic votes and proportional votes of all the members.

(ii) The number of the proportional votes of each member shall be equal to the number of shares of the capital stock of the Bank held by that member.

2.   In voting in the Board of Governors, each Governor shall be entitled to cast the votes of the member he represents. Except as otherwise expressly provided in this Agreement, all matters before the Board of Governors shall be decided by a majority of the voting power represented at the meeting.

3.   In voting in the Board of Directors, each Director shall be entitled to cast the number of votes that counted towards his election which votes need not be cast as a unit. Except as otherwise expressly provided in this Agreement, all matters before the Board of Directors shall be decided by a majority of the voting power represented at the meeting.

Article 34

THE PRESIDENT

1.   The Board of Governors, by a vote of a majority of the total number of Governors, representing not less than a majority of the total voting power of the members, shall elect a president of the Bank. He shall be a national of a regional member country. The President, while holding office, shall not be a Governor or a Director or an alternate for either.

2.   The term of office of the President shall be five (5) years. He may be re-elected. He shall, however, cease to hold office when the Board of Governors so decides by a vote of two-thirds of the total number of Governors, representing not less than two-thirds of the total voting power of the members. If the office of the President for any reason becomes vacant more than one hundred and eighty (180) days before the end of his term, a successor shall be elected for the unexpired portion of such term by the Board of Governors in accordance with the provisions of paragraph 1 of this Article. If such office for any reason becomes vacant one hundred and eighty (180) days or less before the end of his term, a successor may similarly be elected for the unexpired portion of such term by the Board of Governors.

3.   The President shall be Chairman of the Board of Directors but shall have no vote, except a deciding vote in case of an equal division. He may participate in meetings of the Board of Governors but shall not vote.

4.   The President shall be the legal representative of the Bank.

5.   The President shall be chief of the staff of the Bank and shall conduct, under the direction of the Board of Directors, the current business of the

Bank. He shall be responsible for the organization, appointment and dismissal of the officers and staff in accordance with regulations adopted by the Board of Directors.

6. In appointing the officers and staff, the President shall, subject to the paramount importance of securing the highest standards of efficiency and technical competence, pay due regard to the recruitment of personnel on as wide a regional geographical basis as possible.

Article 35

VICE-PRESIDENT(S)

1. One or more Vice-Presidents shall be appointed by the Board of Directors on the recommendation of the President. Vice-President(s) shall hold office for such term, exercise such authority and perform such functions in the administration of the Bank, as may be determined by the Board of Directors. In the absence or incapacity of the President, the Vice-President or, if there be more than one, the ranking Vice-President, shall exercise the authority and perform the functions of the President.

2. Vice-President(s) may participate in meetings of the Board of Directors but shall have no vote at such meetings, except that the Vice-President or ranking Vice-President, as the case may be, shall cast the deciding vote when acting in place of the President.

Article 36

PROHIBITION OF POLITICAL ACTIVITY: THE INTERNATIONAL CHARACTER OF THE BANK

1. The Bank shall not accept loans or assistance that may in any way prejudice, limit, deflect or otherwise alter its purpose or functions.

2. The Bank, its President, Vice-President(s), officers and staff shall not interfere in the political affairs of any member, nor shall they be influenced in their decisions by the political character of the member concerned. Only economic considerations shall be relevant to their decisions. Such considerations shall be weighed impartially in order to achieve and carry out the purpose and functions of the Bank.

3. The President, Vice-President(s), officers and staff of the Bank, in the discharge of their offices, owe their duty entirely to the Bank and to no other authority. Each member of the Bank shall respect the international character of this duty and shall refrain from all attempts to influence any of them in the discharge of their duties.

Article 37

OFFICE OF THE BANK

1.   The principal office of the Bank shall be located in Manila, Philippines.

2.   The Bank may establish agencies or branch offices elsewhere.

Article 38

CHANNEL OF COMMUNICATIONS, DEPOSITORIES

1.   Each member shall designate an appropriate official entity with which the Bank may communicate in connexion with any matter arising under this Agreement.

2.   Each member shall designate its central bank, or such other agency as may be agreed upon with the Bank, as a depository with which the Bank may keep its holdings of currency of that member as well as other assets of the Bank.

Article 39

WORKING LANGUAGE, REPORTS

1.   The working language of the Bank shall be English.

2.   The Bank shall transmit to its members an Annual Report containing an audited statement of its accounts and shall publish such Report. It shall also transmit quarterly to its members a summary statement of its financial position and a profit and loss statement showing the results of its operations.

3.   The Bank may also publish such other reports as it deems desirable in the carrying out of its purpose and functions. Such reports shall be transmitted to the members of the Bank.

Article 40

ALLOCATION OF NET INCOME

1.   The Board of Governors shall determine annually what part of the net income of the Bank, including the net income accruing to Special Funds, shall be allocated, after making provision for reserves, to surplus and what part, if any, shall be distributed to the members.

2.   The distribution referred to in the preceding paragraph shall be made in proportion to the number of shares held by each member.

3.   Payments shall be made in such manner and in such currency as the Board of Governors shall determine.

Chapter VII

WITHDRAWAL AND SUSPENSION OF MEMBERS, TEMPORARY SUSPENSION AND TERMINATION OF OPERATIONS OF THE BANK

Article 41

WITHDRAWAL

1.   Any member may withdraw from the Bank at any time by delivering a notice in writing to the Bank at its principal office.

2.   Withdrawal by a member shall become effective, and its membership shall cease, on the date specified in its notice but in no event less than six (6) months after the date that notice has been received by the Bank. However, at any time before the withdrawal becomes finally effective, the member may notify the Bank in writing of the cancellation of its notice of intention to withdraw.

3.   A withdrawing member shall remain liable for all direct and contingent obligations to the Bank to which it was subject at the date of delivery of the withdrawal notice. If the withdrawal becomes finally effective, the member shall not incur any liability for obligations resulting from operations of the Bank effected after the date on which the withdrawal notice was received by the Bank.

Article 42

SUSPENSION OF MEMBERSHIP

1.   If a member fails to fulfil any of its obligation to the Bank, the Board of Governors may suspend such member by a vote of two-thirds of the total number of Governors, representing not less than three-fourths of the total voting power of the members.

2.   The member so suspended shall automatically cease to be a member of the Bank one (1) year from the date of its suspension unless the Board of Governors, during the one-year period, decides by the same majority necessary for suspension to restore the member to good standing.

3.   While under suspension, a member shall not be entitled to exercise any rights under this Agreement, except the right of withdrawal, but shall remain subject to all its obligations.

Article 43

SETTLEMENT OF ACCOUNTS

1.   After the date on which a country ceases to be a member, it shall remain liable for its direct obligations to the Bank and for its contingent

liabilities to the Bank so long as any part of the loans or guarantees contracted before it ceased to be a member is outstanding, but it shall not incur liabilities with respect to loans and guarantees entered into thereafter by the Bank nor share either in the income or the expenses of the Bank.

2.   At the time a country ceases to be a member, the Bank shall arrange for the repurchase of such country's shares by the Bank as a part of the settlement of accounts with such country in accordance with the provisions of paragraphs 3 and 4 of this Article. For this purpose, the repurchase price of the shares shall be the value shown by the books of the Bank on the date the country ceases to be a member.

3.   The payment for shares repurchased by the Bank under this Article shall be governed by the following conditions:

   (i)   Any amount due to the country concerned for its shares shall be withheld so long as that country, its central bank or any of its agencies, instrumentalities or political subdivisions remains liable, as borrower or guarantor, to the Bank and such amount may, at the option of the Bank, be applied on any such liability as it matures. No amount shall be withheld on account of the contingent liability of the country for future calls on its subscription for shares in accordance with paragraph 5 of Article 6 of this Agreement. In any event, no amount due to a member for its shares shall be paid until six (6) months after the date on which the country ceases to be a member.

   (ii) Payments for shares may be made from time to time, upon surrender of the corresponding stock certificates by the country concerned, to the extent by which the amount due as the repurchase price in accordance with paragraph 2 of this Article exceeds the aggregate amount of liabilities, on loans and guarantees referred to in sub-paragraph (i) of this paragraph, until the former member has received the full repurchase price.

   (iii) Payments shall be made in such available currencies as the Bank determines, taking into account its financial position.

   (iv) If losses are sustained by the Bank on any guarantees or loans which were outstanding on the date when a country ceased to be a member and the amount of such losses exceeds the amount of the reserve provided against losses on that date, the country concerned shall repay, upon demand, the amount by which the repurchase price of its shares would have been reduced if the losses had been taken into account when the repurchase price was determined. In addition, the former member shall remain liable on any call for unpaid subscriptions in accordance with paragraph 5 to Article 6 of this Agreement, to the same extent that it would have been required to respond if the impairment of capital had occurred and the call had been made at the time the repurchase price of its shares was determined.

4.   If the Bank terminates its operations pursuant to Article 45 of this Agreement within six (6) months of the date upon which any country ceases to be a member, all rights of the country concerned shall be determined in accordance with the provisions of Articles 45 to 47 of this Agreement. Such country shall be considered as still a member for purposes of such Articles but shall have no voting rights.

Article 44

TEMPORARY SUSPENSION OF OPERATIONS

In an emergency, the Board of Directors may temporarily suspend operations in respect of new loans and guarantees, pending an opportunity for further consideration and action by the Board of Governors.

Article 45

TERMINATION OF OPERATIONS

1.   The Bank may terminate its operations by a resolution of the Board of Governors approved by a vote of two-thirds of the total number of Governors, representing not less than three-fourths of the total voting power of the members.

2.   After such termination, the Bank shall forthwith cease all activities, except those incident to the orderly realization, conservation and preservation of its assets and settlement of its obligations.

Article 46

LIABILITY OF MEMBERS AND PAYMENT OF CLAIMS

1.   In the event of termination of the operations of the Bank, the liability of all members for uncalled subscriptions to the capital stock of the Bank and in respect of the depreciation of their currencies shall continue until all claims of creditors, including all contingent claims shall have been discharged.

2.   All creditors holding direct claims shall first be paid out of the assets of the Bank and then out of payments to the Bank or unpaid or callable subscriptions. Before making any payments to creditors holding direct claims, the Board of Directors shall make such arrangements as are necessary, in its judgment, to ensure a pro rata distribution among holders of direct and contingent claims.

Article 47

DISTRIBUTION OF ASSETS

1. No distribution of assets shall be made to members on account of their subscriptions to the capital stock of the Bank until all liabilities to creditors have been discharged or provided for. Moreover, such distribution must be approved by the Board of Governors by a vote of two-thirds of the total number of Governors, representing not less than three-fourths of the total voting power of the members.

2. Any distribution of the assets of the Bank to the members shall be in proportion to the capital stock held by each member and shall be effected at such times and under such conditions as the Bank shall deem fair and equitable. The shares of assets distributed need not be uniform as to type of asset. No member shall be entitled to receive its share in such a distribution of assets until it has settled all of its obligations to the Bank.

3. Any member receiving assets distributed pursuant to this Article shall enjoy the same rights with respect to such assets as the Bank enjoyed prior to their distribution.

Chapter VIII

STATUS, IMMUNITIES, EXEMPTIONS AND PRIVILEGES

Article 48

PURPOSE OF CHAPTER

To enable the Bank effectively to fulfil its purpose and carry out the functions entrusted to it, the status, immunities, exemptions and privileges set forth in this Chapter shall be accorded to the Bank in the territory of each member.

Article 49

LEGAL STATUS

The Bank shall possess full juridical personality and, in particular, full capacity:

(i) to contract;

(ii) to acquire, and dispose of, immovable and movable property; and

(iii) to institute legal proceedings.

Article 50

IMMUNITY FROM JUDICIAL PROCEEDINGS

1. The Bank shall enjoy immunity from every form of legal process, except in cases arising out of or in connexion with the exercise of its powers to borrow money, to guarantee obligations, or to buy and sell or underwrite the sale of securities, in which cases actions may be brought against the Bank in a court of competent jurisdiction in the territory of a country in which the Bank has its principal or a branch office, or has appointed an agent for the purpose of accepting service or notice of process, or has issued or guaranteed securities.

2. Notwithstanding the provisions of paragraph 1 of this Article, no action shall be brought against the Bank by any member, or by any agency or instrumentality of a member, or by any entity or person directly or indirectly acting for a deriving claims from a member or from any agency or instrumentality of a member. Members shall have recourse to such special procedures for the settlement of controversies between the Bank and its members as may be prescribed in this Agreement, in the by-laws and regulations of the Bank, or in contracts entered into with the Bank.

3. Property and assets of the Bank, shall, wheresoever located and by whomsoever held, be immune from all forms of seizure, attachment or execution before the delivery of final judgment against the Bank.

Article 51

IMMUNITY OF ASSETS

Property and assets of the Bank, wheresoever located and by whomsoever held, shall be immune from search, requisition, confiscation, expropriation or any other form of taking or foreclosure by executive or legislative action.

Article 52

IMMUNITY OF ARCHIVES

The archives of the Bank, and, in general, all documents belonging to it, or held by it, shall be inviolable, wherever located.

Article 53

FREEDOM OF ASSETS FROM RESTRICTIONS

To the extent necessary to carry out the purpose and functions of the Bank effectively, and subject to the provisions of this Agreement, all property and assets of the Bank shall be free from restrictions, regulations, controls and moratoria of any nature.

Article 54

PRIVILEGE FOR COMMUNICATIONS

Official communications of the Bank shall be accorded by each member treatment not less favourable than that it accords to the official communications of any other member.

Article 55

IMMUNITIES AND PRIVILEGES OF BANK PERSONNEL

All Governors, Directors, alternates, officers and employees of the Bank, including experts performing missions for the Bank:

(i)   shall be immune from legal process with respect to acts performed by them in their official capacity, except when the Bank waives the immunity;

(ii) where they are not local citizens or nationals, shall be accorded the same immunities from immigration restrictions, alien registration requirements and national service obligations, and the same facilities as regards exchange regulations, as are accorded by members to the representatives, officials and employees of comparable rank of other members; and

(iii) shall be granted the same treatment in respect of travelling facilities as is accorded by members to representatives, officials and employees of comparable rank of other members.

Article 56

EXEMPTION FROM TAXATION

1.   The Bank, its assets, property, income and its operations and transactions, shall be exempt from all taxation and from all customs duties. The Bank shall also be exempt from any obligation for the payment, withholding or collection of any tax or duty.

2.   No tax shall be levied on or in respect of salaries and emoluments paid by the Bank to Directors, alternates, officers or employees of the Bank, including experts performing missions for the Bank, except where a member deposits with its instrument of ratification or acceptance a declaration that such member retains for itself and its political subdivisions the right to tax salaries and emoluments paid by the Bank to citizens or nationals of such member.

3.   No tax of any kind shall be levied on any obligation or security issued by the Bank, including any dividend or interest thereon, by whomsoever held:

(i) which discriminates against such obligation or security solely because it is issued by the Bank; or

(ii) if the sole jurisdictional basis for such taxation is the place or currency in which it is issued, made payable or paid, or the location of any office or place of business maintained by the Bank.

4. No tax of any kind shall be levied on any obligation or security guaranteed by the Bank, including any dividend or interest thereon, by whomsoever held:

(i) which discriminates against such obligation or security solely because it is guaranteed by the Bank; or

(ii) if the sole jurisdictional basis for such taxation is the location of any office or place of business maintained by the Bank.

Article 57

IMPLEMENTATION

Each member, in accordance with its juridical system, shall promptly take such action as is necessary to make effective in its own territory the provisions set forth in the Chapter and shall inform the Bank of the action which it has taken on the matter.

Article 58

WAIVER OF IMMUNITIES, EXEMPTIONS AND PRIVILEGES

The Bank at its discretion may waive any of the privileges, immunities and exemptions conferred under this Chapter in any case or instance, in such manner and upon such conditions as it may determine to be appropriate in the best interests of the Bank.

Chapter IX

AMENDMENTS, INTERPRETATION, ARBITRATION

Article 59

AMENDMENTS

1. This Agreement may be amended only by a resolution of the Board of Governors approved by a vote of two-thirds of the total number of Governors, representing not less than three-fourths of the total voting power of the members.

2. Notwithstanding the provisions of paragraph 1 of this Article, the unanimous agreement of the Board of Governors shall be required for the approval of any amendment modifying:

(i) The right to withdraw from the Bank;

(ii) The limitations on liability provided in paragraphs 6 and 7 of Article 5; and

(iii) The rights pertaining to purchase of capital stock provided in paragraph 2 of Article 5.

3.   Any proposal to amend this Agreement, whether emanating from a member or the Board of Directors, shall be communicated to the Chairman of the Board of Governors, who shall bring the proposal before the Board of Governors. When an amendment has been adopted, the Bank shall so certify in an official communication addressed to all members. Amendments shall enter into force for all members three (3) months after the date of the official communication unless the Board of Governors specifies therein a different period.

Article 60

INTERPRETATION OR APPLICATION

1.   Any question of interpretation or application of the provisions of this Agreement arising between any member and the Bank, or between two or more members of the Bank, shall be submitted to the Board of Directors for decision. If there is no Director of its nationality on that Board, a member particularly affected by the question under consideration shall be entitled to direct representation in the Board of Directors during such consideration; the representative of such member shall, however, have no vote. Such right of representation shall be regulated by the Board of Governors.

2.   In any case where the Board of Directors has given a decision under paragraph 1 of this Article, any member may require that the question be referred to the Board of Governors, whose decision shall be final. Pending the decision of the Board of Governors, the Bank may, so far as it deems necessary, act on the basis of the decision of the Board of Directors.

Article 61

ARBITRATION

If a disagreement should arise between the Bank and a country which has ceased to be a member, or between the Bank and any member, after adoption of a resolution to terminate the operations of the Bank, such disagreement shall be submitted to arbitration by a tribunal of three arbitrators. One of the arbitrators shall be appointed by the Bank, another by the country concerned, and the third, unless the parties otherwise agree, by the President of the International Court of Justice or such other authority as may have been prescribed by regulations adopted by the Board of Governors. A majority vote of the arbitrators shall be sufficient to reach a decision which shall be final and binding upon the parties. The third arbitrator shall be empowered to settle all questions of procedure in any case where the parties are in disagreement with respect thereto.

Article 62

APPROVAL DEEMED GIVEN

Whenever the approval of any member is required before any act may be done by the Bank, approval shall be deemed to have been given unless the member presents an objection within such reasonable period as the Bank may fix in notifying the member of the proposed act.

Chapter X

FINAL PROVISIONS

Article 63

SIGNATURE AND DEPOSIT

1.   The original of this Agreement in a single copy in the English language shall remain open for signature at the United Nations Economic Commission for Asia and the Far East, in Bangkok, until 31 January 1966 by Governments of countries listed in Annex A to this Agreement. This document shall thereafter be deposited with the Secretary-General of the United Nations (hereinafter called the "Depository").

2.   The Depository shall send certified copies of this Agreement to all the Signatories and other countries which become members of the Bank.

Article 64

RATIFICATION OR ACCEPTANCE

1.   This Agreement shall be subject to ratification or acceptance by the Signatories. Instruments of ratification or acceptance shall be deposited with the Depository not later than 30 September 1966. The Depository shall duly notify the other Signatories of each deposit and the date thereof.

2.   A Signatory whose instrument of ratification or acceptance is deposited before the date on which this Agreement enters into force, shall become a member of the Bank, on that date. Any other Signatory which complies with the provisions of the preceding paragraph, shall become a member of the Bank on the date on which its instrument of ratification or acceptance is deposited.

Article 65

ENTRY INTO FORCE

This Agreement shall enter into force when instruments of ratification or acceptance have been deposited by at least fifteen (15) Signatories (including not less than ten [10] regional countries) whose initial subscriptions, as set forth in Annex A to this Agreement, in the aggregate comprise not less than sixty-five (65) per cent of the authorized capital stock of the Bank.

Article 66

COMMENCEMENT OF OPERATIONS

1. As soon as this Agreement enters into force, each member shall appoint a Governor, and the Executive Secretary of the United Nations Economic Commission for Asia and the Far East shall call the inaugural meeting of the Board of Governors.

2. At its inaugural meeting, the Board of Governors:

    (i) shall make arrangements for the election of Directors of the Bank in accordance with paragraph 1 of Article 30 of this Agreement; and

    (ii) shall make arrangements for the determination of the date on which the Bank shall commence its operations.

3. The Bank shall notify its members of the date of the commencement of its operations.

DONE at the City of Manila, Philippines, on 4 December 1965, in a single copy in the English language which shall be brought to the United Nations Economic Commission for Asia and the Far East, Bangkok, and thereafter deposited with the Secretary-General of the United Nations, New York, in accordance with Article 63 of this Agreement.

[**Note:** Annex A and Annex B are omitted from this reproduction of the AsDB Charter. Annex A is titled "Initial Subscriptions to the Authorized Capital Stock for Countries Which May Become Members in Accordance with Article 64." Annex B is titled "Election of Directors."]

APPENDIX H

CHARTER OF THE EBRD

Citation: Agreement Establishing the European Bank for Reconstruction and Development, done at Paris, May 29, 1990 (entered into force Mar. 28, 1991), 29 I.L.M. 1077, 1083.

Contents

X. Final provisions
    60. Signature and deposit
    61. Ratification, acceptance or approval
    62. Entry into force
    63. Inaugural meeting and commencement of operations

Agreement Establishing the European Bank for Reconstruction and Development

The contracting parties,

Committed to the fundamental principles of multiparty democracy, the rule of law, respect for human rights and market economics;

Recalling the Final Act of the Helsinki Conference on Security and Co-operation in Europe, and in particular its Declaration on Principles;

Welcoming the intent of central and eastern European countries to further the practical implementation of multiparty democracy, strengthening democratic institutions, the rule of law and respect for human rights and their willingness to implement reforms in order to evolve towards market-oriented economies;

Considering the importance of close and co-ordinated co-operation in order to promote the economic progress of central and eastern European countries to help their economies become more internationally competitive and assist them in their reconstruction and development and thus to reduce, where appropriate, any risks related to the financing of their economies;

Convinced that the establishment of a multilateral financial institution which is European in its basic character and broadly international in its membership would help serve these ends and would constitute a new and unique structure of co-operation in Europe;

Have agreed to establish hereby the European Bank for Reconstruction and Development (hereinafter called "the Bank") which shall operate in accordance with the following:

Chapter I—Purpose, Functions and Membership

Article 1. Purpose

In contributing to economic progress and reconstruction, the purpose of the Bank shall be to foster the transition towards open market-oriented economies and to promote private and entrepreneurial initiative in the central and eastern European countries committed to and applying the principles of multiparty democracy, pluralism and market economics.

Article 2. Functions

1.   To fulfil on a long-term basis its purpose of fostering the transition of central and eastern European countries towards open market-oriented economies and the promotion of private and entrepreneurial initiative, the Bank shall assist the recipient member countries to implement structural and sectoral economic reforms, including demonopolization, decentralization and privatization, to help their economies become fully integrated into the international economy by measures:

(i)   to promote, through private and other interested investors, the establishment, improvement and expansion of productive, competitive and private sector activity, in particular small and medium-sized enterprises;

(ii)   to mobilize domestic and foreign capital and experienced management to the end described in (i);

(iii)   to foster productive investment, including in the service and financial sectors, and in related infrastructure where that is necessary to support private and entrepreneurial initiatives, thereby assisting in making a competitive environment an raising productivity, the standard of living and conditions of labour;

(iv)   to provide technical assistance for the preparation, financing and implementation of relevant projects, whether individual or in the context of specific investment programmes;

(v)   to stimulate and encourage the development of capital markets;

(vi)   to give support to sound and economically viable projects involving more than one recipient member country;

(vii)   to promote in the full range of its activities environmentally sound and sustainable development; and

(viii) to undertake such other activities and provide such other services as may further these functions.

2.   In carrying out the functions referred to in paragraph 1 of this Article, the Bank shall work in close cooperation with all its members and, in such manner as it may deem appropriate within the terms of this Agreement, with the International Monetary Fund, the International Bank for Reconstruction and Development, the International Finance Corporation, the Multilateral Investment Guarantee Agency, and the Organisation for Economic Co-operation and Development, and shall cooperate with the United Nations and its Specialized Agencies and other related bodies, and any entity, whether public or private, concerned with the economic development of, and investment in, Central and Eastern European countries.

Article 3. Membership

1. Membership in the Bank shall be open:

    (i) to (1) European countries and (2) non-European countries which are members of the International Monetary Fund; and

    (ii) to the European Economic Community and the European Investment Bank.

2. Countries eligible for membership under paragraph 1 of this Article, which do not become members in accordance with Article 61 of this Agreement, may be admitted, under such terms and conditions as the Bank may determine, to membership in the Bank upon the affirmative vote of not less than two-thirds of the Governors, representing not less than three-fourths of the total voting power of the members.

Chapter II—Capital

Article 4. Authorized capital stock

1. The original authorized capital stock shall be ten thousand million (10,000,000,000) ECU. It shall be divided into one million (1,000,000) shares, having a par value of ten thousand (10,000) ECU each, which shall be available for subscription only by members in accordance with the provisions of Article 5 of this Agreement.

2. The original capital stock shall be divided into paid-in shares and callable shares. The initial total aggregate par value of paid-in shares shall be three thousand million (3,000,000,000) ECU.

3. The authorized capital stock may be increased at such time and under such terms as may seem advisable, by a vote of not less than two-thirds of the Governors, representing not less than three-fourths of the total voting power of the members.

Article 5. Subscription of shares

1. Each member shall subscribe to shares of the capital stock of the Bank, subject to fulfilment of the member's legal requirements. Each subscription to the original authorized capital stock shall be for paid-in shares and callable shares in the proportion of three (3) to seven (7). The initial number of shares available to be subscribed to by Signatories to this Agreement which become members in accordance with Article 61 or this Agreement shall be that set forth in Annex A. No member shall have an initial subscription of less than one hundred (100) shares.

2. The initial number of shares to be subscribed to by countries which are admitted to membership in accordance with paragraph 2 of Article 3 of

this Agreement shall be determined by the Board of Governors; provided, however, that no such subscription shall be authorized which would have the effect of reducing the percentage of capital stock held by countries which are members of the European Economic Community, together with the European Economic Community and the European Investment Bank, below the majority of the total subscribed capital stock.

3. The Board of Governors shall at intervals of not more than five (5) years review the capital stock of the Bank. In case of an increase in the authorized capital stock, each member shall have a reasonable opportunity to subscribe, under such uniform terms and conditions as the Board of Governors shall determine, to a proportion of the increase in stock equivalent to the proportion which its stock subscribed bears to the total subscribed capital stock immediately prior to such increase. No member shall be obliged subscribe to any part of an increase of capital stock.

4. Subject to the provisions of paragraph 3 of this Article, the Board of Governors, may, at the request of a member, increase the subscription of that member, or allocate shares to that member within the authorized capital stock which are not taken up by other members; provided, however, that such increase shall not have the effect of reducing the percentage of capital stock held by countries which are members of the European Economic Community, together with the European Economic Community and the European Investment Bank, below the majority of the total subscribed capital stock.

5. Shares of stock initially subscribed to by members shall be issued at par. Other shares shall be issued at par unless the Board of Governors, by a vote of not less than two-thirds of the Governors, representing not less than two-thirds of the total voting power of the members, decides to issue them in special circumstances on other terms.

6. Shares of stock shall not be pledged or encumbered in any manner whatsoever, and they shall not be transferable except to the Bank in accordance with Chapter VII of this Agreement.

7. The liability of the members on shares shall be limited to the unpaid portion of their issue price. No member shall be liable, by reason of its membership, for obligations of the Bank.

Article 6. Payment of subscriptions

1. Payment of the paid-in shares of the amount initially subscribed to by each Signatory to this Agreement, which becomes a member in accordance with Article 61 of this Agreement, shall be made in five (5) instalments of

twenty (20) per cent each of such amount. The first instalment shall be paid by each member within sixty (60) days after the date of entry into force of this Agreement, or after the date of deposit of its instrument of ratification, acceptance or approval in accordance with Article 61, if this latter is later than the date of entry into force. The remaining four (4) instalments shall each become due successively one year from the date on which the preceding instalment became due and shall each, subject to the legislative requirement of each member, be paid.

2.   Fifty (50) per cent of payment of each instalment pursuant to paragraph 1 of this Article, or by a member admitted in accordance with paragraph 2 of Article 3 of this Agreement, may be made in promissory notes or other obligations issued by such member and denominated in ECU, in United States dollars or in Japanese yen, to be drawn down as the Bank needs funds for disbursement as a result of its operations. Such notes or obligations shall be non-negotiable, non-interest-bearing and payable to the Bank at par value upon demand. Demands upon such notes or obligations shall, over reasonable periods of time, be made so that the value of such demands in ECU at the time of demand from each member is proportional to the number of paid-in shares subscribed to and held by each such member depositing such notes of obligations.

3.   All payment obligations of a member in respect of subscription to shares in the initial capital stock shall be settled either in ECU, in United States dollars or in Japanese yen on the basis of the average exchange rate of the relevant currency in terms of the ECU for the period from 30 September 1989 to 31 March 1990 inclusive.

4.   Payment of the amount subscribed to the callable capital stock of the Bank shall be subject to call, taking account of Articles 17 and 42 of this Agreement, only as and when required by the Bank to meet its liabilities.

5.   In the event of a call referred to in paragraph 4 of this Article, payment shall be made by the member in ECU, in United States dollars or in Japanese yen. Such calls shall be uniform in ECU value upon each callable share calculated at the time of the call.

6.   The Bank shall determine the place for any payment under this Article not later than one month after the inaugural meeting of its Board of Governors, provided that, before such determination, the payment of the first instalment referred to in paragraph 1 of this Articles shall be made to the European Investment Bank, as trustee for the Bank.

7.   For subscriptions other than those described in paragraphs 1,2 and 3 of this Article, payments by a member in respect of subscription to paid-in

shares in the authorized capital stock shall be made in ECU, in United States dollars or in Japanese yen whether in cash or in promissory notes or in other obligations.

8. For the purpose of this Article, payment or denomination in ECU shall include payment or denomination in any fully convertible currency which is equivalent on the date of payment or encashment to the value of the relevant obligation in ECU.

Article 7. Ordinary capital resources

As used in this Agreement, the term "ordinary capital resources" of the Bank shall include the following:

  (i) authorized capital stock of the Bank, including both paid-in and callable shares, subscribed to pursuant to Article 5 of this Agreement;

 (ii) funds raised by borrowings of the Bank by virtue of powers conferred by sub paragraph (i) of Article 20 of this Agreement, to which the commitment to calls provided for in paragraph 4 of Article 6 of this Agreement is applicable;

(iii) funds received in repayment of loans or guarantees and proceeds from the disposal of equity investment made with the resources indicated in sub paragraphs (i) and (ii) of this Article;

 (iv) income derived from loans and equity investment, made from the resources indicated in sub paragraphs (i) and (ii) of this Article, and income derived from guarantees and underwriting not forming part of the special operations of the Bank; and

  (v) any other funds or income received by the Bank which do not form part of its Special Funds resources referred to in Article 19 of this Agreement.

Chapter III—Operations

Article 8. Recipient countries and use of resources

1. The resources and facilities of the Bank shall be used exclusively to implement the purpose and carry out the functions set forth, respectively, in Articles 1 and 2 of this Agreement.

2. The Bank may conduct its operations in countries from central and eastern Europe which are proceeding steadily in the transition towards market-oriented economies and the promotion of private and entrepreneurial initiative, and which apply, by concrete steps and otherwise, the principles set forth in Article 1 of this Agreement.

3.   In cases where a member might be implementing policies which are inconsistent with Article 1 of this Agreement, or in exceptional circumstances, the Board of Directors shall consider whether access by a member to Bank resources should be suspended or otherwise modified and may make recommendations accordingly to the Board of Governors. Any decision on these matters shall be taken by the Board of Governors by a majority of not less than two-thirds of the Governors, representing not less than three-fourths of the total voting power of the members.

4.   (i)   Any potential recipient country may request that the Bank provide access to its resources for limited purposes over a period of three (3) years beginning after the entry into force of this Agreement. Any such request shall be attached as an integral part of this Agreement as soon as it is made.

(ii) During such a period:

(a) the Bank shall provide to such a country, and to enterprises in its territory, upon their request, technical assistance and other types of assistance directed to finance its private sector, to facilitate the transition of state-owned enterprises to private ownership and control, and to help enterprises operating competitively and moving to participation in the market-oriented economy, subject to the proportion set forth in paragraph 3 of Article 11 of this Agreement.

(b) the total amount of any assistance thus provided shall not exceed the total amount of cash disbursed and promissory notes issued by that country for its shares.

(iii) At the end of this period, the decision to allow such a country access beyond the limits specified in sub paragraphs (a) and (b) shall be taken by the Board of Governors by a majority of not less than three-fourths of the Governors representing not less than eighty-five (85) per cent of the total voting power of the members.

Article 9. Ordinary and special operations

The operations of the Bank shall consists of ordinary operations financed from the ordinary capital resources of the Bank referred to in Article 7 of this Agreement and special operations financed from the Special Funds resources referred to in Article 19 of this Agreement. The two types of operations may be combined.

Article 10. Separation of operations

1.   The ordinary capital resources and the Special Funds resources of the Bank shall at all times and in all respects be held, used, committed, invested

or otherwise disposed of entirely separately from each other. The financial statements of the Bank shall show the reserves of the Bank, together with its ordinary operations and, separately, its special operations.

2.   The ordinary capital resources of the Bank shall, under no circumstances, by charged with, or used to discharge, losses or liabilities arising out of special operations or other activities for which Special Funds resources were originally used or committed.

3.   Expenses appertaining directly to ordinary operations shall be charged to the ordinary capital resources of the Bank. Expenses appertaining directly to the special operations shall be charged to Special Funds resources. Any other expenses shall, subject to paragraph 1 of Article 18 of this Agreement, be charged as the Bank shall determine.

Article 11. Methods of operation

1.   The Bank shall carry out its operations in furtherance of its purpose and functions as set out in Articles 1 and 2 of this Agreement in any or all of the following ways:

   (i)   by making or co-financing together with multilateral institutions, commercial banks or other interested sources, or participating in, loans to private sector enterprises, loans to any state-owned enterprise operating competitively and moving to participation in the market-oriented economy, and loans to any state-owned enterprise to facilitate its transition to private ownership and control; in particular, to facilitate or enhance the participation of private and/or foreign capital in such enterprises;

   (ii) (a) by investment in the equity capital of private sector enterprises;

         (b) by investment in the equity capital of any state-owned enterprise operating competitively and moving to participation in the market-oriented economy, and investment in the equity capital of any state-owned enterprise to facilitate its transition to private ownership and control; in particular to facilitate or enhance the participation of private and/or foreign capital in such enterprises; and

         (c) by underwriting, where other means of financing are not appropriate, the equity issue of securities by both private sector enterprises and such state-owned enterprises referred to in (b) above for the ends mentioned in that sub paragraph;

   (iii) by facilitating access to domestic and international capital markets by private sector enterprises or by other enterprises referred to in sub paragraph (i) of this paragraph for the ends mentioned in that sub paragraph, through the provision of guarantees, where other means of financing are not appropriate, and through financial advice and other forms of assistance;

(iv) by deploying Special Funds resources in accordance with the agreements determining their use; and

(v) by making or participating in loans and providing technical assistance for the reconstruction or development of infrastructure, including environmental programmes, necessary for private sector development and the transition to a market-oriented economy.

For the purposes of this paragraph, a state-owned enterprise shall not be regarded as operating competitively unless it operated autonomously in a competitive market environment and unless it is subject to bankruptcy laws.

2. (i) The Board of Directors shall review at least annually the Bank's operations and lending strategy in each recipient country to ensure that the purpose and functions of the Bank, as set out in Articles 1 and 2 of this Agreement, are fully served. Any decision pursuant to such a review shall be taken by a majority of not less than two-thirds of the Directors, representing not less than three-fourths of the total voting power of the members.

   (ii) The said review shall involve the consideration of, inter alia, each recipient country's progress made on decentralization, demonopolization and privatization and the relative shares of the Bank's lending to private enterprises, to state-owned enterprises in the process of transition to participation in the market-oriented economy or privatization, for infrastructure, for technical assistance, and for other purposes.

3. (i) Not more than forty (40) per cent of the amount of the Bank's total committed loans, guarantees and equity investments, without prejudice to its other operations referred to in this Article, shall be provided to the state sector. Such percentage limit shall apply initially over a two (2) year period, from the date of commencement of the Bank's operations, taking one year with another, and thereafter in respect of each subsequent financial year.

   (ii) For any country, not more than forty (40) per cent of the amount of the Bank's total committed loans, guarantees and equity investments over a period of five (5) years, taking one year with another, and without prejudice to the Bank's other operations referred to in this Article, shall be provided to the state sector.

(iii) For the purposes of this paragraph,

    (a) the state sector includes national and local Governments, their agencies, and enterprises owned or controlled by any of them;

    (b) a loan or guarantee to, or equity investment in, a state-owned enterprise which is implementing a programme to achieve private ownership and control shall not be considered as made to the state sector;

    (c) loans to a financial intermediary for onlending to the private sector shall not considered as made to the state sector.

Article 12. Limitations on ordinary operations

1.   The total amount of outstanding loans, equity investments and guarantees made by the Bank on its ordinary operations shall not be increased at any time, if by such increase the total amount of its unimpaired subscribed capital, reserves and surpluses included in its ordinary capital resources would be exceeded.

2.   The amount of any equity investment shall not normally exceed such percentage of the equity capital of the enterprise concerned as shall be determined, by a general rule, to be appropriate by the Board of Directors. The Bank shall not seek to obtain by such an investment a controlling interest in the enterprise concerned and shall not exercise such control or assume direct responsibility for managing any enterprise in which it has an investment, except in the event of actual or threatened default on any of its investments, actual or threatened insolvency of the enterprise in which such investment shall have been made, or other situations which, in the opinion of the Bank, threaten to jeopardize such investment, in which case the Bank may take such action and exercise such rights as it may deem necessary for the protection of its interests.

3.   The amount of the Bank's disbursed equity investments shall not at any time exceed an amount corresponding to its total unimpaired paid-in subscribed capital, surpluses and general reserve.

4.   The Bank shall not issue guarantees for export credits nor undertake insurance activities.

Article 13. Operating principles

The Bank shall operate in accordance with the following principles:

    (i) the Bank shall apply sound banking principles to all its operations;

(ii)   the operations of the Bank shall provide for the financing of specific projects, whether individual or in the context of specific investment programmes, and for technical assistance, designed to fulfil its purpose and functions as set out in Articles 1 and 2 of this Agreement;

(iii) the Bank shall not finance any undertaking in the territory of a member if that member objects to such financing;

(iv)   the Bank shall not allow a disproportionate amount of its resources to be used for the benefit of any member;

(v)   the Bank shall seek to maintain reasonable diversification in all its investments;

(vi)   before a loan, guarantee or equity investment is granted, the applicant shall have submitted an adequate proposal and the President of the Bank shall have presented to the Board of Directors a written report regarding the proposal, together with recommendations, on the basis of a staff study;

(vii) the bank shall not undertake any financing, or provide any facilities, when the applicant is able to obtain sufficient financing or facilities elsewhere on terms and conditions that the Bank considers reasonable;

(viii) in providing or guaranteeing financing, the Bank shall pay due regard to the prospect that the borrower and its guarantor, if any, will be in a position to meet their obligations under the financing contract;

(ix)   in case of a direct loan made by the Bank, the borrower shall be permitted by the Bank to draw its funds only to meet expenditure as it is actually incurred;

(x)   the Bank shall seek to revolve its funds by selling its investments to private investors whenever it can appropriately do so on satisfactory terms;

(xi)   in its investments in individual enterprises, the Bank shall undertake its financing on terms and conditions which it considers appropriate, taking into account the requirements of the enterprise, the risks being undertaken by the Bank, and the terms and conditions normally obtained by private investors for similar financing;

(xii) the Bank shall place no restriction upon the procurement of goods and services from any country from the proceeds of any loan, investment or other financing undertaken in the ordinary or special operations of the Bank, and shall, in all appropriate cases, make its loans and other operations conditional on international invitations to tender being arranged; and

(xiii) the Bank shall take the necessary measures to ensure that the proceeds of any loan made, guaranteed or participated in by the Bank, or any equity investment, are used only for the purposes for which the loan or the equity investment was granted and with due attention to considerations of economy and efficiency.

Article 14. Terms and conditions for loans and guarantees

1. In the case of loans made, participated in, or guaranteed by the Bank, the contract shall establish the terms and conditions for the loan or the guarantee concerned, including those relating to payment of principal, interest and other fees, charges, maturities and dates of payment in respect of the loan or the guarantee, respectively. In setting such terms and conditions, the Bank shall take fully into account the need to safeguard its income.

2. Where the recipient of loans or guarantees of loans is not itself a member, but is a state-owned enterprise, the Bank may, when it appears desirable, bearing in mind the different approaches appropriate to public and state-owned enterprises in transition to private ownership and control, require the member or members in whose territory the project concerned is to be carried out, or a public agency or any instrumentality of such member or members acceptable to the Bank, to guarantee the repayment of the principal and the payment of interest and other fees and charges of the loan in accordance with the terms thereof. The Board of Directors shall review annually the Bank's practice in this matter, paying due attention to the Bank's creditworthiness.

3. The loan or guarantee contract shall expressly state the currency or currencies, or ECU, in which all payments to the Bank thereunder shall be made.

Article 15. Commission and fees

1. The Bank shall charge, in addition to interest, a commission on loans made or participated in as part of its ordinary operations. The terms and conditions of this commission shall be determined by the Board of Directors.

2. In guaranteeing a loan as part of its ordinary operations, or in underwriting the sale of securities, the Bank shall charge fees, payable at rates and time determined by the Board of Directors, to provide suitable compensation for its risks.

3. The Board of Directors may determine any other charges of the Bank in its ordinary operations and any commission, fees or other charges in its special operations.

Article 16. Special reserve

1. The amount of commissions and fees received by the Bank pursuant to Article 15 of this Agreement shall be set aside as a special reserve which shall be kept for meeting the losses of the Bank in accordance with Article 17 of this Agreement. The special reserve shall be held in such liquid form as the Bank may decide.

2. If the Board of Directors determines that the size of the special reserve is adequate, it may decide that all or part of the said commission or fees shall henceforth form part of the income of the Bank.

Article 17. Methods of meeting the losses of the Bank

1. In the Bank's ordinary operations, in cases of arrears of default on loans made, participated in, or guaranteed by the Bank, and in case of losses on underwriting and in equity investment, the Bank shall take such action as it deems appropriate. The Bank shall maintain appropriate provisions against possible losses.

2. Losses arising in the Bank's ordinary operations shall be charged:

   (i) first, to the provisions referred to in paragraph 1 of this Article;

   (ii) second, to net income;

   (iii) third, against the special reserve provided for in Article 16 of this Agreement;

   (iv) fourth, against its general reserve and surpluses;

   (v) fifth, against the unimpaired paid-in capital; and

   (vi) last, against an appropriate amount of the uncalled subscribed callable capital which shall be called in accordance with the provisions of paragraphs 4 and 5 of Article 6 of this Agreement.

Article 18. Special funds

1. The Bank may accept the administration of Special Funds which are designed to serve the purpose and come within the functions of the Bank. The full cost of administering any such Special Fund shall be charged to that Special Fund.

2. Special Funds accepted by the Bank may be used in any manner and on any terms and conditions consistent with the purpose and functions of the Bank, with the other applicable provisions of this Agreement, and with the agreement or agreements relating to such Funds.

3. The Bank shall adopt such rules and regulations as may be required for the establishment, administration and use of each Special Fund. Such

rules and regulations shall be consistent with the provisions of this Agreement, except for those provisions expressly applicable only to ordinary operations of the Bank.

Article 19. Special funds resources

The term "Special Funds resources" shall refer to the resources of any Special Fund and shall include:

(i) funds accepted by the Bank for inclusion in any Special Fund;

(ii) funds repaid in respect of loans or guarantees, and the proceeds of equity investments, financed from the resources of any Special Fund which, under the rules and regulations governing that Special Fund, are received by such Special Fund; and

(iii) income derived from investment of Special Funds resources.

Chapter IV—Borrowing and other miscellaneous powers

Article 20. General powers

1. The Bank shall have, in addition to the powers specified elsewhere in the Agreement, the power to;

(i) borrow funds in member countries or elsewhere, provided always that;

    (a) before making a sale of its obligations in the territory of a country, the Bank shall have obtained its approval; and

    (b) where the obligations of the Bank are to be denominated in the currency of a member, the Bank shall have obtained its approvals;

(ii) invest or deposit funds not needed in its operations;

(iii) buy and sell securities, in the secondary market, which the Bank has issued or guaranteed or in which it has invested;

(iv) guarantee securities in which it has invested in order to facilitate their sale;

(v) underwrite, or participate in the underwriting of, securities issued by any enterprise for purposes consistent with the purpose and functions of the Bank;

(vi) provide technical advice and assistance which serve its purpose and come within its functions;

(vii) exercise such powers and adopt such rules and regulations as may be necessary or appropriate in furtherance of its purpose and functions, consistent with the provisions of this Agreement; and

(viii) conclude agreements of cooperation with any public or private entity or entities.

2.   Every security issued or guaranteed by the Bank shall bear on its face a conspicuous statement to the effect that it is not an obligation of any Government or member, unless it is in fact the obligation of a particular government or member, in which case it shall so state.

Chapter V—Currencies

Article 21. Determination and use of currencies

1.   Whenever it shall become necessary under this Agreement to determine whether any currency is fully convertible for the purposes of this Agreement, such determination shall be made by the Bank, taking into account the paramount need to preserve its own financial interests, after consultation, if necessary, with the International Monetary Fund.

2.   Members shall not impose any restrictions on the receipt, holding, use or transfer by the Bank of the following;

(i)   currencies or ECU received by the Bank in payment of subscriptions to its capital stock, in accordance with Article 6 of this Agreement;

(ii) currencies obtained by the Bank by borrowing;

(iii) currencies and other resources administered by the Bank as contributions to Special Funds; and

(iv) currencies received by the Bank in payment on account of principal interest, dividends or other charges in respect of loans or investments, or the proceeds of disposal of such investments made out of any of the funds referred to in sub paragraphs (i) to (iii) of this paragraph, or in payment of commission, fees or other charges

Chapter VI—Organization and management

Article 22. Structure

The Bank shall have a Board of Governors, a Board of Directors, a President, one or more Vice-Presidents and such other officers and staff as may be considered necessary.

Article 23. Board of Governors: composition

1.   Each member shall be represented on the Board of Governors and shall appoint one Governor and one Alternate. Each Governor and Alternate shall serve at the pleasure of the appointing member. No Alternate may vote except in the absence of is or her principal. At each of its annual meetings, the Board shall elect one of the Governors as Chairman who shall hold office until the election of the next Chairman.

2.   Governors and Alternates shall serve as such without remuneration from the Bank.

Article 24. Board of Governors: powers

1.   All the powers of the Bank shall be vested in the Board of Governors.

2.   The Board of Governors may delegate to the Board of Directors any or all of its powers, except the power to:

   (i)   admit new members and determine the conditions of their admission;

   (ii)   increase or decrease the authorized capital stock of the Bank;

   (iii)   suspend a member;

   (iv)   decide appeals from interpretations or applications of this Agreement given by the Board of Directors;

   (v)   authorize the conclusion of general agreements for co-operation with other international organizations;

   (vi)   elect the Directors and the President of the Bank;

   (vii)   determine the remuneration of the Directors and Alternate Directors and the salary and other terms of the contract of service of the President;

   (viii) approve, after reviewing the auditors' report, the general balance sheet and the statement of profit and loss of the Bank;

   (ix)   determine the reserves and the allocation and distribution of the net profits of the Bank;

   (x)   amend this Agreement;

   (xi)   decide to terminate the operations of the Bank and to distribute its assets; and

   (xii)   exercise such other powers as are expressly assigned to the Board of Governors in this Agreement.

3.   The Board of Governors shall retain full power to exercise authority over any matter delegated or assigned to the Board of Directors under paragraph 2 of this Article, or elsewhere in this Agreement.

Article 25. Board of Governors: procedure

1.   The Board of Governors shall hold an annual meeting and such other meetings as may be provided for by the Board or called by the Board of Directors. Meetings of the Board of Governors shall be called, by the Board of Directors, whenever requested by not less than five (5) members of the Bank or members holding not less than one quarter of the total voting power of the members.

2.   Two-thirds of the Governors shall constitute a quorum for any meeting of the Board of Governors, provided such majority represents not less than two-thirds of the total voting power of the members.

3.   The Board of Governors may by regulation establish a procedure whereby the Board of Directors may, when the latter deems such action advisable, obtain a vote of the Governors on a specific question without calling a meeting of the Board of Governors.

4.   The Board of Governors, and the Board of Directors to the extent authorized, may adopt such rules and regulations and establish such subsidiary bodies as may be necessary or appropriate to conduct the business of the Bank.

Article 26. Board of Directors: composition

1.   The Board of Directors shall be composed of twenty-three (23) members who shall not be members of the Board of Governors, and of whom:

    (i)   eleven (11) shall be elected by the Governors, representing Belgium, Denmark, France, the Federal Republic of Germany, Greece, Ireland, Italy, Luxembourg, the Netherlands, Portugal, Spain, the United Kingdom, the European Economic Community and the European Investment Bank; and

    (ii) twelve (12) shall be elected by the Governors representing other members, of whom:

        (a) four (4), by the Governors representing those countries listed in Annex A as central and eastern European countries eligible for assistance from the Bank;

        (b) four (4), by the Governors representing those countries listed in Annex A as other European countries;

        (c) four (4), by the Governors representing those countries listed in Annex A as non-European countries.

Directors, as well as representing members whose Governors have elected them, may also represent members who assign their votes to them.

2.   Directors shall be persons of high competence in economic and financial matters and shall be elected in accordance with Annex B.

3.   The Board of Governors may increase or decrease the size, or revise the composition, of the Board of Directors, in order to take into account changes in the number of members of the Bank, by an affirmative vote of not less than two-thirds of the Governors, representing not less than three-fourths of the total voting power of the members. Without prejudice to the exercise of these powers for subsequent elections, the number and com-

position of the second Board of Directors shall be as set out in paragraph 1 of this Article.

4. Each Director shall appoint an Alternate with full power to act for him and her when he or she is not present. Directors and Alternates shall be nationals of member countries. No member shall be represented by more than one Director. An Alternate may participate in meetings of the Board but may vote only when he or she is acting on place of his or her principal.

5. Directors shall hold office for a term of three (3) years and may be re-elected; provided that the first Board of Directors shall be elected by the Board of Governors at its inaugural meeting, and shall hold office until the next immediately following annual meeting of the Board of Governors or, if that Board shall so decide at that annual meeting, until its next subsequent annual meeting. They shall continue in office until their successors shall have been chosen and assumed office. If the office of a Director becomes vacant more than one hundred and eighty (180) days before the end of his or her term, a successor shall be chosen in accordance with Annex B for the remainder of the term, by the Governors who elected the former Director. A majority of the votes cast by such Governors shall be required for such election. If the office of a Director becomes vacant one hundred and eighty (180) days or less before the end of his or her term, a successor may similarly be chosen for the remainder of the term, by the votes cast by such Governors who elected the former Director, in which election majority of the votes cast by such Governors shall be required. While the office remains vacant, the Alternate of the former Director shall exercise the powers of the latter, except that of appointing an Alternate.

Article 27. Board of Directors: powers

Without prejudice to the powers of the Board of Governors as provided in Article 24 of this Agreement, the Board of Directors shall be responsible for the direction of the general operations of the Bank and, for this purpose, shall, in addition to the powers assigned to it expressly by this Agreement, exercise all the powers delegated to it by the Board of Governors, and in particular:

(i) prepare the work of the Board of Governors;

(ii) in conformity with the general directions of the Board of Governors, establish policies and take decisions concerning loans, guarantees, investment in equity capital, borrowing by the Bank, the furnishing of technical assistance and other operations of the Bank;

(iii) submit the audited accounts for each financial year for approval of the Board of Governors at each annual meeting; and

(iv) approve the budget of the Bank.

Article 28. Board of Directors: procedure

1. The Board of Directors shall normally function as the principal office of the Bank and shall meet as often as the business of the Bank may require.

2. A majority of the Directors shall constitute a quorum for any meeting of the Board of Directors, provided such majority represents not less than two-thirds of the total voting power of the members.

3. The Board of Governors shall adopt regulations under which, if there is no Director of its nationality, a member may send a representative to attend, without right to vote, any meeting of the Board of Directors when a matter particularly affecting that member is under consideration.

Article 29. Voting

1. The voting power of each member shall be equal to the number of its subscribed shares in the capital stock of the Bank. In the event of any member failing to pay any part of the amount due in respect of its obligations in relation to paid-in shares under Article 6 of this Agreement, such member shall be unable for so long as such failure continues to exercise that percentage of its voting power which corresponds to the percentage which the amount due but unpaid bears to the total amount of paid-in shares subscribed to by that member in the capital stock of the Bank.

2. In voting in the Board of Governors, each Governor shall be entitled to cast the votes of the member he or she represents. Except as otherwise expressly provided in this Agreement, all matters before the Board of Governors shall be decided by a majority of the voting power of the members voting.

3. In voting in the Board of Directors, each Director shall be entitled to cast the number of votes to which the Governors who have elected him or her are entitled and those to which any Governors who have assigned their votes to him or her, pursuant to section D or Annex B, are entitled. A Director representing more than one member may cast separately the votes of the members he or she represents. Except as otherwise expressly provided in this Agreement, and except for general policy decisions in which cases such policy decisions shall be taken by a majority of not less than two-thirds of the total voting power of the members voting, all matters before the Board of Directors shall be decided by a majority of the voting power of the members voting.

Article 30. The President

1. The Board of Governors, by a vote of a majority of the total number of Governors, representing not less than a majority of the total voting power of the members, shall elect a President of the Bank. The President, while holding office, shall not be a Governor or a Director of an Alternate for either.

2.   The term of office of the President shall be four (4) years. He or she may be re-elected. He or she shall, however, cease to hold office when the Board of Governors so decides by an affirmative vote of not less than two-thirds of the Governors, representing not less than two-thirds of the total voting power of the members. If the office of the President for any reason becomes vacant, the Board of Governors, in accordance with the provisions of paragraph 1 of this Article, shall elect a successor for up to four (4) years.

3.   The President shall not vote, except that he or she may cast a deciding vote in case of an equal division. He or she may participate in meetings of the Board of Governors and shall chair the meetings of the Board of Directors.

4.   The President shall be the legal representative of the Bank.

5.   The President shall be chief of the staff of the Bank. He or she shall be responsible for the organization, appointment and dismissal of the officers and staff in accordance with regulations to be adopted by the Board of Directors. In appointing officers and staff, he or she shall, subject to the paramount importance of efficiency and technical competence, pay due regard to recruitment on a wide geographical basis among members of the Bank.

6.   The President shall conduct, under the direction of the Board of Directors, the current business of the Bank.

Article 31. Vice-President(s)

1.   One or more Vice-Presidents shall be appointed by the Board of Directors on the recommendation of the President. A Vice-President shall hold office for such term, exercise such authority and perform such functions in the administration of the Bank, as may be determined by the Board of Directors. In the absence or incapacity of the President, a Vice-President shall exercise the authority and perform the functions of the President.

2.   A Vice-President may participate in meetings of the Board of Directors but shall have no vote at such meetings, except that he or she may cast the deciding vote when acting in place of the President.

Article 32. International character of the Bank

1.   The Bank shall not accept Special Funds or other loans or assistance that may in any way prejudice, deflect or otherwise alter its purpose or functions.

2.   The Bank, its President, Vice-President(s), officers and staff shall in their decisions take into account only considerations relevant to the Bank's purpose, functions and operations, as set out in this Agreement. Such con-

siderations shall be weighed impartially in order to achieve and carry out the purpose and functions of the Bank.

3. The President, Vice-President(s), officers and staff of the Bank, in the discharge of their offices, shall owe their duty entirely to the Bank and to no other authority. Each member of the Bank shall respect the international character of this duty and shall refrain from all attempts to influence any of them in the discharge of their duties.

Article 33. Location of offices

1. The principal office of the Bank shall be located in London.

2. The Bank may establish agencies or branch offices in the territory of any member of the Bank.

Article 34. Depositories and channels of communication

1. Each member shall designate its central bank, or such other institution as may be agreed upon with the Bank, as a depository for all the Bank's holdings of its currency as well as other assets of the Bank.

2. Each member shall designate an appropriate official entity with which the Bank may communicate in connection with any matter arising under this Agreement.

Article 35. Publication of reports and provision of information

1. The Bank shall publish an annual report containing an audited statement of its accounts and shall circulate to members at intervals of three (3) months or less a summary statement of its financial position and a profit and loss statement showing the results of its operations. The financial accounts shall be kept in ECU.

2. The Bank shall report annually on the environmental impact of its activities and may publish such other reports as it deems desirable to advance its purpose.

3. Copies of all reports, statements and publications made under this Article shall be distributed to members.

Article 36. Allocation and distribution of net income

1. The Board of Governors shall determine at least annually what part of the Bank's net income, after making provisions for reserves and, if necessary, against possible losses under paragraph 1 of Article 17 of this Agreement,

shall be allocated to surplus or other purposes and what part, if any, shall be distributed. Any such decision on the allocation of the Bank's net income to other purposes shall be taken by a majority of not less than two-thirds of the Governors, representing not less than two-thirds of the total voting power of the members. No such allocation, and no distribution, shall be made until the general reserve amounts to at least ten (10) per cent of the authorized capital stock.

2.   Any distribution referred to in the preceding paragraph shall be made in proportion to the number of paid-in shares held by each member; provided that in calculating such number, account shall be taken only of payments received in cash and promissory notes encashed in respect of such shares on or before the end of the relevant fiscal year.

3.   Payments to each member shall be made in such manner as the Board of Governors shall determine. Such payments and their use by the receiving country shall be without restriction by any member.

Chapter VII—Withdrawal and suspension of membership: temporary suspension and termination of operation

Article 37. Right of members to withdraw

1.   Any member may withdraw from the Bank at any time by transmitting a notice in writing to the Bank at its principal office.

2.   Withdrawal by a member shall become effective, and its membership shall cease, on the date specified in its notice but in not event less than six (6) months after such notice is received by the Bank. However, at any time before the withdrawal becomes finally effective, the member may notify the Bank in writing of the cancellation of its notice of intention to withdraw.

Article 38. Suspension of membership

1.   If a member fails to fulfil any of its obligations to the Bank, the Bank may suspend its membership by decision of a majority of not less than two-thirds of the Governors, representing not less than two-thirds of the total voting power of the members. The member so suspended shall automatically cease to be a member one year from the date of its suspension unless a decision is taken by not less than the same majority to restore the member to good standing.

2.   While under suspension, a member shall not be entitled to exercise any rights under this Agreement, except the right of withdrawal, but shall remain subject to all its obligations.

Article 39. Settlement of accounts with former members

1. After the date on which a member ceases to be a member, such former member shall remain liable for its direct obligations to the Bank and for its contingent liabilities to the Bank so long as any part of the loans, equity investments or guarantees contracted before it ceased to be a member are outstanding; but it shall cease to incur such liabilities with respect to loans, equity investments and guarantees entered into thereafter by the Bank and to share either in the income or the expenses of the Bank.

2. At the time a member ceases to be a member, the Bank shall arrange for the repurchase of such former member's shares as a part of the settlement of accounts with such former member in accordance with the provisions of this Article. For this purpose, the purchase price of the shares shall be the value shown by the books of the Bank on the date of cessation of membership, with the original purchase price of each share being its maximum value.

3. The payment for shares repurchased by the Bank under this Article shall be governed by the following conditions:

   (i) any amount due to the former member for its shares shall be withheld so long as the former member, its central bank or any of its agencies or instrumentalities remains liable, as borrower or guarantor, to the Bank and such amount may, at the option of the Bank be applied on any such liability as it matures. No amount shall be withheld on account of the liability of the former member resulting from its subscription for shares in accordance with paragraphs 4, 5 and 7 of Article 6 of this Agreement. In any event, no amount due to a member for its shares shall be paid until six (6) months after the date upon which the member ceases to be a member;

   (ii) payments for shares may be made from time to time, upon their surrender by the former member, to the extent by which the amount due as the repurchase price in accordance with paragraph 2 of this Article exceeds the aggregate amount of liabilities on loans, equity investments and guarantees in sub paragraph (i) of this paragraph until the former member has received the full repurchase price;

   (iii) payments shall be made on such conditions and in such fully convertible currencies, or ECU, and on such dates, as the Bank determines; and

   (iv) if losses are sustained by the Bank on any guarantees, participation in loans, or loans which were outstanding on the date when the member ceased to be a member, or if a net loss is sustained by the Bank on equity investments held by it on such date, and the amount of such losses exceeds the amount of the reserves provided against losses on the date when the member ceased to be a member, such former member shall repay, upon demand, the amount by which repurchase the price of its shares would have been reduced if the losses had been taken into account when the repurchase price was determined. In addition, the former member shall remain liable on any call for unpaid subscriptions under paragraph 4 of Article 6 of this Agreement, to the extent that it would have been required to respond if the impairment of capital had occurred and the call had been made at the time the repurchase price of its shares was determined.

4.   If the Bank terminates its operations pursuant to Article 41 of this Agreement within six (6) months of the date upon which any member ceases to be a member, all rights of such former members shall be determined in accordance with the provisions of Articles 41 to 43 of this Agreement.

Article 40. Temporary suspension of operations

In an emergency, the Board of Directors may suspend temporarily operations in respect of new loans, guarantees, underwriting, technical assistance and equity investments pending an opportunity for further consideration and action by the Board of Governors.

Article 41. Termination of operations

The Bank may terminate its operations by the affirmative vote of not less than two-thirds of the Governors, representing not less than three-fourths of the total voting power of the members. Upon such termination of operations the Bank shall forthwith cease all activities, except those incident to the orderly realization, conservation and preservation of its assets and settlement of its obligations.

Article 42. Liability of members and payments of claims

1.   In the event of termination of the operations of the Bank, the liability of all members for all uncalled subscriptions to the capital stock of the Bank shall continue until all claims of creditors; including all contingent claims, shall have been discharged.

2.   Creditors on ordinary operations holding direct claims shall be paid first out of the assets of the Bank, secondly out of the payments to be made to the Bank in respect of unpaid paid-in shares, and then out of payments to be made to the Bank in respect of callable capital stock. Before making any payments to creditors holding direct claims, the Board of Directors shall

make such arrangements as are necessary, in its judgment, to ensure a pro rata distribution among holders of direct and holders of contingent claims.

Article 43. Distribution of assets

1.   No distribution under this Chapter shall be made to members on account of their subscriptions to the capital stock of the Bank until:

> (i)   all liabilities to creditors have been discharged or provided for; and

> (ii) the Board of Governors has decided by a vote of not less than two-thirds of the Governors, representing not less than three-fourths of the total voting power of the members, to make a distribution.

2.   Any distribution of the assets of the Bank to the members shall be in proportion to the capital stock held by each member and shall be effected at such times and under such conditions as the Bank shall deem fair and equitable. The shares of assets distributed need not be uniform as to type of assets. No member shall be entitled to receive its share in such a distribution of assets until it has settled all of its obligations to the Bank.

3.   Any member receiving assets distributed pursuant to this Article shall enjoy the same rights with respect to such assets as the Bank enjoyed prior to their distribution.

Chapter VIII—Status, immunities, privileges and exemptions
Article 44. Purposes of chapter

To enable the Bank to fulfil its purpose and the functions with which it is entrusted, the status, immunities, privileges and exemptions set forth in this Chapter shall be accorded to the Bank in the territory of each member country.

Article 45. Status of the Bank

The Bank shall possess full legal personality and, in particular, the full legal capacity:

> (i)   to contract;

> (ii) to acquire, and dispose of, immovable and movable property; and

> (iii) to institute legal proceedings.

Article 46. Position of the Bank with regard to judicial process

Actions may be brought against the Bank only in a court of competent jurisdiction in the territory of a country in which the Bank has an office, has appointed an agent for the purpose of accepting service or notice of process, or has issued or guaranteed securities. No actions shall, however, be brought by members or persons acting for or deriving claims from members. The property and assets of the Bank shall, wheresoever located and by whomsoever held, be immune from all forms of seizure, attachment or execution before the delivery of final judgment against the Bank.

Article 47. Immunity of assets from seizure

Property and assets of the Bank, wheresoever located and by whomsoever held, shall be immune from search, requisition, confiscation, expropriation or any other form of taking or foreclosure by executive or legislative action.

Article 48. Immunity of archives

The archives of the Bank, and in general all documents belonging to it or held by it, shall be inviolable.

Article 49. Freedom of assets from restrictions

To the extent necessary to carry out the purpose and functions of the Bank and subject to the provisions of this Agreement, all property and assets of the Bank shall be free from restrictions, regulations, controls and moratoria of any nature.

Article 50. Privilege for communications

The official communications of the Bank shall be accorded by each member the same treatment that it accords to the official communications of any other member.

Article 51. Immunities of officers and employees

All Governors, Directors, Alternates, officers and employees of the Bank and experts performing missions for the Bank shall be immune from legal process with respect to acts performed by them in their official capacity, except when the Bank waives this immunity, and shall enjoy inviolability of all their official papers and documents. This immunity shall not apply, however, to civil liability in the case of damage arising from a road traffic accident caused by any such Governor, Director, Alternate, officer, employee or expert.

Article 52. *Privileges of officers and employees*

1.   All Governors, Directors, Alternates, officers and employees of the Bank and experts of the Bank performing missions for the Bank:

   (i) not being local nationals, shall be accorded the same immunities from immigration restrictions, alien registration requirements and national service obligations, and the same facilities as regards exchange regulations, as are accorded by members to the representatives, official, and employees of comparable rank of other members; and

   (ii) shall be granted the same treatment in respect of travelling facilities as is accorded by members to representatives, officials and employees of comparable rank of other members.

2.   The spouses and immediate dependants of those Directors, Alternate Directors, officers, employees and experts of the Bank who are resident in the country in which the principal office of the Bank is located shall be accorded opportunity to take employment in that country. The spouses and immediate dependants of those Directors, Alternate Directors, officers, employees and experts of the Bank who are resident in a country in which any agency or branch office of the Bank is located should, wherever possible, in accordance with the national law of that country, be accorded similar opportunity in that country. The Bank shall negotiate specific agreements implementing the provisions of this paragraph with the country in which the principal office of the Bank is located and, as appropriate, with the other countries concerned.

Article 53. *Exemption from taxation*

1.   Within the scope of its official activities the Bank, its assets, property, and income shall be exempt from all direct taxes.

2.   When purchases or services of substantial value and necessary for the exercise of the official activities of the Bank are made or used by the Bank and when the price of such purchases or services includes taxes or duties, the member that has levied the taxes or duties shall, if they are identifiable, take appropriate measures to grant exemption from such taxes or duties or to provide for their reimbursement.

3.   Goods imported by the Bank and necessary for the exercise of its official activities shall be exempt from all import duties and taxes, and from all import prohibitions and restrictions. Similarly goods exported by the Bank and necessary for the exercise of its official activities shall be exempt from all export duties and taxes, and from all export prohibitions and restrictions.

4. Goods acquired or imported and exempted under this Article shall not be sold, hired out, lent or given away against payment or free of charge, except in accordance with conditions laid down by the members which have granted exemptions or reimbursements.

5. The provisions of this Article shall not apply to taxes or duties which are no more than charges for public utility services.

6. Directors, Alternate Directors, officers and employees of the Bank shall be subject to an internal effective tax for the benefit of the Bank on salaries and emoluments paid by the Bank, subject to conditions to be laid down and rules to be adopted by the Board of Governors within a period of one year from the date of entry into force of this Agreement. From the date on which this tax is applied, such salaries and emoluments shall be exempt from national income tax. The members may, however, take into account the salaries and emoluments thus exempt when assessing the amount of tax to be applied to income from other sources.

7. Notwithstanding the provisions of paragraph 6 of this Article, a member may deposit, with its instrument of ratification, acceptance or approval, a declaration that such member retains for itself, its political subdivisions or its local authorities the right to tax salaries and emoluments paid by the Bank to citizens or nationals of such member. The Bank shall be exempt from any obligation for the payment, withholding or collection of such taxes. The bank shall not make any reimbursement for such taxes.

8. Paragraph 6 of this Article shall not apply to pensions and annuities paid by the Bank.

9. No tax of any kind shall be levied on any obligation or security issued by the Bank, including any dividend or interest thereon, by whomsoever held:

(i) which discriminates against such obligation or security solely because it is issued by the Bank, or

(ii) if the sole jurisdictional basis for such taxation is the place or currency in which it is issued, made payable or paid, or the location of any office or place of business maintained by the Bank.

10. No tax of any kind shall be levied on any obligation or security guarantied by the Bank, including any dividend or interest thereon, by whomsoever held:

(i) which discriminates against such obligation or security solely because its guarantied by the Bank, or

(ii) if the sole jurisdictional basis for such taxation is the location of any office; place of business maintained by the Bank.

Article 54. Implementation of chapter

Each member shall promptly take such action as is necessary for the purpose of implementing the provisions of this Chapter and shall inform the Bank of the detailed action which it has taken.

Article 55. Waiver of immunities, privileges and exemptions

The immunities, privileges and exemptions conferred under this Chapter are granted in the interest of the Bank. The Board of Directors may waive to such extent and upon such conditions as it may determine any of the immunities, privileges and exemptions conferred under this Chapter in cases where such action would, in its opinion, be appropriate in the best interests of the Bank. The President shall have the right and the duty to waive any immunity, privilege or exemption in respect of any officer, employee or expert of the Bank, other than the President, Vice-President, where, in his or her opinion, the immunity, privilege or exemption would impede the course of justice and can be waived without prejudice to the interests of the Bank. In similar circumstances and under the same conditions, the Board of Directors shall have the right and the duty to waive any immunity, privilege or exemption in respect of the President and each Vice-President.

Chapter IX—Amendments, interpretation, arbitration

Article 56. Amendments

1. Any proposal to amend this Agreement, whether emanating from a member, a Governor or the Board of Directors, shall be communicated to the Chairman of the Board of Governors who shall bring the proposal before that Board. If the proposed amendment is approved by the Board the Bank shall, by any rapid means of communication, ask all members whether they accept the proposed amendment. When not less than three-fourths of the members (including at least two countries from central and eastern Europe listed in Annex A), having not less than four-fifths of the total voting power of the members, have accepted the proposed amendment, the Bank shall certify that fact by formal communication addressed to all members.

2. Notwithstanding paragraph 1 of this Article:

    (i) acceptance by all members shall be required in the case of any amendment modifying:

        (a) the right to withdraw from the Bank;

        (b) the rights pertaining to purchase of capital stock provided from in paragraph 3 of Article 5 of this Agreement;

        (c) the limitations on liability provided for in paragraph 7 of Article 5 of this Agreement; and

(d) the purpose and functions of the Bank defined by Articles 1 and 2 of this Agreement;

(ii) acceptance by not less than three-fourths of the members having not less than eighty-five (85) per cent of the total voting power of the members shall be required in the case of any amendment modifying paragraph 4 of Article 8 of this Agreement.

When the requirements for accepting any such proposed amendment have been met, the Bank shall certify that fact by formal communication addressed to all members.

3.   Amendments shall enter into force for all members three (3) months after the date of the formal communication provided for in paragraphs 1 and 2 of this Article unless the Board of Governors specifies a different period.

Article 57. Interpretation and application

1.   Any question of interpretation or application of the provisions of this Agreement arising between any member and the Bank, or between any members of the Bank, shall be submitted to the Board of Directors for its decision. If there is no Director of its nationality in that Board, a member particularly affected by the question under consideration shall be entitled to direct representation in the meeting of the Board of Directors during such consideration. The representative of such member shall, however, have no vote. Such right of representation shall be regulated by the Board of Governors.

2.   In any case where the Board of Directors has given a decision under paragraph 1 of this Article, any member may require that the question be referred to the Board of Governors, whose decision shall be final. Pending the decision of the Board of Governors, the Bank may, so far as it deems it necessary, act on the basis of the decision of the Board of Directors.

Article 58. Arbitration

If a disagreement should arise between the Bank and a member which has ceased to be a member, or between the Bank and any member after adoption of a decision to terminate the operations of the Bank, such disagreement shall be submitted to arbitration by a tribunal of three (3) arbitrators, one appointed by the Bank, another by the member or former member concerned, and the third, unless the parties otherwise agree, by the President of the International Court of Justice or such other authority as may have been prescribed by regulations adopted by the Board of Governors. A majority vote of the arbitrators shall be sufficient to reach a decision which shall be final and binding upon the parties. The third arbitrator shall have full power to settle all questions of procedure in any case where the parties are in disagreement with respect thereto.

Article 59. *Approval deemed given*

Whenever the approval or the acceptance of any member is required before any act may be done by the Bank, except under Article 56 of this Agreement, approval or acceptance shall be deemed to have been given unless the member presents an objection within such reasonable period as the Bank may fix in notifying the member of the proposed act.

Chapter X—Final provisions

Article 60. *Signature and deposit*

1.   This Agreement, deposited with the Government of the French Republic (hereinafter called "the Depository"), shall remain open until 31 December 1990 for signature by the prospective members whose names are set forth in Annex A to this Agreement.

2.   The Depository shall communicate certified copies of this Agreement to all the Signatories.

Article 61. *Ratification, acceptance or approval*

1.   The Agreement shall be subject to ratification, acceptance or approval by the Signatories. Instruments of ratification, acceptance or approval shall, subject to paragraph 2 of this Article, be deposited with the Depository not later than 31 March 1991. The Depository shall duly notify the other Signatories of each deposit and the date thereof.

2.   Any Signatory may become a party to this Agreement by depositing an instrument of ratification, acceptance or approval until one year after the date of its entry into force or, if necessary, until such later date as may be decided by a majority of Governors, representing a majority of the total voting power of the members.

3.   A Signatory whose instrument referred to in paragraph 1 of this Article is deposited before the date on which this Agreement enters into force shall become a member of the Bank on that date. Any other Signatory which complies with the provisions of the preceding paragraph shall become a member of the Bank on the date on which its instrument of ratification, acceptance or approval is deposited.

Article 62. *Entry into force*

1.   This Agreement shall enter into force when instruments of ratification, acceptance or approval have been deposited by Signatories whose initial

subscriptions represent not less than two thirds of the total subscriptions set forth in Annex A, including at least two countries from central and eastern Europe listed in Annex A.

2. If this Agreement has not entered into force by 31 March 1991, the Depository may convene a conference of interested prospective members to determine the future course of action and decide a new date by which instruments of ratification, acceptance or approval shall be deposited.

Article 63. Inaugural meeting and commencement of operations

1. As soon as this Agreement enters into force under Article 62 of this Agreement, each member shall appoint a Governor. The Depository shall call the first meeting of the Board of Governors within sixty (60) days of entry into force of this Agreement under Article 62 or as soon as possible thereafter.

2. At its first meeting, the Board of Governors:

   (i) shall elect the President;

   (ii) shall elect the Directors of the Bank in accordance with Article 26 of this Agreement;

   (iii) shall make arrangements for determining the date of the commencement of the Bank's operations; and

   (iv) shall make such other arrangements as appear to it necessary to prepare for the commencement of the Bank's operations.

3. The Bank shall notify its members of the date of commencement of its operations.

Done at Paris on 29 May 1990 in a single original, whose English, French, German and Russian texts are equally authentic, which shall be deposited in the archives of the Depository which shall transmit a duly certified copy to each of the other prospective members whose names are set forth in Annex A.

[*Note:* Annexes are not reproduced here. Annex A sets forth initial subscriptions to EBRD capital stock; and Annex B prescribes procedures for selection of Directors.]

CHARTER OF THE WTO

Citation: Marrakesh Agreement Establishing the World Trade Organization, done at Marrakesh, Apr. 15, 1994, 33 ILM 1125 (1994).

Contents

Annexes [Only the List of Annexes is reproduced here]

Agreement Establishing the World Trade Organization

The Parties to this Agreement,

Recognizing that their relations in the field of trade and economic endeavour should be conducted with a view to raising standards of living, ensuring full employment and a large and steadily growing volume of real income and effective demand, and expanding the production of and trade in goods and services, while allowing for the optimal use of the world's resources in accordance with the objective of sustainable development, seeking both to protect and preserve the environment and to enhance the means for doing so in a manner consistent with their respective needs and concerns at different levels of economic development,

Recognizing further that there is need for positive efforts designed to ensure that developing countries, and especially the least developed among them, secure a share in the growth in international trade commensurate with the needs of their economic development,

Being desirous of contributing to these objectives by entering into reciprocal and mutually advantageous arrangements directed to the substantial reduction of tariffs and other barriers to trade and to the elimination of discriminatory treatment in international trade relations,

Resolved, therefore, to develop an integrated, more viable and durable multilateral trading system encompassing the General Agreement on Tariffs and Trade, the results of past trade liberalization efforts, and all of the results of the Uruguay Round of Multilateral Trade Negotiations,

Determined to preserve the basic principles and to further the objectives underlying this multilateral trading system,

Agree as follows:

Article I

Establishment of the Organization

The World Trade Organization (hereinafter referred to as "the WTO") is hereby established.

Article II

Scope of the WTO

1. The WTO shall provide the common institutional framework for the conduct of trade relations among its Members in matters related to the agreements and associated legal instruments included in the Annexes to this Agreement.

2. The agreements and associated legal instruments included in Annexes 1, 2 and 3 (hereinafter referred to as "Multilateral Trade Agreements") are integral parts of this Agreement, binding on all Members.

3.   The agreements and associated legal instruments included in Annex 4 (hereinafter referred to as "Plurilateral Trade Agreements") are also part of this Agreement for those Members that have accepted them, and are binding on those Members. The Plurilateral Trade Agreements do not create either obligations or rights for Members that have not accepted them.

4.   The General Agreement on Tariffs and Trade 1994 as specified in Annex 1A (hereinafter referred to as "GATT 1994") is legally distinct from the General Agreement on Tariffs and Trade, dated 30 October 1947, annexed to the Final Act Adopted at the Conclusion of the Second Session of the Preparatory Committee of the United Nations Conference on Trade and Employment, as subsequently rectified, amended or modified (hereinafter referred to as "GATT 1947").

Article III

Functions of the WTO

1.   The WTO shall facilitate the implementation, administration and operation, and further the objectives, of this Agreement and of the Multilateral Trade Agreements, and shall also provide the framework for the implementation, administration and operation of the Plurilateral Trade Agreements.

2.   The WTO shall provide the forum for negotiations among its Members concerning their multilateral trade relations in matters dealt with under the agreements in the Annexes to this Agreement. The WTO may also provide a forum for further negotiations among its Members concerning their multilateral trade relations, and a framework for the implementation of the results of such negotiations, as may be decided by the Ministerial Conference.

3.   The WTO shall administer the Understanding on Rules and Procedures Governing the Settlement of Disputes (hereinafter referred to as the "Dispute Settlement Understanding" or "DSU") in Annex 2 to this Agreement.

4.   The WTO shall administer the Trade Policy Review Mechanism (hereinafter referred to as the "TPRM") provided for in Annex 3 to this Agreement.

5.   With a view to achieving greater coherence in global economic policy-making, the WTO shall cooperate, as appropriate, with the International Monetary Fund and with the International Bank for Reconstruction and Development and its affiliated agencies.

Article IV

Structure of the WTO

1.   There shall be a Ministerial Conference composed of representatives of all the Members, which shall meet at least once every two years. The

Ministerial Conference shall carry out the functions of the WTO and take actions necessary to this effect. The Ministerial Conference shall have the authority to take decisions on all matters under any of the Multilateral Trade Agreements, if so requested by a Member, in accordance with the specific requirements for decision-making in this Agreement and in the relevant Multilateral Trade Agreement.

2. There shall be a General Council composed of representatives of all the Members, which shall meet as appropriate. In the intervals between meetings of the Ministerial Conference, its functions shall be conducted by the General Council. The General Council shall also carry out the functions assigned to it by this Agreement. The General Council shall establish its rules of procedure and approve the rules of procedure for the Committees provided for in paragraph 7.

3. The General Council shall convene as appropriate to discharge the responsibilities of the Dispute Settlement Body provided for in the Dispute Settlement Understanding. The Dispute Settlement Body may have its own chairman and shall establish such rules of procedure as it deems necessary for the fulfilment of those responsibilities.

4. The General Council shall convene as appropriate to discharge the responsibilities of the Trade Policy Review Body provided for in the TPRM. The Trade Policy Review Body may have its own chairman and shall establish such rules of procedure as it deems necessary for the fulfilment of those responsibilities.

5. There shall be a Council for Trade in Goods, a Council for Trade in Services and a Council for Trade-Related Aspects of Intellectual Property Rights (hereinafter referred to as the "Council for TRIPS"), which shall operate under the general guidance of the General Council. The Council for Trade in Goods shall oversee the functioning of the Multilateral Trade Agreements in Annex 1A. The Council for Trade in Services shall oversee the functioning of the General Agreement on Trade in Services (hereinafter referred to as "GATS"). The Council for TRIPS shall oversee the functioning of the Agreement on Trade-Related Aspects of Intellectual Property Rights (hereinafter referred to as the "Agreement on TRIPS"). These Councils shall carry out the functions assigned to them by their respective agreements and by the General Council. They shall establish their respective rules of procedure subject to the approval of the General Council. Membership in these Councils shall be open to representatives of all Members. These Councils shall meet as necessary to carry out their functions.

6. The Council for Trade in Goods, the Council for Trade in Services and the Council for TRIPS shall establish subsidiary bodies as required. These

subsidiary bodies shall establish their respective rules of procedure subject to the approval of their respective Councils.

7.   The Ministerial Conference shall establish a Committee on Trade and Development, a Committee on Balance-of-Payments Restrictions and a Committee on Budget, Finance and Administration, which shall carry out the functions assigned to them by this Agreement and by the Multilateral Trade Agreements, and any additional functions assigned to them by the General Council, and may establish such additional Committees with such functions as it may deem appropriate. As part of its functions, the Committee on Trade and Development shall periodically review the special provisions in the Multilateral Trade Agreements in favour of the least-developed country Members and report to the General Council for appropriate action. Membership in these Committees shall be open to representatives of all Members.

8.   The bodies provided for under the Plurilateral Trade Agreements shall carry out the functions assigned to them under those Agreements and shall operate within the institutional framework of the WTO. These bodies shall keep the General Council informed of their activities on a regular basis.

Article V

Relations with Other Organizations

1.   The General Council shall make appropriate arrangements for effective cooperation with other intergovernmental organizations that have responsibilities related to those of the WTO.

2.   The General Council may make appropriate arrangements for consultation and cooperation with non-governmental organizations concerned with matters related to those of the WTO.

Article VI

The Secretariat

1.   There shall be a Secretariat of the WTO (hereinafter referred to as "the Secretariat") headed by a Director-General.

2.   The Ministerial Conference shall appoint the Director-General and adopt regulations setting out the powers, duties, conditions of service and term of office of the Director-General.

3.   The Director-General shall appoint the members of the staff of the Secretariat and determine their duties and conditions of service in accordance with regulations adopted by the Ministerial Conference.

4. The responsibilities of the Director-General and of the staff of the Secretariat shall be exclusively international in character. In the discharge of their duties, the Director-General and the staff of the Secretariat shall not seek or accept instructions from any government or any other authority external to the WTO. They shall refrain from any action which might adversely reflect on their position as international officials. The Members of the WTO shall respect the international character of the responsibilities of the Director-General and of the staff of the Secretariat and shall not seek to influence them in the discharge of their duties.

Article VII

Budget and Contributions

1. The Director-General shall present to the Committee on Budget, Finance and Administration the annual budget estimate and financial statement of the WTO. The Committee on Budget, Finance and Administration shall review the annual budget estimate and the financial statement presented by the Director-General and make recommendations thereon to the General Council. The annual budget estimate shall be subject to approval by the General Council.

2. The Committee on Budget, Finance and Administration shall propose to the General Council financial regulations which shall include provisions setting out:

  (a) the scale of contributions apportioning the expenses of the WTO among its Members; and

  (b) the measures to be taken in respect of Members in arrears.

  The financial regulations shall be based, as far as practicable, on the regulations and practices of GATT 1947.

3. The General Council shall adopt the financial regulations and the annual budget estimate by a two-thirds majority comprising more than half of the Members of the WTO.

4. Each Member shall promptly contribute to the WTO its share in the expenses of the WTO in accordance with the financial regulations adopted by the General Council.

Article VIII

Status of the WTO

1. The WTO shall have legal personality, and shall be accorded by each of its Members such legal capacity as may be necessary for the exercise of its functions.

2.   The WTO shall be accorded by each of its Members such privileges and immunities as are necessary for the exercise of its functions.

3.   The officials of the WTO and the representatives of the Members shall similarly be accorded by each of its Members such privileges and immunities as are necessary for the independent exercise of their functions in connection with the WTO.

4.   The privileges and immunities to be accorded by a Member to the WTO, its officials, and the representatives of its Members shall be similar to the privileges and immunities stipulated in the Convention on the Privileges and Immunities of the Specialized Agencies, approved by the General Assembly of the United Nations on 21 November 1947.

5.   The WTO may conclude a headquarters agreement.

Article IX

Decision-Making

1.   The WTO shall continue the practice of decision-making by consensus followed under GATT 1947. [FN1] Except as otherwise provided, where a decision cannot be arrived at by consensus, the matter at issue shall be decided by voting. At meetings of the Ministerial Conference and the General Council, each Member of the WTO shall have one vote. Where the European Communities exercise their right to vote, they shall have a number of votes equal to the number of their member States [FN2] which are Members of the WTO. Decisions of the Ministerial Conference and the General Council shall be taken by a majority of the votes cast, unless otherwise provided in this Agreement or in the relevant Multilateral Trade Agreement. [FN3]

2.   The Ministerial Conference and the General Council shall have the exclusive authority to adopt interpretations of this Agreement and of the Multilateral Trade Agreements. In the case of an interpretation of a Multilateral Trade Agreement in Annex 1, they shall exercise their author-

---

FN1. The body concerned shall be deemed to have decided by consensus on a matter submitted for its consideration, if no Member, present at the meeting when the decision is taken, formally objects to the proposed decision.

FN2. The number of votes of the European Communities and their member States shall in no case exceed the number of the member States of the European Communities.

FN3. Decisions by the General Council when convened as the Dispute Settlement Body shall be taken only in accordance with the provisions of paragraph 4 of Article 2 of the Dispute Settlement Understanding.

ity on the basis of a recommendation by the Council overseeing the functioning of that Agreement. The decision to adopt an interpretation shall be taken by a three-fourths majority of the Members. This paragraph shall not be used in a manner that would undermine the amendment provisions in Article X.

3. In exceptional circumstances, the Ministerial Conference may decide to waive an obligation imposed on a Member by this Agreement or any of the Multilateral Trade Agreements, provided that any such decision shall be taken by three fourths [FN4] of the Members unless otherwise provided for in this paragraph.

> (a) A request for a waiver concerning this Agreement shall be submitted to the Ministerial Conference for consideration pursuant to the practice of decision-making by consensus. The Ministerial Conference shall establish a time-period, which shall not exceed 90 days, to consider the request. If consensus is not reached during the time-period, any decision to grant a waiver shall be taken by three fourths [FN4] of the Members.

> (b) A request for a waiver concerning the Multilateral Trade Agreements in Annexes 1A or 1B or 1C and their annexes shall be submitted initially to the Council for Trade in Goods, the Council for Trade in Services or the Council for TRIPS, respectively, for consideration during a time-period which shall not exceed 90 days. At the end of the time-period, the relevant Council shall submit a report to the Ministerial Conference.

4. A decision by the Ministerial Conference granting a waiver shall state the exceptional circumstances justifying the decision, the terms and conditions governing the application of the waiver, and the date on which the waiver shall terminate. Any waiver granted for a period of more than one year shall be reviewed by the Ministerial Conference not later than one year after it is granted, and thereafter annually until the waiver terminates. In each review, the Ministerial Conference shall examine whether the exceptional circumstances justifying the waiver still exist and whether the terms and conditions attached to the waiver have been met. The Ministerial Conference, on the basis of the annual review, may extend, modify or terminate the waiver.

5. Decisions under a Plurilateral Trade Agreement, including any decisions on interpretations and waivers, shall be governed by the provisions of that Agreement.

FN4. A decision to grant a waiver in respect of any obligation subject to a transition period or a period for staged implementation that the requesting Member has not performed by the end of the relevant period shall be taken only by consensus.

Article X

Amendments

1.   Any Member of the WTO may initiate a proposal to amend the provisions of this Agreement or the Multilateral Trade Agreements in Annex 1 by submitting such proposal to the Ministerial Conference. The Councils listed in paragraph 5 of Article IV may also submit to the Ministerial Conference proposals to amend the provisions of the corresponding Multilateral Trade Agreements in Annex 1 the functioning of which they oversee. Unless the Ministerial Conference decides on a longer period, for a period of 90 days after the proposal has been tabled formally at the Ministerial Conference any decision by the Ministerial Conference to submit the proposed amendment to the Members for acceptance shall be taken by consensus. Unless the provisions of paragraphs 2, 5 or 6 apply, that decision shall specify whether the provisions of paragraphs 3 or 4 shall apply. If consensus is reached, the Ministerial Conference shall forthwith submit the proposed amendment to the Members for acceptance. If consensus is not reached at a meeting of the Ministerial Conference within the established period, the Ministerial Conference shall decide by a two-thirds majority of the Members whether to submit the proposed amendment to the Members for acceptance. Except as provided in paragraphs 2, 5 and 6, the provisions of paragraph 3 shall apply to the proposed amendment, unless the Ministerial Conference decides by a three-fourths majority of the Members that the provisions of paragraph 4 shall apply.

2.   Amendments to the provisions of this Article and to the provisions of the following Articles shall take effect only upon acceptance by all Members:

> Article IX of this Agreement;
> Articles I and II of GATT 1994;
> Article II:1 of GATS;
> Article 4 of the Agreement on TRIPS.

3.   Amendments to provisions of this Agreement, or of the Multilateral Trade Agreements in Annexes 1A and 1C, other than those listed in paragraphs 2 and 6, of a nature that would alter the rights and obligations of the Members, shall take effect for the Members that have accepted them upon acceptance by two thirds of the Members and thereafter for each other Member upon acceptance by it. The Ministerial Conference may decide by a three-fourths majority of the Members that any amendment made effective under this paragraph is of such a nature that any Member which has not accepted it within a period specified by the Ministerial Conference in each case shall be free to withdraw from the WTO or to remain a Member with the consent of the Ministerial Conference.

4.   Amendments to provisions of this Agreement or of the Multilateral Trade Agreements in Annexes 1A and 1C, other than those listed in paragraphs 2 and 6, of a nature that would not alter the rights and obligations of the Members, shall take effect for all Members upon acceptance by two thirds of the Members.

5.   Except as provided in paragraph 2 above, amendments to Parts I, II and III of GATS and the respective annexes shall take effect for the Members that have accepted them upon acceptance by two thirds of the Members and thereafter for each Member upon acceptance by it. The Ministerial Conference may decide by a three-fourths majority of the Members that any amendment made effective under the preceding provision is of such a nature that any Member which has not accepted it within a period specified by the Ministerial Conference in each case shall be free to withdraw from the WTO or to remain a Member with the consent of the Ministerial Conference. Amendments to Parts IV, V and VI of GATS and the respective annexes shall take effect for all Members upon acceptance by two thirds of the Members.

6.   Notwithstanding the other provisions of this Article, amendments to the Agreement on TRIPS meeting the requirements of paragraph 2 of Article 71 thereof may be adopted by the Ministerial Conference without further formal acceptance process.

7.   Any Member accepting an amendment to this Agreement or to a Multilateral Trade Agreement in Annex 1 shall deposit an instrument of acceptance with the Director-General of the WTO within the period of acceptance specified by the Ministerial Conference.

8.   Any Member of the WTO may initiate a proposal to amend the provisions of the Multilateral Trade Agreements in Annexes 2 and 3 by submitting such proposal to the Ministerial Conference. The decision to approve amendments to the Multilateral Trade Agreement in Annex 2 shall be made by consensus and these amendments shall take effect for all Members upon approval by the Ministerial Conference. Decisions to approve amendments to the Multilateral Trade Agreement in Annex 3 shall take effect for all Members upon approval by the Ministerial Conference.

9.   The Ministerial Conference, upon the request of the Members parties to a trade agreement, may decide exclusively by consensus to add that agreement to Annex 4. The Ministerial Conference, upon the request of the Members parties to a Plurilateral Trade Agreement, may decide to delete that Agreement from Annex 4.

10. Amendments to a Plurilateral Trade Agreement shall be governed by the provisions of that Agreement.

Article XI

Original Membership

1.   The contracting parties to GATT 1947 as of the date of entry into force of this Agreement, and the European Communities, which accept this Agreement and the Multilateral Trade Agreements and for which Schedules of Concessions and Commitments are annexed to GATT 1994 and for which Schedules of Specific Commitments are annexed to GATS shall become original Members of the WTO.

2.   The least-developed countries recognized as such by the United Nations will only be required to undertake commitments and concessions to the extent consistent with their individual development, financial and trade needs or their administrative and institutional capabilities.

Article XII

Accession

1.   Any State or separate customs territory possessing full autonomy in the conduct of its external commercial relations and of the other matters provided for in this Agreement and the Multilateral Trade Agreements may accede to this Agreement, on terms to be agreed between it and the WTO. Such accession shall apply to this Agreement and the Multilateral Trade Agreements annexed thereto.

2.   Decisions on accession shall be taken by the Ministerial Conference. The Ministerial Conference shall approve the agreement on the terms of accession by a two-thirds majority of the Members of the WTO.

3.   Accession to a Plurilateral Trade Agreement shall be governed by the provisions of that Agreement.

Article XIII

Non-Application of Multilateral Trade Agreements between Particular Members

1.   This Agreement and the Multilateral Trade Agreements in Annexes 1 and 2 shall not apply as between any Member and any other Member if either of the Members, at the time either becomes a Member, does not consent to such application.

2.   Paragraph 1 may be invoked between original Members of the WTO which were contracting parties to GATT 1947 only where Article XXXV of that Agreement had been invoked earlier and was effective as between those contracting parties at the time of entry into force for them of this Agreement.

3.   Paragraph 1 shall apply between a Member and another Member which has acceded under Article XII only if the Member not consenting to the application has so notified the Ministerial Conference before the approval of the agreement on the terms of accession by the Ministerial Conference.

4.   The Ministerial Conference may review the operation of this Article in particular cases at the request of any Member and make appropriate recommendations.

5.   Non-application of a Plurilateral Trade Agreement between parties to that Agreement shall be governed by the provisions of that Agreement.

Article XIV

Acceptance, Entry into Force and Deposit

1.   This Agreement shall be open for acceptance, by signature or otherwise, by contracting parties to GATT 1947, and the European Communities, which are eligible to become original Members of the WTO in accordance with Article XI of this Agreement. Such acceptance shall apply to this Agreement and the Multilateral Trade Agreements annexed hereto. This Agreement and the Multilateral Trade Agreements annexed hereto shall enter into force on the date determined by Ministers in accordance with paragraph 3 of the Final Act Embodying the Results of the Uruguay Round of Multilateral Trade Negotiations and shall remain open for acceptance for a period of two years following that date unless the Ministers decide otherwise. An acceptance following the entry into force of this Agreement shall enter into force on the 30th day following the date of such acceptance.

2.   A Member which accepts this Agreement after its entry into force shall implement those concessions and obligations in the Multilateral Trade Agreements that are to be implemented over a period of time starting with the entry into force of this Agreement as if it had accepted this Agreement on the date of its entry into force.

3.   Until the entry into force of this Agreement, the text of this Agreement and the Multilateral Trade Agreements shall be deposited with the Director-General to the CONTRACTING PARTIES to GATT 1947. The Director-General shall promptly furnish a certified true copy of this

Agreement and the Multilateral Trade Agreements, and a notification of each acceptance thereof, to each government and the European Communities having accepted this Agreement. This Agreement and the Multilateral Trade Agreements, and any amendments thereto, shall, upon the entry into force of this Agreement, be deposited with the Director-General of the WTO.

4.   The acceptance and entry into force of a Plurilateral Trade Agreement shall be governed by the provisions of that Agreement. Such Agreements shall be deposited with the Director-General to the CONTRACTING PARTIES to GATT 1947. Upon the entry into force of this Agreement, such Agreements shall be deposited with the Director-General of the WTO.

Article XV

Withdrawal

1.   Any Member may withdraw from this Agreement. Such withdrawal shall apply both to this Agreement and the Multilateral Trade Agreements and shall take effect upon the expiration of six months from the date on which written notice of withdrawal is received by the Director-General of the WTO.

2.   Withdrawal from a Plurilateral Trade Agreement shall be governed by the provisions of that Agreement.

Article XVI

Miscellaneous Provisions

1.   Except as otherwise provided under this Agreement or the Multilateral Trade Agreements, the WTO shall be guided by the decisions, procedures and customary practices followed by the CONTRACTING PARTIES to GATT 1947 and the bodies established in the framework of GATT 1947.

2.   To the extent practicable, the Secretariat of GATT 1947 shall become the Secretariat of the WTO, and the Director-General to the CONTRACTING PARTIES to GATT 1947, until such time as the Ministerial Conference has appointed a Director-General in accordance with paragraph 2 of Article VI of this Agreement, shall serve as Director-General of the WTO.

3.   In the event of a conflict between a provision of this Agreement and a provision of any of the Multilateral Trade Agreements, the provision of this Agreement shall prevail to the extent of the conflict.

4.   Each Member shall ensure the conformity of its laws, regulations and administrative procedures with its obligations as provided in the annexed Agreements.

5.   No reservations may be made in respect of any provision of this Agreement. Reservations in respect of any of the provisions of the Multilateral Trade Agreements may only be made to the extent provided for in those Agreements. Reservations in respect of a provision of a Plurilateral Trade Agreement shall be governed by the provisions of that Agreement.

6.   This Agreement shall be registered in accordance with the provisions of Article 102 of the Charter of the United Nations.

DONE at Marrakesh this fifteenth day of April one thousand nine hundred and ninety-four, in a single copy, in the English, French and Spanish languages, each text being authentic.

Explanatory Notes:

The terms "country" or "countries" as used in this Agreement and the Multilateral Trade Agreements are to be understood to include any separate customs territory Member of the WTO.

In the case of a separate customs territory Member of the WTO, where an expression in this Agreement and the Multilateral Trade Agreements is qualified by the term "national," such expression shall be read as pertaining to that customs territory, unless otherwise specified.

LIST OF ANNEXES [Annexes themselves are not reproduced here]

ANNEX 1

    ANNEX 1A: Multilateral Agreements on Trade in Goods
        General Agreement on Tariffs and Trade 1994
        Agreement on Agriculture
        Agreement on the Application of Sanitary and Phytosanitary Measures
        Agreement on Textiles and Clothing
        Agreement on Technical Barriers to Trade
        Agreement on Trade-Related Investment Measures
        Agreement on Implementation of Article VI of the General Agreement on Tariffs and Trade 1994
        Agreement on Implementation of Article VII of the General Agreement on Tariffs and Trade 1994
        Agreement on Preshipment Inspection
        Agreement on Rules of Origin
        Agreement on Import Licensing Procedures
        Agreement on Subsidies and Countervailing Measures
        Agreement on Safeguards

ANNEX 1B: General Agreement on Trade in Services and Annexes
ANNEX 1C: Agreement on Trade-Related Aspects of Intellectual Property Rights

ANNEX 2

Understanding on Rules and Procedures Governing the Settlement of Disputes

ANNEX 3

Trade Policy Review Mechanism

ANNEX 4

Plurilateral Trade Agreements

Agreement on Trade in Civil Aircraft

Agreement on Government Procurement

International Dairy Agreement

International Bovine Meat Agreement

APPENDIX J
DRAFT PROTOCOL TO THE AsDB CHARTER

—Reference in text: Subsection IVG of Chapter Four—

(Draft) Protocol to the Agreement Establishing
the Asian Development Bank

The Parties to this Protocol,

Considering that in order to further achieve the purposes of the Agreement Establishing the Asian Development Bank (hereinafter the Agreement") and to enhance the contribution that the Asian Development Bank (hereinafter "the Bank") can make in facilitating economic development, broadly defined, in the region (as defined in the Agreement), and

Taking into account the initiatives being taken by other multilateral development banks to make similar modifications to their charters and to cooperate in the establishment of certain common policies and institutional arrangements,

Have agreed as follows:

Article 1. Institutional Principles

The Bank shall be governed by the rules of public international law and by the following institutional principles:

1. Transparency, meaning in this context that the greatest practicable degree of disclosure of documents and other information produced by, within, or for the Bank shall be made to the public, and that the proceedings of the Board of Directors and of the Board of Governors shall to the greatest practicable degree be accessible to the public, subject to appropriate respect for confidentiality where necessary to protect legitimate interests of private parties.

2. Participation, meaning in this context that the Bank shall invite public participation in its development and implementation of policies pertinent to the Bank's operations, and to this end shall, inter alia, (i) accept public comment on proposed actions in this regard and (ii) facilitate the participation by, and take into account the views of, nongovernment organizations.

3. Legality and the rule of law, meaning in this context that the Bank (i) shall state its policies clearly and act consistently with them and (ii) shall take into account in its operations and governance the performance of all members of the Bank in honoring their international legal commitments, including the treaty commitments referred to in Articles 2 and 3 of this Protocol.

4. Competence, meaning in this context that the Bank shall (i) place paramount emphasis, in the engagement and advancement of Bank staff, on ensuring their competence as international civil servants in the discharge of their duties and (ii) support efforts by national authorities to ensure that persons appointed as Directors and Governors have suitable professional qualifications necessary to meet their responsibilities.

5. Accountability, meaning in this context that the Bank shall (i) regard itself as accountable to its members and their people, as reflected in part by the establishment of the Tribunal referred to in Article 6 of this Protocol, and (ii) support efforts by national authorities to honor their obligations under the Articles of Agreement of the International Monetary Fund and to adopt and implement the general economic and financial policies prescribed by the Bank in its developing member countries to promote national economic growth and stability.

Article 2. Environmental Protection

1. The Bank shall take all action necessary and appropriate to ensure

   (a) that it follows, and sees that any recipient of Bank financial assistance follows, adequate procedures to assess in advance the environmental impact of any development projects for which Bank financing is used,

   (b) that its operations do not create undue harm to the physical, human, or cultural environment in the region,

   (c) that it observes and promotes, both in its own operations and in its dealings with members, sound principles of environmental management and improvement, and

   (d) that it acts consistently with the rules and principles of international law on environmental protection and management.

2. Each member of the Bank shall comply with the following treaty provisions, subject to (i) any permissible reservation that the member has made pertinent to one or more of those provisions upon becoming a party to the treaty at issue or (ii) if the member is not a party to the treaty in question, any qualifying declaration that the member transmits to the Bank on or before the date that the member deposits with the Secretary-General of the United Nations its instrument of ratification to this Protocol, pro-

vided that such qualifying declaration would be permissible as a reservation under standards used for this purpose by the Secretary-General of the United Nations pursuant to Articles 19 through 23 of the 1969 Vienna Convention on the Law of Treaties.

(a) Articles I through XIV of the Convention on International Trade in Endangered Species of Wild Fauna and Flora (CITES) (1973);

(b) Articles 1 through 4 of the Vienna Convention for the Protection of the Ozone Layer (1985), and pertinent provisions of the Protocols thereto and of the Amendments to those Protocols;

(c) Articles 1 through 9 of the Basel Convention on the Control of Transboundary Movements of Hazardous Wastes and Their Disposal (1989);

(d) Articles 1 through 20 of the Convention on Biological Diversity (1992); and

(e) Articles 2 through 6 of the Kyoto Protocol to the United Nations Framework Convention on Climate Change (1997).

Article 3. Human Rights and Social Dimensions of Development

1. The Bank shall take all action necessary and appropriate to ensure

(a) that it follows, and sees that any recipient of Bank financial assistance follows, adequate procedures to assess in advance the social impact of any development projects for which Bank financing is used,

(b) that no person directly affected by any development project for which Bank financing is used is worse off than before such project was undertaken,

(c) that it observes and promotes, both in its own operations and in its dealings with members, the respect for and protection of human rights and fundamental freedoms; and

(d) that it acts consistently with the rules and principles of international law on human rights.

2. Each member of the Bank shall comply with the following treaty provisions, subject to (i) any permissible reservation that the member has made pertinent to one or more of those provisions upon becoming a party to the treaty at issue or (ii) if the member is not a party to the treaty in question, any qualifying declaration that the member transmits to the Bank on or before the date that the member deposits with the Secretary-General of the United Nations its instrument of ratification to this Protocol, provided that such qualifying declaration would be permissible as a reservation under standards used for this purpose by the Secretary-General of the United Nations pursuant to Articles 19 through 23 of the 1969 Vienna Convention on the Law of Treaties.

(a) Articles 1 through 28 of the International Covenant on Civil and Political Rights (1967);

(b) Articles 1 through 7 of the International Convention on the Elimination of All Forms of Racial Discrimination (1966);

(c) Articles 1 through 16 of the Convention on the Elimination of All Forms of Discrimination Against Women (1979);

(d) Articles 1 through 16 of the Convention Against Torture and Other Cruel Inhuman or Degrading Treatment or Punishment (1984); and

(e) Articles 1 through 41 of the Convention on the Rights of the Child (1989).

Article 4. Governance

1. The Bank shall promote through appropriate means, as determined by regulations adopted by the Board of Governors at the recommendation of the Board of Directors, the development in its regional member countries of effective multi-party representative governance.

2. Pursuant to paragraph 1 above, Article 36(2) of the Agreement is hereby amended to read as follows:

> Except in furtherance of the provisions of Article 4, paragraph 1 of the Protocol to the Agreement Establishing the Asian Development Bank, the Bank, its President, Vice-President(s), officers and staff shall not interfere in the political affairs of any member, nor shall they be influenced in their decisions by the political character of the member concerned. Only those considerations made applicable by this Agreement and by that Protocol shall be taken into account in their decisions. Such considerations shall be weighed impartially in order to achieve and carry out the purpose and functions of the Bank.

3. The Bank shall take all action necessary and appropriate (i) to ensure that its own operations comport with sound practices of good governance and do not involve corruption or bribery and (ii) to promote within its member countries the adoption of practices and policies to combat corruption or bribery.

4. Each member of the Bank shall comply with the provisions of the OECD Convention on Combating Bribery of Foreign Public Officials in International Business Transactions (1997).

SELECTED BIBLIOGRAPHY

Works listed here provide especially helpful information about, or critical assessments of, the GEOs. This is not intended, however, as a comprehensive bibliography of literature in the area. Numerous other works are referred to in footnote citations in the main text of this book and in the survey of literature provided in Appendix A.

Books

Walden Bello, DEGLOBALIZATION: IDEAS FOR A NEW WORLD ECONOMY (2004)

Walden Bello, David Kinley & Elaine Elinson, DEVELOPMENT DEBACLE: THE WORLD BANK IN THE PHILIPPINES (1982)

Raj Bhala, GATT LAW (2005)

Raj Bhala, INTERNATIONAL TRADE LAW: THEORY AND PRACTICE (2d ed. 2001)

Raj Bhala, TRADE, DEVELOPMENT, AND SOCIAL JUSTICE (2003)

Raj Bhala and Kevin Kennedy, WORLD TRADE LAW: THE GATT-WTO SYSTEM, REGIONAL ARRANGEMENTS, AND U.S. LAW (1998)

Graham Bird, IMF LENDING TO DEVELOPING COUNTRIES: ISSUES AND EVIDENCE (1995)

James M. Boughton & K. Sarwar Lateef eds., FIFTY YEARS AFTER BRETTON WOODS: THE FUTURE OF THE IMF AND THE WORLD BANK (1995)

Antonio Cassese, INTERNATIONAL LAW IN A DIVIDED WORLD (1986)

Steve Charnovitz, TRADE LAW AND GLOBAL GOVERNANCE (2002)

Kevin Danaher ed., DEMOCRATIZING THE GLOBAL ECONOMY (2001)

Mac Darrow, BETWEEN THE LIGHT AND SHADOW: THE WORLD BANK, THE INTERNATIONAL MONETARY FUND AND INTERNATIONAL HUMAN RIGHTS LAW (2003)

Erik Denters, *International Monetary Fund, in* INTERNATIONAL ENCYCLOPAEDIA OF LAWS (R. Blanpain ed., 1993)

Erik Denters, LAW AND POLICY OF IMF CONDITIONALITY (1996)

Margaret Garritsen de Vries, THE IMF IN A CHANGING WORLD, 1945–85 (1986)

Paul DeWaart, Paul Peters & Eric Denters, INTERNATIONAL LAW AND DEVELOPMENT (1988)

Richard W. Edwards, Jr., INTERNATIONAL MONETARY COLLABORATION (1985)

Ralph H. Folsom, Michael Gordon Wallace & John A. Spanogle, INTERNATIONAL TRADE AND ECONOMIC RELATIONS IN A NUTSHELL (3d ed. 2004)

Frank J. Garcia, TRADE, INEQUALITY, AND JUSTICE: TOWARD A LIBERAL THEORY OF JUST TRADE (2003)

John W. Head, *Asian Development Bank, in* INTERNATIONAL ENCYCLOPAEDIA OF LAWS (R. Blanpain ed., 2002)

International Monetary Fund, FINANCIAL ORGANIZATION AND OPERATIONS OF THE IMF (IMF Pamphlet Series No. 45, 2d ed. 1991)

Harold James, INTERNATIONAL MONETARY COLLABORATION SINCE BRETTON WOODS (1996)

Kent Jones, WHO'S AFRAID OF THE WTO? (2004)

Peter B. Kenen ed., MANAGING THE WORLD ECONOMY: FIFTY YEARS AFTER BRETTON WOODS (1994)

Frederic L. Kirgis, INTERNATIONAL ORGANIZATIONS IN THEIR LEGAL SETTING (1993)

Timothy Lane & Steven Phillips, MORAL HAZARD: DOES IMF FINANCING ENCOURAGE IMPRUDENCE BY BORROWERS AND LENDERS? (International Monetary Fund, Economic Issues No. 28, 2002)

S. Mansoob Murshed ed., GLOBALIZATION, MARGINALIZATION AND DEVELOPMENT (2002) (in particular, S. Mansoob Murshed, *Perspectives on Two Phases of Globalization,* appearing as chapter 1)

Cheryl Payer, THE WORLD BANK: A CRITICAL ANALYSIS (1982)

Richard Peet, UNHOLY TRINITY: THE IMF, WORLD BANK AND WTO (2003)

Rumu Sarkar, DEVELOPMENT LAW AND INTERNATIONAL FINANCE (1999)

Henry G. Schermers, INTERNATIONAL INSTITUTIONAL LAW: UNITY WITHIN DIVERSITY (2003)

Amartya Sen, DEVELOPMENT AS FREEDOM (1999)

Ibrahim F.I. Shihata, THE WORLD BANK IN A CHANGING WORLD—SELECTED ESSAYS (three volumes) (1991–2000)

Sigrun I. Skogly, THE HUMAN RIGHTS OBLIGATIONS OF THE WORLD BANK AND THE INTERNATIONAL MONETARY FUND (2001)

James Raymond Vreeland, THE IMF AND ECONOMIC DEVELOPMENT (2003)

Friedl Weiss, Erik Denters & Paul De Waart eds., INTERNATIONAL ECONOMIC LAW WITH A HUMAN FACE (1998)

Stephen Zamora & Ronald A. Brand, eds., BASIC DOCUMENTS OF INTERNATIONAL ECONOMIC LAW (two volumes) (1990)

Adam Zwass, GLOBALIZATION OF UNEQUAL NATIONAL ECONOMIES: PLAYERS AND CONTROVERSIES (2002)

Articles

Saladin Al-Jurf, *Good Governance and Transparency: Their Impact on Development*, 9 TRANSNAT'L L. & CONTEMP. PROBS. 193 (1999)

Antony Anghie, *Time Present and Time Past: Globalization, International Financial Institutions, and the Third World*, 32 N.Y.U. J. INT'L L. & POL. 243 (2000)

Jeffrey Atik, *Democratizing the WTO*, 33 GEO. WASH. INT'L L. REV. 455 (2001)

C. Fred Bergsten, *America's Two-Front Economic Conflict*, 80 FOREIGN. AFF., Mar.–Apr. 2001, at 16

Raj Bhala, *Clarifying the Trade-Labor Link*, 37 COLUM. J. TRANSNAT'L L. 11 (1998)

Raj Bhala, *Marxist Origins of the "Anti-Third World" Claim*, 24 FORDHAM INT'L L.J. 132 (2000)

Raj Bhala, *Saudi Arabia, the WTO, and American Trade Law and Policy*, 38 7 J. INT'L LAW. 741 (2004)

Graham Bird, *Reforming the IMF: Should the Fund Abandon Conditionality?*, 7 NEW ECONOMY 214 (2000)

Richard Blackhurst & David Hartridge, *Improving the Capacity of WTO Institutions to Fulfil Their Mandate*, 7 J. INT'L ECON. L. 705 (2004)

Daniel D. Bradlow, *Rapidly Changing Functions and Slowly Evolving Structures: The Troubling Case of the IMF*, 94 AM. SOC'Y INT'L L. PROC. 152 (2000)

Daniel D. Bradlow, *Should the International Financial Institutions Play a Role in the Implementation and Enforcement of International Humanitarian Law?*, 50 U. KAN. L. REV. 695 (2002)

Daniel D. Bradlow, *Stuffing New Wine Into Old Bottles: The Troubling Case of the IMF*, 3 J. INT'L BANKING REG. 9 (2001)

Daniel D. Bradlow, *"The Times They Are A-Chargin'": Some Preliminary Thoughts on Developing Countries, NGOs and the Reform of the WTO*, 33 GEO. WASH. INT'L L. REV. 503 (2001)

Daniel D. Bradlow, *The World Bank, the IMF, and Human Rights*, 6 TRANSNAT'L & CONTEMP. PROBS. 47 (1996)

Daniel D. Bradlow & Claudio Grossman, *Limited Mandates and Intertwined Problems: A New Challenge for the World Bank and the IMF*, 17 HUM. RTS. Q. 411 (1995)

Marco C.E.J. Bronckers, *More Power to the WTO?*, 4 J. INT'L ECON. L. 41 (2001)

Ross P. Buckley, *A Tale of Two Crises: The Search for the Enduring Reforms of the International Financial System*, 6 UCLA J. INT'L L. & FOREIGN AFF. 1 (2001)

Michel Camdessus, *The IMF at the Beginning of the Twenty-First Century: Can we Establish a Humanized Globalization?*, 7 GLOBAL GOVERNANCE 363 (2001)

Timothy A. Canova, *Global Finance and the International Monetary Fund's Neoliberal Agenda: The Threat to the Employment, Ethnic Identity, and Cultural Pluralism of Latina/o Communities*, 33 U.C. DAVIS L. REV. 1547 (2000)

John D. Ciorciari, *The Lawful Scope of Human Rights Criteria in World Bank Credit Decisions: An Interpretive Analysis of the IBRD and IDA Articles of Agreement*, 33 CORNELL INT'L L.J. 331 (2001)

Chi Carmody, *Beyond the Proposals: Public Participation in International Economic Law*, 15 AM. U. INT'L L. REV. 1321 (2000)

Steve Charnovitz, *WTO Cosmopolitics*, 34 N.Y.U. J. INT'L L. & POL. 299 (2002)

Jessica Einhorn, *The World Bank's Mission Creep*, 80 FOREIGN AFF. 22 (2001)

Richard Falk & Andrew Strauss, *Toward Global Parliament*, 80 FOREIGN AFF. 212 (2001)

Gopal Garuda, *Lender of Last Resort: Rethinking IMF Conditionality*, 20 HARV. INT'L L. REV. 36 (1998)

François Gianviti, *The Reform of the International Monetary Fund (Conditionality and Surveillance)*, 34 INT'L LAW. 107 (2003)

Globalization and Its Critics: A Survey of Globalization, THE ECONOMIST, Sept. 29, 2001 (series of articles)

Andrew T. Guzman, *Global Governance and the WTO*, 45 HARV. INT'L L.J. 303 (2004)

Günther Handl, *The Legal Mandate of Multilateral Development Banks as Agents for Change Toward Sustainable Development*, 92 AM. J. INT'L L. 642 (1998)

John W. Head, *Environmental Conditionality in the Operations of International Development Finance Institutions*, 1 KAN. J.L. & PUB. POL'Y 15 (1991)

John W. Head, *For Richer or For Poorer: Assessing the Criticisms Directed at the Multilateral Development Banks*, 52 U. KAN. L. REV. 241 (2004)

John W. Head, *Lessons from the Asian Financial Crisis: The Role of the IMF and the United States*, 7 KAN. J.L. & PUB. POL'Y 70 (1998)

John W. Head, *Seven Deadly Sins: An Assessment of Criticisms Directed at the International Monetary Fund*, 52 U. KAN. L. REV. 521 (2004)

John W. Head, *Supranational Law: How the Move Toward Multilateral Solutions Is Changing the Character of "International" Law*, 42 U. KAN. L. REV. 605 (1994)

John W. Head, *Throwing Eggs at Windows: Legal and Institutional Globalization in the 21st-Century Economy*, 50 U. KAN. L. REV. 731 (2002)

John W. Head, *Suspension of Debtor Countries' Voting Rights in the IMF: An Assessment of the Third Amendment to the IMF Charter*, 33 VA. J. INT'L L. 591 (1993)

Robert Hockett, *From Macro to Micro to "Mission-Creep": Defending the IMF's Emerging Concern with the Infrastructural Prerequisites to Global Financial Stability*, 41 COLUM. J. TRANSNAT'L L. 153 (2002)

Robert Hockett, *Legally Defending Mission Creep*, 13 INT'L LEGAL PERSP. 34 (2002)

John H. Jackson, *The WTO 'Constitution' and Proposed Reforms: Seven 'Mantras' Revisited*, 3 J. INT'L ECON. L. 67 (2001)

Jane Kelsey, *World Trade and Small Nations in the South Pacific Region*, 14 KAN. J.L. & PUB. POL'Y 247 (2005)

Kevin C. Kennedy, *Implications for Global Governance: Why Multilateralism Matters in Resolving Trade-Environment Disputes*, 7 WID. L. SYMP J. 31 (2001)

Kevin C. Kennedy, *The Incoherence of Agricultural, Trade, and Development Policy for Sub-Saharan Africa: Sowing the Seeds of False Hope for Sub-Saharan Africa's Cotton Farmers?*, 14 KAN. J.L. & PUB. POL'Y 307 (2005)

David Kinley & Junko Tadaki, *From Talk to Walk: The Emergence of Human Rights Responsibilities for Corporations at International Law*, 44 VA. J. INT'L L. 931 (2004)

Ross B. Leckow, *The International Monetary Fund and Strengthening the Architecture of the International Monetary System*, 30 LAW & POL'Y INT'L BUS. 117 (1999)

Catherine H. Lee, *To Thine Ownself Be True: IMF Conditionality and Erosion of Economic Sovereignty in the Asian Financial Crisis*, 24 U. PA. J. INT'L ECON. L. 875 (2003)

Eugenia McGill, *Poverty and Social Analysis of Trade Agreements: A More Coherent Approach?*, 27 B.C. INT'L & COMP. L. REV. 371 (2004)

John O. McGinnis and Mark L. Movsesian, *The World Trade Constitution*, 114 HARV. L. REV. 511 (2000)

Herbert V. Morais, *The Globalization of Human Rights Law and the Role of International Financial Institutions in Promoting Human Rights*, 33 GEO. WASH. INT'L L. REV. 71 (2000)

Ernst-Ulrich Petersmann, *Challenges to the Legitimacy and Efficiency of the World Trading System: Democratic Governance and Competition Culture in the WTO*, 7 J. INT'L ECON. L. 585 (2004)

Balakrishnan Rajagopal, *From Resistance to Renewal: The Third World, Social Movements, and the Expansion of International Institutions*, 41 HARV. INT'L L.J. 529 (2000)

Susan Rose-Ackerman, *The Role of the World Bank in Controlling Corruption*, 29 L. & POL'Y INT'L BUS. 93 (1997)

Carlos Santiso, *Good Governance and Aid Effectiveness: The World Bank and Conditionality*, 7 GEO. PUB. POL'Y REV. 1 (2001)

Bruce R. Scott, *The Great Divide in the Global Village*, 80 FOREIGN AFF. 161 (2001)

Gregory Shaffer, *Parliamentary Oversight of WTO Rule-Making: The Political, Normative, and Practical Contexts*, 7 J. INT'L ECON. L. 629 (2004)

Joseph E. Stiglitz, *Failure of the Fund: Rethinking the IMF Response*, 23 HARV. INT'L L. REV. 14 (2001)

Andrés Rigo Sureda, *Informality and Effectiveness in the Operation of the International Bank for Reconstruction and Development*, 6 J. INT'L ECON. L. 565 (2003)

Chantal Thomas, *Trade-Related Labor and Environment Agreements?*, 5 J. INT'L ECON. L. 791 (2002)

James W. Thomson, *Globalization: Its Defenders and Dissenters*, 106 BUS. & SOC'Y REV. 170 (2001)

Ngaire Woods, *Making the IMF and the World Bank More Accountable*, 77 INT'L AFF. 83 (2001)

Websites

Websites of GEOs:

AfDB	www.afdb.org
AsDB	www.adb.org
EBRD	www.ebrd.org
IADB	www.iadb.org
IMF	www.imf.org
World Bank	www.worldbank.org
WTO	www.wto.org

Selected other useful websites:

Bank Information Center	www.bciusa.org
Bretton Woods Project	www.brettonwoodsproject.org
CEE Bankwatch Network	www.bankwatch.org
InterAction	
(American Council for Voluntary	www.interaction.org
International Action)	
Overseas Development Institute	www.odi.org.uk

INDEX

NOTES: *(1)* *Entries are indexed here by reference to the chapter, section, and subsection of the text in which they appear. Corresponding page references may be found in the table of Detailed Contents.*

(2) *This index includes names of a few specific individuals whose contribution to the literature has been noted in the text. Other contributors to the literature are, of course, cited in footnotes and in Appendix A.*

For Reference
Not to be taken from this room